Blackstone's Police Manual

Evidence and Procedure

Blackstone's
Police Manual

Evidence and Procedure

2004 edition

David Johnston

LLB, LLM, Barrister

and

Glenn Hutton

BA, MPhil, FCIPD

OXFORD

UNIVERSITY PRESS

OXFORD

UNIVERSITY PRESS

Great Clarendon Street, Oxford OX2 6DP

Oxford University Press is a department of the University of Oxford.
It furthers the University's objective of excellence in research, scholarship,
and education by publishing worldwide in

Oxford New York

Auckland Bangkok Buenos Aires Cape Town Chennai
Dar es Salaam Delhi Hong Kong Istanbul Karachi Kolkata
Kuala Lumpur Madrid Melbourne Mexico City Mumbai Nairobi
São Paulo Shanghai Taipei Tokyo Toronto

Oxford is a registered trade mark of Oxford University Press
in the UK and certain other countries

Published in the United States
by Oxford University Press Inc., New York

A Blackstone Press Book

© Glenn Hutton and David Johnston, 2004

First published 1998
Second edition, 1999
Third edition, 2000
Fourth edition, 2001
Fifth edition, 2002
Sixth edition, 2004

The moral rights of the author have been asserted
Database right Oxford University Press (maker)

British Library Cataloguing in Publication Data

Data available

Library of Congress Cataloging in Publication Data

Data available

ISBN 0-19-926248-9

1 3 5 7 9 10 8 6 4 2

Typeset by Newgen Imaging Systems (P) Ltd., Chennai, India
Printed in Great Britain
on acid-free paper by
Ashford Colour Press, Gosport, Hampshire

Contents

?

Preface

Since the last edition was published Oxford University Press commissioned an independent review of the Manual by an independent legal expert and also agreed with Centrex for their legal department at Harrogate to validate the legal content. The feedback from the review and validation have been invaluable and resulted in a number of changes to both the content and format of the Manual.

The most significant development in legislation has been the revision of the Police and Criminal Evidence Act 1984, Codes of Practice A to E. The Codes have been amended throughout the Manual and particularly in the chapters within Part 3—police station procedure. Other legislation that has been incorporated includes the provisions of the Police Reform Act 2002 and several commencement orders for recent major pieces of legislation including the Criminal Justice and Police Act 2001, Youth Justice and Criminal Evidence Act 1999 and Access to Justice Act 1999.

All the relevant case law has been included together with consideration of the affect of the Human Rights Act 1998 and European-wide case law.

For police officers intending to sit the police qualifying examination for sergeant and inspector (OSPRE Part I), if the law is not in the latest edition of the Manual it is not in the examination. Certain parts of the Manual will not tested in the 2004 OSPRE examinations. These parts are indicated by a continuous vertical line down the left-hand margin of the text. This applies to all of Chapters 1, 2 and 3 and most of Chapter 9.

Every care has been taken to ensure the accuracy of the contents of this Manual. However, neither the authors nor the publishers can accept any responsibility for any actions taken, or not taken, on the basis of the information contained within it.

We continue to receive useful feedback on the content and style of the book from operational personnel and trainers. It is important to us that this continues and Oxford University Press are always happy to receive written feedback from any reader.

The law is stated as at 20 July 2003.

Acknowledgements

As with the previous five editions of the *Evidence and Procedure Manual* support in its production has come from many quarters across the police service and beyond. However, we would like to thank the Central Police Training and Development Authority and in particular their Harrogate legal team for the irreplaceable monthly Digest and the meticulous way they validated the legal content of the Manual.

Fraser Sampson, our series editor, continues to inspire us with his appetite for work and unerring search for perfection.

Our thanks to the staff in the Higher Education Department at Oxford University Press, especially Jane Kavanagh (Editor-in-Chief), Roxanne Selby, Jane O'Regan and Sean Hutton. Also to Mandy Preece who keeps us on the straight and narrow! Finally, an annual special thanks to RH for her tolerance and forbearance in the hours spent reviewing and updating the Manual.

Foreword

In the 21st century, police officers must demonstrate a wide range of knowledge, skills, and abilities—not only if they are to perform effectively in their current role, but also if they are seeking to gain promotion to higher ranks within the service. The knowledge and understanding of relevant law and procedure remains central to the role of any officer, as does the ability to effectively apply this law and procedure in their day-to-day duties.

The *Blackstone's Police Manuals* are presented in four volumes—crime, evidence and procedure, road traffic and general police duties. The manuals have been fully updated to reflect recent changes in legislation, including the 2003 revisions to the PACE Codes of Practice. Oxford University Press work alongside Centrex to ensure that the books are fully accurate and up-to-date, and reflect the content which is required by a police officer in today's service.

The *Blackstone's Police Manuals* are primarily designed to assist candidates preparing for the Sergeants' and Inspectors' OSPRE Part I Police Promotion Examination. In serving this purpose, the books should be used in combination with official OSPRE Rules & Syllabus document. You may have received a copy of this document when you obtained these manuals. However, additional copies of the Rules & Syllabus can be downloaded from the Employers' Organisation for Local Government website at www.lg-employers.gov.uk.

From a wider perspective, the Manuals are also designed to provide an ongoing reference point for officers seeking to keep their professional knowledge up-to-date. Moreover, the Manuals continue to be widely used by officers seeking a concise explanation of specific aspects of the law they use in their day-to-day duties.

Centrex continues to play a key role within the modern police service through assisting officers in their ongoing professional development. The OSPRE system, developed and delivered by Centrex Examinations & Assessment, not only selects tomorrow's managers and supervisors, but also assists candidates in developing themselves professionally in the knowledge and skills required for these ranks. I believe the Blackstone's Police Manuals continue to play a central role in this process.

If you are using the books to prepare for the OSPRE Promotion Examinations, may I take this opportunity to wish you the best of luck in your studies, and I hope the books will assist you in progressing your career within the service.

Chris Mould
Centrex
Chief Executive

Table of Cases

Table of Statutes

Table Rules, Regulations, Circulars and Codes of Practice

Home Office Circulars

PART ONE

The Criminal Justice System

1 Sources of law

1.1 Introduction

As with most branches of the law in England and Wales, the sources of criminal law are found partly in common law and partly in statute law.

1.2 Common Law

Common law originated from the customs of the early communities, which were unified and developed in the Royal Courts during the three centuries following the Norman Conquest.

There is no authoritative text of the common law (although *Stephen's Digest* is one of the most often cited) and, as a whole, its sources lie in the principles of the law declared by the judges in the course of deciding particular cases. It should be noted that the common law can only be declared authoritatively by the judge(s) of the superior courts (i.e. from the High Court) and then only to the extent that it is necessary to do so for the purpose of deciding a particular case. For this reason, the development of the common law has always been dependent upon the incidence of cases arising for decision, and the particular facts of those cases.

Those decisions are the *authoritative sources* of certain offences and powers, in exactly the same way as an Act (such as the Theft Act 1968) and will be relevant irrespective of how ancient the case is—if anything, the older a case authority is, the more persuasive it is, having stood the test of time. A good example of this would be the decision in *Doodeward* v *Spence* (1907) 6 CLR 406 where it was held that a human body could not be 'property' for the purposes of theft (**see Crime, chapter 12**). Reviewing this decision in 1998, Lord Justice Rose said that he was reluctant to interfere with a decision which had stood the test of time for so long and left the issue for Parliament.

In relation to certain offences which originate in the common law, e.g. murder, theft, rape, robbery and arson, precise definitions were evolved because the severity of the punishment rendered this necessary. As most were punishable by death, the burden of proof on the prosecution (as to which, **see chapter 10**) was also very high—and has remained so ever since. Other offences of similar origin, however, e.g. conspiracy and attempts to commit crime, are notable for the lack of precision in their formulation (**see Crime, chapter 3**), and are still being used to bring new sets of facts within the ambit of the criminal law, as in the decisions of *Shaw* v *DPP* [1962] AC 220 and *Knuller (Publishing, Printing and Promotions) Ltd* v *DPP* [1973] AC 435 on conspiracy to corrupt public morals.

1.3 Legislation

Statutes, in the form of Acts of Parliament, have always been regarded as supplementary to the common law. It is true that the major part of criminal law and procedure is now in statutory form, but it is equally true that the principles of common law, notably in relation to criminal liability generally, homicide and the rules of evidence and procedure at a criminal trial, have not lessened in importance.

Statutes are enacted by Parliament and it is the duty of the court, as and when the occasion arises, to interpret and give effect to the intention of Parliament as expressed in the words of the statute. The courts have the same task in relation to delegated legislation, i.e. in the form of Orders in Council, statutory instruments and bye-laws made by Ministers, heads of Government Departments, local authorities and other bodies under powers delegated to them by Parliament. In looking at the intentions of Parliament, the courts may now consider the content of any debates within either House as reported in *Hansard* (*Pepper* v *Hart* [1993] AC 593).

The only distinction, for practical purposes, between statutes and delegated legislation is that, while the validity of the former cannot be questioned in a court, the latter are valid only within the limits of the powers conferred by the enabling statute, and in the case of bye-laws they must also be reasonable. Consequently, the courts have the power, most notably in the context of judicial review applications (**see para. 2.6.4**), to hold that delegated legislation is invalid because the terms of the statute under which it is made have not been complied with.

A statute is construed so far as possible in conformity with the common law, because of the presumption against the alteration of general common law principles. Where the two cannot be reconciled, the statute prevails.

The Interpretation Act 1978 (which is the main authority for interpreting the effect of statutes), s. 18 states:

> Where an act or omission constitutes an offence under two or more Acts, or both under an Act and at common law, the offender shall, unless the contrary intention appears, be liable to be prosecuted and punished under either or any of those Acts or at common law, but shall not be liable to be punished more than once for the same offence.

1.4 Judicial Precedents

The decision in a criminal trial as to the guilt or innocence of the defendant is a matter for the jury (or the magistrate(s); **see chapter 2**) although this decision will only be left to a jury when the trial judge is satisfied that a verdict of guilty would be proper in law on the facts, and that there is evidence which, if believed, would justify such a verdict.

Juries decide questions of *fact*; judges decide questions of *law* (and, confusingly, magistrates decide both *fact and law*), (**see para. 2.6.2**), although in relation to the latter, they are advised by the court clerk (**see para. 2.8.2**).

Matters of law are solely for the judge who frequently has to rule on these during the course of a trial. Ultimately, the judge directs the jury on the law in summing up. In a trial by jury these rulings and directions alone are important in the development and illustration of the law.

1.4.1 The Courts and Decided Cases

The system of courts in England and Wales is a hierarchy, the various courts being related to one another as superior and inferior. An inferior court is generally bound by the decision and directions of a superior court. For example, judges of the Divisional Court and Crown Courts are bound by the decisions of the Court of Appeal. The Appeal Court is in turn bound by the decisions of the House of Lords, which is also bound—to an extent—by decisions of the European Court of Justice. It should be noted that, although the Crown Court is superior to a magistrates' court and enjoys wider powers (**see para. 2.10**), it is still a 'lower' court and its decisions are not generally binding on other courts.

When it is said that a decision is binding, or more fully, a binding and authoritative precedent, what is meant is that the *principle of law* on which the decision was based, or the reason for the decision, is binding. This principle of the law is known as the *ratio decidendi* of the case. An example of this would be the decision that, once the prosecution have proved that a defendant was carrying a weapon that is 'offensive' *per se*, there is no need to prove any intention to use that weapon offensively (*Ohlson v Hylton* [1975] 1 WLR 724). (For the law on weapons generally, **see General Police Duties, chapter 6.**)

The *ratio decidendi* consists only of the principle(s) of law essential to a decision. A judge, or court as a whole, may sometimes go beyond the facts of a particular case and give an *opinion* on some connected matter, which is intended to be of guidance in future cases. Such an opinion is known as an *obiter dictum*, and may be persuasive, but not binding, on other courts in a future case. Such *obiter dicta* are often made where an important point has arisen from the arguments in an appeal case but that point has not been directly raised by either party to the case.

In some cases, particularly those which go to the House of Lords, the *dissenting* judgment—that is, the speech of a judge who does not agree with his/her fellow judges on the bench—can also be very instructive and it is not uncommon for those judgments to become law through Acts of Parliament at a later date (see, for example, Lord Mustill's speech in the 'Spanner trial' involving sado-masochism (*R v Brown* [1993] 2 All ER 75, at 101)).

Where a case decision becomes authoritative or binding, it is a 'reported' (**see para. 1.4.3**) or 'decided' case. Such cases are often referred to as *stated cases*, a description which is inaccurate and also misleading as stated cases are a very specific form of appeal to the Queen's Bench Divisional Court (**see chapter 2**).

1.4.2 Human Rights Act 1998

Introduction

The Human Rights Act 1998 introduces into English law most of the rights protected by the European Convention for the Protection of Human Rights and Fundamental Freedoms.

The 1998 Act creates a statutory general requirement that all past and future legislation be read and given effect in a way that is compatible with the Convention (s. 3).

Briefly, in relation to evidence and procedure, the 1998 Act will have the following effects. The courts must:

- decide cases having regard to the compatibility of their decision with Convention rights (s. 6(1));

- interpret existing and future legislation in conformity with the Convention (s. 3); and

- take account of Strasbourg case law where relevant (s. 2(1)).

If a statute or statutory instrument is clear in its terms and not compatible with the Convention, the courts will not give effect to the Convention even though this may result in a breach of a Convention right. This in effect preserves Parliamentary sovereignty (s. 3(2)(b) and (c)) and is different from the position with *EU* law where any incompatible domestic legislation will be 'superseded' by EU legislation. However, the higher courts have the power to issue 'declarations of incompatibility', and a fast-track procedure has been put in place so that the government can legislate to remedy any incompatibility (ss. 4 and 10 and sch. 2).

In relation to taking account of Strasbourg case law the obligation on UK courts is considered less than an obligation to adopt or apply it (*R v Davis* [2001] 1 Cr App R 115). In *Tyrer* v *United Kingdom* (1978) 2 EHRR 1 it was recognised that the Convention was a 'living instrument which must be interpreted in the light of present day conditions'. Therefore it may well be that the decision of an earlier case may not be relevant where factors have changed over time. See also *R (Anderson)* v *Secretary of State for the Home Department* (2002) *The Times*, 26 November).

Convention Rights

As indicated in the introduction above, the 1998 Act will have considerable effect on the police but more especially on the courts and their procedures.

This Manual is concerned with those rights that impact directly on 'evidence and procedure'. The Convention rights are contained within sch. 1, part I of the Human Rights Act 1998 (**see General Police Duties**).

1.4.3 | **Law Reports**

The authority of judicial precedents dates from the beginning of modern law reporting in the eighteenth century. Until 1865, there were numerous private reports, each series published under the name of the reporter, and which are still occasionally referred to today. Since 1865, the Incorporated Council of Law Reporting in England and Wales has published the series known as 'The Law Reports'. These are cited according to the court (e.g. Appeal Court; Queen's Bench Divisional Court) in which the case was heard and the year in which the case is reported (e.g. *R* v *Brown* [1994] 1 AC 212; *R* v *Bryant* [1979] QB 108).

These reports are now supplemented by various commercial series, of which the best known are:

- Criminal Appeal Reports (e.g. *R* v *Bray* (1988) 88 Cr App R 354);

- Justice of the Peace Reports (e.g. *R* v *Britzman* (1983) 147 JP 531);

- All England Law Reports (e.g. *R* v *Bryce* [1992] 4 All ER 567);

- Weekly Law Reports (e.g. *R* v *Khan* [1996] 3 WLR 162);

- Criminal Law Review (e.g. *R* v *Deakin* [1972] Crim LR 781).

The examples shown in parenthesis are how cases are usually referenced (cited) in law texts. The numbers which follow the date in a reported case are simply the *volume*, and then the *page* where the report begins, or the page where the relevant speech of the judge can be found. Many important cases can be found in a number of different reports, though decisions of the House of Lords are usually to be found in the Appeal Cases (AC).

When researching a legal reference it is worth remembering that many authors in criminal law texts refer simply to the surname or family name of the defendant (e.g. *Deakin* and not '*R* v *Deakin*').

In relation to the European Court of Human Rights, cases are cited in relation to the appellant and country concerned, e.g. *Campbell and Fell* v *United Kingdom* (1984) 7 EHRR 195.

Individual judgments and decisions are published by the Council of Europe under the title, *Publications of the European Court of Human Rights*. In the UK, the best source available is the *European Human Rights Reports* (EHRR) which publishes all the Court judgments and the important decisions of the Commission.

Current decisions and judgments can be found on the Internet at the Court's website: www.echr.coe.int/

(Note that the European Commission of Human Rights ceased to exist in November 1998 and all cases are now dealt with by the European Court of Human Rights.)

In addition to the above reports, cases are also published in some newspapers, e.g. *The Times* and the *Independent*. All the reports are written by reporters from the Incorporated Council of Law Reporting for England and Wales and may be cited in court as and when necessary.

Other reports of cases which may appear in newspapers for their general news value are *not* 'reported' cases and this often causes frustration when trying to look up a particular case that has appeared in the press.

2 The courts

2.1 ## Introduction

The nature of an offence will determine in which court a case is heard. In England and Wales offences can be tried in either the magistrates' court or the Crown Court. Cases tried in the magistrates' court are tried by either a district judge (magistrates' courts), who is a qualified lawyer, or a panel of lay magistrates (**see para. 2.8**). In the magistrates' court the magistrates decide on questions of law and fact. Cases tried in the Crown Court are presided over by a judge, who is a qualified lawyer; he/she decides on any points of law while questions of fact are decided by a jury (**see para. 2.10**). All cases will start with the defendant appearing at the magistrates' court who will either deal with the matter themselves or commit the case to the Crown Court for trial or, on occasions, for sentence for either way offences. For all indictable only offences, they will send them straight to the Crown Court.

Which court the accused goes before will depend on the offences charged and the seriousness of the offence. The nature of the particular court is also important in terms of sentencing. A magistrates' court can only ever give a maximum prison sentence of 6 months which may be doubled to 12 months when sentencing for two or more either way offences and there are also limits on the size of the fine that can be given. The Crown Court has much wider powers of sentencing, which is another factor when deciding which of the two courts will deal with an either way case.

This chapter also examines the role of both the European Court of Human Rights and the International Criminal Court.

2.2 ## Categories of Trial

Offences are categorised in three groups:

- summary offences
- indictable offences
- either way offences.

2.2.1 ### Summary Offences

These offences tend to be considered as less 'serious' in the eyes of the law (although not in the eyes of the victim!) and can only be tried in the magistrates' court, where the penalties are less severe. When an offender is charged with linked/connected either way or indictable offences, which go to the Crown Court, these lesser offences may also go to the Crown Court where they are not generally pursued.

Indictable Offences

These offences are considered to be the more serious offences and must be dealt with in the Crown Court whether the person pleads guilty or not. There are no committal proceedings for indictable-only offences (ss. 51 and 52 and sch. 3 to the Crime and Disorder Act 1998); a much quicker and simple procedure is followed called 'sending for trial'.

Either Way Offences

Plea Before Venue

Where the offence is an either way offence, the defendant will be asked if he/she is prepared to indicate his/her plea. If the indication is a guilty plea, then as a general rule the case will be dealt with in the magistrates' court and should proceed to sentence. However, the magistrates may commit the defendant to the Crown Court where the offence itself is too serious and/or where the defendant's previous convictions are too serious.

Where the defendant indicates a not guilty plea, or refuses to indicate a plea, the next stage in the procedure is the mode of trial enquiry.

Mode of Trial Hearing

The object of this hearing is to determine whether the case should be dealt with by a magistrates' court or by the Crown Court. The magistrates decide initially whether or not to deal with the case basing their decision mainly on the seriousness of the offence and whether their powers of punishment are adequate. They will hear representations from both the prosecution and the defence. If they decide not to deal with the case it will be committed to the Crown Court. Where the magistrates accept jurisdiction, the defendant has the right to choose/elect between being dealt within the magistrates' court or the Crown Court.

A magistrates' court dealing with the trial of an either way offence may, on conviction of the defendant, commit them to the Crown Court for sentencing in certain circumstances. These circumstances are usually linked to the seriousness of the offence and/or the seriousness of the defendant's previous convictions which the magistrates will not usually be aware of until the end of the trial.

The *Practice Direction (criminal: consolidated)* [2002] 3 All ER 904, para. 51 (mode of trial), provides guidelines in relation to where either way offences should be tried. The guidelines provide that generally either way offences should be tried summarily unless certain conditions set out in the guidelines apply or the magistrates consider their sentencing powers are insufficient.

Jurisdiction to Deal with Offences Summarily

Section 2 of the Magistrates' Courts Act 1980 states:

(1) A magistrates' court for a commission area shall have jurisdiction to try all summary offences committed within the commission area.

(2) Where a person charged with a summary offence appears or is brought before a magistrates' court in answer to a summons issued under paragraph (b) of section 1(2) above, or under a warrant issued under that paragraph, the court shall have jurisdiction to try the offence.

(3) A magistrates' court for a commission area shall have jurisdiction as examining justices over any offence committed by a person who appears or is brought before the court, whether or not the offence was committed within the commission area.

(4) Subject to sections 18 to 22 . . . and any other enactment (wherever contained) relating to the mode of trial of offences triable either way, a magistrates' court shall have jurisdiction to try sum-

marily an offence triable either way in any case in which under subsection (3) above it would have jurisdiction as examining justices.

(5) [Relates to summary trial of indictable offences alleged against juveniles.]

(6) A magistrates' court for any area by which a person is tried for an offence shall have jurisdiction to try him for any summary offence for which he could be tried by a magistrates' court for any other area.

(7) Nothing in this section shall affect any jurisdiction over offences conferred on a magistrates' court by any enactment not contained in this Act.

KEYNOTE

In other words, s. 2 allows a magistrates' court which already has jurisdiction regarding an offence, to deal with any other summary offence alleged against the defendant.

Note that s. 1 of the 1980 Act states:

(2) A justice of the peace for an area to which this section applies may issue a summons or warrant under this section—

. . .

(b) if it appears to the justice necessary or expedient, with a view to the better administration of justice, that the person charged should be tried jointly with, or in the same place as, some other person who is charged with an offence, and who is in custody, or is being or is to be proceeded against, within the area . . .

2.3.1   Jurisdiction to Deal with Offences on Boundaries and Journeys

Section 3 of the Magistrates' Courts Act 1980 states:

(1) Where an offence has been committed on the boundary between two or more areas to which this section applies, or within 500 yards of such a boundary, or in any harbour, river, arm of the sea or other water lying between two or more such areas, the offence may be treated for the purposes of the preceding provisions of this Act as having been committed in any of those areas.

(2) An offence begun in one area to which this section applies and completed in another may be treated for the purposes of the preceding provisions of this Act as having been wholly committed in either.

(3) Where an offence has been committed on any person, or on or in respect of any property, in or on a vehicle or vessel engaged on any journey or voyage through two or more areas to which this section applies, the offence may be treated for the purposes of the preceding provisions of this Act as having been committed in any one of those areas; and where the side or any part of a road or any water along which the vehicle or vessel passed in the course of the journey or voyage forms the boundary between two or more areas to which this section applies, the offence may be treated for the purposes of the preceding provisions of this Act as having been committed in any of those areas.

(4) The areas to which this section applies are any commission areas.

KEYNOTE

Normally an offence takes place where it is completed but, where the special circumstances relating to boundaries and journeys apply, s. 3 extends the jurisdiction.

The 500 yards distance should be measured in a straight line (or as the crow flies).

Other useful points concerning s. 3 include:

- The offence of taking excessive hackney carriage/taxi fares is committed where the taking occurred in the jurisdiction, although the journey may have begun in another jurisdiction.

- A letter posted in one jurisdiction for the purpose of obtaining money by false pretences (**see Crime, chapter 13**), and delivered in another jurisdiction may be prosecuted in either.

- The mere unlawful use of a vehicle such as contravening an operators' licence (see Road Traffic, chapter 13) is not 'an offence . . . committed . . . on or in respect of any property in or on a vehicle' for the purposes of s. 3(3) above. Section 3(3) applies to offences in respect of property (such as theft or damage, see Crime, chapters 12 and 14) in or on a vehicle.

2.4 Offences Committed by Juveniles

Generally offences committed by juveniles are dealt with in the youth court, which is part of the magistrates' court. A juvenile is any person under the age of 18. Apart from homicide (**see Crime, chapter 5**) and a few specific exceptions outlined below, no other charge against such a person can be heard anywhere other than at a youth court. The general principle is that juveniles should be tried in the youth court and as a result they are not given the option of electing trial by jury. The public do not have access to youth courts and there is also a restriction on what the press can publicise about cases involving juveniles. It is for this reason that many news stories carry a section which says that the writer or broadcaster has been unable to identify the defendant (or others) for 'legal reasons'. (For the situation regarding anonymity of victims of sexual offences, **see Crime, chapter 10**.)

Section 24 of the Magistrates' Courts Act 1980 provides three instances where a person under the age of 18 years must be tried on indictment or where the magistrates have a discretion to deal with the accused or commit him/her for trial:

- Where a juvenile is charged with murder or manslaughter they must be tried on indictment in the Crown Court.

- Where a juvenile is charged with an indictable offence and the youth court or magistrates' court consider their sentencing powers insufficient, they may commit the juvenile for trial on indictment in the Crown Court.

- Where a juvenile is jointly charged with an adult and the adult is going to be tried on indictment, the magistrates' court may commit the juvenile for trial with the adult in the Crown Court.

If the adult is committed to the Crown Court, it is for the magistrates to decide whether the juvenile should similarly be committed or whether the case should be dealt with in the youth court.

In *R* v *Uxbridge Youth Court, ex parte H* (1998) *The Times*, 7 April, it was held that s. 48 of the Children and Young Persons Act 1933, as amended, prohibited any charge against a child or young person being heard by a court of summary jurisdiction other than a youth court.

The youth court can deal with a defendant who attains the age of 18 after charge and remit him/her to the magistrates' court for sentence (s. 47 of the Crime and Disorder Act 1998).

Additionally, the youth court can commit a young person to the Crown Court for trial where it is of the opinion that if the young person was found guilty it could not rule out the possibility of a period of detention in accordance with the terms of s. 90 (offenders who commit murder when under 18: duty to detain at Her Majesty's pleasure) and s. 91 (offenders under 18 convicted of certain serious offences: power to detain for specified periods) of the Powers of Criminal Courts (Sentencing) Act 2000.

In relation to s. 24 of the Magistrates' Courts Act 1980 and s. 91 of the Powers of Criminal Courts (Sentencing) Act 2000, it was held in *R (on the application of D)* v *Manchester City Youth Court* (2001) 166 JP 15 that these sections only applied to offences of such gravity that a court was likely to consider a sentence of at least two years' detention.

In *R v Devizes Youth Court, ex parte A* (2000) 164 JP 330, a 12-year-old was committed to the Crown Court for trial as the court considered the allegation came within the terms of s. 53(2)(a) of the Children and Young Persons Act 1933 (as replaced by ss. 90 and 96 of the Powers of Criminal Courts (Sentencing) Act 2000). It was contended that the actions of the youth court were contrary to Article 6 of the European Convention on Human Rights. It was held that this was not the case and that any matters in relation to a breach of Article 6 would be considered by a judge in the Crown Court and could not affect the way in which justices carried out their duty under English law.

In another case it was contended that an 11-year-old boy with learning difficulties, who was convicted in the Crown Court of attempted robbery and sentenced to 30 months' detention, should not have been tried in that court and that this was in contravention of Articles 3 and 6 of the European Convention. It was held that the judge was entitled to exercise his discretion as to whether a 'child' should be tried in the Crown Court and it was not therefore in breach of the Convention (*R v C (A Juvenile)* (2000) *The Times*, 5 July).

2.5 | Limitation on Proceedings

In the law of England and Wales the general rule is that there is no restriction on the time which may elapse between the commission of an offence and the commencement of a prosecution for it. However, there are a number of statutory provisions prohibiting proceedings once a certain time has elapsed. The relevant provisions are outlined below.

2.5.1 | Summary Offences

Section 127 of the Magistrates' Courts Act 1980 states:

(1) Except as otherwise expressly provided by any enactment and subject to subsection (2) below, a magistrates' court shall not try an information or hear a complaint unless the information was laid, or the complaint made, within 6 months from the time when the offence was committed, or the matter of complaint arose.

KEYNOTE

Examples of offences which provide otherwise are the summary offences under s. 143 of the Road Traffic Act 1988 (uninsured use of a motor vehicle) and s. 8 of the Vehicles (Excise) Act 1971 (using and keeping a vehicle without an excise licence), where proceedings can be instituted up to and including three years after the commission of the offence (for both offences, see Road Traffic, chapters 6 and 12).

2.5.2 | Indictable Offences (Either Way and Indictable Only)

Section 127 of the Magistrates' Courts Act 1980 states:

(2) Nothing in—
    (a) subsection (1) above; or
    (b) subject to subsection (4) below, any other enactment (however framed or worded) which, as regards any offence to which it applies, would but for this section impose a time-limit on the power of a magistrates' court to try an information summarily or impose a limitation on the time for taking summary proceedings,

shall apply in relation to any indictable offence.

(3) Without prejudice to the generality of paragraph (b) of subsection (2) above, that paragraph includes enactments which impose a time-limit that applies only in certain circumstances (for

example, where the proceedings are not instituted by or with the consent of the Director of Public Prosecutions or some other specified authority).

(4) Where, as regards any indictable offence, there is imposed by any enactment (however framed or worded, and whether falling within subsection (2)(b) above or not) a limitation on the time for taking proceedings on indictment for that offence no summary proceedings for that offence shall be taken after the latest time for taking proceedings on indictment.

There are a number of other statutory provisions in relation to time-limits and these include:

- The Sexual Offences Act 1956, sch. 2, para. 10, which provides that prosecutions for unlawful sexual intercourse with a girl under 16 contrary to s. 6 of the 1956 Act must be commenced within 12 months.

- The Sexual Offences Act 1967, s. 7, which provides that prosecutions for gross indecency between men and buggery where no assault is involved and the 'victim' is 16 or over must be commenced within 12 months.

(For both offences, **see Crime, chapter 10.**)

In the case of an offence triable either way, where there is no time-limit for taking proceedings on indictment, there is no time-limit for summary proceedings. Where there is a time-limit on indictment, summary proceedings cannot be taken once the time-limit bars proceedings on indictment.

The definition of 'indictable offence' under s. 64(1)(a) of the Criminal Law Act 1977 includes offences triable either way. Section 127 excludes purely indictable offences and offences triable either way from the operation of s. 127(1) of the Magistrates' Courts Act 1980 (which prohibits summary trial where the information is not laid within six months of the offence being committed). Consequently, an offence triable either way such as theft, contrary to ss. 1 to 7 of the Theft Act 1968 (**see Crime, chapter 12**) can still be tried summarily after the six-month limitation has expired.

The day on which the offence etc. arose is not to be included when determining the time-limit.

The time runs from the *commission of the offence*, not from the date of its discovery. A 'month' means a calendar month and a month ends at midnight on the day of the next month which has the same number as the day on which the offence was committed. For example, X commits a driving licence offence at 10 am on 24 September; the information should be laid before midnight on 24 March the following year, i.e. within six months.

2.6 Appeals

2.6.1 Introduction

A person has a right of appeal from the magistrates' court to the Crown Court, following a plea of not guilty, against either conviction and/or sentence and, following a guilty plea, against sentence (Magistrates' Courts Act 1980, s. 108(1)). Both the defence and prosecution have a right to appeal to the Crown Court or Divisional Court of the Queen's Bench Division, by way of 'case stated'; where the magistrates' court proceedings are questioned on the ground that they were wrong in law or in excess of their jurisdiction (Magistrates' Courts Act 1980, s. 111(1)).

Appeals from the Crown Court to the Court of Appeal (Criminal Division) normally require leave to be heard unless it is purely an appeal on a point of law. Leave is also required for appeals to the House of Lords which will usually be granted where the appeal raises a question of law of general public importance.

Whether an appeal, against conviction, to the Court of Appeal will be successful is governed by s. 2 of the Criminal Appeal Act 1968, as amended by the Criminal Appeal Act 1995, which states:

(1) Subject to the provisions of this Act, the Court of Appeal—
    (a) shall allow an appeal against conviction if they think that the conviction is unsafe; and
    (b) shall dismiss such an appeal in any other case.

This does not mean that every time a mistake has been made during a trial that a conviction must be overturned. The ultimate question is whether the conviction is *unsafe* (*Stafford* v *DPP* [1974] AC 878). If the court take the view that it is, and that there has been a 'miscarriage of justice', the conviction will not stand. The approach taken by the Court of Appeal is shown in the judgment of *R* v *Cohen* (1909) 2 Cr App R 197, where the court explained:

> There is such a miscarriage of justice not only where the court comes to the conclusion that the verdict of guilty was wrong, but also when it is of opinion that the mistake of fact or omission on the part of the judge may reasonably be considered to have brought about that verdict, and when, on the whole facts and with a correct direction, the jury might fairly and reasonably have found the appellant not guilty. Then there has been not only a miscarriage of justice but a substantial one, because the appellant has lost the chance which was fairly open to him of being acquitted . . . . If, however, the court in such a case comes to the conclusion that, on the whole of the facts and with a correct direction, the only reasonable and proper verdict would be one of guilty, there is no miscarriage of justice, or at all events no substantial miscarriage of justice . . .

The effect of this approach is that, on occasions, even if it concludes that certain evidence was wrongly admitted or that a judge failed to do something relevant to the defendant's trial, the Court of Appeal may still refuse to overturn the conviction.

Where fresh evidence is received on an appeal against conviction, the correct test to be applied by the Court of Appeal, in determining whether to allow the appeal, was the effect of the evidence on the minds of the members of the court. The question for its consideration was whether the conviction was safe and not whether the accused was guilty (*R* v *Pendleton* [2002] 1 All ER 524).

Where an appellant wishes the Court of Appeal to receive fresh evidence under s. 23 of the Criminal Appeal Act 1968 and the circumstances give rise to the need for a lengthy or complex explanation of why the evidence was not admitted at the original trial, an affidavit or signed statement from the appellant or his/her solicitor, setting out the grounds relied on, should be supplied to the court (*R* v *T* (1998) *The Times*, 30 June).

In *R* v *Hanratty* [2002] 3 All ER 534, it was held that the Court of Appeal could admit fresh evidence if it would assist it to achieve justice irrespective that the evidence was not adduced to rebut fresh evidence introduced by the defence. In this case DNA evidence was admitted under s. 23 which made a strong case even stronger and established beyond doubt that Hanratty was the murderer.

Appeals to the House of Lords, from a decision of the Criminal Division of the Court of Appeal, can be by the prosecution and defence. Before an appeal can be heard in the House of Lords the Court of Appeal must certify that the decision which is sought to appeal involves a point of law of general public importance. In addition either the Court of Appeal or the House of Lords believes the point of law is one that ought to be considered by the House of Lords (Criminal Appeal Act 1968, s. 33).

In relation to appeal proceedings, Article 6 of the European Convention on Human Rights (right to a fair trial) applies. For the purpose of satisfying the requirements of Article 6 it is sufficient, after hearing the evidence and submissions, for the court to determine whether the applicant's convictions were safe and satisfactory. It has also been held that the 'presumption of innocence' does not apply in appeal proceedings (*Callaghan* v *United Kingdom* (1989)

60 DR 296). An appeal can be heard in the absence of the defendant and again this is not in breach of Article 6 (*Prinz* v *Austria* (2001) 31EHRR12).

2.6.2

The Appeals Process

Cases can be appealed for a number of reasons:

- questions of fact
- questions of law
- mixed questions of fact and law
- level of sentence.

Questions of Fact

This is an appeal on the basis that the facts do not support the decision that has been reached. These appeals are unlikely to succeed as an appellate court will not change a decision of fact unless it feels that no reasonable tribunal could have reached the decision made by the trial court.

As magistrates are the judges of questions of *fact* in any summary trial (**see para. 1.4**). their interpretation of what happened may be affected by local conditions and different magistrates' courts may arrive at different decisions on the same facts. Take an example of a person in a street shouting the word 'scab'. A magistrates' court in South Yorkshire may be ready to accept that the word 'scab' is in fact 'insulting' for the purposes of public order legislation (**see General Police Duties, chapter 4**), while a magistrates' court in Suffolk may not. As the decisions of magistrates' courts are not binding on each other and as the decision as to what is 'insulting' is a question of fact, there is little likelihood of a successful appeal against such a decision; there is also little likelihood of that decision being followed by other courts.

The Crown Court is not bound by the findings of fact by the magistrates' court and so where the defendant appeals against sentence to the Crown Court, the Crown Court may determine the appeal on a different factual basis to that accepted by the magistrates. Where the Crown Court is minded to reflect the view taken by the magistrates, and that view was unfavourable to the defendant, the Crown Court should warn the defendant that this is so and give him/her the opportunity to challenge the factual basis the Crown Court wishes to adopt (*Bussey* v *Chief Constable of Suffolk* [1999] 1 Cr App R (S) 125).

Questions of Law

Unlike questions of fact (which are decided by the jury) questions of law are determined by the trial judge or judges. Of course, in a magistrates' court, the magistrate(s) decides on both questions and therefore, to understand an appeal proceeding from a magistrates' court, it is first necessary to understand whether that appeal is based on a question of fact or law. An appeal on a question of law is one where a party to the proceedings wishes a higher court to give a ruling on the *interpretation* or *application* of the law, for instance, what 'recklessness' means in relation to criminal damage (**see Crime, chapter 1**) or, in the example above, i.e. the word 'scab', whether 'insulting' behaviour is covered by the Public Order Act 1986.

Having considered the question of law, the higher court will then give a judgment on the point. This will either allow the original court hearing the case to continue with it or, in some circumstances, allow the appeal court to decide the outcome of the case.

Mixed Questions of Fact and Law

As the heading suggests, this is where a party to the proceedings appeals on an issue which requires the appeal court to consider both a question of fact and a point of law. This often involves the court being asked to make a finding, first on the facts and then to interpret them in relation to the law. This allows parties to take a case to the appeal court on occasions where, if it were just a question of fact, an appeal would not be allowed.

The 'scab' example above might be broken down as follows:

- whether the word 'scab' can be insulting—question of *fact*;
- whether the word 'scab' was in fact used by a defendant on a certain date—question of *fact*;
- whether 'insulting' behaviour is covered by the Public Order Act 1986—question of *law*;
- whether, simply by shouting 'scab' in an empty street, a defendant commits the entire offence under s. 4 of the Public Order Act 1986—question *of fact and law*.

Level of Sentence

The courts will also hear appeals on the level of sentence given to a convicted person.

Where an offender gives information, enabling serious criminal activity to be stopped and serious criminals to be brought to book, after he/she has been sentenced, the Court of Appeal will not normally take account of the information. However, if the offender expresses willingness to help prior to sentence but the value of help thereafter given greatly exceeds the help anticipated by the sentence, the Court of Appeal can adjust the sentence to reflect the value of the help given after sentence (*R v A (Informer: Reduction of Sentence)* [1999] 1 Cr App R (S) 52).

2.6.3 Appeal by Prosecution

The Attorney-General may refer two types of case to the Court of Appeal. The first type is where a person has been acquitted in the Crown Court and the prosecution wish to test the correctness of a ruling of law during the course of the trial (Criminal Justice Act 1972, s. 36). The importance of this is to ensure that a potentially false decision of law does not affect future decisions of other courts (*Attorney-General's Reference (No. 1 of 1975)* [1975] 1 QB 773). In this type of case the accused person remains acquitted whatever the outcome of the appeal. (For the procedure to be adopted on making a reference, see the Criminal Appeal (Reference of Points of Law) Rules 1973 (SI 1973 No. 1114.))

The other type of case, which may be referred to the Court of Appeal, is where the Attorney-General considers an offender was sentenced unduly leniently by the Crown Court and requires a review of the sentence. The Criminal Justice Act 1988, ss. 35 and 36, set out the grounds for this review process. The only cases which can be referred by the Attorney-General are:

- offences which are triable only on indictment;
- offences which are triable either way and which have been specified in a statutory instrument.

The offences specified by statutory instrument at the time of writing are:

- threats to kill;
- indecent assault;
- cruelty to a child under 16 years;
- attempts to commit or incite the offences above.

(See Reviews of Sentencing Order 1994 (SI 1994 No. 119).)

The procedure also includes some serious fraud cases (Reviews of Sentencing Order 1995 (SI 1995 No. 10)).

In each case, leave of the Court of Appeal is required before a referral and the Attorney-General must consider that the offender's sentence was unduly lenient (this would include occasions where the judge failed to impose a sentence as required by the Powers of Criminal Courts (Sentencing) Act 2000).

In addition, the Court of Appeal may increase a sentence despite the fact that the judge had indicated that he/she did not intend to impose a custodial sentence and had not done so (*Attorney-General's Reference (Nos 86 and 87 of 1999)* [2001] 1 Cr App R (S) 141).

2.6.4   Judicial Review

Judicial review is a method of challenging decisions made by administrative bodies and office holders such as the police service. Cases can range from policy decisions made by the organisation—such as the decision not to prosecute someone—to decisions made by individual supervisors (e.g. the cautioning of a juvenile). The circumstances under which a matter can go before the High Court for judicial review are quite limited. Generally, applications for judicial review can only proceed if there is no other method by which to appeal the decision. An application for judicial review must be made as soon as reasonably practicable and generally within three months of the decision. In reviewing the decision the High Court can look at whether the administrative body or individual was acting within the law when making that decision; it will also consider whether the decision was a reasonable one and whether the common law rules of natural justice were applied.

Whether a decision was made within the law will be determined by a number of features surrounding the decision-making process. These would include:

- Whether the organisation or individual actually had the authority or power to make the decision.

- What procedure was followed and whether that procedure observed the requirements of 'natural justice'.

- Whether the decision-maker exercised his/her own discretion or whether he/she delegated or fettered that discretion in a way which was not permitted in law.

This is one reason why the documentation and recording of any significant decision-making procedure is important.

In reviewing whether or not a decision is 'reasonable' the court will consider whether the decision is one that any reasonable person in the position of the decision-maker could have made, applying the *Wednesbury* principles (from the case of *Associated Provincial Picture Houses Ltd* v *Wednesbury Corporation* [1948] 1 KB 223). In reviewing the reasonableness of a decision, the court is not asking whether *it* would have made that decision itself; it is asking whether the decision was lawfully and reasonably made in the circumstances. Therefore it would be possible for conflicting decisions made under similar circumstances to be upheld provided both were lawful and reasonable. If the court considers that a decision is unreasonable or unlawful it can make a declaration to that effect.

The declaration can be made in one of three ways: a mandatory order instructing the administrative body to perform a function that it is required to perform (i.e., a chief officer must consider each case involving officers convicted of drink-driving on its merits and not have a blanket policy requiring them to resign); a quashing order where the court quashes the earlier decision (e.g. a caution given to a juvenile where there was insufficient evidence to obtain a conviction); a prohibiting order directing the administrative body *not* to perform an act which the court has found to be unlawful or outside the body's power (*Practice Direction (Administrative Court: Establishment)* [2000] 1 WLR 1654).

The key points to remember are that applications for judicial review are made to the High Court, they will only be heard if there are no other avenues of appeal available and that the application has been made as soon as reasonably practicable.

Following the case of *Smith and Grady* v *UK* (2000) 29 EHRR 493 where the Court noted that judicial review did not allow the applicants to challenge the armed forces ban as being contrary to the European Convention on Human Rights and the requirement for the courts to apply the Convention, the *Wednesbury* principles will be replaced by more stringent tests under human rights law.

2.7 | Rules of Construction

2.7.1 | Interpretation of Statutes

Statutes are to be construed according to the intentions of Parliament. Such intentions can only be assumed from the words used in the Act, except where there is imprecision or ambiguity.

Where imprecision or ambiguity exists the following rules are applied, which are derived from common law sources, to assist in interpretation:

- The 'ordinary meaning' of words is to be used (as per the dictionary), read in the context of the statute in which they appear.

- The interpretation should suppress the 'mischief' being dealt with by the legislation. (For example, in the Criminal Damage Act 1971, any interpretation issue should be decided in such a way as to prevent criminal damage and provide a punishment for criminal damage.)

- The interpretation should not lead to unreasonable, inconvenient, absurd or inconsistent results.

2.7.2 | *Ejusdem Generis* Rule

Ejusdem generis means of the same kind or nature.

Numerous Acts of Parliament provide lists of specifically named things or places etc. followed by a generalisation, e.g. 'all signals, warning sign posts, direction posts, signs or other devices'. Where such lists are shown in an Act, the 'generalisation' will be construed by the courts in the light of the words which appear alongside it. This rule of construction is known as the *ejusdem* (pronounced 'use-dem') *generis* rule. In the example above, the expression 'other devices' will be interpreted as being in the same class as those other words ('signals, warning posts' etc.) which appear alongside it; the expression could not be construed as meaning *any* 'other device', say, a breathalyser machine, even though a literal interpretation of 'other devices' might.

2.7.3 | *De Minimis* Rule

A further rule of construction commonly used by the courts is the *de minimis* rule. This rule (fully named *de minimis non curat lex*—'the law is not concerned with trifling matters') means that courts will not deal with trivial infringements of the law. An example of the *de minimis* rule might be where a motorist displays a valid 'pay-and-display' parking ticket clearly in the window of their car; although the requirements on the ticket may say that it must be affixed to the *windshield*. It is likely that an attempt to enforce a penalty against the motorist would fail under the *de minimis* rule (it would probably also fail the test of construction looking at the 'mischief' intended to be addressed by the parking regulations, see para. **2.7.1**). Some offences of 'absolute' liability, however, may be prosecuted for even the most minor infringement (**see Crime, chapter 1**).

2.7.4 The Interpretation Act 1978

The Interpretation Act 1978 deals with particular words which are in common usage.

'Month' means calendar month. 'Week' can mean a calendar week beginning on a Sunday and ending on the following Saturday or any period of seven days. The onus is on the court to interpret the word according to the appropriate statute.

'Day' can mean between sunrise and sunset as well as from midnight to midnight. The length of time between sunrise and the next sunset is a question of fact and obviously varies according to locality.

Masculine includes feminine and vice versa, and singular includes plural and vice versa.

Service by post is deemed effective at the time the letter would be delivered in the ordinary course of the post, unless the contrary is proved.

2.8 Magistrates' Courts

Magistrates' courts consist of justices of the peace, the majority of whom are unpaid lay men and women. A minority of justices are paid and are known as district judges (magistrates' courts) and deputy district judges (magistrates' courts) (**see para. 2.8.3**).

The law relating to justices and magistrates' courts is contained principally in the following legislation:

- Justices of the Peace Act 1997 which deals with appointment, removal etc. of justices and the organisation of magistrates' courts.
- Magistrates' Courts Act 1980 which deals with the jurisdiction and powers of the courts.
- Magistrates' Courts Rules 1981 (SI 1981 No. 552) which deals with practice and procedure.

2.8.1 Justices of the Peace

Justices of the peace are appointed to act for a particular county, and are then assigned to the bench for one of the petty sessions areas into which the county is divided. A justice would normally sit only in the magistrates' court for his/her petty sessions area.

The number of justices sitting to deal with a case as a magistrates' court shall not be greater than three but this does not apply when the court is sitting as a youth court, proceedings court or a licensing or betting licensing committee (r. 3 of the Justices of the Peace (Size and Chairmanship of Bench) Rules 2002 (SI 2002 No. 193)).

However, with the intention of enhancing the ability of the magistrates' court to manage business expeditiously, s. 49(1) of the Crime and Disorder Act 1998 provides powers which can be exercised by a single justice, for example, to impose, extend or vary bail conditions, to withdraw an information, to dismiss a case where the prosecution offers no evidence, etc.

Justices are generally appointed by the Lord Chancellor 'on behalf and in the name of Her Majesty' (Justices of the Peace Act 1997, s. 5(1)), following a recommendation from the local advisory committees which are located in each county. They are not required to possess any legal or other qualification though they are obliged to attend a course of basic instruction within 12 months of appointment. In the case of Lancashire, Greater Manchester and Merseyside, justices are appointed by the Chancellor of the Duchy of Lancaster (s. 26 of the 1997 Act, as amended by the Access to the Justice Act 1999).

Justices are not paid a salary for their work but s. 10 of the Justices of the Peace Act 1997 does provide for them to receive travel and subsistence allowance and compensation for loss of earnings, etc.

2.8.2 Justices' Clerks

The duties of a justices' clerk consist of sitting in court with the justices during the conduct of proceedings and advising the justices (whether in court or out of court) on matters of law, practice and procedure (*Practice Direction (criminal: consolidated)* [2002] 3 All ER 904, para. 55). Administrative and accounting functions (including the collection of fines and fees) are the responsibility of the justices' chief executives.

The powers of a single justice provided by s. 49(1) of the Crime and Disorder Act 1998 may also be done by a justices' clerk, with a few exceptions (s. 49(2)(a)):

• to extend, impose or vary bail conditions without the consent of the prosecutor and accused;

• to give an indication of the seriousness of an offence for the purposes of a pre-sentence report;

• to remand an accused in custody for a medical report or, without the consent of the prosecutor and accused, remand an accused on bail for those purposes on conditions other than those (if any) previously imposed;

• to prohibit the publication of matters disclosed or exempted from disclosure in court;

• to give, vary or revoke orders for the separate or joint trials in the case of two or more accused or two or more informations, without the consent of the parties

(s. 49(3)).

A justices' clerk must be a barrister or solicitor of at least five years' standing, or a barrister or solicitor who has served for not less than five years as assistant to a justices' clerk. They are appointed by the magistrates' courts committee for the county and the Lord Chancellor's approval is required.

Some of the functions exercisable by a justices' clerk may also be exercised by a person appointed by the magistrates' court to assist the clerk (s. 45(2) of the Justices of the Peace Act 1997 and the Justices' Clerks Rules 1999 (SI 1999 No. 2784)). Such assistants would normally be senior members of the clerk's staff but there is no necessity for them to have any legal qualifications.

2.8.3 District and Deputy District Judges (Magistrates' Courts)

District and deputy district judges (magistrates' courts) are both paid and legally-qualified barristers or solicitors of at least seven years' standing. Their appointment is by Her Majesty on the recommendation of the Lord Chancellor.

A person appointed as a district or deputy district judge (magistrates' courts) is a justice of the peace for every commission area. One of the district judges (magistrates' courts) is designated as the senior district judge (chief magistrate).

2.9 Youth Courts

The procedures and composition of youth courts are contained in the Children and Young Persons Act 1933. Youth courts are required to sit as often as may be required in order to exercise the jurisdiction conferred on them by the 1933 Act and any other legislation (s. 47(1) of the 1933 Act).

2.9.1 | **Youth Court Panel**

Schedule 2, para. 3 to the Children and Young Persons Act 1933 requires every petty sessions area to form a youth court panel. Such panels consist of justices specially qualified for dealing with juvenile cases. Such qualification is obtained by training which is additional to a justice's ordinary training. It is only these justices who are allowed to sit in the youth court (r. 11 of the Youth Courts (Constitution) Rules 1954 (SI 1954 No. 1711)). No more than three justices can sit in the court (r. 12(1)) and wherever possible one shall be a man and one a woman (r. 12(1) and (2)). A district judge (magistrates' courts) may sit alone (r. 2).

Where the youth court decide to continue with a case and no man or woman is available to sit as a properly constituted court, the decision so to proceed must be made in open court after hearing submissions from all the parties (R v *Birmingham Youth Court, ex parte F (a minor)* [2000] Crim LR 588).

The Judicial Studies Board (JSB) publishes a *Benchbook* providing a comprehensive source of referencing covering all areas of youth court jurisdiction. It is primarily for use by lay magistrates, district judges (magistrates' courts) and youth offending team managers. It is available free on the JSB website—www.jsboard.co.uk.

2.9.2 | **Restrictions on Persons Present**

Restrictions are placed on those persons who may be present during proceedings in the youth court and this is contained in s. 47(2) of the 1933 Act which states:

(2) No person shall be present at any sitting of a youth court except—
  (a) members and officers of the court;
  (b) parties to the case before the court, their solicitors and counsel, and witnesses and other persons directly concerned in that case;
  (c) bona fide representatives of newspapers or news agencies;
  (d) such other persons as the court may specially authorise to be present.

KEYNOTE

Although the press are allowed to attend proceedings they are not permitted to report the name, address or any other detail which may lead to the identity of the juvenile concerned (s. 49(1)). There are a number of exceptions to this rule. These include where the youth court consider it necessary to avoid injustice to the juvenile or where it is necessary to secure his/her apprehension to either appear at court or be returned to custody (s. 49(5)).

The restrictions on the press identifying the juvenile defendant also apply to other juveniles who may have been concerned in the case, i.e. witnesses in the proceedings (s. 49(4)).

2.9.3 | **Attendance of Parent or Guardian**

The youth court has the power to order the juvenile's parent or guardian to attend the proceedings (s. 34A of the 1933 Act). This power equally applies to the attendance of the parent or guardian in the adult magistrates' court and Crown Court.

2.10 | **Crown Court**

The Crown Court is part of the Supreme Court and was created by the Courts Act 1971. It derives its jurisdiction from s. 1 of the Supreme Court Act 1981 which states:

(1) The Supreme Court of England and Wales shall consist of the Court of Appeal, the High Court of Justice and the Crown Court, each having such jurisdiction as is conferred on it by or under this or any other Act.

The Crown Court is a single court though it sits in many locations across England and Wales. The court has exclusive jurisdiction over trials on indictment and will normally hear cases which involve offences committed within its geographical area but there are no territorial restrictions on the cases it can hear. Section 46 of the Supreme Court Act 1981 states:

> (2) The jurisdiction of the Crown Court with respect to proceedings on indictment shall include jurisdiction of the Crown Court with respect to proceedings on indictment for offences wherever committed, and in particular proceedings on indictment for offences within the jurisdiction of the Admiralty of England.

2.10.1 Judges

Section 8 of the Supreme Court Act 1981 states:

> (1) The jurisdiction of the Crown Court shall be exercisable by—
>   (a) any judge of the High Court; or
>   (b) any circuit judge or recorder; or
>   (c) subject to and in accordance with the provisions of sections 74 and 75(2), a judge of the High Court, circuit judge or recorder sitting with not more than four justices of the peace, and any such persons when exercising the jurisdiction of the Crown Court shall be judges of the Crown Court.

All proceedings in the Crown Court must be heard and disposed of by a single judge except where a justice is permitted to sit with such a judge (s. 73(1) of the 1981 Act).

2.10.2 Modes of Address

The following guidelines relate to the address of judges in open court. Other conventions may apply when meeting a judge in chambers.

High Court judges should be addressed as 'My Lord' or 'My Lady'.

Circuit judges, recorders and deputy circuit judges should be addressed as 'Your Honour'. Exceptions to this are:

- a judge is sitting at the Central Criminal Court

- any circuit judge who holds the office of honorary Recorder of Liverpool or honorary Recorder of Manchester

who should be addressed as 'My Lord' or 'My Lady' (*Practice Direction (Judges: Modes of Address)* [1982] 1 WLR 101; *Practice Direction (Judges: Recorder of Cardiff)* [1999] 1 WLR 597).

2.10.3 Right of Audience in the Crown Court

Until the enactment of the Courts and Legal Services Act 1990 only practising barristers had a right of audience in the Crown Court. The 1990 Act introduced a statutory scheme for the definition and regulation of the rights of audience before the courts, preserving all existing rights (ss. 31 and 32) and setting up a framework for the granting of new rights (s. 27). Advocates who are not barristers can now obtain rights of audience in the Crown Court. This includes solicitors, whether employed or in private practice, provided they meet the requirements of s. 27 of the 1990 Act as amended by the Access to Justice Act 1999.

2.10.4 Juries

The general rule is that questions of law must be determined by the judge and questions of fact must be determined by the jury.

All person aged 18 to 70 are eligible for jury service if they are registered either as parliamentary or local government electors and have been ordinarily resident in the UK for any period of at least five years since attaining the age of 13.

Certain groups are ineligible for jury service: the judiciary; members of the legal profession and others concerned with the administration of justice; the clergy; the mentally disordered. Other groups are disqualified from jury service where they have been subject to specified periods of imprisonment or detention, or have been subject to a suspended sentence, community service, probation or who are on bail in criminal proceedings. Police officers are exempt for ten years after leaving the service.

The Lord Chancellor has the responsibility for summoning jurors (s. 2(1) of the Juries Act 1974) and if a person so summoned fails to attend on the date required he/she commits an offence (s. 20(1)).

A jury generally consists of 12 jurors whose role in the Crown Court is to determine the accused's guilt or innocence to which a not guilty plea has been entered. The 12 jurors are selected by ballot in open court from the panel of jurors summoned to attend on a particular date (s. 11 of the 1974 Act).

For offences in relation to the intimidation of jurors and witnesses, **see Crime**.

2.11 | Tribunals and Inquiries

2.11.1 | Tribunals

Tribunals are alternative mechanisms to the courts which provide remedies for decision making in the public sector and grievances in both central and local government.

There are 78 tribunals in England and Wales which are supervised by the courts and directly supervised by the Council on Tribunals which was created by the Tribunals and Inquiries Act 1958 (now 1992). Tribunals cover a wide area of subject matter: those that deal with the issues of the ordinary citizen (e.g. benefits, education of children, fair rents); those that perform a licensing role (e.g. Civil Aviation Authority); and those that deal with a variety of other functions.

The role of the Council of Tribunals is:

- to keep under review the constitution and working of tribunals specified in sch. 1 to the 1992 Act and from time to time report on their constitution and working;

- to consider and report in matters referred to the Council under the 1992 Act with respect to tribunals other than ordinary courts of law, whether or not specified in sch. 1 to the Act; and

- to consider and report on these matters, or matters the Council may consider to be of special importance, with respect to administrative procedures which involve or may involve the holding of a statutory inquiry by or on behalf of a Minister

(s. 1(1) of the Tribunals and Inquiries Act 1992).

This role extends to the Police Appeals Tribunal (as to which, **see General Police Duties, chapter 1**).

Tribunals are subject to the supervisory jurisdiction of the High Court under the application for judicial review procedure (**see para. 2.6.4**). They must act within their powers and are under a duty to act fairly.

2.11.2 | Inquiries

The use of statutory inquiries has grown considerably during the past few decades and are an essential government tool in dealing with large scale public controversy. There are numerous examples of the areas which such inquiries cover, e.g. building nuclear power stations, new airport terminals and extending motorways.

Non-statutory inquiries may also be established by the government to investigate an issue considered to be of public importance. The criminal justice system and particularly the police have recent experience of such non-statutory inquiries, e.g. Lord Justice Scarman's inquiry into the inner city riots of the early 1980s, to the more recent Stephen Lawrence Inquiry by Sir William Macpherson of Cluny (1999, Cm 4262).

In conducting its investigation, the inquiry may be given powers equivalent to the High Court to summon witnesses, send for documents and administer oaths. Inquiries tend to be inquisitorial and they have been formed to apportion blame.

With a view to protecting the position of persons required to give evidence at inquiries a Royal Commission on Tribunals of Inquiry, chaired by Lord Justice Salmon, was set up in 1966. The subsequent report of the Royal Commission contained six cardinal recommendations:

- Before any person becomes involved in an inquiry, the tribunal must be satisfied that there are circumstances which affect him/her and which the tribunal proposes to investigate.

- Before any person who is involved in an inquiry is called as a witness he/she should be informed of any allegations which are made against him/her and the substance of the evidence in support of them.

- Any person called to give evidence should be given an adequate opportunity of preparing his/her case and being assisted by legal advisers. His/her legal expenses should be met out of public funds.

- Any person called should have the opportunity of being examined by his/her own solicitor or counsel and of stating his/her case in public at the inquiry.

- Any material witnesses he/she wishes called at the inquiry should, if reasonably practicable, be heard.

- A witness should have the opportunity of testing, by cross-examination conducted by his/her own solicitor or counsel, any evidence which may affect him/her.

Albeit the six cardinal principles of the Salmon Report are used as the template for inquiries, they are not seen as binding *per se*. In the Matrix Churchill Inquiry, conducted by Sir Richard Scott, it was considered that although the safeguards provided by the principles were designed to protect the witness, they also introduced an 'adversarial' element into the proceedings—the right to call and cross-examine witnesses.

In the Stephen Lawrence Inquiry, Sir William Macpherson stated that although the inquiry was alert to Salmon's six cardinal principles, they accorded with Sir Richard Scott's declared 'golden rule'—'that there should be procedural flexibility, with procedures to achieve fairness tailored to suit the circumstances of each inquiry'.

2.12   The European Court of Human Rights

The Court was established by the European Convention for the Protection of Human Rights and Fundamental Freedoms. It is located in Strasbourg, France, and judges sitting at the court are representatives of those countries who are contracted to the Convention. As the name implies, the Court deals with matters related to human rights referred to it from any of its signatories.

As a matter of international law, the Convention creates rights against States, not against private individuals. Those rights are discussed elsewhere in this series (**see General Police Duties**). Decisions of the court are binding on the country concerned but are not necessarily followed where similar facts arise again.

Section 18 of the Human Rights Act 1998 states that the holder of a judicial office may become a judge of the European Court of Human Rights without being required to relinquish his/her office (s. 18(2)). Such a person is not required to perform the duties of his/her judicial office whilst a judge of the Court (s. 19(3)). However, no such enabling legislation had been enacted, though s. 68 of the Access to Justice Act 1999 has put in place the provisions for appointing judges to hold office in European or international courts apart from the European Court of Human Rights.

The Court is available to those people who believe that their rights under the Convention have been violated and that the domestic courts have not taken this into account in their case.

The European Court of Human Rights should not be confused with the European Court of Justice that is based in Luxembourg. This is the Court of the European Union and exists to enforce the Treaties relating to the Common Market dealing with economic and employment matters.

2.13

International Criminal Court

The International Criminal Court (ICC) was established by the Rome Statute of the International Criminal Court on 17 July 1998, when 120 States participating in the 'United Nations Diplomatic Conference of Plenipotentiaries on the Establishment of an International Criminal Court' adopted the Statute. The ICC is a permanent Court, situated in The Hague, with the remit to try individuals for genocide, crimes against humanity and war crimes. It is 'complementary' to national courts, with countries retaining jurisdiction unless they are unable or unwilling genuinely to investigate and prosecute a crime.

The ICC comprises 18 judges and its own prosecutor, and member States are obliged to cooperate with the Court, including the gathering of evidence and the arresting of suspects.

The International Criminal Court Act 2001 incorporates the offences contained in the ICC Statute into domestic law. This does not preclude domestic authorities from investigating and prosecuting any ICC crimes committed in the UK, or committed overseas by a UK national, a UK resident or UK armed service personnel. The 2001 Act also fulfills the UK's obligation in relation to the arrest and surrender of people wanted by the ICC (**see para. 5.16**) and the provision of assistance with respect to its investigations. It also enables the UK to reach an agreement with the ICC where people convicted can serve terms of imprisonment in the UK.

3 Parties to criminal cases

3.1 | Introduction

The parties generally represented in criminal proceedings are the prosecutor and the accused (*Re Pinochet Ugarte* (2000) *The Times*, 16 February). However, there are also a number of individuals and organisations who may become involved in a case and this chapter sets out their various roles and functions.

3.2 | Attorney-General

The Attorney-General is a member of the government and is responsible to Parliament for the discharge of his/her duties. However, he/she can only be required to account for a decision after a prosecution has reached its conclusion. Although a member of the government, he/she is obliged, by constitutional convention, to exercise an independent discretion when performing non-political functions.

The main functions of the Attorney-General with regard to criminal proceedings are as follows:

- He/she appoints the Director of Public Prosecutions, who discharges his/her functions 'under the superintendence of the Attorney-General' (ss. 2 and 3(1) of the Prosecution of Offences Act 1985, **see para. 3.3**).

- He/she may institute and conduct the prosecution of offences of exceptional gravity or complexity, especially those concerned with the security of the State and/or relationships with other countries.

- He/she may also take over the conduct of a privately-commenced prosecution or require the Director of Public Prosecutions to do so.

- Certain offences may only be prosecuted by or with the consent of the Attorney-General/Solicitor-General.

- To issue guidelines on aspects of prosecution practice which are meant to be observed by prosecutors in general and not just the Director of Public Prosecutions or the Crown Prosecution Service.

- At any time after the bill of indictment against an accused has been signed and before judgment, the Attorney-General may enter a *nolle prosequi*, which terminates the prosecution.

- Appeal against leniency of certain sentences (**see para. 2.6.3**).

Either the prosecution or defence may apply informally to the Attorney-General for entry of a *nolle prosequi*. The usual purpose of this power being exercised is that the defendant is physically or mentally unfit to be produced in court and his/her incapacity is likely to be permanent.

There may be other exceptional situations in which a *nolle prosequi* is the best method to halt proceedings. In *R v Beresford* (1952) 36 Cr App R 1, a coroner's jury found the cause of a cyclist's death in a collision with B's car to have been manslaughter by B, and B was accordingly committed for trial. However, B had already been convicted of, and fined for dangerous driving arising out of the same incident. The trial judge directed that the matter be referred to the Attorney-General and he entered a *nolle prosequi*.

Since the Law Officers Act 1997, the functions of the Attorney-General may be executed by the Solicitor-General and vice versa in many cases.

3.3 | Director of Public Prosecutions

The Director of Public Prosecutions (DPP), a position created in 1879, is a barrister or solicitor of at least ten years' standing. The Director is appointed by the Attorney-General under whose superintendence he/she discharges his/her functions.

The Director's duties are contained in s. 3(2)(a) to (g) of the Prosecution of Offences Act 1985, namely:

- To 'take over the conduct of all criminal proceedings . . . instituted on behalf of a police force (whether by a member of that force or any other person)'. 'Police force', in this context, covers any of the forces maintained by police authorities under the Police Act 1996, plus any other body of constables specified by an order made by the Secretary of State. Those specified include the City of London Police, Metropolitan Police, British Transport Police, Ministry of Defence Police, the Royal Parks Constabulary and numerous harbour police forces.

- To institute and have the conduct of criminal proceedings in any case where it appears appropriate to do so, either on account of the importance or difficulty of the case, or for any other reason.

- To 'take over the conduct of all binding-over proceedings instituted on behalf of a police force'.

- To take over the conduct of all proceedings begun by a summons issued under s. 3 of the Obscene Publications Act 1959 (forfeiture of obscene articles).

- To advise police forces, as appropriate, on all matters relating to criminal offences.

- To appear for the prosecution when directed by the court to do so on:

  - appeals from the High Court to the House of Lords in criminal cases;

  - appeals from the Crown Court to the Court of Appeal (Criminal Division) and thence to the House of Lords; and

  - appeals to the Crown Court against the exercise by a magistrates' court of its powers under s. 12 of the Contempt of Court Act 1981 to deal with offences of contempt of court.

- To take over the conduct of any criminal proceedings instituted by an immigration officer (as defined for the purposes of the Immigration Act 1971) acting in his capacity as such an officer (Immigration and Asylum Act 1999).

- To institute and have the conduct of any criminal proceedings in any case where the proceedings relate to the subject-matter of a report a copy of which has been sent to him/her under para. 23 or 24 of sch. 3 to the Police Reform Act 2002 (reports on investigations into the conduct of persons serving with the police).

- To discharge such other functions as may from time to time be assigned to him/her by the Attorney-General.

The DPP is exempted from taking over criminal proceedings for police forces for various minor road traffic offences dealt with on a plea of guilty or under the fixed penalty procedure (Prosecution of Offences Act 1985 (Specified Proceedings) Order 1999 (SI 1999 No. 904)).

In *R (on the application of Pretty)* v *DPP* [2002] 1 All ER 1 the House of Lords held that the DPP does not have the discretion to give a prior undertaking not to prosecute. His discretion can be exercised only in respect of past events giving rise to a suspicion that a crime has been committed; in this case an 'assisted suicide' offence contrary to s. 2 of the Suicide Act 1961.

In addition to the above, the 1985 Act also imposes further duties on the Director:

- to make an annual report to the Attorney-General, which the latter is required to lay before Parliament (s. 9);

- to issue a code for the guidance of Crown Prosecutors in the performance of various aspects of their duties (s. 10, **see appendix 1**).

Finally, the Director has one other duty, which is to give or refuse his/her consent to a prosecution in those cases where statute provides that the prosecutor may not proceed without it. Examples where such consent is required include:

- offences of theft or criminal damage where the property in question belongs to the defendant's spouse (Theft Act 1968, s. 30(4));

- offences of assisting offenders and wasting police time (Criminal Law Act 1967, ss. 4(4) and 5(3));

- homosexual offences where either party was under the age of 16 (Sexual Offences Act 1967, s. 8);

- aiding and abetting suicide (Suicide Act 1961, s. 2);

- riot (Public Order Act 1986, s. 7);

- offences under the War Crimes Act 1991.

The consent of the Director to a prosecution may be given on his/her behalf by a Crown Prosecutor (s. 1(7) of the Prosecution of Offences Act 1985).

Where an offence requires the consent of the Director before proceedings can be instituted, this does not prevent the arrest of a suspect for the offence in question or his/her initial remand (whether in custody or on bail).

3.4 | **Crown Prosecution Service**

The Prosecution of Offences Act 1985 created the Crown Prosecution Service (CPS) of which the Director of Public Prosecutions is the head. The Service performs the task required of the Director under s. 3(2)(a) of the 1985 Act to 'take over the conduct of all criminal proceedings . . . instituted on behalf of a police force'.

The Director is responsible for dividing England and Wales into areas and appointing a Chief Crown Prosecutor for each area (s. 1(4)).

Since April 1999, following a review of the Service by the Rt. Hon. Sir Iain Glidewell (Cm 3960, 1988), the Service moved from 14 to 42 areas with each area being aligned to existing police force boundaries. The CPS London actually covers two forces: the City of London Police and the Metropolitan Police.

The Service is not instructed by the police but takes over prosecutions commenced by the police, providing an independent judgment in deciding any legal questions which arise.

Every Crown Prosecutor has all the powers of the Director as to the institution and conduct of proceedings (s. 1(6)).

Section 10 of the 1985 Act requires the Director to issue a Code for Crown Prosecutors giving guidance on the general principles to be applied by them in:

- determining whether proceedings for an offence should be instituted or (if already instituted) discontinued;

- determining what charges should be preferred; and

- considering what representations should be made by them to a magistrates' court about the mode of trial suitable for a particular case.

The Code issued by the Director, and which may be changed from time to time, is annexed to the annual report which the Director is required to provide to the Attorney-General, and is reproduced in **appendix 1**.

Paragraph 9 of the Code deals with plea bargaining which is subject to guidelines from the Attorney-General. These guidelines require that, where the prosecution accepts pleas to a reduced number of charges or less serious charges, they should be prepared to explain their reasons in open court (*Attorney-General's Guidelines on the Acceptance of Pleas* [2001] 1 Cr App R 28).

Section 53 of the Crime and Disorder Act 1998 introduced a provision for the Director to designate 'lay staff', under the direction and supervision of Crown Prosecutors, to undertake certain prosecution functions. These functions are provided by s. 7A of the 1985 Act, which states:

(1) The Director may designate, for the purposes of this section, members of the staff of the Crown Prosecution Service who are not Crown Prosecutors.

(2) subject to such exceptions (if any) as may be specified in the designation, a person so designated shall have such of the following as may be so specified, namely—
   (a) the powers and rights of audience of a Crown Prosecutor in relation to—
      (i) applications for, or relating to, bail in criminal proceedings;
      (ii) the conduct of criminal proceedings in magistrates' courts other than trials;
   (b) the powers of such a Prosecutor in relation to the conduct of criminal proceedings not falling within paragraph (a)(ii) above.

(3) A person so designated shall exercise any such powers subject to instructions given to him by the Director.

KEYNOTE

Limitations are placed on the powers of 'lay staff'. They do not extend, even for bail applications, to any proceedings for an offence triable only on indictment, which includes, offences such as murder, manslaughter, wounding with intent, robbery and rape, or an either way offence, such as unlawful wounding, theft and indecent assault:

- for which the accused has elected to be tried by a jury;

- which a magistrates' court has decided is more suitable to be so tried; or

- in respect of which a notice of transfer has been given under s. 4 of the Criminal Justice Act 1987 or s. 53 of the Criminal Justice Act 1991

(s. 7A(6)).

The use of 'lay staff' to undertake specified prosecution functions is designed to speed up the criminal justice process.

3.5   Serious Fraud Office

The only other government department, apart from the Crown Prosecution Service, which exists principally to prosecute crime is the Serious Fraud Office. It was set up by the Criminal Justice Act 1987 and is headed by a Director, who is appointed and superintended by the Attorney-General (s. 1(2) of the 1987 Act).

The Director may appoint such staff as he/she considers necessary for the discharge of his/her functions. Those functions are to 'investigate any suspected offence which appears to [the Director] on reasonable grounds to involve serious or complex fraud', and to initiate and conduct (or take over and then conduct) any criminal proceedings relating to such fraud (s. 1(3) and (5)).

The Serious Fraud Office and Crown Prosecution Service resemble each other in many ways. However, the two organisations differ in that:

- The Serious Fraud Office is concerned only with very serious fraud.

- Section 2 of the Criminal Justice Act 1987 gives the Director of the Serious Fraud Office wide investigatory powers. So, whereas the Serious Fraud Office both *investigates* and *initiates* proceedings, by contrast the Crown Prosecution Service have no investigatory role but merely initiate or take over the conduct of proceedings.

- The Serious Fraud Office comprises, not only lawyers, but also accountants and fraud investigators. Some of the staff are seconded to the Office from police fraud squads and branches of government, e.g. the Department of Trade and Industry.

3.6   Other Prosecuting Bodies

Several governmental departments and quasi-government organisations initiate and conduct prosecutions as one aspect of performing the major functions for which they exist. Such departments include:

- the Department of Trade and Industry for some business frauds and violations of the Companies Acts;

- the Information Commissioner for failure to comply with applicable legislative requirements;

- the Department of Social Security for fraudulent benefit claims;

- the Inland Revenue for tax evasion;

- Customs and Excise for evading import duties, unlawful importation of drugs, and VAT frauds;

- local authorities for violations of food and hygiene and other health regulations;

- the Assets Recovery Agency to deal with the confiscation of the proceeds of crime.

3.7   Prosecutions by Other People

Any individual has the right to bring criminal proceedings where the duty of the Director of Public Prosecutions to take over the conduct of proceedings does not apply (s. 6(1) of the Prosecution of Offences Act 1985).

However, the Director has the discretion of taking over the conduct of proceedings brought by somebody other than himself/herself (s. 6(2)). This means that the Director has the power to discontinue any proceedings by taking them over and then serving a notice of discontinuance. Provided there is evidence to support a private prosecution, the Director is entitled not to intervene to stop it even though he/she would not have instigated proceedings himself/herself (*R* v *DPP, ex parte Duckenfield* [2000] 1 WLR 55).

Where a private prosecution has been brought and an accused has been committed for trial, the police can be compelled to produce all statements and exhibits in their possession (*R* v *Pawsey* [1989] Crim LR 152).

3.8 Local Criminal Justice Boards

In April 2003, 42 Local Criminal Justice Boards were established. Each Board comprised of: chief officers of police, probation, courts, the Crown Prosecution Service, youth offending teams and prisons. Their purpose is to improve co-ordination between criminal justice agencies and be responsible and accountable for the local delivery of key national targets. The main focus will be to bring more offenders to justice, to identify those responsible for causing blockages in the system and to find collaborative solutions.

4 Summonses and warrants

4.1 Introduction

In order to secure the attendance of parties to criminal and civil cases, it is important that courts and tribunals have the relevant powers to bring people—and evidence—before them. Many of those powers are exercised through the issuing of summonses and warrants.

Before examining in detail aspects of summonses and warrants, it is useful to identify the meaning of the terms summons, information and complaint.

4.1.1 Information

Generally, an information means a written or verbal allegation made to a magistrate (known as laying an information) that a person has committed an offence or is suspected of having committed such an offence. This has to be done before a summons or warrant can be issued.

4.1.2 Summons

A summons means a written order issued by a magistrate or a magistrates' clerk, on behalf of the magistrate. It orders the person named therein to appear at a named court at a given time and date to answer an allegation of an offence which is set out in the summons or, in the case of a witness summons, to give evidence and/or produce exhibits.

4.1.3 Complaint *Not criminal*

A complaint is a verbal allegation made before a magistrate to the effect that a person has committed a breach of the law not being a criminal offence (such as breach of the peace, resulting in a common law binding-over to keep the peace). Acts of Parliament sometimes enact that proceedings are to be taken by way of complaint (e.g., under s. 2 of the Dogs Act 1871 where proceedings instituted by 'information' are invalid).

4.2 The Process

The appearance of a defendant before a magistrates' court is secured by:

- his/her arrest without warrant, followed by his/her being charged with an offence at a police station and being bailed to attend at court on a specified day to answer the charge; or
- as above except, instead of being bailed, the person is brought before the court in police custody; or
- the laying of an information by the prosecutor before a magistrate (or a magistrates' clerk) resulting in the issue of a summons requiring the accused to attend at court on a specified day to answer the allegation in the information; or

- as above except that the magistrate issues a warrant for the defendant to be arrested and brought before the court. Alternatively, the warrant may be backed for bail where the defendant is arrested and then released on bail to attend court on a specified day.

For the law relating to powers and procedures for arrest, entry, search and seizure (with and without warrant), **see General Police Duties, chapter 2**; for the law relating to questioning, detention, charge and bail, **see chapters 5 and 15**.

4.3 Laying an Information

Rule 4(2) of the Magistrates' Courts Rules 1981 (SI 1981 No. 552) provides that an information (i.e. an allegation that a person has committed an offence), may be laid orally or in writing. It may be laid either by the prosecutor in person, or by counsel or a solicitor on his/her behalf, or by any other authorised person (r. 4(1)).

Under s. 1(1) of the Magistrates' Courts Act 1980, on an information being laid before him/her, a magistrate may issue either:

- a summons requiring the person named in the information to appear before a magistrates' court to answer thereto; or

- a warrant to arrest that person and bring him/her before a magistrates' court.

An information should provide the following details:

- the name of the informant and his/her address;

- brief particulars of the offence suspected; and

- the law which has been contravened.

A written information is laid when it is received in the office of the clerk of the justices (*R* v *Manchester Stipendiary Magistrate, ex parte Hill* [1983] 1 AC 328). An oral information is laid by the informant going before a magistrate or clerk to make his/her allegation. The information need not be given on oath (r. 4(2) of the Magistrates' Courts Rules 1981) for the issue of a summons. However, in order to obtain the issue of a warrant for arrest, an information must be in writing, and substantiated on oath (s. 1(3) of the Magistrates' Courts Act 1980).

The information must be laid by a named, actual person and must disclose the identity of that person. In *Rubin* v *DPP* [1990] 2 QB 80 it was held that a police force was *not* a named, actual person. Some police forces now have a policy of laying all informations in the name of the Chief Constable or other senior officer.

4.4 Issuing a Summons

Under s. 1(2) of the Magistrates' Courts Act 1980, a justice before whom an information has been laid has jurisdiction to issue a summons requiring the person named in the information to attend court to answer the charge if:

- the offence was committed or is suspected to have been committed within the justice's area; or

- it appears to the justice that it is necessary or expedient for the better administration of justice that the accused should be tried jointly with or in the same place as another person who is charged with an offence and is either in custody in the area or is being proceeded against within the area; or

- the accused resides or is (or is believed to reside or be) within the area; or
- a magistrates' court for the area, by virtue of a statutory provision, has jurisdiction to try the offence alleged; or
- the offence was committed outside England and Wales and (if the offence is summary) a magistrates' court for the area would have jurisdiction to try the offence were the accused before it.

The decision to issue the summons is judicial, not merely administrative (*R* v *Gateshead Justices, ex parte Tesco Stores Ltd* [1981] QB 470). Consequently, the justice or clerk must be satisfied that:

- the information alleges an offence known to the law;
- it was laid within any time-limit applicable to commencing a prosecution for the offence in question;
- any consent necessary for the bringing of the prosecution has been obtained; and
- there is jurisdiction to issue a summons having regard to the provisions of s. 1(2) of the 1980 Act.

Where the above criteria are met it is normal that a summons would be issued. In *R* v *Clerk to the Bradford Justices, ex parte Sykes* (1999) 163 JP 224, it was held that the magistrate and clerk has no obligation to make inquiries before issuing a summons. It would only be in exceptional circumstances where the justice or clerk made use of their residual discretion to refuse a summons. Such refusal applies in applications which appear frivolous or vexatious or to be an abuse of the process of the court. For example, in *R* v *Bros* (1901) 66 JP 54, a summons was not issued against a Jewish baker for Sunday trading in a predominantly Jewish area. In *R* v *Clerk to the Medway Justices, ex parte DHSS* (1986) 150 JP 401, the clerk refused to issue a summons because of the failure of the prosecutor to lay an information within a reasonable time. Four months had been allowed to elapse between the interview of the suspect and the laying of the information.

4.5 Service of the Summons

Rule 98(1) of the Magistrates' Courts Rules 1981, requires that a summons must be signed by the justice or clerk issuing it or (in the case of a summons issued by a justice) must state his/her name and be authenticated by the clerk's signature. It is now common practice for the necessary signature to be affixed by means of a rubber stamp.

Under r. 98(2), a summons should state:

- the substance of the information which has been laid against the person summoned; and
- the time and place at which he/she is required to appear to answer the charge.

One summons may be issued in relation to several informations against a person but it is usual for a separate summons to be issued for each information (r. 98(3)).

Under r. 99(1) of the 1981 Rules, a summons may be served on a person by:

(a) personal delivery; or

(b) leaving it with another person at his/her last known, or usual place of abode; or

(c) posting it to the aforementioned place of abode.

A court can proceed in an accused's absence if the service of the summons can be 'treated as proved' that is, where it can be established that the summons came to the person's knowledge. In relation to a summons being served by (b) or (c) above, r. 99(2) provides that, where the offence alleged is summary and the summons was either left as required or sent by registered letter or recorded delivery to the person's last known or usual place of abode, it is then not necessary to prove that it came to his/her knowledge. (See also **para. 4.6** in relation to the procedure in the event of non-appearance of the defendant.)

A summons for service on a corporation may be undertaken by delivering it at, or sending it by post to its registered office. Where there is no registered office within the UK, it should be delivered or sent to the corporation's place of trade or business (r. 99(3) and s. 436 of the Companies Act 1948).

References to a person's 'last known or usual place of abode' are construed as including any address which he/she gives for the purposes of service (r. 99(8)). This is of particular relevance to the procedure for the conditional power of arrest under s. 25 of the Police and Criminal Evidence Act 1984 (**see General Police Duties, chapter 2**).

Generally, the service of a summons on a member of the armed forces is effected by it being served on the commanding officer in the case of army and RAF personnel, and the commanding officer of a ship or other establishment in the case of Royal Navy or Royal Marines personnel, as well as on the individual concerned.

The Criminal Law Act 1977 deals with the service of summonses issued throughout the UK. Section 39 of the 1977 Act states:

(1) A summons requiring a person charged with an offence to appear before a court in England and Wales may, in such manner as may be prescribed by rules of court, be served on him in Scotland or Northern Ireland.

(2) A summons requiring a person charged with an offence to appear before a court in Northern Ireland may, in such a manner as may be prescribed by rules of court, be served on him in England, Wales or Scotland.

(3) Citation of a person charged with a crime or offence to appear before a court in Scotland may be effected in any part of the United Kingdom in like manner as may be done in Scotland, and for this purpose the persons authorised to effect such citation shall include, in England and Wales and Northern Ireland, constables and prison officers serving in those parts of the United Kingdom.

KEYNOTE

There are occasions where the prosecutor may wish to delay the issue of a summons when laying an information, for example, where the defendant is known to be out of the country. However, an information should be laid with the intention of having the consequent summons served as soon as reasonably possible. Where a prosecutor has not decided to proceed and an information is laid for the purpose of ensuring the prosecution should not be out of time, this amounts to an abuse of the process of the court and the magistrates should stay the proceedings if ultimately he/she does decide to proceed (*R* v *Brentford Justices, ex parte Wong* [1981] QB 445).

4.5.1 Service Elsewhere in the UK

The Scottish term for a summons is a 'citation'. A 'summons' is said to be 'served' in England or Wales and a 'citation' is said to be 'effected' in Scotland.

Postal service of summonses issued in England and Wales is permitted throughout Great Britain, although postal service of a summons is not acceptable to courts in Northern Ireland. Therefore, all service of Northern Ireland summonses in England and Wales must be served in person. The service of a Scottish citation in England and Wales by post is permitted.

4.6   Issue of Warrants

There are several different types of warrants which may be issued by justices, some of which are detailed below. For search warrants, **see General Police Duties, chapter 2.**

4.6.1   Warrant to Arrest an Offender

Section 1(1)(b) of the Magistrates' Court Act 1980 provides that, whenever a justice before whom an information is laid has power to issue a summons, he/she may alternatively issue a warrant for the arrest of the person named in the information, save that:

- the information must be in writing and substantiated on oath (s. 1(3)); and
- either the offence alleged must be indictable or punishable with imprisonment, or the accused's address must be insufficiently established for a summons to be served (s. 1(4)).

Warrants for arrest under s. 1 of the 1980 Act are not commonly issued as many offences will carry a power of arrest without warrant.

Unlike the issue of a summons (**see para. 4.4**), the justices' clerk is not allowed to issue a warrant; the information has to be on oath and made to a justice.

4.6.2   Warrant to Arrest a Witness

Section 97 of the Magistrates' Courts Act 1980 provides that, where a magistrate is satisfied that a person who could give material evidence would not voluntarily attend court, then a warrant may be issued. This course of action would only be used where the magistrate considers a summons would not be effective.

A similar power exists for witness warrants for the High Court and the Crown Court.

4.6.3   Warrant to Arrest in Default

This warrant is issued where a person defaults in payment of a fine or other sum and is a type of commitment warrant.

4.6.4   Warrant to Commit to Prison

This is a warrant of arrest directing that the person be taken to a specified place. On arrest the constable should take the person to the place specified and obtain a receipt. This is one of the very rare occasions where a person need not be taken to a police station after arrest.

4.6.5   Warrant to Distrain Property

This warrant is issued in an effect to collect money. It allows certain goods to be seized and sold as prescribed by the Magistrates' Courts Rules 1981.

4.7   Execution of Warrants

By virtue of s. 125D(1) of the Magistrates' Courts Act 1980 a warrant to which s. 125A(1) applies may be executed by any person entitled to execute it even though it is not in his/her possession at the time.

The warrants to which s. 125A(1) applies are:

(3) ... any warrant of arrest, commitment, detention or distress issued by a justice of the peace—

    (a) under any provision specified for the purposes of this subsection by an order made by the Lord Chancellor and the Secretary of State, acting jointly; or

    (b) for the enforcement of a court order of any description so specified

Section 125D of the 1980 Act provides that in addition to warrants to which s. 125A(1) apply, other types of warrant may be executed by a constable even though it is not in his/her possession at the time. Section 125D(3) provides a list of such warrants as follows:

(a) a warrant to arrest a person in connection with an offence;

(b) a warrant under section 186(3) of the Army Act 1955, section 186(3) of the Air Force Act 1955, section 105(3) of the Naval Discipline Act 1957 or schedule 2 to the Reserve Forces Act 1996 (desertion etc.);

(c) a warrant under section 102 or 104 of the General Rate Act 1967 (insufficiency of distress);

(d) a warrant under section 47(8) of the Family Law Act 1996 (failure to comply with occupation order or non-molestation order);

(e) a warrant under paragraph 4 of schedule 3 to the Crime and Disorder Act 1988 (unwilling witnesses);

(f) a warrant under paragraph 3(2) of schedule 1 to the Youth Justice and Criminal Evidence Act 1999 (offenders referred to court by youth offender panel); and

(g) a warrant under section 55, 76, 93, 97 or 97A above [warrants relating to the non-appearance of a defendant, warrants of commitment, warrants of distress and warrants to arrest a witness].

Where an arrested person demands to see the warrant, it must be shown to them as soon as it is practicable.

In *McGrath* v *Chief Constable of the RUC* [2001] 3 WLR 312, it was held that when enforcing a warrant, a constable has no obligation to question what appeared on the face of the warrant; in this case where the warrant was mistakenly issued in the wrong name. (**See also General Police Duties, chapter 2.**)

'Possession' has been held to include a warrant which was in a police car approximately 60 yards away from the scene of the arrest (*R* v *Purdy* [1974] 3 All ER 465). In *De Costa Small* v *Kirkpatrick* [1979] Crim LR 41, it was held that a warrant for a civil matter was not in the officer's possession when it was at a police station half a mile away.

In order to execute a warrant of arrest issued in connection with, or arising out of criminal proceedings, or a warrant of commitment issued under s. 76 of the Magistrates' Courts Act 1980, a constable may enter and search any premises when he/she has reasonable grounds for believing the person sought is on the premises.

The search may only be to the extent required and is restricted to the parts of the premises where the constable reasonably believes the person may be. Reasonable force may be used when necessary.

These powers are derived from ss. 17(1)(a) and 117 of the Police and Criminal Evidence Act 1984 and the Codes of Practice (**see appendices 5 to 7**). For the law regulating powers of entry, search and seizure, **see General Police Duties, chapter 2**.

For court orders in relation to harassment and domestic violence, **see General Police Duties, chapter 3**.

4.7.1 Execution of Warrants throughout the UK

Section 38 of the Criminal Law Act 1977 states:

(1) A warrant issued in Scotland or Northern Ireland for the arrest of a person charged with an offence may be executed in England or Wales by a constable acting within his police area; and subsection (3) of section 125 of the Magistrates' Courts Act 1980 (execution without possession of the warrant) shall apply to the execution in England or Wales of any such warrant.

(2) A warrant issued in England, Wales or Northern Ireland for the arrest of a person charged with an offence may be executed in Scotland by any constable appointed for a police area in like manner as any such warrant issued in Scotland.

(3) A warrant issued in England, Wales or Scotland for the arrest of a person charged with an offence may be executed in Northern Ireland by any member of the Royal Ulster Constabulary or the Royal Ulster Constabulary Reserve; and subsections (4) and (5) of section 159 of the Magistrates' Courts (Northern Ireland) Act 1964 (execution without possession of the warrant and execution on Sunday) shall apply to the execution in Northern Ireland of any such warrant.

(4) A warrant may be executed by virtue of this section whether or not it has been endorsed under section 12, 14 or 15 of the Indictable Offences Act 1848 or under section 27, 28 or 29 of the Petty Sessions (Ireland) Act 1851.

KEYNOTE

The endorsement of Scottish warrants for execution in England and Wales is dealt with by the Summary Jurisdiction (Process) Act 1881. The 1881 Act provides that any process issued by a court of summary jurisdiction in Scotland may be endorsed by a court of summary jurisdiction in England and Wales and if so endorsed may be executed within the jurisdiction of the endorsing court. The converse also applies in respect of warrants issued in England and Wales for execution in Scotland (*R v Manchester Stipendiary Magistrate and the Lord Advocate, ex parte Granada Television Ltd* [2000] 1 WLR 1).

Section 38A of the 1977 Act provides for Scottish warrants of extract conviction (the Scottish equivalent of a warrant of commitment) to be executed in a similar manner to warrants of arrest for offences except that the former must be in the possession of the constable when executed although they need not be endorsed. Once executed the defaulter may be lodged at a prison in England as though the warrant had been issued in England, as a commitment warrant for non-payment of fine.

Section 38B similarly provides for cross-border execution of such warrants between England and Wales and Northern Ireland. The requirements as to possession of the warrant and the lodging in a prison in England are identical.

Republic of Ireland warrants endorsed for execution in England and Wales charging an applicant with various offences are accepted where the offences correspond with English offences (Backing of Warrants (Republic of Ireland) Act 1965).

4.7.2 Execution of Warrants: Civilian Enforcement Officers

Section 125A of the Magistrates' Courts Act 1980 provides that certain warrants may be executed in England and Wales by civilian enforcement officers.

The civilian enforcement officer requires to be authorised in the prescribed manner (s. 125A(2)).

The warrants that may be executed by such an enforcement officer are any warrant of arrest, commitment, detention or distress, issued by a justice of the peace (s. 125A(3)).

Where such a warrant is executed, the person arrested, committed or detained may demand a written statement from the enforcement officer which must include:

- the officer's name,
- the authority by which he/she is employed, and
- the fact that he/she is authorised to execute warrants

(s. 125A(4)).

Section 31A of the Justices of the Peace Act 1997 enables a magistrates' court to approve enforcement agencies for the purpose of executing warrants. Section 125B of the Magistrates' Courts Act 1980 provides similar provisions for agencies to those described in s. 125A above.

Section 125C of the Magistrates' Courts Act 1980 provides for basic personal information to be disclosed to any person entitled to execute a warrant. 'Basic personal information' means a person's name, date of birth or national insurance number or the address or addresses of a person. Such information may be required from a 'relevant public authority' that includes a government department, local authority or chief officer of police.

Section 125(4) of the 1980 Act will provide that a person who intentionally or recklessly discloses information supplied to them otherwise than in connection with the execution of a warrant commits an offence.

5 | Bail

5.1 Introduction

The Bail Act 1976 is the primary source of legislation in relation to bail both by courts and custody officers. Important amendments to the 1976 Act have been made by the Police and Criminal Evidence Act 1984, the Criminal Justice and Public Order Act 1994, the Crime and Disorder Act 1998 and the Criminal Justice and Police Act 2001. The Human Rights Act 1998 gives further effect to the rights and freedoms guaranteed under the European Convention on Human Rights (particularly Article 5) and the implications of these have been incorporated into this chapter. In addition, the implications in relation to bail are outlined where a person is arrested under the provisions of the International Criminal Court Act 2001.

The meaning of 'bail in criminal proceedings' is contained in s. 1 of the Bail Act 1976 which states:

(1) In this Act 'bail in criminal proceedings' means—
   (a) bail grantable in or in connection with proceedings for an offence to a person who is accused or convicted of the offence, or
   (b) bail grantable in connection with an offence to a person who is under arrest for the offence or for whose arrest for the offence a warrant (endorsed for bail) is being issued.

(2) In this Act 'bail' means bail grantable under the law (including common law) for the time being in force.

(3) Except as provided by section 13(3) of this Act, this section does not apply to bail in or in connection with proceedings outside England and Wales.

   . . .

(5) This section applies—
   (a) whether the offence was committed in England or Wales or elsewhere, and
   (b) whether it is an offence under the law of England and Wales, or of any other country or territory.

(6) Bail in criminal proceedings shall be granted (and in particular shall be granted unconditionally or conditionally), in accordance with this Act.

KEYNOTE

Section 1(5) provides that bail can be granted immaterial of whether the offence was committed in 'England or Wales or elsewhere', and immaterial as to which country's law the offence relates to.

POLICE BAIL

5.2 Bail Without Charge

Where one of the following conditions apply then the custody officer must release a detained person either unconditionally or on bail:

- there is insufficient evidence to charge and the officer is not willing to authorise detention for questioning, etc. (s. 37(1) and (2) of the Police and Criminal Evidence Act 1984);
- the officer conducting the review concludes the detention without charge can no longer be justified (s. 40(8) of the 1984 Act);
- at the end of 24 hours' detention without charge unless the detained person is suspected of a serious arrestable offence and continued detention up to 36 hours is authorised by a superintendent (s. 41(7) of the 1984 Act).

In relation to s. 41(7) above, where continued detention is authorised for up to 36 hours, the detained person must be released with or without bail at or before the expiry of this time. Alternatively, an application can be made to a magistrates' court for a warrant of further detention (s. 42(10) of the 1984 Act).

5.3 Bail After Charge

Where a person is charged at the police station (otherwise than on a warrant backed for bail), the custody officer must make a decision:

- to keep the person in custody until he/she can be brought before a magistrates' court, or to release the person; and
- to release the person either unconditionally or on bail

(s. 38(1) of the 1984 Act).

This is a review of the person's detention and therefore the person or his/her legal representative should be given an opportunity to make representations to the custody officer. The review should be conducted with regard to PACE Code of Practice, Code C, paras 15.1 to 15.16 (**see appendix 5**). Where the detained person is a juvenile, an opportunity to make representations should also be given to the 'appropriate adult'.

Where the decision is made to release a person who has been charged, it would be usual for the person to be released on bail being required to attend at the magistrates' court on a specified day and time.

With the exception of the circumstances set out below in s. 25 of the Criminal Justice and Public Order Act 1994, a person charged with an offence will be given bail unless certain conditions (contained in s. 38 of the 1984 Act) exist allowing the custody officer to refuse bail.

5.4 Bail Restrictions

The decision to deny any unconvicted person bail is a significant one, both personally and constitutionally. Every person has a general right not to be subject to unnecessarily onerous bail conditions, a right which has existed since the Magna Carta in the thirteenth century.

Section 25 of the Criminal Justice and Public Order Act 1994 states:

(1) A person who in any proceedings has been charged with or convicted of an offence to which this section applies in circumstances to which it applies shall be granted bail in those proceedings only if the court or, as the case may be, the constable considering the grant of bail is satisfied that there are exceptional circumstances which justify it.

(2) This section applies, subject to subsection (3) below, to the following offences, that is to say—
  (a) murder;
  (b) attempted murder;
  (c) manslaughter;
  (d) rape; or
  (e) attempted rape.

(3) This section applies to a person charged with or convicted of any such offence only if he has been previously convicted by or before a court in any part of the United Kingdom of any such offence or of culpable homicide and, in the case of a previous conviction of manslaughter or of culpable homicide, if he was then sentenced to imprisonment or, if he was then a child or young person, to long-term detention under any of the relevant enactments.

(4) This section applies whether or not an appeal is pending against conviction or sentence.

(5) In this section—
  'conviction' includes—
  (a) a finding that a person is not guilty by reason of insanity;
  (b) a finding under section 4A(3) of the Criminal Procedure (Insanity) Act 1964 (cases of unfitness to plead) that a person did the act or made the omission charged against him; and
  (c) a conviction of an offence for which an order is made placing the offender on probation or discharging him absolutely or conditionally;

  and 'convicted' shall be construed accordingly; and

  'the relevant enactments' means—

  (a) as respects England and Wales, section 91 of the Powers of Criminal Courts (Sentencing) Act 2000;
  (b) as respects Scotland, sections 205(1) to (3) and 208 of the Criminal Procedure (Scotland) Act 1995;
  (c) as respects Northern Ireland, section 73(2) of the Children and Young Persons Act (Northern Ireland) 1968.

KEYNOTE

Section 25 provides that bail may not be granted where a person is charged with murder, attempted murder, manslaughter, rape or attempted rape if they have been convicted of any of these offences *unless* there are exceptional circumstances.

Section 25 appears to conflict with the European Convention's presumption of an individual's right to liberty. However, the European Commission has suggested that all the factors for and against the granting of bail should be considered, giving special weight to those contained within s. 25 (*CC v United Kingdom* [1999] Crim LR 228, *Caballero v United Kingdom* [2000] Crim LR 587).

In all other cases the custody officer must consider the issue of bail and s. 38(1) of the 1984 Act sets out the occasions where bail can be refused (see para. 5.5). Where bail is refused, the custody officer must inform the detained person of the reasons why and make an entry as to these reasons in the custody record (s. 38(3) and (4)).

In accordance with PACE Code C, para. 1.8 (**see appendix 5**), if one of the following conditions apply to the detained person he/she must be informed of the decision to refuse bail as soon as practicable. The conditions are that the detained person:

- is incapable of understanding what is said;

- is too violent, or likely to become violent; or

- is in need of medical attention.

In reaching a decision as to whether a person should be refused bail the custody officer should consider whether the same objective can be achieved by imposing conditions to the bail, that is, for the person to appear at an appointed place at an appointed time. If conditions attached to a person's bail are likely to achieve the same objective as keeping the person in detention, bail must be given.

In *Gizzonio* v *Chief Constable of Derbyshire* (1998) *The Times*, 29 April, Gizzonio had been remanded in custody in respect of certain charges which had not ultimately been pursued. Damages (for the wrongful exercise of lawful authority) were sought on the basis that the police had wrongly opposed the grant of bail. It was held that the decision regarding bail is part of the process of investigation of crime with a view to prosecution and so the police enjoyed immunity in that respect.

5.5 Grounds for Refusing Bail

Section 38(1) of the Police and Criminal Evidence Act 1984 provides that a custody officer need not grant bail to an unconvicted accused who is charged with an offence if one or more of the following grounds apply.

5.5.1 Name and Address cannot be Ascertained

If there are reasonable grounds for doubting whether the accused's name and address is correct, these doubts would have to be recorded, along with the decision to refuse bail, on the custody record. If the person refuses to give his/her name, this does not automatically satisfy the requirements of s. 38. The actual wording of the section is that the name *or* address *cannot be ascertained* or that which is given is doubted.

5.5.2 Risk of Absconding

If there are reasonable grounds for believing that the accused will fail to appear at court if bailed, there are certain factors which the custody officer should consider when taking a decision to refuse bail under this section. These factors include:

- the nature and seriousness of the offence;
- the character, antecedents, associations and community ties of the accused;
- the accused's 'record' for having answered bail in the past;
- the strength of the evidence against the accused.

5.5.3 Interference with Administration of Justice

There may be reasonable grounds for believing that detention is necessary to prevent the detained person from interfering with the administration of justice or with the investigation of offences or a particular offence.

This ground would not apply for the purpose of the police making further enquiries or where other suspects are still to be arrested. It is generally intended to protect witnesses, keeping them free from fear of intimidation or bribery and enabling other evidence to be properly obtained. For the offences of interfering with witnesses, see **Crime, chapter 15**.

5.5.4 Commission of Further Offences (Imprisonable Offences Only)

If there are reasonable grounds for believing that bail should be refused to prevent the accused committing other offence(s) the custody officer should give due weight to whether the accused had committed offences when previously on bail and also the 'factors' outlined under **para. 5.5.2** above.

5.5.5 Risk of Injury to Another, etc. (Non-imprisonable Offences Only)

There may be reasonable grounds for believing that detention is necessary to prevent the accused causing physical injury to another or causing loss or damage to property.

5.5.6 Own Protection

There may also be reasonable grounds for believing that detention is necessary for the accused's own protection. 'Own protection' can relate to protection from themselves, such as people who are suicidal, alcoholic, drug addicted or mentally unstable, or protection from others, such as in child abuse cases where there is a lot of public anger directed at the suspect.

5.5.7 Juvenile: Welfare

Reasonable grounds for believing that detention is necessary for the juvenile's own welfare provide another reason whereby bail may be denied.

The expression 'welfare' has a wider meaning than just 'protection' and could apply to juveniles who, if released, might be homeless or become involved in prostitution or vagrancy.

In respect of the above conditions, the custody officer must have regard to the same considerations that a court has to consider in taking the corresponding decisions under sch. 1, part I, para. 2 to the Bail Act 1976 (s. 38(2A) of the Police and Criminal Evidence Act 1984). This relates to imprisonable offences where a court need not grant bail if it is satisfied there are *substantial* grounds for believing the accused would:

- fail to surrender to custody;
- commit an offence; or
- interfere with witnesses or otherwise obstruct the course of justice, whether in relation to himself/herself or any other person.

5.6 Bail Consideration by the Custody Officer

The Criminal Justice and Public Order Act 1994 allows the police to impose conditions on bail given to people charged with an offence. These conditions are the same as those which the courts can impose under the Bail Act 1976 with certain modifications outlined below.

5.6.1 General Provisions

The general provisions as to bail are contained in s. 3 of the Bail Act 1976, which states:

(1) A person granted bail in criminal proceedings shall be under a duty to surrender to custody, and that duty is enforceable in accordance with section 6 of this Act.

(2) No recognisance for his surrender to custody shall be taken from him.

(3) Except as provided by this section—
   (a) no security for his surrender to custody shall be taken from him,
   (b) he shall not be required to provide a surety or sureties for his surrender to custody, and
   (c) no other requirement shall be imposed on him as a condition of bail.

(4) He may be required, before release on bail, to provide a surety or sureties to secure his surrender to custody.

(5) He may be required, before release on bail, to give security for his surrender to custody. The security may be given by him or on his behalf.

(6) He may be required to comply, before release on bail or later, with such requirements as appear to the court to be necessary to secure that—

    (a) he surrenders to custody,

    (b) he does not commit an offence while on bail,

    (c) he does not interfere with witnesses or otherwise obstruct the course of justice whether in relation to himself or any other person,

    (d) he makes himself available for the purpose of enabling inquiries or a report to be made to assist the court in dealing with him for the offence,

    (e) before the time appointed for him to surrender to custody, he attends an interview with an authorised advocate or authorised litigator, as defined by section 119(1) of the Courts and Legal Services Act 1990;

and, in any Act, 'the normal powers to impose conditions of bail' means the powers to impose conditions under paragraph (a), (b) or (c) above.

(6ZAA) Subject to section 3AA below, if he is a child or young person he may be required to comply with requirements imposed for the purpose of securing the electronic monitoring of his compliance with any other requirement imposed on him as a condition of bail.

(6ZA) Where he is required under subsection (6) above to reside in a bail hostel or probation hostel, he may also be required to comply with the rules of the hostel.

(6A) In the case of a person accused of murder the court granting bail shall, unless it considers that satisfactory reports on his mental condition have already been obtained, impose as conditions of bail—

    (a) a requirement that the accused shall undergo examination by two medical practitioners for the purpose of enabling such reports to be prepared; and

    (b) a requirement that he shall for that purpose attend such an institution or place as the court directs and comply with any other directions which may be given to him for that purpose by either of those practitioners.

(6B) Of the medical practitioners referred to in subsection (6A) above at least one shall be a practitioner approved for the purposes of section 12 of the Mental Health Act 1983.

(7) If a parent or guardian of a child or young person consents to be surety for the child or young person for the purposes of this subsection, the parent or guardian may be required to secure that the child or young person complies with any requirement imposed on him by virtue of subsection (6), (6ZAA) or (6A) above but—

    (a) no requirement shall be imposed on the parent or the guardian of a young person by virtue of this subsection where it appears that the young person will attain the age of 17 before the time to be appointed for him to surrender to custody; and

    (b) the parent or guardian shall not be required to secure compliance with any requirement to which his consent does not extend and shall not, in respect of those requirements to which his consent does extend, be bound in a sum greater than £50.

(8) Where a court has granted bail in criminal proceedings that court or, where that court has committed a person on bail to the Crown Court for trial or to be sentenced or otherwise dealt with, that court or the Crown Court may on application—

    (a) by or on behalf of the person to whom bail was granted, or

    (b) by the prosecutor or a constable,

vary the conditions of bail or impose conditions in respect of bail which has been granted unconditionally.

(8A) Where a notice of transfer is given under a relevant transfer provision, subsection (8) above shall have effect in relation to a person in relation to whose case the notice is given as if he had been committed on bail to the Crown Court for trial.

(8B) Subsection (8) above applies where a court has sent a person on bail to the Crown Court for trial under section 51 of the Crime and Disorder Act 1998 as it applies where a court has committed a person on bail to the Crown Court for trial.

(9) This section is subject to subsection (3) of section 11 of the Powers of Criminal Courts (Sentencing) Act 2000 (conditions of bail on remand for medical examination).

(10) This section is subject, in its application to bail granted by a constable, to section 3A of this Act.

(10) In subsection (8A) above 'relevant transfer provision' means—

    (a) section 4 of the Criminal Justice Act 1987, or

    (b) section 53 of the Criminal Justice Act 1991.

KEYNOTE

Section 3(6)(e) was added by s. 54(2) of the Crime and Disorder Act 1998 which provides a court granting bail with a further condition not available to the police. This condition, for the accused to attend an interview with an authorised advocate, was introduced to limit the occasions where an accused attended a first hearing and an adjournment was required for such legal advice to be obtained. This condition does not affect the right of an accused to represent himself/herself in court.

Subsection 6ZAA (electronic monitoring) was added by s. 131 of the Criminal Justice and Police Act 2001. A new s. 3AA has also been added by this Act. This section provides the conditions that must be satisfied before a court can order electronic monitoring in relation to a child or young person, i.e. that:

- the alleged offender has attained the age of 12 years; and

- the child or young person has been charged or convicted of a violent or sexual offence, or an offence punishable in the case of an adult with 14 years' imprisonment or more, or has a recent history of repeatedly committing imprisonable offences while remanded on bail or to local authority accommodation; and

- electronic monitoring arrangements are available in that area; and

- the youth offending team has sanctioned its use for the individual.

Section 3A of the Bail Act 1976 applies to bail granted specifically by a custody officer thereby amending s. 3 of the Act:

(1) Section 3 of this Act applies, in relation to bail granted by a custody officer under part IV of the Police and Criminal Evidence Act 1984 in cases where the normal powers to impose conditions of bail are available to him, subject to the following modifications.

(2) Subsection (6) does not authorise the imposition of a requirement to reside in a bail hostel or any requirement under paragraph (d) or (e).

(3) Subsections (6ZAA), (6ZA), (6A) and (6B) shall be omitted.

(4) For subsection (8), substitute the following—

    '(8) Where a custody officer has granted bail in criminal proceedings he or another custody officer serving at the same police station may, at the request of the person to whom it was granted, vary the conditions of bail and in doing so he may impose conditions or more onerous conditions.'.

(5) Where a constable grants bail to a person no conditions shall be imposed under subsections (4), (5), (6) or (7) of section 3 of this Act unless it appears to the constable that it is necessary to do so for the purpose of preventing that person from—

    (a) failing to surrender to custody, or

    (b) committing an offence while on bail, or

    (c) interfering with witnesses or otherwise obstructing the course of justice, whether in relation to himself or any other person.

(6) Subsection (5) above also applies on any request to a custody officer under subsection (8) of section 3 of this Act to vary the conditions of bail.

KEYNOTE

The modifications to s. 3, in relation to bail granted by custody officers, are:

- no authority to order electronic monitoring of a child or young person (s. 3(6ZAA));

- no authority to bail to a bail hostel or probation hostel (s. 3(6ZA));

- no authority to bail for court reports (s. 3(6)(d));
- no authority to bail for medical reports (s. 3(6A)).

5.6.2 Bail Conditions

Section 3A(5) of the Bail Act 1976 provides for the occasions when a custody officer can consider imposing bail conditions. These are where it appears to be necessary to prevent the person from:

- failing to surrender to custody; or
- committing an offence while on bail; or
- interfering with witnesses or otherwise obstructing the course of justice, whether in relation to himself/herself or any other person.

Where the custody officer decides to grant bail and considers one or more of the requirements in s. 3A(5)(a) to (c) apply, one or more of the following conditions can be imposed:

- the accused is to live and sleep at a specified address;
- the accused is to notify any changes of address;
- the accused is to report periodically (daily, weekly or at other intervals) to his/her local police station;
- the accused is restricted from entering a certain area or building or to go within a specified distance of a specified address;
- the accused is not to contact (whether directly or indirectly) the victim of the alleged offence and/or any other probable prosecution witness;
- the accused is to surrender his/her passport;
- the accused's movements are restricted by an imposed curfew between set times (i.e. when it is thought the accused might commit offences or come into contact with witnesses);
- the accused is required to provide a surety or security.

Where conditions are imposed, an accused may make application to the same custody officer or another custody officer serving at the same police station to have the conditions varied or removed. When such an application is received the matter should be considered on its merits at that time. The custody officer can vary the conditions, including making them more onerous, if this can be justified, or leave them the same (s. 5A(2)).

The custody officer either imposing or varying the conditions of bail imposed 'shall include a note of those reasons in the custody record and shall give a copy of that note to the person in relation to whom the decision was taken' (s. 5A(4)).

The application for varying conditions can also be made to a magistrates' court (s. 5A(2)).

A custody officer must record the reasons for imposing and varying bail conditions and indicate details of the relevant risk. Guidance to courts when approaching the decision to grant bail was given in *R* v *Mansfield Justices, ex parte Sharkey* [1985] QB 613, where it was held that any relevant risk (e.g. of absconding, etc.) must be a 'real' risk, not just a fanciful one. *Ex parte Sharkey* concerned the probability of a striking miner during the NUM dispute picketing unlawfully and, it is submitted, any future decision would have to take into account the lawfulness of the person's conduct under the European Convention on Human Rights (as to which, **see General Police Duties**).

5.6.3 Surety and Sureties

Section 3(4) of the Bail Act 1976 provides that before a person is granted bail he/she may be required to provide one or more sureties to secure his/her surrender to custody. A custody officer is entitled (as a court) to require such sureties.

The question of whether or not sureties are necessary is at the discretion of the custody officer (or court) but this condition can be applied only where it is believed the accused may abscond, commit further offences, interfere with witnesses, etc. (sch. 1, part I). It should be noted that sureties have no responsibilities (liability) in relation to an accused committing further offences or interfering with witnesses etc. whilst on bail.

The suitability of sureties is provided by s. 8 of the 1976 Act and provides for the following considerations as to a surety's suitability:

- financial resources
- character and previous convictions
- relationship to the accused.

The decision as to the suitability of individual sureties is a matter for the custody officer.

The normal consequence for a surety if the accused does not answer bail is that the surety is required to forfeit the entire sum in which he/she stood surety. The power to forfeit recognisances is a matter for the court and is contained in s. 120(1) to (3) of the Magistrates' Courts Act 1980 and rr. 21 and 21A of the Crown Court Rules 1982.

It is not necessary to prove that the surety had any involvement in the accused's non-appearance (*R* v *Warwick Crown Court, ex parte Smalley* [1987] 1 WLR 237). However, where a surety has taken all reasonable steps to ensure the appearance of an accused it was held that the recognisance ought not to be forfeited (*R* v *York Crown Court, ex parte Coleman* (1987) 86 Cr App R 151). In *R* v *Stipendiary Magistrate for Leicester, ex parte Kaur* (2000) 164 JP 127, it was held that the means of the surety *at the time of enforcement* must be taken into account when the court decides whether or not to remit the whole or part of the forfeited recognisance. Section 7(3)(c) of the Bail Act 1976 provides for a surety to notify a constable *in writing* that the accused is unlikely to surrender to custody and that for that reason the surety wishes to be relieved of his/her obligations as a surety. Such an action may well be determined to be 'reasonable steps'.

5.6.4 Security

Section 3(5) of the Bail Act 1976 provides that, before a person is granted bail, he/she may be required to give security for his/her surrender to custody. As with sureties, a custody officer is entitled (as a court) to require such security, as far as s. 3(6)(a) to (c) (surrender to custody, not commit an offence on bail, interfere with witnesses, etc.) applies. The security required may be a sum of money or other valuable item and may be given either by the accused or someone on his/her behalf. A third party may make an asset available to an accused for the purpose of providing a security and where the security is forfeited there is no requirement for the third party to be informed (*R (Stevens)* v *Truro Magistrates' Court* [2002] 1 WLR 144).

As with sureties, where an accused absconds this would result in forfeiture of the security. This would not be the case if there appears reasonable cause for the (accused's) failure to surrender to custody (s. 5(7) to (9) of the 1976 Act).

5.6.5 **The Human Rights Act 1998**

Generally, the approach of European Court and Commission is that an accused person should be released unconditionally unless factors that would otherwise lead to a refusal of bail can be met by imposing bail conditions.

Against this background the Court has accepted:

- use of sureties (*Schertenlieb* v *Switzerland* (1980) 23 DR 137)
- surrender of a passport (*Stögmüller* v *Austria* (1969) 1 EHRR 155)
- restrictions on movement (*Schmid* v *Austria* (1985) 44 DR 195).

In the case of *Neumeister* v *Austria* (1968) 1 EHRR 91, the Court considered that it would be a violation of the Convention where the amount of a surety was set by reference to the losses allegedly caused by the person charged.

5.7 Appointment of Court Date

There is a statutory requirement on a custody officer in relation to when a person must appear before a magistrates' court when he/she is being released on bail.

Section 47 of the Police and Criminal Evidence Act 1984 states:

(3A) Where a custody officer grants bail to a person subject to a duty to appear before a magistrates' court, he shall appoint for the appearance—
    (a) a date which is not later than the first sitting of the court after the person is charged with the offence; or
    (b) where he is informed by the clerk to the justices for the relevant petty sessions area that the appearance cannot be accommodated until a later date, that later date.

5.8 Juveniles Refused Bail

Under s. 38(6) of the Police and Criminal Evidence Act 1984, where a juvenile has been refused bail, the custody officer must try and make arrangements for the detained juvenile to be taken into the care of a local authority in order that he/she can be detained pending appearance in court.

Two exceptions are provided:

- where the custody officer certifies that it is impracticable to do so, or
- in the case of a juvenile of at least 12 years of age, where no secure accommodation is available and there is a risk to the public of serious harm from that juvenile which cannot be adequately protected by placing the juvenile in other local authority accommodation.

The certificate signed by the custody officer must be produced when the juvenile first appears at court (s. 38(7)).

PACE Code C, Note 16D (**see appendix 5**), makes it clear that the availability of secure accommodation is only a factor in relation to a juvenile aged 12 or over, when the local authority accommodation would not be adequate to protect the public from serious harm from the juvenile.

The obligation to transfer a juvenile to local authority accommodation applies equally to a juvenile charged during the daytime as it does to a juvenile to be held overnight, subject to a requirement to bring the juvenile before a court in accordance with s. 46 of the 1984 Act (see below).

5.9 Treatment of People Refused Bail

The custody officer must continue to comply with the PACE Codes of Practice in relation to the treatment of the person while detained pending his/her appearance at court or any latter decision to give bail. Even though a decision to refuse bail may have been taken properly at the time, the circumstances may change and bail may become appropriate. It may be that bail has been refused because of the fear that the person may interfere with a witness. If that witness then informs the police that he/she is going to stay with friends abroad, it may be sufficient to protect the witness by granting bail on the condition that the accused surrenders his/her passport.

Section 40 of the 1984 Act requires that a person who has been refused bail must have his/her detention reviewed by the custody officer *within nine hours of the last decision to refuse bail*. This can only be delayed if the custody officer is not available to carry out the review and then it must be carried out as soon as practicable. Any reason for the delay must be recorded in the custody record along with the decision. If detention can no longer be justified, the person should be bailed with or without conditions as appropriate.

A person charged with an offence and refused bail must be brought before a magistrates' court in accordance with s. 46 of the 1984 Act. Section 46 states:

(1) Where a person—
   (a) is charged with an offence; and
   (b) after being charged—
       (i) is kept in police detention; or
       (ii) is detained by a local authority in pursuance of arrangements made under section 38(6) above,
   he shall be brought before a magistrates' court in accordance with the provisions of this section.

(2) If he is to be brought before a magistrates' court for the petty sessions area in which the police station at which he was charged is situated, he shall be brought before such a court as soon as is practicable and in any event not later than the first sitting after he is charged with the offence.

(3) If no magistrates' court for that area is due to sit either on the day on which he is charged or on the next day, the custody officer for the police station at which he was charged shall inform the clerk to the justices for the area that there is a person in the area to whom subsection (2) above applies.

(4) If the person charged is to be brought before a magistrates' court for a petty sessions area other than that in which the police station at which he was charged is situated, he shall be removed to that area as soon as is practicable and brought before such a court as soon as is practicable after his arrival in the area and in any event not later than the first sitting of a magistrates' court for that area after his arrival in the area.

(5) If no magistrates' court for that area is due to sit either on the day on which he arrives in the area or on the next day—
   (a) he shall be taken to a police station in the area; and
   (b) the custody officer at that station shall inform the clerk to the justices for the area that there is a person in the area to whom subsection (4) applies.

(6) Subject to subsection (8) below, where a clerk to the justices for a petty sessions area has been informed—
   (a) under subsection (3) above that there is a person in the area to whom subsection (2) above applies; or
   (b) under subsection (5) above that there is a person in the area to whom subsection (4) above applies,
   the clerk shall arrange for a magistrates' court to sit not later than the day next following the relevant day.

(7) In this section 'the relevant day'—
  (a) in relation to a person who is to be brought before a magistrates' court for the petty sessions area in which the police station at which he was charged is situated, means the day on which he was charged; and
  (b) in relation to a person who is to be brought before a magistrates' court for any other petty sessions area, means the day on which he arrives in the area.

(8) Where the day next following the relevant day is Christmas Day, Good Friday or a Sunday, the duty of the clerk under subsection (6) above is a duty to arrange for a magistrates' court to sit not later than the first day after the relevant day which is not one of those days.

(9) Nothing in this section requires a person who is in hospital to be brought before a court if he is not well enough.

KEYNOTE

The person must be brought before the next available court (it is for the clerk of the court to decide when the next available court is sitting (*R v Avon Magistrates, ex parte Broome* [1988] Crim LR 618)). If no court is sitting on the next day after charging, (other than Sundays, Christmas Day or Good Friday), the custody officer must inform the clerk of the court. If the court in which the person is to appear is in another area, the person must be taken to the area as soon as practicable and then be taken to that court at the next available sitting. Section 46(9) provides an exception to this requirement if the person is in hospital and is not fit to appear.

The Bail Act 1976, sch. 1, Part 1, para. 2 and the Police and Criminal Evidence Act 1984, s. 38(2A) provides that the custody officer need not grant bail if he/she is satisfied there are 'reasonable grounds' for believing the defendant, if released on bail (whether subject to conditions or not) would:

- fail to surrender; or

- commit an offence while on bail; or

- interfere with witnesses or otherwise obstruct the course of justice, whether in relation to himself/herself or any other person.

These factors are the same as those considered by the courts except that a court needs to be satisfied that there are 'substantial grounds' in their belief as opposed to the custody officer's 'reasonable grounds'.

The detained person may also be refused bail for his/her own protection. Where the accused is a juvenile, bail may also be refused if he/she should be kept in custody for his/her own welfare.

5.10 Offence of Absconding

Section 6 of the Bail Act 1976 Act creates an offence of absconding and states:

(1) If a person who has been released on bail in criminal proceedings fails without reasonable cause to surrender to custody he shall be guilty of an offence.

(2) If a person who—
  (a) has been released on bail in criminal proceedings, and
  (b) having reasonable cause therefor, has failed to surrender to custody,
  fails to surrender to custody at the appointed place as soon after the appointed time as is reasonably practicable he shall be guilty of an offence.

KEYNOTE

The burden of proof in relation to showing ' reasonable cause' (s. 6(1)) is a matter for the accused (s. 6(3)).

A person who has 'reasonable cause' still commits the offence if he/she fails to surrender 'as soon after the appointed time as is reasonably practicable'. In *Laidlaw v Atkinson* (1986) *The Times*, 2 August, it was held that being mistaken about the day on which one should have appeared was not a reasonable excuse.

Section 6(4) also states:

> A failure to give to a person granted bail in criminal proceedings a copy of the record of the decision shall not constitute reasonable cause for that person's failure to surrender to custody.

The procedure for prosecuting offences under s. 6 is provided by Practice Direction (criminal: consolidated) [2002] 3 All ER 904, para. 56 (failure to surrender). In relation to a person who has been bailed by the police to attend at a magistrates' court or a police station and fails to attend, proceedings should be initiated by charging the accused or by the laying of an information. For a person granted bail by a magistrates' court, the court initiates proceedings for failure to appear by its own motion where there has been an express invitation to do so by the prosecutor.

5.10.1 Failure to Comply with Police Bail

There are occasions where a person who has been bailed to return to a police station at a later date or to appear at court may be arrested without warrant. These occasions are dealt with by s. 46A of the Police and Criminal Evidence Act 1984 and s. 7 of the Bail Act 1976.

Section 46A of the Police and Criminal Evidence Act 1984 states:

> (1) A constable may arrest without a warrant any person who, having been released on bail under this Part of this Act subject to a duty to attend at a police station, fails to attend at that police station at the time appointed for him to do so.
>
> (2) A person who is arrested under this section shall be taken to the police station appointed as the place at which he is to surrender to custody as soon as practicable after the arrest.
>
> (3) For the purposes of—
>   (a) section 30 above (subject to the obligation in subsection (2) above), and
>   (b) section 31 above,
>   an arrest under this section shall be treated as an arrest for an offence.

KEYNOTE

The offence for which the person is arrested under subsection (1) above is the offence for which he/she was originally arrested (s. 34(7) of the 1984 Act). This power of arrest applies only where the person *has failed* to attend the police station at the appointed time; it does not extend to situations where there is a 'reasonable suspicion' that the person has failed to attend.

5.10.2 Failure to Appear at Court (or Expected Not to Appear)

Section 7 of the Bail Act 1976 states:

> (1) If a person who has been released on bail in criminal proceedings and is under a duty to surrender into the custody of a court fails to surrender to custody at the time appointed for him to do so the court may issue a warrant for his arrest.
>
> (2) If a person who has been released on bail in criminal proceedings absents himself from the court at any time after he has surrendered into the custody of the court and before the court is ready to begin or to resume the hearing of the proceedings, the court may issue a warrant for his arrest but no warrant shall be issued under this subsection where that person is absent in accordance with leave given to him by or on behalf of the court.
>
> (3) A person who has been released on bail in criminal proceedings and is under a duty to surrender into the custody of a court may be arrested without warrant by a constable—
>   (a) if the constable has reasonable grounds for believing that that person is not likely to surrender to custody;
>   (b) if the constable has reasonable grounds for believing that that person is likely to break any of the conditions of his bail or has reasonable grounds for suspecting that that person has broken any of those conditions; or

(c) in a case where that person was released on bail with one or more surety or sureties, if a surety notifies a constable in writing that that person is unlikely to surrender to custody and that for that reason the surety wishes to be relieved of his obligations as a surety.

KEYNOTE

Section 7 therefore provides a power of arrest without warrant if the constable:

- has reasonable grounds for believing that the person is not likely to surrender to custody;

- has reasonable grounds for believing that the person is likely to break, or reasonable grounds for suspecting that the person has broken, any conditions of bail; or

- is notified by a surety in writing that the person is unlikely to surrender to custody and for that reason the surety wishes to be relieved of his/her obligations as a surety.

Where a person is arrested under s. 7 he/she shall be brought before a magistrate in the petty sessions area where he/she was arrested as soon as practicable and in any event within 24 hours (s. 7(4)(a)).

This section requires that a detainee be brought not merely to the court precincts or cells but actually before a justice of the peace within 24 hours of being arrested. This requirement is absolute and since the justice's jurisdiction under s. 7(5) to remand a detainee in custody only arises once s. 7(4) has been complied with; a detainee who is brought before the justices out of time cannot be remanded in custody (*R v Governor of Glen Parva Young Offender Institution, ex parte G (a minor)* [1998] QB 887).

Where a person is arrested within 24 hours of the time appointed for him/her to surrender to custody he/she must be brought before the court at which he/she was to have so surrendered (s. 7(4)(b)). In reckoning the 24 hour period no account is to be taken of Christmas Day, Good Friday or any Sunday (s. 7(4)).

In dealing with a person brought before the court under subsection (4), if the magistrate is of the opinion that the person is not likely to surrender to custody or has broken or is likely to break any bail conditions he/she may:

- remand or commit the person to custody;

- grant bail subject to the same or different conditions.

Where the justice is not of such an opinion, he/she shall grant bail with the same conditions (if any) as were originally imposed (s. 7(5)).

Where the person being dealt with is a child or young person and the justice does not grant bail, he/she should remand such person to the care of the local authority (s. 7(6)).

COURT BAIL

5.11 Courts and Bail

Where a person is accused of an offence and appears before a magistrates' court or Crown Court and applies to the court for bail there is a presumption (under s. 4(1) of the Bail Act 1976) in favour of granting bail:

A person to whom this section applies shall be granted bail except as provided in schedule 1 to this Act.

(See para. 5.12 for sch. 1.)

This presumption is also reinforced by Article 5(1) of the European Convention on Human Rights that states:

1. Everyone has the right to liberty and security of person. No one shall be deprived of his liberty save in the following cases and in accordance with a procedure prescribed by law:
   (a) the lawful detention of a person after conviction by a competent court;
   (b) the lawful arrest or detention of a person for non-compliance with the lawful order of a court or in order to secure the fulfilment of any obligation prescribed by law;

(c) the lawful arrest or detention of a person effected for the purpose of bringing him before the competent legal authority on reasonable suspicion of having committed an offence or when it is reasonably considered necessary to prevent his committing an offence or fleeing after having done so . . .

In addition to a person appearing before the court in connection with proceedings for an offence, s. 4(1) of the 1976 Act also applies to adjournments for reports before sentencing and persons being dealt with for an alleged breach of a requirement in a community rehabilitation, community punishment, community punishment and rehabilitation or curfew order.

With the exception of s. 4(2) (adjournment for report of a convicted person), s. 4(1) does not apply where a person has been convicted and is seeking bail pending an appeal or has been committed to the Crown Court for sentence. In such cases the granting or refusal of bail is at the discretion of the court. If bail were to be granted by the court it would be subject to s. 1(1) of the Bail Act 1976, 'bail in criminal proceedings'.

The Criminal Justice and Police Act 2001 has amended s. 5 of the Bail Act 1976 and now requires that, wherever a magistrates' court or the Crown Court grants bail to a person to whom s. 4 of the Act applies, the court must give reasons for its decision in any case where the prosecutor makes representations against the granting of bail on any conditions (s. 5(2A)). It also requires the court to give the prosecutor, on request, a copy of the note of the reasons for its decision (s. 5(2B)).

5.11.1 Bail by Magistrates' Courts

A magistrates' court may remand an accused person in custody or on bail (ss. 5(1), 10(1) and 18(4) of the Magistrates' Courts Act 1980). In exercising their powers of remand or bail the magistrates must do so in accordance with the Bail Act 1976 (s. 128(1) of the 1980 Act). These provisions relate to the magistrates' jurisdiction to adjourn and remand a case. Such jurisdiction applies when the court is:

- inquiring into an offence as examining justices;
- trying an information summarily; or
- determining mode of trial for an offence triable either way.

The Crime and Disorder Act 1998, s. 49(1) provides that subject to the Bail Act 1976, s. 4 and the Magistrates' Courts Act 1980, s. 41, where magistrates' courts are sending defendants charged with indictable offences forthwith to the Crown Court for trial (a) for that offence; and (b) for an either way offence, or a summary offence punishable with imprisonment or by obligatory or discretionary disqualification, where the offence appears to the court to be related to the indictable-only offence, they may do so:

- by committing the defendants to custody to be safely kept until delivered in due course of law; or
- by releasing the defendants on bail directing them to appear before the Crown Court for trial.

The Bail (Amendment) Act 1993 provides that where a magistrates' court has granted bail, the prosecution may appeal to a judge of the Crown Court against the granting of bail. For this to apply the accused must be charged or have been convicted of an offence punishable by imprisonment of five years or more or offences of taking a conveyance without authority or aggravated vehicle-taking (ss. 12 and 12A of the Theft Act 1968 respectively) and the prosecution must have opposed bail before it was granted.

The prosecution are required to give oral notice of appeal at the end of the proceedings following which the court is required to remand the accused in custody pending the appeal outcome. The prosecution are then required to serve a written notice of appeal on the court and accused within two hours of the conclusion of the proceedings. The appeal must be heard within 48 hours from the date of the oral notice (excluding weekends and public holidays). In *R v Middlesex Guildhall Crown Court, ex parte Okoli* [2001] 1 Cr App R 1, it was held that the 48 hours' period was from the date and not the time the oral notice was given.

5.11.2 Bail by the Crown Court

Section 81(1)(a) to (g) of the Supreme Court Act 1981, lists the persons to whom the Crown Court may grant bail. Section 81(1) states:

(1) The Crown Court may grant bail to any person—
(a) who has been committed in custody for appearance before the Crown Court or in relation to whose case a notice of transfer has been given under section 4 of the Criminal Justice Act 1987 or who has been sent in custody to the Crown Court for trial under section 51 of the Crime and Disorder Act 1998; or
(b) who is in custody pursuant to a sentence imposed by a magistrates' court, and who has appealed to the Crown Court against his conviction or sentence; or
(c) who is in the custody of the Crown Court pending the disposal of his case by that court; or
(d) who, after the decision of his case by the Crown Court, has applied to that court for the statement of a case for the High Court on that decision; or
(e) who has applied to the High Court for an order of quashing to remove proceedings in the Crown Court in his case into the High Court, or has applied to the High Court for leave to make such an application; or
(f) to whom the Crown Court has granted a certificate under section 1(2) or 11(1A) of the Criminal Appeal Act 1968 or under subsection (1B) below; or
(g) who has been remanded in custody by a magistrates' court on adjourning a case under section 11 of the Powers of Criminal Courts (Sentencing) Act 2000 (remand for medical examination) or—
(i) section 5 (adjournment of inquiry into offence);
(ii) section 10 (adjournment of trial); or
(iii) section 18 (initial procedure on information against adult for offence triable either way) of the Magistrates' Courts Act 1980;
and the time during which a person is released on bail under any provision of this subsection shall not count as part of any term of imprisonment or detention or detention under his sentence.

KEYNOTE

Subsection (1)(g) relates to an accused who is remanded in custody by the magistrates' court and makes an application for bail to the Crown Court. The magistrates' court is required to provide a certificate to the Crown Court, that, before refusing bail, it heard full argument. Where such an accused is granted conditional bail by the Crown Court, and they are subsequently arrested under s. 7 of the Bail Act 1976 for a breach of conditions, they should be brought before the magistrates' court who must deal with the matter (*R (Ellison)* v *Teesside Magistrates' Court* (2001) 165 JP 355).

Section 25 of the Criminal Justice and Public Order Act 1994 (occasions where bail cannot be granted) relates to all the powers of the Crown Court to grant bail (see para. 5.4).

5.11.3 Bail by the High Court

The High Court has jurisdiction to grant bail to the following people in the following circumstances:

- people refused bail by the magistrates' court (s. 22(1) of the Criminal Justice Act 1967);

- people who have applied to the Crown Court to state a case for opinion or seeking an order to quash that court's decision (s. 37(1)(b) of the Criminal Justice Act 1948);

- people convicted or sentenced by the magistrates' court and seeking an order to quash that decision (s. 37(1)(d) of the 1948 Act).

There is, therefore, some overlap with applications for bail before a Crown Court judge. In practice such applications to the High Court are rarer than those to the Crown Court because public funding is not available.

As with the Crown Court, s. 25 of the Criminal Justice and Public Order Act 1994 (occasions where bail cannot be granted) applies to bail by the High Court (**see para. 5.4**).

5.11.4   Bail by Court of Appeal

The Court of Appeal may grant bail to a person who has served notice of appeal or notice of application for leave to appeal against conviction and sentence in the Crown Court (s. 19 of the Criminal Appeal Act 1968). People appealing from the Court of Appeal to the House of Lords can also be granted bail (s. 36 of the 1968 Act).

The provisions of s. 25 of the Criminal Justice and Public Order Act 1994 apply equally to the Court of Appeal (**see para. 5.4**).

5.12   Courts Refusing Bail

The considerations of the court in relation to granting bail are similar but not identical to those of the custody officer (**see para. 5.5**) and can be divided into the same two groups, namely:

- those offences that are imprisonable; and
- those offences that do not carry a sentence of imprisonment.

5.12.1   Imprisonable Offences

The Bail Act 1976 (sch. 1, part I, paras 2 to 5) lists the five grounds where a court need not grant bail to an unconvicted accused charged with an imprisonable offence:

2. The defendant need not be granted bail if the court is satisfied that there are substantial grounds for believing that the defendant, if released on bail (whether subject to conditions or not) would—
   (a) fail to surrender to custody, or
   (b) commit an offence while on bail, or
   (c) interfere with witnesses or otherwise obstruct the course of justice, whether in relation to himself or any other person.
2A. The defendant need not be granted bail if—
   (a) the offence is an indictable offence or an offence triable either way; and
   (b) it appears to the court that he was on bail in criminal proceedings on the date of the offence.
3. The defendant need not be granted bail if the court is satisfied that the defendant should be kept in custody for his own protection or, if he is a child or young person, for his own welfare.
4. The defendant need not be granted bail if he is in custody in pursuance of the sentence of a court or of any authority acting under any of the Services Acts.
5. The defendant need not be granted bail where the court is satisfied that it has not been practicable to obtain sufficient information for the purpose of taking the decisions required by this part of this schedule for want of time since the institution of the proceedings against him.

KEYNOTE

The ground outlined in para. 2A is no longer relied on in practice due to the concern of the Law Commission, which it raised in its Consultation Paper on Bail and the Human Rights Act 1998 (Law Com No. 157), that reliance solely on this ground may well violate the European Convention on Human Rights and in particular Article 6(2) (the presumption of innocence). However, the fact that a person has committed an offence whilst on bail may determine that bail should be refused due to the risk of the accused committing further offences on bail.

In para. 3, where the defendant is being kept in custody for his/her own protection, or where the defendant is a child or young person (under the age of 17 (s. 2(2)), the detention is 'for his/her own welfare'.

There are two further grounds where the court need not grant bail:

- where the defendant has been arrested for absconding or breaking conditions of bail (sch. 1, part I, para. 6);

- where the court wishes further inquiries or a report to be made and is satisfied that the only practical way of achieving this is to remand the defendant in custody (sch. 1, part I, para. 7).

5.12.2 Non-imprisonable Offences

The Bail Act 1976 (sch. 1, part II, paras 2 to 4) lists the four grounds where a court need not grant bail to an unconvicted accused charged with an imprisonable offence:

2. The defendant need not be granted bail if—
   (a) it appears to the court that, having been previously granted bail in criminal proceedings, he has failed to surrender to custody in accordance with his obligations under the grant of bail; and
   (b) the court believes, in view of that failure, that the defendant, if released on bail (whether subject to conditions or not) would fail to surrender to custody.

3. The defendant need not be granted bail if the court is satisfied that the defendant should be kept in custody for his own protection or, if he is a child or young person, for his own welfare.

4. The defendant need not be granted bail if he is in custody in pursuance of the sentence of a court or of any authority acting under any of the Services Acts.

KEYNOTE

There is one further ground (the same as for imprisonable offences) where the court need not grant bail. That is:

- where the defendant has been arrested for absconding or breaking conditions of bail (sch. 1, part II, para. 5).
  In addition, s. 58 of the Criminal Justice and Court Services Act 2000, inserted a new subsection (9) into s. 4 of the Bail Act 1976. This new subsection provides that in taking any decisions required by part I or II of sch. 1 the court should also have regard to any misuse of controlled drugs by the defendant.

When considering bail, the courts also need to take account of the provisions of Article 5 of the European Convention on Human Rights (right to liberty and security) as already outlined in relation to bail by the police (**see paras 5.1, 5.4, 5.6.5 and 5.15**).

In *Letellier* v *France* (1991) 14 EHRR 83, it was held that the task of any court in considering bail is to:

... examine all the facts arguing for or against the existence of a genuine requirement of public interest justifying, with due regard to the principle of the presumption of innocence, a departure from the rule of respect for individual liberty and set them out in their decisions on applications for release.

The European Court has also held that where a person is subject to pre-trial detention, this should be reviewed at reasonable intervals. An interval of one month was considered reasonable (*Bezicheri* v *Italy* (1989) 12 EHRR 210).

5.13 Detention of Adults and Juveniles

Where an accused is aged 21 or over and a court refuses bail, that person is detained in prison until the next hearing.

In relation to an accused under 17 years old, where a court remands them or commits them for trial or sentence without bail, that person must be remanded to local authority accommodation unless the criteria laid down in s. 23(5) of the Children and Young Persons Act 1969 are satisfied (s. 23(1)).

Section 23(5) states:

(5) A court shall not impose a security requirement except in respect of a child who has attained the age of twelve, or a young person, who (in either case) is of a prescribed description, and then only if—

    (a) he is charged with or has been convicted of a violent or sexual offence, or an offence punishable in the case of an adult with imprisonment for a term of fourteen years or more; or

    (b) he is charged with or has been convicted of one or more imprisonable offences which, together with any other imprisonable offences of which he has been convicted in any proceedings—

        (i) amount, or

        (ii) would, if he were convicted of the offences with which he is charged, amount, to a recent history of repeatedly committing imprisonable offences while remanded on bail or to local authority accommodation,

and (in either case) the condition set out in subsection (5AA) below is satisfied.

(5AA) The condition mentioned in subsection (5) above is that the court is of the opinion, after considering all the options for the remand of the person, that only remanding him to local authority accommodation with a security requirement would be adequate—

    (a) to protect the public from serious harm from him; or

    (b) to prevent the commission by him of imprisonable offences.

KEYNOTE

Section 23(5) applies to boys and girls aged 12 to 16 (Secure Remands and Committals Prescribed Description of Children and Young Persons) Order 1999 (SI 1999 No. 1265).

In *R v Croydon Crown Court, ex parte G* (1995) *The Times*, 3 May, 'serious harm' was held to be assessed by reference to the nature of the offences charged and the surrounding circumstances.

Section 23A of the Children and Young Persons Act 1969 provides the police with a power of arrest where a constable has reasonable grounds for suspecting that a person is breaking his/her conditions (i.e. remanded or committed to local authority accommodation). Where the arrested person cannot be brought before the court, before which he/she was to have appeared, within 24 hours then he/she must 'be brought as soon as practicable and in any event within 24 hours after his arrest before a justice of the peace for the petty sessions area in which he was arrested' (s. 23A(2)).

5.14 Remands in Police Custody

As outlined in **para. 5.13** above, where a person is remanded in custody it normally means detention in prison. However, s. 128 of the Magistrates' Courts Act 1980 provides that a magistrates' court may remand a person to police custody:

• for a period not exceeding three days (24 hours for persons under 17) (s. 128(7));

• for the purpose of inquiries into offences (other than the offence for which he/she appears before the court) (s. 128(8)(a));

- as soon as the need ceases he/she must be brought back before the magistrates (s. 128 (8)(b));

- the conditions of detention and periodic review apply as if the person was arrested without warrant on suspicion of having committed an offence (s. 128(8)(c) and (d)).

This option is colloquially referred to as a 'three day lie down'.

5.15 The Human Rights Act 1998

Custody officers need to be aware and give consideration to the rights and freedoms guaranteed under the European Convention on Human Rights when reaching a decision as to bail.

Article 5 of the Convention relates to the right to liberty and security. Article 5(3) provides that a person arrested under Article 5(1)(c) is entitled to 'trial within a reasonable time or to release pending trial'. Article 5(1)(c) states:

> ... the lawful arrest or detention of a person effected for the purpose of bringing him before the competent legal authority on reasonable suspicion of having committed an offence or when it is reasonably considered necessary to prevent his committing an offence or fleeing after having done so ...

It should be noted that 'trial within a reasonable time' and 'release pending trial' have been held not to be alternatives (*Wemhoff* v *Germany* (1968) 1 EHRR 55).

The Convention requires that every arrested person be brought 'promptly' before a judge or other judicial officer. The meaning of 'promptly' is not specified but in *Brincat* v *Italy* (1992) 16 EHRR 591, the European Court held that a person who had been detained for four days on blackmail charges before being brought before a court was not treated in accordance with the Article. However it is likely that the periods of detention provided by the Police and Criminal Evidence Act 1984 would be acceptable for most purposes of the Convention.

Article 5(3) provides the right to be released pending trial where a person's continuing detention ceases to be reasonable (*Neumeister* v *Austria* (1968) 1 EHRR 91). Bail should only be refused where there are 'relevant' and 'sufficient' reasons and in all cases these reasons should be provided (*Wemhoff* v *Germany*, above; *Tomasi* v *France* (1992) 15 EHRR 1). In *Yagci and Sargin* v *Turkey* (1995) 20 EHRR 505, the European Court were sceptical about what it referred to as 'stereotyped' reasons for refusing bail and it is likely that our domestic courts will take a similar view to anything other than a genuine consideration of each person's individual circumstances.

In *R (DPP)* v *Havering Magistrates' Court* [2001] 1 WLR 805, no oral evidence was available to prove the breach of bail conditions. It was held that such a hearing does not equate to facing a criminal charge and therefore Article 6 (right to a fair trial) does not apply. Also Article 5 would not necessarily be breached as evidence could be considered which was not admissible in the strict sense and the case did not need to be proved beyond reasonable doubt.

The European Court has identified four grounds where the refusal of bail may be justified under the Convention:

- fear of absconding

- interference with the course of justice

- the prevention of crime

- the preservation of public order.

These will be considered in turn.

5.15.1 Fear of Absconding

The seriousness of the offence alone has been deemed not to be a sufficient reason to suppose a person will necessarily abscond (*Yagci and Sargin* v *Turkey* (1995) 20 EHRR 505). Regard must be taken of other factors including the character of the detained person, their background, financial status, etc. (*W* v *Switzerland* (1993) 17 EHRR 60).

5.15.2 Interference with the Course of Justice

As with s. 38(1) of the Police and Criminal Evidence Act 1984 (**see para. 5.5**), this would apply where there are reasonable grounds for believing that detention is necessary to prevent the interference with the administration of justice or with the investigation of offences or a particular offence.

The approach in some European cases has been that where further evidence is obtained and statements taken, the risk of interference diminishes and further detention under this ground is difficult to justify (*W* v *Switzerland*, above). Also, if the detained person has previously been bailed and there was no evidence of interference with the course of justice, using this ground would be very difficult to justify (*Ringeisen* v *Austria* (1971) 1 EHRR 455).

5.15.3 The Prevention of Crime

Again, this is similar to the condition contained in s. 38(1) of the Police and Criminal Evidence Act 1984, where the custody officer has reasonable grounds for believing that the detained person will commit other offence(s) if bailed. It was held in *Matznetter* v *Austria* (1979–80) 1 EHRR 198 and *Toth* v *Austria* (1991) 14 EHRR 551 that a reasonable risk of the person committing further offences whilst on bail was a valid reason for refusal.

In considering a person's previous convictions, the European Court has held that, where these were not comparable either in nature or seriousness with the offence(s) charged, their use as grounds for refusing bail would not be acceptable for the purposes of Article 5 (*Clooth* v *Belgium* (1991) 14 EHRR 717).

5.15.4 The Preservation of Public Order

This provides for the temporary detention of a person where the particular gravity of the offence(s) and the likely public reaction is that the release may give rise to public disorder (*Letellier* v *France* (1991) 14 EHRR 83). This may be difficult to reconcile with the recent approach of the Court in *Redmond-Bate* v *DPP* (1999) 163 JP 789, where the predicted unlawful acts of others were held not to be a reason for arresting and detaining the individual whose lawful behaviour was antagonising them (**see General Police Duties, chapter 2**).

5.16 International Criminal Court

Sections 16 to 18 of the International Criminal Court Act 2001 provides the requirements for people arrested at the request of the International Criminal Court (ICC) (**see para. 2.13**). These sections incorporate Article 59 of the ICC Statute that deals with the question of interim release pending surrender (i.e. bail).

Section 16 provides that a court may grant bail if an application is made. However, s. 18(1) and (2) provide for compulsory consultation with the ICC.

Section 18(3) requires the court to consider the matters specified in Article 59(4), that is whether, given the gravity of the alleged crime, there are urgent and exceptional circumstances to justify bail and whether necessary safeguards exist to ensure that the State can fulfill its duty to surrender the person to the ICC.

6 Court procedure and witnesses

6.1 Introduction

This chapter deals with the conditions where a defendant can plead guilty by post for certain summary offences, the procedure in dealing with offenders for summary, either way and indictable offences, and the law in relation to witnesses.

6.2 'Statement of Facts' Procedure

The procedure of allowing the defendant to plead guilty be post is provided by s. 12 of the Magistrates' Courts Act 1980 and applies to proceedings only by way of summons in an adult magistrates' court for summary offences for which the accused cannot be sentenced to more than three months' imprisonment. The summons is served on the defendant together with a 'statement of facts' and a prescribed form of explanation. This enables the defendant an opportunity to plead guilty and put forward any mitigation in his/her absence. The magistrates' clerk informs the prosecution of any written guilt plea.

Where service of the summons and 'statement of facts' is proved, and a guilty plea has been received from the defendant, the 'statement of facts' and any mitigation are read out by the magistrates' clerk in open court. Failure to read out any mitigation submitted by the defendant will nullify the proceedings (*R* v *Epping and Ongar Justices, ex parte Breach* [1987] RTR 233). No further facts or evidence can be given by the prosecution. Where the defendant is present in court at this time, he/she must be given an opportunity of giving any mitigation in person (s. 12A).

The magistrates have the discretion to decide that a case is not appropriate to be dealt with under the 'statement of facts' procedure and may adjourn the case for the defendant to appear in court. In these circumstances the guilty plea entered by the defendant is disregarded (s. 12(9)).

At any time before the hearing, a defendant may withdraw his/her guilty plea by notifying the magistrates' clerk in writing. Also the court may allow a defendant to change his/her plea at the hearing and contest the case (*R* v *Bristol Justices, ex parte Sawyers* [1988] Crim LR 754).

6.3 Mode of Trial

Trials are either trials on indictment, which take place in the Crown Court, or summary trials that take place in the magistrates' court. As outlined in **chapter 2 (paras 2.2.1 to 2.2.3)** the classification of the offence determines in which court the trial takes place; generally, summary offences in the magistrates' court and indictable offences in the Crown Court. Either way offences can be tried in both courts and the determination as to which court are outlined in **chapter 2**.

Where an offence is triable on indictment only, the defendant is sent immediately to the Crown Court from a preliminary hearing in the magistrates' court (s. 51 of the Crime and Disorder Act 1998). In the case of an either way offence which the magistrates' court have determined will be tried on indictment in the Crown Court, committal proceedings are held in accordance with s. 2(2) of the Administration of Justice (Miscellaneous Provisions) Act 1933.

There are two types of committal: those where the magistrates consider the evidence and those where they do not. In the former case, no witnesses are called and the prosecutor outlines the case. The evidence, which is tendered in written form, is either read out or summarised. Following this the accused may make a submission of 'no case to answer' though the defence cannot tender any evidence. The court then decides if there is sufficient evidence to commit the accused for trial or to discharge him/her (s. 6(1) of the Magistrates' Courts Act 1980). In committal proceedings where magistrates do not consider the evidence, all the evidence must consist of written statements, the accused must be legally represented and the accused's counsel or solicitor must not have requested the justices to consider a submission of there being insufficient evidence to justify trial by jury. The court do not have to consider the contents of any statements, depositions, other documents or any exhibits before committing the accused for trial (s. 6(2) of the 1980 Act).

6.4 Summary Trial

Summary trials take place in the magistrates' court before at least two lay justices or a single district or deputy district judge.

The prosecution and defence may conduct their own case in person or be represented by counsel or solicitor (Magistrates' Courts Act 1980, s. 122(1)). In the Crown Court the prosecution must appear by legal representative but the accused may still conduct his/her own case. An accused conducting his/her own case may be allowed a friend to accompany them as an advisor though such an advisor may not question witnesses or address the court (*McKenzie* v *McKenzie* [1971] P 33).

Where there is a 'guilty plea' in the magistrates' court, the hearing starts with the prosecution stating the facts of the case and introducing the offender's previous convictions, if there are any that are relevant. The defence then puts any mitigation to the court before sentence is passed.

A 'not guilty' plea in the magistrates' court allows the prosecution to call its evidence. The prosecution will begin proceedings by addressing the court in an opening speech. If the prosecution have established that there is a case to answer, the defendant can then call evidence. Very occasionally this may be followed by rebuttal evidence being called by the prosecution which is confined to unexpected matters raised by the defence. At the end of the evidence for the defence (and the rebuttal evidence, if any), the defence will usually address the court, if they have not already done so, in a closing speech. If the defence considers that the prosecution has not established a case to answer, they may make a submission of 'no case to answer'. There is no clear direction as to what would constitute 'no case to answer' in the magistrates' court, and if the prosecution have provided the necessary minimum amount of evidence on which a reasonable court could convict, the trial should continue. In *Moran* v *DPP* (2002) 166 JP 467 it was held that the justices are not required to give reasons in rejecting a submission of 'no case to answer'.

6.5   Trial on Indictment

Where there is a 'guilty plea', which must be entered personally by the accused (*R* v *Ellis* (1973) 57 Cr App R 571), the only evidence which the prosecution needs to call are details of the accused's antecedents and criminal record. Occasionally, where there is disagreement about the precise facts of the offence, the prosecution may be required to call evidence to support their version of the facts; known as *Newton* hearings (*R* v *Newton* (1982) 77 Cr App R 13).

Where there is a 'not guilty plea', the prosecution are required to satisfy the jury beyond reasonable doubt that the accused committed the offence. Where the prosecution fails to provide sufficient evidence as to *any* element of the offence, the accused is entitled to be acquitted. This acquittal would take place on the direction of the judge, at the end of the prosecution case, following a defence submission of 'no case to answer'.

There are occasions where an accused may plead not guilty to the offence charged but guilty to a lesser offence (s. 6(1)(b) of the Criminal Law Act 1967). If the prosecution accepts the plea of guilty to the lesser offence, the court proceeds to sentence the accused for that lesser offence and treats him/her as being acquitted of the original offence charged (s. 6(5) of the 1967 Act). However, if the prosecution refuses to accept the plea of guilty to the lesser offence, the case proceeds as if the accused had pleaded not guilty (*R* v *Hazeltine* [1967] 2 QB 857).

An accused may be allowed to change his/her plea from not guilty to guilty as long as this occurs before the jury return their verdict. The judge then directs the jury to return a formal verdict of guilty (*R* v *Heyes* [1951] 1 KB 29). Similarly, an accused may be allowed to change his/her plea from guilty to not guilty and the judge has the discretion to allow this at any stage before sentence is passed (*R* v *Plummer* [1902] 2 KB 339).

6.6   Defendant's Non-appearance

Where the defendant fails to appear in the magistrates' court in answer to bail, the court can issue a warrant for his/her arrest under s. 7 of the Bail Act 1976 (**see chapter 5**) or s. 1 of the Magistrates' Courts Act 1980 (**see chapter 4**).

Section 11 of the Magistrates' Courts Act 1980 provides that where at the place and time appointed for the trial or adjourned trial of an information the prosecutor appears but the accused does not, the court may proceed in the accused's absence (s. 11(1)). However, where the accused's appearance was by way of summons, the court must be satisfied by evidence on oath that the summons was served in a prescribed manner before commencing in the accused's absence (s. 11(2)).

Section 13 of the 1980 Act further provides that where the court determines not to proceed in the absence of the accused they may issue a warrant for his/her arrest. Where a summons has been issued again the court must be satisfied by evidence on oath that the summons was served in a prescribed manner before issuing a warrant. Where a summons was not issued, the court must be satisfied that this adjournment was a second or subsequent adjournment of the trial, the accused was present at the last (or only) occasion when the trial was adjourned, and on that occasion the court determined the time for the hearing at which the adjournment is now being made. If they are satisfied that these conditions are fulfilled, they may issue a warrant.

In *R* v *Ealing Magistrates' Court, ex parte Burgess* (2001) 165 JP 82, the defendant had obtained a medical certificate to secure a number of adjournments. The court finally required the defendant to provide a full medical report. This was not sent to the court. At the next hearing another medical certificate was provided for the defendant's absence but the court went ahead with the case. It was held that the court was entitled to proceed in the defendant's absence.

The Crown Court does have the discretion to conduct a trial in the absence, from its commencement, of the defendant and the seriousness of the offence is not a matter which is relevant to the exercise of this discretion. It is generally desirable that the defendant is represented by counsel during the trial, even where he/she had voluntarily absconded. In *R v Jones* [2002] 2 All ER 113, the House of Lords held that in conducting a trial in the defendant's absence, where the defendant was represented by counsel, the defendant had enjoyed his convention right to a fair trial.

The European Court has held that it is for the authorities to satisfy the court that the accused was aware of the proceedings and adequate steps had been taken to trace the accused (*Colozza v Italy* (1985) 7 EHRR 516). In *Re X* [2001] Dalloz Jur 1899, the European Court held that where a judgment was made in the absence of the accused the court must hear the defence counsel and any written plea from the accused.

6.7 Open Court

It has long been established that criminal trials should take place in open court and be freely reported.

Section 4 of the Magistrates' Courts Act 1980 states:

> (2) Examining justices shall sit in open court except where any enactment contains an express provision to the contrary and except where it appears to them as respects the whole or any part of committal proceedings that the ends of justice would not be served by their sitting in open court.

Section 121 of the Magistrates' Courts Act 1980 states:

> (4) Subject to the provisions of any enactment to the contrary, where a magistrates' court is required by this section to sit in a petty-sessional or occasional court-house, it shall sit in open court.

Article 6 of the European Convention on Human Rights (sch. 1, part I, to the Human Rights Act 1998) states:

> 1. In the determination of his civil rights and obligations or of any criminal charge against him, everyone is entitled to a fair and public hearing within a reasonable time by an independent and impartial tribunal established by law. Judgment shall be pronounced publicly ...

KEYNOTE

In *Attorney-General v Leveller Magazine Ltd* [1979] AC 440, three aspects of the principle of open justice were reported, namely:

- the courts should be open to the public;
- evidence communicated to the court should be communicated publicly; and
- the media should not be impeded from reporting what has taken place publicly in court.

For further discussion of Article 6, **see para. 6.10.3.**

6.8   Sitting *in Camera*: Common Law

The following instances are contained within the common law, whereby the public may be excluded from court proceedings.

6.8.1   Possibility of Disorder

In *Scott* v *Scott* [1913] AC 417, it was held that:

> . . . the court may be closed or cleared if such a precaution is necessary for the administration of justice. Tumult or disorder, or the just apprehension of it, would certainly justify the exclusion of all from whom such interruption is expected, and, if discrimination is impracticable, the exclusion of the public in general.

6.8.2   Witnesses who Refuse to Testify Publicly

Scott v *Scott* also held that:

> If the evidence to be given is of such a character that it would be impracticable to force an unwilling witness to give it in public, the case may come within the exception to the principle that . . . a public hearing must be insisted on in accordance with the rules which govern the general procedure in English courts of justice.

This *dictum* (speech) needs to be treated with a degree of caution as to its general applicability. The case in question was one relating to proceedings within the divorce court where the witness was in fear of testifying. It might also be appropriate for a witness, to overcome his/her fears, to write down his/her name and address for the eyes of the court only. Alternatively, the witness's evidence may be admissible under one of the documentary hearsay exceptions (Criminal Justice Act 1988, s. 23 — **see para. 6.12.8**). It may also be more appropriate to deal with a reluctant witness by the threat of contempt proceedings than by depriving the public of their access to the courts.

6.8.3   Effect of Public Hearing on Possible Future Prosecutions

There is limited case law in relation to this particular area. Lord Scarman in *Attorney-General* v *Leveller Magazine Ltd* [1979] AC 440 stated that a court might sit in private, 'if the factor of national safety appears to endanger the due administration of justice, e.g. by deterring the Crown from prosecuting in cases where it should do so'.

A decision to sit *in camera* is not justified solely on the grounds that a witness would find it embarrassing to testify publicly. In *R* v *Malvern Justices, ex parte Evans* [1988] QB 540, it was held to be inappropriate to spare the defendant the ordeal of giving evidence of 'the embarrassing and intimate details' of her personal life.

6.9   *Voir Dire*: Trial within a Trial

In order for a judge to hear applications on matters of law or procedure in the absence of the trial jury, there is a process called a *voir dire*. Colloquially, this is referred to as 'a trial within a trial' and it simply involves the jury being sent out while these matters of law or procedure are determined by the judge; the court otherwise remains 'open' to the public.

6.10 **Statutory Provisions**

6.10.1 **Official Secrets**

Section 8 of the Official Secrets Act 1920 states:

> (4) In addition and without prejudice to any powers which a court may possess to order the exclusion of the public from any proceedings if, in the course of proceedings before a court against any person for an offence under [the Official Secrets Act 1911] or this Act or the proceedings on appeal, or in the course of the trial of a person for [any offence under the Official Secrets Act 1911] or this Act, application is made by the prosecution, on the ground that the publication of any evidence to be given or of any statement to be made in the course of the proceedings would be prejudicial to the national safety, that all or any portion of the public shall be excluded during any part of the hearing, the court may make an order to that effect, but the passing of sentence shall in any case take place in public.

KEYNOTE

Where a prosecutor or a defendant apply for the public to be excluded from some or all of the hearing, a notice of application must be served seven days before the trial. The application is heard, usually *in camera*, at the beginning of the trial before the jury has been sworn. The trial is then adjourned for 24 hours in order that any appeal may be heard (Crown Court Rules 1982 (SI 1982 No. 1109), r. 24A). The notice of application should specify whether the ground relied on was national security or the protection of the identification of a witness or other person, or both. The notice is to be dated and a copy displayed by the court should bear the date on which it was displayed (*Ex parte Guardian Newspapers Limited* [1999] 1 WLR 2130).

6.10.2 **Children**

Sections 36 and 37 of the Children and Young Persons Act 1933 states:

> **36.** No child (other than an infant in arms) shall be permitted to be present in court during the trial of any other person charged with an offence, or during any proceedings preliminary thereto, except during such time as his presence is required as a witness or otherwise for the purposes of justice; and any child present in court when under this section he is not permitted to be so shall be ordered to be removed.
>
> **37.** —(1) Where, in any proceedings in relation to an offence against, or any conduct contrary to, decency or morality, a person who, in the opinion of the court is a child or young person, is called as a witness, the court may direct that all or any persons, not being members or officers of the court or parties to the case, their counsel or solicitors, or persons otherwise directly concerned with the case, be excluded from the court during the taking of the evidence of that witness:
>
> Provided that nothing in this section shall authorise the exclusion of bona fide representatives of a newspaper or news agency.
>
> (2) The powers conferred on a court by this section shall be in addition and without prejudice to any other powers of the court to hear proceedings in camera.

KEYNOTE

'Child' for the purpose of s. 36 means a person under the age of 14 and 'young person' is any person under 18.

There are other provisions which allow for the giving of evidence anonymously or remotely by CCTV link or video (**see paras 6.12.3 and 6.12.4**).

6.10.3   **The European Convention on Human Rights**

Article 6(1) of the Convention states:

> 1. In the determination of his civil rights and obligations or of any criminal charge against him, everyone is entitled to a fair and public hearing within a reasonable time by an independent and impartial tribunal established by law. Judgment shall be pronounced publicly but the press and public may be excluded from all or part of the trial in the interests of morals, public order or national security in a democratic society, where the interests of juveniles or the protection of the private life of the parties so require, or to the extent strictly necessary in the opinion of the court in special circumstances where publicity would prejudice the interests of justice.

KEYNOTE

There are only limited European Court cases that provide an interpretation of Article 6(1) in relation to the exclusion of the public. In *Campbell and Fell* v *United Kingdom* (1984) 7 EHRR 165, which related to prison discipline procedures conducted in a prison, the Court noted that:

. . . ordinary criminal proceedings—which may well concern dangerous individuals or necessitate the production of a prisoner before the court—nearly always take place in public, notwithstanding the attendant security problems, the possible propagation of malicious allegations and the wishes of the accused.

In relation to the requirement that 'judgment shall be pronounced publicly', it was held in *Pretto* v *Italy* (1983) 6 EHRR 182, that there was a requirement for the judgment to be read in open court as well as the outcome being publicly available.

6.11   **Adjournments and Remands**

6.11.1   **Adjournments**

Adjournment of Inquiry into Offence

A magistrates' court may, before beginning to inquire into an offence which may be tried 'either way' as examining justices, or at any time during the inquiry, adjourn the hearing, and if it does so shall remand the accused (s. 5 of the Magistrates' Courts Act 1980).

Adjournment of Trial

A magistrates' court may adjourn a summary trial at any time before or after beginning to try an information. It need not remand the defendant unless one of the following conditions apply:

- the defendant has attained the age of 18 years; and
- the offence is triable 'either way'; and
- the accused has been in custody when first appearing or having been released on bail was surrendering to the custody of the court; or
- the accused has been remanded at any time during the proceedings

(Magistrates' Courts Act 1980, s. 10).

Initial Procedure on Information for Offence Triable Either Way

Where a magistrates' court is hearing an information for an offence, triable either way, against a person who has attained the age of 18 years and they or their representative indicates a not guilty plea they may adjourn the proceedings and may remand that person.

However, they shall remand that person if:

- the accused has been in custody when first appearing or having been released on bail was surrendering to the custody of the court; or
- the accused has been remanded at any time during the proceedings

(Magistrates Courts Act 1980, s. 18).

Where a person aged over 18 years is charged with an offence which may only be tried on indictment, the magistrates' court may adjourn the proceedings but must remand the defendant (Crime and Disorder Act 1998, s. 52(5)).

'Remands' can be either by committing the defendant to custody or to remand on bail in accordance with the provisions of the Bail Act 1976 (**see chapter 5**).

References in ss. 10 and 18 to the trial of an information, or a defendant appearing in answer to an information, extend to cases where the proceedings are brought by way of a police charge. The charge sheet prepared at the police station is conventionally treated as the equivalent of an information laid before a magistrate.

6.11.2 Remands

The Magistrates' Courts Act, s. 128(6) provides that a magistrates' court shall not remand a person for a period exceeding eight clear days except where the person is:

- remanded on bail and the prosecution and defendant consent;
- remanded for inquiries to be made or of determining the most suitable method of dealing with the case; but, if the person is remanded, the remand can be no longer than four weeks on bail or three weeks in custody (s. 10(3) of the 1980 Act);
- remanded for a medical report (s. 11 of the Powers of Criminal Courts (Sentencing) Act 2000); or
- remanded where the court is to try an either way offence summarily and needs to be constituted for that purpose even where the remand is for a period exceeding eight clear days.

A magistrates' court may also remand a person in custody by committing him/her to detention at a police station for a period not exceeding three clear days. This may only occur where there is a need for the person to be so detained for the purpose of inquiries into other offences for which the person has not been charged (Magistrates' Courts Act 1980, s. 128(7)). Where a person is eliminated from an inquiry he/she must be taken back to the magistrates' court even though the permitted period of detention has not expired. Whilst in detention, the requirements of s. 39 of the Police and Criminal Evidence Act 1984 apply (responsibilities in relation to person detained) as do the requirements of s. 40 (review of police detention) (Magistrates' Courts Act 1980, s. 128(8)).

A court may further remand a person where they are unable to appear because of illness or injury (s. 129 of the 1980 Act).

'Eight clear days' in s. 128(6) means, for example, from Monday (when the court remanded a person) to Wednesday of the following week.

Section 128A provides that, in certain circumstances, a magistrates' court may remand a person in custody before conviction for longer than eight days, which in any event cannot exceed 28 days, but the period of time must be stipulated. Failure to stipulate the period of time will result in a person being set free without any conditions being imposed (*Re Szakal* [2000] 1 Cr App R 248). Section 128(3A) to (3E) provides conditions where a person can be remanded in his/her absence for a period up to 32 days though he/she must be brought back before the court at least every fourth application for a remand. These provisions apply to both adults and persons under the age of 17 years.

6.11.3   Time Limits

Youth courts

The Prosecution of Offences (Youth Court Time Limits) Regulations 2003 (SI 2003 No. 917) provide that there are no maximum periods in proceedings in youth courts.

Magistrates' courts

The Prosecution of Offences (Custody Time Limits) (Amendment) Regulations 1999 (SI 1999 No. 2744) provides for a maximum magistrates' court custody time limit (from first appearance to start of trial) of 56 days in relation to those charged with summary offences.

Crown Courts

The Prosecution of Offences (Custody Time Limits) (Amendment) Regulations 2000 (SI 2000 No. 3284) provides a maximum Crown Court custody time limit of 182 days less any period previously spent in custody of a magistrates' court for the relevant offence.

6.12   Witnesses

At the heart of a criminal trial will be the oral testimony provided by witnesses. A witness is a person called by a party in court proceedings with a view to proving a particular matter material to the case. This section examines the key issues in relation to witnesses:

- who can be called to give evidence;
- when a witness can be forced to give evidence;
- exceptions to the competence and compellability rules;
- hostile witnesses.

Under Article 6(3)(d) of the European Convention on Human Rights everyone charged with a criminal offence shall be entitled:

> to examine or have examined witnesses against him and to obtain the attendance and examination of witnesses on his behalf under the same conditions as witnesses against him . . .

The European Court and Commission have considered that specific rules concerning the admissibility, relevance and probity of evidence should be matters for regulation under domestic law (*Schenk* v *Switzerland* (1988) 13 EHRR 242).

6.12.1   Competence and Compellability

In looking at witnesses, it is crucial to consider two related questions:

- Whether there are any restrictions to a witness being called to provide testimony. This question is frequently one of whether a witness is *competent*.
- Whether a witness may be compelled or made to provide testimony. This is a question of whether a witness is *compellable*.

Competence in its simplest interpretation is whether in law a witness is allowed to be a witness. For a witness to be compellable two aspects must be considered:

- the witness must be competent; *and*
- the law requires the witness to give evidence even if the witness would rather not do so.

Failure of a Witness to Attend Court

Should a witness who is compelled to attend court fail to do so, he/she may be found to be in contempt of court and may be punished accordingly. Whilst someone can be physically made to attend court (s. 3 of the Criminal Procedure (Attendance of Witnesses) Act 1965), a witness may refuse to give evidence or to answer some question asked of them. Where a witness is compellable but acts in this way, he/she may also be dealt with for contempt of court. The court has a range of powers to deal with contempt of court and these include imprisonment (*R v Haselden* [2000] All ER (D) 56).

The European Court has taken the view that where repeated and unsuccessful attempts have been made to bring a witness before the court—and in this case where he was forcibly brought before the court but absconded before giving evidence—it is open to domestic courts to have regard to any statement the witness made to the police, particularly where it is corroborated by other evidence (*Doorson* v *Netherlands* (1996) 22 EHRR 330).

General Rule of Competence and Compellability

There is a general rule in English law that: 'All people are competent and all competent witnesses are compellable.' The rule was sanctioned by the provisions of the Youth Justice and Criminal Evidence Act 1999, s. 53. Section 53 states:

> (1) At every stage in criminal proceedings all persons are (whatever their age) competent to give evidence.

Exceptions to the Rule of Competence and Compellability

Section 53(3) of the Youth Justice and Criminal Evidence Act 1999 states:

> (3) A person is not competent to give evidence in criminal proceedings if it appears to the court that he is not a person who is able to—
> (a) understand questions put to him as a witness, and
> (b) give answers to them which can be understood.

The 1999 Act also specifically relates to the competence of an accused to give evidence on behalf of the prosecution and the competence of wives and husbands to give evidence for or against each other.

In essence, the exceptions can be listed as follows:

- the accused
- wives and husbands
- children
- those of defective intelligence
- other special groups.

The European Court of Human Rights has accepted that some categories of witness may not be compellable under a country's domestic law to give evidence, for example, spouses, cohabitees and family members. In *Unterpertinger* v *Austria* (1986) 13 EHRR 175, the Court held that the Convention:

> ...makes allowance for the special problems that may be entailed in a confrontation between someone 'charged with a criminal offence' and a witness from his own family and is calculated to protect such a witness by avoiding his being put in a moral dilemma...

The Accused

Evidence on behalf of the prosecution

The competence of the accused to give evidence on behalf of the prosecution is dealt with under s. 53(4) of the Youth Justice and Criminal Evidence Act 1999, which states:

> (4) A person charged in criminal proceedings is not competent to give evidence in the proceedings for the prosecution (whether he is the only person, or is one of two or more persons, charged in the proceedings).

However, a person charged in criminal proceedings will be competent to give evidence for the prosecution at such time as:

- they plead guilty

- are convicted

- the charges against them are dropped (referred to as entering a *nolle prosequi*—a promise not to prosecute)

(s. 53(5)).

It follows from the application of s. 53(4) and (5) of the 1999 Act, that should the prosecution wish to use the testimony of an accused against a co-accused, they must first make that person competent to be able to give that evidence. The person can only give evidence if that person pleads guilty, or they are convicted of the offence or the charges are dropped against them.

The European Commission of Human Rights held that the admission of the guilty plea of a co-defendant did not violate the accused's rights to a fair trial under Article 6 (*MH* v *United Kingdom* [1997] EHRLR 279).

However, the Commission has directed domestic courts to adopt a 'critical approach' in their assessment of 'accomplice' evidence where the accomplice stood to lose the benefit of sentence reductions if he/she retracted previous statements or confessions. In such cases it was considered crucial that the accomplice evidence could be challenged and that such evidence was not the sole basis for a conviction (*Baragiola* v *Switzerland* (1993) 75 DR 76).

Evidence on behalf of the defence

The Criminal Evidence Act 1898 sets out the position of whether an accused person is competent and compellable for the defence. Section 1 of the 1898 Act states:

> (1) A person charged in criminal proceedings shall not be called as a witness in the proceedings except upon his own application.

> (4) Every person charged in criminal proceedings who is called as a witness in the proceedings shall, unless otherwise ordered by the court, give his evidence from the witness-box or other place from which the other witnesses give their evidence.

KEYNOTE

When an accused elects to give evidence, s. 72 of the Criminal Justice Act 1982 requires that such evidence be given on oath and that the accused is liable to cross-examination.

In being cross-examined, an accused may also be questioned by the prosecution about a co-accused (*R* v *Paul* [1920] 2 KB 183).

Wives and Husbands

A wife or husband (other than when the wife or husband are jointly charged) is competent to give evidence on behalf of the prosecution against their spouse.

A wife or husband is only compellable to give evidence on behalf of the prosecution against their spouse (unless jointly charged) in certain circumstances. These circumstances are provided by s. 80 of the Police and Criminal Evidence Act 1984 as amended by sch. 4 to the Youth Justice and Criminal Evidence Act 1999. The circumstances are:

- the offence charged involves an assault on, or injury or a threat of injury to, the wife or husband of the accused; or
- the offence charged involves an assault on, or injury or a threat of injury to, a person who at the material time is under the age of 16; or
- the offence charged is a sexual offence alleged to have been committed in respect of a person who was at the material time under 16; or
- in the case of attempting or conspiring to commit, or of aiding, abetting, counselling, procuring or inciting the commission of any of the above offences.

A wife or husband is competent and compellable to give evidence on behalf of the *accused*, unless jointly charged.

A wife or husband is competent to give evidence on behalf of any *co-accused*.

Section 80A of the 1984 Act also states:

The failure of a wife or husband of a person charged in any proceedings to give evidence in the proceedings shall not be made the subject of any comment by the prosecution.

KEYNOTE

Cohabitees are not afforded the same concessions as a husband and wife in giving evidence against each other (that of being competent but not compellable). In *R* v *Pearce* [2002] 1 WLR 1553 it was held that the position with cohabitees was not in breach of Article 8 of the European Convention on Human Rights (the right to respect for family life).

In *Bellinger* v *Bellinger* [2002] 1 All ER 311 it was held that a marriage is void if the parties involved are not male and female. Gender is fixed immutably at birth for the purpose of marriage (Matrimonial Causes Act 1973, s. 11) and this even applies to a male who has undergone a sex change operation.

Children

Section 33A of the Criminal Justice Act 1988, which dealt with the position of children to act as witnesses in criminal proceedings, was amended by the Youth Justice and Criminal Evidence Act 1999, s. 55.

Section 55 of the 1999 Act states:

(1) Any question whether a witness in criminal proceedings may be sworn for the purpose of giving evidence on oath, whether raised—
    (a) by a party to the proceedings, or
    (b) by the court of its own motion,
    shall be determined by the court in accordance with this section.

(2) The witness may not be sworn for that purpose unless—
    (a) he has attained the age of 14, and
    (b) he has a sufficient appreciation of the solemnity of the occasion and of the particular responsibility to tell the truth which is involved in taking an oath.

(3) The witness shall, if he is able to give intelligible testimony, be presumed to have sufficient appreciation of those matters if no evidence tending to show the contrary is adduced (by any party).

(4) If any such evidence is adduced, it is for the party seeking to have the witness sworn to satisfy the court that, on a balance of probabilities, the witness has attained the age of 14 and has a sufficient appreciation of the matters mentioned in subsection (2)(b).

KEYNOTE

The statutory provisions require that no witness under the age of 14 is to be sworn. This sets up a presumption that witnesses are to be sworn if they are 14 or over.

Witnesses of 14 or over are only eligible to be sworn if they understand the solemnity of a criminal trial and that by taking the oath they are responsible for telling the truth.

The 1999 Act provides that a person *of any* age who is competent to give evidence, but by virtue of s. 55(2) is not permitted to be sworn, may give unsworn evidence (s. 56(1) and (2)).

In *G* v *DPP* [1997] 2 All ER 755, 'intelligible testimony' was defined as evidence which is capable of being understood. In this case it was also determined that whether a child was capable of giving evidence was within the capacity of the judge and did not require expert evidence.

Witnesses who are under the age of 17 might be allowed 'special measures' to help them with giving evidence in criminal proceedings (s. 16(2) of the 1999 Act) (**see para. 6.12.4**).

Issues of Age

The time when a person is deemed to have reached a particular age is covered by s. 9(1) of the Family Law Reform Act 1969.

The time at which a person attains a particular age expressed in years shall be the commencement of the relevant anniversary of the date of his/her birth.

Section 150 of the Magistrates' Courts Act 1980 states:

(4) Where the age of any person at any time is material for the purposes of any provision of this Act regulating the powers of a magistrates' court, his age at the material time shall be deemed to be or to have been that which appears to the court after considering any available evidence to be or to have been his age at that time.

KEYNOTE

Similar provisions appear in the following Acts:

- s. 1(6) of the Criminal Justice Act 1982 (for the purposes of sentencing young offenders (young offenders institution));

- s. 99 of the Children and Young Persons Act 1933 (parent or guardian assisting in the conduct of the defence);

- s. 28(5) of the Sexual Offences Act 1956 (causing or encouraging prostitution of, intercourse with, or indecent assault on, a girl under 16).

A birth certificate is usually accepted as evidence of age. A statement from a person present at the birth may be useful in difficult cases. If a certificate of birth is produced to prove age, evidence must also be provided to positively identify the person as the person named in the certificate (*R* v *Rogers* (1914) 10 Cr App R 276).

In *R* v *Viazani* (1867) 31 JP 260, it was held that where the statement of an accused as to his/her age is in conflict with his/her appearance the statement of the accused may be disregarded.

People with Impaired Intellect

Under the Youth Justice and Criminal Evidence Act 1999 in determining whether a witness is competent to give evidence, proceedings take place in the absence of any jury (s. 55(5)). Expert evidence can be received as to the witness's competence (s. 55(6)), and the questioning of the witness is conducted by the court in the presence of the prosecution and defence (s. 55(7)).

In considering whether a witness is able to give 'intelligible testimony', s. 55(8) defines this as testimony where the witness is able to:

- understand questions put to him as a witness, and

- give answers to them which can be understood.

The decision in *R v Hayes* [1977] 1 WLR 234 may still apply to a witness's competence, where the courts are likely to take the view that the ability to understand and tell the truth is more important than an understanding of the religious meaning attached to the oath. Where such a person gives evidence, it is for the jury to determine how much weight to attach to the testimony.

Clearly, there is no inherent reason why a person suffering from a mental condition would not make a reliable witness. In *R v Barratt* [1996] Crim LR 495, a witness was suffering from a psychiatric condition and the court considered that her evidence was as reliable as that of any other witness save for certain aspects affected by her condition.

Witnesses suffering from a mental disorder, mental impairment or a learning disability might be allowed 'special measures' to help them with giving evidence in criminal proceedings (s. 16(2) of the 1999 Act) (**see para. 6.12.4**).

Other Groups

In addition to the main exceptions outlined above, other people and groups may be incompetent or not compellable as witnesses. These situations are likely to be less frequent than the earlier exceptions:

- The Sovereign and Heads of State are competent but not compellable.

- Diplomats and consular officers may have total or partial immunity from being compelled.

- Restrictions also apply in respect of bankers and judges.

6.12.2   Hostile Witnesses

A party calling a witness, whether it be the defence or prosecution, would ordinarily do so in the expectation that the witness will be providing testimony that supports a point being advanced by that party. A witness may, however, provide unfavourable testimony to the side calling him/her. In such circumstances, it is said that the witness has failed to come up to proof. In other words, their oral testimony has not been consistent with their original witness statement, e.g. by not proving the matter intended or by proving the opposite. It is a general rule that a party calling a witness does not impeach the credit of his/her witness by asking leading questions and cross-examining the witness on his/her earlier previous inconsistent statement.

However, should a witness not give his/her evidence fairly and show no regard for the truth as against the party calling him/her, the judge may deem that witness to be a hostile witness. In this instance, the party calling the witness may contradict him/her with other evidence or, with the leave of the judge, prove that on an earlier occasion he/she made a statement inconsistent with the present testimony.

Where such cross-examination occurs as a result of a witness being treated as hostile, the jury should be reminded in clear terms what weight should be attached to it namely, that the previous inconsistent statement is not evidence as such, but simply goes to undermine the credibility of the witness's oral testimony. This is the case even where the 'hostile witness' gives evidence that is consistent with his/her previous statement. The rationale for this is that the witness would not otherwise have given evidence if he/she had not been treated as hostile (*R v Ugorji, The Independent*, 5 July 1999).

It is important to distinguish between an unfavourable witness and one who is hostile. Simply because a witness does not provide testimony to prove a matter does not make them hostile. A hostile witness deliberately goes beyond this.

. . . .

EXAMPLE

Consider the situation where the defence calls witness A to provide evidence of a particular issue, e.g. that A saw a particular car at a particular place. However, in giving testimony A, in good faith or as a result of an earlier misunderstanding, believes he was mistaken. In this instance A is an unfavourable witness. If, however, A in fact decides to lie and say he did not in fact see the car when he really did then A may be deemed by the judge to be a hostile witness.

. . . .

6.12.3　Live Television Link

Witnesses will ordinarily give their evidence from the witness box. However, there has been an increasing trend towards allowing some witnesses (particularly vulnerable ones) to give their testimony by other means, e.g., through a live television link. These statutory developments in this area are summarised below.

Criminal Justice Act 1988

The Criminal Justice Act 1988, s. 32 states:

(1) A person other than the accused may give evidence through a live television link on a trial on indictment or an appeal to the criminal division of the Court of Appeal or the hearing of a reference under section 17 of the [1968 c. 19] Criminal Appeal Act 1968 if

(a) the witness is outside the United Kingdom.

KEYNOTE

Where a witness gives evidence through a television link outside the United Kingdom, having made a statement on oath, s. 32(3) provides that such evidence shall be treated for the purposes of s. 1 of the Perjury Act 1911 as having been made in proceedings in which it is given in evidence.

The procedure for evidence to be provided through a television link where the witness is outside the United Kingdom is contained in the Crown Court Rules 1982 (SI 1982 No. 1109) (see *Blackstone's Criminal Practice*, 2003, Appendix 1).

There is no presumption in favour of using a television link and its use has to be justified for displacing the general rule that a witness should give evidence in the presence of the defendant (*R (on the application of DPP)* v *Redbridge Youth Court* [2001] 4 All ER 411).

Crime and Disorder Act 1998

Section 57 of the Crime and Disorder Act 1998 provides for the use of live television links at preliminary court hearings where an accused is being detained in custody in prison or any other institution. The purpose of this provision is to reduce both delays in proceedings and the number of escapees from custody during transportation to and from courts.

Section 57 states:

(1) In any proceedings for an offence, a court may, after hearing representations from the parties, direct that the accused shall be treated as being present in the court for any particular hearing before the start of the trial if, during that hearing—

(a) he is held in custody in a prison or other institution; and

(b) whether by means of a live television link or otherwise, he is able to see and hear the court and to be seen and heard by it.

(2) A court shall not give a direction under subsection (1) above unless—

(a) it has been notified by the Secretary of State that facilities are available for enabling persons held in custody in the institution in which the accused is or is to be so held to see and hear the court and to be seen and heard by it; and

(b) the notice has not been withdrawn.

(3) If in a case where it has power to do so a magistrates' court decides not to give a direction under subsection (1) above, it shall give its reasons for not doing so.

(4) In this section 'the start of the trial' has the meaning given by subsection (11A) or (11B) of section 22 of the 1985 Act.

KEYNOTE

For the purposes of s. 57 no consent is required from either the accused or his/her legal adviser; it is a matter for the discretion of the court.

The phrase 'start of trial' (s. 57(4)) means:

- for cases being tried summarily, at the point where the prosecution start to present their evidence or when a guilty plea is accepted;

- for cases being tried on indictment, when a jury is sworn to consider the issue of guilt or fitness to plead, or, before a jury is sworn, at the time a plea of guilty is accepted by the court.

Youth Justice and Criminal Evidence Act 1999

Section 24 of the Youth Justice and Criminal Evidence Act 1999 provides for the use of a television link as part of a series of special measures designed to help young, disabled or intimidated witnesses give evidence in criminal proceedings. This section came into force on 24 July 2002 in relation to witnesses in the Crown Court but only vulnerable witnesses (s. 16) in the magistrates' court. (**See para. 6.12.4** for the details of vulnerable (s. 16) and intimidated (s. 17) witnesses and other 'special measures'.)

Section 24 of the 1999 Act states:

(1) A special measures direction may provide for the witness to give evidence by means of a live link.

(2) Where a direction provides for the witness to give evidence by means of a live link, the witness may not give evidence in any other way without the permission of the court.

(3) The court may give permission for the purposes of subsection (2) if it appears to the court to be in the interests of justice to do so, and may do so either—

(a) on an application by a party to the proceedings, if there has been a material change of circumstances since the relevant time, or

(b) of its own motion.

(4) In subsection (3) 'the relevant time' means—

(a) the time when the direction was given, or

(b) if a previous application has been made under that subsection, the time when the application (or last application) was made.

KEYNOTE

There are three categories of witness who are eligible to apply for 'special measures' (**see para. 6.12.4**). Where facilities are not available in a magistrates' court, evidence can be given by means of a live link at a place appointed as suitable for the purpose (s. 24(5)).

'Live link' means a live television link where the witness is able to see and hear the proceedings and to be seen and heard by the judge or justices, legal representatives, and any interpreter appointed to assist the witness (s. 24(8)).

6.12.4 Special Measures for Vulnerable or Intimidated Witnesses

The Youth Justice and Criminal Evidence Act 1999 contains a range of measures designed to help young, disabled, vulnerable or intimidated witnesses to give evidence in criminal proceedings.

Eligible Witnesses

There are three categories of witness eligible for assistance and it is for the court to determine whether a witness falls into one of these categories:

- a witness who is under the age of 17 at the time of the hearing (s. 16(1));

- a witness who suffers from a mental or physical disorder or otherwise has a significant impairment of intelligence (s. 16(2));

- a witness whose evidence is likely to be affected on grounds of fear or distress about testifying (s. 17(1)).

The prosecution or defence may apply to the court for a special measure direction to be made or the court may make such a direction of its own motion (s. 19).

There are also special provisions relating to a 'child witness' (i.e. under the age of 17). Section 21 provides that a child witness will be deemed to be 'in need of special protection' if the offence to which the proceedings relate is a proscribed sexual offence or one of kidnapping, assault, etc. In such instances, the court must give a special measures direction for the witness's evidence to be obtained by means of a video recording. Where this is not possible, subject to availability, the evidence must be given by means of a live link.

Screening Witnesses

The court can direct to provide a witness, while giving testimony or being sworn, to be prevented by means of a screen or other arrangement from seeing the accused. However, the witness must be able to be seen by the judge or justices (or both), the jury (if there is one), legal representatives and any interpreter or other person appointed to assist the witness (s. 23). This section came into force on 24 July 2002 in relation to vulnerable and intimidated witnesses in the Crown Court.

Evidence given in Private

A special measures direction may provide for the exclusion of any persons from the court whilst the witness is giving evidence (s. 25(1)). This does not include the exclusion of the accused, legal representatives and any interpreter acting for the witness (s. 25(2)).

This direction may only be used where the proceedings relate to a sexual offence or there are reasonable grounds to believe that the witness has or will be intimidated by any person other than the accused (s. 25(4)).

This section came into force on 24 July 2002 in relation to vulnerable and intimidated witnesses in the Crown Court.

Removal of Wigs and Gowns

A direction may be provided for the wearing of wigs and gowns to be dispensed with whilst a witness gives his/her evidence (s. 26). This special measure direction came into force on 24 July 2002.

Video Recorded Evidence

Section 27 of the Youth Justice and Criminal Evidence Act 1999 provides for video recorded evidence in chief and states:

(1) A special measures direction may provide for a video recording of an interview of the witness to be admitted as evidence in chief of the witness.

(2) A special measures direction may, however, not provide for a video recording, or part of such a recording, to be admitted under this section if the court is of the opinion, having regard to all the circumstances of the case, that in the interests of justice the recording, or that part of it, should not be so admitted.

(3) In considering for the purposes of subsection (2) whether any part of a recording should not be admitted under this section, the court must consider whether any prejudice to the accused which might result from that part being so admitted is outweighed by the desirability of showing the whole, or substantially the whole, of the recorded interview.

KEYNOTE

It was held in *R (on the application of DPP)* v *Redbridge Youth Court* [2001] 4 All ER 411 that an accused could successfully oppose an order under this section if it could be established that the appearance of a witness in court was not likely to impact on the quality of the evidence.

Section 27 came into force on 24 July 2002 in relation to vulnerable witnesses (s. 16) in both the Crown Court and magistrates' court. Section 17 in relation to intimidated witnesses has not yet been introduced.

When in force, s. 28(1) of the Act will provide that where a video recording is admitted as a witness's evidence-in-chief, the direction can provide for any cross-examination or re-examination of the witness before trial to be recorded by means of a video recording (s. 28(1)). The judge or justices and legal representatives, in the absence of the accused, must be able to see and hear the examination of the witness. The accused must also be able to see and hear the examination of the witness probably by use of a live link (s. 28(2)).

For those involved in conducting video recorded interviews with vulnerable and intimidated witnesses, both adult and children, new guidance has been produced for use from May 2002 in the form of *Achieving Best Evidence in Criminal Proceedings: Guidance for Vulnerable or Intimidated Witnesses* (2002). This guidance replaces the *Memorandum of Good Practice* (1992).

No implementation date has been set for s. 28 though a scoping study took place in summer 2002 followed by live pilot projects.

Examination of Witness through Intermediary

When brought into force, a special measures direction may provide for any examination of the witness to be conducted through an interpreter or other person approved by the court (s. 29(1)).

The intermediary's function is to communicate questions to the witness, answers to any person asking such questions and provide an understanding of the questions and answers to the witness or person in question (s. 29(2)).

Aids to Communication

The 1999 Act provides for the provision of any device which will enable questions or answers to be communicated to or by the witness despite any disability or disorder or other impairment which the witness has or suffers from (s. 30).

In relation to all the special measures directions, where such a direction has been used to provide evidence, in a trial on indictment, the judge must warn the jury that the use of such a direction does not prejudice the accused (s. 32).

Section 30 came into force on 24 July 2002 in relation to both vulnerable and intimidated witnesses in the Crown Court.

6.12.5 **Refreshing Memory**

Witnesses are frequently called upon to provide testimony where a considerable time has elapsed between the actual events and their appearance in court. In some instances, this time gap can involve a number of years. For police officers, who will be dealing with many such incidents, the problem is compounded. In addition, it would be unrealistic to expect a witness to provide accurate and reliable evidence without allowing them to refresh their memory by looking at some note or document recording the event.

There are no fixed and immutable rules to be followed before a witness can refresh his/her memory by a document prepared by him/her when his/her memory was clearer. There is a broad fact-sensitive judicial discretion to be exercised in the interests of fairness and justice (*R v Gordon* (2002) *The Times*, 30 January).

A witness may refresh his/her memory by referring to a document that they made or verified providing certain criteria are met. Those criteria are:

- that the document was made or verified at the time of the incident, or shortly after, while the circumstances were fresh in the witness's mind;
- that the document is produced in court for inspection;
- where a witness has no recollection of the events, and is giving evidence as to the accuracy of the contents of the document, that the original document is used.

In the case where a statement was made to the police some time after the event, it is quite reasonable for any witness, whether for the prosecution or defence, to refresh his/her memory prior to giving evidence by being allowed access to their statement. The giving of evidence is about reliability and not a test of memory (*R v Richardson* [1971] 2 QB 484; *Lau Pak Ngarn v R* [1966] Crim LR 443).

There is no duty on either the defence or prosecution to inform the other party that the witness has refreshed his/her memory by reading a statement or other document. It should be assumed that the opponent's witnesses have seen their statements (*Worley v Bentley* [1976] 2 All ER 449; *R v Westwell* [1976] 2 All ER 812).

In *Owen v Edwards* (1983) 77 Cr App R 191, a police officer had refreshed his memory from his notebook outside the court, but had not used it in the witness box. It was held that the accused was entitled to examine the contents of the notebook and crossexamine the officer upon the relevant matters contained in it.

R v Skinner (1994) 99 Cr App R 212 determined that, in refreshing their memory, witnesses should not discuss their evidence with other witnesses. It would also not be proper to discuss or acquaint a witness with the contents of a document made by another witness, so as to refresh his/her memory before he/she gives evidence. In *R v Arif* (1993) *The Times*, 17 June, it was stated that, in criminal trials, pre-trial discussions of evidence between potential witnesses, the rehearsal of evidence and the coaching of witnesses are to be strongly discouraged because of the risk of abuse.

It was held in *R v Bass* [1953] 1 All ER 1064, that two witnesses who have acted together can refresh their memories from notes made in collaboration. A record should be made that the notes were made in collaboration. This is particularly significant for police officers who often witness events while in the company of other officers. The judgment stated:

> The officers' notes were almost identical. They were not made at the time of the interview. One officer made his notes after the appellant had been charged, and the other officer made his an hour later. . . . This court has observed that police officers nearly always deny that they have collaborated

in the making of notes, and we cannot help wondering why they are the only class of society who do not collaborate in such a matter. It seems to us that nothing could be more natural or proper when two persons have been present at an interview with a third person than that they should afterwards make sure that they have a correct version of what was said. Collaboration would appear to be a better explanation of almost identical notes than the possession of a superhuman memory.

In *R v Cheng* [1976] Crim LR 379, it was held that a copy or extract of the original notes etc., can be used in court to refresh the witness's memory if once the witness's memory has been refreshed he/she can swear positively to the facts. Comments may be made regarding the use of a copy.

6.12.6 Evidence of Oral Statement made Through an Interpreter

It is inadmissible for a police officer to give evidence of a conversation held through the use of an interpreter. The only valid witness would be the interpreter (*R v Attard* (1958) 43 Cr App R 90).

6.12.7 Interference with Witnesses

The interference with witnesses or potential witnesses is included in the common law offence of perverting the course of public justice (as to which, **see Crime, chapter 15**).

6.12.8 Witnesses in Fear of Testifying

Section 23 of the Criminal Justice Act 1988 allows a witness statement to be read out where the witness 'does not give oral evidence through fear'. There have been a number of decided cases in relation to s. 23, particularly in attempting to define the term 'through fear'. In *R v Acton Justices, ex part McMullen* (1990) 92 Cr App R 98, it was suggested that the fear induced in the witness should be as a direct result of the crime itself or of something said or done afterwards in relation to the offence. However, in *R v Martin* [1996] Crim LR 589, it was held that there should be no restrictions on the manner in which the witness was put in fear. In *Martin*, the witness was put in fear by the appearance of a silent stranger at his door.

Whatever meaning is given to 'through fear', however, the maker's fear must be established by evidence to the appropriate standard of proof and such evidence must itself be admissible. Also, evidence which satisfies the conditions of admissibility under s. 23 of the 1988 Act may nevertheless be excluded by the exercise of the court's discretion under s. 25 or 26 of the Act, under which provision the court is directed to consider where the interests of justice lie with regard to the admission of the offence.

In order to satisfy the requirements of s. 23, it is necessary for the court to hear oral evidence as to the fear. 'Fear' cannot be provided by a written statement made by a witness (*R v Belmarsh Magistrates' Court, ex parte Gilligan* [1998] 1 Cr App R 14 and *R v Radak* [1999] 1 Cr App R 187).

The European Court of Human Rights, whilst accepting that a genuine fear of reprisals may justify reliance on hearsay evidence in some cases, considers that in such instances there needs to be counterbalancing procedures to preserve the rights of the defence. The Court has held that to convict solely on such hearsay evidence (e.g. reading out witness statements), would not be acceptable and in breach of Article 6(3)(d).

In *Doorson v Netherlands* (1996) 22 EHRR 330, the Court accepted the admission of hearsay evidence even where the two witnesses concerned had not been directly threatened by the defendant. The Court held that:

> Regard must be had to the fact, as established by the domestic courts and not contested by the applicant, that drug dealers frequently resorted to threats or actual violence against persons who gave evidence against them.

In a later application the Court considered that, where the witness was a police officer, the position may well be different in accepting his/her evidence as hearsay (*Van Mechelen* v *Netherlands* (1997) 25 EHRR 647).

6.12.9   Oaths and Affirmations

It is the general rule that every witness who gives evidence must be sworn, that is, take the oath or make an affirmation.

The manner in which the oath is administered is provided by s. 1 of the Oaths Act 1978. This requires the witness to hold the New Testament (Old Testament in the case of a Jew) in his uplifted hand and repeat, after the person administering the oath, the words 'I swear by Almighty God that . . .', followed by the oath prescribed by law.

Where the witness is neither a Christian nor a Jew they can object to taking the oath in the prescribed manner. Alternatively, they may affirm or take an oath upon a holy book appropriate to their religious belief. For example, Hindus are sworn on the Vedas and Muslims are sworn on the Koran (*R* v *Morgan* (1764) 1 Leach 54).

An affirmation may be made by a witness who objects to being sworn or where his/her request for an alternative form of oath is not reasonably practicable and would delay or inconvenience the proceedings (s. 5 of the 1978 Act). The witness repeats after the person administering the affirmation, the words 'I [name] do solemnly, sincerely and truly declare and affirm', followed by the words of the oath prescribed by law (s. 6 of the 1978 Act).

There are two exceptions to the general rule:

- children may give unsworn evidence (s. 55 of the Youth Justice and Criminal Evidence Act 1999);

- witnesses merely producing a document need not be sworn (*Perry* v *Gibson* (1834) 1 A & E 48).

Where a compellable witness refuses to take an oath or make an affirmation in the Crown Court, he/she can be held in contempt of court and where appropriate face a penalty of imprisonment (s. 45(4) of the Supreme Court Act 1981).

Where a witness refuses, without just excuse, to be sworn or give evidence in the magistrates' court, he/she can be committed to custody for a period not exceeding one month and/or be fined to an amount not exceeding £2,500 (s. 97(4) of the Magistrates' Court Act 1980).

6.13   Examination-in-Chief

The party who calls a witness (prosecution or defence) is entitled to examine the witness by asking questions with a view to providing evidence which is favourable to that party's case. This is known as 'examination-in-chief'.

All witnesses are examined in chief with one exception; where the prosecution determine not to examine its witness in chief but allow the witness to be cross-examined by the defence. This is common in the case of police officers whose evidence-in-chief will be identical. Consequently, one police officer can give the evidence-in-chief but other officers involved may be required for cross-examination by the defence.

Cross-examination and re-examination are discussed in more detail below (**see paras 6.14 and 6.15**).

6.13.1   **Leading Questions**

The general rule is that leading questions, i.e. those which suggest the desired answer, may not be asked of a party's own witness. However, it is quite common practice for a party to lead a witness through certain parts of his/her evidence which are not in dispute.

There are two forms of leading questions; those which indicate to a witness the answer required and those which assume something to be true when it has not been established.

The first form is where a question puts words into the witness's mouth. For example, if evidence is given that A assaulted B and the question for the court is whether the defendant did in fact assault B, a prosecution witness should not be asked 'Did you see the defendant assault B?', but should be asked 'What did you see A do?

6.13.2   **Exceptions to the Leading Questions Rule**

Where leading questions are asked of a witness, these do not nullify proceedings but the judge will stop a party asking questions in the prohibited form. Evidence obtained from leading questions is not *inadmissible* but may affect the *weight* placed on it by the judge or jury.

Leading questions are admissible in the following circumstances:

- To refresh a witness's memory (**see para. 6.12.5**).
- Where the witness is deemed 'hostile' (**see para. 6.12.2**).
- For identification purposes (**see chapter 16**).
- Usually in matters accepted as being uncontroversial.
- In cross-examination.

6.14   **Cross-examination**

Cross-examination is the process by which one party may ask questions of the other party's witnesses. This examination is usually focused on either undermining their evidence or supporting that of the party's own witnesses.

Cross-examination, like any other form of questioning, is subject to the rules of evidence. The answers elicited from witnesses must be directly relevant to an issue in the case, or indirectly so, concerning evidence of collateral issues which means that although all witnesses (except generally the defendant) may be asked credit questions, as a general rule, their answers to such questions will be final. A collateral issue is one which is only relevant to the credibility of the witness. In *Attorney-General* v *Hitchcock* (1847) 1 Exch 91, the court determined the general rule preventing a party from calling evidence on collateral issues. However, there are five exceptions to this general rule. These relate to where a witness:

- is biased;
- has previous convictions;
- has a reputation for untruthfulness;
- is unreliable because of some physical or mental disability or illness;
- has made a statement inconsistent with what he/she has said in the witness box.

If any of these exceptions apply, then further questions can be asked of the witness to disprove his/her answer to the credit question.

The rules in relation to cross-examination do not prevent a party from asking the other party's witnesses about any matter which, if accepted by the witness, will undermine the witness's evidence.

Where a party decides not to cross-examine an opponent's witness, this is held to be an *acceptance* of the witness's evidence-in-chief. Consequently, it is not open to the party that failed to cross-examine to criticise, in a closing speech, the unchallenged evidence of the witness (*R v Bircham* [1972] Crim LR 430).

In *R v Bingham* [1999] 1 WLR 598, it was held that a defendant who goes into the witness box and is sworn thereby exposes himself/herself to cross-examination by the prosecution and any co-accused, even if he/she does not give any evidence-in-chief. The prosecution is entitled to cross-examine the defendant even where no questions have been put to him/her by the defence counsel and adverse inferences can be drawn if the defendant does not answer those questions (**see chapter 10**).

6.14.1 **Protection of Witnesses from Cross-examination**

The Youth Justice and Criminal Evidence Act 1999 prohibits defendants from personally cross-examining complainants and particular witnesses in certain circumstances. The Act also creates a new statutory framework in relation to questioning witnesses about their previous sexual behaviour.

Complainants

Section 34 of the 1999 Act states:

> No person charged with a sexual offence may in any criminal proceedings cross-examine in person a witness who is the complainant, either—
> (a) in connection with that offence, or
> (b) in connection with any other offence (of whatever nature) with which that person is charged in the proceedings.

Section 35 of the 1999 Act states:

> (1) No person charged with an offence to which this section applies may in any criminal proceedings cross-examine in person a protected witness, either—
> (a) in connection with that offence, or
> (b) in connection with any other offence (of whatever nature) with which that person is charged in the proceedings.

KEYNOTE

A 'protected witness' for the purposes of s. 35(1) is the complainant, a witness to the commission of the offence or a child, i.e. a person under the age of 17 (s. 35(2)).

The offences to which s. 35 apply are any offence under:

- the Sexual Offences Act 1956

- the Indecency with Children Act 1960

- the Sexual Offences Act 1967

- s. 54 of the Criminal Law Act 1977 (incitement to have sexual intercourse with a girl under 16 who is his granddaughter, daughter or sister)

- the Protection of Children Act 1978.

The following offences are also included in s. 35(3):

- kidnapping, false imprisonment or an offence under s. 1 or 2 of the Child Abduction Act 1984

- any offence under s. 1 of the Children and Young Persons Act 1933

- any offence which involves an assault on, or injury or a threat of injury to, any person.

Particular Witnesses

Section 36 of the 1999 Act states:

(1) This section applies where, in a case neither of sections 34 and 35 operates to prevent an accused in any criminal proceedings from cross-examining a witness in person—

    (a) the prosecutor makes an application for the court to give a direction under this section in relation to the witness, or

    (b) the court of its own motion raises the issue whether such a direction should be given.

(2) If it appears to the court—

    (a) that the quality of evidence given by the witness on cross-examination—

        (i) is likely to be diminished if the cross-examination (or further cross-examination) is conducted by the accused in person, and

        (ii) would be likely to be improved if a direction were given under this section, and

    (b) that it would not be contrary to the interests of justice to give such a direction, the court may give a direction prohibiting the accused from cross-examining (or further cross-examining) the witness in person.

KEYNOTE

Where an accused is prohibited from cross-examining the complainant or a witness, he/she must appoint a legal representative to conduct the cross-examination on his/her behalf. If the accused refuses or fails to appoint a legal representative, the court must consider appointing one on his/her behalf in order to test the witness's evidence.

Witness's Previous Sexual Behaviour

Section 41 of the 1999 Act states:

(1) If at a trial a person is charged with a sexual offence, then, except with the leave of the court—

    (a) no evidence may be adduced, and

    (b) no question may be asked in cross-examination,

    by or on behalf of the accused at the trial, about any sexual behaviour of the complainant.

KEYNOTE

It is for the defence to apply to the court if it wishes to introduce evidence or ask questions about the complainant's previous sexual behaviour (s. 41(2)).

Evidence will only be allowed if it is relevant to an issue in the case or is necessary to rebut prosecution evidence. It will also be allowed if it is an issue of consent and relates to sexual behaviour alleged to have taken place at or about the same time as the event which is the subject matter of the charge (s. 41(3)).

No evidence or question will be regarded as relating to a relevant issue where it is designed to impugn the credibility of the complainant as a witness (s. 41(4)).

Where the defence makes application under s. 41, the application is heard in private and in the absence of the complainant (s. 43(1)).

Following the hearing in private, the court must state in open court the reasons for giving or refusing the application (s. 43(2)).

In *R v Y* [2001] 2 WLR 1546, it was held that the complainant could be questioned about her sexual history with the defendant as otherwise s. 41 was in danger of being found to be in breach of Article 6 of the Convention (right to a fair trial). The House of Lords considered that it is common sense that a prior sexual relationship between a complainant and defendant could be relevant to the defence of consent.

Questions or evidence about false statements in the past by a complainant relating to sexual assaults, or about a failure, while complaining of other sexual assaults, to complain of the alleged assault charged, are not normally questions 'about' any sexual behaviour of the complainant. Therefore, s. 41 was not intended to exclude questions or evidence about previous false complaints (*R* v *T* [2002] 1 All ER 683).

6.15   Re-examination

Following cross-examination, the party calling the witness is entitled to re-examine. The questions put to the witness at this time may only relate to those matters upon which there was a cross-examination. No leading questions are allowed within the re-examination of a witness.

After the defendant has been re-examined it is open to the judge to ask questions to clear up uncertainties, to fill gaps, or to answer queries which might be lurking in the jury's mind. It is not appropriate for the judge to cross-examine the witness (*R* v *Wiggan* (1999) *The Times*, 22 March).

6.16   Further Evidence

It is the general rule that the prosecution must call the whole of their evidence before closing their case (*R* v *Francis* [1991] 1 All ER 225).

However, there are three well established exceptions to the general rule:

- evidence in rebuttal of defence evidence, that is, matters arising *ex improviso* (i.e. evidence which becomes relevant in circumstances which the prosecution could not have foreseen at the time when they presented their case) (*R* v *Owen* [1952] 2 QB 362);
- evidence not called by reason of oversight or inadvertence (*Royal* v *Prescott-Clarke* [1966] 2 All ER 366 and *Hammond* v *Wilkinson* [2001] Crim LR 323);
- evidence not previously available (*R* v *Pilcher* (1974) 60 Cr App R 1).

New evidence may be admitted in appeals for criminal cases as provided by s. 23(1) of the Criminal Appeal Act 1968. Section 23 allows the Court of Appeal, 'if they think it necessary or expedient in the interests of justice' *inter alia* to receive the evidence, if tendered, of any competent but not compellable witness or to order any compellable witness to attend for examination, whether or not that witness was called at the trial. In *R* v *Ahluwalia* [1992] 4 All ER 889, s. 23 was used to admit fresh evidence of the accused's alleged endogenous depression which, if put forward at the trial, may have provided an arguable defence to the charge of murder. Similarly, in *R* v *O'Brien* [2000] Crim LR 676, expert psychiatric evidence was admitted as fresh evidence to show that a defendant's abnormal disorder might render a confession or evidence unreliable. However, in *R* v *Horsman* (2001) *The Times*, 14 December, the Court of Appeal held that generally, at a re-trial, a defendant could not adduce as fresh evidence a statement which he/she had withheld for tactical reasons during his/her first trial.

6.17   Presence of Witnesses in Court

It is the general rule for all witnesses not to be present in court until called to give evidence. An exception to the rule relates specifically to expert witnesses who are never excluded from court. The police officer in charge of the case is also allowed to remain in court at least until the start of police evidence. If a witness is in the court, he/she may be required by the judge to withdraw until called to give evidence. If a witness deliberately remains in court after being required to withdraw, the evidence of the witness may not be admitted. However, a judge has no grounds to exclude a witness's testimony solely on the grounds that the witness had been in court before giving evidence (*R* v *Briggs* (1930) 22 Cr App R 68; *Tomlinson* v *Tomlinson* [1980] 1 WLR 322).

6.18 Contempt of Court

This section is not intended to provide full details of criminal contempt of court but to consider occasions where police officers may be involved or required to take action.

Section 12 of the Contempt of Court Act 1981 deals with criminal contempt in the magistrates' court and states:

(1) A magistrates' court has jurisdiction under this section to deal with any person who—
   (a) wilfully insults the justice or justices, any witness before an officer of the court or any solicitor or counsel having business in the court, during his or their sitting or attendance in court or in going to or returning from the court; or
   (b) wilfully interrupts the proceedings of the court or otherwise misbehaves in court.

(2) In any such case the court may order any officer of the court, or any constable, to take the offender into custody and detain him until the rising of the court; and the court may, if it thinks fit, commit the offender to custody for a specified period not exceeding one month or impose on him a fine not exceeding £2,500, or both.

KEYNOTE

Contempt of court in the High Court and Crown Court is provided for by the Rules of the Supreme Court 1965, ord. 52 and penalties for contempt by s. 14 of the Contempt of Court Act 1981. The 1981 Act provides for an offender to be committed to custody for a fixed term; not exceeding two years in the case of committal by a superior court and one month by an inferior court.

---

7 Youth justice

7.1 Introduction

Sections 6 and 7 of the Crime and Disorder Act 1998 seek to create a framework of partnership between agencies for the reduction of crime and fear of insecurity.

The 1998 Act places the responsibility for formulating a strategy for the reduction of crime and disorder resting jointly on local authorities and chief officers of police. The councils and police have equal stakes in this process and both are under a mutual duty to co-operate with every police authority, probation committee and health authority whose areas of responsibility coincide with any part of the relevant local government area (s. 5(1)).

The Home Secretary may also prescribe, by order, other bodies or persons to co-operate or participate in the formulation and implementation of the strategy (s. 5(2) and (3)).

7.2 Youth Justice Scheme

Section 37 of the Crime and Disorder Act 1998 states the aim of the youth justice scheme:

(1) It shall be the principal aim of the youth justice system to prevent offending by children and young persons.

(2) In addition to any other duty to which they are subject, it shall be the duty of all persons and bodies carrying out functions in relation to the youth justice system to have regard to that aim.

KEYNOTE

The 'persons and bodies' referred to in s. 37(2) are those working within the youth justice system. This includes local authorities, health authorities, probation services, voluntary agencies, the police and the courts.

Local authorities have a duty, acting in co-operation with these persons and bodies, to provide all youth justice services (s. 38(1)). These services are determined by national standards drawn up by the Youth Justice Board **(see para. 7.5)**. The duty is performed in co-operation with every chief officer of police or police authority and every local probation board or health authority (s. 38(2)).

Section 37(1) provides a 'principal aim' and this should not have an effect on other considerations such as: the duty a lawyer owes to his/her client; the duty a Crown Prosecutor has with regard to the Code of Crown Prosecutors **(see appendix 1)**; and the means by which re-offending may be dealt with, i.e. the use of a custodial order. The sentencing courts principal aim is the prevention of re-offending generally by children and young persons.

7.3   Youth Offending Teams

The provisions of s. 39 of the Crime and Disorder Act 1998 formalises this multi-agency approach with the introduction of youth offending teams. Section 39 states:

(1) Subject to subsection (2) below, it shall be the duty of each local authority, acting in co-operation with the persons and bodies mentioned in subsection (3) below, to establish for their area one or more youth offending teams.

(2) Two (or more) local authorities acting together may establish one or more youth offending teams for both (or all) their areas; . . .

The 'persons and bodies' referred to in subsection (1) differ from those found in s. 38(2) and are contained in s. 39(3) which states:

(3) It shall be the duty of—
    (a) every chief officer of police any part of whose police area lies within the local authority's area; and
    (b) every local probation board or health authority any part of whose area lies within that area, to co-operate in the discharge by the local authority of their duty under subsection (1) above.

KEYNOTE

Youth offending teams carry out those functions which are required of the team within the local authority's youth justice plan (see para. 7.4).

The primary work of the youth offending teams include:

- a 'responsible officer' role in relation to parenting and child safety orders;

- assessment and intervention work;

- supervision of community sentences;

- an 'appropriate adult' service for police interviews;

- bail information, supervision and support;

- placement of young offenders;

- court work and preparation of reports.

The Powers of Criminal Courts (Sentencing) Act 2000 provides two more requirements of youth offending teams in relation to referral orders (see para. 9.4.14): to establish youth offender panels (s. 21); and their responsibilities in relation to such panels (s. 29).

7.3.1   Youth Offender Panels

Section 21 of the Powers of Criminal Courts (Sentencing) Act 2000 states:

(1) Where a referral order has been made in respect of an offender (or two or more associated referral orders have been so made), it is the duty of the youth offending team specified in the order (or orders)—
    (a) to establish a youth offender panel for the offender;
    (b) to arrange for the first meeting of the panel to be held for the purposes of section 23 below; and
    (c) subsequently to arrange for the holding of any further meetings of the panel required by virtue of section 25 below (in addition to those required by virtue of any other provision of this Part).

(2) A youth offender panel shall—
(a) be constituted,
(b) conduct its proceedings, and
(c) discharge its functions under this Part (and in particular those arising under section 23 below), in accordance with guidance given from time to time by the Secretary of State.

KEYNOTE

Each meeting of the panel will be made up of a member of the youth offending team and two members who are not from the youth offending team (s. 21(3)). The other two members are volunteers from the local community.

Panel members will have such qualifications or satisfy such criteria as determined by the Secretary of State (s. 21(4)).

Section 23 of the 2000 Act relates to a youth offender contract and the first meeting of the panel where a programme of behaviour to prevent re-offending will be agreed with the offender. The terms of the programme may include a number of provisions such as: financial or other reparation to the victim; attendance at mediation sessions; unpaid work or service; curfew requirements; educational attendance; rehabilitation for drugs and alcohol misuse; etc.

7.3.2 Youth Offender Panels: Youth Offender Teams' Functions

In respect of referral orders, the youth offender teams are responsible for providing administrative support, accommodation and other facilities required by the youth offender panel (s. 29(1) of the 2000 Act).

The team will also arrange for supervising the offender's compliance with the terms of the contract and the member of the team, who is part of the youth offender panel, will ensure records are kept of the offender's compliance or non-compliance (s. 29(2)).

7.4 Youth Justice Plans

The purpose of youth justice plans is to prevent re-offending by children and young persons.

A duty to produce these plans is provided by s. 40 of the Crime and Disorder Act 1998 which states:

(1) It shall be the duty of each local authority, after consultation with the relevant persons and bodies, to formulate and implement for each year a plan (a 'youth justice plan') setting out—
(a) how youth justice services in their area are to be provided and funded; and
(b) how the youth offending team or teams established by them (whether alone or jointly with one or more other local authorities) are to be composed and funded, how they are to operate, and what functions they are to carry out.

KEYNOTE

The youth justice plans are a similar provision to those statutory requirements to produce plans already placed upon the police (s. 8 of the Police Act 1996—annual policing plan), local authorities (Children Act 1989—children's services plan) and education (s. 9 of the Education Act 1997—plan to deal with behaviourally difficult pupils, truants, etc.).

7.5 Youth Justice Board

The Youth Justice Board, which is a body corporate, was created by s. 41(1) of the Crime and Disorder Act 1998. The Board consists of 10, 11 or 12 members appointed by the Secretary of State (s. 41(2)) and these members have extensive experience of the youth justice system (s. 41(4)). Members are appointed for a fixed period no longer than five years and may be re-appointed provided the total length of service does not exceed ten years (sch. 2, para. 2(5)).

The functions of the Board are provided by s. 41(5) which states:

(5) The Board shall have the following functions, namely—
  (a) to monitor the operation of the youth justice system and the provision of youth justice services;
  (b) to advise the Secretary of State on the following matters, namely—
    (i) the operation of that system and the provision of such services;
    (ii) how the principal aim of that system might most effectively be pursued;
    (iii) the content of any national standards he may see fit to set with respect to the provision of such services, or the accommodation in which children and young persons are kept in custody; and
    (iv) the steps that might be taken to prevent offending by children and young persons;
  (c) to monitor the extent to which that aim is being achieved and any such standards met;
  (d) for the purposes of paragraphs (a), (b) and (c) above, to obtain information from relevant authorities;
  (e) to publish information so obtained;
  (f) to identify, to make known and promote good practice in the following matters, namely—
    (i) the operation of the youth justice system and the provision of youth justice services;
    (ii) the prevention of offending by children and young persons; and
    (iii) working with children and young persons who are or are at risk of becoming offenders.
  (g) to make grants, with the approval of the Secretary of State, to local authorities or other bodies for them to develop such practice, or to commission research in connection with such practice; and
  (h) themselves to commission research in connection with such practice.

KEYNOTE

The Board provides the framework, context and information base within which local authorities and youth offending teams operate. It is also responsible for providing advice on the national standards used by youth offending teams and youth justice services.

The Youth Justice Board for England and Wales Order 2000 (SI 2000 No. 1160), reg. 3, introduced a further function of the board, that is, to enter into agreements for the provision of secure accommodation and accommodation for young offenders.

7.6 Reprimands and Warnings

Reprimands and warnings for young offenders are provided by s. 65 of the Crime and Disorder Act 1998 and Home Office Circular 9/99 which is included in **appendix 4** sets out the purpose of the new system and it will be important to follow the set procedure for the force area where the child or young person is being dealt with.

7.6.1 Reprimand

Section 65(1) and (2) of the 1998 Act provide a constable with a power to reprimand an offender where:

(a) a constable has evidence that a child or young person ('the offender') has committed an offence;

(b) the constable considers that the evidence is such that, if the offender were prosecuted for the offence, there would be a realistic prospect of his being convicted;

(c) the offender admits to the constable that he committed the offence;

(d) the offender has not previously been convicted of an offence; and

(e) the constable is satisfied that it would not be in the public interest for the offender to be prosecuted.

KEYNOTE

An offender may only be reprimanded where he/she has not previously been reprimanded or warned (s. 65(2)).

7.6.2 Warning

Section 65(3) of the 1998 Act provides a constable with a power to warn an offender where:

(a) the offender has not previously been warned; or

(b) where the offender has previously been warned, the offence was committed more than two years after the date of the previous warning and the constable considers the offence to be not so serious as to require a charge to be brought;
but no person may be warned under paragraph (b) above more than once.

7.6.3 Reprimand and Warning: Police Powers

In relation to the giving of a reprimand or warning s. 65(5) of the 1998 Act provides that a police officer must:

(a) where the offender is under the age of 17, give any reprimand or warning in the presence of an appropriate adult; and

(b) explain to the offender and, where he is under that age, the appropriate adult in ordinary language—
  (i) in the case of a reprimand, the effect of subsection 5(a) of section 66 below;
  (ii) in the case of a warning, the effect of subsections (1), (2), (4) and (5)(b) and (c) of that section, and any guidance issued under subsection (3) of that section.

KEYNOTE

In relation to s. 65(5)(b)(i) above, s. 66(5)(a) provides that a reprimand may be cited in criminal proceedings in the same way as a conviction.

In relation to s. 65(5)(b)(ii) above, explanations of each of the subsections referred to are provided in brackets:

- s. 66(1) (referral to youth offending team);

- s. 66(2) (participation in a rehabilitation programme);

- s. 66(4) (restrictions on a court to impose a conditional discharge);

- s. 66(5)(b) and (c) (citation as a criminal conviction).

In *R (on the application of U)* v *Metropolitan Police Commissioner* (2002) *The Times*, 29 November, it was held that where the full and informed consent from the offender and the appropriate adult were not obtained, the administration of a reprimand or warning could be considered a breach of Article 6 of the European Convention on Human Rights (the right to a fair trial).

---

8 Youth crime and disorder

8.1 Introduction

This chapter details the provisions contained in the Crime and Disorder Act 1998 that were enacted to address the causes of youth crime. These provisions are contained in Part I of the 1998 Act and relate to:

- parenting orders
- child safety orders
- local child curfew schemes
- removal of truants to designated premises, etc.

8.2 Parenting Orders

These orders are about influencing parental responsibility and control and the importance placed upon this by the government. The orders were introduced to give parents more help and support to change the criminal and/or anti-social behaviour of their children in providing a framework where parents participate in their child's supervision. The strategy here is one of prevention in attempting to dissuade a recurrence of criminality or truancy.

Parenting orders are defined by s. 8 of the Crime and Disorder Act 1998:

(4) A parenting order is an order which requires the parent—
    (a) to comply, for a period not exceeding twelve months, with such requirements as are specified in the order; and
    (b) ... to attend, for a concurrent period not exceeding three months and not more than once in any week, such counselling and guidance sessions as may be specified in directions given by the responsible officer; ...

In considering the requirements of an order s. 9 of the 1998 Act states:

(4) Requirements specified in, and directions given under, a parenting order shall, as far as practicable, be such as to avoid—
    (a) any conflict with the parent's religious beliefs; and
    (b) any interference with the times, if any, at which he normally works or attends an educational establishment.

KEYNOTE

For the purpose of the 1998 Act, 'child' is someone under the age of 14 and 'young person' is someone of 14 years or over but under 18 (s. 117).

'Parenting order' should not be confused with 'parental responsibility order' (Children Act 1989) and 'parental order' (Human Embryology and Fertilisation Act 1990) which are available for other purposes.

8.2.1 Counselling and Guidance

Counselling and guidance sessions referred to in s. 8(4)(b) of the 1998 Act are intended to educate parents in how to respond more effectively to the demands of their child. These sessions could include the setting and enforcement of consistent standards of behaviour or a requirement that the child be escorted to school by a responsible adult.

Where a parent has attended counselling and guidance sessions under an earlier parenting order the court may waive this requirement (s. 8(5)).

The requirements provided by s. 8(4)(a) above are not specified but in drafting the legislation certain examples were given. These included a parent escorting their child to school and a child being supervised by a responsible adult during the evenings.

8.2.2 Responsible Officer

The definition of 'responsible officer' is provided in s. 8(8) of the 1998 Act which states:

> In this section and section 9 below 'responsible officer', in relation to a parenting order, means one of the following who is specified in the order, namely—
>
> (a) an officer of a local probation board;
> (b) a social worker of a local authority social services department; and
> (bb) a person nominated by a person appointed as chief education officer under section 532 of the Education Act 1996;
> (c) a member of a youth offending team

8.2.3 The Parenting Order

Section 8 of the 1998 Act states:

> (1) This section applies where, in any court proceedings—
>   (a) a child safety order is made in respect of a child;
>   (b) an anti-social behaviour order or sex offender order is made in respect of a child or young person;
>   (c) a child or young person is convicted of an offence; or
>   (d) a person is convicted of an offence under section 443 (failure to comply with a school attendance order) or section 444 (failure to secure regular attendance at a school of registered pupil) of the Education Act 1996.
>
> (2) Subject to subsection (3) and section 9(1) below and to section 19(5) of, and paragraph 13(5) of Schedule 1 to, the Powers of Criminal Courts (Sentencing) Act 2000, if in the proceedings the court is satisfied that the relevant condition is fulfilled, it may make a parenting order in respect of a person who is a parent or guardian of the child or young person or, as the case may be, the person convicted of the offence under section 443 or 444 ('the parent').

KEYNOTE

An order may be made against:

- One or both biological parents (this could include an order against a father who may not be married to the mother).

- A person who is a guardian.

Guardians are defined as any person who, in the opinion of the court, has for the time being the care of a child or young person (s. 117(1)).

The court will be required to establish whether or not the making of an order is 'desirable' in the circumstances of a particular case. This is seen as an entirely subjective test (except for the requirement in s. 9(1)(a) below), following on from s. 8(2) above which states that the court *may* make an order. Consequently, the court generally retains a discretion not to impose an order.

Child Safety orders and anti-social behaviour orders are discussed in **paras 8.3** and **8.4** respectively. For the law in relation to sex offenders, **see Crime, chapter 10.**

8.2.4   **Parenting Order: Statutory Requirement**

Section 9 of the 1998 Act states:

(1) Where a person under the age of 16 is convicted of an offence, the court by or before which he is so convicted—
   (a) if it is satisfied that the relevant condition is fulfilled, shall make a parenting order; and
   (b) if it is not so satisfied, shall state in open court that it is not and why not.

KEYNOTE

Section 9(1) provides a statutory requirement in favour of making an order where the relevant condition relates to where a child or young person (under 16) is convicted of an offence (s. 8(1)(c)).

In determining the legislation the government decided to provide a distinction between offenders under 16 and those of 16 and 17. The decision appears to have been made on advice concerning the differences in emotional, intellectual and physical development between juveniles aged 16 and 17 and younger children. It was considered that parents of those under 16 who are subject to criminal proceedings must be involved in preventing a further commission of an offence. For 16 and 17 year olds the court should determine any parental involvement.

8.2.5   **Procedure**

Apart from considering information about the family circumstances of each case, whatever the age of the child or young person, s. 9(3) of the 1998 Act places the following requirement on the court:

(3) Before making a parenting order, a court shall explain to the parent in ordinary language—
   (a) the effect of the order and of the requirements proposed to be included in it;
   (b) the consequences which may follow (under subsection (7) below) if he fails to comply with any of those requirements; and
   (c) that the court has power (under subsection (5) below) to review the order on the application either of the parent or of the responsible officer.

KEYNOTE

The parent or responsible officer can apply for the discharge or variation of an order and the court can agree to cancel, add or substitute any of its provisions. This can only be done by the court making the original order.

8.2.6   **Breach of a Parenting Order**

Section 9(7) of the 1998 Act states:

If while a parenting order is in force the parent without reasonable excuse fails to comply with any requirement included in the order, or specified in directions given by the responsible officer, he shall be liable on summary conviction to a fine not exceeding level 3 on the standard scale.

KEYNOTE

The section does not specify who would be responsible for instituting proceedings but it is assumed this will be the 'responsible officer' and that the normal processes will be followed whereby the Crown Prosecution Service will make decisions as to a prosecution applying the usual test of public interest.

8.3   Child Safety Orders

These orders have been introduced to help prevent children under 10 from turning to crime. Such orders are concerned with the child's potential offending behaviour and in practice are likely to be used in conjunction with parenting orders under s. 8 of the Crime and Disorder Act 1998.

Section 11 of the 1998 Act states:

(1) Subject to subsection (2) below, if a magistrates' court, on the application of a local authority, is satisfied that one or more of the conditions specified in subsection (3) below are fulfilled with respect to a child under the age of 10, it may make an order (a 'child safety order') which—

    (a) places the child, for a period (not exceeding the permitted maximum) specified in the order, under the supervision of the responsible officer; and

    (b) requires the child to comply with such requirements as are so specified.

KEYNOTE

In order to ensure any such proceedings are not viewed as 'criminal', jurisdiction for making the order rests with the magistrates' family proceedings court.

The section provides evidence of the government's determination to deliver crime prevention through a partnership approach. A local authority with social services responsibilities must make the application for such an order. However, it would probably be the police who first become aware of the misconduct which triggers such an application.

8.3.1   Child Safety Order: Conditions

The court must be satisfied that one or more of four conditions are fulfilled before making an order. These are provided by s. 11(3) of the 1998 Act:

    (a) that the child has committed an act which, if he had been aged 10 or over, would have constituted an offence;

    (b) that a child safety order is necessary for the purpose of preventing the commission by the child of such an act as is mentioned in paragraph (a) above;

    (c) that the child has contravened a ban imposed by a curfew notice; and

    (d) that the child has acted in a manner that caused or was likely to cause harassment, alarm or distress to one or more persons not of the same household as himself.

KEYNOTE

The civil standard of evidence (the 'balance of probabilities') is the standard of proof in determining whether a condition is fulfilled. There is no minimum age for an order. The permitted maximum period of supervision of such an order is three months. If the court is satisfied that the circumstances of the case are exceptional it can extend the order up to a maximum of 12 months (s. 11(4)).

8.3.2 **Breach of Child Safety Order**

Section 12(6) of the 1998 Act states:

(6) Where a child safety order is in force and it is proved to the satisfaction of the court which made it or another magistrates' court acting for the same petty sessions area, on the application of the responsible officer, that the child has failed to comply with any requirement included in the order, the court—
    (a) may discharge the order and make in respect of him a care order under subsection 1(a) of section 31 of the 1989 Act; or
    (b) may make an order varying the order—
        (i) by cancelling any provision included in it; or
        (ii) by inserting in it (either in addition to or in substitution for any of its provisions) any provision that could have been included in the order if the court had then had power to make it and were exercising the power.

KEYNOTE

'Section 31 of the 1989 Act' relates to the Children Act 1989. The provisions in this subsection provides a new route into care. Although the section does not provide the court with the power to make a supervision order in response to a breach, there is nothing to stop an application being made for such an order by a local authority or other authorised person in the ordinary way.

8.4 **Anti-social Behaviour Orders**

Anti-social behaviour orders (ASBO) are provided by the Crime and Disorder Act 1998, s. 1 which states:

(1) An application for an order under this section may be made by a relevant authority if it appears to the authority that the following conditions are fulfilled with respect to any person aged 10 or over, namely—
    (a) that the person has acted, since the commencement date, in an anti-social manner, that is to say, in a manner that caused or was likely to cause harassment, alarm or distress to one or more persons not of the same household as himself; and
    (b) that such an order is necessary to protect relevant persons from anti-social acts by him.

The 'relevant authority' was amended by the Police Reform Act 2002 which inserted a new s. 1(1A) which states:

(1A) In this section and sections 1B and 1E 'relevant authority' means—
    (a) the council for a local government area;
    (b) the chief officer of police of any police force maintained for a police area;
    (c) the Chief Constable of the British Transport Police Force; or
    (d) any person registered under section 1 of the Housing Act 1996 (c 52) as a social landlord who provides or manages any houses or hostel in a local government area.

By virtue of s. 1B of the 1998 Act an order can be applied for and obtained by a relevant authority in county court proceedings. Where the relevant authority is not a party to those proceedings it can apply to the court to be joined to the proceedings in order to apply for an ASBO against the relevant party. This also includes the application for an interim ASBO (s. 1D).

An application for an ASBO can be made by way of complaint to a magistrates' court (s. 1(3)) or an order can be issued on conviction in criminal proceedings, either on an application or by the court's own initiative (s.1C).

Section 1E of the 1998 Act requires that consultation must take place between the council for a local government area and the chief officer of police of any police force maintained for a police area before an application is made for an ASBO. If the application is being made by the British Transport Police or a Registered Social Landlord, they must consult with both the council and chief officer of police for their respective areas.

If the conditions set out in s. 1(1) of the Act are fulfilled, the court may make an anti-social behaviour order prohibiting the defendant from doing anything described in the order (s. 1(4)). The prohibitions that may be imposed by an order are those necessary for the purpose of protecting persons (whether relevant persons or persons elsewhere in England and Wales) from further anti-social acts by the defendant.

These orders have effect for periods of not less than two years though the applicant or defendant may apply by complaint to the court for it to be varied or discharged by a further order (s. 1(8)). However, no order may be discharged without the consent of both parties (s. 1(9)).

Where a person is in breach of an ABSO, s. 1(10) provides:

(10) If without reasonable excuse a person does anything which he is prohibited from doing by an anti-social behaviour order, he shall be liable—
  (a) on summary conviction, to imprisonment for a term not exceeding six months or to a fine not exceeding the statutory maximum, or to both; or
  (b) on conviction on indictment, to imprisonment for a term not exceeding five years or to a fine, or to both.

KEYNOTE

Proceedings under s. 1(1) for the imposition of an ABSO are civil and not criminal proceedings, both as a matter of domestic law and for the purposes of Article 6 of the European Convention on Human Rights (right to a fair trial). However, magistrates are required to apply the criminal and not the civil standard of proof, i.e. beyond reasonable doubt (*R (on the application of McCann)* v *Crown Court of Manchester* [2002] 4 All ER 593).

8.5   Child Curfew Schemes

Child curfew schemes are designed to tackle the problem of unsupervised young children committing crime, anti-social activities and causing real harm and misery to local communities. The age of the young child was raised by the Criminal Justice and Police Act 2001 from under 10 to under 16. The 2001 Act also gives the police the power to initiate a local child curfew scheme in addition to local authorities.

Section 14 of the Crime and Disorder Act 1998 states:

(1) A local authority or a chief officer of police may make a scheme (a 'local child curfew scheme') for enabling the authority—
  (a) subject to and in accordance with the provisions of the scheme; and
  (b) if, after such consultation as is required by the scheme, the authority or as the case may be the officer considers it necessary to do so for the purpose of maintaining order,
  to give a notice imposing, for a specified period (not exceeding 90 days), a ban to which subsection (2) below applies.

(2) This subsection applies to a ban on children of specified ages (under 16) being in a public place within a specified area—
  (a) during specified hours (between 9 pm and 6 am); and
  (b) otherwise than under the effective control of a parent or a responsible person aged 18 or over.

KEYNOTE

The local authority or chief officer of police are required to consult with each other and such people or other bodies as are considered appropriate (s. 14(3)). The extent of the consultation with other people or bodies is totally discretionary but if appropriate community groups are not consulted the Home Secretary may decide not to confirm the scheme (see below).

Most schemes should come into force one month after confirmation of their introduction by the Home Secretary (s. 14(5)).

'Public place' for the purpose of the section has the same meaning as in Part II of the Public Order Act 1986 (s. 14(8)) (**see General Police Duties, chapter 4**).

8.5.1 Contravention of Curfew Notices

Section 15 of the 1998 Act states:

(1) Subsections (2) and (3) below apply where a constable has reasonable cause to believe that a child is in contravention of a ban imposed by a curfew notice.

(2) The constable shall, as soon as practicable, inform the local authority for the area that the child has contravened the ban.

(3) The constable may remove the child to the child's place of residence unless he has reasonable cause to believe that the child would, if removed to that place, be likely to suffer significant harm.

KEYNOTE

This provision does not give the constable a power to use force. However, in applying common law principles, a constable may use reasonable force in exercising a lawful power (**see General Police Duties, chapter 2**).

Section 15(3) does not state what a constable should do with a child if he/she does not remove the child to its home. However, it would seem appropriate to use the power under s. 46 of the Children Act 1989 in removing the child to suitable accommodation, i.e. a police station or care of social services (**see Crime, chapter 11**).

Where a constable has informed the local authority about a contravention of the curfew notice s. 15(4) places a duty on the local authority to enquire into the circumstances of the child and to initiate the investigation within 48 hours of receiving such notification.

8.6 Removal of Truants to Designated Premises, etc.

Section 16 of the Crime and Disorder Act 1998 states:

(1) This section applies where a local authority—
    (a) designates premises in a police area ('designated premises') as premises to which children and young persons of compulsory school age may be removed under this section; and
    (b) notifies the chief officer of police for that area of the designation.

(2) A police officer of or above the rank of superintendent may direct that the powers conferred on a constable by subsection (3) below—
    (a) shall be exercisable as respects any area falling within the police area and specified in the direction; and
    (b) shall be so exercisable during a period specified;
    and references in that subsection to a specified area and a specified period shall be construed accordingly.

KEYNOTE

'Designated premises' are not defined in the 1998 Act and are a matter for the local authority. In drafting the legislation it was considered that in many cases children would ultimately be removed to their own schools.

8.6.1   **Police Powers**

Section 16(3) provides the police powers in relation to dealing with truants:

> (3) If a constable has reasonable cause to believe that a child or young person found by him in a
> public place in a specified area during a specified period—
> (a) is of compulsory school age; and
> (b) is absent from school without lawful authority,
> the constable may remove the child or young person to designated premises, or to the school
> from which he is so absent.

KEYNOTE

Again 'public place' has the same meaning as in part II of the Public Order Act 1986.

'Without lawful authority' is qualified by subsection (4) in that lawful authority will be that which falls within s. 444 of the Education Act 1996—leave, sickness, unavoidable cause or day set apart for religious observation.

The power of a constable to remove a child or young person to 'designated premises' is not an arrest in the traditional sense of detention and statutory powers relating to arrests will not apply. However, the duty to explain the reason for a persons 'seizure' may well apply in such cases (as to which, **see General Police Duties, chapter 2**).

As with the powers conferred in relation to curfew notices (**see para. 8.5**), it appears probable that the common law rule entitling a constable to use reasonable force would apply. However, legal commentators are not convinced this is the case as the use of force could be seen as having a damaging effect on relations between the police and young persons and the possibility of criminal or civil action against individual officers.

The requirement for the officer to have 'reasonable cause to believe' that the person meets the criteria at (a) and (b) is more stringent than mere suspicion (**see General Police Duties, chapter 2**).

---

9 | Sentencing

9.1 | Introduction

This chapter is intended to provide an overview of the powers of the courts in relation to sentencing offenders. It deals with the range of available sentences by reference to the concept of seriousness and includes, custody, community-based penalties, financial penalties and discharge.

9.2 | Custody

9.2.1 | Custody of Adults

Custodial Sentence

A court's powers to impose a custodial sentence on an offender is provided by s. 79 of the Powers of Criminal Courts (Sentencing) Act 2000, which states:

(1) This section applies where a person is convicted of an offence punishable with a custodial sentence other than one—
   (a) fixed by law; or
   (b) falling to be imposed under section 109(2), 110(2) or 111(2) below.

(2) Subject to subsection (3) below, the court shall not pass a custodial sentence on the offender unless it is of the opinion—
   (a) that the offence, or the combination of the offence and one or more offences associated with it, was so serious that only such a sentence can be justified for the offence; or
   (b) where the offence is a violent or sexual offence, that only such a sentence would be adequate to protect the public from serious harm from him.

(3) Nothing in subsection (2) above shall prevent the court from passing a custodial sentence on the offender if he fails to express his willingness to comply with—
   (a) a requirement which is proposed by the court to be included in a community rehabilitation order or supervision order and which requires an expression of such willingness; or
   (b) a requirement which is proposed by the court to be included in a drug treatment and testing order or an order under section 52(4) above (order to provide samples).

KEYNOTE

Where a court imposes a custodial sentence, it is required to state in open court that it is of the opinion that either or both of paragraphs (a) and (b) of subsection (2) above apply and why it is of that opinion. Additionally, the court is required to explain to the offender in open court and in ordinary language why it is passing a custodial sentence (s. 79(4)).

In relation to a magistrates' court, this explanation needs to be specified in the commitment warrant and be entered in the court register (s. 79(5)).

Generally, before imposing a custodial sentence, a court would obtain a 'pre-sentence report' in order to ascertain if the grounds outlined in s. 79(2) are met (s. 81(1)).

A 'custodial sentence' under the 2000 Act means:

- a sentence of imprisonment (s. 89(1)(a));
- a sentence of detention (ss. 90 or 91));
- a detention and training order (s. 100).

(s. 76(1)).

Pre-sentence Report

A 'pre-sentence report' is a written report to assist the court and is prepared by one of the following: probation officer; social worker; member of a youth offending team for persons under 18 (s. 81).

Where a court obtains a pre-sentence report, it is required to give a copy of the report to the offender or his/her legal representative and to the prosecutor (s. 156).

Persons not Legally Represented

There is a restriction on imposing custodial sentences on persons not legally represented by the Powers of Criminal Courts (Sentencing) Act 2000. Section 83 of the 2000 Act states:

(1) A magistrates' court on summary conviction, or the Crown Court on committal for sentence or on conviction on indictment, shall not pass a sentence of imprisonment on a person who—
    (a) is not legally represented in that court, and
    (b) has not been previously sentenced to that punishment by a court in any part of the United Kingdom,

unless he is a person to whom subsection (3) below applies.

...

(3) This subsection applies to a person if either—
    (a) he was granted a right to representation funded by the Legal Services Commission as part of the Criminal Defence Service but the right was withdrawn because of his conduct; or
    (b) having been informed of his right to apply for such representation and having had the opportunity to do so, he refused or failed to apply.

KEYNOTE

A person is treated as having been legally represented if he/she has assistance of counsel or a solicitor to represent him/her at some time after he/she is found guilty and before sentence is passed (s. 83(4)).

Seriousness of the Offence

In determining whether an offence 'was so serious that only such a sentence [custodial] can be justified for the offence' (s. 79(2)(a) of the 2000 Act), guidance is provided by a number of decided cases, the most recent of which being *R* v *Howells* [1998] Crim LR 836. It was argued in this case that laying down prescriptive rules as to what constituted 'serious' was both 'dangerous and wrong'.

However, a number of issues were discussed as to what factors might be considered in determining whether an offence was serious. These included:

- deliberate and premeditated actions as opposed to spontaneous and unpremeditated;
- where personal injury or mental trauma were inflicted as opposed to solely financial loss;
- the offender's previous convictions and response to previous sentences;
- whether the offence was committed while the defendant was on bail.

In borderline cases, it was considered appropriate for the court to take into account the:

- early admission of the offence;
- genuine remorse shown by the offender;
- youth and immaturity of the offender;
- good character of the offender;
- offender's family responsibilities;
- physical or mental disability of the offender;
- offender not previously having served a custodial sentence.

When considering passing a severe sentence on a person the court must also give consideration to Article 3 of the European Convention on Human Rights (prohibition of torture), which includes inhuman punishment and degrading punishment. In *Weeks* v *United Kingdom* (1987) 10 EHRR 293, it was held that to sentence a 17 year old to life imprisonment for punitive purposes for an offence of robbery would potentially violate Article 3.

Article 7 of the Convention (no punishment without law) also has a bearing on sentencing and states: 'Nor shall a heavier penalty be imposed than the one that was applicable at the time the criminal offence was committed.'

Seriousness of the Offence: Racially or Religiously Aggravated Offences

In gauging issues relevant to the seriousness of the offence a further factor is provided by s. 153 of the Powers of Criminal Courts (Sentencing) Act 2000. Section 153 states:

(1) This section applies where a court is considering the seriousness of an offence other than one under sections 29 to 32 of the Crime and Disorder Act 1998 (racially-aggravated assaults, racially-aggravated criminal damage, racially-aggravated public order offences and racially-aggravated harassment etc).

(2) If the offence was racially aggravated, the court—
   (a) shall treat that fact as an aggravating factor (that is to say, a factor that increases the seriousness of the offence); and
   (b) shall state in open court that the offence was so aggravated.

(3) Section 28 of the Crime and Disorder Act 1998 (meaning of 'racially aggravated') applies for the purposes of this section as it applies for the purposes of sections 29 to 32 of that Act.

KEYNOTE

For the racially or religiously aggravated offences under ss. 29 to 32 of the 1998 Act, **see Crime** and **General Police Duties**.

Violent or Sexual Nature

In determining whether an offence 'is of a violent or sexual nature, that only such a sentence would be adequate to protect the public from serious harm' (s. 79(2)(b)), guidance is provided by s. 161 of the 2000 Act.

Under s. 161(3) 'violent offence' means:

an offence which leads, or is intended or likely to lead, to a person's death or to physical injury to a person, and includes an offence which is required to be charged as arson...

Under s. 161(2) 'sexual offence' means:

(a) an offence under the Sexual Offences Act 1956, other than an offence under section 30 [living on immoral earnings], 31 [woman exercising control over a prostitute] or 33 to 36 [keeping brothels and related offences] of that Act;

(b) an offence under section 128 of the Mental Health Act 1959 [sexual intercourse with patients];

(c) an offence under the Indecency with Children Act 1960;

(d) an offence under section 9 of the Theft Act 1968 of burglary with intent to commit rape;

(e) an offence under section 54 of the Criminal Law Act 1977 [incitement to have sexual intercourse with granddaughter, daughter, sister, under 16];

(f) an offence under the Protection of Children Act 1978;

(g) an offence under section 1 of the Criminal Law Act 1977 of conspiracy to commit any of the offences in paragraphs (a) to (f) above;

(h) an offence under section 1 of the Criminal Attempts Act 1981 of attempting to commit any of those offences;

(i) an offence of inciting another to commit any of those offences.

KEYNOTE

For a full discussion of these offences, see Crime, chapter 10.

9.2.2 | Maximum Sentences

Maximum custodial sentences are reserved for the gravest examples of the offence for which a person has been convicted (*R* v *Carroll* (1995) 16 Cr App R (S) 488). In *R* v *Ambler* [1976] Crim LR 266), it was directed that those responsible for sentencing, in determining the gravity of an offence, should consider the particular case 'within the broad bands of that type'.

9.2.3 | Reduction for Guilty Plea

It is a well established principle that the length of a prison sentence is normally reduced in light of the offender entering a plea of guilty (*R* v *Greene* (1993) 14 Cr App R (S) 682). The extent of the reduction appears to vary between one-fifth and one-third of the maximum sentence.

Section 152 of the Powers of Criminal Courts (Sentencing) Act 2000 makes specific provision for reducing sentences for guilty pleas. It requires the court to take into account when the plea of guilty was indicated, and the circumstances in which the plea was made. If the court then passes a less severe sentence than would normally have been the case, it must state in open court that it has done so.

This 'reduction' of sentence can equally apply to the level of a fine, or reducing the duration of a community sentence (Magistrates' Association Guidelines (2000)).

9.2.4 | Life Sentences

Life sentences can be categorised into three specific types: mandatory, automatic and discretionary.

Mandatory Life Sentences

Mandatory life sentences are those where an offender, aged 21 or over, is convicted of murder and must be sentenced to imprisonment for life (s. 1(1) of the Murder (Abolition of Death Penalty) Act 1965). Since the sentence is mandatory, there is no right of appeal (s. 9 of the Criminal Appeal Act 1968).

Section 1(2) of the 1965 Act empowers the court to, 'declare the period which it recommends to the Secretary of State as the minimum period which in its view should elapse' before the offender is released on licence. Similarly, with the life sentence, there is no right of appeal against the recommendation (*R* v *Leaney* [1996] 1 Cr App R (S) 30). The *Practice Direction (criminal: consolidated)* [2002] 3 All ER 904, para. 49 (life sentences), provides guidance on the setting of minimum terms with its primary purpose being to give effect to the advice of the Sentencing Advisory Panel.

In *Dennis Stafford* v *United Kingdom* (2002) 35 EHRR 32, the European Court on Human Rights held that the Home Secretary's power to impose a fixed tariff to a mandatory life sentence was incompatible with Article 6 of the European Convention on Human Rights and the right to a fair trial (which includes the element of sentencing). This decision of the European Court was followed in *R* v *Secretary for the Home Department, ex parte (1) Anthony Anderson (2) John Hope Taylor* (2002) *The Times*, 29 November.

The House of Lords held in *R* v *Lichniak* [2002] 4 All ER 1122, that mandatory life sentences were compatible with Article 3 (the prohibition on inhuman or degrading treatment or punishment) and Article 5(1) (the right to liberty) of the European Convention on Human Rights.

Automatic Life Sentences

Section 109 of the Powers of Criminal Courts (Sentencing) Act 2000 requires the Crown Court to impose a sentence of imprisonment for life on an offender who is convicted of a serious offence where the offender is aged 18 or over and has already been convicted of another serious offence.

The offences which qualify as 'serious offences' for the purposes of s. 109 include:

- attempted murder, conspiracy to murder or incitement to murder;

- soliciting murder;

- manslaughter;

- wounding or causing grievous bodily harm with intent;

- rape or attempted rape;

- sexual intercourse with a girl under 13;

- an offence under the following sections of the Firearms Act 1968: s. 16 (possession with intent to endanger life), s. 17 (use to resist arrest), s. 18 (carrying to commit indictable offence or resist arrest);

- robbery (does not include attempted robbery) where the offender had in his/her possession a firearm or imitation firearm.

For a full discussion of these offences, **see Crime** and **General Police Duties**.

Where s. 109 above applies, it is only in exceptional circumstances that the court may decide not to impose a life sentence. In so doing the court must state in open court what these exceptional circumstances are (s. 109(3)).

The provision of a life sentence for a second previous offence was originally introduced by the Crime (Sentences) Act 1997. In *R* v *Kelly* [1999] 2 WLR 346, it was held that 'exceptional' was not a term of art but a familiar adjective describing a circumstance which was unusual or uncommon, not regularly or routinely encountered, but which need not be unique or unprecedented. In the case stated, the defendant's youth at the time of the first serious offence, the dissimilarity between the two serious offences, and the abstention from crime during the intervening period were not so out of the ordinary as to amount to exceptional circumstances.

In *R* v *Offen* [2001] 1 WLR 253 the Court of Appeal again considered the issue of 'exceptional circumstances' and this case is now the leading authority on the interpretation of s. 109. Emphasising that the purpose of automatic life sentences was for the protection of the public Lord Woolf CJ went on to say:

> The policy and intention of Parliament was to protect the public against a person who had committed two serious offences. It therefore can be assumed that the section was not intended to apply to someone in relation to whom it was established that there would be no need for protection in the future. In other words, if the facts showed the statutory assumption was misplaced, then this, in the statutory context was not the normal situation and, in consequence, for the purpose of the section the position was exceptional.

Lord Woolf CJ further commented that 'exceptional circumstances' might relate to the time that had elapsed between the commission of the two serious offences but consideration needed to focus on any danger against which the public required protection. Similarly, when considering whether the two offences were of a different character, or where the first offence was committed by the accused when he/she was young, the court's concern must remain as to any continuing danger to the safety of the public.

A defendant's acute mental illness at the time of committing a 'serious offence was held to be not of itself an exceptional circumstance which justified the court in not passing a life sentence under section [109] of the Act' (*R v Newman* [2000] 2 Cr App R 227).

As the court indicated in the *Bulger* case, the purpose of sentencing in these cases is to protect society. Whilst the effect of the crime on the victim's family was a relevant consideration to the period of the tariff by way of punishment and deterrence, the main issue is whether the offenders could safely be released back into the community on licence.

Discretionary Life Sentences

A court may only pass a discretionary life sentence in respect to an offence for which life imprisonment is provided as the maximum penalty. The statutory criteria outlined in s. 109 of the Powers of Criminal Courts (Sentencing) Act 2000 above apply to these sentences, in that they can only be imposed in cases involving an offence of such seriousness or of a violent or sexual offence (*R v Robinson* [1997] 2 Cr App R (S) 35).

In relation to the use of discretionary life sentences the Court of Appeal has provided principles whereby such sentences should only be imposed in exceptional circumstances. In *R v Wilkinson* (1983) 5 Cr App R (S) 105 it was stated that, with few exceptions, these sentences would only be used for offenders whose mental state was such that they are a danger to the 'life or limb of members of the public'. Obviously, this is where the provisions of the Mental Health Act 1983 cannot be used to deal with the offender.

9.2.5 Mandatory Minimum Sentences

Class A Drug Trafficking Offence

Section 110 of the Powers of Criminal Courts (Sentencing) Act 2000 requires the court to impose a sentence of imprisonment of at least seven years on a person who:

- is convicted of a class A drug trafficking offence; and

- was aged 18 or over at the time of the offence; and

- has been previously convicted for two or more similar offences, one committed after the conviction for the other.

However, the court need not impose the mandatory minimum sentence if it is of the opinion that there are particular circumstances relating to any of the offences or the offender that would make such a sentence unjust in all the circumstances. Such 'particular circumstances' must be stated in open court.

Domestic Burglary

Section 111 of the Powers of Criminal Courts (Sentencing) Act 2000 requires the court to impose a sentence of imprisonment of at least three years on a person who:

- is convicted of a domestic burglary; and

- was aged 18 or over at the time of the offence; and

- had been previously convicted on two or more occasions of domestic burglary, one committed after the conviction for the other.

As with s. 110 of the 2000 Act, the court need not impose the mandatory minimum sentence if it is of the opinion that there are particular circumstances relating to any of the offences or the offender that would make such a sentence unjust in all the circumstances. Again, such 'particular circumstances' must be stated in open court.

In relation to s. 110, the drug trafficking offence subject of the conviction must have been committed after 30 September 1997 (s. 110(1)(a)), and for s. 111, the domestic burglary must have been committed after 30 November 1999 (s. 111(1)(a)).

For offences of drug trafficking and burglary, **see Crime, chapters 6 and 12.**

Mandatory minimum sentences were originally introduced by the Crime (Sentences) Act 1997 following which Home Office Circulars 54/1997 and 55/1999 were published to provide appropriate guidance to the police and Crown Prosecution Service.

Police Action

Where a person is charged with burglary of a dwelling the police should:

- obtain information about any previous convictions or matters outstanding arising from police action; and

- where there is verifiable and reliable information/evidence (e.g. from PNC records) that the alleged offender has received two convictions of domestic burglary since the implementation of s. 111 of the 2000 Act, they should make the Crown Prosecution Service aware of this when passing them the relevant case.

Crown Prosecution Service Action

Where a person is charged with burglary of a dwelling the prosecutor should:

- inform the magistrates' court at the earliest possible opportunity (and by the first hearing at the latest) of a case involving an alleged third-time domestic burglary; and

- when drafting relevant indictments, include in the 'Particulars of Offence' the term 'dwelling' to denote that a dwelling house was the subject of the offence.

9.2.6   **Suspended Sentences**

The power for a court to impose a suspended sentence is provided by s. 118 of the Powers of Criminal Courts (Sentencing) Act 2000, which states:

(1) A court which passes a sentence of imprisonment for a term of not more than two years for an offence may (subject to subsection (4) below) order that the sentence shall not take effect unless, during a period specified in the order, the offender commits in Great Britain another offence punishable with imprisonment and thereafter a court having power to do so orders under section 119 below that the original sentence shall take effect.

(2) The period specified in an order under subsection (1) above must be a period of not less than one year nor more than two years beginning with the date of the order.

(3) In this Act—

'suspended sentence' means a sentence to which an order under subsection (1) above relates; and 'operational period', in relation to such a sentence, means the period specified in the order under subsection (1).

(4) A court shall not deal with an offender by means of a suspended sentence unless it is of the opinion—

(a) the case is one in which a sentence of imprisonment would have been appropriate even without the power to suspend the sentence, and

(b) that the exercise of that power can be justified by the exceptional circumstances of the case.

(5) A court which passes a suspended sentence on any person for an offence shall consider whether the circumstances of the case are such as to warrant in addition the imposition of a fine or the making of a compensation order.

KEYNOTE

Section 119 of the 2000 Act provides a court with powers to deal with an offender convicted of an offence punishable with imprisonment during the period of the suspended sentence. The court may deal with the offender in one of four ways:

- order that the suspended sentence take effect (usually consecutively) with the original term unaltered;

- order that the suspended sentence take effect with a lesser term;

- vary the original order by extending the operational period of the suspended sentence expiring not later than two years;

- make an order with respect to the suspended sentence.

The longest sentence which can be imposed is two years, therefore, if consecutive sentences are imposed totalling more than two years, a suspended sentence cannot be used (*R v Coleman* [1969] 2 QB 468).

Suspended Sentence Supervision Orders

Section 122 of the Powers of Criminal Courts (Sentencing) Act 2000 states:

(1) Where a court passes on an offender a suspended sentence for a term of more than six months for a single offence, the court may make a suspended sentence supervision order, that is to say, an order placing the offender under the supervision of a supervising officer for a period which is specified in the order and does not exceed the operational period of the suspended sentence.

...

(3) An offender in respect of whom a supervision order is in force shall keep in touch with the supervising officer in accordance with such instructions as he may from time to time be given by that officer and shall notify him of any change of address.

KEYNOTE

Where an offender, without reasonable cause, fails to comply with the requirements of a supervision order, he/she may be fined up to £1,000 (s. 123(3) of the 2000 Act).

9.2.7 | **Sentencing Guidelines**

Section 80 of the Crime and Disorder Act 1998 enables the Court of Appeal to provide guidance in relation to the principles courts should apply in determining sentences for particular categories of offences. The purpose of these guidelines is not to remove the element of judicial discretion open to a court but to provide greater consistency in passing sentences appropriate to the level of seriousness of the offence.

In framing or revising guidelines, the court is obliged to have regard to various matters. Section 80(3) provides that the court must have regard to:

(a) the need to promote consistency in sentencing;

(b) the sentences imposed by courts in England and Wales for offences of the relevant category;

(c) the cost of different sentences and their relative effectiveness in preventing re-offending;

(d) the need to promote public confidence in the criminal justice system; and

(e) the views communicated to the Court . . . by the Sentencing Advisory Panel.

KEYNOTE

The guidelines are intended to provide criteria for assessing:

- the seriousness of the offence;

- the weight to be given to previous convictions; and

- the failure of the accused to respond to previous sentences (s. 80(4)).

A sentencing court also needs to take account of Article 14 of the European Convention on Human Rights (prohibition of discrimination), which provides that Convention rights must be secured 'without discrimination on any grounds such as sex, race, colour, language, religion, political or other opinion, national or social origin, association with a national minority, property, birth or other status'. Article 14 has been described as a parasite right since it needs to be pleaded in conjunction with another Convention right, though it is not necessary to establish a violation of the substantive right concerned. It would be necessary for a person to show that there had been a difference in treatment in the delivery of the right in comparison with another person similarly dealt with.

Sentencing Advisory Panel

Where the Court of Appeal decides to frame or revise any guidelines as outlined above, it must notify the Panel (s. 81(1)). The Panel must propose guidelines if directed to do so by the Home Secretary (s. 81(3)).

The composition of the Sentencing Advisory Panel is determined by the Lord Chancellor and consists of about 12 people usually appointed for a five-year period. There is no restriction as to whom the Lord Chancellor may appoint but it may include:

- sentencers (including a magistrate)

- people with experience of the prison service

- people with experience of the probation service

- people with academic experience

- people with research experience

- people who are independent of the criminal justice system.

The Lord Chancellor has the power to provide remuneration for Panel members (s. 81(5)).

9.2.8 **Victim Personal Statements**

The victim personal statements scheme provides victims of crime with an opportunity to prove a statement saying how the crime has affected them and enables the court to take such statements into account when determining sentence. Guidance on the relevance of victim personal statements is provided by *Practice Direction (criminal: consolidated)* [2002] 3 All ER 904, para. 28 (personal statements of victims) and the decision of the Court of Appeal in *R v Perks* [2001] 1 Cr App R (S) 66.

When taking a statement from a victim a police officer is required to inform the victim of the scheme. The decision as to whether to make such a statement is entirely a matter for the victim. A victim personal statement may be made or updated at any time prior to the disposal of the case.

9.2.9 Release of Short-term Prisoners on Licence and Subject to Home Curfew

Release of Short-term Prisoners on Licence

Section 34A of the Criminal Justice Act 1991 (introduced by s. 99 of the Crime and Disorder Act 1998), provides the Secretary of State with the power to release a prisoner on licence where the prisoner has served the 'requisite period' for the term of his/her sentence. The 'requisite period' for prisoners with terms of imprisonment of four months or more but less than 12 months is one quarter of their term, and for those with terms of imprisonment of 12 months or more is a period that is 90 days less than one half of their term (Release of Short-Term Prisoners on Licence (Amendment of Requisite Period) Order 2002 (SI 2002 No. 2933)).

Release may be subject to conditions that may include conditions for either securing the electronic monitoring of his/her compliance with any other conditions of his/her release or securing the electronic monitoring of his/her whereabouts (s. 62(1) and (2) of the Criminal Justice and Court Services Act 2000).

Certain categories of prisoners are not eligible for release under this section. One such category are prisoners covered by the notification requirements of the Sex Offenders Act 1997 (as to which, **see Crime, chapter 10**) (s. 65 of the Criminal Justice and Court Services Act 2000).

Release of Short-term Prisoners Subject to Home Curfew

The release of short-term prisoners subject to home curfews is provided by s. 37A of the Criminal Justice Act 1991 (introduced by s. 100(1) of the Crime and Disorder Act 1998).

The home detention curfew is set up for a prisoner to complete their sentence and runs for a minimum period of 14 days and a maximum period of 60 days. The prisoner is required to agree to the curfew conditions. The governor at the relevant prison determines the details of the curfew. This will normally be from 7 pm to 7 am and may be varied. The minimum period of curfew is nine hours but there is no maximum. HM Prison Service Parole Unit is responsible for the management and monitoring of home detention curfews. The curfew equipment is operated and monitored by an approved private contractor. The contractor installs a home monitoring unit at the approved address and fits the prisoner with the personal identification device at this address on the day of release. Although there is no involvement in the release process, the police are notified of all prisoners subject to home detention curfew 14 days prior to release. The police may request information from the monitoring contractor as to the offender's compliance, or otherwise, with the curfew, including any short-term 'unexplained' absences. Such requests for information are authorised by an officer of the rank of superintendent or above. Electronic monitoring contractors are obliged to provide such information within 24 hours of the request being made.

Breaches of Curfew

The breach of a curfew condition is provided by s. 38A of the 1991 Act (introduced by s. 100(2) of the Crime and Disorder Act 1998), which states:

(2) If it appears to the Secretary of State, as regards a person released on licence under section 34A(3) above—
   (a) that he has failed to comply with the curfew condition;
   (b) that his whereabouts can no longer be electronically monitored at the place for the time being specified in that condition; or

(c) that it is necessary to do so in order to protect the public from serious harm from him,
the Secretary of State may, if the curfew condition is still in force, revoke the licence and
recall the person to prison.

KEYNOTE

The reporting of any breaches of a home detention curfew is the responsibility of the independent contractor. Minor infringements are dealt with by way of a warning but two warnings constitute a failure to comply with the curfew conditions. Any reports of a breach are made to HM Prison Service Parole Unit. This Unit may make a decision to revoke or vary the curfew order. The relevant prison governor may also make variations to the order.

There is no power to arrest any person solely found breaching his/her curfew and local policy should be followed.

On the revocation of a person's licence following a breach of curfew conditions that person, 'shall be liable to be detained in pursuance of his sentence and, if at large, shall be deemed to be unlawfully at large' (s. 38A(5)).

Police Arrests

The guidance provided to police forces in relation to persons who are subject of a home detention curfew is as follows:

Where arrested:

- custody officer to notify the monitoring contractor immediately of:
  - details of the prisoner
  - details of the offence
  - whether the prisoner is to be bailed or retained in custody
  - whether the prisoner continues to wear the electronic tag;
- custody officer to notify the monitoring contractor when the prisoner is released.

Where charged:

- custody officer to immediately inform HM Prison Service Parole Unit;
- custody officer to inform contractor *if* the prisoner is to be returned to prison to remove and collect the monitoring unit.

Where a person is charged with an offence whilst subject to a home detention curfew the PACE Code C in relation to detention following charge continues to apply.

Where a prisoner has been charged with an offence, the decision to revoke the prisoner's licence is a matter for HM Prison Service Parole Unit and not the police.

Police Requests for Revocation

Where the police consider that a prisoner subject to a home detention curfew represents a serious risk to the public they may make a request for it to be revoked. Any such request should be authorised by an officer of the rank of superintendent or above and made to HM Prison Service Parole Unit at the Home Office.

'Serious risk' means:

- Offenders convicted of a sexual or violent offence: death or serious injury (physical or psychological) occasioned by further offences committed by the offender. Sexual and violent offences are considered the same in that a prisoner convicted of an offence of violence may be recalled following concerns about offences of a sexual nature.
- Offenders convicted of a non-sexual or violent offence: death or serious injury, etc. The offence which may cause that risk need not be the same as the original offence.

- It is only necessary to demonstrate that the prisoner has acted in such a way as to give *reasonable cause for belief* that recall is necessary to protect the public.

The chief of police and local parole board for an area also have a statutory duty to make suitable arrangements for managing dangerous offenders (**see Crime**).

9.3 | Custody of Young Offenders

The detention and custody of young offenders is provided by the Powers of Criminal Courts (Sentencing) Act 2000. There are three forms of custodial sentence applicable to young offenders: detention during Her Majesty's pleasure, detention for specific periods, and detention and training orders.

9.3.1 | Detention during Her Majesty's Pleasure

This is confined to murder cases where s. 90 of the Powers of Criminal Courts (Sentencing) Act 2000 provides a mandatory sentence of detention during Her Majesty's pleasure for an offender who is under 18 at the time of the offence.

A person sentenced to be detained during Her Majesty's pleasure will be detained in a place and under such conditions as directed or arranged by the Secretary of State (s. 92(1)).

9.3.2 | Detention for Specific Periods

Section 91 of the 2000 Act applies to young offenders who are convicted of certain serious offences. These offences are provided by s. 91(1) and (2) which states:

(1) Subsection (3) below applies where a person aged under 18 is convicted on indictment of—
    (a) an offence punishable in the case of a person aged 21 or over with imprisonment for 14 years or more, not being an offence the sentence for which is fixed by law; or
    (b) an offence under section 14 of the Sexual Offences Act 1956 (indecent assault on a woman); or
    (c) an offence under section 15 of that Act (indecent assault on a man) committed after 30th September 1997.

(2) Subsection (3) below also applies where a person aged at least 14 but under 18 is convicted of an offence under—
    (a) section 1 of the Road Traffic Act 1988 (causing death by dangerous driving); or
    (b) section 3A of that Act (causing death by careless driving while under influence of drink or drugs).

KEYNOTE

The court may sentence the offender to be detained for such a period not exceeding the maximum term of imprisonment with which the offence is punishable if it is of the opinion that there is no other suitable way in dealing with the case (s. 91(3)).

9.3.3 | Detention and Training Orders

Detention and training orders are provided by s. 100 of the Powers of Criminal Courts (Sentencing) Act 2000, which states:

(1) Subject to sections 90 and 91 above and subsection (2) below, where—
    (a) a child or young person (that is to say, any person aged under 18) is convicted of an offence which is punishable with imprisonment in the case of a person aged 18 or over, and

(b) the court is of the opinion that either or both of paragraphs (a) and (b) of section 79(2) above apply or the case falls within section 79(3),

the sentence that the court is to pass is a detention and training order.

(2) A court shall not make a detention and training order—
   (a) in the case of an offender under the age of 15 at the time of the conviction, unless it is of the opinion that he is a persistent offender;
   (b) in the case of an offender under the age of 12 at that time, unless—
      (i) it is of the opinion that only a custodial sentence would be adequate to protect the public from further offending by him; and
      (ii) the offence was committed on or after such date as the Secretary of State may by order appoint.

KEYNOTE

In *Aldis* v *DPP* (2002) *The Times*, 6 March, it was held that a court was entitled to impose a detention and training order on a youth who had attained the age of 18 prior to his conviction and sentence for the relevant offence.

The court is required to take account of any period for which the offender has been remanded in custody in determining the term of the order (s. 101(8)). This includes where the offender is held in police detention for the purposes of the Police and Criminal Evidence Act 1984 (s. 101(11) and (12)).

Period of Detention and Training

The term of a detention and training order is 4, 6, 8, 10, 12, 18 or 24 months (s. 101(1)), and the period of detention and training is served in secure accommodation (s. 102(1)). This period is one-half of the term of the order (s. 102(2)) and for the second half of the term the person is subject to a period of supervision.

Period of Supervision

A person who is subject to a detention and training order is subject to a period of supervision. This begins with the offender's release at the half-way point of the order or otherwise and ends when the term of the order ends (s. 103(1)).

For the purpose of supervision s. 103(3) provides that the offender shall be under the supervision of an officer of a local probation board, social worker or a member of the youth offending team. The offender is to be given a notice informing him/her of the person responsible for the supervision and any requirements with which the offender needs to comply (s. 103(6)).

Breaches of Supervision

Where an offender fails to comply with the requirements of his/her supervision, an information can be laid before a justice who may issue a summons or warrant for the offender to appear before a youth court (s. 104(1)).

Where it is proved to the satisfaction of the youth court that an offender has failed to comply with the terms of the supervision order, the court may order the offender:

- to be detained in secure accommodation for a period not exceeding the shorter of three months or the remainder of the term of the order, as the court may specify (s. 104(3)(a));

- to pay a fine not exceeding level 3 on the standard scale (s. 104(3)(b)).

Where a person subject to a detention and training order commits a further offence(s) which is punishable with imprisonment in the case of a person aged 18 or over, the court may order the offender to serve a term of detention in secure accommodation. This is in addition to any other disposal (s. 105(2)).

9.4 | **Community-based Penalties**

Community orders are provided by s. 33(1) of the Powers of Criminal Courts (Sentencing) Act 2000, which states:

(1) In this Act, 'community order' means any of the following orders—
   (a) a curfew order;
   (aa) an exclusion order;
   (b) a community rehabilitation order;
   (c) a community punishment order;
   (d) a community punishment and rehabilitation order;
   (e) a drug treatment and testing order;
   (ee) a drug abstinence order;
   (f) an attendance centre order;
   (g) a supervision order;
   (h) an action plan order.

KEYNOTE

In imposing a community order, the court is required to justify its decision in terms of the seriousness of the offence(s). The order or orders shall be the most suitable for the offender and where there is a restriction on liberty this should be commensurate with the seriousness of the offence(s) (s. 35).

A community order may include requirements for securing the electronic monitoring of the offender's compliance subject to arrangements being available in the relevant area (s. 36B of the Powers of Criminal Courts (Sentencing) Act 2000).

Sections 26 to 34 of the Criminal Justice and Court Services Act 2000 have also introduced a new power for the Crown Court. This is to impose a *disqualification order* on a person who has committed an offence against a child and is receiving a qualifying sentence, i.e. imprisonment for 12 months or more, detention in a young offender institution for 12 months, a detention training order for 12 months or more, a hospital order or a guardianship order. The effect of the order will be to disqualify that person from working with children in the future. (**See General Police Duties.**)

9.4.1 | **Curfew Orders**

The power of a court to make a curfew order is provided by s. 37 of the Powers of Criminal Courts (Sentencing) Act 2000, which states:

(1) Where a person is convicted of an offence, the court by or before which he is convicted may (subject to sections 34 to 36 above) make an order requiring him to remain, for periods specified in the order, at a place so specified.

(2) An order under subsection (1) above is in this Act referred to as a 'curfew order'.

(3) A curfew order may specify different places or different periods for different days, but shall not specify—
   (a) periods which fall outside the period of six months beginning with the day on which it is made; or
   (b) periods which amount to less that two hours or more than twelve hours in any one day.

KEYNOTE

Where the offender is under the age of 16, the six-month period referred to in subsection (3)(a) above should read three months (s. 37(4)).

Arrangements for monitoring an offender's whereabouts need to be available for the court to make a curfew order. Such availability is notified by the Secretary of State (s. 37(7)).

Section 37(1) refers to s. 34 (sentence fixed by law and custodial sentence requirement), s. 35 (seriousness of offence to impose community order) and s. 36 (requirement for pre-sentence reports).

9.4.2 Exclusion Orders

The power of a court to make an exclusion order is provided by s. 40A of the Powers of Criminal Court (Sentencing) Act 2000, which states:

(1) Where a person is convicted of an offence, the court by or before which he is convicted may (subject to section 34 to 36 above) make an order prohibiting him from entering a place specified in the order for a period so specified of not more than two years.

(2) An order under subsection (1) above is in this Act referred to as an 'exclusion order'.

(3) An exclusion order—
(a) may provide for the prohibition to operate only during the periods specified in the order;
(b) may specify different places for different periods or days.

(4) In relation to an offender aged under 16 on conviction, subsection (1) above shall have effect as if the reference to two years were a reference to three months.

KEYNOTE

A court shall not make an exclusion order unless it has been notified by the Secretary of State that arrangements for monitoring the offender's whereabouts are available in the area in which the place proposed in the order is situated.

An exclusion order includes the provision for making a person responsible for monitoring the offender's whereabouts during the periods when the prohibition operates. The description of a 'responsible person' will be specified in an order made by the Secretary of State.

Section 40A refers to ss. 34 to 36 of the Act; see para. 9.4.1.

9.4.3 Community Rehabilitation Orders

The power of a court to make a community rehabilitation order is provided by s. 41 of the Powers of Criminal Courts (Sentencing) Act 2000, which states:

(1) Where a person aged 16 or over is convicted of an offence and the court by or before which he is convicted is of the opinion that his supervision is desirable in the interests of—
(a) securing his rehabilitation, or
(b) protecting the public from harm from him or preventing the commission by him of further offences,
the court may (subject to sections 34 to 36 above) make an order requiring him to be under supervision for a period specified in the order of not less than six months nor more than three years.

(2) An order under subsection (1) above is in this Act referred to as a 'community rehabilitation order'.

(3) A community rehabilitation order shall specify the petty sessions area in which the offender resides or will reside.

(4) If the offender is aged 18 or over at the time when the community rehabilitation order is made, he shall, subject to paragraph 18 of schedule 3 to this Act (offender's change of area), be required to be under the supervision of an officer of a local probation board appointed for or assigned to the petty sessions area specified in the order.

(5) If the offender is aged under 18 at that time, he shall, subject to paragraph 18 of schedule 3, be required to be under the supervision of—
(a) an officer of a local probation board appointed for or assigned to the petty sessions area specified in the order; or
(b) a member of a youth offending team established by a local authority specified in the order; and if an order specifies a local authority for the purposes of paragraph (b) above, the

authority specified must be the local authority within whose area it appears to the court that the offender resides or will reside.

KEYNOTE

Before it makes a community rehabilitation order, the court is required to explain to the offender, in ordinary language: the effect of the order; the consequences of failure to comply with the order; and the court's power to review the order on application from the offender (s. 41(7)).

Requirements

Schedule 2 to the 2000 Act provides requirements which *may* be included in a community rehabilitation order, i.e. a requirement to:

- reside in an approved hostel or other institution (para. 1(3));
- present himself/herself to a person or persons at a place or places so specified, and to participate or refrain from participating in activities specified in the order for not more than 60 days (para. 2);
- attend a community rehabilitation centre for no more than 60 days (para. 3);
- where the offender is convicted of a sexual offence, the 60 days specified in paras 2 and 3 above can be increased and will be specified in the order (para. 4);
- obtain treatment for a mental condition (para. 5);
- obtain treatment for drug or alcohol dependency (para. 6);
- follow curfew requirements (para. 7).

9.4.4 | **Community Punishment Orders**

The power of a court to make a community punishment order is provided by s. 46 of the Powers of Criminal Courts (Sentencing) Act 2000, which states:

> (1) Where a person aged 16 or over is convicted of an offence punishable with imprisonment, the court by or before which he is convicted may (subject to sections 34 to 36 above) make an order requiring him to perform unpaid work in accordance with section 47 below.
>
> (2) An order under subsection (1) above is in this Act referred to as a 'community punishment order'.

KEYNOTE

Before it makes a community punishment order, the court is required to explain to the offender, in ordinary language: the effect of the order; the consequences of failure to comply with the order; the court's power to review the order on application from the offender or the responsible officer (s. 46(10)).

The 'responsible officer' can include an officer of a local probation board, social worker or member of a youth offending team (s. 46(5)).

Requirements

Under the 2000 Act, the following requirements *may* be included in a community punishment order:

- to keep in touch with the responsible officer (s. 47(1)(a));
- to notify the responsible officer of any change of address (s. 47(1)(a));
- to perform the number of hours required doing such work at such times as instructed (s. 47(1)(b)).

The number of hours which a person may be required to work will be in the aggregate:

- not less than 40, and

- not more than 240

(s. 46(3)).

Where an offender is sentenced to consecutive community punishment orders, the total number of hours must not exceed 240 (s. 46(8)).

The work required is to be completed within 12 months from the date the order was made (s. 47(3)).

The court can only make an order if it is satisfied that the offender is a suitable person to perform work under such an order (s. 46(4)).

9.4.5 Community Punishment and Rehabilitation Orders

The power of a court to make a community punishment and rehabilitation order is provided by s. 51 of the Powers of Criminal Courts (Sentencing) Act 2000, which states:

(1) Where a person aged 16 or over is convicted of an offence punishable with imprisonment and the court by or before which he is convicted is of the opinion mentioned in subsection (3) below, the court may (subject to sections 34 to 36 above) make an order requiring him both—
   (a) to be under supervision for a period specified in the order, being not less than twelve months nor more than three years; and
   (b) to perform unpaid work for a number of hours so specified, being in the aggregate not less than 40 nor more than 100.

(2) An order under subsection (1) above is in this Act referred to as a 'community punishment and rehabilitation order'.

(3) The opinion referred to in subsection (1) above is that the making of a community punishment and rehabilitation order is desirable in the interests of—
   (a) securing the rehabilitation of the offender; or
   (b) protecting the public from harm from him or preventing the commission by him of further offences.

KEYNOTE

The requirements in relation to community punishment and rehabilitation orders are the same as those described for the individual orders.

9.4.6 Drug Treatment and Testing Orders

The power of a court to make a drug treatment and testing order is provided by s. 52 of the Powers of Criminal Courts (Sentencing) Act 2000, which states:

(1) Where a person aged 16 or over is convicted of an offence, the court by or before which he is convicted may (subject to sections 34 to 36 above) make an order which—
   (a) has effect for a period specified in the order of not less than six months nor more than three years ('the treatment and testing period'); and
   (b) includes the requirements and provisions mentioned in sections 53 and 54 below; but this section does not apply in relation to an offence committed before 30th September 1998.

(2) An order under subsection (1) above is in this Act referred to as a 'drug treatment and testing order'.

(3) A court shall not make a drug treatment and testing order in respect of an offender unless it is satisfied—
   (a) that he is dependent on or has a propensity to misuse drugs; and
   (b) that his dependency or propensity is such as requires and may be susceptible to treatment.

KEYNOTE

Although treatment for drug and alcohol dependency may be provided as a condition within a community rehabilitation order, s. 52 has introduced a testing requirement without any causal link between drugs and the offence.

Section 52(4) states:

(4) For the purpose of ascertaining for the purposes of subsection (3) above whether the offender has any drug in his body (in a case where, at the time of his conviction, he was aged under 18), the court may by order require him to provide samples of such description as it may specify; but the court shall not make such an order unless the offender expresses his willingness to comply with its requirements.

KEYNOTE

Before making a requirement under s. 52(4), the offender must state a willingness to comply. If not, the order cannot be imposed.

Requirements

Under the 2000 Act the following requirements *may* be included in a drug treatment and testing order, i.e. a requirement:

- that the offender submit to treatment (s. 53(1));
- to provide such treatment as a resident in an institution or place specified (s. 53(2)(a));
- to provide such treatment as a non-resident in an institution or place specified and at such intervals specified (s. 53(2)(b));
- that the offender provide samples of such description as determined by the treatment provider (s. 53(4));
- specifying for each month the minimum number of occasions where samples are to be provided (s. 53(5));
- specifying in the order the petty sessions area in which the offender resides or will reside (s. 54(1));
- that the offender be under the supervision of an officer of a local probation board (s. 54(2));
- that the offender keep in touch with the officer of a local probation board as specified (s. 54(4)(a));
- that the offender communicate to the officer of a local probation board the results of tests carried out on the samples (s. 54(4)(b)).

Supervision by the officer of a local probation board should be for the purpose of reporting to the court on the offender's progress, and any failure to comply with the order (s. 54(5)).

The offender's progress is reviewed by the court at intervals of less than one month (s. 54(6)(a)). Initially, the offender is required to attend these hearings (s. 54(6)(c)), but if progress is satisfactory subsequent reviews can be carried out without a full review hearing (s. 55(6)).

9.4.7 **Drug Abstinence Orders**

The power of a court to make a drug abstinence order is provided by s. 58A of the Powers of Criminal Courts (Sentencing) Act 2000, which states:

(1) Where a person aged 18 or over is convicted of an offence, the court by or before which he is convicted may (subject to sections 34 to 36 above) make an order which requires the offender—

(a) to abstain from misusing specified Class A drugs; and

(b) to provide, when instructed to do so by the responsible officer, any sample mentioned in the instruction for the purpose of ascertaining whether he has any specified Class A drug in his body.

(2) An order under subsection (1) above is in this Act referred to as a 'drug abstinence order'.

KEYNOTE

The court can only make an order if it is of the opinion that the offender is dependent on or has a propensity to use class A drugs *and* the offence in question is a 'trigger' offence or the misuse by the offender caused or contributed to the offence in question (s. 58A(3)).

A 'trigger' offence is any offence under the Theft Act 1968, ss. 1 (theft), 8 (robbery), 9 (burglary, including s. 10 aggravated burglary), 12 (taking a conveyance), 12A (aggravated vehicle-taking), 15 (criminal deception) and 25 (going equipped); class A drug offences under the Misuse of Drugs Act 1971 and ss. 4 (production and supply), 5(2) (possession), and 5(3) (possession with intent to supply) (sch. 6 to the Criminal Justice and Court Services Act 2000).

A 'responsible officer' is the person responsible for the offender's supervision (s. 58A(5)). Officers of local probation boards are specified as persons responsible for the supervision of offenders subject to these orders (Drug Abstinence Order (Responsible Officer) (No. 2) Order 2001 (SI 2001 No. 3494)).

A drug abstinence order can have effect for not less than six months nor more than three years (s. 58A(7)).

For the power to require people in police custody to undergo drug tests, **see chapter15.**

Pre-sentence Drug Testing

Section 36A of the Powers of Criminal Courts (Sentencing) Act 2000 provides the court with the power to make an order for the offender to provide samples of any description to ascertain whether the offender has any class A drugs in his body. The offender must be aged 18 or over and have been convicted of an offence (s. 36A(1) and (2)).

If the offender fails, without reasonable excuse, to comply with the order, the court may impose a fine of an amount not exceeding level 4 (s. 36A(3)).

A drug abstinence order can also be included in a community rehabilitation order if two sets of conditions are satisfied. The first set of conditions are: where the offender was aged 18 or over when convicted, is dependent or has a propensity to misuse class A drugs and the offence if a trigger offence. The second set of conditions contain one additional element; the misuse by the offender of any specified class A drug caused or contributed to the offence. (Section 42(2), (2A), (2B) and (2C) of the 2000 Act.)

9.4.8   **Orders for Persistent Petty Offenders**

Section 59 of the Powers of Criminal Courts (Sentencing) Act 2000 provides the court with the power to make curfew orders and community punishment orders for persistent petty offenders. Section 59 states:

(1) This section applies where—
   (a) a person aged 16 or over is convicted of an offence;
   (b) the court by or before which he is convicted is satisfied that each of the conditions mentioned in subsection (2) below is fulfilled; and
   (c) if it were not so satisfied, the court would be minded to impose a fine in respect of the offence.

(2) The conditions are that—
   (a) one or more fines imposed on the offender in respect of one or more previous offences have not been paid; and
   (b) if a fine were imposed in an amount which was commensurate with the seriousness of the offence, the offender would not have sufficient means to pay it.

KEYNOTE

As to whether an offender is a 'persistent offender' should be judged on the facts of the case and the word 'persistent' is to be given its ordinary meaning rather than any definition contained in a government circular (*R v C* (*A Juvenile: Persistent Offender*) (2000) *The Times*, 11 October).

Where the conditions under subsection (2) are met, the court can make either a curfew order (**see para. 9.4.1**) or a community punishment order (**see para. 9.4.3**) instead of imposing a fine (s. 59(3)).

The restrictions on imposing community sentences contained in subsections (1) and (3)(b) of s. 35 do not apply in relation to s. 59 and a curfew order or community punishment order can still be made (s. 59(4)).

9.4.9   **Breach of Curfew, Exclusion, Community Rehabilitation, Community Punishment, Community Punishment and Rehabilitation, Drug Treatment and Testing and Drug Abstinence Orders**

Schedule 3 to the 2000 Act provides for the breach of community orders.

Paragraph 3, sch. 3 states:

(1) If at anytime while a relevant order is in force in respect of an offender it appears on information to a justice of the peace acting for the petty sessions area concerned that the offender has failed to comply with any of the requirements of the order, the justice may—
   (a) issue a summons requiring the offender to appear at the place and time specified in it; or
   (b) if the information is in writing and on oath, issue a warrant for his arrest.

(2) Any summons or warrant issued under this paragraph shall direct the offender to appear or be brought—
   (a) in the case of a drug treatment and testing order or a drug abstinence order, before the court responsible for the order;
   (b) in the case of any other relevant order which was made by the Crown Court and included a direction that any failure to comply with any of the requirements of the order be dealt with by the Crown Court, before the Crown Court; and
   (c) in the case of a relevant order which is neither a drug treatment and testing order or a drug abstinence order nor an order to which paragraph (b) above applies, before a magistrates' court acting for the petty sessions area concerned.

KEYNOTE

Where it is proved to the satisfaction of the Crown Court or magistrates' court that an offender has failed without reasonable excuse to comply with any of the requirements of the relevant order the court may:

- impose a fine not exceeding £1,000

- make a community punishment order

- deal with the offender for the offence in respect of which the order was made

(sch. 3, paras 4(1) and 5(1)).

The court will also revoke any relevant order if it is still in force (paras 4(3) and 5(3)).

9.4.10   **Attendance Centre Orders**

The power of a court to make an attendance centre order is provided by s. 60 of the Powers of Criminal Courts (Sentencing) Act 2000, which states:

(1) Where—
   (a) (subject to sections 34 to 36 above) a person aged under 21 is convicted by or before a court of an offence punishable with imprisonment, or
   (b) a court has power or would have power, but for section 89 below (restrictions on imprisonment of young offenders and defaulters), to commit a person aged under 21 to prison in

default of payment of any sum of money or for failing to do or abstain from doing anything required to be done or left undone, or

(c) a court has power to commit a person aged at least 21 but under 25 to prison in default of payment of any sum of money,

the court may, if it has been notified by the Secretary of State that an attendance centre is available for the reception of persons of his description, order him to attend at such a centre, to be specified in the order, for such number of hours as may be so specified.

(2) An order under subsection (1) above is in this Act referred to as an 'attendance centre order'.

KEYNOTE

The aggregate number of hours for attendance is dependent on the age of the offender as follows:

- Under 14—not less than 12 hours, except where the court determines that 12 hours would be excessive (s. 60(3)).

- Under 16—must not exceed 24 hours where the court considers 12 hours inadequate (s. 60(4)(a)).

- Under 21—must not exceed 36 hours (s. 60(4)(b)).

Breach of Attendance Centre Orders

Schedule 5 to the 2000 Act provides for the breach of attendance centre orders.

Paragraph 1, sch. 5 states:

(1) Where an attendance centre order is in force and it appears on information to a justice acting for a relevant petty sessions area that the offender—
   (a) has failed to attend in accordance with the order, or
   (b) while attending has committed a breach of rules made under section 62(3) of this Act which cannot be adequately dealt with under those rules,

the justice may issue a summons requiring the offender to appear at the place and time specified in the summons before a magistrates' court acting for the area or, if the information is in writing and on oath, may issue a warrant for the offender's arrest requiring him to be brought before such a court.

KEYNOTE

As with a breach of other community-based sentences, the court may impose a fine not exceeding £1,000 and deal with the offender for the original offence in respect of which the order was made (sch. 5, para. 2(1)).

The court will also revoke the attendance centre order if it is still in force.

9.4.11 **Supervision Orders**

The power of a court to make a supervision order is provided by s. 63 of the Powers of Criminal Courts (Sentencing) Act 2000, which states:

(1) Where a child or young person (that is to say, any person aged under 18) is convicted of an offence, the court by or before which he is convicted may (subject to sections 34 to 36 above) make an order placing him under the supervision of—
   (a) a local authority designated by the order;
   (b) an officer of a local probation board; or
   (c) a member of a youth offending team.

(2) An order under subsection (1) above is in this Act referred to as a 'supervision order'.

KEYNOTE

A supervision order lasts for three years or such shorter period as specified (s. 63(7)), and during the period of the order the supervisor *shall advise, assist and befriend the offender* (s. 64(4)).

Requirements

Under sch. 6 to the 2000 Act, the following requirements may be included in a supervision order, i.e. a requirement to:

- reside with an individual named in the order (para. 1);
- live at a place or places so specified (para. 2(1)(a));
- present himself/herself to a person or persons, at a place or places, on a day or days so specified (para. 2(1)(b));
- participate in activities so specified (para. 2(1)(c));
- impose a 'night restriction' requirement (para. 3(2)(e)), for no longer than ten hours on any one night (para. 4(2));
- reside in local authority accommodation for a specified period (para. 5);
- comply with arrangements to receive treatment for a mental condition (para. 6);
- comply with arrangements for his/her education (para. 7).

Breach of Supervision Orders

Schedule 7 to the 2000 Act provides for the breach of supervision orders.

Paragraph 2, sch. 7 states:

(1) This paragraph applies if while a supervision order is in force in respect of an offender it is proved to the satisfaction of a relevant court, on the application of the supervisor, that the offender has failed to comply with any requirement included in the supervision order in pursuance of paragraph 1, 2, 3, 5 or 7 of Schedule 6 to this Act or section 63(6)(b) of this Act.

KEYNOTE

As with other community-based sentences, the court may order the offender to pay a fine not exceeding £1,000 (para. 2(2)(a)(i)).

Unlike the other community-based sentences, the court may make a curfew order in respect of the offender or an attendance centre order (para. 2(2)(a)(ii) and (iii)).

The court may also revoke the supervision order and deal with the offender for the offence in respect of which the order was made (para. 2(2)(b)).

9.4.12   **Action Plan Orders**

The power of a court to make an action plan order is provided by s. 69 of the Powers of Criminal Courts (Sentencing) Act 2000, which states:

(1) Where a child or young person (that is to say, any person aged under 18) is convicted of an offence and the court by or before which he is convicted is of the opinion mentioned in subsection (3) below, the court may (subject to sections 34 to 36 above) make an order which—
   (a) requires the offender, for a period of three months beginning with the date of the order, to comply with an action plan, that is to say, a series of requirements with respect to his actions and whereabouts during that period;
   (b) places the offender for that period under supervision of the responsible officer; and
   (c) requires the offender to comply with any directions given by the responsible officer with a view to the implementation of that plan;
   and the requirements included in the order, and any directions given by the responsible officer may include requirements authorised by section 70 below.

(2) An order under subsection (1) above is in this Act referred to as an 'action plan order'.

(3) The opinion referred to in subsection (1) above is that the making of an action plan order is desirable in the interests of—
   (a) securing the rehabilitation of the offender; or
   (b) preventing the commission by him of further offences.

KEYNOTE

'A responsible officer' for the purpose of action plan orders include officers of a local probation board, social workers or members of a youth offending team (s. 69(4)).

An action plan order cannot be made where the offender is already subject to such an order or the court propose to impose a custodial sentence, community rehabilitation order, community punishment order, community punishment and rehabilitation order, attendance centre order, supervision order or referral order (s. 69(5)).

Requirements

Under s. 70 of the 2000 Act, the following requirements *may* be included in action plan orders directing the offender:

- to participate in activities at a specified time or times (s. 70(1)(a));
- to present himself/herself at a place or places at a specified time or times (s. 70(1)(b));
- to attend an attendance centre (s. 70(1)(c));
- to stay away from a specified place or places (s. 70(1)(d));
- to comply with any arrangement for his/her education (s. 70(1)(e));
- to make reparation to a specified person or persons or to the community at large (s. 70(1)(f));
- to attend court within 21 days of the order to consider its effectiveness (ss. 70(1)(g) and 71(1)).

In relation to reparation (s. 70(1)(f) above) 'make reparation' means make reparation for the offence otherwise than by the payment of compensation (s. 70(3)).

Breach of Action Plan Orders or Reparation Orders

Schedule 8 to the 2000 Act provides for the breach of both action plan orders and reparation orders.

Paragraph 2, sch. 8 states:

> (1) This paragraph applies if while an action plan order or reparation order is in force in respect of an offender it is proved to the satisfaction of the appropriate court, on the application of the responsible officer, that the offender has failed to comply with any requirement included in the order.

KEYNOTE

For breaching an action plan order or reparation order the penalties are exactly the same as those for a supervision order: a fine not exceeding £1,000, or a curfew order, or an attendance centre order (para. 2(2)).

Again the court may deal with the offender for the original offence and revoke the action plan order or reparation order if one is still in force (para. 2(2)(b), (4)(b) and (5)).

9.4.13 | **Reparation Orders for Young Offenders**

Reparation orders for an offender under 18 are provided by s. 73 of the Powers of Criminal Courts (Sentencing) Act 2000, which states:

> (1) Where a child or young person (that is to say, any person aged under 18) is convicted of an offence other than one for which the sentence is fixed by law, the court by or before which he is convicted may make an order requiring him to make reparation specified in the order—
> (a) to a person or persons so specified; or
> (b) to the community at large;
>
> and any person so specified must be a person identified by the court as a victim of the offence or a person otherwise affected by it.

KEYNOTE

'Make reparation' means make reparation otherwise than by the payment of compensation (s. 73(3)).

A reparation order cannot be made where the court proposes to pass a custodial sentence or to make a community punishment order, community punishment and rehabilitation order, supervision order, an action plan order or a referral order (s. 73(4)).

Unless the Secretary of State has made arrangements for implementing reparation orders, such orders cannot be made (para. 73(6)).

The court must give reasons for not making a reparation order where it has the power to do so (s. 73(8)).

Requirements

Section 74 of the 2000 Act provides for the requirements of reparation orders and states:

(1) A reparation order shall not require the offender—
   (a) to work for more than 24 hours in aggregate; or
   (b) to make reparation to any person without the consent of that person.

(2) Subject to subsection (1) above, requirements specified in a reparation order shall be such as in the opinion of the court are commensurate with the seriousness of the offence, or the combination of the offence and one or more offences associated with it.

KEYNOTE

For breach of reparation orders, see para. 9.4.12.

9.4.14

Referral Orders

Referral orders were introduced to tackle offending behaviour and its causes. In certain circumstances, a youth court (and in exceptional circumstances an adult magistrates' court), is required to sentence a young offender by ordering them to be referred to a youth offender panel.

Section 16 of the Powers of Criminal Courts (Sentencing) Act 2000 provides the circumstances which must exist before the court is required to make a referral order and states:

(1) This section applies where a youth court or other magistrates' court is dealing with a person aged under 18 for an offence and—
   (a) neither the offence nor any connected offence is one for which the sentence is fixed by law;
   (b) the court is not, in respect of the offence or any connected offence, proposing to impose a custodial sentence on the offender or make a hospital order (within the meaning of the Mental Health Act 1983) in his case; and
   (c) the court is not proposing to discharge him absolutely in respect of the offence.

(2) If—
   (a) the compulsory referral conditions are satisfied in accordance with section 17 below, and
   (b) referral is available to the court,
   the court shall sentence the offender for the offence by ordering him to be referred to a youth offending panel.

Section 17(1) of the 2000 Act sets out the compulsory referral conditions. Section 17 states:

(1) For the purposes of section 16(2) above the compulsory referral conditions are satisfied in relation to an offence if the offender—
   (a) pleaded guilty to the offence and to any connected offence;
   (b) has never been convicted by or before a court in the United Kingdom of any offence other than the offence and any connected offence; and
   (c) has never been bound over in criminal proceedings in England and Wales or Northern Ireland to keep the peace or to be of good behaviour.

Section 17(2) provides for the circumstances which must exist before a court has the power to make a referral order. Section 17 states:

> (2) For the purposes of section 16(3) above the discretionary referral conditions are satisfied in relation to an offence if—
>> (a) the offender is being dealt with by the court for the offence and one or more connected offences;
>> (b) although he pleaded guilty to at least one of the offences mentioned in paragraph (a) above, he also pleaded not guilty to at least one of them;
>> (c) he has never been convicted by or before a court in the United Kingdom of any offence other than the offences mentioned in paragraph (a) above; and
>> (d) he has never been bound over in criminal proceedings in England and Wales or Northern Ireland to keep the peace or to be of good behaviour.

KEYNOTE

Referral orders are available for an offender under the age of 18 but only on his/her first conviction. A conditional discharge in relation to a previous offence does count as a conviction (s. 17(5)).

The referral order will specify the youth offending team responsible for implementing the order and the period during which the contract is to have effect. The minimum period of an order is three months and the maximum 12 months (s. 18(1)).

Where an offender is being dealt with for associated offences, more than one referral order can be made and their compliance periods can run concurrently or consecutively but must not exceed 12 months (s. 18(6)).

A court making a referral order may make an order requiring the attendance of parents or another appropriate person at meetings of the youth offender panel. Where the offender is under 16, the making of such an order is compulsory (s. 20(1) and (2)).

For youth offender panels, see para. 7.3.

Offender Referred Back to Court

The youth offender panel may refer the offender back to court if they consider there has been non-compliance with the agreed contract (sch. 1, para. 2 of the 2000 Act).

If the court accepts the referral, they may revoke the referral order and deal with the offender for the original offence (sch. 1, para. 5(1), (2) and (5)).

The court may disagree with the decision of the youth offender panel and refer the offender back to the panel or if they consider that the offender has satisfactorily completed the contract, discharge the order (sch. 1, paras 7 and 8).

Where a person subject to a referral order is convicted of an offence, this would normally revoke the order. However, where the offence was committed prior to the referral order being made, the court may sentence the offender by extending the period of compliance up to a maximum of 12 months (sch. 1, paras 10 and 11).

In 'exceptional circumstances', where the offence was committed after the order was made, the court may also decide to extend the period of compliance (sch. 1, para. 12).

9.5 Financial Penalties

9.5.1 Fines

The imposition of a fine is the most commonly encountered penalty in criminal courts and amounts to an order that the offender shall pay a sum of money to the State.

The principles for the fixing of fines for both the Crown Court and magistrates' courts are contained in s. 128 of the Powers of Criminal Courts (Sentencing) Act 2000, which states:

> (1) Before fixing the amount of any fine to be imposed on an offender who is an individual, a court shall inquire into his financial circumstances.

(2) The amount of any fine fixed by a court shall be such as, in the opinion of the court, reflects the seriousness of the offence.

(3) In fixing the amount of any fine to be imposed on an offender (whether an individual or other person), a court shall take into account the circumstances of the case including, among other things, the financial circumstances of the offender so far as they are known, or appear, to the court.

(4) Subsection (3) above applies whether taking into account the financial circumstances of the offender has the effect of increasing or reducing the amount of the fine.

(5) Where—
  (a) an offender has been convicted in his absence in pursuance of section 11 or 12 of the Magistrates' Courts Act 1980 (non-appearance of accused), or
  (b) an offender—
    (i) has failed to comply with an order under section 126(1) above, or
    (ii) has otherwise failed to cooperate with the court in its inquiry into his financial circumstances,
  and the court considers that it has insufficient information to make a proper determination of the financial circumstances of the offender, it may make such determination as it thinks fit.

KEYNOTE

Two key principles therefore help determine the level of fine a court may impose on an offender: first, the seriousness of the offence; and secondly, the offender's ability to pay the fine based on his/her financial circumstances.

Section 126 of the 2000 Act gives the court the power to order a statement as to the offender's financial circumstances. This order may require an offender to give the court *such a statement of his/her financial circumstances as the court may require*. Individuals who fail to provide such a statement, make a false statement or fail to disclose any material fact commit an offence (s. 126(4) and (5)).

The standard scale of *maximum* fines in the magistrates' court (s. 37(2) of the Criminal Justice Act 1982) is:

Level on the scale	Amount of fines
1	£200
2	£500
3	£1,000
4	£2,500
5	£5,000

For a person under the age of 18, the amount of any fine imposed by the court shall not exceed £1,000 (s. 135(1) of the 2000 Act).

For a person under the age of 14, the fine shall not exceed £250 (s. 135(2) of the 2000 Act).

In practice it is unusual for a court to impose the maximum fine.

The court may order the parent or guardian of a person under the age of 18 to pay the young offender's fine, costs or compensation (s. 137 of the 2000 Act) and order a statement as to the financial circumstances of a parent or guardian (s. 136 of the 2000 Act).

9.5.2 | **Compensation Orders**

The power of a court to make compensation orders against convicted persons is provided by s. 130 of the Powers of Criminal Courts (Sentencing) Act 2000, which states:

(1) A court by or before which a person is convicted of an offence, instead of or in addition to dealing with him in any other way, may, on application or otherwise, make an order (in this Act referred to as a 'compensation order') requiring him—
  (a) to pay compensation for any personal injury, loss or damage resulting from that offence or any other offence which is taken into consideration by the court in determining sentence; or
  (b) to make payments for funeral expenses or bereavement in respect of a death resulting from any such offence, other than a death due to an accident arising out of the presence of a motor vehicle on a road;
  but this is subject to the following provisions of this section and to section 131 below.

(2) Where a person is convicted of an offence the sentence for which is fixed by law or falls to be imposed under section 109(2), 110(2) or 111(2) above, subsection (1) above shall have effect as if the words 'instead of or' were omitted.

(3) A court shall give reasons, on passing sentence, if it does not make a compensation order in a case where this section empowers it to do so.

(4) Compensation under subsection (1) above shall be of such amount as the court considers appropriate, having regard to any evidence and to any representations that are made by or on behalf of the accused or the prosecutor.

KEYNOTE

Section 130(2) relates to: s. 109(2) (sentence of imprisonment for life); s. 110(2) (seven years' imprisonment for a third class A drug trafficking offence); s. 111(2) (three years' imprisonment for a third domestic burglary).

A compensation order can be made following an accident due to the presence of a motor vehicle on a road if there was damage to a vehicle which was subject to an offence under the Theft Act 1968; or the offender is uninsured in relation to the use of the vehicle and compensation is not payable under any arrangements to which the Secretary of State is a party (s. 130(6)).

There is no restriction on the Crown Court to the amount of compensation it may order, though it must take into account the offender's means. The maximum sum that the magistrates' court may order by way of compensation is £5,000 (s. 131(1)).

The powers under ss. 136 and 137 of the 2000 Act in relation to a parent or guardian's liability in relation to a young offender are the same as for fines (**see para. 9.5.1**).

Compensation orders may also be made to compensate for distress and anxiety (*Bond v Chief Constable of Kent* [1983] 1 WLR 40; *R v Godfrey* (1994) 15 Cr App R (S) 536).

The starting point for measuring the level of compensation is the loss to the victim rather than the benefit to the offender and where there has been no damage or loss no compensation can be made (*R v Hier* (1976) 62 Cr App R 233; *R v Tyce* (1994) 15 Cr App R (S) 415).

In *R v Callum* [2000] All ER (D) 53, the Crown Court sentenced the offender to 180 hours' community service and ordered him to pay compensation of £22,750 to the victim at a rate of £150 per month. The Court of Appeal held that a compensation order should not be made to last over a long period of time and that, in this instance, the order was oppressive and manifestly excessive.

9.6 Discharge

9.6.1 Absolute and Conditional Discharge

Section 12 of the Powers of Criminal Courts (Sentencing) Act 2000 provides the court with the power to grant absolute and conditional discharges. Section 12 states:

(1) Where a court by or before which a person is convicted of an offence (not being an offence the sentence for which is fixed by law or falls to be imposed under section 109(2), 110(2) or 111(2) below) is of the opinion, having regard to the circumstances including the nature of the offence and the character of the offender, that it is inexpedient to inflict punishment, the court may make an order either—
   (a) discharging him absolutely; or
   (b) if the court thinks fit, discharging him subject to the condition that he commits no offence during such period, not exceeding three years from the date of the order, as may be specified in the order.

(2) Subsection (1)(b) above has effect subject to section 66(4) of the Crime and Disorder Act 1998 (effect of reprimands and warnings).

(3) An order discharging a person subject to such a condition as is mentioned in subsection (1)(b) above is in this Act referred to as an 'order for conditional discharge'; and the period specified in any such order is in this Act referred to as 'the period of conditional discharge'.

(4) Before making an order for conditional discharge, the court shall explain to the offender in ordinary language that if he commits another offence during the period of conditional discharge he will be liable to be sentenced for the original offence.

KEYNOTE

Absolute Discharge

An absolute discharge may be used in all criminal courts granted irrespective of the age of the offender. Such a power is normally used to reflect the trivial nature of the offence, the circumstances in which the offender came to be before the court or special factors concerning the offender himself/herself.

Conditional Discharge

As with absolute discharge, a conditional discharge may be used in all criminal courts and granted irrespective of the age of the offender. The only 'condition' is that the offender does not commit any further offences during the period of the discharge fixed by the court. This period must not exceed three years.

Section 13 of the 2000 Act provides that a conditional discharge can only be breached where, during the period of the discharge, a person is convicted by a court in Great Britain of a further offence (s. 13(1)). Where a person is in breach of a conditional discharge, the court may sentence the offender for the original offence at the same time it sentences the offender for the further offences (s. 13(6)).

If the Crown Court is dealing with a breach where the conditional discharge was imposed in a magistrates' court, it can only deal with the original offence subject to the lower courts sentencing powers (s. 13(7)). If the breach is being dealt with in a magistrates' court and the conditional discharge was originally imposed in another magistrates' court, the consent of the original court is required first (s. 13(8)).

- Breach of an anti-social behaviour order (s. 1(11) of the Crime and Disorder Act 1998), where the offender has been, without reasonable excuse, doing anything prohibited by the order. (**See General Police Duties, chapter 3.**)

- Breach of a sex offender order (s. 2(9) of the 1998 Act), where the offender has been, without reasonable excuse, doing anything prohibited by the order. (**See Crime, chapter 10.**)

- Other than in exceptional circumstances, where an offender is convicted of an offence within two years of receiving a warning from a police officer (ss. 65 and 66 of the 1998 Act). (**See chapter 7.**)

9.6.2 | ### Binding Over to Keep the Peace

The power of the magistrates' court to bind over to keep the peace or be of good behaviour is provided by:

- s. 115 of the Magistrates' Courts Act 1980 (in relation to a complaint);
- common law powers (of the court's own motion);
- various statutes but particularly the Justices of the Peace Act 1361.

An order under s. 115 of the 1980 Act can only be made following a full hearing of the complaint. However, where the court binds over of its own motion it may do so in any of the following circumstances:

- before the end of the proceedings
- where the case is withdrawn by the prosecution

- where the prosecution offer no evidence
- where the case is adjourned
- where the defendant is acquitted
- where the justice believes there may be a breach of the peace in the future
- where the person's behaviour was against public morality

(*Hughes* v *Holley* [1987] Crim LR 253).

In *Veater* v *Glennon* [1981] 1 WLR 567 it was held that these wide powers were available to the court as a 'measure of preventive justice'.

Powers of Magistrates' Court, Crown Court and Court of Appeal

Section 1 of the Justices of the Peace Act 1968 extends the powers to bind over to be of good behaviour and states:

> (7) It is hereby declared that any court of record having a criminal jurisdiction has, as ancillary to that jurisdiction, the power to bind over to be of good behaviour, a person who or whose case is before the court, by requiring him to enter into his own recognisances or to find sureties or both, and committing him to prison if he does not comply.

KEYNOTE

This power relates to 'any court of record' which includes magistrates' courts, the Crown Court and the Court of Appeal (Criminal Division).

This power does not limit itself to the defendant but includes 'a person who . . . is before the court'. It can therefore relate to the following:

- a defendant who is acquitted (*R* v *Inner London Crown Court, ex parte Benjamin* (1986) 85 Cr App R 267);
- a defendant whose prosecution has not been proceeded with (*R* v *Lincoln Crown Court, ex parte Jude* [1998] 1 WLR 24);
- a person who is a witness before the court (*Sheldon* v *Bromfield Justices* [1964] 2 QB 573);
- a person who is a complainant (*R* v *Wilkins* [1907] 2 KB 380).

The general rule as to who may be subject of a binding over appears to be that the person must have given evidence before the court (*R* v *Swindon Crown Court, ex parte Pawitter Singh* [1984] 1 WLR 449; *R* v *Kingston-upon-Thames Crown Court, ex parte Guarino* [1986] Crim LR 325).

Where a court is considering binding over a person other than a person charged with an offence, that person must be given an opportunity to make representations to the court (*R* v *Hendon Justices, ex parte Gorchein* [1973] 1 WLR 1502). There is no set period that a binding over order may run, it is at the discretion of the court. In binding a person over to be of good behaviour, the court may require that person to enter into a recognisance that is, to bind over a person in a sum of money which would be forfeited upon breach of the order. Again, there is no set figure but the court is expected to be reasonable and, where appropriate, undertake a means enquiry (*R* v *Lincoln Crown Court, ex parte Jude* [1998] 1 WLR 24). In *Hasham and Harrup* v *UK* (2000) 30 EHRR 241 it was held that the conditions imposed on a person bound over to be of good behaviour were a breach of Article 10(2), a 'restriction—prescribed by law', as they were insufficiently precise.

Refusal and Failure to be Bound Over

The following apply to cases of refusal or failure to enter into a recognisance:

- People aged 21 or over, in a magistrates' court, can be sentenced to a term of imprisonment for up to six months or until they agree to comply (s. 115(3) of the Magistrates' Courts Act 1980).

- People aged 18 to 20 inclusive, can be committed to prison for contempt of court (s. 108 of the Powers of Criminal Courts (Sentencing) Act 2000).

- People under the age of 21 may be ordered to attend at an attendance centre but there is no power of detention (s. 60(1) of the Powers of Criminal Courts (Sentencing) Act 2000).

Failure to Comply

Where a person fails to comply with the conditions of a binding order the court may forfeit the whole or part of the recognisance in its discretion. The court cannot impose a term of imprisonment (*R* v *Finch* (1962) 47 Cr App R 58; *R* v *Gilbert* (1974) CSP D10–3A01).

Binding Over of Parent or Guardian

Section 150 of the Powers of Criminal Courts (Sentencing) Act 2000 provides for the binding over of a parent or guardian and states:

(1) Where a child or young person (that is to say, any person aged under 18) is convicted of an offence, the powers conferred by this section shall be exercisable by the court by which he is sentenced for that offence, and where the offender is aged under 16 when sentenced it shall be the duty of the court—

    (a) to exercise those powers if it is satisfied, having regard to the circumstances of the case, that their exercise would be desirable in the interests of preventing the commission by him of further offences; and

    (b) if it does not exercise them, to state in open court that it is not satisfied as mentioned in paragraph (a) above and why it is not so satisfied;

but this subsection has effect subject to section 19(5) above and paragraph 13(5) of Schedule 1 to this Act (cases where referral orders made or extended).

(2) The powers conferred by this section are as follows—

    (a) with the consent of the offender's parent or guardian, to order the parent or guardian to enter into a recognizance to take proper care of him and exercise proper control over him; and

    (b) if the parent or guardian refuses consent and the court considers the refusal unreasonable, to order the parent or guardian to pay a fine not exceeding £1,000;

and where the court has passed a community sentence on the offender, it may include in the recognizance provision that the offender's parent or guardian ensure that the offender complies with the requirements of that sentence.

KEYNOTE

The recognisance can be imposed on the parent or guardian for up to three years or until the offender is aged 18, whichever is the shorter (s. 150(4)).

For the purposes of s. 150, taking 'care' of a person includes giving him/her protection and guidance and 'control' includes discipline (s. 150(11)).

9.6.3   **Travel Restriction Orders**

Section 33 of the Criminal Justice and Police Act 2001 provides that, where a person is convicted of a drug trafficking offence (as defined by s. 34 of the Act) and the court imposes a sentence of four years or more, a court may impose a travel restriction order for a minimum period of two years from the date of the offender's long-term release from custody. The court may also order the surrender of any UK passport held by the individual. (**See Crime, chapter 6.**)

The Law of Evidence

10 | Evidence

10.1 Introduction

Evidence can be described as information that may be presented to a court so that it may decide on the probability of some facts asserted before it, that is information by which facts in issue tend to be proved or disproved. There are several types of evidence by which facts are open to proof—or disproof—and these are discussed later in the chapter.

10.2 Weight and Admissibility of Evidence

The two questions that need to be applied to any evidence are:

- admissibility; and
- weight.

The question of admissibility, to be decided by the judge in all cases, is whether the evidence is relevant to a fact in issue. All evidence of facts in issue and all evidence which is sufficiently relevant to prove (or disprove) facts in issue are potentially admissible.

The admissibility of evidence is very important to the outcome of any trial as it is from this that a person's guilt is decided. When collecting evidence in a case it should always be a consideration whether the evidence being collected is the best available (although, **see para. 10.8**) and whether it will be admissible.

Once it is established that the evidence is admissible, it is put before the court to determine what weight it will attach to the evidence; that is, how much effect does it have on proving or disproving the case.

10.2.1 Evidence Gathering

The word evidence must not be confused with information. In relation to preparing an offence file, the investigation of the offence will result in the collection of information. What is and what is not evidence can be decided at a later stage with the help of the Crown Prosecution Service. The importance of this distinction is that rules of evidence should not restrict the initial collection of information, otherwise a fact vital to the outcome of the case may be disregarded as irrelevant and/or inadmissible.

10.2.2 Reasons for Excluding Admissible Evidence

Even though evidence may be admissible in criminal cases, at common law, the trial judge has a general discretion to exclude legally admissible evidence tendered by the prosecution. This can be seen in *R v Sang* [1980] AC 402, where it was held that:

- A trial judge, as part of his/her duty to ensure that an accused receives a fair trial, always has a discretion to exclude evidence tendered by the prosecution if in his/her opinion its prejudicial effect outweighs its probative value. In deciding if the evidence should be admitted, the question the judge asks himself/herself is whether it is fair to allow the evidence not whether it is obtained fairly or by unfair means.

- With the exception of admissions and confessions (here s. 76 of the Police and Criminal Evidence Act 1984 applies) and generally with regard to evidence obtained from the accused after the commission of the offence, the judge generally has no discretion whether to exclude relevant admissible evidence on the ground that this was obtained by improper or unfair means.

If the evidence is relevant to the matters in issue then it is admissible and the court is not concerned with how the evidence was obtained (*Kuruma, Son of Kaniu* v *The Queen* [1955] AC 197). This proposition was upheld in *Jeffrey* v *Black* [1978] QB 490 where evidence was admissible concerning the unlawful search of premises.

Evidence may also be excluded for the following reasons:

- the incompetence of the witness;
- it relates to previous convictions, the character or disposition of the accused;
- it falls under hearsay;
- it is non-expert opinion evidence;
- it is privileged information;
- it is withheld as a matter of public policy.

There are also powers to exclude evidence under ss. 76 and 78 of the Police and Criminal Evidence Act 1984 (**see chapter 13**).

10.3   Facts in Issue

In a criminal case, facts in issue are those facts which must be proved by the prosecution in order to establish the defendant's guilt, or in exceptional cases those facts which are the essential elements of a defence, where the burden of proof is on the defendant to prove the defence.

Such facts will include:

- the identity of the defendant;
- the *actus reus* (**see Crime, chapter 2**);
- the *mens rea* (**see Crime, chapter 1**).

The relevant criminal conduct (*actus reus*) and state of mind (*mens rea*) will always be facts in issue, and it is therefore essential that these features are understood, both as general concepts and also in relation to the particular offence being investigated.

10.4   Burden of Proof

The facts in issue fall into two distinct categories:

- the facts that the *prosecution* bear the burden of proving or disproving in order to establish the defendant's guilt;
- the facts which, in exceptional circumstances, the *defence* need to prove to show that the defendant is not guilty.

10.4.1 **Duty of the Prosecution**

'Throughout the web of the English criminal law one golden thread is always to be seen; that is the duty of the prosecution to prove the prisoner's guilt.' This famous passage is taken from the House of Lords' decision in *Woolmington* v *DPP* [1935] AC 462. The underlying principle was perhaps best explained by Geoffrey Lawrence QC in an address to the jury in a murder trial:

The possibility of guilt is not enough, suspicion is not enough, probability is not enough, likelihood is not. A criminal matter is not a question of balancing probabilities and deciding in favour of probability.

If the accusation is not proved beyond reasonable doubt against the man accused in the dock, then by the law he is entitled to be acquitted, because that is the way our rules work. It is no concession to give him the benefit of the doubt. He is entitled by law to a verdict of not guilty.

(See Brian Harris, *The Literature of the Law*, Blackstone Press, 1998.)

Therefore the general rule is that the prosecution have the legal (or persuasive) burden of proving all the elements of the offence in order to prove guilt.

In *Evans* v *DPP* (2001) *The Times*, 9 July, it was held that the justices had wrongly applied *the balance of probabilities* in finding the defendant guilty rather than the full criminal standard of proof.

Where the defendant enters a plea of not guilty to the charge, the onus is on the prosecution to prove the whole of their case. This includes 'the identity of the accused, the nature of the act and the existence of any necessary knowledge or intent' (*R* v *Sims* [1946] KB 531).

Generally the onus is on the prosecution in the first instance to establish particular facts to prove the accused's guilt beyond all reasonable doubt. However, once a prima facie case is made out, the defence has to establish particular facts in order to rebut the prosecution evidence. Here there is a shift of the onus to establish particular facts.

10.4.2 **Duty on the Defence**

Exceptionally, the defence may have the burden of proof. In such circumstances the standard of proof for the defence is less rigorous than for the prosecution when establishing guilt (beyond all reasonable doubt). The defence will succeed if the court or jury are satisfied that the defence evidence is more probably true than false. This standard of proof is referred to as *the balance of probabilities*, the same standard of proof that operates in a civil trial.

Generally the prosecution bear the duty of proving or disproving certain facts and, if they fail to do so, the defence need say nothing; the prosecution fails and the defendant is acquitted.

Exceptionally, the common law (e.g. the defence of insanity), or a statute (e.g. diminished responsibility (s. 2 of the Homicide Act 1952)), may impose a burden on the defence to prove the defence.

The law relating to the carrying of weapons is a good illustration of where the defence may have a burden of proof. Once the prosecution have proved (beyond a reasonable doubt) that a defendant was carrying an offensive weapon, the burden then shifts to the defence to prove (on the balance of probabilities) that the defendant had lawful authority or reasonable excuse (**see General Police Duties, chapter 6**).

There will also be occasions where the defence has what is called an *evidential burden* in relation to certain specific defences they intend to rely on. Common examples of defences that only place an evidential burden on the defence are defences relating to alibis, self-defence, accident and provocation. In contrast to the evidential burden borne by the prosecution (to show that there is a case to answer by the end of the prosecution evidence), the defence's evidential burden arises somewhat differently. Unlike those defences that place a full legal burden of proof on the defence, the defence does not have to satisfy the judge of anything as such. All that the defence has to do is to ensure that there is enough evidence relating to the defence that is to be raised to enable the judge to direct the jury upon that defence as a live issue. In other words, the defence cannot invite the jury merely to speculate what there might have been, e.g. provocation or self-defence, or accident. There has to be some firm evidence about a defence before the judge will direct the jury in relation to it. This does not in any sense mean that the judge has to believe the evidence. Very little evidence in fact will do because if a judge does wrongly withdraw a defence from the jury any resulting conviction is likely to be quashed. All that the judge has to find is that there has been some evidence, however flimsy, of a given defence so that he/she can direct the jury about it. Of course, once the defence has satisfied this evidential burden, the legal burden of proof is with the prosecution to disprove the defence beyond a reasonable doubt.

With the incorporation of the European Convention of Human Rights into UK law, there was some argument that placing a full legal burden of proof on the defence violated the defendant's right to a fair trial under Article 6(2), which deals with the presumption of innocence. There has now been some clear guidance given by the House of Lords on this issue in *R* v *Lambert* [2001] 3 WLR 206.

The *Lambert* case involved an allegation of possession with intent to supply cocaine contrary to s. 5 of the Misuse of Drugs Act 1971. Section 28(2) of the Act provides a defence on the following basis:

> ... in any proceedings for an offence to which this section applies it shall be a defence **for the accused to prove** that he neither knew of nor suspected nor had reason to suspect the existence of some fact alleged by the prosecution which it is necessary for the prosecution to prove if he is to be convicted of the offence charged.

One of the certified points that went to the House of Lords was whether the defence under s. 28 imposed a legal rather than an evidential burden. Lord Steyn accepted the defence argument that s. 28(2), if read in isolation, imposed a legal burden of proof on the accused and went on to acknowledge that if this was the case it gave rise to serious arguments as to whether this was justified or so disproportionate that it amounted to a violation of Article 6(2) of the Convention. He also accepted that this was a very difficult question when balancing the interests of the individual in achieving justice on the one hand and the needs of society to protect against abuse of drugs on the other. Lord Steyn was however inclined to the view that such a burden would not be justified under Article 6(2) of the Convention. However, what he and the other three members of the majority of the House were prepared to do was read s. 28(2) in light of s. 3 of the Human Rights Act 1988. Section 3(1) provides that:

> So far as it is possible to do so, primary legislation and subordinate legislation must be read and given effect in a way which is compatible with the Convention rights.

On this basis, the House of Lords were prepared to read the wording of s. 28(2) as imposing only an evidential burden of proof on the accused and not a persuasaive burden of proof. However, this judgment does not mean that all statutory defences that place a full legal burden of proof on the defence will violate the right to a fair trial. In *Lambert*, the House of Lords acknowledged that in certain circumstances statutes may legitimately place a legal burden of proof on the defence such as for offences involving strict liability, defences such as diminished responsibility and insanity and other defences covered by, for example, s. 101 of the Magistrates' Courts Act 1980.

In the more recent case of *L* v *DPP* [2002] 2 All ER 854 it was held that the reverse onus provision, where the defence were required to give good reason why the defendant had with him in a public place a blade or sharp point, did not conflict with Article 6 of the Convention.

Section 101 of the Magistrates' Courts Act 1980 places a legal burden of proof on the accused either expressly or by implication. Section 101 of the 1980 Act states:

> Where the defendant to an information or complaint relies for his defence on any exception, exemption, proviso, excuse or qualification, whether or not it accompanies the description of the offence or matter of complaint in the enactment creating the offence or on which the complaint is founded, the burden of proving the exception, exemption, proviso, excuse or qualification shall be on him; and this notwithstanding that the information or complaint contains an allegation negativing the exception, exemption, proviso, excuse or qualification.

KEYNOTE

Although s. 101 applies to summary trials, it has now been established that where the burden of proof is placed on an accused then that burden relates whether the offence is being tried summarily or on indictment (*R* v *Hunt* [1987] AC 352).

An example of a summary offence where the burden of proof is on the defence is driving without insurance where the accused is required to prove he/she is insured (*Williams* v *Russell* (1933) 149 LT 190). An example of an indictable offence is where the accused was convicted on indictment of selling intoxicating liquor without a licence and the Court of Appeal held that it was for the accused to prove that he was the holder of a licence (*R* v *Edwards* [1975] QB 27).

10.5 Formal Admissions

Where a fact is accepted by the defence, there is a process by which this can be formally admitted under s. 10 of the Criminal Justice Act 1967. In such formal admissions the fact ceases to be an issue.

Section 10 states:

(1) Subject to the provisions of this section, any fact of which oral evidence may be given in any criminal proceedings may be admitted for the purpose of those proceedings by or on behalf of the prosecutor or defendant, and the admission by any party of any such fact under this section shall as against that party be conclusive evidence in those proceedings of the fact admitted.

(2) An admission under this section—
   (a) may be made before or at the proceedings;
   (b) if made otherwise than in court, shall be in writing;
   (c) if made in writing by an individual, shall purport to be signed by the person making it and, if so made by a body corporate, shall purport to be signed by a director or manager, or the secretary or clerk, or some other similar officer of the body corporate;
   (d) if made on behalf of a defendant who is an individual, shall be made by his counsel or solicitor;
   (e) if made at any stage before the trial by a defendant who is an individual, must be approved by his counsel or solicitor (whether at the time it was made or subsequently) before or at the proceedings in question.

(3) An admission under this section for the purpose of proceedings relating to any matter shall be treated as an admission for the purpose of any subsequent criminal proceedings relating to that matter (including any appeal or retrial).

(4) An admission under this section may with the leave of the court be withdrawn in the proceedings for the purpose of which it is made or any subsequent criminal proceedings relating to the same matter.

KEYNOTE

Where the accused enters a not guilty plea at a plea and directions hearing in the Crown Court, both the prosecution and defence are expected to inform the court of facts which are to be admitted and which are then accepted in written form in accordance with s. 10(2)(b) of the 1967 Act (see *Practice Direction (Crown Court: Plea and Directions Hearings)* [1995] 1 WLR 1318, para. 10(f)).

Formal admission may be made by counsel or a solicitor during court proceedings. In such cases the admission is written down and signed by or on behalf of the party making the admission. This procedure applies for the purpose of summary trial or proceedings before magistrates acting as examining justices (r. 71 of the Magistrates' Courts Rules 1981).

10.6 Inferences from Silence

At common law, when being questioned about involvement in a criminal offence, a suspect is under no obligation to answer any of the questions. This is another key feature of the criminal justice system in England and Wales and is the reason behind the cautioning of suspects required by the Police and Criminal Evidence Act 1984 (**see General Police Duties, chapter 2**). However, ss. 34 to 38 of the Criminal Justice and Public Order Act 1994 have a potentially important impact on the law in relation to the accused's silence.

Sections 34 to 37 permit the court to draw 'such inferences as appear proper' against the accused in the circumstances contained within the sections.

10.6.1 Inferences from Silence when Questioned or Charged

Section 34 of the Criminal Justice and Public Order Act 1994 provides that inferences can be drawn if, when questioned by the police under caution, charged or officially informed that he/she may be prosecuted, the accused fails to mention a fact on which he/she later relies in his/her defence, and which he/she could reasonably have been expected to mention at the time.

Section 34 states:

(1) Where, in any proceedings against a person for an offence, evidence is given that the accused—
    (a) at any time before he was charged with the offence, on being questioned under caution by a constable trying to discover whether or by whom the offence had been committed, failed to mention any fact relied on in his defence in those proceedings; or
    (b) on being charged with the offence or officially informed that he might be prosecuted for it, failed to mention any such fact,
being a fact which in the circumstances existing at the time the accused could reasonably have been expected to mention when so questioned, charged or informed, as the case may be, subsection (2) below applies.

(2) Where this subsection applies—
    (a) a magistrates' court, in deciding whether to grant an application for dismissal made by the accused under section 6 of the Magistrates' Courts Act 1980 (application for dismissal of charge in course of proceedings with a view to transfer for trial);
    (b) a judge, in deciding whether to grant an application made by the accused under—
        (i) section 6 of the Criminal Justice Act 1987 (application for dismissal of charge of serious fraud in respect of which notice of transfer has been given under section 4 of that Act); or
        (ii) paragraph 5 of schedule 6 to the Criminal Justice Act 1991 (application for dismissal of charge of violent or sexual offence involving child in respect of which notice of transfer has been given under section 53 of that Act);
    (c) the court, in determining whether there is a case to answer; and

(d) the court or jury, in determining whether the accused is guilty of the offence charged, may draw such inferences from the failure as appear proper.

(2A) Where the accused was at an authorised place of detention at the time of the failure, subsections (1) and (2) above do not apply if he had not been allowed an opportunity to consult a solicitor prior to being questioned, charged or informed as mentioned in subsection (1) above.

(3) Subject to any directions by the court, evidence tending to establish the failure may be given before or after evidence tending to establish the fact which the accused is alleged to have failed to mention.

(4) This section applies in relation to questioning by persons (other than constables) charged with the duty of investigating offences or charging offenders as it applies in relation to questioning by constables; and in subsection (1) above 'officially informed' means informed by a constable or any such person.

(5) This section does not—
  (a) prejudice the admissibility in evidence of the silence or other reaction of the accused in the face of anything said in his presence relating to the conduct in respect of which he is charged, in so far as evidence thereof would be admissible apart from this section; or
  (b) preclude the drawing of any inference from any such silence or other reaction of the accused which could properly be drawn apart from this section.

(6) This section does not apply in relation to a failure to mention a fact if the failure occurred before the commencement of this section.

KEYNOTE

A judgment of the European Court of Human Rights in the case of *Murray* v *United Kingdom* (1996) 22 EHRR 29 directly lead to s. 34(2A) being added by the Youth Justice and Criminal Evidence Act 1999. In this case the court held that an inference being drawn from silence, where an accused was denied access to legal advice, constituted a breach of Article 6(1) in conjunction with Article 6(3) of the European Convention on Human Rights (right to a fair trial).

Section 34 deals with the 'failure to mention any fact' and the word 'fact' is given its normal dictionary definition of 'something that is actually the case' (*R* v *Milford* [2001] Crim LR 330). Where an accused alleges that they did mention the relevant fact when being questioned it is for the prosecution to prove the contrary before any adverse inference can be drawn.

In *R* v *Daniel* (1998) 162 JP 578 the accused received legal advice not to answer questions when interviewed. It was held that the accused was entitled to give evidence of the conversation with the solicitor prior to interview to rebut any allegation of post-interview fabrication. The accused was also entitled to call the solicitor to give evidence of the advice given. (This action may have the effect of waiving legal professional privilege; see para. 11.3.5). However, where an accused, acting on legal advice, declines to answer any question or give or call any evidence at trial, no inferences can be drawn in accordance with this section (*R* v *Moshaid* [1998] Crim LR 420).

In relation to s. 34, the accused cannot be convicted solely on an inference drawn from silence. In *Condron* v *UK* [2000] Crim LR 679, the European Court of Human Rights, although accepting that there are cases which clearly call for an accused to provide an explanation, the court are required to apply 'particular caution' before invoking the accused's silence against him.

In *R* v *Argent* [1997] 2 Cr App R 27, the court stated that personal factors which might be relevant to an assessment of what an individual could reasonably have been expected to mention were age, experience, mental capacity, state of health, sobriety, tiredness and personality.

In *R* v *Flynn* (2001) *The Times*, 8 June, the court held that the police are entitled to conduct a second interview with a suspect, having obtained evidence from their witnesses which was not available in the first interview, and adverse inference could be drawn from the suspect's silence.

Section 34 differs from the other 'inference' sections in that the questioning need not occur at a police station and therefore the presence of a legal representative is not required. However, it appears clear that, should the prosecution seek to draw any inferences of an accused's silence where such questioning has occurred, the questions would need to be asked of the suspect again once he/she had access to legal advice.

A requirement to caution the person is contained in s. 34(1)(a) to make it clear of the risks connected with a failure to mention facts which later form part of the defence (see General Police Duties, chapter 2).

Guidance has been provided by the government (Home Office Circular 53/1998). This requires that where access to legal advice has been delayed in accordance with Annex B of PACE Code C (**see appendix 5**), the procedures for conducting the interview at the police station should be as follows:

- the interviewing officer should conduct any interview with the suspect at the police station in accordance with PACE Code C (**see appendix 5**);

- the interviewing officer should make a written note of those questions which the suspect has failed or refused to answer;

- once the suspect has had the opportunity of access to legal advice, the interviewing officer should put these questions to the suspect again; and ask the suspect whether he/she wishes to say/add anything further.

10.6.2   Inferences from Silence: Failure to Account for Objects, Substances and Marks

Section 36 of the Criminal Justice and Public Order Act 1994 provides that inferences can be drawn from an accused's failure to give evidence or refusal to answer any question about any object, substance or mark which may be attributable to the accused in the commission of an offence.

Section 36 states:

(1) Where—
    (a) a person is arrested by a constable, and there is—
        (i)   on his person; or
        (ii) in or on his clothing or footwear; or
        (iii) otherwise in his possession; or
        (iv) in any place in which he is at the time of his arrest,
    any object, substance or mark, or there is any mark on any such object; and
    (b) that or another constable investigating the case reasonably believes that the presence of the object, substance or mark may be attributable to the participation of the person arrested in the commission of an offence specified by the constable; and
    (c) the constable informs the person arrested that he so believes, and requests him to account for the presence of the object, substance or mark; and
    (d) the person fails or refuses to do so,
    then if, in any proceedings against the person for the offence so specified, evidence of those matters is given, subsection (2) below applies.

(2) Where this subsection applies—
    (a) a magistrates' court, in deciding whether to grant an application for dismissal made by the accused under section 6 of the Magistrates' Courts Act 1980 (application for dismissal of charge in course of proceedings with a view to transfer for trial);
    (b) a judge, in deciding whether to grant an application made by the accused under—
        (i)   section 6 of the Criminal Justice Act 1987 (application for dismissal of charge of serious fraud in respect of which notice of transfer has been given under section 4 of that Act); or
        (ii) paragraph 5 of schedule 6 to the Criminal Justice Act 1991 (application for dismissal of charge of violent or sexual offence involving child in respect of which notice of transfer has been given under section 53 of that Act);
    (c) the court, in determining whether there is a case to answer; and
    (d) the court or jury, in determining whether the accused is guilty of the offence charged, may draw such inferences from the failure or refusal as appear proper.

(3) Subsections (1) and (2) above apply to the condition of clothing or footwear as they apply to a substance or mark thereon.

(4) Subsections (1) and (2) above do not apply unless the accused was told in ordinary language by the constable when making the request mentioned in subsection (1)(c) above what the effect of this section would be if he failed or refused to comply with the request.

(4A) Where the accused was at an authorised place of detention at the time of the failure or refusal, subsections (1) and (2) do not apply if he had not been allowed an opportunity to consult a solicitor prior to the request being made.

(5) This section applies in relation to officers of customs and excise as it applies in relation to constables.

(6) This section does not preclude the drawing of any inference from a failure or refusal of the accused to account for the presence of an object, substance or mark or from the condition of clothing or footwear which could properly be drawn apart from this section.

(7) This section does not apply in relation to a failure or refusal which occurred before the commencement of this section.

KEYNOTE

As with s. 37 below, an inference may only be drawn where four conditions are satisfied:

- the accused has been arrested;
- a constable reasonably believes that the object, substance or mark (or the presence of the accused (s. 37)) may be attributable to the accused's participation in a crime (s. 36 (an offence 'specified by the constable') or s. 37 (the offence for which he/she was arrested));
- the constable informs the accused of his/her belief and requests an explanation (by giving a special warning (see below));
- the constable tells the suspect (in ordinary language) the effect of a failure or refusal to comply with the request.

It is considered that the request for information under both s. 36 and s. 37 are a form of questioning and should be undertaken during the interview at the police station. The request for such information prior to this would be an exception to the rule.

The interviewing officer is required to give the accused a 'special warning' for an inference to be drawn from a suspect's failure or refusal to answer a question about one of these matters or to answer it satisfactorily. This 'special warning' is provided by PACE Code C, para. 10.11, (**see appendix 5**) which states that the interviewing officer must first tell the suspect *in ordinary language*:

- what offence is being investigated;
- what fact the suspect is being asked to account for;
- that the interviewing officer believes this fact may be due to the suspect's taking part in the commission of the offence in question;
- that a court may draw a proper inference if the suspect fails or refuses to account for the fact about which he/she is being questioned;
- that a record is being made of the interview and that it may be given in evidence at any subsequent trial.

As with s. 34, in relation to s. 36 the accused cannot be convicted solely on an inference drawn from a failure or refusal (s. 38(3)) (**see para. 10.6.5**).

10.6.3   Inferences from Silence: Failure to Account for Presence

Section 37 of the Criminal Justice and Public Order Act 1994 provides that inferences can be drawn from an accused's failure to give evidence or refusal to answer any question about his/her presence at a place or time when the offence for which he/she was arrested was committed.

Section 37 states:

(1) Where—
  (a) a person arrested by a constable was found by him at a place at or about the time the offence for which he was arrested is alleged to have been committed; and
  (b) that or another constable investigating the offence reasonably believes that the presence of the person at that place and at that time may be attributable to his participation in the commission of the offence; and
  (c) the constable informs the person that he so believes, and requests him to account for that presence; and
  (d) the person fails or refuses to do so,
  then if, in any proceedings against the person for the offence, evidence of those matters is given, subsection (2) below applies.

(2) Where this subsection applies—
  (a) a magistrates' court, in deciding whether to grant an application for dismissal made by the accused under section 6 of the Magistrates' Courts Act 1980 (application for dismissal of charge in course of proceedings with a view to transfer for trial);
  (b) a judge, in deciding whether to grant an application made by the accused under—
    (i) section 6 of the Criminal Justice Act 1987 (application for dismissal of charge of serious fraud in respect of which notice of transfer has been given under section 4 of that Act); or
    (ii) paragraph 5 of schedule 6 to the Criminal Justice Act 1991 (application for dismissal of charge of violent or sexual offence involving child in respect of which notice of transfer has been given under section 53 of that Act);
  (c) the court, in determining whether there is a case to answer; and
  (d) the court or jury, in determining whether the accused is guilty of the offence charged,
  may draw such inferences from the failure or refusal as appear proper.

(3) Subsections (1) and (2) do not apply unless the accused was told in ordinary language by the constable when making the request mentioned in subsection (1)(c) above what the effect of this section would be if he failed or refused to comply with the request.

(3A) Where the accused was at an authorised place of detention at the time of the failure or refusal, subsections (1) and (2) do not apply if he had not been allowed an opportunity to consult a solicitor prior to the request being made.

(4) This section applies in relation to officers of customs and excise as it applies in relation to constables.

(5) This section does not preclude the drawing of any inference from a failure or refusal of the accused to account for his presence at a place which could properly be drawn apart from this section.

(6) This section does not apply in relation to a failure or refusal which occurred before the commencement of this section.

KEYNOTE

Section 37 appears somewhat restrictive in that it is only concerned with the suspect's location at the time of arrest and applies only when he/she was found at that location at or about the time of the offence.

PACE Code C (**see appendix 5**) also applies to s. 37 in relation to the 'special warning' required to be given by the interviewing officer.

Unlike s. 36, here the officer that sees the person at or near the scene of the alleged offence must be the arresting officer.

As with ss. 34 and 36, in relation to s. 37 the accused cannot be convicted solely on an inference drawn from a failure or refusal (s. 38(3)) (**see para. 11.6.5**).

10.6.4 **Inferences from Silence at Trial**

Section 35 of the Criminal Justice and Public Order Act 1994 provides that inferences can be drawn from an accused's failure to give evidence or refusal to answer any question, without good cause, where the person has been sworn. Section 35 states:

(1) At the trial of any person for an offence, subsections (2) and (3) below apply unless—
  (a) the accused's guilt is not in issue; or
  (b) it appears to the court that the physical or mental condition of the accused makes it undesirable for him to give evidence;
  but subsection (2) below does not apply if, at the conclusion of the evidence for the prosecution, his legal representative informs the court that the accused will give evidence or, where he is unrepresented, the court ascertains from him that he will give evidence.

(2) Where this subsection applies, the court shall, at the conclusion of the evidence for the prosecution, satisfy itself (in the case of proceedings on indictment, in the presence of the jury) that the accused is aware that the stage has been reached at which evidence can be given for the defence and that he can, if he wishes, give evidence and that, if he chooses not to give evidence, or having been sworn, without good cause refuses to answer any question, it will be permissible for the court or jury to draw such inferences as appear proper from his failure to give evidence or his refusal, without good cause, to answer any question.

(3) Where this subsection applies, the court or jury, in determining whether the accused is guilty of the offence charged, may draw such inferences as appear proper from the failure of the accused to give evidence or his refusal, without good cause, to answer any question.

(4) This section does not render the accused compellable to give evidence on his own behalf, and he shall accordingly not be guilty of contempt of court by reason of a failure to do so.

(5) For the purposes of this section a person who, having been sworn, refuses to answer any question shall be taken to do so without good cause unless—
  (a) he is entitled to refuse to answer the question by virtue of any enactment, whenever passed or made, or on the ground of privilege; or
  (b) the court in the exercise of its general discretion excuses him from answering it.

(6) [repealed]

(7) This section applies—
  (a) in relation to proceedings on indictment for an offence, only if the person charged with the offence is arraigned on or after the commencement of this section;
  (b) in relation to proceedings in a magistrates' court, only if the time when the court begins to receive evidence in the proceedings falls after the commencement of this section.

KEYNOTE

In *R* v *Friend* [1997] 1 WLR 1433 (in considering s. 35(1)(b) of the Act), the accused was aged 15 with a mental age of nine and an IQ of 63. It was held that the accused's mental condition did not make it 'undesirable' for him to give evidence and it was right that inferences be drawn under s. 35(3).

As with s. 34, in relation to s. 35 the accused cannot be convicted solely on an inference drawn from a failure or refusal (s. 38(3)) (**see para. 10.6.5**).

It must be made clear to the accused that when the prosecution case has finished he/she may give evidence if he/she so wishes. The court must inform the accused that if he/she fails to give evidence or, being sworn, refuses to answer any question without good cause, then the jury may infer such inferences that appear proper from such a failure to give evidence or a refusal to answer any question (*Practice Direction (criminal: consolidation)* [2002] All ER 904, para. 44, (defendant's rights to give or not give evidence)). In *R* v *Gough* [2002] 2 Cr App R 121, it was held that it is mandatory for the court to inform the accused of his/her right to give or not to give evidence even where the accused has absconded.

10.6.5 Inferences from Silence: No Conviction on Silence Alone

Section 38 of the Criminal Justice and Public Order Act 1994 applies to all of the four provisions relating to inferences from silence (ss. 34, 35, 36 and 37) and provides that an inference cannot be the sole basis for a finding of a case to answer, issue or dismissal of a notice to transfer, or for a finding of guilt. Nothing in s. 38 prejudices the courts general powers to exclude evidence (**see chapter 13**).

In *R* v *Gowland-Wynn* [2002] 1 Cr App R 569, the Court of Appeal held that in cases involving directions under s. 34, the burden of proof remained on the Crown despite the fact that a defendant chose to make no comment.

10.7 Relevant Facts

The cardinal rule of the law of evidence is that, subject to the exclusionary rules, all evidence which is sufficiently relevant to the facts in issue is admissible, and all evidence which is irrelevant or insufficiently relevant to the facts in issue should be excluded.

In *DPP* v *Kilbourne* [1973] AC 729, Lord Simon of Glaisdale stated that: 'relevant... evidence is evidence which makes the matter which requires proof more or less probable'.

Evidence of the *facts in issue* (**see para. 10.3**) might include a statement that the witness saw the accused hit the victim over the head with a bottle. This is directly relevant to the charge of assault. Other *relevant facts*, on the other hand, might require the court to put together pieces of evidence in order to come to the conclusion that some other relevant incidents occurred. For instance, that the witness saw the accused walk past the victim, heard a scream, looked round to see blood coming from a cut on the victim's head and the accused running away. In these circumstances, the witness does not actually see the assault but there may be sufficient circumstantial evidence from that witness for the court to draw the conclusion that the accused assaulted the victim.

10.8 The Best Evidence Rule

This rule of evidence covers the best evidence that the nature of the case will allow. The rule was propounded in 1745 and generally required that only the people having immediate personal knowledge of a fact in issue (**see para. 10.3**) could give evidence as to that fact. With the social and technological changes since the rule was introduced this rule is all but defunct.

Nevertheless, for the purpose of evidence gathering, the general principle to produce evidence from the best practicable source still holds good.

10.9 Sources of Evidence

For the purpose of this chapter evidence is categorised into the following two groups: the ways in which evidence can be proved and the main evidential rules.

Evidence can be proved in the following ways:

- original (primary) evidence
- real evidence
- secondary evidence
- documentary evidence.

The main evidential rules are:

- hearsay evidence
- circumstantial evidence
- presumptions
- character
- opinion
- corroboration
- judicial notice.

Each of these categories is considered in detail below.

10.9.1   Original Evidence

This is where a witness gives evidence to the court directly from the witness box. The evidence is presented to the court *as evidence of the truth of what he/she states* (contrast this with the exceptions to hearsay; **see para. 10.9.5**). Here the witness is giving direct testimony about a fact of which he/she has personal or first-hand knowledge and therefore can be challenged on the truth of that fact in cross-examination (**see chapter 6**).

10.9.2   Real Evidence

Real evidence usually takes the form of a material object for inspection by the court. This evidence is to prove, either that the material object in question exists, or to enable the court to draw an inference from its own observation as to the object's value and physical condition (an example would be pornographic material to determine whether it is 'obscene'). Such material objects, referred to as exhibits, produced to the court would normally be accompanied by written testimony and identified by a witness. This testimony usually includes an explanation of the connection between the exhibit and the facts in issue or the relevance to an issue.

Little if any weight can attach to real evidence in the absence of accompanying testimony identifying the object and connecting it with the facts in issue. So, in the example of the assault (**see para. 10.7**) simply producing a bottle without an accompanying statement identifying it as the one actually used would prove nothing.

There is no rule of law that an object must be produced, or its non-production excused, before oral evidence may be given about it. For example, it is not necessary for the police to produce the very breath test device used by them on a particular occasion (see *Castle* v *Cross* [1984] 1 WLR 1372). However, the weight of the oral evidence may be adversely affected by the non-production of the object in question (*Armory* v *Delamirie* (1722) 1 Str 505).

In addition to material objects, behaviour, appearance and demeanour may be regarded as real evidence. Examples would be:

- Behaviour (e.g. a person's misconduct in a court of law for the purposes of contempt of court).
- Appearance (e.g. a person's physical appearance in relation to evidence of identification or on the question of the existence or causation of personal injuries).
- Demeanour (e.g. a person's attitude may be relevant to the weight to be attached to his/her evidence, or whether he/she is to be treated as a hostile witness (**see chapter 6**).

The court has the responsibility to preserve and retain exhibits until the conclusion of the trial. It is usual for the court to entrust the exhibits to the police or Crown Prosecution

Service and this places a duty on them to:

- take all proper care to preserve the exhibits safe from loss or danger;
- co-operate with the defence in order to allow them reasonable access to the exhibits for the purpose of inspection and examination; and
- produce the exhibits at the trial (*R v Lambeth Metropolitan Stipendiary Magistrate, ex parte McComb* [1983] QB 551). (**See chapter 14** for the general rules on disclosure.)

10.9.3 Secondary Evidence

Secondary evidence is evidence of an inferior kind, e.g. a copy of a document or a copy of such a copy. Such evidence can be admissible, e.g. in *Butler* v *Board of Trade* [1971] Ch 680 where a copy of a letter from the claimant's solicitor to the claimant had been accidentally included in papers handed over to the Official Receiver. It was held that, although the original letter was privileged, a copy was admissible in the criminal proceedings. (See also *Calcraft* v *Guest* [1898] 1 QB 759.)

Secondary documentary evidence is admissible by way of exception in the following cases (although the list is not exhaustive):

- Where the other party fails to produce a document at court after being served with a notice to do so.
- Where a stranger to the case lawfully refuses to produce a document, e.g. where he/she could claim privilege.
- Where a document has been lost and after due search cannot be found or has been destroyed.
- Where the production of the original document is impossible, such as, writing on a wall or where the law requires the document to remain where it is for reasons of security.
- Where a public document is concerned, on the grounds that its production would be illegal or inconvenient.

Nowadays the court is not confined to the best evidence rule but can admit all relevant evidence (*Kajala* v *Noble* (1982) 75 Cr App R 149).

10.9.4 Documentary Evidence

Documentary evidence consists of documents produced for inspection by the court, either as items of real evidence or as hearsay or original evidence. Here the word 'document' includes maps, plans, graphs, drawings, photographs, discs, tapes, video tapes and films. This would include CCTV recordings and tapes from police control rooms. The contents of a document may be admissible *as evidence of their truth* or *for some other purpose*. Documents produced to the court are usually accompanied by some testimony and identified by a witness.

Evidence by Certificate of Plan or Drawing

Section 41 of the Criminal Justice Act 1948 states:

(1) In any criminal proceedings, a certificate purporting to be signed by a constable, or by a person have the prescribed qualifications, and certifying that a plan or drawing exhibited thereto is a plan or drawing made by him of the place or object specified in the certificate, and that the plan or drawing is correctly drawn to a scale so specified, shall be evidence of the relative position of the things shown on the plan or drawing.

...

(4) Nothing in this section shall be deemed to make a certificate admissible as evidence in proceedings for an offence except in a case where and to the extent to which oral evidence to the like effect would have been admissible in those proceedings.

(5) Nothing in this section shall be deemed to make a certificate admissible as evidence in proceedings for any offence unless a copy thereof has, not less than seven days before the hearing or trial, been served in the prescribed manner on the person charged with the offence; or if that person, not later than three days before the hearing or trial or within such further time as the court may in special circumstances allow, serves notice in the prescribed form and manner on the prosecutor requiring the attendance at the trial of the person who signed the certificate.

(6) In this section the expression prescribed means prescribed by rules made by the Secretary of State.

KEYNOTE

Police officers are quite often required to produce plans or drawings, the most common example of this being the road layout and positions of vehicles following a road traffic accident.

Prescribed qualification as mentioned in s. 41(1) refers to registered architects, chartered surveyors, civil engineers, municipal engineers and members of the Land Agents Society.

Where a witness makes a statement to the police and video footage of the events subsequently becomes available, it is acceptable for the witness to be permitted to see the video and to be allowed to correct or modify his/her statement in the light of the video evidence (*R* v *Rebuts* (1998) *The Times*, 2 May).

Computer Records

Computer printouts containing records produced without human intervention, for example, printout of an Intoximeter that has performed an analysis of specimens of breath, are generally admissible in evidence (*R* v *Minors* [1989] 1 WLR 441). However, printouts containing information implanted by a human will be considered as hearsay and be inadmissible (*R* v *Coventry Justices, ex parte Bullard* (1992) 95 Cr App R 175).

Proof of Public Documents and By-laws

Where necessary the proof of a public document can be made as follows. A certified copy of an entry under the hand of the deputy superintendent registrar of births, deaths and marriages, is admissible evidence provided he/she also certifies the register was in his/her lawful custody (s. 14 of the Evidence Act 1851).

10.9.5 Hearsay Evidence

The rule against hearsay is that any statement, other than one made by a witness while giving evidence, is inadmissible *as evidence of the facts stated*. Hearsay evidence may, on some limited occasions, be admissible *for other, specific purposes*.

In *Subramanium* v *Public Prosecutor* [1956] 1 WLR 965, it was stated that evidence of a statement made to a witness by a person who is not himself called as a witness may or may not be hearsay. It is hearsay and inadmissible when the object of the evidence is to the truth of what is contained in the statement.

When dealing with hearsay evidence you should consider:

- Is the evidence *admissible*?

- If so, *for what purpose*?

- How much *weight* will it carry?

EXAMPLE

Kingsley tells Gurinder that Ronald stole a cheque book. If Gurinder tells the court that Ronald stole a cheque book this would constitute hearsay because Gurinder is presenting the statement (that Ronald stole a cheque book) as being evidence of that fact (that Ronald actually *did* steal a cheque book).

If, however, the statement is used in court for some reason other than proving the truth of its contents, then this is not hearsay. For example, if Gurinder were to give evidence that Kingsley spoke to him about Ronald stealing a cheque book and that conversation was relevant to show that Kingsley was with Gurinder at that particular time, then the statement would be admissible for *that purpose only*. It would not be admissible to prove what was actually said.

A good test for deciding whether a statement is hearsay is to ask yourself whether the witness giving the evidence of the statement can be cross-examined as to the truth of its contents (**see chapter 6**). If the witness is unable to support the truth of the *content* of a statement that he/she is making to a court (as opposed to whether it was actually said or not) then it is probably hearsay.

Exceptions

There are a number of common law and statutory exceptions to the hearsay rule when evidence will be admissible for certain purposes.

Common Law Exceptions

Statement by the accused
Statement(s) made by an accused person are admissible as to their factual content provided they are made in compliance with PACE Code of Practice C (**see appendix 5**).

Statements made in the presence and hearing of the accused
The rule against hearsay is partly based on the fact that when a statement is made in the accused's absence he/she has no opportunity to deny or question its truth. Therefore statements made in the presence of an accused are an exception to the rule but *only to prove the reaction of the accused*. Therefore, when getting a victim or witness to repeat an allegation in the presence and hearing of a suspect the most important thing to record is the reaction of the suspect. Statements made in the presence and hearing of an accused are *not* admissible as evidence of the truth of what was said.

Dying declarations
These are admissible in trials for murder or manslaughter provided that:

- the declarant was in 'hopeless expectation of death';
- the death was the subject of the charge; and
- the circumstances of the death were the subject of the declaration (i.e. identifying who or what killed them).

Statements made by deceased
These are generally inadmissible. Exceptions to this general rule include:

- where the deceased was under a duty to make declarations contemporaneously in the course of his/her business (either written or oral), e.g. a verbal statement to an inspector made by a police constable to the effect that he was going to keep observations on a prisoner who later killed him, has been admitted (*R* v *Buckley* (1873) 13 Cox CC 293); and
- declarations against one's own pecuniary interest (*R* v *Rogers* [1995] 1 Cr App R 374).

The approach of the European Court of Human Rights to hearsay caused by death is contained in its judgment in *Ferrantelli and Santangelo* v *Italy* (1996) 23 EHRR 288. The application related to Article 6(3)(d) (right to examine witnesses), where the applicant complained that he did not have an opportunity of examining the witness who had died. The Court held that there was no breach of the Article as the authorities had not been responsible for the death and the deceased's evidence was corroborated by other evidence (see s. 26 of the Criminal Justice Act 1988 below for further commentary on this area).

Entries in public documents

These are exceptions to the hearsay rule provided:

- the statements and entries have been made by the authorised agents of the public in the course of official duties; and

- the facts recorded are of public interest or notoriety, or required to be recorded for the benefit of the public.

This exception is largely superseded by the effects of the Criminal Justice Act 1988 (see below).

Besides the exceptions above, the practical problems of proving such facts by the production of witnesses would be in some cases insurmountable.

Res gestae

These are statements which are so closely associated with an action or state of affairs which is relevant to a fact in issue that they become part of that action or state of affairs. These statements may be admissible as evidence *of the truth of their contents* if they concern contemporaneous actions, physical sensations or state of mind, or they are closely associated with a dramatic event.

These statements fall into four main categories, i.e. statements relating to:

- a specific event;
- the maker's physical state;
- the maker's state of mind;
- the maker's performance of an act.

A specific event This principle can best be explained by use of the case of *R v Andrews* [1987] 2 WLR 413. Two men entered M's flat and attacked him with knives and stole some property. Shortly afterwards M, grievously wounded, made his way to the flat below his own to get help. Two police officers arrived within minutes and M told them that O and the defendant had been the assailants. Two months later M died as a result of his injuries. The defendant was jointly charged with O with aggravated burglary and the murder of M.

The prosecution sought to have the deceased's statement admitted, not as a dying declaration (see above), but *as evidence of the truth of the facts that he had asserted*, namely that he had been attacked by O and the defendant. Ordinarily the rule against hearsay would exclude such a statement from being used for that purpose. The prosecution argued that the statement made by the deceased was *so closely connected with the specific event (the stabbing) that it ought to be admitted in evidence under the res gestae exception.*

The case went to the House of Lords who held that, where the victim of an attack informed a witness of what had occurred, such a statement may be admitted in evidence if the circumstances in which it was made satisfy the trial judge that:

- the event was so unusual or startling or dramatic as to dominate the thoughts of the victim; and

- that very effect on the thoughts of the victim excluded the possibility of their lying or being mistaken; and

- the statement was made at approximately (although not *exactly*) the same time as the event.

Under these conditions evidence of what the victim said would be admissible as to the truth of the facts recounted.

In *R v Ward* [2001] Crim LR 316 it was held that evidence tending to confirm a suspect's presence at a scene might be admissible, despite it being *prima facie* hearsay, providing a clear direction is given to the jury.

The maker's physical state   A statement concerning its maker's physical sensations, made at the time when he/she felt them is admissible to prove that he/she did in fact experienced that sensation.

If, for example, a person states 'my hand hurts' or 'my hand really hurt yesterday', both statements would be admissible by another to show that the person's hand had hurt.

Similarly, 'I feel really embarrassed', might be admissible to show that the person felt embarrassed at the time.

Such statements are only admissible to prove that *the sensation* existed; they may not be used to show what *caused* the sensation and must, as with all evidence, be relevant to a fact in issue in the case.

The maker's state of mind   Statements concerning the maker's state of mind at the time when he/she made it are admissible to prove what the maker *intended* or *believed* at that time. Such statements *are not admissible as evidence of the truth of the maker's beliefs*.

In *Ratten* v *The Queen* [1972] AC 378, the defendant's wife had been shot dead in her home. The defendant, in his defence to the charge of murder, claimed that the shooting was an accident. He also denied that any telephone call had been made from his house, where only he and his wife and small children were present, before the shooting. In these circumstances evidence of a telephone call made by the wife to an emergency operator was held to be admissible.

In deciding that the telephone call was admissible, Lord Wilberforce said:

> ...[the operator's statement] can be analysed into the following elements. (1) At about 1.15 pm the number Echuca 1494 rang. I plugged into that number. (2) I opened the speak key and said 'number please'. (3) A female voice answered. (4) The voice was hysterical and sobbed. (5) The voice said 'Get me the police please.'
>
> The factual items numbered (1)–(3) were relevant in order to show that, contrary to the evidence of the appellant, a call was made, by a woman only some 3–5 minutes before the fatal shooting. It not being suggested that there was anybody in the house other than the appellant, his wife and small children, this woman, the caller, could only have been the deceased. Items (4) and (5) were relevant as possibly showing...that the deceased woman was at this time in a state of emotion or fear. They were relevant and necessary evidence in order to explain and complete the fact of the call being made...

The longer the time gap between the making of the statement and the performance of the act, the lower the probative value of the statement and the likelihood of its being admissible.

The maker's performance of an act   Where an act carried out by a person needs to be proved, the statement of the person undertaking the act is likely to be the best evidence of why that act was completed. In order to amount to an exemption under the *res gestae rule,* the statement must be reasonably contemporaneous with the act; it must also be *related to* the act. For example, a person (X) boarding a plane saying 'I'm leaving the country to avoid being arrested' may be admissible as evidence of the reason why X got on the plane or why X left the country.

An example of this principle in practice is the case of *R* v *McCay* [1990] 1 WLR 645. Here a witness was asked to attend an identification parade to see if he could identify the defendant who was suspected of an attack on another man. The witness, a police inspector, and the appellant's solicitor watched the parade from behind a screen. The witness identified the defendant and said, 'It is number 8'. The defendant was charged with the assault and, at the trial, the witness gave evidence that he had attended the parade, made an identification but that he was unable to recall the number of the person whom he identified. The inspector was then called and gave evidence that the appellant had occupied position number 8 on the parade and that the witness had said 'It is number 8'. The defence argued that what the inspector said should be inadmissible hearsay. It was held that, although the words spoken by the witness at the parade were said in the absence of the appellant, they accompanied the relevant act of identification and therefore were contemporaneous with, and necessary to explain, the act of identification.

Statutory Exceptions

Admissibility of Written Statements in Summary Proceedings

Section 9 of the Criminal Justice Act 1967 states:

(1) In any criminal proceedings, other than committal proceedings, a written statement by any person shall, if such of the conditions mentioned in the next following subsection as are applicable are satisfied, be admissible as evidence to the like extent as oral evidence to the like effect by that person.

(2) The said conditions are—
   (a) the statement purports to be signed by the person who made it;
   (b) the statement contains a declaration by the person to the effect that it is true to the best of his knowledge and belief and that he made the statement knowing that, if it were tendered in evidence, he would be liable to prosecution if he wilfully stated in it anything which he knew to be false or did not believe to be true;
   (c) before the hearing at which the statement is tendered in evidence, a copy of the statement is served, by or on behalf of the party proposing to tender it, on each of the other parties to the proceedings; and
   (d) none of the other parties or their solicitors, within seven days from the service of the copy of the statement, serves a notice on the party so proposing objecting to the statement being tendered in evidence under this section:

   Provided that the conditions mentioned in paragraphs (c) and (d) of this subsection shall not apply if the parties agree before or during the hearing that the statement shall be so tendered.

KEYNOTE

The statement must be signed by the person making it but the declaration outlined at s. 9(2)(b) need not be separately signed.

The procedure for serving a statement under s. 9 is set out in Form 14 of the Magistrates' Courts (Forms) Rules 1981 (SI 1981 No. 553) which provides for a notice to be sent to the defendant, or if legally represented, their solicitor. The notice informs the defendant of the effect of the procedure and requires them, within seven days, to inform the prosecutor if they wish the witness to attend court. Failure to inform the prosecutor will deprive the defendant of his/her right to insist on the witness's attendance.

Statements that are admitted under s. 9 are either read out in full to the court or parts of it may be summarised at the court's discretion.

The court may still require a witness to attend and give oral evidence even where there has been no objection from the other parties (s. 9(4)(b)).

Although under s. 9(1) the statement is 'admissible as evidence' the statement itself does not have to be accepted as the truth. Even where the defence have failed to serve notice of a witness being required to give oral evidence they may still present evidence in court which might be inconsistent with a witness's written statement (*Lister* v *Quaife* [1983] 1 WLR 48). In these circumstances the prosecution may seek an adjournment of the case for the witness to attend court and give evidence.

Section 9 goes on to state:

(3) The following provisions shall also have effect in relation to any written statement tendered in evidence under this section, that is to say—
   (a) if the statement is made by a person under the age of 18, it shall give his age;
   (b) if it is made by a person who cannot read it, it shall be read to him before he signs it and shall be accompanied by a declaration by the person who so read the statement to the effect that it was so read; and
   (c) if it refers to any other document as an exhibit, the copy served on any other party to the proceedings under paragraph (c) of the last foregoing subsection shall be accompanied by a copy of that document or by such information as may be necessary in order to enable the party on whom it is served to inspect that document or a copy thereof.

(4) Notwithstanding that a written statement made by any person may be admissible as evidence by virtue of this section—

    (a) the party by whom or on whose behalf a copy of the statement was served may call that person to give evidence; and

    (b) the court may, of its own motion or on the application of any party to the proceedings, require that person to attend before the court and give evidence.

(5) ...

(6) So much of any statement as is admitted in evidence by virtue of this section shall, unless the court otherwise directs, be read aloud at the hearing and where the court so directs an account shall be given orally of so much of any statement as is not read aloud.

(7) Any document or object referred to as an exhibit and identified in a written statement tendered in evidence under this section shall be treated as if it had been produced as an exhibit and identified in court by the maker of the statement.

(8) A document required by this section to be served on any person may be served—

    (a) by delivering it to him or to his solicitor; or

    (b) by addressing it to him or leaving it at his usual or last known place of abode or place of business or by addressing it to his solicitor and leaving it at his office; or

    (c) by sending it in a registered letter or by recorded delivery service or by first class post addressed to him at his usual or last known place of abode or place of business or addressed to his solicitor at his office; or

    (d) in the case of a body corporate, by delivering it to the secretary or clerk of the body at its registered or principal office or sending it in a registered letter or by the recorded delivery service or by first class post addressed to the secretary or clerk of that body at that office; and in paragraph (d) of this subsection references to the secretary, in relation to a limited liability partnership, are to any designated member of the limited liability partnership.

KEYNOTE

The provisions of s. 9 of the Criminal Justice Act 1967, had a major impact on both witness's time (particularly the police) and the cost of court cases. The section allows for evidence to be admitted without the necessity of physically calling the witness who gave the statement.

Documentary Records

Section 23 of the Criminal Justice Act 1988 states:

(1) Subject—

    (a) to subsection (4) below; and

    (b) to paragraph 1A of schedule 2 to the Criminal Appeal Act 1968 (evidence given orally at original trial to be given orally at retrial),

    a statement made by a person in a document shall be admissible in criminal proceedings as evidence of any fact of which direct oral evidence by him would be admissible if—

    (i) the requirements of one of the paragraphs of subsection (2) below are satisfied; or

    (ii) the requirements of subsection (3) below are satisfied.

(2) The requirement mentioned in subsection (1)(i) above are—

    (a) that the person who made the statement is dead or by reason of his bodily or mental condition unfit to attend as a witness;

    (b) that—

        (i) the person who made the statement is outside the United Kingdom; and

        (ii) it is not reasonably practicable to secure his attendance; or

    (c) that all reasonable steps have been taken to find the person who made the statement, but that he cannot be found.

(3) The requirements mentioned in subsection (1)(ii) above are—

    (a) that the statement was made to a police officer or some other person charged with the duty of investigating offences or charging offenders; and

(b) that the person who made it does not give oral evidence through fear or because he is kept out of the way.

(4) Subsection (1) above does not render admissible a confession made by an accused person that would not be admissible under section 76 of the Police and Criminal Evidence Act 1984.

KEYNOTE

For the purposes of s. 23 a 'statement' means anything in which information of any description is recorded (sch. 2, para. 5) and has included the use of a video recording.

If the prosecution or defence can establish that one of the statutory reasons exist for the unavailability of the witness it does not matter that the other reasons cannot be made out (*Farrand* v *Galland* [1989] Crim LR 573).

In relation to a witness's unfitness to attend court, in *R* v *Setz-Dempsey* (1994) 98 Cr App R 23 it was held that this does not just apply to their physical fitness to attend but also to unfitness through any mental condition. In a European case, where an elderly witness's statement was read out due to his deteriorating intellect, it was held not to be a violation of Article 6 of the European Convention on Human Rights (right to a fair trial) (*Trivedi* v *United Kingdom* (1997) 89 DRI 36).

R v *Castillo* [1996] 1 Cr App R 438 provides the three considerations that should apply when determining whether or not it is reasonably practicable to secure the attendance of a witness from outside the United Kingdom. These considerations are:

- the importance of the evidence which the witness would a provide;

- both the expense and inconvenience of securing the witness's attendance;

- the weight which should be attributed to the reasons given for the witness's failure to attend court.

In addition, the court also suggested a consideration of prejudice to the defence if evidence were admitted for the prosecution under s. 23(2)(b). The words 'reasonably practicable' used in the *Castillo* case have been construed to mean whether the normal steps were taken in securing the witness's appearance and that cost was a relevant factor (*R* v *Hurst* [1995] 1 Cr App R 82). In *R* v *Bray* (1988) 99 Cr App R 354 it was held that the provisions of s. 23(2)(b) were not to be used where the prosecution should have been aware of a witness's absence abroad.

In relation to s. 23(2)(c), where a witness cannot be found and his/her statement is read out in court, the judge is required to make the jury aware of the drawbacks for the defence and to explain the significance of having the evidence tested and the importance of cross-examination (*R* v *McCoy* [1999] All ER (D) 1410).

In relation to a witness who does not give oral evidence through fear, a statement made by the witness to a police officer or other individual with a duty to investigate crime is admissible under s. 23(3)(b) (*R* v *H* (2001) *The Times*, 6 July). The subsection is of important consideration in cases of domestic violence where witnesses often prefer to be held in contempt rather than give evidence in court (*R* v *Bird* (1997) 161 JP 96).

Business Documents

Section 24 of the Criminal Justice Act 1988 states:

(1) Subject—
    (a) to subsections (3) and (4) below; and
    (b) to paragraph 1A of schedule 2 to the Criminal Appeal Act 1968,
    a statement in a document shall be admissible in criminal proceedings as evidence of any fact of which direct oral evidence would be admissible, if the following conditions are satisfied—
        (i) the document was created or received by a person in the course of a trade, business, profession or other occupation or as the holder of a paid or unpaid office; and
        (ii) the information contained in the document was supplied by a person (whether or not the maker of the statement) who had, or may reasonably be supposed to have had, personal knowledge of the matters dealt with.

(2) Subsection (1) above applies whether the information contained in the document was supplied directly or indirectly but, if it was supplied indirectly, only if each person through whom it was supplied received it—

(a) in the course of a trade, business, profession or other occupation; or

(b) as the holder of a paid or unpaid office.

(3) Subsection (1) above does not render admissible a confession made by an accused person that would not be admissible under section 76 of the Police and Criminal Evidence Act 1984.

(4) A statement prepared otherwise than in accordance with section 3 of the Criminal Justice (International Co-operation) Act 1990 below or an order under paragraph 6 of schedule 13 to this Act or under section 30 or 31 ... for the purposes—

(a) of pending or contemplated criminal proceedings; or

(b) of a criminal investigation,

shall not be admissible by virtue of subsection (1) above unless—

(i) the requirements of one of the paragraphs of subsection (2) of section 23 above are satisfied; or

(ii) the requirements of subsection (3) of that section are satisfied; or

(iii) the person who made the statement cannot reasonably be expected (having regard to the time which has elapsed since he made the statement and to all the circumstances) to have any recollection of the matters dealt with in the statement.

(5) This section shall not apply to proceedings before a magistrates' court inquiring into an offence as examining justices.

KEYNOTE

The term 'business document' is not included in the section itself but includes documents created or received by a person in the course of a trade, business, profession or other occupation. Such documents have been held to include hospital's records of examinations, the transcript of evidence given by a witness (*R* v *Lockley* [1995] 2 Cr App R 554), or a police custody record (*R* v *Hogan* [1997] Crim LR 349).

Although it is not generally necessary to show why a witness should not be called before tendering his/her statement, this is not the case if the statement has been obtained for criminal proceedings or for a criminal investigation to which s. 24(4) applies (*R* v *Murphy* [1992] Crim LR 883). In the latter case it is necessary to prove that one of the reasons apply in the case of a s. 23 statement or, that as a result of the time that has elapsed since the statement was made, the witness could not reasonably be expected to have any recollection of the events. In *R* v *Carrington* [1994] Crim LR 438 it was held that s. 24(4)(iii) applied where a witness was able to recollect part of a longer statement but not the part in relation to a car registration number she had forgotten.

Under s. 24 it is the 'statement' and not the 'document' that is admitted. For example, in *R* v *Derodra* [2000] 1 Cr App R 41 a police officer was given information about a burglary and the officer made a record of the incident. The court held that it is the 'statement' made to the police officer, then recorded, which would be admitted under s. 24.

Subject to the provisions of s. 24(1)(a) and (b), a statement in a document will be admissible if both conditions (i) and (ii) of subsection (1) are satisfied. Also, a statement:

- other than a statement obtained on request outside the United Kingdom (s. 3 of the Criminal Justice (International Co-operation) Act 1990),

- for use in a Service court (sch. 13 of the 1988 Act),

- an expert's report (s. 30), or

- provision of material to help members of a jury to understand complicated issues or technical terms (s. 31),

will only be admissible if one of the requirements of (i) to (iii) of s. 24(4) are satisfied.

Admission and Exclusion of Statements

Section 25 of the Criminal Justice Act 1988 states:

(1) If, having regard to all the circumstances—
   (a) the Crown Court—
      (i)   on a trial on indictment;
      (ii) on an appeal from a magistrates' court;
      (iii) on the hearing of an application under section 6 of the Criminal Justice Act 1987 (applications for dismissal of charges of fraud transferred from magistrates' court to Crown Court); or
      (iv) on the hearing of an application under paragraph 5 of schedule 6 to the Criminal Justice Act 1991 (applications for dismissal of charges in certain cases involving children transferred from magistrates' court to Crown Court); or
   (b) the criminal division of the Court of Appeal; or
   (c) a magistrates' court on a trial of an information,
   is of the opinion that in the interest of justice a statement which is admissible by virtue of section 23 or 24 above nevertheless ought not to be admitted, it may direct that the statement shall not be admitted.

(2) Without prejudice to the generality of subsection (1) above, it shall be the duty of the court to have regard—
   (a) to the nature and source of the document containing the statement and to whether or not, having regard to its nature and source and to any other circumstances that appear to the court to be relevant, it is likely that the document is authentic;
   (b) to the extent to which the statement appears to supply evidence which would otherwise not be readily available;
   (c) to the relevance of the evidence that it appears to supply to any issue which is likely to have to be determined in the proceedings; and
   (d) to any risk, having regard in particular to whether it is likely to be possible to controvert the statement if the person making it does not attend to give oral evidence in the proceedings, that its admission or exclusion will result in unfairness to the accused or, if there is more than one, to any of them.

Section 26 of the Criminal Justice Act 1988 states:

Where a statement which is admissible in criminal proceedings by virtue of section 23 or 24 above appears to the court to have been prepared, otherwise than in accordance with section 29 below or an order under paragraph 6 of schedule 13 to this Act or under section 30 or 31 below, for the purposes—
   (a) of pending or contemplated criminal proceedings; or
   (b) of a criminal investigation,
the statement shall not be given in evidence in any criminal proceedings without the leave of the court, and the court shall not give leave unless it is of the opinion that the statement ought to be admitted in the interests of justice; and in considering whether its admission would be in the interests of justice, it shall be the duty of the court to have regard—
   (i)   to the contents of the statement;
   (ii) to any risk, having regard in particular to whether it is likely to be possible to controvert the statement if the person making it does not attend to give oral evidence in the proceedings, that its admission or exclusion will result in unfairness to the accused or, if there is more than one, to any of them; and
   (iii) to any other circumstances that appear to the court to be relevant.

KEYNOTE

Although there are similarities between ss. 25 and 26 the emphasis of each is different: s. 25 poses the question that the court must be made to hold the opinion that the statement ought not to be admitted; in s. 26 the court is not to admit the statement unless made to hold the opinion that in the interests of justice it ought to be admitted.

The purpose of the provisions of ss. 25 and 26 were explained in *R* v *Cole* [1990] 1 WLR 866, at 875D–E:

... to widen the power of the court to admit documentary hearsay evidence while ensuring that the accused receives a fair trial. In judging how to achieve the fairness of the trial a balance must on occasions be struck between the interests of the public in enabling the prosecution case to be properly presented and the interest of a particular defendant in not being put in a disadvantageous position, for example by the death or illness of a witness. The public of course also has a direct interest in the proper protection of the individual accused. The point of balance, as directed by Parliament, is set out in the sections.

The Court of Appeal have held that the procedures set out in ss. 25 and 26 accord fully with the obligations of the European Convention on Human Rights particularly in relation to Article 6, the right to a fair trial (*R* v *Gokal* [1997] 2 Cr App R 266). In *R* v *Montgomery* [2002] EWCA Crim 1655 it was considered that the Convention right might pose a difficulty in cases where a statement is the only evidence relating to a crucial part of a case. However, the court held that if the witness's failure to give evidence was as a result of intimidation by the accused then they should not be able to profit from this wrongful act.

Under s. 27 of the 1988 Act, where a statement contained in a document is admissible as evidence in criminal proceedings, it may be proved by the production of that document, or a copy authenticated to the court's approval.

10.9.6   Circumstantial Evidence

In contrast to direct evidence which is evidence of facts in issue, circumstantial evidence is evidence of relevant facts *from which the facts in issue may be presumed with more or less certainty*.

An example would be where a bank robbery has occurred and a witness sees the defendant hurriedly climbing into a vehicle near to the bank at the relevant time and carrying bank cash bags. The witness has not actually *seen* the defendant inside the bank committing the offence, but can still provide circumstantial evidence from which it can be proved that the witness saw the bank robber.

Pollack CB in *R* v *Exall* (1866) 4 F & F 922 described circumstantial evidence as:

... a combination of circumstances, no one of which would raise a reasonable conviction, or more than a mere suspicion; but the whole, taken together, may create a strong conclusion of guilt....

Circumstantial evidence may be admissible if it is relevant to a fact in issue and examples of circumstantial evidence include:

- evidence of facts which supply a motive;
- facts which tend to suggest that a person made plans or preparations relevant to a subsequent action performed;
- evidence of a person's mental or physical capacity to do a particular act;
- evidence of opportunity—or lack of opportunity to act in a certain way;
- evidence of identity, e.g. fingerprints (**see chapter 16**);
- inferences from silence, e.g. s. 35 of the Criminal Justice and Public Order Act 1994;
- presumptions of fact (**see para. 10.9.7**).

10.9.7   Presumptions

Facts in issue and relevant facts must generally be proved before a court by admissible evidence before they can be accepted by the court as being true. There are occasions, however, when the courts will allow the proof of a fact or number of facts which lead it to presume the existence of a further fact, without any evidence of that fact being given in evidence. That is, from the facts that have been given in evidence, the court will then presume another fact for which no direct evidence has been given. A presumption is normally a conclusion which can be drawn until, where permissible, the contrary is proved.

There are three types of these 'presumptions':

- irrebuttable presumptions of law;
- rebuttable presumptions of law;
- presumptions of fact.

Irrebuttable Presumptions of Law

This is also known as a conclusive presumption. In these cases, where the courts accept the existence of certain basic fact(s) then they must also assume the existence of another fact and the other party to the proceedings cannot produce evidence questioning its existence.

For instance, s. 50 of the Children and Young Persons Act 1933 states:

It shall be conclusively presumed that no child under the age of ten years can be guilty of any offence.

Where the defence produce a birth certificate for the accused showing he/she is only nine then, from that basic fact, the courts *must* presume that the child is not guilty of the offence charged. It is an irrebuttable presumption that a child under ten can never be guilty of an offence and matters not what other evidence the prosecution call. Once the birth certificate is accepted as being that of the child, the court will find him/her not guilty.

Rebuttable Presumptions of Law

In these cases, once one party has satisfied the court of the basic fact from which a presumption about other facts must be made, it is for the other party to prove that the presumed fact does not exist. That is, the other party can *rebut* the presumption but, if he/she is unable to do so, the court will draw the appropriate inference from it.

Where the prosecution have to disprove an assumption they must do so beyond reasonable doubt but the defence only have to show on a balance of probabilities that the fact (the presumption) exists (**see para. 10.4**).

There are a number of rebuttable presumptions but the most likely to apply to criminal cases are 'presumptions of regularity'.

Presumption of regularity

It is presumed that where evidence shows that a person acted in a public or official capacity, in the absence of contrary evidence, that that person was regularly and properly appointed and the act was regularly and properly performed. A typical example is on a charge of assaulting a police officer in the course of his/her duty (**see Crime, chapter 8**). Evidence that the police officer acted in that capacity is sufficient proof of his/her due appointment (*R* v *Gordon* (1789) 1 Leach 515; and see *Cooper* v *Rowlands* [1971] RTR 291).

There is also a presumption that mechanical and other instruments were in working order at the time of their use. For example, automatic traffic signals are presumed to be in proper working order unless the contrary is proved (*Tingle Jacobs & Co.* v *Kennedy* [1964] 1 WLR 638). However, there must be evidence of usually correct operation, for example, in relation to the admissibility of evidence of the results of a breath test in excess alcohol cases, where the reliability of the testing device is in question (*Cracknell* v *Willis* [1988] AC 450 and *Newton* v *Woods* [1987] RTR 41).

Presumptions of Fact

The court may, after evidence is given about certain facts, presume (in the absence of sufficient evidence to the contrary), that another fact exists. This differs from rebuttable presumptions of law in that here the court *may* presume the fact exists from other facts presented to the court. With rebuttable presumptions of fact the court *must* presume the fact exists unless it is proved to the contrary. In reality this is just another way of showing that the courts use circumstantial evidence to infer that a fact is true.

Cases where the courts regularly infer the existence of facts from other circumstantial evidence are labelled 'presumptions of fact'. The following are examples of presumptions of fact:

Presumption of intention

Section 8 of the Criminal Justice Act 1967 states:

A court or jury in determining whether a person has committed an offence—
  (a) shall not be bound in law to infer that he intended or foresaw a result of his actions by reason only of its being a natural and probable consequence of those actions; but
  (b) shall decide whether he did intend or foresee that result by reference to all the evidence, drawing such inferences from the evidence as appear proper in the circumstances.

(For further discussion on this area, **see Crime, chapter 1**.)

Presumption of life

Where evidence that a person was alive on a certain date is given to the court, it may be presumed that he/she was still alive on some subsequent date. Of course, where additional evidence is provided showing that the person was in good health and spirits, the chances of such an inference being made will be greater.

10.9.8 **Character**

Credit Questions

Where a witness is being cross-examined they may be asked questions about matters which were not raised during the examination-in-chief. Such questions may relate to any fact in issue or to the credibility of the witness.

During cross-examination, witnesses may be asked leading questions even where they appear to be more favourable to the cross-examining party than to the party which called them (*Parkin* v *Moon* (1836) 7 C & P 408).

Judges have the power to restrain unnecessary, improper or oppressive questions in cross-examination and the exclusionary rules of evidence relating to hearsay, opinion and privilege etc. all apply to cross-examination as they apply to examination-in-chief.

What is known as 'cross-examination as to credit' is where the credibility of a witness is questioned under cross-examination. These questions may relate to the witness's previous convictions, bias, mental or physical disability affecting his/her reliability, reputation for untruthfulness, and previous inconsistent statements relative to the subject matter of the indictment. Where a witness denies any of these matters the cross-examining party is entitled to prove them (see 'Previous Inconsistent Statements' below).

Any cross-examination of a witness designed to impugn his/her credibility should comply with the rules contained in the Code of Conduct of the Bar of England and Wales but although the rules have a strong persuasive force they are not binding on the courts (*R* v *McFaden* (1975) 62 Cr App R 187).

The extent to which police officers may be cross-examined about their behaviour was considered in the case of *R* v *Edwards* [1991] 1 WLR 207. The evidence against the accused consisted of a witness, who was an accomplice, and of certain police officers, who produced interview notes and spoke about interviews with the accused. At these interviews the accused had made admissions but had refused to sign the interview notes, two of which had been certified by senior officers. The accused denied making the admissions and claimed that the interview was a charade, that the interrogating officers had written down what suited them, that it was unrelated to what he had said and that he had been 'fitted up' with false evidence.

The prosecution had been asked to supply the names of any police officers subject to investigation for fabricating evidence. They failed to provide the details of one of the certifying officers who had recently been disciplined internally in relation to another case. In this case the officer had certified interview notes which, to his knowledge, had been wrongly re-written; resulting in the case against the defendants failing.

The Court of Appeal held that a police officer giving evidence, who had allegedly fabricated an admission, could properly be cross-examined to make the jury aware of the fact that his evidence of an admission in a previous case was demonstrably disbelieved; it would have been relevant and admissible to put to the officers concerned that they had given evidence in the earlier trials involving an issue whether alleged confessions had been fabricated and that the trials had ended as they had; that the cross-examination would have been as to credit alone. (See also **para. 10.9.11** with regard to uncorroborated police evidence.)

Where the defence introduce evidence alleging misconduct on the part of the prosecution witnesses, it is not open to the Crown to introduce evidence of good character to boost the testimony of these witnesses (*R* v *Hamilton* (1998) *The Independent*, 6 July).

Rule of Finality

The general rule is that evidence is not admissible to contradict answers given by a witness to questions put in cross-examination that concern collateral matters. These are matters which merely go to credit but which are otherwise irrelevant to the issues in the case (*Harris* v *Tippett* (1811) 2 Camp 637; *Palmer* v *Trower* (1852) 8 Exch 247).

The test whether a matter is collateral or not is that if the answer of a witness is a matter which the cross-examining party would be allowed to prove in evidence, that is, if it has such a connection with the issues that it would be allowed to be given in evidence, then it is a matter on which the witness may be contradicted (*Attorney-General* v *Hitchcock* (1847) 1 Exch 91). In *R* v *Bisby* (1981) 75 Cr App R 79 police officers were cross-examined to the effect that they had fabricated statements attributed to the accused and threatened a potential defence witness to stop them testifying. The judge ruled that the defence could not call the witness who had been allegedly threatened because this would solely go to the credit of the defence. The Court of Appeal held that the evidence of the potential defence witness was relevant to an issue that had to be tried because, if true, the statements attributed to the accused had been fabricated.

Previous Inconsistent Statements

Where a witness makes a previous inconsistent statement (oral or written) and the inconsistency relates to the witness's standing after cross-examination, by ss. 4 and 5 (s. 5 only applies to written statements) of the Criminal Procedure Act 1865, the witness may be asked about these earlier statements and if he/she denies making them or denies their inconsistency the earlier statement can then become admissible evidence.

Convictions of Witnesses

Section 6 of the Criminal Procedure Act 1865 states:

> A witness may be questioned as to whether he has been convicted of any [offence], and upon being so questioned, if he either denies or does not admit the facts, or refuses to answer, it shall be lawful for the cross-examining party to prove such conviction.

KEYNOTE

Previous convictions may be proved by the production of a certificate of the court of conviction. The certificate must be properly signed by the appropriate officer and deal with the substance and effect of the charge and the conviction recorded, coupled with evidence of the identity of the witness as the person so convicted (see s. 73 of the Police and Criminal Evidence Act 1984).

In *Martin* v *White* [1910] 1 KB 665 it was held that evidence of identity need not be conclusive and only be such that the court can properly draw the inference that it has been established.

The Rehabilitation of Offenders Act 1974 and s. 16 of the Children and Young Persons Act 1963 govern and restrict the use of certain previous convictions. In other words, s. 6 of the 1865 Act must be read as relating to those previous convictions which may properly be put to a witness.

Where an accomplice is giving evidence for the Crown, his/her previous convictions should normally be disclosed by the prosecution to the jury at the outset of a trial unless counsel for the defence indicates otherwise (*R* v *Taylor* [1999] 2 Cr App R 163).

The circumstances in which the *accused* may be asked about his/her previous convictions are provided for in s. 1(2) and (3) of the Criminal Evidence Act 1898 (see below).

10.9.9   **Character Evidence of the Accused**

Character evidence in relation to the accused may be admissible to show:

- good character

- bad character.

Good character
The accused is allowed to call evidence of his/her good character provided that it is confined to evidence of general reputation.

The leading case on the use of the good character of an accused is *R* v *Vye* [1993] 1 WLR 471. Evidence of good character is relevant to two issues:

- the accused's credibility as a witness, assuming he/she gives evidence in his/her defence;

- the accused's propensity to commit an offence. In other words, the fact that the accused has not done this type of thing before is relevant when deciding whether he/she has done it on this occasion.

Good character in itself cannot amount to a defence.

Bad character
Evidence of the accused's bad character may be admissible either at common law or under statute.

At common law the prosecution may call evidence of the accused's bad character:

- where the evidence is admissible under the similar facts doctrine (**see chapter 12**);

- where the defence adduces evidence of the accused's good character when this is in fact not the case.

There are also specific statutory powers that may permit the prosecution to adduce evidence of the accused's bad character. Examples of this would include proof of an earlier disqualification in a trial on driving whilst disqualified and guilty knowledge in cases of handling and theft.

Guilty knowledge in cases of handling and theft
Section 27(3) of the Theft Act 1968 allows for the admissibility of previous misconduct and states:

(3) Where a person is being proceeded against for handling stolen goods (but not for any offence other than handling stolen goods), then at any stage of the proceedings, if evidence has been given of his having or arranging to have in his possession the goods the subject of the charge, or of his undertaking or assisting in, or arranging to undertake or assist in, their retention, removal, disposal or realisation, the following evidence shall be admissible for the purpose of proving that he knew or believed the goods to be stolen goods—

    (a) evidence that he has had in his possession, or has undertaken or assisted in the retention, removal, disposal or realisation of, stolen goods from any theft taking place not earlier than 12 months before the offence charged; and

    (b) (provided that seven days' notice in writing has been given to him of the intention to prove the conviction) evidence that he has within the five years preceding the date of the offence charged been convicted of theft or of handling stolen goods.

KEYNOTE

This provision applies to all forms of handling (*R* v *Ball* [1983] 1 WLR 801) and can be used where handling is the only offence involved in the proceedings.

    The question as to what constitutes recent possession is a matter of fact and degree dependent on the circumstances of each case. This presumption can be rebutted by the person offering a true explanation for the possession (*R* v *Schama* (1914) 84 LJ KB 396, *R* v *Garth* [1949] 1 All ER 773, *R* v *Aves* [1950] 2 All ER 330 and *R* v *Williams* [1962] Crim LR 54).

    The term 'recent possession' is not defined and so is a question of fact in each case. In *R* v *Smythe* (1980) 72 Cr App R 8, the Court of Appeal held that property found in the possession of an accused, stolen two or three months earlier during some robberies and burglaries, did not amount to recent possession for the offence of handling stolen goods generally (**see Crime, chapter 12**).

Unlike any other witness, the defendant, as a general rule cannot be cross-examined about his bad character. However, there are four exceptions to this rule contained in s. 1 of the Criminal Evidence Act 1898 which states:

(2) A person charged in criminal proceedings who is called as a witness in the proceedings may be asked any question in cross-examination notwithstanding that it would tend to criminate him as to any offence with which he is charged in the proceedings.

(3) A person charged in criminal proceedings who is called as a witness in the proceedings shall not be asked, and if asked shall not be required to answer, any question tending to show that he has committed or been convicted of or been charged with any offence other than one with which he is then charged, or is of bad character, unless—

    (i) the proof that he has committed or been convicted of such other offence is admissible evidence to show that he is guilty of an offence with which he is then charged; or

    (ii) he has personally or by his advocate asked questions of the witnesses for the prosecution with a view to establish his own good character, or has given evidence of his good character, or the nature or conduct of the defence is such as to involve imputations on the character of the prosecutor or the witnesses for the prosecution or the deceased victim of the alleged crime; or

    (iii) he has given evidence against any other person charged in the same proceedings.

KEYNOTE

Section 1(2) permits questions which tend *directly* to incriminate the accused, whereas s. 1(3) protects the accused from being asked questions which would tend *indirectly* to incriminate the accused (i.e. questions which refer to his/her misconduct on other occasions or his/her commission of other offences or his/her bad character generally), unless s. 1(3)(i), (ii) or (iii) applies.

    This gives the accused a 'shield' against being cross-examined by the prosecution (or a co-accused) about his/her previous bad character which is lost if any of the conditions in s. 1(3) are met. The accused will lose the shield if he/she puts his/her good character in issue either:

- by cross-examination of witnesses; or

- by giving evidence about his/her own good character or by attacking the character of prosecution witnesses.

    The provisions of s. 1(3)(ii) are best described by the case of *Selvey* v *DPP* [1970] AC 304 where the accused alleged that the man with whom he was alleged to have committed buggery was in fact a male prostitute and that the allegation was false and being made because he had declined his services. In making this allegation Selvey lost his 'shield' and the prosecution were able to put to him details of his previous convictions for homosexual offences.

The shield will not be lost if the accused merely asserts his/her innocence or emphatically denies the allegation. If the accused is of previous good character, attacking prosecution witnesses will be of less detriment.

However, where the accused elects to give evidence and has embarked on doing so, he/she cannot avoid evidence of his/her own character going before the jury simply by refusing to return to the witness box so that he/she cannot be cross-examined. In such circumstances the Crown is entitled to adduce evidence as to his/her bad character (*R* v *Forbes* [1999] 2 Cr App R 501).

Where a defendant renders himself/herself liable to cross-examination as to his/her previous convictions under s. 3(ii), the court has an overriding discretion in the interests of fairness to disallow such cross-examination; but the fact that the defendant has no previous convictions for dishonesty is a factor for the court to consider but not an automatic bar to disallowing the cross-examination (*Fearon* v *DPP* (1995) 159 JP 649).

In *Barley* v *DPP* (1998) *The Times*, 30 July, the defendant contended that a memorandum of conviction bearing his name and address did not relate to him. Evidence had to be adduced to disprove the suggestion that some other person had given the defendant's details to the police and court in respect of the earlier offence. Section 16 of the Children and Young Persons Act 1963 prevents an accused who is over the age of 21 from being asked about any offences that he/she may have committed when under the age of 14.

In relation to police cautions, as it is a pre-requisite of a caution that the offender admits the offence, the court is entitled to have regard to them when character is in issue (*R* v *Maikin* [1999] All ER (D) 1482).

In relation to s. 1(3)(iii) it is often the case that an accused can only assert his/her innocence by placing the blame on a co-accused and in such instances the accused loses the shield against cross-examination. The position of this subsection was summarised by the Court of Appeal in *R* v *Varley* [1982] 2 All ER 519:

> Mere denial of participation in a joint venture is not of itself sufficient to rank as evidence against the co-defendant. For the proviso to apply, such denial must lead to the conclusion that if the witness did not participate then it must have been the other who did. . . . Where the one defendant asserts or in due course would assert one view of the joint venture which is directly contradicted by the other such contradiction may be evidence against the co-defendant.

10.9.10 Opinion

The general rule is that the opinion of a witness is inadmissible. However, where it is admissible it can be divided into two groups:

- non-expert evidence;
- expert evidence.

Non-expert Evidence

The courts have allowed the following non-expert opinion evidence from a witness:

- identification of a person or object;
- the speed of a moving vehicle;
- evidence as to temperature or time;
- the value of an item (provided it does not require specialist knowledge to estimate the price).

Two examples of non-expert evidence that are likely to be given by police officers are provided by the following two cases:

- *R* v *Davies* [1962] 1 WLR 1111: any competent witness may give evidence that in his/her opinion a person is drunk provided that he/she describes the facts on which his/her opinion is based.
- *R* v *Hill* (1993) 96 Cr App R 456: police officers could identify substances as prohibited drugs (as to which, **see Crime, chapter 6**).

Expert Evidence

There will be instances in which the issues that the court will need to decide on are beyond its knowledge. In such instances it may be necessary to call on witnesses who, through their own experience or training or both, have the necessary expertise. It is for the judge to decide whether a witness is competent to give expert opinion. The expert witness is only there to assist the court in deciding the facts of the case.

Where more than one expert witness is called and their opinions differ, it will be for the tribunal of fact to decide which evidence they prefer. It must be remembered that expert evidence is not admissible where the issue before the court is one that should fall within the experiences of those deciding the case.

Where the parties have instructed a single joint expert it is not permissible for one party to have a conference with the expert in the absence of the other party without the latter's prior written consent (*Peet* v *Mid-Kent Area Healthcare NHS Trust* [2002] 3 All ER 688).

Expert evidence has been held appropriate in the following areas:

- medical issues and science;

- determining mental illness and the effects of a mental condition on mental processes;

- handwriting samples and facial mapping.

Section 81 of the Police and Criminal Evidence Act 1984 provides for regulations to be made requiring pre-trial disclosure. These rules, contained within Crown Court (Advance Notice of Expert Evidence) Rules 1987 (SI 1987 No. 716), require any party intending to produce expert evidence to furnish to the other parties in the proceedings a statement in writing of the expert finding. This allows the other parties to review the statement and, if necessary, call a countering expert witness. (Note that this applies equally to the defence as it does to the prosecution.)

High standards of accuracy and objectivity are required of an expert witness. An expert witness should provide independent assistance to the court by way of objective unbiased opinion in relation to the matters within his/her expertise (*National Justice Compania Naviera* v *Prudential Assurance Co. Ltd* [1993] 2 Lloyd's Rep 68 and *Liverpool Roman Catholic Archdiocesan Trust* v *Goldberg* [2001] 4 All ER 950). If a witness provides evidence of an opinion that he/she does not genuinely believe, he/she may commit an offence of perjury (**see Crime, chapter 15**).

In *R* v *Okolie* (2000) *The Times*, 16 June, it was held that in establishing matters of foreign law, s. 15 of the the Administration of Justice Act 1920 clearly provides that expert evidence was to be given in person unless it could be agreed or no issue taken. The case involved an accused charged with handling cars stolen in Germany. The evidence produced to prove the cars were in fact stolen were German crime reports that had not been translated. There was a requirement that an expert witness should have given evidence in relation to the theft of the vehicles in Germany.

Even where the evidence given is considered to be hearsay, a court is entitled to deem a police officer an expert witness where the officer has a considerable wealth of experience and knowledge on a specific topic (*R* v *Hodges* (2003) *The Times*, 22 January).

10.9.11   **Corroboration**

The classic definition of corroboration is to be found in *R* v *Baskerville* [1916] 2 KB 658 (per Lord Reid):

> ... evidence in corroboration must be independent testimony which affects the accused by connecting or tending to connect him with the crime. In other words, it must be evidence which implicates him, that is, which confirms in some material particular not only the evidence that the crime has been committed, but also that the prisoner committed it.

In order to satisfy the full technical meaning of the term corroboration, evidence must be:

- admissible in itself;
- from a source independent of the evidence required to be corroborated; and
- such as to tend to show, by confirmation of some material particular, not only that the offence charged was committed, *but also that it was committed by the accused.*

Although a conviction may be based on the testimony of a single prosecution witness who swears that he/she saw the accused commit the crime, it was recognised by Lord Morris in *DPP* v *Hester* [1973] AC 296 that:

> Any risk of the conviction of an innocent person is lessened if conviction is upon the testimony of more than one acceptable witness.

Where possible, supporting evidence should be collected while offences are being investigated to strengthen the prosecution case (or, where appropriate, to support the case the suspect has put forward).

The corroborating evidence does not have to confirm *all* the evidence already given by the witness requiring corroboration. In *R* v *Hill* (1988) 86 Cr App R 337, Lord Lane said:

> For example, in a rape case where the defendant denies he ever had sexual intercourse with the complainant, it may be possible to prove (1) by medical evidence that she had had sexual intercourse within an hour or so prior to the medical examination, (2) by other independent evidence that the defendant and no other man had been with her during that time, (3) that her underclothing was torn and that she had injuries to her private parts. None of these items of evidence on their own would be sufficient to provide the necessary corroboration, but the judge would be entitled to direct the jury that if they were satisfied so as to feel sure that each of those three items had been proved the combined effect of the three items would be capable of corroborating the girl's evidence.

When Corroboration or Other Supporting Evidence is Needed

The general rule is that a court's decision can be based on the evidence of one witness but there are some exceptions to the general rule. These are:

- where corroboration is required as a matter of law;
- obligatory care warnings;
- discretionary care warnings;
- in relation to identification evidence.

Corroboration required as a matter of law
A conviction in the following cases can only be successful if the evidence is corroborated. There are three offences that fall into this category:

- treason;
- perjury;
- speeding (corroboration as to the speed the vehicle was travelling).

Obligatory care warnings
There used to be a number of cases that fell into this group but with recent legislation it now only applies to cases involving persons who are mentally handicapped where they have made a confession which was not witnessed by an independent person. This is now covered by s. 77 of the Police and Criminal Evidence Act 1984, which states:

> (1) Without prejudice to the general duty of the court at a trial on indictment to direct the jury on any matter on which it appears to the court appropriate to do so, where at such a trial—

(a) the case against the accused depends wholly or substantially on a confession by him;

(b) and the court is satisfied—

(i) that he is mentally handicapped; and

(ii) that the confession was not made in the presence of an independent person,

the court shall warn the jury that there is special need for caution before convicting the accused in reliance on the confession, and shall explain that the need arises because of the circumstances mentioned in paragraphs (a) and (b) above.

(2) In any case where at the summary trial of a person for an offence it appears to the court that a warning under subsection (1) above would be required if the trial were on indictment, the court shall treat the case as one in which there is a special need for caution before convicting the accused on his confession.

(3) In this section—

'independent person' does not include a police officer or a person employed for, or engaged on, police purposes;

'mentally handicapped' in relation to a person, means that he is in a state of arrested or incomplete development of mind which includes significant impairment of intelligence and social functioning...

Discretionary care warnings

Sections 32 and 33 of the Criminal Justice and Public Order Act 1994 abolished the rule requiring a corroboration warning be given in relation to the evidence of accomplices and the evidence of complainants in sexual offences and the requirement for corroboration in certain offences under the Sexual Offences Act 1956 (i.e. ss. 2 to 4, 22 and 23).

As a direct result of the provisions of ss. 32 and 33 of the 1994 Act it was recognized by the Court of Appeal that there was still a need to retain a discretion to warn the jury about convicting on the evidence of an unreliable witness (*R* v *Makanjuola* [1995] 1 WLR 1348). Although there is no set form of warning, it is seen as good practice for a judge to warn the jury of any reason(s) why a witness's testimony should be treated with caution (*R* v *R* [1996] Crim LR 815), and to point out to the jury any evidence that potentially corroborates the witness's evidence.

In *R* v *Isham* (1998) 162 JP 391 it was held that in cases involving sexual offences, where the prosecution adduces evidence of complaints made by the complainant after the alleged assault, the jury must be directed that the evidence of the complaint is only of limited relevance and, since it does not come from a source which is independent of the complainant, does not amount to independent confirmation of the complainant's evidence.

Identification evidence

R v *Turnbull* [1976] 3 WLR 445 is the leading case on how the court should approach disputed visual identification evidence. In this case the Court of Appeal outlined those factors that should be considered when identification evidence is presented to the court and therefore those factors that should be considered by police when investigating offences.

In the *Turnbull* case the Court of Appeal laid down important guidelines, reproduced below, for judges in trials where identification evidence was disputed:

First, whenever the case against an accused depends wholly or substantially on the correctness of one or more identifications of the accused which the defence alleges to be mistaken, the judge should warn the jury of the special need for caution before convicting the accused in reliance on the correctness of the identification or identifications. In addition he should instruct them as to the reason for the need for such a warning and should make some reference to the possibility that a mistaken witness can be a convincing one and that a number of such witnesses can all be mistaken. Provided this is done in clear terms the judge need not use any particular form of words.

Secondly, the judge should direct the jury to examine closely the circumstances in which the identification by each witness came to be made. How long did the witness have the accused under observation? At what distance? In what light? Was the observation impeded in any way, as for example, by passing traffic or a press of people? Had the witness ever seen the accused before? How often? If only occasionally, had he any special reason for remembering the accused? How long elapsed between the original observation and the subsequent identification to the police? Was there any material discrepancy between the description of the accused given to the police by the witness when first seen by them and his actual appearance? If in any case, whether it is being dealt with summarily or on indictment, the prosecution have reason to believe that there is such a material discrepancy they should supply the accused or his legal advisors with particulars of the description the police were first given. In all cases if the accused asks to be given particulars of such descriptions, the prosecution should supply them. Finally, he should remind the jury of any specific weaknesses which had appeared in the identification evidence.

Recognition may be more reliable than identification of a stranger; but even when the witness is purporting to recognise someone whom he knows, the jury should be reminded that mistakes in recognition of close relatives and friends are sometimes made.

All these matters go to the quality of the identification evidence. If the quality is good and remains good at the close of the accused's case, the danger of a mistaken identification is lessened; but the poorer the quality, the greater the danger.

In our judgment when the quality is good, as for example when the identification is made after a long period of observation, or in satisfactory conditions by a relative, a neighbour, a close friend, a workmate and the like, the jury can safely be left to assess the value of the identifying evidence even though there is no other evidence to support it; provided always, however, that an adequate warning has been given about the special need for caution. . . .

When, in the judgment of the trial judge, the quality of the identifying evidence is poor, as for example when it depends solely on a fleeting glance or on a longer observation made in difficult conditions, the situation is very different. The judge should then withdraw the case from the jury and direct an acquittal unless there is other evidence which goes to support the correctness of the identification. . . .

The trial judge should identify to the jury the evidence which he adjudges is capable of supporting the evidence of identification. If there is any evidence or circumstances which the jury might think was supporting when it did not have this quality, the judge should say so.

In relation to corroboration of identification evidence, the court made it clear that this is wider than corroboration in the strict legal sense. The court held:

This may be corroboration in the sense lawyers use that word; but it need not be so if its effect is to make the jury sure that there has been no mistaken identification: for example, X sees the accused snatch a woman's handbag; he gets only a fleeting glance of the thief's face as he runs off but he does see him entering a nearby house. Later he picks out the accused on an identity parade. If there was no more evidence than this, the poor quality of the identification would require the judge to withdraw the case from the jury; but this would not be so if there was evidence that the house into which the accused was alleged by X to have run was his father's.

An example of supporting identification evidence is *R* v *Long* (1973) 57 Cr App R 871. Here the defendant was charged with robbery. He had been identified by three witnesses in different places on different occasions but each had only a momentary opportunity for observation. Immediately after the robbery the accused had left his home and could not be found by the police. When he was later seen by the police he claimed to know who had done the robbery and offered to help to find the robbers. At his trial he put forward an alibi which the jury rejected. The court considered that it was an odd coincidence that the eye-witnesses should have identified a man who had behaved in this way and without some explanation by the defence this was admissible as supporting the identification.

The *Turnbull* guidelines should always be followed by judges where the possible mistaken identification of an accused is in issue. Even where an accused has admitted being present at the scene of an offence, there will still be occasions where a judge should give such a direction as required by the guidelines (*R* v *Thornton* [1995] 1 Cr App R 578).

It has been held that in cases where voice identification evidence is an issue the *Turnbull* guidelines should be used to direct the jury as to the 'quality' of the evidence (*R* v *Hersey* [1998] Crim LR 281).

Within the PEACE model used to train police officers, in relation to the taking of both witness statements and suspect statements, the mnemonic **ADVOKATE** is used as an *aide-memoire*:

A—Amount of time under observation

D—Distance between suspect and witness

V—Visibility at time

O—Any Obstructions

K—Known or seen before

A—Any reason to remember

T—Time lapse since witness saw suspect

E—Error or material discrepancy.

For an examination of the law relating to identification, **see chapter 16**.

10.9.12 Judicial Notice

The courts may take judicial notice of various matters that are so well known or clearly established that proof thereof is not required. Judicial notice is another way of saying that a court accepts a fact or facts without formal proof.

Examples of the operation of the exception to the burden of proof include matters which are common knowledge, Acts of Parliament, and custom such as the Home Secretary's approval of certain breath test devices (**see Road Traffic, chapter 5**).

11 Privilege and public policy

11.1 Introduction

This chapter deals with another exception to the general principle that evidence which is relevant to the issues in legal proceedings should be admitted. There are occasions where the courts will allow a person or body of people to refuse to disclose information or documents (and, sometimes, prevent others disclosing such evidence), *even though the evidence in question is reliable and clearly relevant to the issues in a particular case.*

This chapter looks at two main categories which may justify the exclusion of otherwise relevant evidence

- **Privilege**—where a person has a specific *right* in respect of non-disclosure. This includes legal professional privilege.

- **Public policy**—where there is no specific right in respect of non-disclosure but it is nevertheless accepted that public policy justifies the non-disclosure of certain evidence.

11.2 Privilege

11.2.1 Privilege against Self-incrimination

This privilege may be claimed generally by any person in any proceedings (civil or criminal). Any person, when called upon to answer questions or disclose documents, may refuse to do so on the grounds that they may incriminate themselves. This was recognised in *Blunt* v *Park Lane Hotel* [1942] 2 KB 253 where it was said that:

> The rule is that no-one is bound to answer any question if the answer thereto would, in the opinion of the judge, have a tendency to expose [him/her] to any criminal charge, penalty or forfeiture which the judge regards as reasonably likely to be preferred or sued for.

This privilege has been developed by the courts and means that a witness may refuse to answer questions in court and refuse to produce documents if this would have a tendency to incriminate him/her or lead to a criminal charge. While this principle is still seen as another fundamental right (alongside the right to silence), there are many exceptions which are set out below. It is also important to see what use can be made of such testimony. The right to claim this privilege *is for the witness himself/herself*; it does not include the right to claim the privilege in order to protect others, even the accused's spouse. If the courts demand that a person comply with an order to disclose certain evidence, he/she may substitute a different protection in place of the privilege, provided the alternative gives sufficient protection to the witness (as when the prosecuting authorities unequivocally agree not to make use of the information—*AT & T Istel* v *Tully* [1992] 3 WLR 344).

11.2.2   **Exceptions to the Rule against Self-incrimination**

The exceptions to the rule against self-incrimination include:

- s. 31 of the Theft Act 1968
- s. 9 of the Criminal Damage Act 1971
- s. 98 of the Children Act 1989
- s. 2 of the Criminal Justice Act 1987
- s. 1(2) of the Criminal Evidence Act 1898.

Section 31 of the Theft Act 1968

Section 31 of the Theft Act 1968 states:

> (1) A person shall not be excused, by reason that to do so may incriminate that person or the wife or husband of that person of an offence under this Act—
>   (a) from answering any question put to that person in proceedings for the recovery or administration of any property, for the execution of any trust or for an account of any property or dealings with property; or
>   (b) from complying with any order made in any such proceedings;
>   but no statement or admission made by a person in answering a question put or complying with an order made as aforesaid shall, in proceedings for an offence under this Act, be admissible in evidence against that person or (unless they married after the making of the statement of admission) against the wife or husband of that person.
> (2) Notwithstanding any enactment to the contrary, where property has been stolen or obtained by fraud or other wrongful means, the title to that or any other property shall not be affected by reason only of the conviction of the offender.

KEYNOTE

Section 31 simply requires questions to be answered and orders to be complied with in proceedings for the recovery or administration of any property or dealing with property. Where such answers may incriminate the witness or his/her spouse and leave them liable to a charge for an offence under the Theft Act 1968, the answers may not be used in proceedings for any such offence.

In *Renworth* v *Stephansen* [1996] 3 All ER 244, it was held that the fact that the witness might incriminate himself/herself in respect of a non-Theft Act offence (as well as a Theft Act offence) will not necessarily preclude the application of s. 31.

Even though compliance may expose the witness or his/her spouse to a charge for an offence under the Theft Act 1968, the answers may not be used in proceedings for any such offence but might be useful in pointing towards areas where evidence might be found linking the witness to the offence.

For Theft Act offences, see Crime, chapter 12.

Section 9 of the Criminal Damage Act 1971

Section 9 of the Criminal Damage Act 1971 states:

> A person shall not be excused, by reason that to do so may incriminate that person or the wife or husband of that person of an offence under this Act—
>   (a) from answering any question put to that person in proceedings for the recovery or administration of any property, for the execution of any trust or for an account of any property or dealings with property; or
>   (b) from complying with any order made in any such proceedings;

but no statement or admission made by a person in answering a question put or complying with an order made as aforesaid shall, in proceedings for an offence under this Act, be admissible in evidence against that person or (unless they married after the making of the statement or admission) against the wife or husband of that person.

KEYNOTE

This provision is virtually identical to s. 31 of the Theft Act 1968 except the offences relate to those under the Criminal Damage Act 1971.

Wife or husband for the purpose of this section includes: where a man and woman have acquired the reputation of being man and wife by cohabitation, a valid marriage between them will generally be presumed.

For Criminal Damage Act offences, see Crime, chapter 14.

Section 98 of the Children Act 1989

Section 98 of the Children Act 1989 states:

(1) In any proceedings in which a court is hearing an application for an order under Part IV or V [relating to the care, supervision and protection of children], no person shall be excused from—
   (a) giving evidence on any matter; or
   (b) answering any question put to him in the course of his giving evidence,
   on the ground that doing so might incriminate him or his spouse of an offence.

(2) A statement or admission made in such proceedings shall not be admissible in evidence against the person making it or his spouse in proceedings for an offence other than perjury.

KEYNOTE

A statement or admission made in such proceedings shall not be admissible in evidence against the person making it or his/her spouse in proceedings for an offence other than perjury. A statement or admission could include a filed statement of the evidence for use at a hearing, an oral admission made by a parent or guardian or, after proceedings have started, an oral admission to a social worker who is involved in the investigation of a child protection case (see *Oxfordshire County Council* v P [1995] Fam 161 and *Cleveland County Council* v F [1995] 1 WLR 785).

Section 2 of the Criminal Justice Act 1987

This section gives the Serious Fraud Office powers to require people in some circumstances to produce documents and answer any questions relevant to an investigation being conducted by that office (a notable example being the case against the family of Robert Maxwell in the mid-1990s).

Section 1 of the Criminal Evidence Act 1898

Section 1 of the Criminal Evidence Act 1898 amended by the Youth Justice and Criminal Evidence Act 1999: Section 1 states

Every person charged with an offence shall be a competent witness for the defence at every stage of the proceedings, whether the person so charged is charged solely or jointly with any other person.

(1) A person charged in criminal proceedings shall not be called as a witness in the proceedings except upon his own application.

(2) A person charged in criminal proceedings who is called as a witness in the proceedings may be asked any question in cross-examination notwithstanding that it would tend to criminate him as to any offence with which he is charged in the proceedings.

(3) A person charged in criminal proceedings who is called as a witness in the proceedings shall not be asked, and if asked shall not be required to answer, any question tending to show that he has committed or been convicted of or been charged with any offence other than one with which he is then charged, or is of bad character, unless—

    (i) the proof that he has committed or been convicted of such other offence is admissible evidence to show that he is guilty of an offence with which he is then charged; or

    (ii) he has personally or by his advocate asked questions of the witnesses for the prosecution with a view to establish his own good character, or has given evidence of his good character, or the nature or conduct of the defence is such as to involve imputations on the character of the prosecutor or the witnesses for the prosecution or the deceased victim of the alleged crime; or

    (iii) he has given evidence against any other person charged in the same proceedings.

(4) Every person charged in criminal proceedings who is called as a witness in the proceedings shall, unless otherwise ordered by the court, give his evidence from the witness box or other place from which the other witnesses give their evidence.

KEYNOTE

Section 1(2) means that should a defendant decide to give evidence from the witness box, he/she may be cross-examined about matters that might incriminate him/her and removes the privilege against self-incrimination.

Section 1(3) allows this cross-examination to include questions about the defendant's conviction, commission or charge with other offences or the defendant's bad character. However, the defendant is not required to answer these questions unless the conviction or commission of other offences is admissible to show that he/she is guilty of the offence charged, the defence has raised the issue of the defendant's good character or, the defence has raised the issue of the character of a prosecution witness.

11.3   Legal Professional Privilege

At common law, no privilege attaches to communications made in confidence except communications:

- between a client and a legal adviser made *for the purpose of the obtaining and giving of legal advice* (advice privilege); and

- between a client or his/her legal adviser and third parties, *the dominant purpose of which was preparation for contemplated or pending litigation* (litigation privilege).

11.3.1   Extent of the Privilege

The privilege which applies to communications between client and legal adviser is considered by the courts to be of great importance. If legal professional privilege applies to a piece of evidence, this overrides all other considerations. This view was highlighted in *R v Derby Magistrates' Court, ex parte B* [1996] AC 487 where the appellant was acquitted of murder. His step-father was subsequently charged with the murder and, at his committal proceedings, the appellant was called as a prosecution witness. Counsel for the defence sought to cross-examine the appellant on certain factual instructions that he had given to his solicitors when he had been charged with the offence. The appellant declined to waive his privilege and refused to answer the question.

The issue was whether a witness summons could properly be issued to compel production by a prosecution witness in committal proceedings of proofs of evidence and attendance notes giving factual instructions to his solicitor in earlier criminal proceedings, arising out of the same event in which he had been acquitted. Lord Taylor of Gosforth CJ stated:

> The principle ... is that a man must be able to consult his lawyer in confidence, since otherwise he might hold back half the truth. The client must be sure that what he tells his lawyer in confidence will never be revealed without his consent. Legal professional privilege is thus much more than an ordinary rule of evidence, limited in its application to the facts of a particular case. It is a fundamental condition on which the administration of justice as a whole rests. ... But it is not for the sake of the applicant alone that the privilege must be upheld. It is in the wider interests of all those hereafter who might otherwise be deterred from telling the whole truth to their solicitors.

In relation to the European Convention on Human Rights, lawyer/client communications are protected by Article 6(3)(c) and Article 8.

The European Court has held:

> ... an accused's right to communicate with his advocate out of the hearing of a third person is one of the basic requirements of a fair trial in a democratic society and follows from Article 6(3)(c) of the Convention. If a lawyer were unable to confer and receive confidential instructions from him without such surveillance, his assistance would lose much of its usefulness, whereas the Convention is intended to guarantee rights that are practical and effective.

(*S* v *Switzerland* (1991) 14 EHRR 670.)

11.3.2 Scope of Privilege

As discussed above, a client *may*, and his/her legal adviser *must* (subject to the client's waiver), refuse to give oral evidence or to produce documents relating to:

- advice privilege—communications between the client and his/her legal adviser made for the purpose of enabling the client to obtain or the adviser to give legal advice about any matter, whether or not litigation was contemplated at the time;

- litigation privilege—communications between the client or his/her legal adviser and third parties, the sole or dominant purpose of which was to enable the legal adviser to advise or act in relation to litigation that was pending or in the contemplation of the client.

A legal adviser, for the purposes of legal professional privilege, includes:

- a solicitor; or
- a barrister;
- employed advisers; and
- overseas advisers.

In the case of communications with third parties, the privilege can be claimed in respect of a document brought into existence before deciding to instruct a solicitor, provided that litigation was reasonably in prospect and the document was prepared for the sole or dominant purpose of enabling the solicitor to advise whether a claim should be made or resisted.

A document that is not privileged in the hands of the client does not become privileged if given into the custody of a lawyer for the purposes of obtaining legal advice (or if sent by the lawyer to a third party in connection with pending or contemplated litigation). If the item could be seized from a suspect it would not become privileged just because it has been sent to his/her lawyer.

In *R (on the application of Bozkurt)* v *Thames Magistrates' Court* [2002] RTR 15, it was held that an interpreter can interpret in defence interviews, and be called by the prosecution to give evidence on matters of procedure (in this case drink drive procedures) without it being a breach of professional privilege, or resulting in an unfair trial (Article 8 of the European Convention on Human Rights).

11.3.3 Exceptions to Legal Privilege

An exception to the principle of legal professional privilege are communications in furtherance of crime or fraud. This would apply where a client asks to a legal adviser for advice in the commission of a crime or fraud. Where the legal adviser is ignorant of the purpose for which his/her advice is sought, the communication between the two is not privileged.

The exception can be relied upon only if there is *prima facie* evidence that it was the client's intention to obtain advice in furtherance of his/her criminal or fraudulent purpose.

11.3.4 Items Subject to Legal Privilege

This principle of legal professional privilege is set out in s. 10 of the Police and Criminal Evidence Act 1984. Section 10 is intended to reflect the common law and states:

(1) Subject to subsection (2) below, in this Act 'items subject to legal privilege' means—
    (a) communications between a professional legal adviser and his client or any person representing his client made in connection with the giving of legal advice to the client;
    (b) communications between a professional legal adviser and his client or any person representing his client or between such an adviser or his client or any such representative and any other person made in connection with or in contemplation of legal proceedings and for the purposes of such proceedings; and
    (c) items enclosed with or referred to in such communications and made—
        (i) in connection with the giving of legal advice; or
        (ii) in connection with or in contemplation of legal proceedings and for the purposes of such proceedings,
    when they are in the possession of a person who is entitled to possession of them.

(2) Items held with the intention of furthering a criminal purpose are not items subject to legal privilege.

KEYNOTE

In *R v Crown Court at Manchester, ex parte R* [1999] 4 All ER 35, a solicitor refused to disclose any records or logs concerning the time of arrival of a client at the solicitor's office on a particular date. It was held that such records or logs had nothing to do with obtaining legal advice and therefore were not protected by legal professional privilege.

For the law governing the search for, and seizure of 'privileged' material, **see General Police Duties, chapter 2.**

11.3.5 By-passing the Privilege and Waiver of Privilege

Often there will be facts which are subject to legal professional privilege which would be useful to the prosecution case. While the rule of privilege is absolute, the facts can still be put to the courts in certain cases, namely:

• by-passing the privilege; and

• waiving the privilege.

By-passing the Privilege

Legal professional privilege prevents facts being proved in a particular way (i.e. through the client or through the lawyer or certain third parties). However, if enquiries reveal *other sources* by which the same fact(s) can be proved, the privilege is not breached. This could be achieved by obtaining a copy of the communication or by making use of documents legally coming in to the hands of police even if by accident.

Waiving the Privilege

The privilege is that of the client and he/she can waive it. However, he/she must take care to mark clearly the *extent* of any waiver otherwise communications which relate to the same subject matter may be taken to have been waived by implication.

Privilege is not taken to be waived where communications are disclosed for a limited purpose (e.g. to assist the police with enquiries).

In *R* v *Bowden* [1999] 1 WLR 823, the Court of Appeal considered the waiver of legal professional privilege. It was held that, if in the course of questioning by the police, a suspect went beyond saying that he declined to answer on legal advice and explained the basis on which he had been so advised, legal professional privilege would be waived. Such waiver would similarly apply if a solicitor, acting as the authorised representative, gave such an explanation. It therefore follows that, if a defendant gave evidence at his/her trial of the grounds on which the advice to make no comment was given, this would be construed as the defendant voluntarily withdrawing his/her protection to confidential information between client and legal adviser. Again, the same waiver would apply to the solicitor required to give evidence. Such waiver of legal privilege would enable questioning directed to the nature of the advice and the factual premises on which it was based.

11.4 Exclusion on Grounds of Public Policy

This is an area of disclosure and needs to be read in conjunction with the Criminal Procedure and Investigations Act 1996 (**see chapter 14**).

Generally, it is in the public interest that all relevant information should be made available to the court. However, it is also important on occasions to withhold material, the disclosure of which would harm the nation or the proper functioning of the public service. At times the needs of justice conflict with the needs of public policy and the courts have to balance these competing needs in deciding whether relevant information should be disclosed.

When public policy is claimed as a reason for not disclosing evidence in a trial, the process is known as claiming *public interest immunity*.

11.4.1 Public Interest Immunity

Public interest immunity may be raised by:

- The relevant minister or the Attorney-General (or Solicitor-General) intervening in a case.
- The party seeking to withhold the evidence either on his/her own initiative or at the request of the relevant government minister or department.
- The judge in the case.

11.4.2 Effect of Immunity

Where the claim is successful:

- A person entitled to claim such immunity may refuse to answer the question(s) put or disclose the document sought.
- The facts may be proved by other evidence, if available.
- No adverse inferences may be drawn against a party or witness claiming such immunity.

If a person entitled to claim privilege fails to do so or waives his/her privilege, no other person may object. In *Wentworth* v *Lloyd* (1864) 10 HL Cas 589, it was held that where a witness claims privilege no adverse inferences may be drawn against them.

11.4.3   **How Immunity is Claimed**

This was set out in *R* v *Ward* [1993] 1 WLR 619:

> If, in a criminal case, the prosecution wish to claim public interest immunity for documents helpful
> to the defence, the prosecution are in law obliged to give notice to the defence of the asserted right
> to withhold the documents so that, if necessary, the court can be asked to rule on the legitimacy of
> the prosecution's claim. If the prosecution, in an exceptional case, are not prepared to have the issue
> determined by a court, the prosecution must be abandoned.

In *R* v *Keane* [1994] 1 WLR 746, Lord Taylor CJ held that it is for the prosecution to put before
the court only those documents which it regards as material but wishes to withhold.
However, if, in an exceptional case, the prosecution are in doubt about the materiality of
some documents or information, the court may be asked to rule on that issue.

In assessing the interests of justice, the court must ask whether a document to which the
immunity relates is *material* (i.e. relevant) to the proceedings. Its materiality will depend on
the purpose for which it is sought to be deployed. If the disputed material may prove the
defendant's innocence or avoid a miscarriage of justice, then the balance will usually come
down in favour of disclosing it.

Evidence which may be affected by a claim of public interest immunity might be a specific
piece of evidence (such as an internal memorandum) which falls under one of the recognised
heads (**see para. 11.4.4**); alternatively, it may fall within a *class* of documents which are
generally protected (such as communications between government ministers and advisers—
see below). In 1996 the Lord Chancellor directed that the focus of excluding evidence on the
ground of public policy should be based on the damage any disclosure would cause. Immunity
should be claimed only where there would be real damage or harm to the public interest.

11.4.4   **Types of Public Interest Immunity**

The types of material under the heads of public interest immunity which are recognised by
the courts are:

- national security and diplomatic relations;
- the proper functioning of the public service;
- police communications;
- informers and information for the detection of crime;
- judges and jurors;
- sources of information contained in publications.

Whether or not withholding information from the defence on the grounds of public interest
immunity is compatible with Article 6 of the European Convention on Human Rights (right
to a fair trial) has yet to be clarified. There is only limited European case law in this area and
at present the Court appears to accept domestic practice and law.

National Security and Diplomatic Relations

A claim here will normally be successful where a ministerial certificate is presented to the
court. In *Balfour* v *Foreign and Commonwealth Office* [1994] 1 WLR 681 it was held that, once
there is an actual or potential risk to national security demonstrated by an appropriate
ministerial certificate, the court should not exercise its right to inspect the material in question.

The Proper Functioning of Public Service

Public interest immunity may be claimed for correspondence and communications between
ministers and high-level government officials, regarding the formulation of government policy.

Such communications were involved in the case against the directors of Matrix-Churchill, the company at the heart of the allegations that a 'supergun' had been sold and exported to Iraq.

Police Communications

Public interest immunity also attaches to police communications relating to the investigation of crime, such as:

- Documents or information upon the strength of which search warrants have been obtained.
- Reports sent by the police to the Director of Public Prosecutions.
- Police complaints and disciplinary files (see *Halford* v *Sharples* [1992] 1 WLR 736). (There is no immunity, however, for written complaints against the police prompting investigations under Part IX of the Police and Criminal Evidence Act 1984, **see General Police Duties, chapter 1**.)
- Working papers and reports prepared by investigating officers involved in complaints against police (production will be ordered where the public interest in disclosure of the contents outweighs the public interest in preserving confidentiality).
- In *Goodridge* v *Chief Constable of Hampshire* [1999] 1 All ER 896, a malicious prosecution case brought by a person charged with murder where the case was later discontinued, it was held that reports and correspondence passing between the police and the Director of Public Prosecutions and a report sent to the Police Complaints Authority were not subject to public interest immunity.

For a discussion of the police complaints system, **see General Police Duties, chapter 1**. (See also *Police Conduct, Complaints and Efficiency*, Blackstone Press (OUP) 2001.)

Public interest immunity does not attach to statements made during the course of a police grievance procedure, initiated by an officer, alleging either racial or sexual discrimination (*Commissioner of Police of the Metropolis* v *Locker* [1993] 3 All ER 584). For the law relating to equality of opportunity and discrimination, **see General Police Duties, chapter 12**.

There is no 'class' immunity (**see para. 11.4.3**) for statements obtained for the purposes of investigations concerning complaints against police. However, immunity may be claimed in the case of a particular document by reason of its contents (*R* v *Chief Constable of the West Midlands Police, ex parte Wiley* [1995] 1 AC 274).

Informers and Information for the Detection of Crime

The Regulation of Investigatory Powers Act 2000 consolidated the law on the use of investigatory powers to ensure that they are exercised in accordance with human rights.

The 2000 Act addresses the regulation of six investigatory powers which includes both the use of covert surveillance in the course of specific operations (observation points) and the use of covert human intelligence sources (informants) (s. 26 of the 2000 Act).

Part II of the 2000 Act creates a statutory framework to ensure that the use of the powers is properly regulated and a full discussion of this framework and its effect on police operations can be found in **Crime, chapter 3**.

Judges and Jurors

A judge cannot be compelled to give evidence of matters of which he/she became aware *as a result of the performance of his/her judicial functions*. However, the judge remains 'competent' to give evidence and, if a situation arises where his/her evidence is vital, the judge should be able to be relied on not to allow his/her non-compellability to stand in the way of giving evidence. Of course, if a judge's evidence is entirely unrelated to his/her judicial office (e.g. if he/she were to witness someone breaking into a neighbour's house), the normal rules regarding compellability and competence will generally apply.

A jury's verdict cannot be impeached by the testimony of a juror as to what happened in the jury room. Unlike some other countries—notably the USA—it is a contempt of court to question a juror about the deliberations within the jury room, even after the trial.

Sources of Information Contained in Publications

Section 10 of the Contempt of Court Act 1981 states:

> No court may require a person to disclose, nor is any person guilty of contempt of court for refusing to disclose, the source of information contained in a publication for which he is responsible, unless it be established to the satisfaction of the court that disclosure is necessary in the interests of justice or national security or for the prevention of disorder or crime.

KEYNOTE

Section 10 applies to information which has been communicated and received for the purposes of publication, even if it is not 'contained in a publication', because the purpose underlying the statutory protection of sources of information is as much applicable before as after publication.

Disclosure will be ordered if it is shown to be necessary, either for the prevention of crime generally, or for the prevention of a particular and identifiable future crime.

---

12 Similar fact evidence

12.1 Introduction

This chapter looks at similar fact evidence. This can be a complex area of the law of evidence and the aim of this chapter is to give the reader an understanding of the subject. The chapter also considers what evidence should be collected against a suspect where the similar fact rule may apply.

As discussed earlier, evidence is admissible if it is relevant to a fact in issue necessary to prove or disprove the case against the accused. Normally such evidence will be directly related to the offence in question, for instance the defendant was seen hitting the victim using a bottle. But what if the victim described the bottle as being a green lager bottle with a German name on it? What relevance would this have if a suspect has been convicted of previous assaults using a green lager bottle from a German brewer or where there are several victims all of whom have been assaulted in the same way? Should this evidence be admissible at the defendant's trial or is there too big a risk that such evidence will be prejudicial to his/her case? Throughout this particular aspect of the law of evidence there is a common theme; balancing the usefulness of the evidence in proving the case in question (its 'probative value') against the possible detrimental effects of that evidence on the defendant (its 'prejudicial effect').

Thus this chapter is concerned with when evidence of the defendant's previous convictions or conduct on other occasions may be admissible as evidence of his/her guilt in relation to the present offence.

12.2 The Similar Fact Principle

This principle was recognised as far back as 1894 in *Makin* v *Attorney-General for New South Wales* [1894] AC 57, where Lord Herschell LC said that:

> It is undoubtedly not competent for the prosecution to adduce evidence tending to show that the accused has been guilty of criminal acts other than those covered by the indictment, for the purpose of leading to the conclusion that the accused is a person likely from his criminal conduct or character to have committed the offence for which he is being tried. On the other hand, the mere fact that the evidence adduced tends to shew the commission of other crimes [or similar actions of the accused] does not render it inadmissible if it be relevant to an issue before the jury, and it may be so relevant if it bears upon the question whether the acts alleged to constitute the crime charged in the indictment were designed or accidental, or to rebut a defence which would otherwise be open to the accused.

This passage sets out the two key propositions surrounding the similar fact doctrine. The first proposition is that evidence which shows that the accused has a *particular disposition* to commit crimes in general, or to commit the kind of crime with which he/she has been charged, is *not* admissible. This is because, although it may appear to be relevant to a case, there is no direct link between the crime committed and the past actions of the accused. Such evidence is excluded, not because it does not support the fact that the accused might have committed the offence, but because of the danger that the jury might attach a disproportionate importance to this evidence compared with other evidence directly concerning the commission of the offence charged.

The second proposition really takes us back to the question of what facts are admissible in court. The answer is those facts which are relevant to prove or disprove the offence(s) charged. Evidence is likely to be admissible if it goes beyond mere evidence of a propensity to commit crime and has a crucial bearing upon the question whether the offence charged was committed by this defendant. In these cases the evidence of previous offences or actions of the accused *may be* admissible because they *connect* the defendant with the offence charged. If so, the evidence that he/she has a disposition to commit that kind of offence or act in a particular way *is* relevant because it makes it more likely that he/she committed the offence charged. Therefore the probative value of that evidence may outweigh any prejudicial effect it might have on the defendant's case.

....

EXAMPLE

An example of such a case is the infamous one of *R* v *Smith* (1915) 11 Cr App R 229 where a man was charged with the murder of his wife who was found dead in the bath. There was evidence of two further marriages where his former wives had been found dead in a bath, along with other similarities including the defendant's profiting financially from the death on each occasion. Lord Reading approved the direction given by the trial judge to the jury:

> If you find an accident which benefits a person and you find that the person has been fortunate to have that accident happen to him a number of times, benefiting each time, you draw a very strong, frequently irresistible inference that the occurrence of so many accidents benefiting him is such a coincidence that it cannot have happened unless it was designed.

Generally, evidence of prior incidents in respect of which a defendant has been acquitted are not admissible in evidence (*R* v *X* [1999] All ER (D) 1373). However, in *R* v *Z* [2000] 3 WLR 117 similar fact evidence in relation to previous sexual conduct was held to be admissible to help disprove the accused's claim that he believed that the victim was consenting to sexual intercourse on this occasion (**see para. 12.4.7**).

....

12.3 Evidence of Similar Facts

As the cases above illustrate, it is a common law rule that evidence which merely shows a similarity to the fact in issue is irrelevant and just because a person has acted in a particular way previously, does not make it probable that he/she so acted on a given occasion. This is one of the reasons why, generally, a person's previous convictions may not be put before a court because its prejudicial effect will generally outweigh any probative value of such evidence (**see chapter 10**).

An exception to this exclusionary rule is when such evidence is positively probative (helpful or evidential) of the offence before the court. Similar fact evidence is not just evidence of previous crimes; it can include evidence of non-criminal misconduct and evidence of a disposition to behave in a particular way. The categories falling within the doctrine of similar fact evidence could be relevant to any case where the courts feel that the evidence has probative value which outweighs any potential prejudicial effect in deciding an issue before them.

12.4 Admissibility of Similar Fact Evidence

Similar fact evidence is admissible in a number of ways:

- striking similarity;
- non-criminal behaviour;
- probative force without striking similarity;

- multiple offence cases;
- possession of objects by the accused;
- association with an event;
- previous sexual conduct and the 'same transaction' rule;
- use of similar fact evidence by a co-accused.

Each of these is examined in detail below.

12.4.1 Striking Similarity

Here the court will look for something more than some feature which is common place. Offences may be identical without being 'striking', e.g. where the *modus operandi* of a burglary is common to thousands of other offences of burglary. However, if a burglar has used a blow torch to crack the window of a building before entering in the past, that feature may be admissible against him/her if charged with similar burglaries in the future (*R* v *Mullen* [1992] Crim LR 735). So it may be better to think in terms of similarities which are really peculiarities to the accused. Lord Hailsham gave a very extreme but memorable example in *DPP* v *Boardman* [1975] AC 421. This example was of a man who commits repeated homosexual offences and whose victims all state that he was attired in 'ceremonial head-dress . . . or other eccentric garb'. If a victim of an offence of gross indecency described the assailant as being dressed in a North American native 'war bonnet', that fact may be so similar to previous offences committed by the defendant that the courts would accept evidence of those earlier offences as 'similar fact' evidence. Whether or not evidence of similar facts will be accepted under this head will depend on the likelihood or otherwise of repetition being attributable to mere coincidence.

In assessing similar fact evidence the question is one of relevance; it does not matter whether similar fact evidence displays its relevance by revealing features of a striking similarity with the offence itself, or simply with its surrounding circumstances.

Probably the best example of such evidence is the case against Rosemarie West. Here, Mrs West was accused of assisting her husband who had been convicted of ten murders before killing himself in prison. In seven of the murders the bodies had been naked, bound and mutilated and had been found under the defendant's house. Evidence from witnesses that the defendant actively engaged in violent sexual assaults with her husband at that address was admitted under the striking similarity rule (*R* v *West* [1996] 2 Cr App R 374).

Dissimilarities in the evidence, which detract from its probative value, must be taken into account and should be presented to the prosecutor along with the other evidence (**see chapter 14**).

In determining the admissibility of similar fact evidence the question, as always, is whether the probative value outweighs the prejudicial effect the evidence could have on the accused.

12.4.2 Non-criminal Behaviour

Evidence of non-criminal behaviour of the accused is admissible if such behaviour has a sufficient degree of probative force linking that behaviour and the circumstances surrounding the commission of the offence charged.

In *R* v *Barrington* [1981] 1 WLR 419, the accused was charged with indecently assaulting three girls. The prosecution alleged that the girls had been lured to the house of a co-accused as baby-sitters, had been shown pornographic photographs, had been asked to pose for photographs in the nude and had then been indecently assaulted. Evidence was also admitted from three other girls concerning another incident. They had not been indecently assaulted, but they had been lured to the house on the same pretext, had been shown the photographs and had been asked to pose in the nude. The Court of Appeal held that the evidence had been properly admitted on the grounds that, although it included no evidence of the commission of offences, it was logically probative of guilt because it was *inexplicable on the basis of coincidence*. Consequently, while the actions were not part of the offence itself, the evidence went to link all the cases together and would assist the jury in deciding the case.

12.4.3 Probative Force without Striking Similarity

In *DPP* v *P* [1991] 2 AC 447 it was held that where the court is dealing with the issue of an offender's identity similar fact evidence must always provide something in the nature of a 'signature or other special feature'. However, in addition to a signature or special feature which identifies the accused, similar fact evidence can also be used to link an offence to an accused by a chain of reasoning which does not include this feature. In *R* v *W (John)* [1998] 2 Cr App R 289 two offences took place within two weeks where, in both cases, the female victim was detained for a short time by the offender. One of the females was indecently assaulted but the other scared the offender away by screaming. The descriptions of the attacker fitted the accused, he was shown to be in the vicinity at the time of both incidents, and his clothing was torn in a way consistent with an injury suffered by the attacker when escaping. The Court of Appeal deduced that a 'relationship in time and circumstances' sufficient to satisfy the required degree of probative value was present and rejected an argument that striking similarity had to be present.

12.4.4 Multiple Offence Cases

Where a defendant faces more than one charge of a similar nature or where evidence of similar allegations is tendered in support of one charge, the evidence of one accuser may be admissible to support the evidence of another. Often this point becomes an issue before a trial starts, when the defence apply to the court to have counts which are of a similar nature tried separately to avoid the overall evidence being heard at one time. This type of evidence has also been used where corroboration used to be in issue.

The underlying principle here is that the probative value of multiple accusations may depend in part on their similarity, but also on the unlikely probability that the same person would find himself/herself falsely accused on different occasions by different and independent individuals. The making of multiple accusations may be a coincidence in itself, which has to be taken into account in deciding admissibility.

The use of similar fact evidence in this area was considered in *R* v *Sims* [1946] KB 531, where it was observed that the evidence of a number of accusations taken together is much greater than one alone, for:

> whereas the jury might think one man might be telling an untruth, three or four are hardly likely to tell the same untruth unless they were conspiring together.

In cases of multiple complainants/witnesses there is always a chance of collusion and this should be borne in mind when taking witness statements.

12.4.5 Possession of Objects by the Accused

There may be occasions where a suspect is arrested and during subsequent searches articles are found which could be used in the type of offence suspected. Such items may be admitted as similar fact evidence *provided the evidence goes beyond mere criminal disposition*. In the assault case referred to above (**see para. 12.1**), if the bottle used was a distinctive or unusual one, the defendant's previous possession of a similar bottle might be used to identify him/her as the offender.

In *Thompson* v *The King* [1918] AC 221 the accused, a homosexual pederast, assaulted two young boys and their identification on him was confirmed by his possession of powder puffs and indecent photographs. Although these items were not used in the offence, or constituted the accused's 'signature' they were admitted as evidence in the light of the probative value they possessed to rebut the accused's claims of mistaken identity.

12.4.6 Association with an Event

Another function which similar fact evidence may be called upon to perform is to show an event involving an accused person in its true light. For instance, it may be relevant in deciding whether an event occurred by accident or innocently or intentionally. It may also be relevant against an alibi, i.e. to show that the accused committed another crime in the vicinity shortly before or after the offence charged. In such cases the evidence may not relate to the actual offence but to the background leading up to the incident.

Makin v *Attorney-General for New South Wales* [1894] AC 57 (**see para. 12.2**) is a good example of 'association with an event'. A husband and wife were accused of murdering a small child who they were looking after for payment. The child's body was found buried at their home along with the bodies of other children. Evidence of the bodies of the other children was admitted as similar fact evidence as this was relevant to the issue of how the child had died.

12.4.7 Previous Sexual Conduct and the 'Same Transaction' Rule

Evidence of sexual or other behaviour which is not the subject of the charge may also be admissible to show the true nature of the relationship between the relevant parties (i.e. the defendant and the victim). In *DPP* v *Boardman* [1975] AC 421, evidence of the accused's previous approaches to a boy with whom he was alleged to have committed buggery was admitted, including evidence of an indecent assault taking place several months before. Similar evidence was given by another complainant of indecent conduct leading over a period of time to incitement to buggery.

There is also a general rule which allows evidence of continuing behaviour to be adduced as part of the 'same transaction', for instance, where a nine-year-old girl gave evidence of indecent assaults, rapes and threats by the defendant, leading up to a final offence of rape which was the subject of the charge against him. The court held that the preliminary behaviour was all part of the 'same transaction' and therefore admissible (*R* v *Rearden* (1864) 4 F & F 76).

Similarly, in *R* v *M* [2000] 1 All ER 148, evidence that M had been taught from a young age to abuse his sisters sexually was admitted where the prosecution contended that this would assist the jury in understanding S's evidence by explaining why she had not sought help and why M had felt able to carry out the alleged offences without fear.

In *R* v *Z* [2000] 3 WLR 117, the accused was charged with rape and there were four similar previous incidents involving the accused and four different women. He had been found guilty on one occasion, but had been acquitted on the other three. It was held that the evidence would be allowed as the evidence of the earlier complaints was relevant to the issue of the accused's belief in consent and such evidence was not inadmissible simply because the accused had been previously acquitted.

Strictly speaking, the 'same transaction' rule is not part of similar fact evidence and therefore does not require the same safeguards when deciding on its prejudicial effect on the defendant (*R* v *Bond* [1906] 2 KB 389).

12.4.8   **Use of Similar Fact Evidence by Co-accused**

A co-accused can also rely on similar fact evidence if it is relevant to an issue before the court. This will normally be to support the accused's defence or damage his/her co-accused's case.

12.5   **Discretionary Exclusion of Similar Fact Evidence**

It will always be for the judge to decide whether in a particular case similar fact evidence should be admissible. It is for the prosecution, based on the evidence provided by the police, if it feels that the evidence is relevant to the case, to raise the issue of admissibility for the judge to rule on. The discretion to exclude similar fact evidence may be used where its prejudicial effect may be so disproportionate to its probative value (i.e. it will do more harm than good) that it ought not to be admitted (*R* v *Straffen* [1952] 2 QB 911).

12.6   **Handling Stolen Goods**

Section 27(3) of the Theft Act 1968 states:

(3) Where a person is being proceeded against for handling stolen goods (but not for any offence other than handling stolen goods), then at any stage of the proceedings, if evidence has been given of his having or arranging to have in his possession the goods the subject of the charge, or of his undertaking or assisting in, or arranging to undertake or assist in, their retention, removal, disposal or realisation, the following evidence shall be admissible for the purpose of proving that he knew or believed the goods to be stolen goods—

(a) evidence that he had in his possession, or has undertaken or assisted in the retention, removal, disposal or realisation of, stolen goods from any theft taking place not earlier than 12 months before the offence charged; and

(b) (provided that seven days' notice in writing has been given to him of the intention to prove the conviction) evidence that he has within five years preceding the date of the offence charged been convicted of theft or of handling stolen goods.

KEYNOTE

This section can only be relied on where handling stolen goods is the only offence in the proceedings and to prove guilty knowledge or belief. It cannot be used to prove any issues of dishonesty or possession of the goods in question (*R* v *Duffas* (1994) 158 JP 224).

The previous conviction of a defendant can be proved by the production of a certificate of the court of conviction in accordance with s. 73(2) of the Police and Criminal Evidence Act 1984. It was held in *R* v *Hacker* [1994] 1 WLR 1659 that the substance of the previous conviction contained within the certificate could be read out, in this instance the fact that the accused, charged with handling the bodyshell of a car, had previously been convicted of receiving stolen cars, was relevant to help prove guilty knowledge or belief. (For offences in relation to handling stolen goods, see **Crime, chapter 12.**)

---

13 Exclusion of admissible evidence

13.1 Introduction

Under the law, every person is presumed innocent until proven guilty. The duty of the courts is not only to decide on the guilt or innocence of a person, but also to ensure that the person has a fair hearing. When considering the second question, the courts will consider the evidence that the prosecution intend to use in the case and how that evidence was obtained.

In ensuring that a person has a fair trial the court may exclude evidence, *even though the evidence itself is admissible*. The court may exclude any evidence in certain circumstances and has additional powers in relation to evidence obtained by confession. The courts' powers to exclude evidence comes generally from s. 78 of the Police and Criminal Evidence Act 1984 (and specifically in relation to confession evidence from s. 76(2) of that Act), although the courts also have common law powers to exclude evidence. The exclusion of confession evidence is the most common and occupies the bulk of this chapter. However, the exclusion of evidence generally will also be discussed here.

The courts bear a substantial responsibility in deciding what evidence should be admitted. Clearly this can have a huge impact on the fairness of the trial. The Human Rights Act 1998 introduced the European Convention for the Protection of Human Rights and Fundamental Freedoms into domestic law in October 2000. When determining an issue which has arisen in connection with a Convention right, courts must consider Convention law which includes judgments, declarations and opinions of the European Court of Human Rights (and previously the European Commission of Human Rights) and all domestic legislation, as far as possible must be interpreted in a way which is compatible with the Convention rights (**see General Police Duties, chapter 2**).

13.2 Confessions

There are three general ways in which you can prove a person's involvement in an offence:

- confessions (or admissions);
- witnesses;
- forensic science.

In some cases where the suspect initially confesses to the offence, he/she may still plead not guilty alleging that the confession was obtained by oppression and/or in circumstances that would render it unreliable or that it should be excluded as having been unfairly obtained. The courts are concerned with the reliability of evidence and often regard confessions as the least reliable way to prove a person's involvement in an offence.

A confession, which is defined by s. 82 of the Police and Criminal Evidence Act 1984 (see below), is an out of court statement made by a person and therefore falls into the category of evidence known as 'hearsay' evidence. Hearsay evidence is admissible unless it falls within one of the statutory or common law exceptions which are considered in **chapter 10**.

Confessions are such an exceptional category and are admissible in evidence as outlined in s. 76(1) of the 1984 Act. However, evidence of confession may be excluded by a court under either s. 76(2) or 78 of the 1984 Act.

Section 76 of the Police and Criminal Evidence Act 1984 states:

> (1) In any proceedings a confession made by an accused person may be given in evidence against him insofar as it is relevant to any matter in issue in the proceedings and is not excluded by the court in pursuance of this section.

A 'confession' is defined by s. 82 of the 1984 Act, which states:

> (1) In this Part of this Act—
> 'confession' includes any statement wholly or partly adverse to the person who made it, whether made to a person in authority or not and whether made in words or otherwise; . . .

KEYNOTE

A confession, therefore, is a positive action by the person making it. The person must use words or some other method of communication (e.g. nodding his/her head to a question, or a video tape of the suspect taking police to a murder weapon). Therefore confessions do not include silence by a person (although this may be relevant to special warnings, **see chapter 17**).

The confession does not have to be a pure statement of guilt and can include the answers to questions asked in interview which are *adverse to the defendant*. In *R v Z* [2003] EWCA Crim 191 the Court of Appeal considered the meaning of 'confession' for the purposes of PACE in light of the Human Rights Act 1998. The court held that the decision as to whether or not a statement was a confession was to be made at the time it was sought to give the statement in evidence as opposed to at the time the statement was made by the person.

With the introduction of the Human Rights Act 1998 and the inclusion of the European Convention on Human Rights directly into domestic legislation, this area is becoming very important, particularly in relation to the way a detained person is treated, the length of his/her detention and the manner in which a confession is obtained. Not only may it lead to the exclusion of evidence, but also to a stay of proceedings or a claim for damages or compensation. For the effects of the 1998 Act generally, **see General Police Duties**.

13.2.1   The Exclusion of Confession Evidence

Section 76(2) of the Police and Criminal Evidence Act 1984 gives the courts a responsibility to exclude confessions where they have been obtained by oppression (s. 76(2)(a)), or where the court considers they are unreliable (s. 76(2)(b)). There is also a general power (under s. 78 of the 1984 Act and at common law) to exclude any evidence that the court considers would be detrimental to the fairness of the trial if allowed, which can also be applicable to the exclusion of confessions. These powers are dealt with at **para. 13.3.1**. In relation to s. 76(2), the court is more concerned about the circumstances in which the confession was obtained than the truthfulness of what was said. Once the defence raise the issue of oppression and/or unreliability it is for the prosecution to prove the confession was not obtained in such circumstances (*R v Allen*, 10 July 2001, (CA), unreported).

The European Court of Human Rights has held that the admission of confession evidence is a matter for domestic courts where procedures and safeguards exist for examining such evidence (*Austria v Italy* (1963) 6 YB 740). It was considered that in the UK there were sufficient procedures and safeguards with the *voir dire* procedure (**see para. 6.9**) and the fact that the burden of proof that any statement had been obtained voluntarily was on the prosecution.

Oppression

Section 76 of the Police and Criminal Evidence Act 1984 states:

> (2) If, in any proceedings where the prosecution proposes to give in evidence a confession made by an accused person, it is represented to the court that the confession was or may have been obtained—
>
> (a) by oppression of the person who made it; or
>
> . . .
>
> the court shall not allow the confession to be given in evidence against him except in so far as the prosecution proves to the court beyond reasonable doubt that the confession (notwithstanding that it may be true) was not obtained as aforesaid.

KEYNOTE

A court is under a duty to exclude a confession where it has been, or may have been, obtained by the oppression of the person making the confession. This means that there must be some link between the oppressive behaviour and the confession. So for instance, if the confession was made *before* the oppressive behaviour, this would not justify exclusion *under this subsection* (it may, however, justify exclusion under the general power of the courts; **see chapter 13**). It does not matter whether the confession is true or not; the issue under s. 76(2)(a) is *how* the person has been treated and whether any mistreatment led, or might have led, the person to make the confession. This issue is of particular importance in the interviewing of suspects (**see chapter 17**). In looking at this the courts seem to take into account the nature of the person being interviewed. It was said in *R* v *Gowan* [1982] Crim LR 821, that hardened criminals must expect vigorous police interrogation.

What is Oppression?

Section 76(8) of the Police and Criminal Evidence Act 1984 gives some guidance as to what oppression means and it includes torture (**see Crime, chapter 9**), inhuman or degrading treatment and the use or threat of violence (whether or not amounting to torture).

In *R* v *Fulling* [1987] QB 426, the Court of Appeal held that oppression is:

> [The] exercise of authority or power in a burdensome, harsh or wrongful manner; unjust or cruel treatment of subjects, inferiors etc., the imposition of unreasonable or unjust burdens.

It is suggested by some commentators that oppression involves some kind of impropriety on the part of the police, which might be suggested by a deliberate failure to follow the PACE Codes of Practice, although a failure to follow the Codes is not of itself an automatic reason for excluding evidence. Given that the courts have occasionally excluded evidence even where the relevant Code of Practice *has* been followed, the converse does not appear to be true and it is possible that a court might conclude that treatment had been 'oppressive' under all the circumstances even though the Codes of Practice had been followed.

The oppression must have been against the person who makes the confession.

As already mentioned, when the defence raise the issue of oppression it will be for the prosecution to show beyond reasonable doubt (*R* v *Miller* (1992) *The Times*, December) (**see chapter 11**) that this was not the case. For these reasons (as well as those of professional ethics) it is of great importance to comply with the PACE Codes of Practice. It is also important to keep records of how a case is investigated, together with the reasons for taking decisions during the course of the investigation so that the prosecution can present a case which demonstrates that there was no oppressive or improper conduct in obtaining the confession.

It is a question of fact on each occasion whether a person's treatment was oppressive and whether there was any link between that person's treatment and his/her decision to make the confession. The legislation itself gives little guidance as to what will amount to oppression.

For this reason it is necessary to look at the case law. Below are examples where the courts have held that the treatment of a person was 'oppressive'. Where:

- A person who was on the border of being mentally impaired admitted the offence after denying it over 300 times because of the bullying manner of the questioning (*R* v *Paris* (1993) 97 Cr App R 99). This case does not mean that interviewers cannot go over the same point several times or even suggest to the interviewee that he/she is lying. However, *Paris* does suggest that this should be done in moderation and not to the point where it becomes oppressive.

- A person confessed but had been kept in custody longer than the court felt was justified and therefore lawful (*R* v *Davison* [1988] Crim LR 442).

- The suspect was wrongly informed that he/she had been recognised when this was not true (*R* v *Heron* (1993), unreported).

- There was a failure to have an appropriate adult present (*R* v *Silcott* (1991) *The Times*, 9 December).

- The defendant was a choir master and the police had told him that if he did not make a statement they would have to interview all the members of the choir and this could disclose other offences on his part (*R* v *Howden-Simpson* [1991] Crim LR 49).

- A confession was obtained where the person was being held without access to a solicitor (*Barbera* v *Spain* (1988) 11 EHRR 360).

- Where interviews had extended over a three-hour period and were conducted in a manner that was persistent, aggressive and calculated to get a conviction as opposed to necessarily getting to the truth (*R* v *Ridley*, 17 December 1999, unreported). The court went on to comment that the manner in which the interviews were conducted was to be deplored and was an exploitation of a naïve man by methods which were unacceptable and had prejudiced the fair conduct of the trial.

Unreliability

Section 76 of the Police and Criminal Evidence Act 1984 states:

> (2) If, in any proceedings where the prosecution proposes to give in evidence a confession made by an accused person, it is represented to the court that the confession was or may have been obtained—
>
> . . .
>
> > (b) in consequence of anything said or done which was likely, in the circumstances existing at the time, to render unreliable any confession which might be made by him in consequence thereof,
> >
> > the court shall not allow the confession to be given in evidence against him except in so far as the prosecution proves to the court beyond reasonable doubt that the confession (notwithstanding that it may be true) was not obtained as aforesaid.

KEYNOTE

A court is under a duty to exclude a confession where it is, has been or may have been obtained in consequence of anything which was likely, in the circumstances that existed at the time, to render it *unreliable*.

When looking at whether a confession is reliable, the court will consider the circumstances as they actually were at the time and not as they were believed to be. For instance, if it was believed that a suspect was in a fit state to be interviewed but it later transpires that he/she was medically unfit, there is likely to be some doubt as to whether a confession made at that time is reliable. (The belief of the officers at the time of acting, however, may be relevant to any disciplinary matters.)

For instance in *R v Walker* [1998] Crim LR 211 the court held that the defendant's mental state may be taken into account when considering the surrounding circumstances, regardless of whether it was known to the police. The prosecution bore the burden of proof to show that the confession was *admissible*. The court went further and said that s. 76(2)(b) was not restricted in its application to use by the police of oppression. It was not necessary to show that the confession was unreliable by reference to the old common law test of 'threat or inducement'. A successful submission under s. 76(2)(b) does not require a breach of a Code of Practice.

It is not for the defendant to prove that his/her confession is unreliable; it is for the prosecution to show (beyond reasonable doubt) that the confession is reliable once the question of unreliability has been raised by the defence.

In *R v Fulling* [1987] QB 426 it was suggested that:

> . . . questioning which by its nature, duration, or other attendant circumstances (including the fact of custody) excites hopes (such as the hope of release) or fears, or so affects the mind of the subject that his will crumbles and he speaks when otherwise he would have stayed silent.

Thus the circumstances of a case can affect the reliability of the accused's statement.

What is Unreliable?

It is a question of fact on each occasion whether the reliability of a person's confession is in question as a result of something said or done. Below are examples where the courts have held that a confession was unreliable. Where:

- No caution was given to the suspect, the suspect was not asked if he wanted his solicitor present and was not shown the note of the interview (*R v Trussler* [1998] Crim LR 446).

- The PACE Codes of Practice were flagrantly breached (*R v Delaney* (1988) 88 Cr App R 338).

- A suspect who had just vomited was interviewed (any medical condition could affect the reliability of a confession; if in doubt have the person examined by a doctor) (*R v McGovern* (1991) 92 Cr App R 228).

- The appropriate adult had a low IQ and was unable to assist the detained person (*R v Silcott*).

- It was suggested to a suspect of a sexual assault that it would be better for them to receive treatment than go to prison (*R v Delaney*).

- A person had been kept in custody for 14 hours, had been interviewed four times before confessing and had been refused any visits from family (*R v Silcott*).

- The officers had a 'warm up chat' with the suspect before the interview, and the 'chat' lasted over two hours (*R v Trussler*).

- An offer of bail is made subject to the suspect admitting the offence or conversely, telling the suspect that he/she will be kept in custody until he/she admits the offence (*R v Barry* (1992) 95 Cr App R 384).

- Psychiatric evidence suggested that the suspect suffered from a severe personality disorder and that her admissions in her interview were unreliable (*R v Walker* [1998] Crim LR 211).

- A suspect had been forcibly overcome, and a confession was obtained in response to a question designed to elicit details of the offence from him without any prior caution having been administered (*R v Allen*, 10 July 2001, unreported).

13.2.2 Effect of Excluding Confessions

The exclusion of a confession may have implications on the value of other evidence.

Often further evidence is obtained after a person makes a confession. If a court excludes all or any part of a confession, then this may impact on the value of the additional evidence obtained by the prosecution.

While the additional evidence obtained after a confession may be admissible, much of the value of the evidence may be lost because s. 76(5) of the 1984 Act prevents the prosecution from linking the discovery of the additional evidence to any confession which has been excluded.

If the additional evidence cannot be linked to the confession then it might not be possible to link the evidence to the suspect (and the evidence may also be excluded under s. 78 of the 1984 Act or at common law).

....

EXAMPLE

For instance, in the case of a murder, if a suspect confesses to the murder and tells the investigators where he/she has hidden the murder weapon, this would be good evidence that the person committed the offence. If the confession is excluded then, although evidence can be given that the weapon found is in fact the murder weapon, it will not be possible to show any connection between the suspect and the weapon. Therefore, unless there is some other evidence to link the weapon to the suspect (e.g. fingerprint evidence), the case may fail. The reason is that it would not be possible to say that the police went to the location where the weapon was hidden without at least implying that the suspect had indicated that it was there when interviewed. All that can be said is that the weapon was found at the particular location, which could be accessible to any number of people.

Section 76(4) of the Police and Criminal Evidence Act 1984 provides that the exclusion of such additional evidence is not affected by the exclusion of the confession. Even where a confession is excluded, it may still be admissible for other matters such as the fact that the accused speaks in a certain way or writes or expresses himself/herself in a particular fashion. In such a case it would only be that part of the confession which is necessary to prove the point that will be admissible. Once again, this illustrates the point that evidence is often only admissible for a specific purpose.

....

13.3 Exclusion of Evidence Generally

Although there is no equivalent of the American doctrine of 'due process' whereby any evidence which is not obtained by proper procedures is rendered inadmissible, the courts in England and Wales can exclude any evidence under certain circumstances.

Those circumstances will usually be concerned with the way in which the evidence has been obtained (as with confessions above) or with the potential effect of allowing it to be adduced at trial.

Again, the European Convention does influence the courts' approach in applying ss. 76 and 78, in particular Article 6(1) which deals with the right to a fair trial.

13.3.1 Exclusion of Unfair Evidence

Section 78 of the Police and Criminal Evidence Act 1984 states:

(1) In any proceedings the court may refuse to allow evidence on which the prosecution proposes to rely to be given if it appears to the court that, having regard to all the circumstances, including the circumstances in which the evidence was obtained, the admission of the evidence would have such an adverse effect on the fairness of the proceedings that the court ought not to admit it.

(2) Nothing in this section shall prejudice any rule of law requiring a court to exclude evidence.

(3) This section shall not apply in the case of proceedings before a magistrates' court inquiring into an offence as examining justices.

KEYNOTE

Section 78 is wider than s. 76 and applies to *all evidence that the prosecution intend to produce in court*.

When applying s. 78, the courts will look at the fairness of allowing the evidence to be admitted against the defendant.

Compliance with the Codes of Practice is vital. In *Batley* v *DPP* (1998) *The Times*, 5 March, the court said that where steps required by the Codes were not observed and where material was entered as evidence, without those checks which formed an important aspect of the case, there was a real risk to the fairness of the proceedings against the defendant.

In *R* v *Allen*, 10 July 2001, unreported, the Court of Appeal held that where significant and substantial breaches of the Act were likely to lead to the exercise of the court's discretion to exclude evidence under s. 78 of the Act, in particular where that evidence was an admission or confession obtained following such breaches.

In *R* v *Samuel* [1988] QB 615 the court stated that it is undesirable to attempt any general guidance as to the way in which a judge's discretion under s. 78 should be exercised. It is a question of fact in each case and, while s. 76 requires links with the treatment of the person spoken to, the only issue under s. 78 is whether it would be unfair to admit the evidence in court. It is therefore difficult to give specific guidance but the following are examples of evidence that has been excluded.

What will be Excluded?

- Evidence of a driver being over the prescribed limit where the officer did not suspect the driver had alcohol in his/her body (**see Road Traffic, chapter 5**).

- Some cases of 'entrapment' where the court are not satisfied that the person would have committed such an offence had it not been for the action of the police/customs officers. The court may look to see whether the person was pressurised into committing the offence/providing information or whether by some ruse, the person was given an opportunity of so doing (**see para. 13.3.3**).

- Informing the suspect and his/her solicitor that the suspect's fingerprints had been found on items at the scene of the offence when this was not true.

- Undercover operations where the officers failed to record conversations in accordance with the PACE Codes of Practice.

- Failure by custody officers to inform a detained person of his/her rights.

- Interviewing a suspect without informing the person of his/her rights.

- Failing to provide the detained person with adequate meals.

- 'Off the record' interviews that were not recorded as required by the PACE Codes of Practice.

- Failing to make a contemporaneous note of a conversation.

- Failing to get an interpreter or appropriate adult.

- Interviewing a person suffering from schizophrenia without an appropriate adult being present (*R* v *Aspinall* [1999] 2 Cr App R 115).

- Identification of a suspect by police officers who had seen the person after he had been arrested and in handcuffs (*R* v *Bazil*, 6 April 1996, unreported).

- Failing to inform a suspect arrested in respect of one offence that it is proposed to question him/her in respect of another more serious offence or ensure they are aware of the true nature of the investigation (*R* v *Kirk* [1999] 4 All ER 698).

13.3.2 **Exclusion at Common Law**

Section 82(1) of the Police and Criminal Evidence Act 1984 retained the courts' common law power to exclude evidence at its discretion (as to which, see *R* v *Sang* [1980] AC 402). For evidence to be excluded at common law the court will not so much concern itself with *how* evidence is obtained, but rather the *effect* that the evidence will have at trial. The court can exclude evidence at common law where the prejudicial effect of the evidence on the defendant greatly outweighs its probative value.

In these cases the courts are looking at the trial process itself, as opposed to the investigation, and therefore this power has less impact on how investigations should be conducted.

13.3.3 **Entrapment**

The issue of entrapment falls into two categories: that is to say, trying to obtain evidence relating to offences that have already been committed; and those cases where evidence is obtained of offences yet to be committed.

In relation to investigations concerning offences already committed, the House of Lords in *R* v *Sang* [1980] AC 402 held that:

> Save with regard to admissions and confessions and generally with regard to evidence obtained from the accused after commission of the offence, [the judge] has no discretion to refuse to admit relevant admissible evidence on the ground that it was obtained by improper or unfair means. The court is not concerned with how it was obtained. It is no ground for the exercise of discretion to exclude that the evidence was obtained as the result of the activities of an *agent provocateur*.

(This is now subject to s. 78 of the 1984 Act but the principle still applies.)

The issues surrounding entrapment are considered by some to be an infringement of a person's human rights. In *Teixeira de Castro* v *Portugal* (1998) 28 EHRR 101, the European Court of Human Rights (subject to the following two qualifications) held that the use of undercover agents is not incompatible with Article 6 of the European Convention (right to a fair trial). Those qualifications were that:

* their use must be restricted and safeguards observed to prevent abuse;

* their actions must not exceed passive surveillance.

This is an area where the substantive criminal law overlaps with evidence and procedure. For the relevant considerations on police operations, **see Crime, chapter 3.**

Evidential factors to consider in running an operation that involves forms of entrapment include:

* The nature of the offence, as some offences are difficult to detect otherwise. Therefore, the more difficult the offence is to detect without intrusive inducement from the police, the more such intrusion will be justifiable.

* What suspicion officers have that an offence of that kind would be committed in the locality. For example, the setting up of a van containing cigarettes to see if someone takes the opportunity to steal them (*Williams and O'Hare* v *DPP* (1994) 98 Cr App R 209). 'If the trick had been the individual enterprise of a policeman in an area where such crime was not suspected to be prevalent, it would have been an abuse of State power.' (Lord Hoffmann in *Attorney-General's Reference (No. 3 of 2000)* [2001] 1 WLR 2060.)

The key question is whether the suspects voluntarily applied themselves to 'the trick' and that they were not enticed or provoked into committing a crime which they would otherwise have not committed.

An example of a case where evidence was not excluded is *R* v *Breen* [2001] EWCA Crim 1213. In this case police officers had attended the suspect's address unannounced and asked for 'blow'. The suspect gave the police his mobile telephone number and they returned the following day and were supplied with £20 worth of cannabis resin. The officers were invited to return at any time and they were supplied with drugs on subsequent visits. The Court of Appeal held that the judge had been entitled to find that the undercover officers had done no more than give the appellants an opportunity to break the law, of which each of them freely took advantage.

14 Disclosure of evidence

14.1 Introduction

The need for the prosecution to provide the defence with material relating to the charge(s) in a case has been recognised by the courts and the government to be crucial in ensuring that defendants get a fair trial. This point is further enforced with the introduction of the Human Rights Act 1998 which incorporates the European Convention on Human Rights and in this area brings in Article 6.

Article 6(3):

3. Everyone charged with a criminal offence has the following minimum rights:
   (a) to be informed promptly, in a language which he understands and in detail, of the nature and cause of the accusation against him;
   (b) to have adequate time and facilities for the preparation of his defence;
   (c) to defend himself in person or through legal assistance of his own choosing or, if he has no sufficient means to pay for legal assistance, to be given it free when the interests of justice so require;
   (d) to examine or have examined witnesses against him and to obtain the attendance and examination of witnesses on his behalf under the same conditions as witnesses against him . . .

In *Rowe and Davis* v *UK* (2000) 30 EHRR 1, the European Court of Human Rights emphasised that the right to a fair trial means that the prosecution authorities should disclose to the defence all material evidence in their possession for and against the accused. Only such measures restricting the rights of the defence to disclosure as are strictly necessary are permissible under Article 6(1). *Rowe and Davis* is an important decision in relation to the disclosure of material in criminal cases and the principles that apply. This can be summarised as follows:

- It is a fundamental aspect of the right to a fair trial that criminal proceedings, including the elements of such proceedings which relate to procedure, should be adversarial and that there should be equality of arms between the prosecution and defence.

- The right to an adversarial trial means, in a criminal case, that both the prosecution and defence must be given the opportunity to have knowledge of and comment on the observations filed and the evidence adduced by the other party.

- Article 6(1), in common with English law, requires that the prosecution authority should disclose to the defence all material evidence in their possession for or against the accused.

- The entitlement of disclosure of relevant evidence is not an absolute right.

- Only such measures restricting the right of the defence which are strictly necessary are permissible under Article 6(1).

- Moreover, to ensure that the accused receives a fair trial, any difficulties caused to the defence by limitation on its rights must be sufficiently counter balanced by the procedures followed by the judicial authorities.

- Decision-making procedure must, so far as is possible, comply with the requirements to provide adversarial proceedings and equality of arms, and incorporate adequate safeguards to protect the interests of the accused.

The requirement to provide the defence with material can be divided between that required prior to the person pleading, which is known as advanced information and that which is required once the defendant has pleaded not guilty in the magistrates' court or is committed/transferred to the Crown Court. The second stage assumes that the defence has been provided with the prosecution case and therefore any evidence that is left is unused material and that it will remain unused by the prosecution. This is usually referred to as 'disclosure'. These two stages are considered below.

Within this chapter reference will be made to the Criminal Procedure and Investigations Act 1996, the Code of Practice for the 1996 Act (the Code), the Attorney-General's Guidelines: Disclosure of Information in Criminal Proceedings (which provides further guidance/interpretation to the Act and Codes) and the Joint CPS/Police Project JOPI Guidelines which set out in detail actions required to meet the disclosure requirements of the 1996 Act.

14.2   **Advanced Information**

Advance information refers to the material that the defence are entitled to have in order to consider whether to plead guilty or not guilty. In some cases it is not a question of whether the defendant committed the crime but whether the prosecution are in a position to prove the offence and, in order to consider this, the defence are unlikely to agree to plead or decide on the mode of trial without knowing the strength of the prosecution case. It is clearly in the public interest that guilty pleas are entered or indicated as soon as possible (*R* v *Calderdale Magistrates' Court, ex parte Donahue* [2001] Crim LR 141) and often this cannot be achieved unless advanced information has been provided. The need to know as early as possible whether a defendant is going to plead not guilty can be particularly important as there are time limits by which the courts have to set trials and committals. Often these can be delayed because the prosecution have not complied with their disclosure duties.

The prosecution is required, on request, to supply the defence with a summary of the prosecution case and/or copies of the statements of the proposed prosecution witnesses. (In indictable and either way offences this is covered by the Magistrates' Courts (Advance Information) Rules 1985 and in summary only cases by the Attorney-General's Guidelines: Disclosure of Information in Criminal Proceedings (see **appendix 2**).) Whilst the rules state that advanced information is only required when requested by the defence, in practice, this should, where possible be made available to the CPS at the first hearing.

It is suggested that Article 6 of the European Convention supports the need to provide advanced information to the defence and that this should be done as soon as possible:

Article 6(3)(a) states that a person is:

> . . . to be informed promptly. . . and in detail, of the nature and cause of the accusation against him;

Article 6(3)(b), states that an accused is entitled to:

> . . . have adequate time. . . for the preparation of his defence.

The point concerning advanced information in summary cases was considered in *R* v *Stratford Justices, ex parte Imbert* [1999] 2 Cr App R 276 where the court gave their opinion that Article 6 does not give an absolute right to pre-trial disclosure, it will be a question of whether the defendant can have a fair trial. Clearly it will be easier to satisfy this test where advanced information as been provided to the defence.

Advanced information might also include the following and so consideration should be had to providing this material to the prosecutor so that he/she can forward it to the defence where appropriate (ensuring the addresses and other details of witnesses and victims are protected):

- copy of the custody record;
- copies of any interview tape(s);
- copy of any first descriptions where relevant;
- significant information that might affect a bail decision or that might enable the defence to contest the committal proceedings (A-G's Guidelines, para. 34);
- any material which is relevant to sentence (e.g. information which might mitigate the seriousness of the offence or assist the accused to lay blame in whole or in part upon a co-accused or another person) (A-G's Guidelines, para. 44);
- statements and/or a summary of the prosecution cases;
- copy of any video evidence.

Where a person has made several statements but all the relevant evidence for the prosecution case is contained in one statement, it is only that one statement which needs to be disclosed. In order to comply with advanced information the defence needs to be either given a copy of the document or allowed to inspect the document (or a copy of it).

Where the OIC considers that providing advanced information might lead to a witness being intimidated or some other interference with the course of justice he/she should consult with the CPS as the rules allow the prosecutor to limit disclosure of some or all the prosecution case.

14.3 Disclosure and the Criminal Procedure and Investigations Act 1996

As stated above this stage assumes that the defence has already been informed of the details of the prosecution case. In most investigations there will be material that has come to the attention of the police which will not be used as evidence to prove the prosecution case but which might be useful to the defence. It is through the disclosure rules that this information will be provided to the defendant. The rules of disclosure are governed by the Criminal Procedure and Investigations Act 1996. The 1996 Act puts the prosecution duty to disclose information to the defence on a statutory footing, and also introduced a new concept in criminal law where the defence have a duty to advise the prosecution of certain matters relating to their case. This is also supported by the 1996 Act Code of Practice, the Attorney-General's Guidelines on Disclosure and the Joint Police and CPS Disclosure Project (JOPI) publication (extracts from which appear in **appendix 2**).

The 1996 Act is further recognition of the need to disclose material to each side to allow the case to be dealt with fairly. This point as well as the need for timely disclosure of material, is further reinforced by Article 6(3) of the European Convention on Human Rights.

In *Jasper* v *United Kingdom* (2000) 30 EHRR 441 the Court expressed the importance of equality of arms being a fundamental aspect of a fair trial; both the defence and the prosecution must be given the opportunity to have knowledge of and comment on filed observations and evidence adduced by the other party. The Court did recognise that the entitlement to disclosure of relevant evidence was not an absolute right but could be restricted as was strictly necessary (**see para. 14.6.4**).

14.3.1 The Criminal Procedure and Investigations Act 1996

The Criminal Procedure and Investigations Act 1996 is made up of seven parts. It is the first two parts which are of interest to the police:

- part I sets out the procedures for disclosure and the effects of failing to comply with the Act; and

- part II sets out the duties of police officers in relation to the disclosure provisions.

14.3.2 Aims of the 1996 Act

The aim of the disclosure rules within the Criminal Procedure and Investigations Act 1996 is to make sure that a defendant gets a fair trial and speeds up the whole trial process. This was confirmed by *R v Stratford Justices, ex parte Imbert* [1999] 2 Cr App R 276, where the court said that the legislation was to try to ensure that nothing which might assist the defence was kept from the accused.

Paragraph 2 of A-G's Guidelines states that:

> The scheme set out in the Criminal Procedure and Investigations Act 1996 (the Act) is designed to ensure that there is fair disclosure of material which may be relevant to an investigation and which does not form part of the prosecution case. Disclosure under the Act should assist the accused in the timely preparation and presentation of their case and assist the court to focus on all the relevant issues in the trial. Disclosure which does not meet these objectives risks preventing a fair trial taking place.

The Act places a responsibility on the prosecution to make *primary* disclosure of material to the defence; a responsibility for the defence—under certain conditions—to disclose their case to the prosecution with a further responsibility on the prosecution to make a *secondary* disclosure to the defence. As a 'catch all' the prosecution also have a continuing duty to review the material they have disclosed.

There is a duty placed on the prosecutor to disclose to the defence material which may prove helpful to defendant's case. This has to be balanced against the risk of disclosing so much material under their duty to disclose that the defence collapses under the sheer volume of paperwork. Alternatively, allowing the defence relentless requests for material which may be of no real value ('fishing expeditions') could lead to situations where a guilty person is acquitted.

While the duty of disclosure is placed on the prosecutor, the police have a responsibility to assist in this process. It is therefore vital that police officers understand, not only the statutory requirements made of them, but also the extent of their role within the whole disclosure process. This view is supported by the A-G's Guidelines. Paragraph 5 states:

> Investigators and disclosure officers must be fair and objective and must work together with prosecutors to ensure that disclosure obligations are met.

14.3.3 Jurisdiction of the 1996 Act

The Criminal Procedure and Investigations Act 1996 is primarily concerned with the disclosure of material which does not form part of the prosecution case resulting from a criminal investigation (i.e. 'unused material'). A criminal investigation is defined by s. 1(4) of the 1996 Act and para. 2.1 of the Code of Practice. In order to satisfy the disclosure requirements police officers should consider recording and retaining material in the early stages of an investigation, including investigations:

- to detect a crime *after* it has been committed and in order to bring a prosecution;

- to discover *whether* a crime has been committed, for instance where a motorist is stopped and then enquiries are made as to whether the car has been stolen;

- that are the result of a belief/information that an offence *might be* committed.

In these cases the investigation may well have started some time before the defendant became a suspect. In such cases all the material from the investigation/operation would have to be considered to see if it was relevant to the defence case. In cases where there is a surveillance operation or observation point, it may be that the details of the observation point and the surveillance techniques would not be revealed but it would be necessary to retain material generating from it (**see para. 14.6.4**).

14.3.4 Failure to Comply

Compliance with the rules of disclosure, by both the defence and prosecution, is essential if the 1996 Act is to have any real value. First, in cases where the defence are obliged to make disclosure to the prosecution, failure to do so may lead to the court or jury drawing such inferences as appear proper in deciding the guilt or innocence of the accused (s. 11(3)). Should the prosecution fail to comply with their obligations then an accused does not have to make defence disclosure and no such inference can be made. Secondly, failure by the prosecution to comply with the rules could lead to the court staying the proceedings on the grounds that there has been an abuse of process (s. 5(1)(b) and s. 10). It could also lead to an action for damages or such other relief as the court sees fit under the Human Rights Act 1998, particularly in relation to Article 6 of the European Convention and the right to a fair trial.

Additionally, where the prosecution have not made disclosure on time or fully, a stay on the proceedings or a further adjournment is possible. It is suggested that the more adjournments in a case, the more likely that witnesses will get fed up with the delays and will fail to attend on the next occasion and the case could therefore be lost!

Even if there has been a failure to comply with disclosure the case will not automatically be stayed and therefore any failings should be brought to the attention of the CPS so that the matter can be considered. In *R (Ebrahim)* v *Feltham Magistrates' Court* [2001] 1 WLR 1293 the court stated that:

> It must be remembered that it is a commonplace in criminal trial for the defendant to rely on holes in the prosecution case. If in such a case, there is sufficient credible evidence, apart from the missing evidence, which, if believed, would justify safe conviction then the trial should proceed, leaving the defendant to seek to persuade the jury or magistrates not to convict because evidence might otherwise have been available was not before the court through no fault of the defendant.

Failure to disclose may result in convictions being overturned, for instance in *R* v *Poole* (2003) *The Times*, 26 June, the Court of Appeal allowed appeals against convictions for murder because the non-disclosure of prosecution evidence influenced the jury's assessment of the reliability of the evidence of a key eye-witness. In this case the witness gave an account that was false in a material particular. However, the police did not follow up those inconsistencies and they failed to inform the CPS that his evidence was unreliable.

14.4 Part I of the 1996 Act: Rules of Disclosure

14.4.1 Application of the Disclosure Provisions

Section 1 of the Criminal Procedure and Investigations Act 1996 defines in which type of cases the disclosure provisions apply. In reality this applies to all cases other than those where the defendant pleads guilty at the magistrates' court. These rules only apply where no criminal investigation into the alleged offence took place before 1 April 1997. If an investigation began before 1 April 1997, then it will be necessary to refer to the common law rules, however ACPO have stated that the 1996 Act should be followed in all cases when considering disclosure.

Some guidance is given by the case of *R* v *Uxbridge Magistrates' Court, ex parte Patel* (2000) 164 JP 209, as to the time an investigation begins. There it was said that the phrase 'criminal investigation' in s. 1(3) of the 1996 Act means that a criminal investigation could begin into an offence before it was committed. This could be so in a surveillance case or where a series of cases was committed, some before and some after the appointed day. Whether in any given case that was the correct view would be a question of fact for the court to determine.

Section 1 also defines a criminal investigation and states:

(4) For the purposes of this section a criminal investigation is an investigation which police officers or other persons have a duty to conduct with a view to it being ascertained—
    (a) whether a person should be charged with an offence, or
    (b) whether a person charged with an offence is guilty of it.

Consequently, this part of the Act also applies to other people, besides the police, who carry out investigations where they have a duty to ascertain whether criminal offences have been committed (e.g. HM Customs and Excise; Benefits Agency investigators). It does not apply to those whose primary responsibility does not relate to criminal offences (e.g. local authorities and schools). It also includes the situation where an investigation is started before any offence has been committed, for instance where a surveillance operation is being conducted with a view to gathering prosecution evidence. In this case it is only the information obtained and not the surveillance operation that is disclosable.

14.4.2   Primary Disclosure by Prosecutor

This is covered by s. 3 of the Criminal Procedure and Investigations Act 1996. This section talks about material which '*might undermine the prosecution case against the accused*'. The courts are likely to consider this to include material which has an adverse affect on the strength of the prosecution case.

Prior to the Criminal Procedure and Investigations Act 1996, in cases where disclosure was required the prosecution had to disclose all material that was relevant to the case. Under the 1996 Act, while a schedule of all relevant material must be provided, only material that undermines the prosecution case must be disclosed at the primary disclosure stage. There is only limited case law in this area but it is likely that such material will consist mainly of material which raises question marks over the strength of the prosecution case, the value of evidence given by witnesses and issues relating to identification. If officers feel that the material is not relevant to the prosecution case but may be useful to the defence in cross-examination, it may well come within the category of material which undermines the prosecution case. Disclosure of previous convictions and other matters that might affect the credibility of a witness may 'undermine the prosecution case' as it may limit the value of the witness's testimony. This factor may not be apparent at the time but may come to light after primary disclosure, such as where it becomes known that the witness has a grudge against the defendant. This is one reason why the 1996 Act requires the decision as to whether material undermines the prosecution case to be continuously monitored throughout the case.

The Code of Practice at para. 3.4 states that:

In conducting an investigation, the investigator should pursue all reasonable lines of inquiry, whether these point towards or away from the suspect. What is reasonable in each case will depend on the particular circumstances.

In *R (Ebrahim)* v *Feltham Magistrates' Court* [2001] 1 WLR 1293 the court stated that the extent of the investigation should be proportionate to the seriousness of the matter being investigated. What is reasonable in a case may well depend on such factors as the staff and resources available, the seriousness of the case, the strength of evidence against the suspect and the nature of the line of inquiry to be pursued. If in doubt it is suggested the CPS are contacted for guidance.

Paragraph 2.19 of the JOPI Guidelines makes important observations concerning negative results when making enquiries 'negative results can sometimes be as significant to an investigation as positive ones'. It is impossible to define precisely when a negative result may be significant, as every case is different. However it will include the result of any enquiry that differs from what might be expected, given the prevailing circumstances. Not only must material or information which points towards a fact or an individual be retained, but also that which casts doubt on the suspect's guilt, or implicates another person. Examples of negative information include:

- where a number of people present at a particular location at the particular time that an offence is alleged to have taken place state they saw nothing unusual;

- where a fingermark from a crime scene cannot be identified as belonging to a known suspect, or is of insufficient value to determine identity;

- any other failure to match a crime scene sample with one taken from a known suspect.

The prosecution only have to disclose material relevant to the prosecution in question. For instance, surveillance logs concerning another matter would not need to be disclosed (*R* v *Dennis*, 13 April 2000, unreported). It is up to the prosecutor to decide on the format in which material is disclosed to the accused. If material is to be copied, s. 3(3) leaves the question of whether this should be done by the prosecutor or the police open. The prosecutor must also provide the defence with a schedule of all non-sensitive material (s. 4(2)). This includes all other information in police possession, or material that has been examined by the police other than 'sensitive material' (this is disclosed to the prosecutor separately). 'Sensitive material' (**see para. 14.6.4**) is material which is not in the public interest to disclose and material obtained as a result of a warrant under the Interception of Communications Act 1985 (now repealed) or Regulation of Investigatory Powers Act 2000, s. 5. Such material must not be disclosed to the accused or his/her representatives (s. 3(6) and (7)). At this stage the defence is not entitled to inspect items on the schedule that have not been disclosed.

Material must not be disclosed to the extent that the court concludes it is not in the public interest to disclose it and orders accordingly or it is material whose disclosure is prohibited by s. 17 of the Regulation of Investigatory Powers Act 2000 unless it falls within the exception provided by s. 18 of the Act.

Time Period for Primary Disclosure

While there are provisions to set specific time periods by which primary disclosure must be met none currently exist. Until such times primary disclosure must be made as soon as practicable after the duty arises. Where disclosure is not made within a reasonable period it could lead to the case being lost. In *R* v *Bourimech* [2002] EWCA Crim 2089 the defendant sought disclosure following the service of his defence statement of a previous crime report made by the victim. One day before the trial was scheduled to begin the crime report relating to that incident was served amongst other papers on the defence. This report escaped the notice of the defence until the final day of the trial. The court held that the defect in disclosure amounted to unfairness in the proceedings and the court could not be confident that if the victim had been cross-examined in relation to the previous allegation the jury might have been influenced by the credit and credibility of the witness.

The 1996 Act in effect only applies once the defendant has been committed/transferred to the Crown Court or is proceeding to trial in the magistrates'/youth court. In most cases prosecution disclosure can wait until after this time without jeopardising the defendant's right to a fair trial. However, the prosecutor must always be alive to the need to make advance disclosure of material that should be disclosed at an earlier stage (*R* v *DPP, ex parte Lee* [1999] 2 All ER 737). Examples include:

- previous convictions of a complainant or a deceased if that information could reasonably be expected to assist the defence when applying for bail;

- material that might enable a defendant to make a pre-committal application to stay the proceedings as an abuse of process;

- material that might enable a defendant to submit that he/she should only be committed for trial on a lesser charge, or perhaps that he/she should not be committed for trial at all;

- depending on what the defendant chooses to reveal about his/her case at this early stage, material that would enable the defendant and his/her legal advisers to make preparations for trial that would be significantly less effective if disclosure were delayed; for example, names of eye witnesses whom the prosecution did not intend to use.

It should be noted that any disclosure by the prosecution prior to committal would not normally exceed the primary disclosure which, after committal, would be required by s. 3 of the 1996 Act (material which in the prosecutor's opinion might undermine the case for the prosecution (*R* v *DPP, ex parte Lee*)).

14.4.3 Disclosure by the Defence

The duty on the defence to make disclosure only arises *after* the prosecution has made the primary disclosure (s. 5(1)). This duty falls into two categories:

- compulsory;
- voluntary.

The disclosure required by the defence is limited to material that they intend to use at trial.

Compulsory Disclosure by Defence (s. 5)

The duty for the defence to make disclosure does not apply to cases being tried summarily. The duty on the defence, whether the accused is represented or not, is to provide a defence statement to the court and the prosecutor within 14 days of the prosecution making primary disclosure (this period can be extended by the courts).

The defence statement should outline the defence case in general terms. In addition, those issues, relevant to the case, which the accused disputes with the prosecution must be set out with reasons. This requirement to give reasons is intended to stop the defence going on a 'fishing expedition' to speculatively look at material in order to find some kind of defence.

Where the defence case involves an alibi, the statement must give details of the alibi, including the name and address of any alibi witness. In cases where there are co-accused, there is no duty to disclose this information to the other defendants, although this could be done voluntarily.

Voluntary Disclosure by Defence (s. 6)

The purpose of s. 6 of the 1996 Act is to allow the defence, in cases where the case is being tried summarily, to obtain further disclosure from the prosecution after the primary disclosure. This is only likely to happen where:

- the defence is not satisfied with the material disclosed at the primary disclosure stage or where they wish to examine items listed in the schedule of non-sensitive material;

- the defence wish to show the strength of their case in order to persuade the prosecution not to proceed.

If the defence decide to make a defence statement they must comply with the same conditions imposed on compulsory defence disclosure.

Effect of Failure in Defence Disclosure

If the defence fails to give a defence statement under s. 5 or where a defence statement is provided it is:

- outside the time limits;
- sets out inconsistent defences in a defence statement or at trial puts forward a different defence; or
- at trial adduces evidence in support of an alibi without having given particulars of the alibi in a defence statement, or calls a witness in support of an alibi without providing details of the witness or information that might help trace the witness;

then following sanctions may apply:

- the court or, with the leave of the court, any other party may make such comment as appears appropriate;
- the court or jury may draw such inferences as appear proper in deciding whether the accused is guilty of the offence concerned (but there must also be other evidence to convict the defendant).

14.4.4   Secondary Disclosure by Prosecutor (s. 7)

Once a defence statement has been provided (whether compulsorily or voluntarily), the prosecution must disclose any prosecution material that:

- might be reasonably expected to assist the accused's defence; and
- has not already been disclosed.

It will be a question of fact whether material in police possession might be reasonably expected to assist the defence case. If the court feels that material that was not disclosed would to any reasonable person have been expected to help the defence case, the case may fail. The test for secondary disclosure is wider than primary disclosure in that this test is objective in that it requires disclosure where any reasonable person would expect the material to assist the defence whereas primary disclosure talks of 'the prosecutor's opinion'.

If there is no additional material to be disclosed then the prosecutor must give a written statement to this effect. It is not the responsibility of the prosecutor or the police to examine material held by third parties which the defence have stated they wish to examine (the defence can request this from the third party or apply for a witness summons). However, there may be occasions where matters disclosed in the defence statement lead investigators to look at material held by third parties as it might impact on the prosecution case. This stage of the disclosure process may require further inquiries prompted by the defence statement. The result of those enquiries may then have to be disclosed because it either undermines the prosecution case or it assists the accused's defence.

If the defence is not satisfied that the prosecution have disclosed all they should have, s. 8 of the 1996 Act allows for the defence to apply to the court for further disclosure.

Material must not be disclosed to the extent that the court concludes it is not in the public interest to disclose it and orders accordingly or it is material whose disclosure is prohibited by s. 17 of the Regulation of Investigatory Powers Act 2000.

14.4.5   **Continuing Duty of Prosecutor to Disclose (s. 9)**

There is duty on the prosecution to continue to review the disclosure of prosecution material right up until the case is completed (acquittal, conviction or discontinuance of the case).

The duty to review is in two stages:

- after primary disclosure the prosecutor must review material not disclosed in terms of whether it might undermine the prosecution case (s. 9); and

- after secondary prosecution disclosure (s. 7).

The review of the material must also be in terms of whether material might be reasonably expected to assist the accused's defence as disclosed by the defence statement. This responsibility is mirrored in the Code of Practice. This is a continuous duty even after secondary disclosure has been made, failure to review could lead to an acquittal, abuse of process or even acquittal at a later appeal.

14.5   **Roles and Responsibilities under the 1996 Act**

The Code of Practice (**see appendix 2**) identifies certain roles within the disclosure process:

- prosecutor;
- officer in charge of the case (OIC);
- disclosure officer;
- investigator;
- supervisor of OIC and disclosure officer.

In addition, it is the responsibility of the chief officer of police of each force to put arrangements in place to ensure that the identity of the OIC and disclosure officer is recorded for each criminal investigation (Code of Practice, para. 3.2). Force policy should be followed in recording this information.

The MG6 series should be used when complying with disclosure to the CPS.

The roles described within the 1996 Act are independent of each other but all must be completed for the disclosure provisions to work (para. 3.1). All police officers involved in an investigation are likely to have to comply with the role of investigator.

Some investigations may involve a large quantity of material, both used and unused. Examples of cases where this may occur include substantial frauds; large-scale conspiracies; drug related offences involving manufacture, importation or supply; homicide or other major enquiries. These are often large or complex cases and additional guidance for these cases is provided in the CPS/Police Joint Operational Instructions (JOPI) Guidelines (2003), paras 2.113 to 2.117.

Although the police roles are independent they may be combined, the OIC may also be an investigator and, depending on the complexity of the case, may also be the disclosure officer. Whether there is one officer involved in the case or several, each role can be considered separately and must be completed fully in order that the right information can be given to the prosecutor who, ultimately, is responsible for the disclosure of material to the defence. It is important that all officers consult fully in order that the disclosure officer can complete his/her task properly. Each role is considered below as if undertaken by a different person.

14.5.1   **Prosecutor**

This role is defined by s. 2(3) of the 1996 Act as being 'any person acting as prosecutor whether an individual or a body'. In other words, the person who will be taking the case to court. On most occasions this will be the Crown Prosecution Service. It would also apply to the Serious Fraud Office or the Data Protection Registrar. In the case of private prosecutions, the prosecutor is obliged to comply with the disclosure provisions of the 1996 Act but does not have to comply with the Code of Practice. The prosecutor is responsible for ensuring that primary disclosure is made to the defence and, where appropriate, secondary disclosure. The prosecutor should also be available to advise the OIC, disclosure officer and investigators on matters relating to the relevance of material recorded and retained by police, sensitive material and on any other disclosure issues that might arise.

Should there need to be an application to the court to withhold material because of public interest (**see para. 14.6.4**), this will be done through the prosecutor.

A more detailed explanation of the roles and responsibilities of the prosecutor are set out in the CPS/Police Joint Operational Instructions (JOPI) Guidelines (2003).

14.5.2   Officer in Charge of the Case (OIC)

This role may be performed by a person directly involved in the investigation or by person who has been given the role of overseeing the investigation (Disclosure Code, paras 3.1 and 3.3). Whoever has this role is both responsible and accountable for the investigation (para. 3.3). (See also JOPI Guidelines, para. 2.4).

The Attorney-General's Guidelines state that an individual must not be appointed as disclosure officer, or continue in that role, if that is likely to result in a conflict of interest, for instance, if the disclosure officer is the victim of the alleged crime which is the subject of criminal proceedings. It is suggested that the same approach should also be taken when identifying the OIC. This is an important consideration as it should be remembered that the officer is a victim and may be in need of support.

The OIC is responsible for ensuring that proper procedures are in place for the recording of information and that records and materials are retained for the required period (**see para. 14.6.3**). Paragraph 4.1 of the Code requires that the material is recorded in a durable and retrievable form and that, where possible, the record is made contemporaneously. If not, the record must be made as soon as practicable. Guidance is given in para. 5.4 of the Code and para. 6 of the A-G's Guidelines. These requirements to record information should be paramount in the mind of all investigators, as well as the OIC.

The need for contemporaneous records is also required under the Police and Criminal Evidence Act 1984 and if not complied with could affect the admissibility of important evidence (see s. 78 of the 1984 Act). Note that, under para. 4.3, relevant material to be recorded includes *negative* material. Such material might include the fact that several people at the scene of a crime were spoken to and claimed to have seen nothing, or that they saw several other people at the scene as well. This last point reiterates the position at common law; that police officers have a duty to get to the truth and allow a suspect a fair trial, a duty which includes recording and retaining material which helps the defence (this also assists in complying with Article 6 of the European Convention).

Having made sure that material is recorded and retained by the investigators in the case, the OIC must make the material available to the disclosure officer (Code, para. 3). Where the function of disclosure officer is carried out by the OIC, there is little problem as the OIC should have a full understanding of the case and the implication of all the material collected, in terms of it being adverse to the case or being of a sensitive nature. In cases where the roles are performed by different people, it is important that the OIC and the disclosure officer consult fully about the material in order that the disclosure officer has as full an understanding of the case as he/she can in order to carry out his/her functions properly (para. 3.1). This must be done in order that the disclosure officer can complete the certification stage (paras 3.1 and 9). These responsibilities can be delegated to other police officers or non-police staff but it remains the responsibility of the OIC to ensure that the tasks are completed (para. 3.3). It may be necessary to demonstrate to the court that these powers have been carried out.

As with all people involved in the disclosure process, s. 9 of the 1996 Act places a duty on the OIC to review material in the case. This duty is emphasised by para. 5.3 of the Code so that, where the OIC becomes aware that previously examined material which has not been disclosed has since become relevant to the case, he/she must take steps to ensure that the material is retained and inform the prosecutor so that disclosure can be made to the defence. At this stage it will be for the OIC to decide in which format that material should be retained (para. 4.1) considering the need to be able to produce it for inspection by the court.

14.5.3   Disclosure Officer

The disclosure officer creates the link between the investigation team and the prosecutor (Crown Prosecution Service) and is therefore very important to the disclosure process. For investigations carried out by the police, generally speaking there is no restriction on who performs this role. It could be the OIC or, equally, it could be performed by unsworn support staff (Code, paras 2.1 and 3.3), or the disclosure officer is responsible for providing information and material to the prosecutor at the primary disclosure stage (para. 7.1) and, where necessary, carrying out any additional work requested by the prosecutor before the primary disclosure is made (para. 7.4). It is important that the disclosure officer does not have a conflict of interest, this is set out in the A-G's Guidelines at para. 7:

> An individual must not be appointed as disclosure officer, or continue in that role, if that is likely to result in a conflict of interest, for instance, if the disclosure officer is the victim of the alleged crime which is the subject of criminal proceedings. The advice of a more senior officer must always be sought if there is doubt as to whether a conflict of interest precludes an individual acting as the disclosure officer. If thereafter the doubt remains, the advice of a prosecutor should be sought.

In some cases it will be desirable to appoint a disclosure officer at the outset of the investigation. In making this decision, the OIC should have regard to the nature and seriousness of the case, the volume of material which may be obtained or created, and the likelihood of a committal or a not guilty plea. If not appointed at the start of an investigation, a disclosure officer must be appointed in sufficient time to be able to prepare the unused material schedules for inclusion in the full file submitted to CPS (JOPI Guidelines, para. 2.9).

The disclosure officer is responsible for examining all material retained by the police during the investigation (Code, para. 2.1). The first step is to establish that all material which has been retained in relation to the case has been recorded and made available for examination. The disclosure officer should verify with the OIC that all material has been made available to him/her.

Disclosure officers, or their deputies, must inspect, view or listen to all material that has been retained by the investigator, and the disclosure officer must provide a personal declaration to the effect that this task has been done. The obligation does not apply in circumstances as set out in para. 9 of the A-G's Guidelines. In such cases a Section 9 statement must be made explaining why the material has not been examined (A-G's Guidelines, para. 8).

There will occasionally be cases where the police investigation has been intelligence led, there may be an additional disclosure officer appointed just to deal with intelligence material which, by its very nature, is likely to be sensitive (**see para. 14.6.4**). In cases where more than one disclosure officer has been appointed to deal with different aspects of the case, a principal disclosure officer should be identified as the single point of contact for the prosecutor. Where an officer other than the principal disclosure officer submits a disclosure schedule to the prosecutor, that officer should inform the principal disclosure officer (JOPI Guidelines, paras 2.140 and 2.141).

Should the disclosure officer fail to provide information to the prosecutor within a reasonable time or to comply with any requests made by the prosecutor for additional material, this could lead to the defence not having to provide a defence statement or adverse remarks being made in court. At worse it could lead to a stay of proceedings for an abuse of process (s. 10 of the 1996 Act; see s. 5(4)).

Duties of the Disclosure Officer: Primary Disclosure

Under s. 3 of the 1996 Act all previously undisclosed material that might undermine the prosecution case must be disclosed to the defence. If there is no such material, then the accused must be given a written statement to that effect. This applies to all material in possession of the police or that has been inspected under the provisions of the Disclosure Code of Practice. This therefore requires the disclosure officer to know what material exists and what material has already been made available to the defence.

Where disclosure is required, the first task is to create a schedule of all *non-sensitive material*, which has been retained by the police and which does not form part of the prosecution case, which may be relevant to the investigation (Code, para. 6.3). If in doubt, the prosecutor should be consulted so that he/she can advise on the relevance of material (para. 6.1). This schedule must be endorsed by the disclosure officer to the effect that, to his/her best ability, it does not contain any sensitive material.

Initially, these schedules only have to be produced where the person is charged with an indictable offence, where the offence is triable either way or where the defendant will be tried summarily and is likely to plead not guilty. If the offence is witnessed by a police officer, or the person has admitted an either way or summary offence, then a schedule is not required unless the person then pleads not guilty. This provision has been added to avoid preparing material which will never be needed. If the person then pleads not guilty the schedule must be prepared as soon as practicable (Code, para. 6.8). However, some forces may require the schedule to be prepared in all cases.

The next step is to create a separate schedule of all sensitive material, which must include the reasons why the disclosure officer believes the material is of a sensitive nature (para. 6.4). Paragraph 6.12 gives examples of the type of material that would be classed as sensitive. If all material has been disclosed and there is no sensitive material, then a statement to that effect should be included on the main schedule. The schedule(s) should include all material, excluding that which forms part of the prosecution case (para. 6.2).

There may be cases where material is so sensitive that the disclosure officer or other investigators consider that it should not even appear on the schedule (**see para. 14.6.4**). In these cases the prosecutor should be informed of these separately (para. 6.4). It is the responsibility of the investigator who knows the details of the sensitive material to inform the prosecutor.

Once the schedules have been completed, the disclosure officer must decide what material, if any (whether listed on the schedules or not), might undermine the prosecution case. There will be a great reliance placed on the opinion of the disclosure officer as to what material might undermine the prosecution case. It is only material that falls into this category that the defence can inspect at this stage. Should the defence wish to inspect any other material on the schedule, this can only happen after the defence statement (outlining the defence case and giving reasons why they wish to inspect other items on the schedule) has been received. The disclosure officer must draw this information to the attention of the prosecutor and the reasons why he/she believes that the material undermines the prosecution case (para. 7.2). This creates a catch all provision and presumably requires the disclosure officer to make enquires of the other officers in the case to ensure all material is included.

The A-G's Guidelines give guidance as to what material might potentially undermine the prosecution case. Paragraph 36 states that:

This will include anything that tends to show a fact inconsistent with the elements of the case that must be proved by the prosecution. Material can have an adverse effect on the strength of the prosecution case:
    (a) by the use made of it in cross-examination; and
    (b) by its capacity to suggest any potential submissions that could lead to:
        (i)   the exclusion of evidence;
        (ii) a stay of proceedings;
        (iii) a court or tribunal finding that any public authority had acted incompatibly with the defendant's rights under the ECHR.

This would include any material individually or when viewed with other factors. Examples are material which:

- casts doubt upon the accuracy of any prosecution evidence;

- may point to another person, whether charged or not (including a co-accused) having involvement in the commission of the offence;

- casts doubt upon the reliability of a confession;

- might go to the credibility of a prosecution witness;

- might support a defence that is either raised by the defence or apparent from the prosecution papers;

- which may have a bearing on the admissibility of any prosecution evidence;

- relates to the defendant's mental or physical health, his/her intellectual capacity;

- relates to any ill-treatment which the defendant may have suffered when in the investigator's custody;

(A-G's Guidelines, paras 37 and 38).

However, what needs to be disclosed should be balanced by A-G's Guidelines, para. 3.

Completing the Schedules

It is important that the schedules themselves are completed fully. Guidance is given by paras 6.9 to 6.11 of the Code and in detail in the JOPI Guidelines, paras 2.45 to 2.73. The schedule should have each item numbered consecutively with a description of the item in sufficient detail to allow the prosecutor, when examining the schedule to make an informed decision about the importance of the item, and whether it needs to be disclosed to the defence, in addition to the items suggested by the disclosure officer, as undermining the prosecution case (A-G's Guidelines, para. 10). Whilst items should be listed separately, there may be occasions where items are similar or the same, in which case these may be listed together (A-G's Guidelines, para. 9). This also applies to sensitive schedules, in so far as is possible without compromising the confidentiality of the information (see also JOPI Guidelines, paras 2.74 to 2.76). Paragraph 9 of the A-G's Guidelines also allow in some circumstances, because of the large volumes of material, not to examine all the material. If such material is not examined by the investigator or disclosure officer, and it is not intended to examine it, its existence should be made known to the accused in general terms. A Section 9 statement must be completed by the investigating officer or disclosure officer describing the material by general category and justifying it not having been examined.

The schedules and copies of any material which is considered to undermine the prosecution case should be given to the prosecutor (Code, paras 7.1 to 7.3). The disclosure officer should include an explanation as to why they consider that the material should be disclosed (para. 7.2). As it is unlikely that the prosecutor will have a chance to examine all the material, it is important that the disclosure officer gives clear reasons in his/her report. For the type of material which might undermine the prosecution case, **see para. 14.6.2**.

In addition to the schedules and copies of material which undermine the prosecution case, para. 7.3 requires the disclosure officer to provide a copy of any material, *whether or not they consider it to undermine the prosecution case*, which is:

- a record of the first description of a suspect given to the police by a potential witness, *whether or not the description differs from that of the alleged offender*;

- information provided by an accused person which indicates an explanation for the offence with which he/she has been charged;

- any material casting doubt on the reliability of a confession;

- any material casting doubt on the reliability of a witness.

The following items should also be considered when deciding on primary disclosure in cases where the disclosure is in the public interest (that is where they are not '*sensitive material*'). The material is (A-G's Guidelines, para. 40):

    (i)   those recorded scientific or scenes of crime findings retained by the investigator which: relate to the defendant; and are linked to the point at issue; and have not previously been disclosed;

   (ii)   where identification is or may be in issue, all previous descriptions of suspects, however recorded, together with all records of identification procedures in respect of the offence(s) and photographs of the accused taken by the investigator around the time of his arrest;

  (iii)   information that any prosecution witness has received, has been promised or has requested any payment or reward in connection with the case;

  (iv)   plans of crime scenes or video recordings made by investigators of crime scenes;

   (v)   names, within the knowledge of investigators, of individuals who may have relevant information and whom investigators do not intend to interview;

  (vi)   records which the investigator has made of information which may be relevant, provided by any individual (such information would include, but not be limited to, records of conversation and interviews with any such person).

The disclosure officer must certify that, to the best of his/her knowledge, all material which has been retained by police and made available to them has been revealed to the prosecutor in accordance with the para. 9.1 of the Code. While the disclosure officer may not always be able to know if all material has been made available to him/her, he/she should consult with the OIC to verify as far as possible that it has been (para. 3.1). Guidance as to primary disclosure revelation is also given in the JOPI Guidelines from para. 2.90 onwards. The disclosure officer should be mindful of the need to demonstrate that he/she has taken all reasonable steps should it transpire that full disclosure had not been made.

Often the police may not possess all the material that could become relevant in a case. It may be that this material has been inspected and a decision made that the material is not relevant to the case at this stage, or that it was not necessary to inspect the material. To cover the risk of material being lost, the disclosure officer should inform third parties of the investigation and invite them to retain material. The disclosure officer should inform the prosecutor that third parties may have such material (para. 3.1). (**See para. 14.6.5** for third party material.)

Under para. 8 of the Code, information provided by the disclosure officer may be accepted by the prosecutor or might be returned with requests for additional information or for amendments to be made to the schedule or items to be disclosed to the defence. The disclosure officer should comply with any instructions given by the prosecutor and any request for the inspection or copying of material should be met (para. 7.4). If the disclosure officer and OIC consider that material is so sensitive it should not be copied, the disclosure officer should inform the prosecutor and make arrangements for the prosecutor to inspect the material instead (para. 7.4). If copies of materials which are not in writing are requested, the disclosure officer and prosecutor must agree on the format of how it will be provided to the prosecutor (para. 7.5).

It should be remembered that the prosecutor is required to advise the disclosure officer of any omissions or amendments or where there are insufficient or unclear descriptions, or where there has been a failure to provide schedules at all. The disclosure officer must then take all necessary remedial action and provide properly completed schedules to the prosecutor. Failure to do so may result in the matter being raised with a senior officer (JOPI Guidelines, para. 2.86). There may also be occasions where schedules need to be edited, this is covered in the JOPI Guidelines at para. 2.83.

Once this stage is complete, the prosecutor is able to make primary disclosure to the defence. It will be the responsibility of the disclosure officer to disclose material to the defence if requested to do so by the prosecutor (Code, para. 10.1).

The defence do not have to provide a defence statement until such times as primary disclosure has been made, they then (subject to an extension from the court) have 14 days in which to serve their defence statement. Clearly the sooner primary disclosure is made the more time, in theory, the disclosure officer will have to complete his/her responsibilities under secondary disclosure before the next effective court date.

Duties of the Disclosure Officer: Secondary Disclosure

Once primary disclosure has been made the defence may provide a defence statement setting out their case, together with reasons why they wish to inspect additional items on the schedule which have not been disclosed. Under para. 8.2 of the Code, once the defence statement has been provided, the disclosure officer must:

- review the material which is contained on the schedules; and
- inform the prosecutor of any material which might reasonably be expected to assist the defence as disclosed by the defence statement.

This role will often be performed in conjunction with the prosecutor and, at times, may even be undertaken by the prosecutor. However, the Code of Practice does require the disclosure officer to carry out this function and as such there is a duty to review this material even if it is also done by the prosecutor. This responsibility remains with the disclosure officer and must be complied with. It should be remembered that the review of disclosure is based on the defence statement, not a full investigation.

After the material has been reviewed, secondary disclosure can be made to the defence. As with the primary disclosure stage, the disclosure officer must certify that, to the best of his/her knowledge, all material which has been retained by the police and made available to them has been revealed to the prosecutor in accordance with para. 9.1 of the Code. Again, while the disclosure officer may not always know if all material has been made available to him/her, he/she should consult with the OIC to verify as far as possible that it has been (Code, para. 3.1). Guidance as to secondary disclosure revelation is also given in the JOPI Guidelines from para. 2.104 onwards.

Where the defence statement points the prosecution to other lines of inquiry, e.g. the investigation of an alibi, or where forensic expert evidence is involved, the disclosure officer should inform the officer in charge of the investigation and copy the defence statement to him/her, together with any CPS advice provided if appropriate (JOPI Guidelines, para. 2.110).

Continuing Duty of Disclosure Officer

Once primary disclosure has been made, the disclosure officer has a continuing duty to review material for items that should be disclosed to the defence as undermining the prosecution case. This continuing duty also applies after secondary disclosure in relation to material which might assist the defence case as disclosed in the defence statement (Code, para. 8.3).

Disclosing Material to the Defence

The disclosure officer may also be involved in the actual disclosure of material to the defence which is covered in para. 10 of the Code of Practice. This is material which the prosecutor has agreed that the disclosure officer will disclose to the defence because it falls within the material disclosed:

- at the primary disclosure stage (adverse to prosecution case);
- at the secondary disclosure stage (it assists the defence case); or
- where the court has ordered disclosure after an application by the defence; or
- where, through the continuing duty to review material, it has been disclosed because it has been decided it might undermine the prosecution case or assist the defence case.

The court can also order disclosure of material which the prosecution contend is sensitive. In such cases it may be appropriate to seek guidance on whether to disclose the material or offer no evidence thereby protecting the sensitive material or the source of that material (e.g. where informants or surveillance techniques are involved).

The disclosure officer can make disclosure to the defence by either:

- providing copies of the material; or
- allowing the defence to inspect the material.

Where a request is made for copies, the material must be provided unless it is not practicable or desirable to do so. Examples of such occasions are given in para. 10.3 of the Code. In cases where the material is not recorded in a written format (for instance an audio or video tape) then the disclosure officer has a discretion whether to provide a copy of the item or transcript of what is contained on the tape. This must be certified as a true copy of the tape (para. 10.4). For further guidance, see the JOPI Guidelines from para. 2.122 onwards. Forces may have instructions as to providing further copies when requested by the defence in relation to procedures and costs. It is suggested that where copies are provided, some proof of delivery should be obtained.

14.5.4   **Duties of Investigators**

The roles of investigator may involve just one officer or several officers. An 'investigation' may be completed in a very short time, e.g. from stopping a car, discovering it was stolen, arresting the suspect, obtaining a victim statement and charging the suspect. Alternatively, the case may involve a long, protracted enquiry with several officers, various witnesses and numerous suspects, arrests and interviews.

An officer who is classed as an investigator must make all reasonable lines of enquiry (Code, para. 3.4) and having done so retain all material which is relevant to the case (**see para. 14.6.3**), whether or not it is helpful to the prosecution (Code, para. 5.1). The investigator also has a responsibility to identify material that could be sensitive and bring this to the attention of the CPS (**see para. 14.6.4**). Where material is identified steps must be taken to record and retain the material. For information recorded on computers see the JOPI Guidelines from para. 2.29 onwards.

The issue of sensitive material is discussed below (**see para. 14.6.4**). Often it is only the investigator who obtained the evidence who will be fully aware of the sensitive nature of the material. In order to balance the need to protect sensitive material yet give the prosecutor full details of why the material is sensitive, para. 6.14 of the Code places the responsibility of informing the prosecutor of details of sensitive material on the investigator. The investigator must take steps to ensure the prosecutor can inspect the material. This does not mean that the disclosure officer or any other officer cannot carry out this function; simply that the investigator must ensure that it is carried out.

When completing the disclosure schedules the investigating officer must be mindful that there may be cases where material is so sensitive that he/she or other investigators consider that it should not even appear on the schedule (such as where disclosure would be likely to lead directly to the loss of life or directly threaten national security (para. 6.13)). It is the responsibility of the investigator who knows the details of the sensitive material to inform the prosecutor.

Continuing Duty of Investigators

The continuing duty of disclosure imposed by ss. 7 and 9 of the 1996 Act means that investigators have a corresponding duty to keep under review the revelation of material which meets the test for disclosure. It is therefore important that investigators are aware of which material might undermine the prosecution case and which might assist the defence case. It is also important therefore that investigators are aware of the content of defence statements provided after primary disclosure. This will therefore require consultation between OICs, disclosure officers and investigators. If investigators do not carry out their function properly, this has an impact on all the others involved in the disclosure process and may lead to disclosure on the defence being defective, which in turn could lead to a miscarriage of justice or stay of proceedings.

14.5.5 **Supervisor of OIC and Disclosure Officer**

In all cases there must be an OIC and a disclosure officer. If for any reason, either the OIC or the disclosure officer can no longer perform their respective tasks, para. 3.6 of the Code places a responsibility on that person's supervisor to assign another person to take over that role. It is suggested, that this requires a supervisor to know what cases their staff are involved in and who the OIC and disclosure officer is in each of those cases.

14.6 **Definitions**

Paragraph 2.1 of the Code provides definitions to be used when considering the Code and some additional guidance is provided below.

14.6.1 **Relevant Material**

The 1996 Act is concerned with the disclosure of material which is obtained during the course of a criminal investigation and which may be relevant to the investigation. Material can be in any form and should be widely interpreted. This applies to any material coming to the knowledge of officers involved in the case at any stage of the investigation or even after a suspect has been charged. This is material which the investigator, OIC or disclosure officer consider has some bearing on any offence being investigated or any people being investigated for those offences or any of the surrounding circumstances.

The material will be *relevant* whether it is beneficial to the prosecution case, weakens the prosecution case or assists the defence case. It is not only material that will become 'evidence' in the case that should be considered, any information, record or thing which may have a bearing on the case can be material for the purposes of disclosure. The way in which evidence has been obtained in itself may be relevant.

What is relevant to the offence is once again a question of fact and will not include everything. In *DPP* v *Metten*, 22 January 1999, unreported, it was claimed that the constables who had arrested the defendant had known the identities of potential witnesses to the arrest and these had not been disclosed. The court said that this was not relevant to the case as it did not fall within the definition of an investigation in s. 2(1) of the Criminal Proceedings and Investigations Act 1996 in that it concerned the time of arrest not what happened at the time the *offence* was committed. Paragraph 5.4 of the Code gives guidance on items that might be considered to be relevant material in a case, they include:

- crime reports (including crime report forms, relevant parts of incident report books or police officers' notebooks);
- custody records;
- records which are derived from tapes of telephone messages (for example, 999 calls) containing descriptions of an alleged offence or offender;
- final versions of witness statements (and draft versions where their content differs from the final version), including any exhibits mentioned (unless these have been returned to their owner on the understanding that they will be produced in court if required);
- interview records (written records, or audio or video tapes, of interviews with actual or potential witnesses or suspects);
- communications between the police and experts such as forensic scientists, reports of work carried out by experts, and schedules of scientific material prepared by the expert for the investigator, for the purposes of criminal proceedings;
- any material casting doubt on the reliability of a confession;
- any material casting doubt on the reliability of a witness.

Relevant material may relate to the credibility of witnesses such as previous convictions, the fact that they have a grudge against the defendant or even the weather conditions for the day if relevant to the issue of identification. It may include information that house to house inquiries were made and that no one witnessed anything.

It should be noted that where material is available to police from a particular source, e.g. local authority records, a decision that some of the material is relevant does not mean that it all has to be disclosed. This point is reinforced by the case of *R* v *Abbott* where the Court of Appeal held that the defendant was not entitled to blanket disclosure of all the files. He was certainly not entitled to documents which were not relevant to the case.

14.6.2 Material that Undermines the Prosecution Case

There is only limited case law in this area but it is likely that such material will consist mainly of material which raises question marks over the strength of the prosecution case, the value of evidence given by witnesses and issues relating to identification. If officers feel that the material is not relevant to the prosecution case but may be useful to the defence in cross-examination, it may well come within the category of material which undermines the prosecution case.

Disclosure of previous convictions and other matters that might affect the credibility of a witness may 'undermine the prosecution case' as it may limit the value of the witness's testimony. This factor may not be apparent at the time but may come to light after primary disclosure, such as where it becomes known that the witness has a grudge against the defendant. This is one reason why the 1996 Act requires the decision as to whether material undermines the prosecution case to be continuously monitored throughout the case. If in doubt advice should be sought from the CPS.

14.6.3 Retention of Material

Clearly in order to disclose material to the defence there is a need first to find it and secondly retain it. Retention of material applies to documents and other evidence including videos. Failure to retain material could lead to the prosecution losing the case, particularly where the court feel its absence will lead to the defendant not being able to receive a fair trial (Article 6 of the European Convention). In *Mouat* v *DPP* [2001] 1 WLR 1293 the defendant had been charged with speeding. Police officers had recorded a video of the defendant driving at speed and had showed the video to the defendant prior to charge but had later recorded over it. The defendant contended that he had been intimidated by the unmarked police car being driven only inches from his rear bumper. The policy of the force was to keep videos for 28 days, unless they recorded an offence, in which case they were kept for 12 months. The court held that the police were under a duty to retain the video tapes at least until the end of the suspended enforcement period, during which time the defendant was entitled to consider whether he wished to contest his liability in court.

In considering what material should be retained in an investigation consideration should be given to any force orders, what powers there are to seize and retain the said material, as well as the Disclosure Code and the A-G's Guidelines. Where an investigator discovers material that is relevant to the case, he/she must record that information or retain the material (Code, para. 4.1). Once again, this duty to record and retain material relevant to the case includes material that would be regarded as negative to the prosecution case (Code, para. 4.3). This does not just mean witness statements and evidence from inquiries but would include arrest notes, custody records, forensic reports, records of interview and all other material the investigator is aware of that might be relevant to the investigation. To this end, para. 5.1 of the Code places a duty on the investigator to retain all relevant material. Paragraph 5.1 of the Code states that:

> The investigator must retain material obtained in a criminal investigation which may be relevant to the investigation. This includes not only material coming into the possession of the investigator (such as documents seized in the course of searching premises) but also material generated by him (such as interview records). Material may be photographed, or retained in the form of a copy rather than the original, if the original is perishable, or was supplied to the investigator rather than generated by him and is to be returned to its owner.

Often, particularly at the early stages of an investigation (sometimes not until the defence statement is provided outlining the defence case), it will not be possible to know whether material is relevant. If in doubt it should be recorded and placed on the schedule of undisclosed material. Throughout the case, investigators and all others involved should continually review the material in the light of the investigation. Any material which becomes relevant and which has not been disclosed should be disclosed and, where it has not been retained, the OIC should be informed in order that he/she can decide what action to take (Code, para. 5.3).

When deciding if the material should be retained the A-G's Guidelines provide that: 'investigators should always err on the side of recording and retaining material where they have any doubt as to whether it may be relevant' (para. 6).

It is important to note that the material itself does not have to be admissible in court for it to undermine the prosecution case. This point was made in *R* v *Preston* (1994) 98 Cr App R 405, where it was said that:

> In the first place, the fact that an item of information cannot be put in evidence by a party does not mean that it is worthless. Often, the train of inquiry which leads to the discovery of evidence which

is admissible at a trial may include an item which is not admissible, and this may apply, although less frequently, to the defence as well as the prosecution.

In cases where officers are in doubt as to whether material should be recorded and retained, the prosecutor should be consulted. If this cannot be done, the material should be retained and recorded. If the material is not in a format that it can be retained (for instance because it was said orally), it should be recorded in a durable and retrievable form (Code, paras 4.1 and 4.2).

If during the lifetime of a case, the OIC becomes aware that material which has been examined during the course of an investigation, but not retained, becomes relevant as a result of new developments, para. 5.3 of the Code will apply. That officer should take steps to recover the material wherever practicable, or ensure that it is preserved by the person in possession of it (JOPI Guidelines, para. 2.33).

CCTV

CCTV is becoming more prevalent in towns and cities, both from 'in store' cameras and those run through local authorities. The likelihood of an incident being caught on CCTV can be quite strong, which raises the question as to the responsibility of the police to investigate the possibility of there being a tape and retaining the tape. This point was considered in *R (Ebrahim)* v *Feltham Magistrates' Court* [2001] 1 WLR 1293. These cases related to the obliteration of video evidence. In coming to their judgment, the court considered a number of previous decisions where the police were not required to retain CCTV evidence. The general question for the court was whether the prosecution had been under a duty to obtain or retain video evidence. If there was no such duty, the prosecution could not have abused the process of the court simply because the material was no longer available, i.e. it was a reasonable line of enquiry (as to whether they were under a duty to obtain the evidence, **see para. 14.5.4**). *Ebrahim* shows that CCTV does not necessarily have to be retained in all cases. *R* v *Dobson* [2001] All ER (D) 109 (Jul) followed *Ebrahim*. Dobson had been convicted of arson with intent to endanger life, his defence being that he was elsewhere at the time. There had been a strong possibility that the route that Dobson claimed to have taken would have been covered by CCTV but it would have depended on which side of the road he had been using and which way the cameras were pointing at the time. Dobson's solicitors had not asked for the tapes to be preserved at interview and the police confirmed that the possibility of investigating the tapes had been overlooked. The tapes had been overwritten after 31 days. In following the principles set down in *Ebrahim*, the police, by their own admissions, had failed in their duty to obtain and retain the relevant footage. Whilst there was plainly a degree of prejudice in Dobson being deprived of the opportunity of checking the footage in the hope that it supported his case, that prejudice was held not to have seriously prejudiced his case given the uncertainty of the likelihood that it would assist and the fact that Dobson had equally been in a position to appreciate the possible existence and significance of the tapes. The fact that there was no suggestion of malice or intentional omission by the police was also an important consideration for the court.

Complaints Against Police Officers Involved in a Case

Not only might the credibility of witnesses undermine the prosecution case, but so too might complaints against officers involved in the case, together with any occasions where officers have not been believed in court in the past. In these cases, it will be necessary to decide whether this information should be disclosed to the defence and if disclosed, in how much detail. This question is probably best answered by the following extract from advice given to prosecutors by the Director of Public Prosecutions:

> It is, of course, necessary in the first instance for the police to bring such matters to the notice of the prosecutor, but it is submitted that the prosecutor should have a greater element of discretion than

with the disclosure of previous convictions. With convictions against prosecution witnesses, disclosure normally follows, whereas in relation to disciplinary findings regard should be had to the nature of the finding and its likely relevance to the matters in issue. Findings which involve some element of dishonesty should invariably be disclosed, while matters such as disobedience to orders, neglect of duty and discreditable conduct will often have no relevance to the officer's veracity or the guilt or otherwise of a defendant. Certainly, there should be no duty on the prosecution to disclose details of unsubstantiated complaints even though this is a popular type of inquiry from some defence representatives. The imposition of such a duty would only encourage the making of false complaints in the hope that they might be used to discredit an officer in the future.

The prosecutor should be informed if officers involved in a case have discipline matters on their record. This may well appear on the schedule in order that the prosecutor can consider the matter and amend the schedule if necessary. It is suggested that advice should be sought from the prosecutor as to what information is included on the schedule and if disclosure is to be made, advice on what information to be included should also be sought.

Some guidance is given by the courts. In *R v Edwards* [1991] 2 All ER 266 the court held that a disciplinary finding and reprimand of a DCI for countersigning interview notes which had been wrongly re-written in another case should have been disclosed to the defence. *R v Guney* [1998] Cr App.R 242 followed *Edwards*, in *Guney* six police officers went to the defendant's home with a warrant to search for drugs. Three of the officers had formerly been members of No. 3 Area Drugs Squad based at Stoke Newington, which had been subject to 'considerable internal police interest'. The court held that the defence was not entitled to be informed of every occasion when any officer had given evidence 'unsuccessfully' or whenever allegations were made against him/her. In this case the information should have been disclosed. The court went on to say that the records available to the CPS should include transcripts of any decisions of the Court of Appeal Criminal Division where convictions were quashed because of the misconduct or lack of veracity of identified police officers as well as cases stopped by the trial judge or discontinued on the same basis. The systematic collection of such material was preferable to the existing haphazard arrangement.

Once again, if in doubt advice should be sought from the Crown Prosecution Service.

Disclosure of Statements in Cases of Complaints against the Police

Statements made by witnesses during an investigation of a complaint against a police officer are disclosable, however the timing of the disclosure may be controlled. In *R v Police Complaints Authority, ex parte Green* (2002) *The Times*, 6 May) the Court of Appeal stated that there is no requirement to disclose witness statements to eyewitness complainants during the course of an investigation. The evidence of such complainants could be contaminated and, therefore, disclosure would risk hindering or frustrating the very purpose of the investigation. A complainant's legitimate interests were appropriately and adequately safeguarded by his/her right to a thorough and independent investigation, to contribute to the evidence, to be kept informed of the progress of the investigation and to be given reasoned conclusions on completion of the investigation. However, a complainant had no right to participate in the investigation as though he/she was supervising it. The general rule was that complainants, whether victims or next of kin, were not entitled to the disclosure of witness statements used in the course of a police investigation until its conclusion at the earliest.

Police complaints and disciplinary files may also fall within sensitive material that does not have to be disclosed (*Halford* v *Sharples* [1992] 1 WLR 736). However this would not apply to written complaints against the police prompting investigations or the actual statements obtained during the investigations, although immunity may be claimed in the case of a particular document by reason of its contents (*Chief Constable of the West Midlands Police, ex parte Wiley* [1995] 1 AC 274). However, the working papers and reports prepared by the investigating officers do form a class which is entitled to immunity, and therefore production of such material should be ordered only where the public interest in disclosure of their contents outweighs the public interest in preserving confidentiality (*Taylor* v *Anderton* [1995] 1 WLR 447).

See also JOPI, Annex A (**see appendix 2**).

14.6.4   **Sensitive Material**

This is material which the investigator believes is not in the public interest to disclose. While the general principle that governs the 1996 Act and Article 6 of the European Convention is that material should not be withheld from the defence, sensitive material is an exception to this. In *Van Mechden* v *Netherlands* (1997) 25 EHRR 647, the court stated that in some cases it may be necessary to withhold certain evidence from the defence so as to preserve the fundamental rights of another individual or to safeguard an important public interest. However, only such measures restricting the rights of the defence which are strictly necessary are permissible under Article 6. It should be noted that the court did recognise that the entitlement of disclosure of relevant evidence was not an absolute right but could only be restricted as was strictly necessary. In *R* v *Keane* [1994] WLR 746 Lord Taylor CJ stated that 'the judge should carry out a balancing exercise, having regard both to the weight of the public interest in non-disclosure and to the importance of the documents to the issues of interest, present and potential, to the defence, and if the disputed material might prove a defendant's innocence or avoid a miscarriage of justice, the balance came down resoundingly in favour of disclosure'.

Decisions as to what should be withheld from the defence is a matter for the court and where necessary an application to withhold the material must be made to the court (*R* v *Ward* [1993] 1 WLR 619). Such applications will usually be made at the primary or secondary disclosure stages. Once material is considered to be sensitive then it should be disclosed only if the pubic interest application fails (unless abandoning the case is considered more appropriate) or with the express written approval of the Treasury Solicitor. Such material is not as wide as it seems, for instance it does not mean evidence which might harm the prosecution case. This category is quite limited and the Code of Practice, at para. 6.12, gives a number of examples of such material. It will be for the disclosure officer to decide what material, if any, falls into this category.

Paragraph 6.12 states that depending on the circumstances, examples of such material may include the following among others:

— material relating to national security;

— material received from the intelligence and security agencies;

— material relating to intelligence from foreign sources which reveals sensitive intelligence gathering methods;

— material given in confidence;

— material which relates to the use of a telephone system and which is supplied to an investigator for intelligence purposes only;

— material relating to the identity or activities of informants, or under-cover police officers, or other persons supplying information to the police who may be in danger if their identities are revealed;

— material revealing the location of any premises or other place used for police surveillance, or the identity of any person allowing a police officer to use them for surveillance;

— material revealing, either directly or indirectly, techniques and methods relied upon by a police officer in the course of a criminal investigation, for example covert surveillance techniques, or other methods of detecting crime;

— material whose disclosure might facilitate the commission of other offences or hinder the prevention and detection of crime;

— internal police communications such as management minutes;

— material upon the strength of which search warrants were obtained;

— material containing details of persons taking part in identification parades;

— material supplied to an investigator during a criminal investigation which has been generated by an official of a body concerned with the regulation or supervision of bodies corporate or of persons engaged in financial activities, or which has been generated by a person retained by such a body;

— material supplied to an investigator during a criminal investigation which relates to a child or young person and which has been generated by a local authority social services department, an Area Child Protection Committee or other party contacted by an investigator during the investigation.

Many of these items are included within the common law principles of public interest immunity. The case law in this area will still apply to decisions regarding the disclosure of such material. These groups are not exclusive and the areas most likely to apply will be those concerning the protection of intelligence and intelligence methods. In any consideration as to what should be withheld the provisions of Part II of the Regulation of Investigatory Powers Act 2000 should be referred to. Part II of the Act will make provision, not only for the gathering and recording of intelligence, but also disclosure of any material gained and methods used. Claims to withhold material may be made by parties other than the prosecutor (who would do so on behalf of the police). In some cases, the relevant minister or the Attorney-General may intervene to claim immunity. Alternatively, the claim to immunity may be made by the party seeking to withhold the evidence, either on its own initiative or at the request of the relevant government department.

Guidance is also provided in paras 41 and 42 of the A-G's Guidelines, even where an application is made to the court to withhold material a prosecutor should aim to disclose as much of the material as he/she properly can (by giving the defence redacted or edited copies of summaries). *R* v *Davis* (1993), unreported, sets out further guidance when applying for immunity from disclosure. The court said that the procedure to be adopted in such cases depended upon the sensitivity of the material for which public interest immunity was claimed. In most cases where the prosecution sought to avoid disclosure the matter could be resolved by an *inter partes* hearing but in ultra sensitive cases the prosecution should notify the defence of an *ex parte* application which it would make. Where however disclosure of the category of material for which immunity was to be claimed would 'let the cat out of the bag' the prosecution might apply to the court without putting the defence on notice. Where the court ruled for non-disclosure before the hearing, the decision was not necessarily final as the situation might change and issues might emerge so that the public interest in non-disclosure was eclipsed by the need to secure fairness for the defendant. The court would therefore have to continually monitor the issue and it was desirable that the same judge who made the ruling, heard the whole case or, if that was impossible, the court must continually keep in mind the ruling which had been made. If there was such a change the prosecution must be told so that it could decide whether to disclose or offer no further evidence.

Where police consider that material should not be disclosed due to the sensitive nature the JOPI Guidelines should be followed. These are covered at paras 2.77 to 2.82.

Some of the key points from these paragraphs include:

• Consultation should take place at a senior level, and a senior officer (who may be independent of the investigation) should be involved.

• The consultation should cover:
  • the reasons why the material is said to be sensitive;
  • the degree of sensitivity said to attach to the material, i.e. why it is considered that real harm would be caused to the public interest by disclosure;

- the consequences of revealing to the defence:
  - the material itself,
  - the category of the material,
  - the fact that an application is being made;
- the significance of the material to the issues in the trial;
- the involvement of any third parties in bringing the material to the attention of the police;
- where the material is likely to be the subject of an order for disclosure, what police views are regarding continuance of the prosecution.

- Any submission that is to be made to the court will be signed by the prosecutor, and by the senior officer, who will state that to the best of his/her knowledge and belief the assertions of fact on which the submission is based are correct.

Informants

The courts recognise the need to protect the identity of informants to ensure that the supply of information about criminal activities does not dry up and for their own safety. However there may be occasions where if the case is to continue the identity of the informant will have to be disclosed.

> ... if the judge should be of opinion that the disclosure of the name of the informant is necessary or right in order to show the prisoner's innocence, then one public policy is in conflict with another public policy, and that which says that an innocent man is not to be condemned when his innocence can be proved is the policy that must prevail. (*Marks* v *Beyfus* (1890) 25 QBD 494, per Lord Esher MR at p. 498.)

This is particularly so where there is a suggestion that an informant has participated in the events constituting, surrounding or following the crime, the judge must consider whether this role so impinges on an issue of interest to the defence, present or potential, as to make disclosure necessary (*R* v *Turner* [1995] 1 WLR 264).

In *R* v *Agar* [1990] 2 All ER 442 the court held that if a defence was manifestly frivolous and doomed to failure, a trial judge might conclude that it must be sacrificed to the general public interest in the protection of informers. But if there was a tenable defence the rule of public policy protecting informants was outweighed by the stronger public interest in allowing a defendant to put forward a case. In this case the defendant alleged that the police had arranged with an informer to ask the accused to go to the informer's house, where drugs allegedly found on him had been planted by the police and the court ruled that the disclosure of the informant should have been made.

The need to disclose details of informants has been considered by the Court of Appeal in two recent cases. The first case, *R* v *Denton* [2002] EWCA Crim 72, concerned a defendant who was a police informer. The defendant was charged with murder and alleged that he had been told by his police handlers not to tell his lawyers about his status. The Court held that there was no duty for the Crown to disclose to the defence, nor to seek a ruling from the judge, as to any information regarding an accused being a police informer. On any common sense view the material had already been disclosed to the defendant and the Crown had no duty to supply the defendant with information with which he was already familiar. This last point may also be relevant to other situations. The second case, *R* v *Dervish* [2002] 2 Cr App R 105 concerned an undercover operation that was commenced after an informant gave information. The court held in this case that the public interest in protecting the identification of an informant had to be balanced against the right of the defendant to a fair trial, if there was material that might assist the defence, the necessity for the defendant to have a fair trial would outweigh the other interests in the case and the material would have to be disclosed or the prosecution discontinued. There had been no such material in this case.

Observation Points and the *Johnson* Ruling

R v Rankine [1986] 2 WLR 1075 considering previous cases stated that it was the rule that police officers should not be required to disclose sources of their information, whether those sources were paid informers or public spirited citizens, subject to a discretion to admit to avoid a miscarriage of justice and that observation posts were in this rule.

In *R v Johnson* [1988] 1 WLR 1377, the appellant was convicted of supplying drugs. The only evidence against him was given by police officers, who testified that, while stationed in private premises in a known drug-dealing locality, they had observed him selling drugs. The defence applied to cross-examine the officers on the exact location of the observation posts, in order to test what they could see, having regard to the layout of the street and the objects in it. In the jury's absence the prosecution called evidence as to the difficulty of obtaining assistance from the public, and the desire of the occupiers, who were also occupiers at the time of the offence, that their names and addresses should not be disclosed because they feared for their safety.

The judge ruled that the exact location of the premises need not be revealed. The appeal was dismissed; although the conduct of the defence was to some extent affected by the restraints placed on it, this led to no injustice. The jury were well aware of the restraints, and were most carefully directed about the very special care they had to give to any disadvantage they may have brought to the defence. *Johnson* was applied and approved in *R v Hewitt* (1992) 95 Cr App R 81 (see also *R v Grimes* [1994] Crim LR 213).

In *Johnson* Watkins LJ at pp. 1385–6 gave the following guidance as to the minimum evidential requirements needed if disclosure is to be protected:

(a) The police officer in charge of the observations to be conducted, no one of lower rank than a sergeant should usually be acceptable for this purpose, must be able to testify that beforehand he visited all observation places to be used and ascertained the attitude of occupiers of premises, not only to the use to be made of them, but to the possible disclosure thereafter of the use made and facts which could lead to the identification of the premises thereafter and of the occupiers. He may of course in addition inform the court of difficulties, if any, usually encountered in the particular locality of obtaining assistance from the public.

(b) A police officer of no lower rank than a chief inspector must be able to testify that immediately prior to the trial he visited the places used for observations, the results of which it is proposed to give in evidence, and ascertained whether the occupiers are the same as when the observations took place and whether they are or are not, what the attitude of those occupiers is to the possible disclosure of the use previously made of the premises and of facts which could lead at the trial to identification of premises and occupiers.

Such evidence will of course be given in the absence of the jury when the application to exclude the material evidence is made. The judge should explain to the jury, as this judge did, when summing up or at some appropriate time before that, the effect of his ruling to exclude, if he so rules.

The guidelines in *Johnson* do not require a threat of violence before protection can be afforded to the occupier of an observation post; it suffices if the occupier is in fear of harassment (*Blake* v *DPP* (1993) 97 Cr App R 169).

This extended the rules established in *R v Rankine* [1986] QB 861 and is based on the protection of the owner or occupier of the premises, and not on the identity of the observation post. Thus, where officers have witnessed the commission of an offence as part of a surveillance operation conducted from an unmarked police vehicle, information relating to the surveillance and the colour, make and model of the vehicle should not be withheld (*R v Brown* (1987) 87 Cr App R 52). Hodgson J said in *Brown*:

We do not rule out the possibility that with the advent of sophisticated methods of criminal investigation, there may be cases where the public interest immunity may be successfully invoked in criminal proceedings to justify the exclusion of evidence as to police techniques and methods. But if and when such an argument is to be raised, it must, in the judgment of this court, be done properly....It would seem clear that if such a contention is put forward the judge must be given as much information as possible and the application will have to be supported, not by the instructions of the junior officer in charge of the case, but by the independent evidence of senior officers.

14.6.5   **Third Party Material**

Third party material can be considered in two categories:

(a) that which is or has been in the possession of the police or which has been inspected by the police;

(b) all other material not falling under (a).

Material that which falls into the first category is covered by the same rules of disclosure as any other material the police have. Where police do not have material that they believe may be relevant to the case, para. 3.5 of the Code provides that:

> If the officer in charge of an investigation believes that other persons may be in possession of material that may be relevant to the investigation, and if this has not been obtained under paragraph 3.4 above, he should ask the disclosure officer to inform them of the existence of the investigation and to invite them to retain the material in case they receive a request for its disclosure. The disclosure officer should inform the prosecutor that they may have such material. However, the officer in charge of an investigation is not required to make speculative enquiries of other persons: there must be some reason to believe that they may have relevant material. That reason may come from information provided to the police by the accused or from other inquiries made or from some other source.

In the vast majority of cases the third party will make the material available to the investigating officer. However there may be occasions where the third party refuses to hand over the material and/or allow it to be examined.

If the OIC, the investigator or the disclosure officer believes that a third party holds material that may be relevant to the investigation, that person or body should be told of the investigation. They should be alerted to the need to preserve relevant material. Consideration should be given as to whether it is appropriate to seek access to the material, and if so, steps should be taken to obtain such material. It will be important to do so if the material or information is likely to undermine the prosecution case, or to assist a known defence. A letter should be sent to the third party together with the explanatory leaflet, specimens of which are provided in the JOPI Guidelines at Annex J.

Where access to the material is declined or refused by the third party and it is believed that it is reasonable to seek production of the material before a suspect is charged, the investigator should consider making an application under sch. 1 to the Police and Criminal Evidence Act 1984 (special procedure material). The investigator may seek advice of the prosecutor before such an application is made (JOPI Guidelines, para. 2.40a).

Where the suspect has been charged and the third party refuses to produce the material, application will have to be made to the court for a witness summons. In the magistrates' court this is covered by s. 97(1) of the Magistrates' Courts Act 1980 and in the Crown Court it is covered by s. 2(2) of the Criminal Procedure (Attendance of Witnesses) Act 1965. The third party may still wish to resist the requirement to produce the material and the point was considered in *R* v *Brushett* [2001] Crim LR 471 (this was a case that concerned Social Services Department files relating to a children's home). The court considered a number of earlier cases and established some central principles as follows:

- To be material evidence documents must be not only relevant to the issues arising in the criminal proceedings, but also documents admissible as such in evidence.

- Documents which are desired merely for the purpose of possible cross-examination are not admissible in evidence and, thus, are not material for the purposes of s. 97.

- Whoever seeks production of documents must satisfy the justices with some material that the documents are 'likely to be material' in the sense indicated, likelihood for this purpose involving a real possibility, although not necessarily a probability.

- It is not sufficient that the applicant merely wants to find out whether or not the third party has such material documents. This procedure must not be used as a disguised attempt to obtain discovery.

- Where social services documents are supplied to the prosecution, the prosecution should retain control of such material as part of the disclosure regime. That is envisaged by the rules. It cannot be acceptable to return material to social services to avoid the obligations arising under the rules. In any event, the obligation would arise in relation to the notes taken and retained.

- The obligation laid on the prosecution by statute and rules cannot be avoided by a third party making an agreement with the prosecution that the prosecution will abrogate any duties laid upon it by either common law or statute.

- If circumstances arise where it would be unjust not to allow disclosure of certain other material, so a defendant would not receive a fair trial, in the sense that he/she could not establish his innocence where he/she might otherwise do so, then that material must be disclosed.

- The fact that the prosecution have knowledge of the third party material may be a relevant factor to allow the defence access.

- Material concerning false allegations in the past may be relevant material.

- If the disputed material might prove the defendant's innocence or avoid a miscarriage of justice, the weight came down resoundingly in favour of disclosing it (*R* v *Reading Justices, ex parte Berkshire County Council* (1996) 1 Cr App R 239).

The A-G's Guidelines also deal with materials held by third parties (including government agencies) in paras 29 to 33. Paragraph 29 deals with material held by Government departments or other Crown bodies and suggests that reasonable steps should be taken to identify and consider material that may be relevant to an issue in the case. Paragraph 30 examines the circumstances in which the prosecution should take steps to obtain access to material or information in the possession of other third parties. In such cases consideration should be given to take steps to obtain such material or information. It will be important to do so if the material or information is likely to undermine the prosecution case, or assist a known defence. Paragraph 31 deals with the situation where the police or prosecutor meet with a refusal by the third party to supply such material or information. If, despite the reasons put forward for refusal by the third party, it still appears reasonable to seek its production, a witness summons requiring the third party to produce the material should be applied for (such an application can also be made by the defence). The third party can then argue at court that it is not material, or that it should not be disclosed on grounds of public interest immunity.

14.6.6 Confidentiality

The defence may only use material disclosed to them under the 1996 Act for purposes related to the defence case; any other use will be a contempt of court. Once evidence has been given in open court, however, the material is available for other purposes.

14.6.7 Retention Periods

Material must be retained in all cases until a decision is taken whether to institute proceedings against a person for an offence. Where a decision is taken to institute proceedings material must then be retained until the case has been dealt with. The Code gives specific guidance in cases where a person is convicted as to how long material must be retained for. Paragraphs 5 to 5.10 set out the retention periods where a person has been convicted. All material which may be relevant must be retained at least until:

- the person is released from custody or discharged from hospital in cases where the court imposes a custodial sentence or hospital order;
- in all other cases, for six months from the date of conviction.

If the person is released from the custodial sentence or discharged from hospital earlier than six months from the date of conviction, the material must be retained for at least six months from the date of conviction. If an appeal is in progress at the end of one of these periods, or an application is being considered by the Criminal Cases Review Commission, the period is extended until:

- the appeal is concluded; or
- the Commission decide not to refer the application to the Court of Appeal; or
- the Court of Appeal determines the appeal resulting from the reference.

In these cases, if material was seized from its owner it may be returned (Code, para. 5.10).

Where material has been seized under the powers provided by the Police and Criminal Evidence Act 1984, para. 5.2 confirms that retention of the material should reflect the provisions of s. 22 of the 1984 Act.

PART THREE

Police Station Procedure

15 Custody officer's duties

15.1 Introduction

The powers to detain people who have been arrested and the manner in which they must be dealt with are primarily contained in the Police and Criminal Evidence Act 1984 and the PACE Codes of Practice whose creation and status come from s. 66 of the Act. The 1984 Act provides directions to police officers in how detained persons should be treated. The main responsibility for detained persons lies with the custody officer, however it is important that *all* officers, including supervisors involved in investigations or those dealing with detained persons, are aware of the provisions of the Act and the Codes. Failure to follow the requirements of the law could lead to prosecutions failing because evidence is excluded (**see chapter 13**), civil claims against forces, bad publicity and the possibility of disciplinary action or even criminal proceedings against officers.

The Human Rights Act 1998 makes it even more important to comply with the 1984 Act and its associated Codes of Practice. This can be seen from the case of *R* v *Chief Constable of Kent Constabulary, ex parte Kent Police Federation Joint Branch Board* [2000] 2 Cr App R 196, where it was held that while Article 5 of the European Convention on Human Rights was not then part of the domestic law of England and Wales, the Article embodied important and basic rights which English law recognised and protected, and any deprivation of liberty must be in accordance with the law. The court went on to say that the 1984 Act and the Codes of Practice represented the balance between the important duty of the police to investigate crime and apprehend criminals and the rights of the private citizen. A breach of Code C is fundamental in affecting the fairness of the evidence (*R* v *Aspinall* [1999] 2 Cr App R 115).

The Human Rights Act 1998 incorporates the European Convention into UK legislation and as such domestic legislation still applies, but will be interpreted so as to incorporate the Articles of the Convention and the relevant case law. Where there is a conflict between domestic law and the Convention, it will be for Parliament to change domestic legislation to come into line with the Convention. The main Articles which need to be considered for the custody officer and others involved in the detention of a person include Articles 3, 5, 6 and 8, **see General Police Duties, chapter 2**.

The custody officer carries the main responsibility towards prisoners who are brought to the police station. Initially it must be decided whether the person should be detained as a prisoner at the police station. If there are grounds to detain him/her, the detention period must be *for those reasons only*. Once a decision to detain a person has been made, the manner in which he/she must be treated while in detention is set out in the PACE Codes (**see appendices 5 to 7**). These Codes are intended to protect the basic rights of detained people. If these Codes are followed it is more likely that evidence obtained while people are in custody will be admissible. The provisions of the 1984 Act give guidance in numerous areas including:

- length of time in detention;
- information about the detained person's arrest;

- searching;

- taking of samples;

- interviewing of suspects;

- identification methods;

- charging; and

- bail.

The PACE Codes set out the minimum standard of treatment that a detained person can expect. These requirements may be extended with the incorporation of the European Convention on Human Rights and its associated case law. The maximum length of detention is also prescribed by the 1984 Act, as are the requirements for charging, bailing and appearances at court.

The following chapter outlines some of the requirements of the legislation and the powers police have in relation to detained people. The chapter is aimed at providing guidance when using the legislation and it is intended to point the reader to the correct sections of the 1984 Act and the PACE Codes of Practice when dealing with detained people and investigations.

Whilst it is common practice for custody officers to have gaolers to assist in managing detained people, it is still the custody officer's responsibility to ensure that PACE is complied with. However, the Police Reform Act 2002 allows the role of support staff to be expanded in this regard (see below).

15.1.1 Designated Support Staff

Sections 38 and 39 of the Police Reform Act 2002 allow persons employed by the police or persons employed by a contractor of the police authority (in relation to detention and escort officers) to be designated as investigating officers, detention officers and escort officers.

Designated officers are given powers to carry out certain functions that would up to this time have been carried out by police officers only. Before a person can be given the powers of a designated officer, the chief officer of police must be satisfied that the person is a suitable person to carry out the functions for which he/she is designated, is capable of effectively carrying out those functions, and has received adequate training in the carrying out of those functions and in the exercise and performance of the powers and duties of a designated officer. It should be noted that not all designated officers will be designated with the same range of powers and it will be important to know what powers a particular designated officer has been given and therefore what their role will be. Schedule 4 to the Police Reform Act 2002 outlines these powers, some of which are set out below.

Investigating Officers

- To act as the supervisor of any access to seized material to which a person is entitled, to supervise the taking of a photograph of seized material, or to photograph it himself/herself.

- To arrest a detainee for a further offence if it appears to him/her that the detainee would be liable to arrest for that further offence if released from their initial arrest.

- Power for the custody officer to transfer to a designated civilian investigating officer responsibility for a detainee. This power includes a duty for the person investigating the offence, once the detainee is returned to the custody of the custody officer, to report back to the custody officer on how the Codes were complied with.

- To question an arrested person under ss. 36 and 37 of the Criminal Justice and Public Order Act 1994 about facts which may be attributable to the person's participation in an offence. The designated person may also give the suspect the necessary warning about the capacity of a court to draw inferences from a failure to give a satisfactory account in response to questioning.

Detention Officers

- Powers to search detained persons, to take fingerprints and certain samples without consent and to take photographs.

- To require certain defined categories of persons who have been convicted, cautioned, reprimanded or warned in relation to recordable offences to attend a police station to have their fingerprints taken.

- To carry out non-intimate searches of persons detained at police stations or elsewhere and to seize items found during such searches.

- To carry out searches and examinations in order to determine the identity of persons detained at police stations. Identifying marks found during such processes may be photographed.

- To carry out intimate searches in the same very limited circumstances that are applicable to constables.

- To take fingerprints without consent in the same circumstances that a constable can.

- To take non-intimate samples without consent and to inform the person from whom the sample is to be taken of any necessary authorisation by a senior officer and of the grounds for that authorisation.

- To require certain defined categories of persons who have been charged with or convicted of recordable offences to attend a police station to have a sample taken.

- To inform a person that intimate samples taken from him/her may be the subject of a speculative search (i.e. this will satisfy the requirement that the person must be informed that the sample will be the subject of a speculative search).

- To photograph detained persons in the same way that constables can.

Escort Officers

- To transport arrested persons to police stations and escort detained persons from one police station to another or between police stations and other locations specified by the custody officer.

- To carry out the duty of taking a person arrested by a constable to a police station as soon as practicable.

- With the authority of the custody officer, to escort detainees between police stations or between police stations and other specified locations.

- To conduct non-intimate searches of the detainee; and to seize or retain, or cause to be seized or retained, anything found on such a search (restrictions on power to seize personal effects are the same as for police officers, as is the requirement that the search be carried out by a member of the same sex).

Where any of the powers allow for the use of reasonable force when exercised by a police constable, a designated person has the same entitlement to use reasonable force as a constable.

The Police Reform Act 2002 creates offences of assaulting, obstructing or impersonating designated persons which mirror offences in ss. 89 and 90 of the Police Act 1996 for such offences against police officers.

Guidance is provided within the various PACE Codes of Practice and in detail in Code C, paras 1.13 to 1.16. It should be noted that the guidance makes it clear that any reference to a police officer includes a designated person acting in the exercise or performance of the powers and duties conferred or imposed on them by their designation.

It is important to note that not all support staff will be designated for the purposes of the Police Reform Act 2002 and non-designated staff will not have the additional powers as outlined above. Code C, para. 1.15 provides that nothing in the Code prevents the custody officer, or other officer given custody of the detainee, from allowing civilian support staff who are not designated persons to carry out individual procedures or tasks at the police station if the law allows. Where staff are used in this way to support the custody officer, the officer remains responsible for making sure that the procedures and tasks are carried out correctly in accordance with the Codes of Practice. Designated persons and other civilian support staff must have regard to any relevant provisions of the Codes (Code C, para. 1.16).

15.2 Designated Police Stations

Section 30 of the Police and Criminal Evidence Act 1984 requires that a person who has been arrested must be taken to a police station *as soon as practicable* after arrest. However, not all police stations have charge rooms or facilities for dealing with prisoners, so the 1984 Act requires that prisoners who will be detained (or who are likely to be detained) for more than six hours must go to a 'designated' police station. A designated police station is one that has enough facilities for the purpose of detaining arrested people. Section 35 requires the Chief Officer of Police to designate sufficient police stations to deal with prisoners. It is for the Chief Officer to decide which stations are to be designated stations and these details are then published. Police stations can be designated permanently or for any specified periods provided that they are not designated for part of a day.

15.3 Custody Officers

Custody officers are responsible for the reception and treatment of prisoners detained at the police station.

The role of the custody officer is to act independently of those conducting the investigation, thereby ensuring the welfare and rights of the detained person. This requirement is contained in s. 36(5) of the 1984 Act. PACE Code C, para. 3.4 also supports this point in that it makes it clear that the custody officer must not ask a detained person any questions regarding his/her involvement in any offence. The custody officer should not make any comment which may be seen as placing a value judgment on what the person is alleged to have done, nor should he/she make any other comment which in any way casts doubt on his/her impartiality.

Section 36 requires that one or more custody officers must be appointed for each designated police station. However, in *Vince* v *Chief Constable of Dorset* [1993] 1 WLR 415, it was held that there does not have to be a custody officer available all the time at such a police station. The provision of the facility of a custody officer must be reasonable. Section 36(3) states that a custody officer must be an officer of at least the rank of sergeant. However, s. 36(4) allows constables to perform the functions of a custody officer if a sergeant is not readily available to perform them. The effect of s. 36(3) and (4) is that the practice of allowing constables to perform the role of custody officer where a sergeant (*who has no other role to perform*) is in the police station must therefore be unlawful. Should a decision be made to use acting sergeants or untrained custody officers, this may lead to a claim in negligence by the officer or the detained person where there is a breach of the Codes or someone is injured as a result of the failure to manage the custody suite effectively.

For cases where arrested people are taken to a non-designated police station, s. 36(7) states that an officer of any rank not involved in the investigation should perform the role of custody officer. If no such person is at the station, the arresting officer (or any other officer involved in the investigation) should perform the role. In these cases, an officer of at least the rank of inspector at a designated police station must be informed. It is suggested that once informed, that officer should consider the circumstances of the detained person.

The role of the custody officer is crucial to the effective and fair operation of the criminal justice system. In addition to protecting the rights of detained people the role, if performed properly, should also prevent evidence being declared inadmissible because of a violation of the rules. In order to provide as full a record as possible about the detention of a person, the custody officer is required to open a custody record for each detained person (Code C, para. 2.1) and entries should be recorded *as soon as practicable*. Guidance on the completion of custody records is given in Code C, paras 2.1 to 2.7. Custody officers must become very familiar with this guidance, as they are responsible for the accuracy and completeness of the custody record (Code C, para. 2.3). It is important that all entries (subject to Code C, para. 2.6A) in the custody record are timed and signed by the maker (Code C, para. 2.6). If a person is requested to sign an entry in accordance with the Codes and refuses, this too should be recorded (Code C, para. 2.7).

It is also recognised that the role of custody officer is very demanding and, on occasions, the time restraints created by the legislation can become unrealistic. For this reason Code C, para. 1.1A states that a custody officer will not be in breach of the Codes if a delay in taking some action was justifiable and steps had been taken to prevent the delay.

However, if that delay was not 'reasonable', it could lead to actions for unlawful detention and false imprisonment and any evidence obtained as a result may be held to be inadmissible (*Roberts* v *Chief Constable of Cheshire Constabulary* [1999] 1 WLR 662).

Where a custody officer feels that he/she is unable to comply with the minimum standards of detention as required by PACE, it is suggested that he/she should draw this to the attention of the line manager and/or the superintendent responsible for the custody suite. Custody officers should be mindful of Article 5 of the European Convention in considering whether they are able to manage the number of detained persons in their custody to ensure that their detention is not any longer than needed.

15.4   Police Detention and the Treatment of Detained Persons

Depriving a person of his/her liberty is a serious step (**see General Police Duties, chapter 2**). The legislation and the PACE Codes of Practice are intended to ensure that where a person's liberty is taken it is for no longer than is necessary. There is a growing trend towards civil claims against the police for unlawful detention and false imprisonment, some of which is as a result of a failure to follow the guidelines. There are strict limits on a person's detention period and the best defence to such cases is to ensure that the 1984 Act and its Codes of Practice are followed.

15.4.1 **Meaning of Police Detention**

Police detention is defined by s. 118 of the Police and Criminal Evidence Act 1984 which states:

(2) A person is in police detention for the purposes of this Act if—
(a) he has been taken to a police station after being arrested for an offence or after being arrested under section 41 of the Terrorism Act 2000, or
(b) he is arrested at a police station after attending voluntarily at the station or accompanying a constable to it,

and is detained there or is detained elsewhere in the charge of a constable, except that a person who is at a court after being charged is not in police detention for those purposes.

(2A) Where a person is in another's lawful custody by virtue of paragraph 22, 34(1) or 35(3) of Schedule 4 to the Police Reform Act 2002, he shall be treated as in police detention.

KEYNOTE

Paragraph 22 of sch. 4 to the Police Reform Act 2002 refers to power to transfer persons into custody of investigating officers, para. 34(1) relates to designated escort officers taking an arrested person to a police station, and para. 35(3) deals with a designated escort officer transferring a detainee from one police station to another.

PACE Code of Practice C also states:

1.10 ... Section 15 applies solely to people in police detention, e.g. those brought to a police station under arrest or arrested at a police station for an offence after going there voluntarily.

1.11 People in police custody include anyone detained under the Terrorism Act 2000, schedule 8 and section 41, having been taken to a police station after being arrested under the Terrorism Act 2000, section 41. In these cases, reference to an offence in this Code includes the commission, preparation and instigation of acts of terrorism.

1.12 This Code's provisions do not apply to people in custody:
(i) arrested on warrants issued in Scotland by officers under the Criminal Justice and Public Order Act 1994, section 136(2), or arrested or detained without warrant by officers from a police force in Scotland under section 137(2). In these cases, police powers and duties and the person's rights and entitlements whilst at a police station in England or Wales are the same as those in Scotland;
(ii) arrested under the Immigration and Asylum Act 1999, section 142(3) in order to have their fingerprints taken;
(iii) whose detention is authorised by an immigration officer under the Immigration Act 1971;
(iv) who are convicted or remanded prisoners held in police cells on behalf of the Prison Service under the Imprisonment (Temporary Provisions) Act 1980;
(v) detained for examination under the Terrorism Act 2000, schedule 7 and to whom the Code of Practice issued under that Act, schedule 14, paragraph 6 applies;
(vi) detained for searches under stop and search powers except as required by Code A.

The provisions on conditions of detention and treatment in sections 8 and 9 must be considered as the minimum standards of treatment for such detainees.

KEYNOTE

The last two lines of Code C, para. 1.12 above, make it clear that the way such prisoners are treated should be of no lower standard than that for other detained people. If in doubt as to whether a person falls within the definition of a detained person, it is suggested that he/she should be afforded all the rights and privileges outlined in the Codes of Practice. A similar approach should be adopted when it comes to reviewing a detainee's detention (see 15.5.6).

With the exception of those groups listed in Code C, para. 1.12, Code C applies to people in custody at police stations in England and Wales, whether or not they have been arrested, and to those removed to a police station as a place of safety under the Mental Health Act 1983, ss. 135 and 136.

15.4.2   **Right to Have Someone Informed**

Section 56 of the Police and Criminal Evidence Act 1984 provides that a person arrested and held in custody at a police station or other premises may, on request, have one person known to him/her or who is likely to take an interest in his/her welfare, informed at public expense of his/her whereabouts as soon as practicable (Code C, para. 5.1). (If the detainee's first choice cannot be contacted, see Code C, para. 5.1 and Notes 5C and 5D.) This fundamental human right is known as the right not to be held *incommunicado* and guidance on this right is contained in Code C, paras 5.1 to 5.7. If a person transfers to another police station, the same right applies at the next police station (Code C, para. 5.3), even if they have already had someone informed at the previous places of detention.

This right can only be delayed if the offence is a 'serious arrestable offence' (**see General Police Duties, chapter 2**) and an officer of the rank of inspector or above (whether or not connected to the investigation) authorises the delay (see Code C, Annex B) (**see para. 15.4.3**). Where a person has to be given information under the Code but is not in a fit state to understand it, it is to be given to him/her as soon as practicable but only when he/she is in a fit state to understand it (Code C, para. 1.8). The delay can only be for a maximum of 36 hours (48 hours in cases involving terrorism), and the 36-hour period is calculated from the 'relevant time' (**see para. 15.4.5**). In the case of a juvenile, the power to authorise the delay does not apply to the person responsible for their welfare, but only to any other person the juvenile wishes to have informed (Code C, para. 3.13).

There may be occasions where officers wish to conduct a search under s. 18 of the 1984 Act (**see General Police Duties, chapter 2**) and the detained person has requested to have someone informed. Clearly if such a person is informed before the search is conducted, vital evidence or property may be lost. Often the custody officer has two methods by which he/she can inform the person requested about the detained person's detention; either in person or on the phone. Contacting the person by telephone is likely to be the quickest, however, there is no requirement to use the quickest method in order to pass on this information. While there is no case law on this point, Code C, Note 5D, supports the view that, where the s. 18 search is to be conducted relatively quickly after the request is made by the detained person, it would be permissible to inform that person at the time the s. 18 search is conducted. Where the search is not to be conducted straight away, it is suggested that consideration would have to be given to obtaining the authority of an officer of at least the rank of inspector to delay the notification as outlined in **para. 15.4.4**. A lengthy delay may be seen as a breach of this right which may lead to a stay of proceedings or a claim for damages as a breach of the detained person's human rights.

Detained people may also be allowed to speak to a person on the telephone for a reasonable time or send letters. If a person has an interpreter, he/she can do this on the detained person's behalf. This right can be denied or delayed in the case of arrestable and serious arrestable offences by an officer of the rank of inspector or above (Code C, para. 5.6). The grounds are the same as those regulating the holding of people *incommunicado* (**see para. 15.4.4**). Where a person is allowed to make a telephone call or send a letter, the procedure in Code C, para. 5.7 should be followed. Should there be any delay in complying with a request by a detained person to have someone informed of his/her detention or to communicate with someone, the detained person should be informed of this and a record kept (s. 56(6) of the 1984 Act). The custody officer also has a discretion to allow visits to the detained person at the police station (Code C, para. 5.4 and Note 5B). It is suggested that with the Codes of Practice outlining the limited rights for the detained person to make telephone calls and the right to restrict these calls, that if the person has a mobile telephone it can be seized for the period of their detention. There is no case law on this point and any force policy should be followed.

There are also special requirements for juveniles and detained people from other countries.

Juveniles

In the case of juveniles, where practicable, a person who is responsible for a juvenile's welfare must be informed of his/her arrest. This person may be the appropriate adult (see Code C, para. 1.7(a)) but if not, an adult must also be arranged to attend the police station to look after the interests of the juvenile. This action must be undertaken regardless of whether the juvenile wishes to have someone informed or has requested that some other person other than the appropriate adult be informed.

Code C, para. 3.13 states:

If the detainee is a juvenile, the custody officer must, if it is practicable, ascertain the identity of a person responsible for their welfare. That person:

- may be:
  - the parent or guardian;
  - if the juvenile is in local authority or voluntary organisation care, or is otherwise being looked after under the Children Act 1989, a person appointed by that authority or organisation to have responsibility for the juvenile's welfare;
  - any other person who has, for the time being, assumed responsibility for the juvenile's welfare.

- must be informed as soon as practicable that the juvenile has been arrested, why they have been arrested and where they are detained. This right is in addition to the juvenile's right in s. 5 not to be held incommunicado. See Code C, Note 3C.

KEYNOTE

If a juvenile known to be subject to a court order under which a person or organisation is given any degree of statutory responsibility to supervise or otherwise monitor them, reasonable steps must also be taken to notify that person or organisation (the 'responsible officer'). The responsible officer will normally be a member of a Youth Offending Team, except for a curfew order which involves electronic monitoring when the contractor providing the monitoring will normally be the responsible officer (Code C, para. 3.14).

Detained persons—special groups

If the detainee appears to be deaf or there is doubt about his/her hearing or speaking ability or ability to understand English, and the custody officer cannot establish effective communication, the custody officer must, as soon as practicable, call an interpreter for assistance to go through the detainee's rights under Code C, paras 3.1–3.5 (Code C, para. 3.12).

If the detainee is a mentally disordered or otherwise mentally vulnerable, the custody officer must, as soon as practicable, inform the appropriate adult of the grounds for their detention and their whereabouts. The appropriate adult should also be asked to come to the police station to see the detainee (Code C, para. 3.15). In managing mentally disordered or otherwise mentally vulnerable persons detained under the Mental Health Act 1983, s. 136, the custody officer must be mindful that it is imperative that the detainee is assessed as soon as possible (Code C, para. 3.16).

Detained People from Other Countries

Citizens of independent commonwealth countries or foreign nationals may communicate with their High Commission, Embassy or Consulate as soon as practicable (Code C, para. 7.1). If the country is included on the list at Annex F to Code C, the High Commission, Embassy or Consulate must be informed unless the detained person is a political refugee or is seeking political asylum (para. 7.1).

Where a person who is a friend, relative or a person with an interest in the detained person's welfare, makes enquires about that person, the detained person should be asked whether he/she agrees to the person being informed prior to any information being given (Code C, para. 5.5). The information must not be given if a delay has been authorised.

15.4.3   Right to Legal Advice

Section 58 of the Police and Criminal Evidence Act 1984 provides an almost inalienable right for a person arrested and held in custody at a police station or other premises to consult privately with a solicitor free of charge if he/she requests it (or the appropriate adult makes the request (Code C, para. 3.19)). This provision is very similar to that of s. 56 of the 1984 Act; the right to have a person informed of the arrest. This right to consult a solicitor is considered to be so important that a detained person must be informed of the right when he/she first arrives at the police station and asked for reasons if he/she declines to exercise this right. Detainees are also reminded of this right at other times, e.g. prior to interview and when detention is being reviewed. In *R* v *Alladice* (1988) 87 Cr App R 380 the Court of Appeal made it clear that:

> no matter how strongly and however justifiably the police may feel that their investigation and detection of crime is being hindered by the presence of a solicitor ... they are nevertheless confined to the narrow limits imposed by section 58.

In *R* v *Aspinall* [1999] 2 Cr App R 115 the court stated that the right to access to legal advice was a fundamental right under Article 6 of the European Convention on Human Rights and even greater importance had to be attached to advice for a vulnerable person.

Code C, Annex B provides only two exceptions to this right to legal advice:

- Cases where an officer of the rank of superintendent or above (whether or not connected to the investigation) authorises the exercise of the right to be delayed. This only applies if the offence is a serious arrestable offence (**see General Police Duties, chapter 2**) and Code C, Annex B applies.

- Where the person is held under the prevention of terrorism legislation (Terrorism Act 2000) and the conditions in Code C, Annex B apply. Here a uniformed officer of at least the rank of inspector not connected with the case may be present if authorised by an Assistant Chief Constable or Commander.

The delay can only be for a maximum of 36 hours (48 hours from the time of arrest in terrorism cases) or until the time the person will first appear at court, which ever is the sooner (see below). The 36-hour period is calculated from the 'relevant time' (**see para. 15.4.5**). The authorisation can initially be made orally either in person or by telephone but must be recorded in writing as soon as practicable. Where a delay is authorised then this restricts the drawing of adverse inferences from silence (see Code C, para. 6.6).

The consultation with a solicitor can be either on the telephone, in person or in writing and it must be in private (Code C, para. 6.1). This right to have a private consultation is a good example of where a person's rights under the European Convention need to be considered. In many custody suites this is difficult to comply with (see Code C, Note 6J) but could lead to adverse comment, particularly if officers act on what they heard the detained person say whilst consulting with their legal representative. Code C, Note 6J gives clear indication that the normal expectation should be that facilities will be available for the detainee to speak in private to a solicitor. This right to have a private consultation also apples to juveniles who, should they wish to have a private consultation without the appropriate adult being present, must be permitted to do so (Code C, Note 1E). This point was considered in *R (on the application of M (A Child))* v *Commissioner of the Police of the Metropolis* [2002] Crim LR 215, where the court said that ideally there ought be a consultation room at every police station and facilities for private telephone calls to be made for legal consultations. However, there was no breach of Article 6(3) of the European Convention where it could not be shown that a detainee had been denied adequate facilities for the preparation of his defence.

Once a person has indicated a wish to have a solicitor, and has not yet been advised by a solicitor, he/she can only be interviewed in limited circumstances as set out in Code C, para. 6.6, but it is not necessary to delay taking breath, blood or urine samples from a motorist until a solicitor arrives nor delay searching the detainee or the taking of non-intimate samples without consent for evidential purposes (Code C, Note 3D and **Road Traffic, chapter 5**). Of particular note is Code C, para. 6.6(b). This allows an officer of the rank of superintendent or above to allow an interview to take place or continue without a solicitor being present, if he/she has reasonable grounds for believing that:

(i) the consequent delay might:
   - lead to interference with, or harm to, evidence connected with an offence;
   - lead to interference with, or physical harm to, other people;
   - lead to serious loss of, or damage to, property;
   - lead to alerting other people suspected of having committed an offence but not yet arrested for it;
   - hinder the recovery of property obtained in consequence of the commission of an offence.

(ii) when a solicitor, including a duty solicitor, has been contacted and has agreed to attend, awaiting their arrival would cause unreasonable delay to the process of investigation.

Another exception is in relation to the drink drive procedure for s. 7 of the Road Traffic Act 1988. In *DPP* v *Noe* [2000] RTR 351 a request to see a solicitor or alternatively to consult a law book to verify the legality of the police request for a specimen of breath was not a reasonable excuse under s. 7. This decision has not been affected by the enactment of the Human Rights Act 1998. This is confirmed by *Campbell* v *DPP* [2003] Crim LR 118 who held that it was entirely proportionate to allow a police officer to require a member of the community to provide a specimen albeit that legal advice had not been obtained.

Where Code C, para. 6.6 is used it will have to be justified at court if the interview is to be admissible. This power might prove useful in circumstances where there are 'delaying tactics' by legal representatives, particularly where they are aware that the detained person's relevant time is due to expire within a short period.

Code C, para. 6.6 provides two further occasions where the interview may go ahead without a solicitor being present provided the consent of an officer of inspector rank or above has been obtained. Paragraph 6.6(c) deals with the situation where the solicitor the detainee has nominated or selected from a list cannot be contacted, has previously indicated they do not wish to be contacted, or having been contacted, has declined to attend; and the detainee has been advised of the Duty Solicitor Scheme but has declined to ask for the duty solicitor. Paragraph 6.6(d) deals with the situation where the detainee changes his/her mind, about wanting legal advice. In these circumstances the interview may be started or continued provided that the detainee agrees to do so, in writing or on tape. In this case the officer of inspector rank or above must inquire about the detainee's reasons for their change of mind. Paragraph 6.6(d) outlines what information must be recorded in the taped or written interview record.

Where an interview has started without the solicitor being present and access has not been refused under Code C, Annex B, the solicitor must be allowed to be present when he/she arrives at the station unless Code C, para. 6.6(b) applies or he/she has been excluded because of his/her conduct (Code C, para. 6.10).

In considering whether to conduct an interview in these circumstances, guidance is given Code C, Note 6A.

A solicitor for these purposes means a solicitor who holds a current practising certificate, a trainee solicitor, a duty solicitor representative or an accredited representative included on the register of representatives maintained by the Legal Services Commission (Code C, para. 6.12). A non-accredited or probationary representative may also attend and give advice unless an officer of the rank of inspector or above considers that such a visit will hinder the investigation of crime and directs otherwise and once admitted he/she should be treated as any other legal adviser (Code C, para. 6.12A).

In deciding whether to admit a non-accredited or probationary representative, the officer should take into account in particular whether the identity and status of the non-accredited or probationary representative have been satisfactorily established; whether he/she is of suitable character to provide legal advice (a person with a criminal record is unlikely to be suitable unless the conviction was for a minor offence and is not of recent date); and any other matters in any written letter of authorisation provided by the solicitor on whose behalf the person is attending the police station (Code C, para. 6.13). The Law Society has advised solicitors that if a non-accredited or probationary representative is refused admission, a written reason for the decision should be requested. If access is refused or a decision is taken that such a person should not be permitted to remain at an interview, the inspector must forthwith notify a solicitor on whose behalf the non-accredited or probationary representative was to have acted or was acting, and give him/her an opportunity to make alternative arrangements. The detained person must also be informed and the custody record noted (Code C, para. 6.14 and Note 6F).

15.4.4 Authority to Delay Rights under ss. 56 or 58 (Code C, Annex B)

An officer of the rank of superintendent or above for s. 58 of the Police and Criminal Evidence Act 1984 and inspector or above for s. 56 of the 1984 Act can only authorise a delay if he/she has reasonable grounds for believing that by exercising the right it will:

- lead to interference with or cause harm to evidence connected with a serious arrestable offence or lead to interference with or cause physical injury to other people; or
- lead to alerting other people suspected of having committed a serious arrestable offence but not yet arrested for it; or
- hinder the recovery of property obtained as a consequence of the commission of such an offence.

The delay may also re-authorised under s. 56 and/or s. 58 where the person is detained for a serious arrestable offence and has benefited from his criminal conduct in circumstances where the recovery of the value of the property constituting the benefit will be hindered by telling the named person of the arrest or his/her right of access to legal advice (s. 56(5A) for delay in notification and s. 58(8A) for access to legal advice).

For these purposes whether a person has benefited from his/her criminal conduct is to be decided in accordance with Part 2 of the Proceeds of Crime Act 2002. Briefly, criminal conduct is conduct which constitutes an offence in England and Wales, or would constitute such an offence if it occurred in England and Wales. A person benefits from conduct if he/she obtains property as a result of or in connection with the conduct.

In cases where the person is detained under the Terrorism Act 2000 an officer of the rank of superintendent or above may delay the exercise of either right or both if he/she has reasonable grounds for believing that the exercise of the right will lead to any of the consequences of:

- interference with, or harm to, evidence connected with a serious arrestable offence;
- interference with, or physical harm to, other people;

- the alerting of other people suspected of having committed a serious arrestable offence but not yet arrested for it;

- hinder the recovery of property obtained as a result of a serious arrestable offence or in respect of which a forfeiture order could be made;

- interference with the gathering of information about the commission, preparation or instigation of acts of terrorism;

- the alerting of any person, making it more difficult to prevent an act of terrorism;

- the alerting of a person and thereby making it more difficult to secure the apprehension, prosecution or conviction of any person in connection with the commission, preparation or instigation of an act of terrorism;

- the detained person has benefited from his/her criminal conduct, and the recovery of the value of the property constituting the benefit will be hindered by informing the named person of the detained person's detention or access to legal advice. For these purposes whether a person has benefited from his/her criminal conduct is to be decided in accordance with Part 2 of the Proceeds of Crime Act 2002. Briefly, criminal conduct is conduct which constitutes an offence in England and Wales, or would constitute such an offence if it occurred in England and Wales. A person benefits from conduct if he/she obtains property as a result of or in connection with the conduct

(Code C, Annex B, paras 8 and 9).

These powers were amended on 24 March 2003 where the Proceeds of Crime Act 2002 amended ss. 56 and 58 of the 1984 Act. These changes are not reflected in the latest Codes of Practice which must be read in conjunction with the above sections.

If the delay is authorised the detained person must be given the reason for the delay which must correspond to one of the above grounds and an entry must be made in the custody record.

Once the reason for authorising the delay has ceased, the detained person must be allowed to exercise his/her rights. Once this point has been reached, the detained person must as soon as practicable be asked if he/she wishes to exercise the right (or rights), the custody record must be noted accordingly, and the relevant action taken (Code C, Annex B, para. 6).

The fact that the grounds for delaying notification of arrest may be satisfied does not automatically mean that the grounds for delaying access to legal advice will also be satisfied (Code C, Annex B, para. 5).

When considering whether to deny access to a solicitor the fact that he/she might advise the person not to answer any questions or that the solicitor was initially asked to attend the police station by someone else, provided that the person himself/herself then wishes to see the solicitor, is not a reason for delaying access to a solicitor (Code C, Annex B, para. 4). When considering the delay of access to a solicitor the authorising officer must bear in mind that access to a solicitor is 'a fundamental right of a citizen' (*R v Samuel* [1988] 2 WLR 920). The authorising officer must actually believe that by allowing access to the solicitor he/she will intentionally or inadvertently alert other suspects. There must also be objective reasons upon which the officer authorising the delay can base his/her beliefs. If the reason for authorising the delay of access to a solicitor is because there are concerns with the particular solicitor who has been requested or is offering his/her services to the detained person the officer should offer the detained person access to a solicitor (who is not the specific solicitor referred to above) on the Duty Solicitor Scheme (Code C, Annex B, para. 3). Annex B, Note B3 suggests that occasions where this delay will be authorised in such circumstances will be rare and only when it can be shown that the suspect is capable of misleading that particular solicitor. In deciding whether such an interview will be admissible the court will consider how reliable it is and will consider how the refusal to allow that particular detained person access to a solicitor affected their decision to make a confession. One such case where the confession was excluded is *R* v *Sanusi* [1992] Crim LR 43, where a person from another country was denied access to a solicitor and the court held that his right to advice was particularly significant due to his lack of familiarity with police procedures.

In terrorism cases a direction may be given by an officer of at least the rank of Commander or Assistant Chief Constable which may provide that a detained person who wishes to exercise the right to consult a solicitor may do so only in the sight and hearing of a qualified officer, this person being a uniform officer of at least the rank of inspector not connected with the investigation from the authorising officer's force.

15.4.5   Relevant Time

As discussed above, there are limits on how long a person can be detained. The Police and Criminal Evidence Act 1984 and the Codes of Practice talk of the 'relevant time'. This is the time from which the limits of detention are calculated. The relevant time of a person's detention starts in accordance with s. 41(2) to (5) of the 1984 Act. Section 41 states:

> (2) The time from which the period of detention of a person is to be calculated (in this Act referred to as 'the relevant time')—
>   (a) in the case of a person to whom this paragraph applies, shall be—
>   (i) the time at which that person arrives at the relevant police station; or
>   (ii) the time 24 hours after the time of that person's arrest,
>   whichever is the earlier;
>   (b) in the case of a person arrested outside England and Wales, shall be—
>   (i) the time at which that person arrives at the first police station to which he is taken in the police area in England or Wales in which the offence for which he was arrested is being investigated; or
>   (ii) the time 24 hours after the time of that person's entry into England and Wales,
>   whichever is the earlier,
>   (c) in the case of a person who—
>   (i) attends voluntarily at a police station; or
>   (ii) accompanies a constable to a police station without having been arrested, and is arrested at the police station, the time of his arrest;
>   (d) in any other case, except where subsection (5) below applies, shall be the time at which the person arrested arrives at the first police station to which he is taken after his arrest.
>
> (3) Subsection (2)(a) above applies to a person if—
>   (a) his arrest is sought in one police area in England and Wales;
>   (b) he is arrested in another police area, and
>   (c) he is not questioned in the area in which he is arrested in order to obtain evidence in relation to an offence for which he is arrested;
>   and in sub-paragraph (i) of that paragraph 'the relevant police station' means the first police station to which he is taken in the police area in which his arrest was sought.
>
> (4) Subsection (2) above shall have effect in relation to a person arrested under section 31 above as if every reference in it to his arrest or his being arrested were a reference to his arrest or his being arrested for the offence for which he was originally arrested.
>
> (5) If—
>   (a) a person is in police detention in a police area in England and Wales ('the first area'); and
>   (b) his arrest for an offence is sought in some other police area in England and Wales ('the second area'); and
>   (c) he is taken to the second area for the purposes of investigating that offence, without being questioned in the first area in order to obtain evidence in relation to it,
>   the relevant time shall be—
>   (i) the time 24 hours after he leaves the place where he is detained in the first area; or
>   (ii) the time at which he arrives at the first police station to which he is taken in the second area,
>   whichever is the earlier.

KEYNOTE

Note that under s. 41(5) the relevant time may vary depending on whether the detainee is interviewed in relation to the offence whilst still in the first police area.

For those detained under the Terrorism Act 2000 (**see para. 16.7.6**) the detention clock starts from the time the person is arrested; not the time they arrive at the police station.

For the provisions of s. 31 relating to people who have been arrested for one offence and if released from the police station would be liable to arrest for some other offence, **see General Police Duties, chapter 2.**

Some situations occur where a person is arrested at one police station and has been circulated as wanted by another police station in the same force area. In these cases, where the person is not wanted on warrant, the detention clock for the second offence starts at the same time as for the original offence for which they were arrested. Consideration will need to be given as to how to protect the detention period for the second offence while officers are dealing with the first matter. Options that might be considered would include bailing the person for one of the offences or conducting both investigations at the same station Here there may be a risk of 'confusing' the suspect, which may allow him/her to retract or qualify any confession he/she might make.

In *Henderson* v *Chief Constable of Cleveland* [2001] 1 WLR 1103 the court considered the policy of not executing a court warrant until after other matters for which the person had been detained were completed. The court held that, once a warrant was executed, there was a requirement to follow the directions of the warrant. The police however had a discretion as to *when* to execute the warrant. This may be relevant where a person has been arrested for one offence and it is discovered that he/she is also wanted for another offence or where there are warrants in existence for that person at more than one court. In such cases, if the warrant is executed immediately, the direction on the warrant tells officers to take the person before the next available court, an action which could interfere with the investigation. If *Henderson* is followed there is no requirement to execute the warrant straightaway and the other matters can be dealt with before the requirement to produce the person at court under the warrant applies.

15.4.6   **Detention of People under Arrest**

People who have been arrested, or voluntarily given themselves up at a police station, will be brought before a custody officer who must decide whether the person should be detained at the police station or released. People who attend police stations voluntarily to assist the police with their investigations are not subject to this procedure; their treatment is dealt with by s. 29 of the 1984 Act and PACE Code C, paras 3.21 and 22 (**see General Police Duties, chapter 2**).

The arresting officer informs the custody officer of the reasons for arrest. This will include *what* offence the person was arrested for and brief details of the *grounds* for the arrest, e.g. the arrest is for robbery and the accused was seen to punch the victim in the face and steal his holdall. In the case of a non-arrestable offence, an example might be that the detained person was seen to drive his car through a red light and has refused to give his name and address, thereby making it impossible to serve a summons (**see General Police Duties, chapter 2**). As this information must be given to the person on arrest—in most cases—the details given to the custody officer should be fresh in the mind of the arresting officer; they should also accord with the reasons and grounds given to the person on arrest! If the grounds were not given at the time of arrest (under justifiable grounds) the custody officer should consider whether the arrested person is now in a position to be given the reasons for the arrest (as being the first practicable opportunity (s. 28(3) of the 1984 Act)). If the grounds for arrest were not given when they should have been the arrest is unlawful regardless of what information is given later (*Wilson* v *Chief Constable of Lancashire* (2000) LTL 23 November).

Having heard the details of and for the arrest, the custody officer must then decide whether or not there are reasons which justify authorising that person's detention (s. 37 of the Police and Criminal Evidence Act 1984 deals with the procedures to be followed before a person is charged). Some commentators have suggested that it is also the role of the custody officer to establish that the arrest itself was lawful. While this would seem to be sensible and good practice, the custody officer's duty is confined to acting in accordance with the requirements set out in s. 37 of the 1984 Act. These duties do not appear to include considering whether the arrest was lawful unless this is relevant to the main question of whether there is sufficient evidence to charge the suspect. The view is supported by the decision of the Divisional Court in *DPP* v *L* [1999] Crim LR 752, where the court held that there was no express or implied requirement imposing a duty on a custody officer to inquire into the legality of an arrest and in that case the custody officer was therefore entitled to assume that it was lawful. A subsequent finding that the arrest was unlawful did not invalidate the decision of the custody officer to hold the person in custody. However, where the custody officer is aware that the arrest is unlawful, he/she will need to consider whether continued detention is justifiable, particularly in light of the Human Rights Act 1998.

Section 37 of the 1984 Act states:

(1) Where—
   (a) a person is arrested for an offence—
      (i) without a warrant; or
      (ii) under a warrant not endorsed for bail,
   the custody officer at each police station where he is detained after his arrest shall determine whether he has before him sufficient evidence to charge that person with the offence for which he was arrested and may detain him at the police station for such period as is necessary to enable him to do so.

(2) If the custody officer determines that he does not have such evidence before him, the person arrested shall be released either on bail or without bail, unless the custody officer has reasonable grounds for believing that his detention without being charged is necessary to secure or preserve evidence relating to an offence for which he is under arrest or to obtain such evidence by questioning him.

(3) If the custody officer has reasonable grounds for so believing, he may authorise the person arrested to be kept in police detention.

(4) Where a custody officer authorises a person who has not been charged to be kept in police detention, he shall, as soon as is practicable, make a written record of the grounds for the detention.

(5) Subject to subsection (6) below, the written record shall be made in the presence of the person arrested who shall at that time be informed by the custody officer of the grounds for his detention.

(6) Subsection (5) above shall not apply where the person arrested is, at the time when the written record is made—
   (a) incapable of understanding what is said to him;
   (b) violent or likely to become violent; or
   (c) in urgent need of medical attention.

KEYNOTE

If the person is arrested on a warrant (see General Police Duties, chapter 2), any directions given by the court in the warrant must be followed. Consideration can always be given to contacting the court to get a variation on the conditions of the warrant. (If the warrant was issued for the arrest of a person who has not yet been charged or summonsed for an offence, he/she should be dealt with as any other person arrested for an offence without warrant unless there are any additional directions on the warrant that must be followed.)

15.4.7 **Authorising a Person's Detention**

A custody officer can authorise the detention of a person when there is sufficient evidence to charge and, more commonly, when there is *not* sufficient evidence to charge the suspect. If there is insufficient evidence to charge, the custody officer must decide if the detention is necessary to secure or preserve evidence relating to an offence for which the person is under arrest or to obtain such evidence by questioning him/her.

If a person representing the detained person does not feel the detention is lawful he/she can apply to the court for the detainee's release (*habeas corpus*). A detainee may also be able to make an application for release or damages following the incorporation of the European Convention on Human Rights. Article 5(4) states:

> Everyone who is deprived of his liberty by arrest or detention shall be entitled to take proceedings by which the lawfulness of his detention shall be decided speedily by a court and his release ordered if the detention is not lawful.

Sufficient Evidence to Charge

Here the custody officer is looking at the evidence in order to satisfy himself/herself that no further investigation is needed before the person can be charged. If this is the case, detention may be authorised. In considering whether this position has been reached it is worth considering Code C, para. 16.1 which states:

> When the officer in charge of the investigation reasonably believes there is sufficient evidence to provide a realistic prospect of the detainee's conviction, ... they shall ... inform the custody officer who will be responsible for considering whether the detainee should be charged. ...

KEYNOTE

Code C, para. 16.1 suggests that a charge should not be brought until there is sufficient evidence for a realistic prospect of a successful prosecution. This might require the person being bailed while advice is sought from the Crown Prosecution Service.

Where there is sufficient evidence to provide a realistic prospect of conviction, under s. 37(7) of the Police and Criminal Evidence Act 1984, the custody officer must charge the person or release him/her without charge, either on bail or without bail. Often the reason for not charging the person will be to allow a decision to be made by the Crown Prosecution Service as to whether to charge the person, caution them or not to proceed with the case. In these circumstances s. 37(8) requires the custody officer to inform the person that a decision to charge has not yet been made.

Where there is sufficient evidence to charge, a delay in bringing charges may be seen to be unreasonable under Article 6 of the European Convention on Human Rights (*D* v *HM Advocate* (2000) *The Times*, 14 April).

In deciding whether there is sufficient evidence to charge for the purposes of authorising detention or when a person's detention is reviewed; where there is a conflict between the detained person's account and victims' or witnesses' accounts it is reasonable to be in possession of at least one witness statement in the English language before preferring charges (*R* v *Chief Constable of Hertfordshire, ex parte Wiles* [2002] EWHC Admin 387). There is no breach of the Police and Criminal Evidence Act in keeping the detained person in police detention while a statement is translated. It is suggested that the translation needs to be completed expeditiously.

Under s. 37(9) release can be delayed if the person is not in a fit state to be released (e.g. he/she is drunk), until he/she is fit. Where a person is detained for charge, the custody officer should record the grounds for detention in the custody record in the presence of the detained person if practicable (Code C, para. 3.23). For the situation relating to drunk drivers, **see Road Traffic, chapter 5.**

Insufficient Evidence to Charge

This creates two separate criteria for detention, that is to say, where detention is necessary to:

- secure and preserve evidence relating to an offence for which the person is arrested; and/or
- obtain such evidence by questioning the detained person.

If the custody officer has determined that there is not sufficient evidence to charge the person, the person must be released unless the custody officer has *reasonable grounds* for believing that the person's detention is necessary to preserve or to obtain such evidence by questioning the person. 'Reasonable grounds for believing' requires a greater amount of evidence than 'reasonable cause to suspect' (**see General Police Duties, chapter 2**) and the custody officer must be able to justify any decision not to release a person from detention.

When deciding if detention should be authorised in order to preserve evidence by questioning, the case of *R* v *McGuinness* [1999] Crim LR 318 should be considered. There the court held that the words 'sufficient evidence to prosecute' and 'sufficient evidence for a prosecution to succeed', in Code C, para. 16.1 (this was the wording under the previous PACE Code of Practice), had to involve some consideration of any explanation, or lack of one, from the suspect. While an interview may not be needed in all cases, questioning of detained people before they are charged may be necessary, particularly where intention or dishonesty (**see Crime, chapter 1**) is involved or where there may be a defence (**see Crime, chapter 4**). It may also be important to put questions to the person about the offence or his/her explanation, as this may be important to negate any defence the person raised at court (see s. 34 of the Criminal Justice and Public Order Act 1994).

Where initial suspicion rests on several people, it may be appropriate to hold all suspects until they all are interviewed before deciding whether there is enough evidence to warrant a charge against any of them. Detention for questioning where there are reasonable grounds for suspecting that an offence has been committed is lawful so long as the suspicion has not been dispelled in the interim and the questioning is not unnecessarily delayed (*Clarke* v *Chief Constable of North Wales, The Independent*, 22 May 2000).

Article 5 of the European Convention on Human Rights makes the decision to authorise detention even more crucial, as it states:

1. Everyone has the right to liberty and security of person. No one shall be deprived of his liberty save in the following cases and in accordance with a procedure prescribed by law:
    (a) the lawful detention of a person after conviction by a competent court;
    (b) the lawful arrest or detention of a person for non-compliance with the lawful order of a court or in order to secure the fulfilment of any obligation prescribed by law;
    (c) the lawful arrest or detention of a person effected for the purpose of bringing him before the competent legal authority on reasonable suspicion of having committed an offence or when it is reasonably considered necessary to prevent his committing an offence or fleeing after having done so . . .

For a full discussion of the Convention, **see General Police Duties, chapter 2**.

The custody officer can detain the person for such period as is necessary in order to make this decision (s. 37(1) of the 1984 Act). Clearly any such period must be 'reasonable' in all the circumstances. For instance, where there are several prisoners waiting to be dealt with it may be reasonable that the last prisoner is not dealt with for 30 minutes because the custody officer is busy with the other prisoners (Code C, para. 1.1A and Note 1H). For the custody officer to be able to make this decision, the arresting officer needs to give sufficient detail about the offence. The account given by the arresting officer should be made in the presence of the arrested person and any comment made by that person in response should be recorded in the custody record (Code C, para. 3.4) (unless the person is violent or it is impractical to do so for some other reason, in which case this fact should also be recorded).

The mere fact that a person needs to be interviewed about the offence is not of itself justification for authorising detention. The question that has to be asked is whether the person can be bailed prior to the interview. Factors which might be relevant in making this decision include whether the person may interfere with witnesses; whether he/she is likely to return if bailed; where there is more than one suspect, that they would have an opportunity to confer before their interviews; whether there is outstanding property; whether the person's name and address is verified. The fact that the officers and any legal representative will be ready to start the interview shortly may also be relevant when making this decision.

Section 37(4) and (5) of the 1984 Act require the custody officer to make a written record of the grounds of detention and to make that record in the presence of the detained person, informing him/her at the same time of the grounds of his/her detention (unless s. 37(6) applies). It is suggested that the custody officer record all the reasons for authorising the person's detention. For example: 'To obtain statements from the victim and witnesses as this information will be needed before interview to fully put the allegation to the suspect and then to allow the suspect to be interviewed about the allegation. If bailed prior to interview he/she may interfere with the witnesses, who are known to the suspect.' It is suggested that detail of at least this minimal level should be included, as it may be necessary in any criminal or civil proceedings. Indeed, it will be difficult for the custody officer to explain his/her decision without such information.

Section 37(6) states:

> (6) Subsection (5) above shall not apply where the person arrested is, at the time when the written record is made—
>   (a) incapable of understanding what is said to him;
>   (b) violent or likely to become violent; or
>   (c) in urgent need of medical attention.

15.4.8 Additional Action to be Taken by the Custody Officer

The action to be taken by the custody officer when receiving detained people is set out in Code C, paras 3.1 to 3.11. For the action relating to special groups, **see para. 15.9.**

Paragraph 3.1 sets out the information the detained person is entitled to. These are *continuing* entitlements and can be requested at any time during the person's detention.

Paragraph 3.2 deals with written notices which must be given to the detained person in relation to his/her rights. (Code C, para. 1.2 requires that a copy of the Codes of Practice must also be readily available to detained persons should they request it.) There should be versions of these rights in languages other than English available in the custody suite.

Paragraph 3.5 requires the custody officer to establish whether the detained person wishes to have a solicitor at this stage. If he/she declines, the custody officer should ask the person the reason why and, if any reasons are given, these should be recorded in the custody record (Code C, para. 6.5). The detained person must still be asked if they require a solicitor even if they are to be held *incommunicado*.

15.5 Limits on Detention and Review

Once detention has been authorised this does not mean that a person can be detained indefinitely. Section 34 of the Police and Criminal Evidence Act 1984 requires the custody officer to release a person if he/she becomes aware that the grounds for detention no longer apply and that no other grounds exist for the continuing detention (unless the person appears to be unlawfully at large). If there are additional grounds, these should be recorded in the custody record and the person informed of these additional grounds in the same way as when a person is first detained. For example, this could be for new offences or it could be that it becomes necessary to preserve evidence by questioning the detained person.

It is only the custody officer who can authorise the release of a detained person (s. 34(3)). In addition to the requirement to release a person should the grounds for detention no longer exist, there are also maximum time limits for which a person can be detained without charge (**see para. 15.5.1**). Once this limit has been reached, it will be necessary to proceed by summons or by warrant. There are also limits on the time a person can be kept in custody after being charged, refused bail and appearing at court (see below).

15.5.1 Time Limits: Without Charge

While a person is in police detention there is a requirement that his/her continuing detention is reviewed. This is dealt with below. There are minimum time requirements for when these reviews must be conducted, with the timing of the first review being calculated from the time detention is authorised. This time can be considered as the 'review time'. The question of whether a person should be kept in custody is a continuous one and the review process is intended as an added protection to the detained person.

The maximum period that a person can be detained without charge (with the exception of suspected acts of terrorism, in which case it is seven days) is 96 hours. The necessity for the continued detention of the person must be reviewed throughout this time. The period of detention is calculated from the 'relevant time' (**see para. 15.4.5**) which can be calculated from the chart below (**see para. 15.5.3**). (*Do not confuse the relevant time with the time from which reviews are due.*) The relevant time 'clock' will always start before, or at the same time as the review 'clock'. This is because the review clock does not start until detention has been authorised which clearly cannot happen until the person is brought before the custody officer which, as can be seen from the chart below, is at the very latest, the time the prisoner walks into the custody suite (*with the exception of where the person has been under arrest for 24 hours but has not yet been taken to a police station*).

This relevant time period (that is, the maximum period a person can be detained for) relates to the actual time spent in custody and not a 24-hour period in time. This means that every time the person is bailed the clock stops and usually continues from the time that the person returns to custody for the offence(s) for which he/she was bailed.

Where a person has been released and re-arrested for an offence, it is possible that the relevant time will start again. This is covered by s. 47(7) of the 1984 Act:

> (7) Where a person who was released on bail subject to a duty to attend at a police station is re-arrested, the provisions of this Part of this Act shall apply to him as they apply to a person arrested for the first time but this subsection does not apply to a person who is arrested under section 46A above or has attended a police station in accordance with the grant of bail (and who accordingly is deemed by section 34(7) above to have been arrested for an offence).

KEYNOTE

In cases where this subsection applies, the relevant time starts again and a fresh clock starts. This will apply where the person has been re-arrested for the same offence because of some new evidence (except at such time as when he/she is returning on bail at the appointed time) under s. 41(9) or 47(2).

Section 41 states:

> (9) A person released under subsection (7) above shall not be re-arrested without a warrant for the offence for which he was previously arrested unless new evidence justifying a further arrest has come to light since his release; but this subsection does not prevent an arrest under section 46A below.

Section 47 states:

> (2) Nothing in the Bail Act 1976 shall prevent the re-arrest without warrant of a person released on bail subject to a duty to attend at a police station if new evidence justifying a further arrest has come to light since his release.

KEYNOTE

The issue will be whether new evidence has come to light since the grant of bail and it will be a question of fact as to what the new evidence is. It is suggested that this must be evidence which was not available at the time the person was last in detention or which would not have been available even if all reasonable enquiries had been conducted.

It will always be important to check how much time is left on the person's 'relevant time' and when his/her next review is due.

15.5.2 The Three Stages of Pre-charge Detention

After the custody officer has authorised detention but before a person has been charged there are three distinct stages of detention. These are distinguished by the level at which authorisation for continuing detention is required.

The three stages of detention under the 1984 Act are:

- The basic period of detention, which is the period of detention up to 24 hours, as first authorised by the custody officer.
- Those authorised by an officer of the rank of superintendent or above (s. 42) up to 36 hours (**see para. 15.5.4**).
- Those authorised by a magistrates' court (ss. 43 and 44) up to a maximum of 96 hours (**see para. 15.5.5**).

Each of these is examined in detail below.

15.5.3 The Basic Period of Detention

The majority of people detained by the police are detained for less than six hours; most other cases are dealt with within 24 hours. If a person's continued detention is not authorised beyond 24 hours and the person is not charged with an offence, he/she *must* be released (with or without bail) and cannot be re-arrested for the offence unless new evidence comes to light (s. 41(7) and (9) of the 1984 Act). New evidence is not defined by the 1984 Act but it is suggested that it covers evidence which was not available at the time the person was detained, or which would not have been available if the investigating officers had conducted reasonable enquiries.

During this period of detention the custody officer has a responsibility to monitor whether the grounds for detention still exist. An officer of at least the rank of inspector not involved in the investigation (s. 40(1)(b)) must review the person's detention *at least once in the first six hours* and then, after the first review, *within nine hours of that review*. Further reviews must then be conducted *no later than nine hours after the last review* was conducted, until the person is either charged or released. The detention of persons in police custody not subject to the statutory review requirement in Code C, para. 15.1 should still be reviewed periodically as a matter of good practice (Code C, Note 15B); **see also para. 15.5.6**.

If a detained person is taken to hospital for medical treatment, the time at hospital and the period spent travelling to and from the hospital does not count towards the relevant time unless the person is asked questions for the purpose of obtaining evidence about an offence. Where questioning takes place, this period would count towards the relevant time and therefore the custody officer must be informed of it (s. 41(6)).

15.5.4 **Detention Authorised by an Officer of the Rank of Superintendent**

Under s. 42(1) of the Police and Criminal Evidence Act 1984, detention can only be authorised beyond 24 hours and up to a maximum of 36 hours from the relevant time if:

- an offence being investigated is a 'serious arrestable offence' (see s. 116 of the 1984 Act and **General Police Duties, chapter 2**); *and*
- an officer of the rank of superintendent or above who is responsible for the station at which the person is detained (referred to here as the authorising officer); *and*
- that that senior officer is satisfied that:
  - there is not sufficient evidence to charge; *and*
  - the investigation is being conducted diligently and expeditiously; *and*
  - that the person's detention is necessary to secure or preserve evidence relating to the offence or to obtain such evidence by questioning that person.

At this stage if the authorising officer considers that there is sufficient evidence to charge, he/she cannot authorise further detention beyond 24 hours unless the detained person is in custody for another serious arrestable offence for which further detention can be, authorised (*R v Samuel* [1988] QB 615 and Code C, para. 16.1).

The grounds for this continuing detention are the same as those when the custody officer made the initial decision to detain, with the additional requirements that the case has been conducted diligently and expeditiously. It is suggested that Article 5 of the European Convention requires this to be a consideration at all times of detention as a person's right to freedom is one of his/her human rights and any unnecessary periods of detention might be considered actionable. To be able to satisfy the senior officer of this, it will be necessary for the custody record to be available for inspection and details of what inquiries have been made and evidence that the investigation has been moving at a pace that will satisfy the senior officer that the inquires should not already have been completed.

The authorising officer (which here must be an officer of the rank of superintendent or above who is responsible for the station at which the person is detained) can authorise detention up to a maximum of 36 hours from the 'relevant time' of detention. The period can be shorter than this and can then be further authorised by that officer or any other officer of the rank of superintendent or above who is responsible for the station at which the person is detained to allow the period to be further extended up to the maximum 36-hour period (s. 42(2)). Code C, Note 15E gives guidance as to which officers this would include.

The extension of a person's detention by a superintendent or above must be made within 24 hours of the relevant time and cannot be made before at least two reviews have been carried out by a review officer under s. 40 of the 1984 Act (i.e. those normally carried out by an inspector) (s. 42(4)) (Code C, para. 15.2).

If an extension to the period of detention is authorised, a record must be made and shall state the number of hours and minutes by which the detention period is extended or further extended (Code C, para. 15.16).

For the situation regarding 'acting' ranks, **see General Police Duties, chapter 2**.

Section 42(5) to (8) mirrors the responsibility on the authorising officer at this stage with those of the review officer during the 'general period' of detention with regard to allowing representations, informing the detained person of the decision to authorise further detention and the need to record the decision. The main difference here is that the authorising

MAXIMUM PERIODS OF DETENTION FOR NON TERRORISM ACT OFFENCES

Arrest	Relevant time starts starts	Review clock relevant time	24 hours from detention	24 to 36 hours' detention	36 to 42 hours' detention	42 to 78 hours' detention	up to 96 hours'
Arrested locally.	24 hours from arrest or arrival at police station whichever earliest.		All offences other than serious arrestable offences.	Only serious arrestable offences.	Only serious arrestable offences.	Only serious arrestable offences.	Only serious arrestable offences.
Arrested outside England and Wales.	Time first arrives at police station in police area where matter being investigated or 24 hours after first entered England or Wales, whichever earliest.	Time custody officer authorises detention.	Release unless s. 41(1) applies.	Detention authorised by superintendent or above (s. 42).	Where delay in applying for warrant of further detention is reasonable (s. 43(5)).	First warrant for further detention issued by magistrates' court (s. 42).	Further warrants of detention issued by magistrates' court (s. 43).
Arrested for an offence in one police area in England or Wales then transferred to another police area for separate offence in that second police area which is also in England or Wales.	24 hours from time he/she leaves the police station in the first police area or the time he/she arrives at the first police station in second police area where the crime is being investigated provided not interviewed about the offence whilst detained in the first police area, whichever is the earliest.	This timing applies where the person was in detention for an offence in the first police area (s. 41(5)).			**See para. 15.5.5** for the dangers of not applying within the 36-hour period.	Remember the warrant can be applied for at any stage of detention.	

Voluntarily attends police station or accompanies constable to station but not under arrest.	Time of arrest.
Arrested in one police area in England or Wales for an offence in another police area in England or Wales, there being no 'local' offence(s) for which he/she has been arrested.	From time the suspect arrives at the first police station in the area he/she is being sought or from 24 hours after the time he/she is arrested or if questioned about the offence whilst in the first police area the relevant time starts from the time he/she first arrived at a police station in the first police area, whichever is the earliest.

officer must look into how the case is being investigated and whether this is being done diligently and expeditiously. Consequently, the authorising officer must also consider any representations on these points and these points should also be covered in any record as to whether detention should continue. When considering whether to authorise further detention the authorising officer must check whether the detained person has exercised his/her right to have someone informed and to consult with a legal representative. If these options have not been taken, s. 42(9) requires the authorising officer to inform the detained person of these rights and also whether he/she will be allowed to exercise these rights if it is a serious arrestable offence and the right has so far been delayed as per Code C, Annex B. The authorising officer should record the detainee's decision in the custody record and the grounds for denying the person those rights where appropriate.

If it is proposed to transfer a detained person from one police area to another for the purpose of investigating the offences for which he/she is detained, the authorising officer may take into consideration the period it will take to get to the other police area when deciding whether detention can go beyond 24 hours (s. 42(3)).

15.5.5   **Detention Authorised by a Magistrates' Court**

Once the 36-hour limit has been reached, a person's detention can only continue with the authority of the courts through the issuing of a warrant of further detention. If a person's continued detention is not authorised beyond 36 hours by a court and the person is not charged with an offence, he/she must be released with or without bail and cannot be re-arrested for the offence unless new evidence comes to light (as to new evidence, **see para. 15.5.1**).

Warrants of Further Detention

Applications for warrants of further detention are made at the magistrates' court. Initially, the magistrates can issue a warrant for further detention for a period of up to 36 hours. This can be extended by the courts on further applications by police up to a maximum total period of detention of 96 hours. The warrant will specify what period of further detention the court has authorised. If detention of the person is required for any longer period, further applications can be made to the court up to a maximum of 96 hours' detention. The grounds on which the court must decide whether to grant a warrant authorising further detention are the same as those that must be considered by a 'superintendent's review' (**see para. 15.5.4**).

Should it be necessary to apply for a warrant it is important that the time restraints are kept in mind at all times and the application procedure followed closely.

Procedure

The application is made in the magistrates' court and both the detained person and the police must be in attendance (s. 43(1) and (2) of the Police and Criminal Evidence Act 1984). The application is made by laying an information before the court. The officer making the application does so on oath and is subject to cross-examination (**see chapter 6**). Under s. 43(14) the information must set out:

- the nature of the offence;
- the general evidence on which the person was arrested;
- what inquiries have been made;
- what further inquiries are proposed; and
- why it is believed that continuing detention is necessary for the proposed inquiries.

It will be important to be able to demonstrate why the person needs to remain in detention while additional inquiries are made, for instance, that further facts need to be verified before further questioning of the suspect can continue and that this cannot be done effectively if the person is released. The detained person must be provided with a copy of the information before the matter can be heard (s. 43(2)). He/she is also entitled to be legally represented. If the person is not legally represented but then requests legal representation at court, the case must be adjourned to allow representation (s. 43(3)). In cases where the person is not represented it may be prudent to remind the person of his/her right to legal representation prior to the court hearing and to make a record of this in the custody record. Should the detained person choose to be legally represented at court, and thereby try and delay the police investigation, s. 43(3)(b) allows the person to be taken back into police detention during the adjournment.

Timing of the application

If it appears likely that the investigation of the serious arrestable offence requires the person's detention to go beyond 36 hours, then thought must be given as to when to make the application to the magistrates' court. Section 43(5) allows the application to be made before the expiry of the 36-hour period (calculated from the relevant time) or, where it has not been practicable for the court to sit within the 36-hour period, the application can be made within the next six hours. There are dangers in applying outside the 36-hour period in that if the court feels that it would have been reasonable to make the application within the 36-hour period then it must refuse the application for the warrant regardless of the merits of the case (s. 43(7)).

The court may either refuse the application or adjourn the hearing until such time as it specifies up to the end of the 36-hour period of detention (s. 43(8)). If the application is refused, the person must be charged or released with or without bail at the expiry of the current permissible period of detention (s. 43(15)).

The application for the warrant can be made at any time, *even before a superintendent's review has been carried out.* If the application is made within the 36-hour period and it is refused, it does not mean the person must be released straight away. Section 43(16) allows the person to be detained until the end of the current detention period (24 hours or 36 hours). The benefit of an early application has to be set against the risk that, once the court has refused an application, it is not allowed to hear any further applications for a warrant of further detention unless new evidence has come to light since the application was refused (s. 43(17)). Code C, Note 15D gives guidance on when an application should be made to the court. Note 15D states:

> An application to a magistrates' court under PACE, sections 43 or 44 for a warrant of further detention or its extension should be made between 10 am and 9 pm, and if possible during normal court hours. It will not usually be practicable to arrange for a court to sit specially outside the hours of 10 am to 9 pm. If it appears a special sitting may be needed outside normal court hours but between 10 am and 9 pm, the clerk to the justices should be given notice and informed of this possibility, while the court is sitting if possible.

In *R v Slough Justices, ex parte Stirling* [1987] Crim LR 576, the 36-hour period expired at 12.53 pm. The case was not heard by the justices until 2.45 pm. The Divisional Court held that the police should have made their application between 10.30 am and 11.30 am, even though this was before the 36-hour time limit had been reached.

In monitoring a person's detention, officers should be mindful of whether a warrant for further detention may be required and, if it is, consider whether a court will be available to hear the application. If a court will not be available then consideration should be given to making an earlier application. The process the magistrates go through in deciding the merits of the application also provides some safeguards in that the person's continued detention has been considered by the courts and therefore may reduce the likelihood of the defence suggesting that detention was not justified. If a warrant for further detention, or extension, is granted under s. 43 or 44, a record shall be made stating the detention period authorised by the warrant and the date and time it was granted (Code C, para. 15.16).

Applying to Extend Warrants of Further Detention

Under s. 44 of the 1984 Act, the process for applying to extend the warrant follows the same procedure as for the initial warrant, with the exception that the application *must be* made before the expiry of the extension given in the previous warrant. Once the period of detention that has been authorised has expired, and no other applications have been made, the detained person must be charged or released with or without bail.

Terrorism Cases

In terrorism cases the application to the magistrates' court is very similar except that the application must be made by a superintendent. The officer who makes the application may also apply to the court for an order that specified information upon which he/she intends to rely should be withheld from the person to whom the application relates and anyone representing him/her. Section 75 of the Criminal Justice and Police Act 2001 allows for the use of video links for proceedings about Terrorism Act 2000 detention. The order to withhold information can only be made if one of the following applies:

- evidence of an offence under any of the provisions mentioned in s. 40(1)(a) of the Terrorism Act 2000 (**see para. 16.7.6**) would be interfered with or harmed;
- the recovery of property obtained as a result of an offence under any of those provisions would be hindered;
- the recovery of property in respect of which a forfeiture order could be made under s. 23 of the Terrorism Act 2000 would be hindered;
- the apprehension, prosecution or conviction of a person who is suspected of committing offences under the Terrorism Act 2000 would be made more difficult as a result of his/her being alerted;
- the prevention of an act of terrorism would be made more difficult as a result of the person being alerted;
- the gathering of information about the commission, preparation or instigation of an act of terrorism would be interfered with; or
- a person would be interfered with or physically injured;
- the detained person has committed an offence to which Part VI of the Criminal Justice Act 1988 applies (any indictable offence and others listed in sch. 4 to the Criminal Justice Act 1988), has benefited from the offence, and the recovery of the value of that benefit would be hindered if the information were disclosed

(sch. 8, pt III to the Terrorism Act 2000).

15.5.6   The Review

While a person is in police detention (**see para. 15.4.1**) before charge, his/her detention must be reviewed by an officer of the rank of inspector or above (inspector reviews). This review acts as another safeguard to protect the detained person's right to be detained for only such periods as are necessary to allow for the investigation of an offence. Reviews of police detention are covered by s. 40 of the Police and Criminal Evidence Act 1984.

Section 40(3) sets out the times when reviews must be conducted:

(3) Subject to subsection (4) . . . —
    (a) the first review shall be not later than six hours after the detention was first authorised;
    (b) the second review shall be not later than nine hours after the first;
    (c) subsequent reviews shall be at intervals of not more than nine hours.

KEYNOTE

Review officer for the purposes of ss. 40 and 40A of the 1984 Act means, in the case of a person arrested but not charged, an officer of at least inspector rank not directly involved in the investigation and, if a person has been arrested and charged, the custody officer. In cases under the Terrorism Act 2000, the review officer means an officer not directly involved in the investigation connected with the detention and of at least inspector rank, for reviews within 24 hours of the detainee's arrest or a superintendent for all other reviews.

It is suggested that even where a detainee is not in police detention as defined by s. 118 of the 1984 Act, consideration should be given to reviewing his/her detention. A case that supports this view is *Chief Constable of Cleveland Police v McGrogan* [2002] 1 FLR 707. This was a case involving a person detained at a police station overnight after having been arrested for breach of the peace, the Court of Appeal held the need to regularly review the person's detention was required even though breach of the peace was not an 'offence' for the purpose of s. 118.

The periods set out in s. 40(3) are the *maximum* periods that a review can be left; should the review officer wish to review before this time for operational reasons etc., the review could be brought forward. The first review must be made within six hours of the custody officer authorising detention (this, it must be remembered, is not the time from which the 24-hour clock starts, i.e. the time the detainee came into the station, but the time at which the custody officer authorised detention). Thereafter, each review must be made within nine hours of the last review.

For the situation regarding 'acting' ranks, **see General Police Duties, chapter 2.**

Section 40(4) does allow reviews to be delayed if it is not practicable to carry out the review. Conducting late reviews should be avoided where at all possible (*see Roberts v Chief Constable of Cheshire Constabulary* [1999] 1 WLR 662). If delayed, the grounds for and extent of any delay must be recorded (Code C, para. 15.13).

Section 40(4) provides two other occasions where it may be justified to delay the review:

- if at that time the person in detention is being questioned by a police officer and the review officer is satisfied that an interruption of the questioning for the purpose of carrying out the review would prejudice the investigation in connection with which he/she is being questioned;

- if at that time no review officer is readily available.

It is suggested that it will be necessary to justify why no review officer was available and it is suggested that where it is known that a review may fall during an interview that it is conducted prior to the interview where appropriate.

In *Roberts*, the defendant had his first review conducted 8 hours, 20 minutes after his detention had been authorised. The Court of Appeal held that under s. 40(1)(b) of the 1984 Act a review of his detention should have taken place by an officer of the rank of inspector or above six hours after detention was first authorised. Section 34(1) was mandatory and provided that a person must not be kept in police detention except in accordance with the relevant provisions of the Act. Therefore, the respondent's detention had been unlawful unless some event occurred to have made it lawful.

The court made it clear that the 1984 Act existed in order to ensure members of the public were not detained except in certain defined circumstances. In the absence of a review, the time spent in detention between 5.25 am, and 7.45 am meant that for that period the defendant's detention was unlawful and amounted to a false imprisonment.

Where a review is due under s. 40 and the detainee has not been charged, the review officer, in limited circumstances, may conduct the review by telephone. The conditions where this is permissible are: that the use of video conferencing facilities does not apply or it is not reasonably practicable to use such facilities (s. 45A of the 1984 Act but not yet in force) and it is not reasonably practicable for the review officer to attend the station holding the detainee, e.g. when severe weather conditions or an unforeseen operational emergency prevent the review officer form attending (Code C, para. 15.9 and Note 15F). Where this review is done by telephone, an officer at the station holding the detainee must fulfil the reviewing officer's obligations under PACE (see Code C, para. 15.10). Code C, para. 15.11 identifies the methods that can be used to ensure that the right of the detainee, appropriate adult and solicitor to make representations to the reviewing officer under Code C, para. 15.3 are satisfied: for example by fax, email message or orally by telephone. The use of telephone to conduct reviews does not include reviews to extend the period of detention beyond the 24-hour clock. Where the review is conducted by telephone, a record must be made of the following: the reason the review officer did not attend the station holding the detainee; the place the review officer was; and the method representations were made to the review officer (Code C, para. 15.14).

Telephone reviews do not apply to reviews of detention after charge by the custody officer or to reviews under the Terrorism Act 2000, sch. 8, pt II in terrorism cases (Code C, Note 15F).

If the review is delayed then it must still be conducted as soon as practicable and the reason for the delay must be recorded in the custody record by the review officer. In these circumstances the nine-hour period until the next review is calculated from the latest time the review should have been carried out and not from the time it was actually carried out. For instance, if the review was due at 3.15 pm and was delayed until 4 pm, the next review would have to be conducted no later than 12.15 am and not 1 am. When the review is conducted the review officer does not have to authorise detention for the full nine-hour period; he/she could decide that the case should be reviewed again within a shorter period and the review decision would reflect this.

When reviewing the detention of a person the review officer goes through the same process as the custody officer did when detention was first authorised (s. 40(8)), namely by asking:

- Is there sufficient evidence to charge? If 'yes', charge or release the person with or without bail. If 'no', then:
- Is detention necessary in order to secure or preserve evidence or is it necessary to detain the person in order to obtain such evidence by questioning him/her? If 'yes', authorise continued detention. If 'no', release the person with or without bail.

The situation may arise where the review officer considers that there is sufficient evidence to charge and authorises detention to charge even though the custody officer disagrees. In this case it is suggested that the custody officer must either charge or release the person with or without bail. The custody officer may wish to refer the matter to an officer of the rank of superintendent or above responsible for the station for advice.

It is suggested that the reviewing officer (or any other officer other than a superintendent or above) cannot tell the custody officer what they must do. The reviewing officer may wish to give advice but it will be for the custody officer to decide whether to take that advice. Clearly failure to do so could lead to internal criticism but legally there is no requirement to follow that advice.

If there is not sufficient evidence to charge, the review officer may want to consider the question: 'If this person is bailed what evidence will be lost'? If the answer is none, continued detention would seem unlawful.

As stated above, it is suggested that Article 5 of the European Convention requires that an investigation must be conducted diligently and expeditiously in order to minimise the time a person is deprived of his/her liberty (particularly where the case does not lead to a prosecution). In order to monitor the effectiveness of the investigation and the time spent in custody, the reviewing officer should consider the period of detention since the last review to ensure that any defect in the person's treatment is corrected, and where necessary, take steps to speed up the investigation.

In cases where it has been decided that a person should be charged but he/she has been detained because he/she is not in a fit state to be charged (s. 37(9)), the review officer must determine whether the person is yet in a fit state. If the detainee is in a fit state, the custody officer should be informed that the person should be charged or released. If the detainee is not in a fit state, detention can be authorised for a further period (s. 40(9)). In such cases, if the person is still unfit, it may be prudent to consider the welfare of the detained person.

During the process of reviewing a person's detention, the review officer must give the detained person (unless he/she is asleep) or any solicitor representing the detained person who is available at the time of the review, an opportunity to make representations about his/her continued detention (s. 40(12)). If the detained person is likely to be asleep at the time the review is to be carried out, the review should be brought forward to allow the detained person to be present at the time of the review (Code C, Note 15C). If the detainee is asleep when the reviewing officer authorises his/her continued detention, the detainee must be informed of the decision when he/she wakes (Code C, para. 15.7) and the details of the officer that informed the detainee of the decision should also be recorded (Code C, para. 15.16). If the detainee makes a comment it may be necessary to inform the reviewing officer (or his/her replacement) of the comment (Code C, para. 15.5). The review officer must also ensure that the detained person is reminded of his/her right to free legal advice and that this reminder is recorded in the custody record (Code C, para. 15.4). In the case of juveniles, the appropriate adult should also be allowed to make representations and the review officer has the discretion to allow other people having an interest in the welfare of the detained person to make representations (Code C, para. 15.3). These representations may be in writing or oral (s. 40(13)). If made in writing, the document should be retained (Code C, para. 15.15). The review officer can refuse to hear oral representations from the detained person if the review officer considers that the person is unfit to make such representations, either because of his/her condition or behaviour (e.g. drunk or violent) (Code C, para. 15.3B). A detainee who is not asleep during the review must be present when the grounds for his/her continued detention are recorded and must at the same time be informed of those grounds unless the review officer considers the person is incapable of understanding what is said, is violent or likely to become violent or in urgent need of medical attention (Code C, Note 15C); any comment made by the detainee should be recorded (Code C, para. 15.5). However, the review officer must not put any questions to the person about his/her comments (Code C, para. 15.6). Also, as the role of review officer is intended to be independent of the investigation, he/she should not put any questions to the person about his/her involvement in any offence; this mirrors the instruction to custody officers (Code C, para. 15.6).

If at any stage an officer of a rank higher than the review officer gives directions which are at variance with a decision made or action taken by the review officer, or which would have been made by the review officer but for the directions by the more senior officer, then s. 40(11) requires the matter to be referred *at once* to an officer of the rank of superintendent or above who is *responsible for the police station*.

It is important to understand the difference between the action of authorising an extension to the 'detention clock' and the role of the review officer. These are two distinct roles and both need to be carried out. When an officer of the rank of superintendent or above extends the 'relevant time' period this is not automatically a review (although there is nothing to stop that officer from conducting the review). This means that the 'reviewing' officer may still have to conduct a review even though the relevant time has only recently been extended, unless the officer of the rank of superintendent or above extending the relevant time has shown the review as having been conducted in the custody record.

Terrorism Act Reviews

(See also General Police Duties, chapter 4.)

In cases where the person has been detained under the Terrorism Act 2000 the first review should be conducted as soon as reasonably practicable after his/her arrest and then at least every 12 hours; after 24 hours it must be conducted by an officer of the rank of superintendent or above. Once a warrant of further detention has been obtained there is no requirement to conduct further reviews. If an officer of higher rank than the review officer gives directions relating to the detained person, and those directions are at variance with the performance by the review officer of a duty imposed on him/her then he/she must refer the matter at once to an officer of at least the rank of superintendent.

A review officer may only authorise a person's continued detention if he/she is satisfied that it is necessary:

- in order to obtain relevant evidence whether by questioning the person or otherwise;
- to preserve relevant evidence;

- pending a decision whether to apply to the Secretary of State for a deportation notice to be served on the detained person;

- pending the making of an application to the Secretary of State for a deportation notice to be served on the detained person;

- pending consideration by the Secretary of State whether to serve a deportation notice on the detained person; or

- pending a decision whether the detained person should be charged with an offence.

In all cases the review officer must be satisfied that the matter is being dealt with diligently and expeditiously. Where the detained person's rights to a solicitor have been withheld or he/she is being held *incommunicado* at the time of the review, the review officer must consider whether the reason or reasons for which the delay was authorised continue to exist. If in his/her opinion the reason or reasons no longer exist, he/she must inform the officer who authorised the delay of his/her opinion. When recording the grounds for the review the officer must also include his/her conclusion on whether there is a continuing need to withhold the detained person's rights.

In cases where the person is detained under the Terrorism Act 2000 and the review officer does not authorise continued detention, the person does not have to be released if an application for a warrant for further detention is going to be applied for or if an application has been made and the result is pending (s. 41 and sch. 8).

15.6   Cautioning, Reprimands and Final Warnings

There are occasions where a person for whom there is sufficient evidence to charge may be cautioned as an alternative method of disposing with the case. *R* v *Chief Constable of Lancashire Constabulary, ex parte Atkinson* (1998) 162 JP 275 is a case which considered the level of evidence required before a caution can be considered. There the court said that, provided it was clear that there had been an admission of guilt, it was not necessary, for the purposes of administering a caution, to show that the admission had been obtained in circumstances which satisfied the Codes of Practice. That was not to say that police authorities would not be well advised to take precautions which would satisfy the Code, but it did not follow that in every case there had to be a formal interview. However, police officers would be well advised to take precautions that would satisfy Code C. It would be both fairer and more reliable for a formal interview to take place.

Before making a case disposal decision it is essential that the matter has been fully investigated in order to reach an informed decision. In *Omar* v *Chief Constable of Bedfordshire Constabulary* (2002) unreported, the Divisional Court quashed a caution that had been administered in order to allow a prosecution to be pursued. The court held that a number of reasonable lines of enquiry had not been made, for instance, the police had failed to take a statement from the victim's friend or obtained CCTV that was available or fully investigated the victim's injuries. Further, that the length of time in custody (17 hours) should not have been a relevant consideration and that the suspect's admission was ambiguous. Therefore it was in the public interest that a decision to caution rather that to change should not prevent the subsequent pursuit of the prosecution of the offender.

While there is no general obligation on the police to disclose material prior to charge, there may be a need to make some disclosure to a suspect's legal representative in order that he/she can advise on whether a caution should be accepted (*DPP* v *Ara* [2001] 4 All ER 559). In *Ara*, the suspect had been interviewed without a legal representative being present but the officers refused to disclose the terms of the interview.

Guidance as to the use of cautioning is provided by Home Office Circular 18/94 and the relevant sections are reproduced in **appendix 4**. The guidelines should be considered carefully in all cases as any decision can be challenged by judicial review (**see para. 2.6.4**).

Sections 65 and 66 of the Crime and Disorder Act 1998 have made new provisions for reprimands and final warnings for children and young persons (**see chapter 7**) which the custody officer must take into account as alternatives to prosecution.

In order to show consistency and, if necessary, to justify the decision to give or refuse to give a caution, the grounds for the decision should be recorded.

There is only one exception to the rule that reprimands and warnings replace cautions, and that is in respect of prostitutes' cautions. This approach to dealing with child prostitutes recognises that they are victims of abuse, and do not consent freely to prostitution. Joint guidance issued by the Home Office and the Department of Health sets out the appropriate way to deal with children in prostitution. That treatment aims to divert children away from prostitution, rather than to prosecute them (**see Crime, chapter 10**).

15.7 Charging

The custody officer must decide whether there is sufficient evidence to charge a person when he/she is first brought to the police station (s. 37(1) of the 1984 Act) and when an officer informs them that he/she considers there is sufficient evidence to provide a realistic prospect of the detainee's conviction (Code C, para. 16.1). If the custody officer decides that there is sufficient evidence to charge, then he/she must charge that person or release him/her without charge, unless officers are still investigating other offences for which the person is in police detention. Similarly, if the custody officer considers that detention is not required, or is no longer required in order to obtain or secure evidence, the person should be released with or without bail attached to the release (s. 37(2)).

It is the custody officer's responsibility to ensure that there is sufficient evidence to charge the person. Where a person is charged in the absence of sufficient evidence (particularly if they are kept in custody), this could lead to a breach of Article 5 of the European Convention, as well as a breach of the PACE Codes of Practice.

Where a detained person is not in a fit state to be charged or released in accordance with s. 34(7) (for instance because he/she is drunk), he/she may be kept in custody until fit (but medical care may have to be considered).

(See also the provisions relating to drunk drivers in **Road Traffic, chapter 5**.)

Even where there is sufficient evidence to prosecute successfully, the detained person may be released without charge because it is felt that a charge is not in the public interest or the person has been cautioned or a decision has not yet been made about prosecuting the person. In this case, the person must be informed when he/she is released that the decision to prosecute has not yet been made (s. 37(8)).

In cases where a person is bailed without being charged, the custody officer cannot impose conditions on that bail (s. 47(1A)).

If a decision is taken to charge the detained person, Code C, para. 16 sets out the procedures to be followed by the custody officer. When a detained person is charged with, or informed that he/she may be prosecuted for an offence, para. 16.2 requires him/her to be cautioned. The caution varies slightly from that when arrested or interviewed (**see General Police Duties, chapter 2**) and is as follows:

You do not have to say anything. But it may harm your defence if you do not mention now something which you later rely on in court. Anything you do say may be given in evidence.

The above caution should not be used in circumstances where the detained person has been denied access to a solicitor (**see para. 17.3**) in which case the following cautions should be used:

> You do not have to say anything, but anything you do say may be given in evidence.

At the time a person is charged, he/she shall be given a written notice as set out in Code C, para. 16.3 and a record shall be made of anything the person says when charged (para. 16.8). Where the person being charged is a juvenile or is mentally disordered or mentally impaired, the appropriate adult should be present and the notice given to him/her (paras 16.3 and 16.6).

Once the person has been charged with or informed that he/she may be prosecuted for an offence, fingerprints can be taken if it is a recordable offence and he/she has not had his/her fingerprints taken during the course of the investigation (s. 61(3)(b)) (**see chapter 16**). Photographs may also be taken and in some cases DNA samples may be taken (**see para. 16.7**).

If fingerprints are taken, the person must be informed of the reason why and that those prints may be used for a speculative search concerning other crimes (**see para. 16.5**). The reasons should also be recorded in the custody record, along with confirmation that the detained person has been given the required information. If the person's photograph is taken, this should also be recorded in the custody record.

Once a person has been charged or informed that he/she may be prosecuted for an offence (which does not include the service of the Notice of Intended Prosecution under ss. 1 and 2 of the Road Traffic Offenders Act 1988; **see Road Traffic, chapter 3**), generally the person cannot be questioned or spoken to about the matter. Code C, paras 16.4 and 16.5 set out occasions where further investigation involving the person may be allowed and para. 16.9 sets out the procedure to be adopted. It should only be in these circumstances that the custody officer allows any further inquiries involving the detained person to be made. Paragraphs 16.4 and 16.5 deal with:

- written statements made by other people which the investigating officers may wish to show to another person charged;

- questions necessary for the purpose of preventing or minimising harm or loss to some other person or to the public or for clearing up an ambiguity in a previous answer or statement;

- where it is in the interests of justice that the person should have put to him/her—and have an opportunity to comment on—information concerning the offence which has come to light since he/she was charged or informed that he/she might be prosecuted.

15.8 **Bail**

If the person is charged then the custody officer has to decide whether the person is going to be bailed to appear at court or whether bail will be refused and the person kept in custody until the next available court. This is a review of the person's detention and therefore the person or his/her solicitor should be given an opportunity to make representations to the custody officer. The review should be conducted with regard to Code C, paras 15.1, 15.3–15.3B, 15.5 to 15.7.

Where bail has been refused this decision must be reviewed by the custody officer at least every nine hours until the person is taken to court in the same manner required by a review officer.

In addition to the grounds for refusing bail covered in **chapter 5**, the custody officer may also detain the person after charge if he/she has reasonable grounds for believing that the detention of the person is necessary to enable a sample to be taken from him/her under s. 63B of the Police and Criminal Evidence Act 1984 (**see para. 15.9**). The custody officer may not authorise a person to be kept in police detention for a period exceeding six hours beginning when the person was charged with the offence.

For occassions where the custody officer refuses bail of a juvenile after charge, see Code C, para. 16.7.

For a full discussion of bail, **see chapter 5**.

In *Williamson* v *Chief Constable of West Midlands, The Times*, 11 March 2003, the Court of Appeal clarified the point that breach of the peace is not a criminal offence. Consequently, as there is no power in the Bail Act 1976 to grant bail except in criminal proceedings, no power exists to grant bail for breach of the peace. This means that if the person is bailed, there is no power to arrest the person or obtain a warrant for his/her failure to appear at court under the Bail Act 1976.

15.9 Custody Officer's Checklist

The following provides a guide to be followed when a person is brought to the police station. The PACE Code of Practice C applies throughout and custody officers should be conversant with its contents.

Throughout the period of detention of a person there are occasions where information must be given to that person. The Codes do allow these requirements to be delayed in certain circumstances, i.e. the detained person is violent or likely to become violent, or is incapable of understanding what is being said or is in need of urgent medical treatment (Code C, para. 1.8). If the detained person is not informed at the time, he/she must be informed as soon as practicable. Where the person is incapable of understanding what is being said because of a language or hearing barrier, action must be taken to obtain an interpreter so that the information can be relayed to the detained person (Code C, para. 3.12).

Initial Action when Commencing Custody Officer's Duties

- Ensure a poster as set out in Code C, para. 6.3 and Note 6H is displayed in the charge room and copies of the Codes of Practice are readily available (para. 1.2).

- Ensure cells that might be used comply with paras 8.2 and 8.4.

- Ensure that suitable blankets etc. will be available (para. 8.3).

- If video cameras are installed in the custody areas, notices of such cameras must be prominently displayed (para. 3.11). (Any request to turn the cameras off shall be refused.) Any audio or video recording made in the custody area does not form part of the custody record (para. 2.1).

On Arrival of the Arrested Person (including people transferred from other police stations)

- Begin custody record even if detention is not authorised (para. 2.1).

- Inform the arrested person of his/her rights (para. 3.1).

- If an appropriate adult is present or required, follow the guidance in paras 3.15 and 3.17.

- Provide the detained person with a written notice setting out his/her rights (para. 3.2 and Note 3A).

- Ask the person to sign the custody record to acknowledge receipt of the notice or note refusal to sign in the custody record (para 3.2).

- Undertake a risk assessment for the detainee (para. 3.6).

When making records concerning a detained person, all entries must be made in the custody record unless otherwise specified (para. 2.1). Action taken by a person must be noted in the custody record with the person's name and rank, except for officers dealing with persons detained under the Terrorism Act 2000 (para. 2.2) or where para. 2.6A applies.

Risk Assessments

The Custody Officer is responsible for initiating a risk assessment to consider whether the detainee is likely to present specific risks to custody staff or themselves (Code C, para. 3.6). Although the risk assessment is the responsibility of the custody officer, he/she may need to consult with others such as the arresting officer or an appropriate health care professional. The risk assessment, which includes a check on the Police National Computer, should be carried out as soon as practicable and reasons for delaying the completion of the assessment must be recorded. (Code C, para. 3.6). This process is ongoing and further assessments must be undertaken if circumstances change (Code C, paras 3.9 and 3.10). The risk assessment must follow a structured process which clearly defines the categories of risk to be considered, guidance is given in Home Office Circular 32/2000, Annex A (**See appendix 9**). The result of the risk assessment must be included within the custody record and the custody officer is responsible for making sure that those responsible for the detainee's custody are appropriately briefed about the risks (Code C, para. 3.8). The custody officer is also responsible for ensuring action is taken to minimise any risks that are identified (Code C, para. 3.9). For this reason it is suggested that the risk assessment should be completed prior to the detainee being placed in a cell or detention room.

Where the custody officer consults an appropriate health care professional and he/she has any doubts or is in any way uncertain about any aspect of the clinical directions given, he/she must ask for clarification. It is particularly important that directions concerning the frequency of visits are clear, precise and capable of being implemented (Code C, para. 9.14).

Special Groups

- If the person is deaf or there is doubt over his/her hearing or understanding of English refer to para. 3.12 and paras 13.1 to 13.11 of Code C (use of interpreters). The custody officer, or any other interviewing officer, must ensure that there is a proper mutual understanding between the detained person and the interpreter (or interpreters, if it is necessary to have more than one interpreter to allow the detained person to understand and be understood) (*R* v *West London Youth Court, ex parte J* [2000] 1 All ER 823).

- If the person is blind or seriously visually impaired or is unable to read, refer to para. 3.20.

- If the detained person could be a juvenile (para. 1.5), obtain the services of an appropriate adult.

- If the person is mentally disordered or vunerable (for people that fall in to this group, see Note 1G), obtain the services of an appropriate adult.

Decision to Authorise Detention? (see para. 15.4.7)

- Arresting officer to give the reasons of arrest (in the presence of the arrested person) (para. 3.4).

- Record any comment made by that person in response to the arresting officer's account (para. 3.4).

- Make a decision whether to authorise detention or release with or without bail (para. 3.4).

- Note any comment made by the detained person (para. 3.4).

If detention is authorised, record the reasons in the custody record and inform the detained person of the decision (paras 3.4 and 3.23). (If the detained person is violent, likely to become violent or incapable of understanding what is being said (but if due to hearing/language barriers consider para. 3.12), or is in need of urgent medical treatment he/she *must* be informed as soon as practicable (para. 1.8 and s. 37(6) of the 1984 Act).)

If the person has already been in custody for the offence for which he/she has been arrested and a new detention clock has not started, it will be necessary to confirm that the person still has time left within his/her 'detention period'. The review clock is also relevant in terms of when the next review is due. (If the person has been arrested for an offence for which he/she has been bailed and there is 'new evidence', the detention clock starts again (s. 41(9)) unless this person is returning to answer his/her bail on time.)

New evidence may be described as evidence that was not in existence at the time of arrest or when the detained person was granted bail (e.g. the results of fingerprint analysis sent off for comparison).

Ascertain whether Detained Person requires Legal Advice

- Ask the detained person if he/she wants legal advice (para. 3.5) and point out that legal advice is free (para. 6.1).

- Ask the detained person to sign the custody record to indicate whether he/she requires legal advice and ensure he/she signs it in the right place (para. 3.5).

- If legal advice is requested it must be given unless Annex B to Code C applies or delay would hinder the investigation (para. 6.6). If any delay occurs, record the reason (para. 1.1A).

- If delay is not authorised, the custody officer must act without delay to secure the provision of legal advice (para. 6.5).

- If the offer of legal advice is declined, point out the right to speak to a solicitor on the phone (para. 6.5).

- If legal advice is still declined, ask the detained person for reasons why and record any reasons given in the custody record (if during interview this can be recorded in the interview record) (para. 6.5). Once it is clear that the detained person does not wish to have any contact with a legal adviser, the custody officer should cease to ask why (para. 6.5).

When complying with the need to provide legal advice the following should be considered:

- For the treatment of the detained person who is to be interviewed or continue to be interviewed once he/she has requested legal advice, see para. 6.6.

- Remember that this is a continuing right that can be exercised at any time during police detention (para. 6.1).

- Note 6B provides guidance on how much choice the detained person has in choosing a solicitor.

- For those persons who can provide legal advice under the Codes of Practice, see para. 6.12. Refer to paras 6.12A to 6.14 if refusing an adviser access.

- If a solicitor arrives to provide legal advice, inform the detained person unless Annex B applies (para. 6.15).

- If the detained person cannot understand the solicitor because of a language barrier refer to para. 13.9 (people who can act as interpreters).

- Consultation with a solicitor must be in private (para. 6.1) with the exception of those detained on terrorism charges. See Note 6J.

Right to Inform Third Party

In addition to a request to have someone informed, the following action must be taken:

- Contact must be made with a juvenile's appropriate adult (para. 3.13).
- For detained persons who are citizens of independent commonwealth countries or foreign nationals, see paras 7.1 to 7.5.

Ascertain whether the detained person wants a third party informed of his/her detention. Should the detained person at any stage request that a person be informed of his/her arrest, consider whether this right should be delayed. This right can only be delayed in circumstances outlined in Annex B to Code C, otherwise paras 5.1 to 5.3 and 5.8 must be followed. If the detained person has no one to contact, see Note 5C for guidance.

The detained person has the right to send letters and make phone calls (paras 5.6 to 5.8) but this can be delayed (para. 5.6).

If a person inquires about a detained person, refer to para. 5.5 and Note 5D. Consideration should also be given to the Data Protection Act 1998 when information is being given to third parties.

Visits are covered by para. 5.4 and Note 5B.

Searching

The proper searching of a detained person is very important, particularly with the introduction of the Human Rights Act 1998. It may lead to the discovery of new evidence, it may also avoid people being injured or even escaping from police detention. The law governing the searching of people on arrest and searches under warrant is discussed elsewhere (**see General Police Duties, chapter 2**).

Section 54 of the Police and Criminal Evidence Act 1984 details the duties and powers relating to the searching of detained persons:

(1) The custody officer at a police station shall ascertain and record or cause to be recorded everything which a person has with him when he is—
  (a) brought to the station after being arrested elsewhere or after being committed to custody by an order or sentence of a court; or
  (b) arrested at the station or detained there, as a person falling within section 34(7), under section 37 above.

(2) In the case of an arrested person the record shall be made as part of his custody record.

(3) Subject to subsection (4) below, a custody officer may seize and retain any such thing or cause any such thing to be seized and retained.

(4) Clothes and personal effects may only be seized if the custody officer—
  (a) believes that the person from whom they are seized may use them—
    (i) to cause physical injury to himself or any other person;
    (ii) to damage property;
    (iii) to interfere with evidence; or
    (iv) to assist him to escape; or
  (b) has reasonable grounds for believing that they may be evidence relating to an offence.

(5) Where anything is seized, the person from whom it is seized shall be told the reason for the seizure unless he is—
  (a) violent or likely to become violent; or
  (b) incapable of understanding what is said to him.

(6) Subject to subsection (7) below, a person maybe searched if the custody officer considers it necessary to enable him to carry out his duty under subsection (1) above and to the extent that the custody officer considers necessary for that purpose.
  (6A) A person who is in custody at a police station or is in police detention otherwise than at a police station may at any time be searched in order to ascertain whether he has with him anything which he could use for any of the purposes specified in subsection(4)(a) above.

(6B) Subject to subsection (6C) below, a constable may seize and retain, or cause to be seized and retained, anything found on such a search.

(6C) A constable may only seize clothes and personal effects in the circumstances specified in subsection (4) above.

(7) An intimate search may not be conducted under this section.

(8) A search under this section shall be carried out by a constable.

(9) The constable carrying out a search shall be of the same sex as the person searched.

KEYNOTE

Section 54 places a duty on a custody officer to ascertain and make a record of what property a person has with him/her when:

- arrested and brought to the station;

- committed to police custody by order of the court;

- arrested at the station;

- detained after surrendering to bail;

- arrested after failing to surrender to bail.

The custody officer must also consider what property the detained person might have in his/her possession for an unlawful or harmful purpose while in custody. The safekeeping of any property taken from the detained person and kept at the police station, is the responsibility of the custody officer.

The custody officer must record in the custody record, all property brought to the police station or which was taken from the detained person at the time of arrest (Code C, para. 4.4). The only exceptions to this requirement are items which, by virtue of their nature, quantity or size, it was not practicable to bring to the police station (Code C, Note 4B).

The Search

While the custody officer has a duty to ascertain what property a person has with them (often by means of searching the person), there is also a need to consider the rights of that detained person. The custody officer may authorise a constable to search a detained person, or may search the detained person themselves in order to ascertain what property the detained person has with them (s. 54(6)). It should be noted that the custody officer must first authorise any search and the extent of the search; officers should not search a person until this authority has been given. Therefore the custody officer may only authorise a search to the extent that he/she considers necessary to comply with this duty. In order to safeguard the rights of the detained person there are three levels to which searches can be conducted:

- searches that do not involve the removal of more than the detained person's outer clothing (this includes the removal of shoes and socks (Code C, Annex A, para. 9));

- strip searches;

- intimate searches.

Each of these is examined below.

If the detained person is not going to be placed in a cell and is only going to be kept in detention for a short period, the custody officer has the option not to search (Code C, Note 4A). If no search is conducted the custody record should be endorsed 'not searched'. Under health and safety it may be appropriate for the custody officer to complete a risk assessment in order to consider whether to search the detained person and balance the risk of injury to staff—this is likely to form part of the risk assessment required by Code C, para. 3.6. The duty to ascertain what property a person has with them is a continuing duty and therefore the custody officer can have the person searched at a later time if he/she feels it is necessary to comply with his/her responsibility under the 1984 Act or the Codes.

The extent of the search is determined by the custody officer on the basis of what he/she honestly believes is necessary in order to comply with the above duties. Both the decision to search the detained person and the extent of the search must be decided on the facts of the case in question. It may be important to consider cultural issues that might affect the detained person, for instance would it be necessary and justifiable to search a Seikh's turban? Force standing orders are not an automatic right to search all detained persons (*Brazil* v *Chief Constable of Surrey* [1983] Crim LR 483). A custody officer can authorise a strip search but an intimate search can only be authorised by an officer of the rank of inspector or above (see below).

Searches that do not involve the removal of more than the detained person's outer clothing

In effect this is any search that does not become a strip search or an intimate search. This type of search applies to almost every person coming before the custody officer unless Code C, Note 4A applies. Typically this will involve emptying out all items that are in the person's pockets, removing jewellery and the searching of other areas that can be conducted without the need to remove more than outer garments such as coats and possibly items such as jumpers. This type of authorisation would also lend itself to a 'pat down' of the detained person. If there is any doubt as to whether the search goes beyond one that falls into this category, it is suggested that it should be treated as a strip search. Where metal detectors are used in custody suites an indication from the device may give the grounds for authorising a strip search.

Strip searches

Strip searches are dealt with in Code C, Annex A, paras 10 to 12. A strip search is a search involving the removal of more than outer clothing. Although a person's mouth may be examined during a strip search, the examination of any other body orifice would amount to an intimate search. It must be remembered that a strip search is the search of any part of a person that requires the removal of more than that person's outer clothing. For instance, where a person is told to take his/her shoes and socks off when being searched, this would amount to a strip search which must be authorised by the custody officer. Where the custody officer authorises a strip search this does not automatically mean a search of the whole person and it will be for the custody officer to decide what parts of the detained person need to be searched.

A strip search may take place only if the custody officer reasonably considers that the detained person might have concealed an article which he/she would not be allowed to keep, such as those items which the detained person may use to:

- cause harm to himself/herself or others;
- damage property;
- effect an escape; or
- which might be evidence of an offence; *and*

that if such an item were found it would be necessary to remove it.

Reasons for the search, the extent of the authorised search, details of the people present and the results of the search must be recorded in the custody record (Annex A, para. 12). The search must be conducted in accordance with Annex A, para. 11. The custody officer may be required to justify why he/she considered that a strip search was necessary. It is suggested that 'I authorise a strip search in case the person may have a weapon hidden' would not be sufficient!

Intimate searches

Intimate searches are dealt with in Code C, Annex A. An intimate search is a search which consists of the physical examination of a person's body orifices other than the mouth. Such searches can only be carried out in two circumstances and then only if they are authorised by an officer of the rank of inspector or above.

The circumstances mentioned above are that the authorising officer has reasonable grounds for believing:

- that an article which could cause physical injury to the detained person or others at the police station has been concealed; or
- that the detained person has concealed a Class A drug which he/she intended to supply to another or to export.

Not only must the authorising officer have reasonable grounds for believing that one or both of the above grounds are satisfied but he/she must also believe that an intimate search is the only practicable means of removing an item. Before authorising the search the authorising officer needs to consider Code C, Annex A, Notes A1 and A2.

The custody officer must record which parts of the person's body were searched (Annex A, para. 7), who carried out the search, who was present, the reasons for the search, why the item could not be removed by some other means and its result.

Conduct of a search

The manner in which a search must be conducted is set out in Code C, paras 4.1 to 4.5. Some relevant practical matters are set out below:

- Before the search begins the detained person should be informed of the reasons for the search, unless it is impracticable to do so (*Brazil* v *Chief Constable of Surrey* [1983] Crim LR 483).
- The search must be conducted by an officer (s. 54(8) of the 1984 Act) of the same sex (s. 54(9) and Code C, para. 4.1).
- Reasonable force may be used (s. 117 of the 1984 Act).
- The custody officer should specify the level of the search to be conducted and must be recorded in the person's record.
- Reference to Code A, para. 3.1 may be useful when considering how to conduct the search: 'Every reasonable effort must be made to minimise the embarrassment that a person being searched may experience.'
- For cases where the intimate search has been authorised to search for a concealed Class A drug which the detained person intended to supply to another or to export:
  - The search may only be carried out by a registered medical practitioner or registered nurse unless Code C, Annex A, paras 3 and 3A apply.
  - The search must take place at a hospital, surgery or other medical premises.
  - No person of the opposite sex who is not a medical practitioner or nurse should be present.
  - A minimum of two people, other than the person searched, must be present during the search.

What property can be retained?

Once a person has been searched and the custody officer has ascertained what property the detained person has with him/her, a decision must be made as to what property will be returned to the detained person and what property will be retained by the police.

The basic position is that, with the exception of articles subject to legal privilege (**see chapter 11**), all property in the possession of a detained person may be retained by the police. However, in the case of clothing and personal items (as defined by Code C, para. 4.3), these may only be retained if the custody officer believes that the item(s) may be used by the detained person to:

- cause harm to himself/herself or others;
- damage to property;
- effect an escape; or
- that they might be evidence of an offence (Code C, para. 4.2).

Where personal items are retained by the custody officer, he/she must inform the person of the reasons why they have been retained.

It is suggested that the custody officer may authorise the seizure of an article of clothing under s. 54(4)(b) of the 1984 Act, where he/she has reasonable grounds for believing that such clothing may be evidence relating to an offence. For instance, if the detained person is wearing a pair of trainers of the same type as those which are reasonably believed to have made impressions at the scene of a recent burglary and the detained person has a burglary record then, unless the custody officer knows of other facts clearly putting the suspect at some other place at the time of the offence, he/she is plainly justified in having those shoes forensically examined. However, it is submitted that this does not authorise the custody officer to seize footwear on the off-chance that some officer or some other police force may have obtained impressions at a burglary site which might match the trainers of the detained person.

Where it is necessary to retain items of clothing that the detained person is wearing, replacement clothing of a reasonable standard of comfort and cleanliness must be provided (Code C, para. 8.5). What is 'reasonable' clothing will be a question of fact. At the time of writing there is no available case law on this point but the dignity of the person will be a consideration the court might take into account if the detained person's detention is alleged to have breached his/her 'human rights'. It is also important to make a record of any offer of replacement clothing (Code C, para. 8.9). It may be appropriate to collect the detained person's own clothes or arrange to have some delivered.

Where the person is searched and a record of his/her property is made, the detained person should be allowed to check the property list and be invited to sign the list as correct. If he/she declines, this should be recorded in the custody record (Code C, para. 4.4).

Unless the property has been seized and retained as evidence under s. 22 of the 1984 Act, it must be returned to the detained person on his/her release. If property is rightfully seized but retained unnecessarily this would be unlawful and could lead to a claim for damages (*Martin* v *Chief Constable Nottingham*, 1 May 1998, unreported). The seizure of a person's property is also protected by the European Convention on Human Rights, First Protocol, Article 1, which states:

> Every natural or legal person is entitled to the peaceful enjoyment of his possessions. No one shall be deprived of his possessions except in the public interest and subject to the conditions provided for by law and by the general principles of international law....

If property is retained the reasons for this should be recorded.

(See also General Police Duties, chapter 2.)

Juveniles

Juveniles are provided with the additional safeguard of an appropriate adult to look out for their interests while in police detention. The Codes of Practice state that where a juvenile or a mentally disordered/mentally vunerable person is the subject of a strip search or an intimate search, in most cases, an appropriate adult must be present (Code C, Annex A, paras 6 and 11). The Codes do not make any mention of this requirement for an ordinary search and therefore searches other than strip and intimate searches may be conducted without an appropriate adult being present. Where an appropriate adult is required:

- the appropriate adult may be of the opposite sex;

- where there is a risk of serious harm to the detained person or to others the search may be conducted without the appropriate adult being present;

- a search of a juvenile may take place in the absence of the appropriate adult only if the juvenile signifies in the presence of the appropriate adult that he/she prefers the search to be done in his/her absence and the appropriate adult agrees. In such cases a record shall be made of the juvenile's decision and signed by the appropriate adult.

Well-being of Detained Person

The custody officer should be mindful at all times for the well-being of the detained person. Code C, para. 12.2 provides a requirement for a detained person to have a rest period:

Except as below, in any period of 24 hours a detainee must be allowed a continuous period of at least 8 hours for rest, free from questioning, travel or any interruption in connection with the investigation concerned. This period should normally be at night or other appropriate time which takes account of when the detainee last slept or rested. If a detainee is arrested at a police station after going there voluntarily, the period of 24 hours runs from the time of their arrest and not the time of arrival at the police station. The period may not be interrupted or delayed, except:

(a) when there are reasonable grounds for believing not delaying or interrupting the period would:
   (i)   involve a risk of harm to people or serious loss of, or damage to, property;
   (ii) delay unnecessarily the person's release from custody;
   (iii) otherwise prejudice the outcome of the investigation;

(b) at the request of the detainee, their appropriate adult or legal representative;

(c) when a delay or interruption is necessary in order to:
   (i)   comply with the legal obligations and duties arising under section 15;
   (ii) to take action required under section 9 or in accordance with medical advice.

If the period is interrupted in accordance with (a), a fresh period must be allowed. Interruptions under (b) and (c), do not require a fresh period to be allowed.

KEYNOTE

If a complaint is made by or on behalf of the detained person, or the person is treated improperly, follow Code C, para. 9.2.

When must health care professional be called

A health care professional is defined by Code C, Note 9A. When arrangements are made to secure clinical attention for a detainee, the custody officer must make sure all relevant information which might assist in the detainee's treatment is made available to the responsible health care professional. Any officer or civilian support staff with relevant information must inform the custody officer of that information as soon as practicable.

The custody officer should call an appropriate health care professional in any of the following circumstances:

- If a complaint is made by, or on behalf of, a detainee concerning a possible assault or the possibility of the unnecessary or unreasonable use of force (Code C, para. 9.2).

- The detainee:
  - appears to be suffering from physical illness; or
  - is injured; or
  - appears to be suffering from a mental disorder (see Code C, para. 9.6);
  - appears to need clinical attention (Code C, para. 9.5).

- If it appears to the custody officer, or they are told, that a person brought to a station under arrest may be suffering from an infectious disease or condition, then advice must be sought from an appropriate health care professional (Code C, para. 9.7).

- The detainee requests a clinical examination (Code C, para. 9.8).

- If a detainee is required to take or apply any medication in compliance with clinical directions prescribed before their detention, the custody officer must consult the appropriate health care professional before the use of the medication (Code C, para. 9.9).

- Where the custody officer would like the advice of an appropriate health care professional to decide whether the detainee is fit for interview (Code C, para. 12.3).

The police surgeon or, if appropriate, some other health care professional should also be called if needed to examine a detainee for the purposes of obtaining evidence relating to any offence in which the detainee is suspected of being involved (Code C, para. 9.1).

Code C, para. 9.5 does not apply to minor ailments or injuries which do not need attention. However, all such ailments or injuries must be recorded in the custody record and any doubt must be resolved in favour of calling the appropriate health care professional. If a safe and appropriate care plan for the detainee cannot be provided, the police surgeon's advice must be sought (Code C, para. 9.8).

Any information that is available about the detained person should be considered in deciding whether to request a medical examination. In *R v HM Coroner for Coventry, ex parte Chief Constable of Staffordshire Police* (2000) 164 JP 665 the detained person had been drunk on arrest and was detained to be interviewed. The detained person made no complaint of his condition but his sister called the police to advise them that he would get the shakes. It was clear at interview and the following morning that he did have the shakes but no complaint was made and no doctor was called. A verdict of accidental death aggravated by neglect was an option in the case as the deceased had died whilst in police custody. The court considered the facts, such as the deceased's withdrawal and the warning as to his condition, from which a properly directed jury could have concluded that had certain steps been taken it was at least possible that the deceased would not have died. In this case a verdict of accidental death aggravated by neglect was left open to the jury, even though a doctor at the inquest gave evidence that he doubted whether calling a doctor would have made any difference to the eventual outcome.

Medical record forming part of the custody record

A record must be made in the custody record of the injury, ailment, condition or other reason which made it necessary to call an appropriate health care professional. Once the detainee has been seen by the health care professional any clinical directions and advice, including any further clarifications, given to police by the health care professional concerning the care and treatment of the detainee must be recorded in the custody record (Code C, para. 9.15). This does not, however, require the health care professional to record his/her clinical findings in the custody record, provided information which is necessary to custody staff to ensure the effective ongoing care and well being of the detainee is openly recorded in the custody record (Code C, para. 9.16). There is no requirement to include within the custody record any information about the cause of any injury, ailment or condition to be recorded on the custody record if it appears capable of providing evidence of an offence (Code C, Note 9G).

A solicitor or appropriate adult must be permitted to consult a detainee's custody record as soon as practicable after their arrival at the station and at any other time whilst the person is detained (Code C, para. 2.4). Therefore details required to be included in the custody record concerning the detainee's injuries and ailments will be accessible to both the solicitor and appropriate adult. It is therefore important to bear in mind the guidance of Code C, Note 9E with regard to not disclosing any more information than is required to be recorded in the custody record. Note 9E states:

> It is important to respect a person's right to privacy and information about their health must be kept confidential and only disclosed with their consent or in accordance with clinical advice when it is necessary to protect the detainee's health or that of others who come into contact with them.

As the Codes specify matters which must be included within the custody record, it is suggested that all other matters recorded by the appropriate health care professional do not form part of the custody record and therefore do not need to be made available to the solicitor or appropriate adult under Code C, para. 2.4, i.e. the notes made by the health care professional.

At least two light meals and one main meal shall be offered in any period of 24 hours. Drinks should be provided at meal times and upon reasonable request between meal times (Code C, para. 8.6). Meals should so far as practicable be offered at recognised meal times (Code C, Note 8B) but consider any religious variations.

Detainees should be visited at least every hour. If no reasonably foreseeable risk was identified in a risk assessment, there is no need to wake a sleeping detainee. Those suspected of being intoxicated through drink or drugs or whose level of consciousness causes concern must, subject to any clinical directions given by the appropriate health care professional, be visited and roused at least every half hour. When rousing the detainee, the checklist provided at Code C, Annex H should be used.

Brief outdoor exercise must be given if practicable (Code C, para. 8.7).

Under Article 2 of the European Convention on Human Rights the State is under a duty to provide a plausible explanation of events that lead to a death in police custody where the person had originally been detained in good health (*Velikova* v *Bulgaria*, application no. 41488/98 (27 April 2000)). This is another good reason why all events that affect the detained person are recorded in the custody record.

Section 51 of the Police Reform Act 2002 introduces independent custody visitors on a statutory basis. The arrangements may confer on independent custody visitors such powers as the police authority considers necessary to enable them to carry out their functions under the arrangements and may, in particular, confer on them powers to:

- require access to be given to each police station;

- examine records relating to the detention of persons;

- meet detainees for the purposes of a discussion about their treatment and conditions while detained; and

- inspect the facilities including, in particular, cell accommodation, washing and toilet facilities and the facilities for the provision of food.

Other Events involving the Detained Person

- Where the detained person is delivered to the custody of another officer, the fact must be recorded and the reason why. Any refusal to hand over the detained person must also be recorded with the reasons why (para. 12.10).

- When handing over the custody of a detained person to another police officer, the custody officer ceases to have responsibility for ensuring that the detained person is treated in accordance with the Codes of Practice and the responsibility passes to the person to whom the detained person is handed (s. 39(2)). However, the custody officer is responsible for deciding whether the detainee should be handed over (Code C, para. 12.1).

- When the detained person is returned to the care of the custody officer, the person returning the detained person must report to the custody officer as to the manner in which the Codes of Practice have been complied with (s. 39(3)). This information must be recorded in the custody record along with any reported breaches of the Codes.

If a police officer wishes to interview, or conduct enquiries which require the presence of a detained person, the custody officer is responsible for deciding whether to deliver him/her into the officer's custody (Code C, para. 12.1). In considering this decision, the custody officer should bear in mind the following factors:

- Whether the person is in need of a rest period (Code C, para. 12.2).

- Whether the detained person is fit to be interviewed. This should be reviewed where necessary in consultation with the officer in the case and/or the appropriate health care professional (Code C, para. 12.3).

- Whether the right of access to legal advice is being complied with as required by Code C, paras 6.1 to 6.17.

If the detained person is to be interviewed, the custody officer should consider the following questions under Code C:

- Will the interview room be adequately heated, lit and ventilated? (para. 12.4)
- Is seating available in the interview room? (para. 12.6)
- If an interpreter is required, will he/she be available for the interview? (paras 13.2, 13.5 and 13.6)
- The guidance contained in Code C, Annex G.

- Where the detained person is a juvenile or a person who is mentally disordered or impaired, whether suspected or not, do not hand over the detained person to the interviewing officer without an appropriate adult being present unless paras 11.1 and 11.18 to 11.20 apply (para. 11.15).

In *Butcher* v *DPP* (2003) unreported, the custody officer physically escorted the detainee's appropriate adult from the custody suite as she had entered the custody suite without being invited and had been verbally abusive and aggressive. The court held that the custody sergeant had not detained the appropriate adult, but had merely used reasonable force to remove her in order to maintain the operational effectiveness of the custody suite. The court held that the custody sergeant was entirely entitled to ask her to leave and use reasonable force when she failed to comply with that request.

- The PACE Codes of Practice do not specifically prevent placing more than one prisoner in a cell. However, Code C, para. 8.1 states that so far as practicable this should not be done. The Codes go on to say that in no circumstances must a juvenile be placed in a cell or detention room with an adult and that where detained people have to share a cell they must be of the same sex. Where the custody officer is considering placing more than one person in a cell, he/she must be mindful of the following points:
  - that there must be sufficient bedding available for each person;
  - he/she is responsible for the safety of all the prisoners and there may be a risk of assault in the cells;
  - he/she is responsible for the safety of police staff and other visitors to the police station who could be over-powered by more than one prisoner;
  - the dignity of the prisoners (e.g. should they have to go to the toilet with someone else watching);
  - security of evidence.

- Allow private consultation with a legal adviser (para. 6.1).

- Allow visits (para. 5.4).

- Release either with or without bail.

It is suggested that the custody officer should undertake a further risk assessment which should be recorded in the custody record before more than one person is placed in a cell. Any steps taken to minimise the risk should also be included in the custody record. (Paragraph 2.3 requires the time of release to be recorded. This is relevant in calculating any period of detention which may still be remaining if the person has been bailed and periods in police detention also count towards the period a person serves in custody.)

Section 117 of the 1984 Act provides that 'reasonable force' may be used if necessary for the following purposes:

- to secure compliance with reasonable instructions, including instructions given in pursuance of the provisions of a Code of Practice; or

- to prevent escape, injury, damage to property or the destruction of evidence.

This is not a blanket power to use force. In *R* v *Jones* (1999) *The Times*, 21 April, the court said that s. 117 should not be interpreted as giving a right to police to exercise force whenever the consent of a suspect was not required.

Code C, para. 8.2 recognises that in using force there may be occasions where additional restraints need to be used on a detainee whilst he/she is in a locked cell. Such restraints should only be used when absolutely necessary and then only restraint equipment approved for use in that force by the Chief Officer, which is reasonable and necessary in the circumstances having regard to the detainee's demeanour and with a view to ensuring their safety and the safety of others. When such restraints are used the reasons for it and, if appropriate, the arrangements for enhanced supervision of the detainee whilst restrained, must be recorded (Code C, para. 8.11).

A further important duty is placed upon a custody officer where a person is to be handed over to prison custody. The custody officer must complete a form in respect of every prisoner handed over for prison custody who is reasonably suspected of:

- being likely to try to escape;

- being associated with a dangerous gang who may attempt rescue;

- against whom other serious charges may be brought;

- being of a violent nature;

- any other reason which may help the governor in deciding whether this prisoner represents a special security risk, e.g. having suicidal tendencies, being ill, being liable to take drugs into prison, etc.

(See Home Office Circular 32/2000, Annexes B and C (**see appendix 9**) which includes this form and fully describes how it should be completed.)

15.10 Taking Photographs of Detained Persons

The Anti-terrorism, Crime and Security Act 2001 inserted s. 64A into the Police and Criminal Evidence Act 1984. This means that a person who is detained at a police station may be photographed with his/her consent; or if it is withheld or it is not practicable to obtain it, without his/her consent (guidance is provided in Code D, paras 5.12 to 5.18). It is suggested that it would be necessary to ask the person for his/her consent before taking the photograph or justify why this was not possible (Code D, paras 5.12 and 5.14 and Note 5E). A photograph may be taken only by either a constable or a person who is designated for the purposes of s. 64A by the chief officer of police for the police area in which the police station in question is situated. For the purpose of obtaining a photograph, a person taking a photograph may require the removal of any item or substance worn on or over the whole or any part of the head or face of the person to be photographed. If the requirement is not complied with, the officer may remove the item or substance using powers of force under s. 117 of the 1984 Act.

A photograph taken under s. 64A may be used by, or disclosed to, any person for any purpose related to the prevention or detection of crime, the investigation of an offence or the conduct of a prosecution. Code D, Note 5B gives examples where such photographs may be of use. The use of the photograph is for any conduct which constitutes a criminal offence (whether under UK law or in another country). This therefore allows the photograph to be used in the preparation of any identification procedure that is being arranged involving the suspect (Code D, para. 3.30).

When there are reasonable grounds for suspecting the involvement of a person in a criminal offence, but that person is at a police station voluntarily and not detained, that person may be photographed subject to the modifications set out in Code D, paras 5.20 to 5.24.

15.10.1 Searches and Examination to Ascertain Identity

The Anti-terrorism, Crime and Security Act 2001 inserted s. 54A into the Police and Criminal Evidence Act 1984. This section will assist officers in obtaining the true identity of a detained person and will allow officers to search the person for marks that may link him/her to the offence. Guidance is given in the Codes at Code D, paras 5.1 to 5.11.

If an officer of at least the rank of inspector authorises it, a detained person may be searched and/or examined, without his/her consent, in order to ascertain whether he/she has any mark that would tend to identify him/her as a person involved in the commission of an offence or to assist to identify him/her (this would include showing that he/she is not a particular person). Mark includes features and injuries; and a mark is an identifying mark for the purposes of s. 54A if it assists to identify the person or his/her involvement in the commission of an offence. While the search may be detailed, the extent is likely to have to be justified and it does not permit officers to carry out an intimate search.

The circumstances under Code D, para. 5.3 where authority may be given are:

- the person in question has refused to identify himself/herself; or

- the authorising officer has reasonable grounds for suspecting that that person is not who he/she claims to be; and

- consent to a search or examination has been withheld or it is not practicable to obtain such consent (as to meaning of appropriate consent, see **para. 16.5.2** keynote).

A person detained at a police station to be searched under a stop and search power is not a detainee for the purposes of these powers.

Authorisation may be given orally or in writing, but if given orally it must be confirmed in writing as soon as is practicable.

All the procedures under s. 54A (except the authorisation), must be conducted by a person of the same sex (Code D, para. 5.5). Should it be necessary, the person carrying out any of these procedures may use powers of force under s. 117 of the 1984 Act. If it is established that a person is unwilling to co-operate sufficiently to enable a search and/or examination to take place or a suitable photograph to be taken, an officer may use reasonable force to search and/or examine a detainee without his/her consent and/or photograph any identifying marks without his/her consent (Code D, para. 5.9).

Where a mark is found, it may be photographed (or recorded by some other method). The person should first be asked if he/she consents to the photograph; if he/she declines the photograph can still be taken (Code D, para. 5.4).

A photograph taken under s. 54A may be used by, or disclosed to, any person for any purpose related to the prevention or detection of crime, the investigation of an offence or the conduct of a prosecution. The use of the photograph is for any conduct which constitutes a criminal offence (whether under UK law or in another country). Code D, Note 5B gives examples where such photographs may be of use.

For a similar provision to obtain a person's identify from fingerprints, **see para. 16.5.1.**

15.11   **Special Groups and Appropriate Adults**

In cases where the detained person is a juvenile or a person who is mentally vulnerable or appears to be suffering from mental disorder, the custody officer must inform an appropriate adult as soon as possible (this must be done in the case of a juvenile regardless of whether he/she is held *incommunicado* (Code C, para. 3.15). In the case of a juvenile who is the subject of a supervision order, the person supervising the juvenile should also be informed. If the custody officer has any doubt as to the mental state or capacity of a person detained, an appropriate adult should be called (Code C, Note 1G).

A juvenile for the purpose of the 1984 Act is any person who is under the age of 17 or who appears to be under the age of 17 until it is established that he/she is 17 or over (Code C, para. 1.5).

Code C, Note 1G defines 'mentally vulnerable' as applying to any detainee who, because of their mental state or capacity, may not understand the significance of what is said, of questions or of their replies. 'Mental disorder' is defined in the Mental Health Act 1983, s. 1(2) as 'mental illness, arrested or incomplete development of mind, psychopathic disorder and any other disorder or disability of mind'. Code C, para. 1.4 also states:

> If an officer has any suspicion, or is told in good faith, that a person of any age may be mentally disordered or otherwise mentally vulnerable, in the absence of clear evidence to dispel that suspicion, the person shall be treated as such for the purposes of this Code. See Note 1G.

An appropriate adult is defined by Code C, para. 1.7. Paragraph 1.7 states:

> 'The appropriate adult' means, in the case of a:
> (a) juvenile:
>   (i) the parent, guardian or, if the juvenile is in local authority or voluntary organisation care, or is otherwise being looked after under the Children Act 1989, a person representing that authority or organisation;
>   (ii) a social worker of a local authority social services department;
>   (iii) failing these, some other responsible adult aged 18 or over who is not a police officer or employed by the police.
> (b) person who is mentally disordered or mentally vulnerable: See Note 1D:
>   (i) a relative, guardian or other person responsible for their care or custody;
>   (ii) someone experienced in dealing with mentally disordered or mentally vulnerable people but who is not a police officer or employed by the police;
>   (iii) failing these, some other responsible adult aged 18 or over who is not a police officer or employed by the police.

KEYNOTE

The role of the appropriate adult is to assist and advise the detained person. Care should be taken when considering the suitability of an appropriate adult. Code C, Note 1D gives guidance for choosing the appropriate adult. Evidence obtained whilst a person is in custody where the person called as an appropriate adult does not have that person's best interests in mind or is not capable of assisting them could be excluded.

An appropriate adult is not required for a 17 year old (*R* v *Stratford Youth Court, ex parte Harding* [2001] EWHC Admin 615).

In *R* v *Aspinall* [1999] 2 Cr App R 115, the Court of Appeal emphasised the importance of appropriate adults. There it was held that an appropriate adult played a significant role in respect of a vulnerable person whose condition rendered him/her liable to provide information which was unreliable, misleading or self-incriminating.

It is also important to consider the welfare of the appropriate adult. This is demonstrated by the case of *Leach* v *Chief Constable of Gloucestershire Constabulary* [1999] 1 All ER 215. Here L was asked by a police officer to attend police interviews of a murder suspect who was also thought to be mentally disordered, as an 'appropriate adult' per the requirement of the Codes. She was told only that the suspect was a 52-year-old male, and was not informed of the nature of the case. The suspect was in fact Frederick West, who was being questioned in connection with murders committed in particularly harrowing and traumatic circumstances. For many weeks L acted as an appropriate adult, accompanying the officer and suspect to murder scenes and on many occasions being left alone in a locked cell with the suspect. She claimed to be suffering from post-traumatic distress and psychological injury as well as a stroke as a result of her experiences. The Court of Appeal said that the Fred West case was notorious amongst modern crimes and it was forseeable that psychiatric harm might arise. Whilst there was no requirement to pre-select or warn appropriate adults as to the nature of the case, however in some cases, counselling or trained help should be offered.

15.12 Interpreters

Where the detained person is unable to speak effectively in English, an interpreter must be called to safeguard the rights of the person and to allow him/her to communicate. The interpreter is there for the benefit of the detained person and should not be considered to be part of the prosecution team. The case of *Bozkurt* v *Thames Magistrates' Court* (2001) *The Times*, 26 June, demonstrates the importance of the interpreter's role. In *Bozkurt*, the police arranged for an interpreter to attend the custody suite and interpret for the drink-drive procedure at the police station. The police then arranged for the interpreter to attend court. The interpreter translated for the defendant while he took advice from the duty solicitor at court. The interpreter failed to inform the solicitor that he had translated for the drink-drive procedure at the police station. The court held that an interpreter was under an equal duty to that of the solicitor to keep confidential what he might hear during a conference. In these circumstances it would have been preferable for a different interpreter to be used, or at least for the interpreter to have obtain the permission of the solicitor to interpret for the conference.

Guidance as to the use of interpreters is provided by Code C, paras 13.2 to 13.11. Should there be any difficulty in obtaining an interpreter this should be brought to the attention of the senior management responsible for arranging access to interpreters (Code C, para. 13.1).

16 Identification

16.1 Introduction

A critical issue in the investigation and prosecution of offences is the identification of the offender and this, like all other facts in issue, must be proved beyond a reasonable doubt. Many different methods of identification exist but the main feature which must be considered in relation to each is its *reliability*.

16.2 Code D

Identification evidence is governed by Code D of the PACE Codes of Practice (**see appendix 6**). These Codes were amended on 1 April 2003.

Generally, the methods of identification covered by Code D can be divided into two:

- occasions where the identity of the suspect is known; and
- occasions where the identity of the suspect is not known.

Although a breach of Code D (or any of the other Codes of Practice) will not automatically result in the evidence being excluded (*R v Khan* [1997] Crim LR 584), the judge or magistrate(s) will consider the effects of any breach on the fairness of any subsequent proceedings. The Codes are intended to provide protection to suspects and, if it is felt that the breach of Code D has resulted in unfairness or other prejudicial effect on the defendant, the court may exclude the related evidence under s. 78 of the Police and Criminal Evidence Act 1984 (**see chapter 13**).

The Police Reform Act 2002 has introduced designated support staff who have some of the powers that police officers have (**see para 15.1.1**).

16.3 Check 'This'

Conversely, even if Code D is followed, that is no guarantee that evidence obtained will be admissible. In each case the ultimate purpose of any identification procedure should be borne in mind and the 'this' list used elsewhere in the series (**see General Police Duties** and **Road Traffic**) should be applied to any proposed procedure by asking:

> How reliable is *this* piece of evidence in proving, or disproving, *this* person's involvement in *this* offence?

This approach should be adopted even if the provisions of Code D are followed. A good example of a situation where such an approach may have helped is *R v Hickin* [1996] Crim LR 584. This case was decided under the old Codes of Practice before it was necessary to obtain a first description from a witness. In the case, a group of some 14 suspects were arrested following an attack on two men at night. Clearly it would have been impracticable to arrange identification parades or group identifications for each suspect at that time, thereby allowing for a direct confrontation (**see para. 16.4.2**). However, witnesses could have been asked to provide initial descriptions of suspects before being used in the confrontation. The witnesses' comments at the time of the confrontation could also have been noted and some witnesses might have been asked to remain behind to take part in some later identification parades. As these things were not done, the Court of Appeal held that the identification evidence obtained by the confrontation procedure was unfairly prejudicial, *even though the provisions of Code D had been followed*.

16.4 Methods of Identification

16.4.1 Visual

The visual identification of suspects by witnesses is one of the most common forms of identification; it is also one of the most unreliable. Even under research conditions, the recall of eye witnesses is inconsistent; where the witness sees or experiences the spontaneous commission of a crime, that reliability is reduced even further.

It was for these reasons that the *Turnbull* guidelines (**see chapter 10**) were set out, together with the provisions of Code D (**see appendix 6**).

Problems of reliability in identification can arise even where the person accused is known to the witness. See, for example, *R v Conway* (1990) 91 Cr App R 143 (**see para. 16.4.2**).

A lot will depend on the individual circumstances of each case but it is essential that these issues are covered in any interview or other evidence gathering process.

'Dock identifications', where the witness's first identification of the accused involves pointing out the person in the dock, are often dramatised by film makers but, in practice, are generally disallowed as being unreliable and unfair.

The rules for identification differ between cases where the suspect *is known* and those where suspect is *not known*. Code D, para. 3.4 defines the terms as:

> . . . a suspect being 'known' mean there is sufficient information known to the police to justify the arrest of a particular person for suspected involvement in the offence. A suspect being 'available' means they are immediately available or will be within a reasonably short time and willing to take an effective part in at least one of the following which it is practicable to arrange;

- video identification;
- identification parade; or
- group identification.

Code D requires that a first description provided of a person suspected of a crime (regardless of the time it was given) must be recorded (para. 3.1). This must also be disclosed to the defence in the pre-trial procedure in all cases and, in particular, before any identification procedures take place. This record must be made and kept in a form which enables details of that description to be accurately produced from it, in a visible and legible form (Code D, para. 3.1), which can be given to the suspect or the suspect's solicitor. Such a record could be made electronically or paper based. The Code also makes provision for the disclosure of materials previously released to the media in relation to an enquiry and for witnesses to be asked if they saw such material before any identification procedure.

16.4.2   **Identification where there is a Known Suspect**

Where the suspect is known, there are four possible methods of identification provided for in Code D (paras 3.4 to 3.23). These are:

- video identification;
- identification parades;
- group identification; and
- confrontation (this is only of limited use and value).

The modifications to the PACE Codes of Practice alter the hierarchy of identification procedures in cases of disputed identification. Under the previous provisions, the preferred method of identification was the identification parade. Only in cases where an identification parade had been refused by the suspect, or was considered impracticable, could a group identification be considered. It was only if that form of identification was refused or impracticable, that a video identification could be considered, and, as a last resort, a confrontation could be held.

It is crucial that once the person becomes a known suspect, any witnesses, *including police officers*, who might be used at an identification parade, are kept apart from the suspect, as any contact could jeopardise a conviction. In *R* v *Lennon*, 28 June 1999, unreported, a suspect was arrested for public order offences after his description was circulated by the police officers that witnessed the offence. The suspect was placed in a van and the officers accidentally went in the van and identified the suspect. The court held that the person was a known suspect and the identification evidence should have been excluded. Paragraph 3.4 gives guidance as to when a suspect will become 'known' or 'available'. Code D, Note 3D gives guidance where a person deliberately makes themselves unavailable.

The Code also makes provision for the disclosure of materials previously released to the media in relation to an enquiry and for witnesses to be asked if they saw such material before any identification procedure. When a witness has previously been shown photographs or computerised or artist's composite or similar likeness, the suspect and their solicitor must be informed of this fact before the identification procedure takes place. It is the responsibility of the officer in charge of the investigation to make the identification officer aware that this is the case (Code D, Annex E, para. 9).

The Codes recognise that the showing of films or photographs to the public through the national or local media, or to police officers for the purposes of recognition and tracing suspects, may be necessary. However, Code D, para. 3.28, provides that when such material is shown to potential witnesses, including police officers, to obtain identification evidence, it shall be shown on an individual basis to avoid any possibility of collusion, and, as far as possible, the showing shall follow the principles for video identification if the suspect is known, or identification by photographs if the suspect is not known (see Code D, paras 3.4 and 3.3.).

When a broadcast or publication is made, a copy of the relevant material released to the media for the purposes of recognising or tracing the suspect must be kept. The suspect or their solicitor, provided it is practicable and would not unreasonably delay the investigation, must be allowed to view such material before any identification procedure is carried out. Each witness involved in the procedure shall be asked, after they have taken part, whether they have seen any broadcast or published films or photographs relating to the offence or any description of the suspect and their replies shall be recorded. This paragraph does not affect any separate requirement under the Criminal Procedure and Investigations Act 1996 to retain material in connection with criminal investigations (Code D, para. 3.29).

Where it has been decided that an identification procedure is to be held (see Code D, para. 3.12), the identification officer and the officer in charge of the investigation must consult each other to determine which procedure is to be offered (Code D, para. 3.14). The suspect shall initially be offered a video identification unless:

- an identification parade is both practicable and more suitable than a video identification; or
- a video identification is not practicable; or
- the officer in charge of the investigation considers a group identification is more satisfactory than a video identification or an identification parade and the identification officer considers it practicable to arrange (Code D, para. 3.16).

An identification parade may not be practicable because of factors relating to the witnesses, such as their number, state of health, availability and travelling requirements. A video identification would normally be more suitable if it could be arranged and completed sooner than an identification parade.

If a suspect refuses the identification procedure first offered, the suspect shall be asked to state their reason for refusing and may get advice from their solicitor and/or if present, their appropriate adult. The suspect, solicitor and/or appropriate adult may make representations about why another procedure should be used. A record should be made of the reasons for refusal and any representations made. If appropriate, the identification officer will arrange for the suspect to be offered an alternative which the officer considers suitable and practicable. If the officer decides it is not suitable and practicable to offer an alternative identification procedure, the reasons for that decision must be recorded (Code D, para. 3.15).

Where a suspect is identified by witnesses, other evidence should still be sought to strengthen the case (or to prove the person's innocence) as identification evidence is often challenged at court. Such supporting evidence may include admissions by the suspect that links him/her to the identification evidence; for example, that he/she owns the vehicle that was driven at the time of the offence (*R* v *Ward* [2001] Crim LR 316).

The photographing of a person in police detention or voluntarily at a police station is covered in **chapter 15 (at para. 15.11)** and Code D, paras 5.1 to 5.24. Such photographs might prove useful for an identification procedure process.

When must an Identification Procedure be Held?

Identification procedures should be held for the benefit of the defence as well as the prosecution (*R* v *Waile* [1998] Crim LR 68). The Codes give guidance on when an identification parade must or may be held. Code D, paras 3.12 and 3.13 state:

3.12 Whenever:
  (i) a witness has identified a suspect or purported to have identified them prior to any identification procedure set out in paragraphs 3.5 to 3.10 having been held; or
  (ii) there is a witness available, who expresses an ability to identify the suspect, or where there is a reasonable chance of the witness being able to do so, and they have not been given an opportunity to identify the suspect in any of the procedures set out in paragraphs 3.5 to 3.10, and the suspect disputes being the person the witness claims to have seen, an identification procedure shall be held unless it is not practicable or it would serve no useful purpose in proving or disproving whether the suspect was involved in committing the offence. For example, when it is not disputed that the suspect is already well known to the witness who claims to have seen them commit the crime.

3.13 Such a procedure may also be held if the officer in charge of the investigation considers it would be useful.

Code D, para. 3.12(ii) provides that there is no need to go through any of the identification procedures where, in all the circumstances, it would serve no useful purpose in proving or disproving whether the suspect was involved in committing the offence. This view is supported by the Court of Appeal decision *R v Chen* (2001) *The Times*, 17 April. The defence in that case was one of duress but the appeal was based on the failure of the police to hold identification parades. The Court of Appeal stated that this was not a case about identification as none of the defendants denied their presence at the scene. What they denied was their criminal participation in the activities that took place. It followed, therefore, that Code D did not apply. Other examples would be where it is not in dispute that the suspect is already well-known to the witness who saw the suspect commit the crime or where there is no reasonable possibility that a witness would be able to make an identification.

There have been a number of Court of Appeal cases recently concerning the requirement to hold identification parades. It is suggested that these should be applied to the revised Code regardless of which form of identification procedure is used. The leading case is *R v Forbes* [2001] 2 WLR 1, which was based on the previous Code of Practice. The House of Lords held that if the police are in possession of sufficient evidence to justify the arrest of a suspect, and that suspect's identification depends on eye-witness identification evidence, even in part, then if the identification is disputed, the Code requires that an identification parade should be held with the suspect's consent, unless one of the exceptions applies. The exceptions are set out in Code D, para. 3.12. This is particularly so where the suspect disputes identification.

The House of Lords went on to say that this mandatory obligation to hold an identification parade applies even if there has been a 'fully satisfactory', 'actual and complete' or 'unequivocal' identification of the suspect.

Despite the wording of Code D, it has been held that a suspect's right to have an identification parade is not confined to cases where a dispute over identity has already arisen; that right also applies where such a dispute might reasonably be anticipated (*R v Rutherford* (1993) 98 Cr App R 191). Similarly, a suspect's failure to request an identification parade does not mean that the police may proceed without one (*R v Graham* [1994] Crim LR 212).

It is important to consider the distinction between identification of a suspect and the suspect's clothing or other features. In *D v DPP* (1998) *The Times*, 7 August, a witness had observed two youths for a continuous period of five to six minutes and then informed the police of what he had seen, describing the age of the youths and the clothes that they were wearing. The court held that there had not been an identification within the terms of the Codes of Practice because the witness had at no stage identified the defendant or the co-accused. He had described only their clothing and their approximate ages and the police, acting on that information, had made the arrests. An identification parade could have served no useful purpose since the clothing would have been changed and those persons used for the parade would have been the same approximate age.

The *key factor* to consider when deciding whether to hold an identification parade is whether *a failure to hold a parade could be a matter of genuine potential prejudice to the suspect*. If it is decided to hold an identification procedure, it should be held as soon as practical (Code D, para. 3.11).

The question for the court will be whether it is fair to admit the identification evidence. When looking at this issue the court will consider how reliable that identification evidence is.

Any decision to proceed without an identification parade must be capable of justification later to the relevant court. The courts have taken different approaches to justification based on practical difficulties. In an early case, the submissions of the identification officer that it was impracticable to find enough people who sufficiently resembled the defendant were treated fairly dismissively by the trial judge (*R v Gaynor* [1988] Crim LR 242). In later cases, however, the courts have been more lenient, accepting that the time scales involved in arranging identification parades may render them 'impracticable' (see *R v Jamel* [1993]

Crim LR 52 where the court refused an objection by the defence to a group identification). A group identification was used in *Jamel* because a parade using mixed-race volunteers would have taken too long to arrange. All reasonable steps must be taken to investigate the possibility of one identification option before moving on to an alternative, and an offer from a suspect's solicitor to find volunteers to stand on a parade is such a 'reasonable' step (*R v Britton and Richards* [1989] Crim LR 144).

Recognition Cases

Recognition cases, that is to say, those cases where the witness states that they know the person who committed the offence as opposed to only being able to give a description, need to be carefully considered. In *R v Ridley* (1999) *The Times*, 13 October, the Court of Appeal stated that there has never been a rule that an identification parade had to be held in all recognition cases and that it will be a question of fact in each case whether or not there is a need to do so. The view that an identification procedure is not required in these cases is supported by para. 3.12(ii).

The facts in *Ridley*, which it is suggested is not uncommon amongst patrolling officers, were that two police officers in a marked police vehicle noticed a car, which had been stolen earlier that day, drive past them. Both officers said that they recognised the defendant driving the car. The officers gave chase and gave evidence that the car was speeding and being driven dangerously. They decided that it was unsafe to continue pursuit, but arrested the suspect six days later. One of the officers claimed to have recognised the suspect because she had interviewed him for some 20 minutes five months previously and had seen him about town. She gave evidence that she had a view of the suspect in the car for about nine seconds. The other officer said that he recognised the suspect from a photograph but could not say when he had seen that photograph. He said that he had seen the suspect in the car for about two seconds. The Court found that the female police officer's identification had been complete and there was no requirement for her to have further identified the suspect.

Ridley can be contrasted with *R v Conway* (1990) 91 Cr App R 143, where the witnesses' evidence was not as strong. There the witnesses stated that they recognised the accused simply because they knew him. The defence argument was that the witnesses did not actually know the accused and so could not have recognised him at the time of the offence. His conviction was quashed because of the prejudice caused by the absence of a parade.

A case can still amount to one of recognition even where the witness does not know the name of the suspect but later obtained those details from a third party, for example where the witness and the suspect went to the same school and the witness became aware of the suspect's full names from other pupils at the school (*R v C; R v B* (2003) unreported).

In *H v DPP* (2003) unreported, the court accepted that it was reasonable for the police not to undertake an identification procedure. In the circumstances of the case the police had every reason to believe that the claimant and the victim were well known to each other. The claimant had accepted that the victim knew her. There was no question of doubt as to the victim's ability to recognise the claimant and as such this was a case of pure recognition where it was futile to hold an identification parade.

Care must be taken in cases where it is believed that the case is one of recognition not requiring an identification procedure. In *R v Harris* [2002] EWCA Crim 174 the witness stated that he recognised the suspect as being someone he went to school with. The suspect gave a prepared statement in which he disputed the suggestion that he was well known to the witness. Here the court held that an identification procedure should have been undertaken, as the circumstances of the case did not fall within the general exception of the Code, that it would serve no useful purpose in proving or disproving whether the suspect had been involved in committing the offence.

When a suspect is filmed committing an offence, it is admissible to give evidence of identification by way of recognition from a witness not present at the scene but who knew the defendant and who, having seen the film, identified the suspect as being the defendant (*Attorney-General's Reference (No. 2 of 2002)* [2003] Crim LR 192).

Another common identification problem is that of disqualified drivers and being able to satisfy the court that the person charged with disqualified driving is the same person who was disqualified by the court. This is because s. 73 of the Police and Criminal Evidence Act 1984 requires proof that the person named in a certificate of conviction as having been convicted is the person whose conviction is to be proved. There has been some guidance from the courts as to how this can be achieved. In *R v Derwentside Justices, ex parte Heaviside* [1996] RTR 384, the court stated that this could be done by:

- fingerprints under s. 39 of the Criminal Justice Act 1948;

- the evidence of a person who was present in court when the disqualification order was made;

- admission of the defendant (preferably in interview) (*Moran v CPS* (2000) 164 JP 562).

The methods outlined in *Ex parte Heaviside*, are not exhaustive, but just suggested methods (*DPP v Mansfield* [1997] RTR 96). A good example of where the police were able to satisfy s. 73 of the 1984 Act came in the case of *Olakunori v DPP* [1998] COD 443. In this case Olakunori was charged with driving whilst disqualified. He had been stopped by police officers and gave a false name and a false date of birth. At the police station, after he was arrested, he gave a different false name and false date of birth to the custody officer. When he was interviewed, he confirmed his surname was Olakunori. A man named Olatokubo Olakunori, born 20 July 1974, had previously been disqualified from holding and obtaining a driving licence for an offence of driving without a valid certificate of insurance. Olakunori denied all knowledge of the previous disqualification. The prosecution argued that Olakunori had given false names in order to avoid detection for the offence and there was sufficient evidence to establish that Olakunori was the person who had been previously disqualified. This included the court register of the previous convictions, Olakunori's birth certificate which was in the name of Olatunji Olatokunbo Adeola Olakunori, showing his date of birth as 20 July 1974, and his passport which was in the name of Olatokunbo Olakunori. The Court held that the justices had been entitled to find that the false names which the appellant had given were a deliberate attempt to avoid the charge, were relevant to the material issues and that there was no innocent explanation why they had been given. The lies supported the conclusion that the appellant was guilty and accordingly the justices had been entitled to take them into account. Such evidence would be useful to obtain from suspects being investigated for offences of disqualified driving. For the offence of disqualified driving, **see Road Traffic, chapter 11**.

Control of the Identification Process

The arrangements for and conduct of identification procedures is the responsibility of an officer not below the rank of inspector who is not involved with the investigation ('the identification officer'). However, except where the Codes expressly state otherwise, the identification officer may allow another officer or civilian support staff to make arrangements for, and to conduct any of the identification procedures in paras 3.11 and 2.21. When the identification officer delegates these procedures, he/she must be able to supervise effectively and either intervene or be available to be contacted for advice.

It is important to note that no officer or any other person involved with the investigation of the case against the suspect, may take any part in these procedures or act as the identification officer. However, the identification officer may consult the officer in charge of the investigation in order to determine which procedure to use.

If the identification officer considers that it is not practicable to hold a video identification or identification parade, the reasons shall be recorded and explained to the suspect (para. 3.26). Should the suspect fail or refuse to co-operate in a video identification, identification parade or group identification, a record should be made including any reasons (paras 3.15 and 3.27).

Before a video identification, an identification parade or group identification is arranged, para. 3.17 outlines a number of matters that must be explained to the suspect and must be recorded in a written notice and handed to the suspect. Paragraph 3.17 must be completed by the identification officer or if it is proposed to hold an identification procedure at a later date and an inspector is not available to act as the identification officer, it can be performed by the custody sergeant before the suspect leaves the station.

Which Identification Procedure should be Used?

Initially the choice should be between a video identification or an identification parade (para. 3.14). However, a group identification could be used where the officer in charge of the investigation considers that in the particular circumstances it is more satisfactory (para. 3.16). The identification officer and the officer in charge of the investigation shall consult each other to determine which of these two options is the most suitable and practicable in the particular case. Paragraphs 3.14 to 3.16 gives guidance as to factors to consider.

Whilst the choice of procedure is for the police, the suspect, solicitor and/or appropriate adult shall be allowed to make representations as to why another procedure should be used (para. 3.15). If a suspect refuses the identification procedure which is first offered, he/she must be asked to state his/her reasons for refusing and may obtain advice from his/her solicitor and appropriate adult if present (para. 3.15).

Even where a person refuses to take part in an identification procedure, it is still possible to use covert video identification, covert group identification or confrontation (paras 3.21 to 3.24). If the identification officer and the officer in charge of the investigation have reasonable grounds to suspect that the person will take steps to avoid being seen by a witness in any identification procedure, the identification officer has a discretion to arrange for images of him/her to be obtained for use in a video identification procedure. If images of the suspect are obtained in these circumstances, the suspect may, for the purposes of a video identification procedure, co-operate in providing suitable images which shall be used in place of those previously taken (para. 3.20).

Section 64A of the Police and Criminal Evidence Act 1984 provides powers to take photographs and images of suspects at police stations and allows the photographs and images so taken to be used to assist with arranging the identification process (**see para. 15.11**). After being so used or disclosed, they may be retained but must not be used or disclosed for any purpose other than that related to the prevention or detection of crime, the investigation of offences or the conduct of prosecutions by, or on behalf of, police or other law enforcement and prosecuting authorities inside and outside the United Kingdom. After being so used or disclosed, they may be retained but can be used or disclosed only for the same purposes (Code D, para. 3.30).

Code D, paras 3.31 to 3.33 provide further guidance on the destruction and retention of photographs and images taken for the purpose of or in connection with identification procedures. It should be noted that the powers to retain photographs of suspects who have not be detained and moving images of anyone whether detained or not are limited to the situations set out in Code D, para. 3.31.

Where a known suspect is not available (or has ceased to be available for any reason), the identification officer has a discretion to make arrangements for a video identification to be conducted. This must be done in accordance with the provisions applicable to covert video identification (para. 3.21 and Note 3D).

If necessary, the identification officer may follow the video identification procedures but using still images. Any suitable moving or still images may be used and these may be obtained covertly if necessary. Any covert activity should be strictly limited to that necessary to test the ability of the witness to identify the suspect. Alternatively, the identification officer may make arrangements for a group identification. These provisions may be applied to juveniles where the consent of their parent or guardian is either refused or reasonable efforts to obtain that consent have failed (Code D, paras 3.21 and 3.22).

It is only if none of the other options are practicable that the identification officer may arrange for the suspect to be confronted by the witness. A confrontation does not require the suspect's consent. In *R* v *McCulloc*, 6 May 1999, unreported, the Court of Appeal made it clear that confrontations between suspects and witnesses should only be carried out if no other procedure is practicable (see below).

Conduct of Identification Parades

Identification evidence can be crucial to the success of a prosecution. There are clear guidelines that must be followed. Where such guidelines are not followed it is likely that the defence will strongly attempt to have the identification evidence excluded. In *R* v *Jones* (1999) *The Times*, 21 April, identification evidence was excluded as the officers told the suspect that if he did not comply with the procedure, force would be used against him.

The conduct of identification parades was criticised in the Stephen Lawrence Inquiry Report. The Report stated that the timing of any identification parade during an investigation must also be considered carefully:

> Where there are a number of suspects and witnesses and where identification evidence may be crucial this can only emphasise the extreme need for careful planning and foresight. . . . The ID parades were delayed until about the middle or end of May partly because of the delay in making the arrests of the suspects. If the arrests had been made earlier it can be said that there would have been more prospect of successful identification, since the passage of time inevitably blunts the memory of the features or look of somebody who has been seen committing a crime.

The need for the identification procedure to be conducted as soon as practical is now recognised by the Codes (para. 3.11).

Annexes A to E of Code D set out in detail the procedures and requirements which must be followed in conducting identification procedures. There is also guidance concerning documentation and retention of material.

Although the courts are aware of the many practical difficulties involved in organising and running identification procedures (see e.g. *R* v *Jamel* above), any flaws in the procedure will be considered in the light of their potential impact on the defendant's trial. Serious or deliberate breaches (such as the showing of photographs to witnesses before the parade), will invariably lead to any evidence so gained being excluded (*R* v *Finley* [1993] Crim LR 50). The key question for the court will be whether the breach of the Codes is likely to have made the identification less reliable. Officers must therefore fully understand and follow the Codes of Practice and relevant Annex for the procedure being used.

Breaches which appear to impact on the safeguards imposed by Annexes A to E to separate the functions of investigation and identification (e.g. where the investigating officer becomes involved with the running of the parade in a way which allows him/her to talk to the witnesses (*R* v *Gall* (1989) 90 Cr App R 64)) will also be treated seriously by the court.

The case of *R* v *Marrin* (2002) *The Times*, 5 March provides some guidance as to methods that could be used to get a suitable pool of participants for an ID parade. The court held that there was nothing inherently unfair or objectionable in some colouring or dye being used on the facial stubble of some volunteers to make them look more like the suspect. However, care needed to be taken with such measures because the procedure would be undermined if it was obvious to the witness that make-up had been used. Another point raised was that it may sometimes be appropriate for those on parade to wear hats, but if possible the wearing of hats should be avoided if hats had not been worn during the offence because this would make it more difficult for a witness to make an identification. However, there could be circumstances where the wearing of hats could help to achieve a resemblance and might be desirable to minimise differences. Finally an identification of a suspect was not invalidated by the witness's request for the removal of a hat. There was nothing unfair in that taking place and there was no breach of any code either. Under para. 18 of Annex B, a witness could ask for any parade member to adopt any specified posture or that he/she should move.

It is important to follow the guidance in the Codes regardless of what agreement is obtained from the suspect or his/her solicitor. In *R* v *Hutton* [1999] Crim LR 74, at the suggestion of the suspect's solicitor, all the participants in the identification parade wore back to front baseball caps and had the lower part of their faces obscured by material. That identification was the only evidence against the defendant on that count. The court excluded the evidence and did not accept the fact that the decision had been agreed by the defence.

It will be essential that any photographs, photofits or other such material is stored securely in a manner that restricts access so as to be able to demonstrate to the court that the material cannot have been viewed by any of the witnesses and that copies have not been made that have not been accounted for.

16.4.3   Identification where there is No Suspect

Where the police have no suspect, Code D provides for witnesses (including police officers) to be shown photographs (Annex E) or taken to a place where the suspect might be (paras 3.2 and 3.3).

If photographs are to be shown, the procedure set out at Annex E must be followed. Once a witness has made a positive identification from the photographs, computerised or artist's composite, no further witnesses should be shown photographs (para. 3.3) (unless the person identified is eliminated from the enquiry (Annex E, para. 6)).

Using photographs from police criminal records can affect the judgment of a jury and nothing should be done to draw their attention to the fact that the defendant's photograph was already held by the police (*R* v *Lamb* (1979) 71 Cr App R 198). This rule does not apply if the jury are already aware of the defendant's previous convictions (*R* v *Allen* [1996] Crim LR 426).

The showing of a CCTV film used for security purposes is addressed at para. 3.28 of Code D.

If a film which has been shown to a witness is later lost or unavailable, the witness may give evidence of what he/she saw on that film but the court will have to consider all the relevant circumstances in deciding whether to admit that evidence *and* what weight to attach to it. (For a discussion of those circumstances, see *Taylor* v *Chief Constable of Cheshire* [1986] 1 WLR 1479.) This is particularly so as the Codes require that the film is retained (Annex A, para. 15 and para. 3.29).

Videos or photographs can be shown to the public at large through the national or local media, or to police officers for the purposes of recognition and tracing suspects. However, when such material is shown to potential witnesses (including police officers) it should be shown on an individual basis so as to avoid any possibility of collusion, and the showing shall, as far as possible, follow the principles for video identification if the suspect is known (paras 3.28, 3.29 and Annex A) or identification by photographs if the suspect is not known (see paras 3.4, 3.3 and Annex E).

16.4.4 Identification at the Scene

There are occasions where the identification is made immediately after the alleged offence. This usually happens when the witness is taken round a particular area to try and find the suspect (in which case Code D, para. 3.2 must be complied with). The need for 'scene identifications' was recognised by Lord Lane CJ in *R* v *Oscar* [1991] Crim LR 778 and by the Court of Appeal in *R* v *Rogers* [1993] Crim LR 386.

In *Oscar*, the court held that there had been no requirement for an identity parade in that case and Lord Lane pointed out that, in any case, a later parade where the suspect was dressed differently would be of no value at all. In *Rogers*, the suspect was found near a crime scene and was confronted by a witness who positively identified him. The court held that the identification in that case was necessary for an arrest to be made, although the court felt a later parade could have been carried out.

In such cases, where the meeting of the suspect and the witness takes place soon after the event, wherever possible the officers should comply with para. 3.2. Matters to consider before doing a 'scene identification' include:

- where practicable, a record shall be made of any description of the suspect given by the witness as in para. 3.1(a);
- care should be taken not to direct the witness's attention to any individual unless, having regard to all the circumstances, this cannot be avoided;
- if there is more than one witness, try to keep them separate;
- once there is sufficient information to justify the arrest of a suspect, a formal identification procedure must be adopted;
- the officer or civilian support staff accompanying the witness must make a record in his/her pocket book of the action taken as soon as practicable and in as much detail as possible.

The admissibility of identification evidence obtained when carrying out a 'scene identification' may be compromised if before a person is identified, the witness's attention is specifically drawn to that person.

Careful consideration must be given before a decision to identify a suspect in this manner is used. If there is sufficient evidence to arrest the suspect without using a witnesses identification, then it is likely the courts will find that an identification method outlined at **para. 16.4.2** should have been used and the evidence may be excluded. Confrontations between witnesses and suspects on the street can be useful at times, but where this takes place it defeats the formal identification process and needs to be carefully considered. The reason for this is that, even if the suspect is picked out on the identification parade by that witness, the defence will be able to argue that the identification was from the confrontation after the incident and not at the time of the commission of the offence. If there is more than one witness available and a decision is taken to use a witness to try and identify a suspect at the scene, other witnesses should be moved away, so as to reduce the possibility of a chance encounter with the suspect. Where possible, these witnesses should be kept apart until the identification parade and ideally should not discuss the matter between themselves.

An example where a street identification was appropriate is *R* v *El-Hannachi* [1998] 2 Cr App R 226. Here an affray took place in the car park of a public house. A witness had seen the man earlier in the pub and she had had an unobstructed view in good light before the attack. The witness described the attacker's clothing to the police and then identified a group of men who had been stopped by other officers a short distance away. The court accepted that this was the correct approach. The defendants were not known suspects when they were stopped by the police prior to the witness's identification. The court also accepted that it had not been practicable for a record to have been made of the witness's description, as required by Code D, para. 3.1, prior to the identification. Where a record has been made prior to the identification this may support the identification itself. It should be remembered, however, that the description does not now have to be recorded in writing and could be recorded by some quicker method (e.g. tape recording) (para. 3.1).

A not uncommon situation is where police officers chase a suspect who is arrested by other officers on the description circulated by the chasing officer, who then attends the scene to confirm the person's identity. The case of *R* v *Nunes*, 31 October 2001, unreported covers this point and points out the dangers of this practice. The facts of the case were that a police officer saw a man inside a house and circulated a description on his radio. A person fitting the description was seen and arrested. The first officer arrived on the scene and identified the arrested person as the man he had earlier seen in the house. The Court of Appeal held that on the particular facts of this case the identification amounted to a breach of the Code. By the time of the identification, the man had been arrested for suspected involvement in the offence and, on his arrest, the identity of the suspect was known to the police. Therefore, by the time the witnessing officer arrived on the scene, the case involved 'disputed identification evidence' because the suspect had said that he had not done anything while the police had told him he matched the description of a suspected burglar. That said, the court did go on to hold that the judge had the discretion to allow the identification evidence to be adduced notwithstanding the breach of the Codes.

16.4.5 Photographs, Image and Sound Reproduction Generally

The use of photographic and computer-generated images (such as E-Fit) to identify suspects has increased considerably over the last few years. Although the courts will exercise considerable caution when admitting such evidence (see *R* v *Blenkinsop* [1995] 1 Cr App R 7), these methods of identification are particularly useful. Expert evidence (**see chapter 10**) may be admitted to interpret images on film (see e.g. *R* v *Stockwell* (1993) 97 Cr App R 260) and police officers who are very familiar with a particular film clip (e.g. of crowd violence at a football match) may be allowed to assist the court in interpreting and explaining events shown within it (see *R* v *Clare* (1995) 159 JP 142).

Logically E-Fit and other witness-generated images would be treated as 'visual statements', in that they represent the witness's recollection of what he/she saw. However, the Court of Appeal has decided that they are not to be so treated (*R* v *Cook* [1987] QB 417) and therefore the restrictions imposed by the rule against hearsay (**see chapter 10**) will not apply (see also *R* v *Constantinou* (1989) 91 Cr App R 74 where this ruling was followed in relation to a photofit image).

Voice identification from what a suspect on an identification parade says, is dealt with under para. 18 of Annex B to Code D. The Codes do not preclude the police making use of aural identification procedures such as a 'voice identification parade', where they judge that appropriate.

Generally, a witness may give evidence identifying the defendant's voice (*R* v *Robb* (1991) 93 Cr App R 161), while expert testimony may be admitted in relation to tape recordings of a voice which is alleged to belong to the defendant. In the latter case, the jury should be allowed to hear the recording(s) so that they can draw their own conclusions (*R* v *Bentum* (1989) 153 JP 538).

16.5   **Fingerprints**

Fingerprint is defined by Code D, para. 4.1 and s. 65(1) of the Police and Criminal Evidence Act 1984 as any record, produced by any method, of the skin pattern and other physical characteristics or features of a person's fingers or palms. Fingerprints can be taken electronically provided that they are taken using such devices as the Secretary of State has approved for the purposes of electronic fingerprinting (s. 61(8A) of the 1984 Act). Where a person's fingerprints are to be taken without their consent, under the powers set out in Code D, paras 4.3 and 4.4, reasonable force may be used if necessary.

16.5.1   **Before Conviction**

The taking of finger and palm prints is governed by ss. 61 and 63A of the Police and Criminal Evidence Act 1984.

Section 61 states:

(1) Except as provided by this section no person's fingerprints may be taken without the appropriate consent.

(2) Consent to the taking of a person's fingerprints must be in writing if it is given at a time when he is at a police station.

KEYNOTE

Fingerprints of a person detained at a police station may be taken without that person's consent in the following circumstances:

- where an officer of at least the rank of inspector authorises them to be taken; or

- where the person has been charged or reported for a recordable offence (see Code D, Note 4A);

- the person's fingerprints have not already been taken in the course of the investigation of the offence by the police or the fingerprints taken do not constitute a complete set of fingerprints or some, or all, of the fingerprints are not of sufficient quality to allow satisfactory analysis, comparison or matching; and

- from a person who has been bailed to appear at a court or a police station if the person has answered to bail for a person whose fingerprints were taken previously and there are reasonable grounds for believing they are not the same person; or who has answered to bail claims to be a different person from a person whose fingerprints were previously taken (the court or an officer of inspector rank or above, authorises the fingerprints to be taken at the court or police station), s. 61(4A)

(s. 61(3) and Code D, para. 4.3).

A inspector may only give authority for fingerprints to be taken if he/she has reasonable grounds:

- for suspecting the person is involved in a criminal offence;

- for believing that the person's fingerprints will tend to confirm or disprove his/her involvement;

- will facilitate ascertaining his/her identity (for what this means see s. 54A of the Police and Criminal Evidence Act 1984, **see 15.11**)

(s. 61(4) and Code D, para. 4.3(a)).

However, an authorisation shall not be given for the purpose only of facilitating the person's identity except where he/she has refused to identify themselves or the officer has reasonable grounds for suspecting that he/she is not who he/she claims to be.

The inspector's authority may be given orally or in writing, but if given orally he/she shall confirm it in writing as soon as is practicable (s. 61(5) and Code D, para. 4.8).

Before any fingerprints are taken the person must be informed of the reason their fingerprints are to be taken, if para. 4.3(a) or (c) apply the grounds on which the relevant authority has been given, that their fingerprints may be retained and may be subject of a speculative search (unless destruction of the fingerprints is required in accordance with Annex F, Part (a)), and that if their fingerprints are required to be destroyed, they may witness their destruction as provided for in Annex F, Part (a) Code D, para. 4.7).

A record must be made when a person has been informed of the possibility that their fingerprints may be subject of a speculative search (Code D, para. 4.9). A record must also be made, as soon as possible, of the reason for taking a person's fingerprints without consent and if force is used, the circumstances and those present (Code D, para. 4.8).

Where the suspect does consent to their fingerprints being subject of such a speculative search, the consent must be in writing. Note 6E provides an example of a basic form of words. Once the suspect has given consent for the sample to be retained and used, he/she cannot withdraw this consent. See **para. 16.7.5** and Code D, Annex F regarding the retention and use of fingerprints and samples taken with consent for elimination purposes.

Note 4B explains what a speculative search means. Code D, paras 4.10 to 4.15 deal with the taking of fingerprints in connection with immigration enquires and Annex F, para. 5 deals with their retention and destruction.

16.5.2   ## After Conviction

Fingerprints may be taken with the appropriate consent, where a person refuses to give that consent, fingerprints can only be taken if s. 61(6) of the 1984 Act applies, i.e. from a person who has been:

- convicted of a recordable offence;
- given a caution in respect of a recordable offence which, at the time of the caution, the person admitted; or
- warned or reprimanded under s. 65 of the Crime and Disorder Act 1998 for a recordable offence.

For the purposes of taking fingerprints, the meaning of appropriate consent is in relation to:

- a person 17 or over, his/her consent;
- a person 14 to 17, the consent of that person or his/her parent or guardian;
- a person under 14, the consent of his/her parent or guardian.

Section 27 of the 1984 Act provides that a person may be required to attend a police station to have his/her fingerprints taken if he/she:

- has been convicted of a recordable offence; given a caution in respect of a recordable offence which, at the time of the caution, the person admitted; or warned or reprimanded under s. 65 of the Crime and Disorder Act 1998, for a recordable offence; and
- the fingerprints taken on the previous occasion do not constitute a complete set of his/her fingerprints; or some or all of the fingerprints taken on the previous occasion are not of sufficient quality to allow satisfactory analysis, comparison or matching.

The requirement must be made within one month of the date the person is convicted, cautioned, warned or reprimanded and the person must be given a period of at least seven days within which to attend. This seven-day period need not fall during the month allowed for making the requirement. If a person fails to comply with the requirement, he/she can be arrested without warrant (Code D, para. 4.4).

Before any fingerprints are taken with or without consent as above, the person must be informed of the reason his/her fingerprints are to be taken. Before any fingerprints are taken at the police station, the person must also be informed that his/her fingerprints may be retained and may be subject of a speculative search against other fingerprints. Code D, Note 4B explains what a speculative search means (Code D, para. 4.7). A record must be made when a person has been informed of the possibility that his/her fingerprints may be subject of a speculative search (Code D, para. 4.9). A record must also be made, as soon as possible, of the reason for taking a person's fingerprints without consent and if force is used, a record must be made of the circumstances and those present (Code D, para. 4.8).

KEYNOTE

In terms of the disposal of the case, cautioning a person for an offence is the equivalent of a conviction at court. Therefore if the person has been in police detention and has not had his/her fingerprints taken prior to the caution, there is no power to take that person's fingerprints under the 1984 Act (see 16.5.1). This is also the case where a person is released and subsequently summonsed.

It should be noted that s. 64 of the 1984 Act, as amended by the Criminal Justice and Police Act 2001, has removed the requirement to destroy fingerprints of suspects who are not convicted and custody officers should no longer inform detained persons of the right to destruction (see Code D, Annex F). The Act removes this obligation in relation to fingerprints and samples where the person is cleared of the offence for which they were taken or a decision is made not to prosecute (see para. 16.7.5). The obligation to destroy is replaced by a rule to the effect that any fingerprints or samples retained can only be used for the purposes related to the prevention and detection of crime, the investigation of any offence or the conduct of any prosecution. This means that if a match is established between an individual who has been cleared of an offence at a subsequent crime scene the police are able to use this information in the investigation of the crime. The system of retaining DNA samples and fingerprint evidence after a suspect had been cleared of the offence that gave rise to the collection of those items of evidence is compatible with both Article 8 and Article 14 of the European Convention on Human Rights (R v Chief Constable of South Yorkshire, ex parte Marper (2002) The Times, 4 April).

Fingerprints and samples taken from a person suspected of committing a recordable offence but not arrested, charged or informed they will be reported for it, may be subject to a speculative search only if the person consents in writing. Code D, Note 4B gives an example of the wording to be used for the consent. Once taken, the sample or fingerprints will be retained and used for purposes related to the prevention and detection of a crime, the investigation of an offence or the conduct of a prosecution either nationally or internationally. Once the person gives consent for the sample to be retained, it cannot be withdrawn.

Where a person, who is not a suspect, provides a sample or fingerprints voluntarily, e.g. for the purposes of elimination, there is no obligation for him/her to allow the samples or fingerprints to be retained or used other than for the purpose for which they were taken. Where consent is not given the fingerprints or samples must be destroyed and the information derived from them cannot be used in evidence against the person concerned or for the purposes of investigation of any offence. When seeking consent from a person for elimination samples and fingerprints the consents should be obtained separately and whether the person is consenting to their use and retention needs to be fully explained. Code D, Annex F, Note F1 should be followed when consent is being requested.

Expert evidence on fingerprints is admissible from suitably qualified individuals who have at least five years' experience in that field.

Whether fingerprint evidence is admissible as evidence tending to prove guilt, depends on:

- the experience and expertise of the witness,
- the number of similar ridge characteristics (if there are fewer than eight ridge characteristics matching the fingerprints of the accused with those found by the police, it is unlikely that a judge would exercise his/her discretion to admit such evidence),
- whether there are dissimilar characteristics,
- the size of print relied on, and
- the quality and clarity of print relied on.

The jury should be warned that expert evidence is not conclusive in itself and that guilt has to be proved in the light of all evidence (R v Buckley (1999) 163 JP 561).

16.5.3 Criminal Record and Conviction Certificates

Under s. 118 Police Act 1997, in certain circumstances the Secretary of State issues certificates concerning an individual's previous convictions. In some cases the Secretary of State will not do this until he/she has been able to verify the person's identity, which can be done through the taking of their fingerprints. Where this is the case, the Secretary of State may require the police officer in charge of the specified police station, or any other police station he/she reasonably determines, to take the applicant's fingerprints at the specified station at such reasonable time as the officer may direct and notify to the applicant.

If fingerprints are taken in these circumstances they must be destroyed as soon as is practicable after the identity of the applicant is established to the satisfaction of the Secretary of State. The destruction can be witnessed by the person giving the fingerprints if he/she requests and/or the person can ask for a certificate stating the fingerprints have been destroyed. The certificate must be issued within three months of the request.

In the case of an individual under the age of 18 years the consent of the applicant's parent or guardian to the taking of the applicant's fingerprints is also required.

16.6 Body Samples and Impressions

The taking of samples and impressions is governed by ss. 62 to 63A of the Police and Criminal Evidence Act 1984, together with Code D (paras 6.1 to 6.12) (**see appendix 6**).

Inferences from a defendant's refusal to consent to the taking of certain samples may be drawn by a court.

16.6.1 DNA Profiles

The purpose behind the taking of many samples is to enable the process of DNA profiling. Very basically, this involves an analysis of the sample taken from the suspect (the first sample), an analysis of samples taken from the crime scene or victim (the second sample) and then a comparison of the two. Both the process and the conclusions which might be drawn from the results are set out by Lord Taylor CJ in *R v Deen* (1994) *The Times*, 10 January.

The matching process involves creating 'bands' from each sample and then comparing the number of those bands which the two samples share. The more 'matches' that exist between the first and second samples, the less probability there is of that happening by pure chance. A 'good match' between the two samples does not of itself prove that the second sample came from the defendant. In using such samples to prove identification the prosecution will give evidence of:

- the *probability* of such a match happening by chance; and

- the *likelihood* that the person responsible was in fact the defendant.

When applying the 'this' rule (**see para. 16.3**) a jury must consider the second issue, that is, the likelihood of the defendant's being responsible.

The jury's task was set out by Phillips LJ in *R v Doheny* [1997] 1 Cr App R 369. In that case, involving a semen sample, his Lordship said:

> If you accept the scientific evidence called by the Crown, that indicates there are probably only four or five white males in the United Kingdom from whom that semen stain could have come. The defendant is one of them. The decision you have to reach, on all the evidence, is whether you are sure

that it was the defendant who left that stain or whether it is possible that it is one of that other small group of men who share the same DNA characteristics.

(See also *Blackstone's Criminal Practice*, 2003, paragraph F18.31.)

In most cases there will be other evidence against the defendant, evidence which clearly increases the likelihood of his/her having committed the offence.

It will be for the prosecution to produce other facts to the court which reduces the 'chance' of the DNA sample belonging to someone other than the defendant. This may require further enquiries linking the suspect to the area or circumstances of the crime or may come from questions put to the suspect during interview. In *R v Lashley*, 25 February 2000, unreported, the sole evidence against the defendant for a robbery was DNA evidence from a half-smoked cigarette found behind the counter of the post office. The DNA matched a sample obtained from the suspect and would have matched the profile of seven to ten other males in the United Kingdom. The court held that the significance of DNA evidence depended critically upon what else was known about the suspect. Had there been evidence that the suspect was in the area, or normally lived there, or had connections there, at the material time, then the jury could have found that the case was compelling. This, the court said, would be because it may have been almost incredible that two out of seven men in the United Kingdom were in the vicinity at the relevant time.

It is also important to ensure that there is no cross-contamination of DNA evidence between crime scenes, victims and suspects as was seen in the infamous American case of OJ Simpson's murder trial. It will be important to ensure that any allegations that officers may have contaminated evidence through handling/being present at several crime scenes can be successfully challenged. It is suggested that the best evidence here will be through records of crime scene logs and, where suspects have are being held in custody, records of who visited the custody suite. It will also be important that suspects and victims are kept apart.

16.7 Intimate and Non-intimate Samples

As discussed earlier, there are three key ways to prove a person's involvement in a criminal offence:

* witnesses
* confessions
* scientific evidence.

Given the inherent problems and weaknesses of the first two (**see chapters 6 and 13**), together with the advances being made in scientific procedures, the last of these is becoming more and more important in criminal evidence.

The analysis of intimate and non-intimate samples may provide essential evidence in showing or refuting a person's involvement in an offence. However, the courts have made it clear that DNA evidence alone will not be sufficient for a conviction and that there needs to be other supporting evidence to link the suspect to the crime. Such evidence may include confessions, that the suspect was near the crime scene at the time of the offence, that the suspect lived in the locality or had connections in the area.

The police powers to obtain intimate and non-intimate samples are provided by the Police and Criminal Evidence Act 1984 and were extended by amendments made by the Criminal Justice and Public Order Act 1994. Further guidance as to the exercise of these powers is contained within Code D of the PACE Codes of Practice.

16.7.1 Intimate and Non-intimate Samples Defined

Code D, para. 6 1 provides the definition of intimate and non-intimate samples:

(a) an 'intimate sample' means, a dental impression or sample of blood, semen or any other tissue fluid, urine, or pubic hair, or a swab taken from a person's body orifice other than the mouth;

(b) a 'non-intimate sample' means:
   (i) a sample of hair, other than pubic hair, which includes hair plucked with the root, see Note 6A;
   (ii) a sample taken from a nail or from under a nail;
   (iii) a swab taken from any part of a person's body including the mouth but not any other body orifice;
   (iv) saliva;
   (v) a skin impression which means any record, other than a fingerprint, which is a record, in any form and produced by any method, of the skin pattern and other physical characteristics or features of the whole, or any part of, a person's foot or of any other part of their body.

Code D, Note 6A sets out advice for taking non-intimate hair samples and states:

When hair samples are taken for the purpose of DNA analysis (rather than for other purposes such as making a visual match), the suspect should be permitted a reasonable choice as to what part of the body the hairs are taken from. When hairs are plucked, they should be plucked individually, unless the suspect prefers otherwise and no more should be plucked than the person taking them reasonably considers necessary for a sufficient sample.

16.7.2 Intimate Samples

Section 62 of the Police and Criminal Evidence Act 1984 sets out police powers to take intimate samples. Code D of the PACE Codes of Practice provides additional guidance as to the exercise of the powers. The provisions of s. 62 together with Code D describe the circumstances and manner in which intimate samples can be taken. These can be understood by considering a number of key issues.

Consent

Before an intimate sample can be taken from a person in police detention, the consent of an officer of at least the rank of inspector is necessary, *together with the consent of the person*. Without the consent of *both*, such a sample cannot be taken (Code D, para. 6.2).

Taking a sample without the relevant authority may amount to inhuman or degrading treatment under Article 3 of the European Convention on Human Rights (as to which, **see General Police Duties, chapter 2**). It may also amount to a criminal offence of assault (**see Crime**) and give rise to liability at civil law.

Where a person is not in police detention, an intimate sample may be taken where that person has already provided two (or more) non-intimate samples in the course of the investigation of the offence, which have proved insufficient for *the same means of analysis*. Should this pre-condition apply then the consent of both a police officer of at least the rank of inspector and the person concerned is necessary, as in the case of a person in police detention (Code D, para. 6.2).

Note 6C of Code D recognises that a sample may be taken from a person not in police detention, for the purposes of elimination, providing his/her consent is given.

In all cases where an intimate sample is to be taken from a young person aged 14 but under 17, the consent of his/her parents or guardian is also necessary. If the person is a child under 14, the consent of his/her parents or guardian is necessary only.

Grounds for Authorisation

Regardless of whether the person is in police detention or not, a inspector may only give his/her authorisation if he/she has reasonable grounds:

- for suspecting the involvement of the person from whom the sample is to be taken in a recordable offence; *and*
- for believing that the sample will tend to confirm or disprove the person's involvement in the offence.

For further discussion on the meaning of 'reasonable grounds to suspect', **see General Police Duties, chapter 2**).

Information to be Given to the Suspect

Where an authorisation has been given and it is proposed to take a sample, an officer shall inform the suspect that the authorisation has been given *and* of the grounds for it being given (including the nature of the offence which the person is suspected of committing). If the person is at a police station then, in addition to the above, an officer must also inform the person, before the sample is taken, that the sample may be subject to a 'speculative search' (Code D, para. 6.8).

(A speculative search is a check made against other samples and information derived from other samples contained in records or held by or on behalf of the police or held in connection with or as a result of an investigation of an offence.)

Paragraph 6.3 of Code D also requires that, before the sample is given, the suspect must be warned that if he/she refuses without good cause, that refusal may harm his/her case if it comes to trial. Where the suspect is in police detention, or is at the police station voluntarily, the officer shall also explain the entitlement to legal advice (as to which, **see chapter 15**).

Recording the Authorisation

An inspector's authorisation may be given orally but, if so given, it must be confirmed in writing as soon as practicable. The consent from the suspect must be given in writing (Code D, para. 6.10).

Other Information to be Recorded

Where an intimate sample is taken, certain information should be recorded. This information includes:

- the reasons for taking a sample or impression and if applicable, of its destruction must be made as soon as practicable;
- if force is used, the circumstances of the use of force and those present;
- whether the person gave written consent;
- if they are a suspect that they have been warned that if they refuse without good cause, their refusal may harm their case if it comes to trial (see para. 6.3);
- if they are in police detention that they have been reminded of their right to legal advice;
- that the person has been informed as in para. 6.8(c) that samples may be subject of a speculative search.

This information shall be recorded as soon as possible after the sample has been taken. Where a suspect is in police detention the information shall be recorded in the custody record.

Refusal of a Suspect to Give Consent

Where a suspect refuses, without good cause, to provide an intimate sample, then, in proceedings against that person for an offence, the court may draw such inferences as appear proper. The court may use such an inference for the purposes of determining:

- guilt;
- whether there is a case to answer;
- whether to commit for trial;
- whether an application to dismiss charges should be granted (where a notice of transfer from a magistrates' court to a Crown Court has been given earlier).

Taking an Intimate Sample

Dental impressions may only be taken by a registered dentist. Intimate samples, other than urine, may only be taken by a registered medical practitioner or a registered health care professional (Code D, para. 6.4).

Paragraph 6.9 of Code D sets out the provisions to be followed where clothing needs to removed in circumstances likely to cause embarrassment. These are:

- no person of the opposite sex may be present (other than a registered medical practitioner or registered health care professional);
- only people whose presence is necessary for the taking of the sample should in fact be present;
- in the case of a juvenile or mentally disordered or mentally vulnerable person, an appropriate adult of the opposite sex may be present *if specifically requested by the person and the person is readily available*;
- in the case of a juvenile, clothing may only be removed in the absence of an appropriate adult if the person signifies (in the presence of the appropriate adult) that he/she prefers his/her absence and the appropriate adult agrees.

16.7.3 Non-intimate Samples

The taking by police of non-intimate samples is governed by s. 63 of the Police and Criminal Evidence Act 1984. Additional guidance in the exercise of the powers is provided by Code D. The key requirements of these provisions are:

Consent

A person may consent to the taking of a non-intimate sample. If he/she does so, the consent must be given in writing.

A non-intimate sample may be taken without consent under the following conditions:

- where a person is in police detention or being held in custody by the police under the authority of a court and an officer of at least the rank of inspector authorises it to be taken;
- where a person has been charged with a recordable offence (or told he/she is to be reported for such an offence) and has not provided a non-intimate sample in the course of the investigation of the offence *or* where the person *has* had an non-intimate sample taken but that sample has either proved not suitable for the same means of analysis, or it has proved insufficient;
- where a person has been convicted of a recordable offence.

'Recordable offences' are generally those offences punishable by imprisonment, together with several others designated by statutory instrument (see Code D, Note 4A).

In order to close a gap in the legislation, the Criminal Evidence (Amendment) Act 1997 was passed, allowing the taking of non-intimate samples without consent in the case of people serving sentences for certain sexual, violent or other specified offences.

The effect of ss. 1 and 2 of the 1997 Act is to allow the taking of such samples from people serving a sentence of imprisonment or being detained under a hospital order (under the Mental Health Act 1983) if they were convicted of a recordable offence listed at sch. 1 before 10 April 1995. The provisions also extend to people who were not convicted by reason of their insanity or their unfitness to plead but who were detained at the relevant time under the Mental Health Act 1983.

For the main offences to which these provisions apply, **see Crime**.

Grounds for Authorisation

An officer of at least the rank of inspector may only give authority for the taking of a non-intimate sample if he/she has reasonable grounds:

- for suspecting the involvement of the person from whom the sample is to be taken in a recordable offence; *and*

- for believing that the sample will tend to confirm *or disprove* the person's involvement in the offence; *and*

- where the sample consists of a skin impression that a skin impression of the same part of the body has not already been taken from that person in the course of the investigation of the offence and if one has already been taken that it had not proved to be sufficient.

Information to be Given to the Suspect

Where an authorisation has been given by an officer of at least the rank of inspector and it is proposed to take a sample, an officer shall inform the suspect that the authorisation has been given *and* of the grounds for it being given (including the nature of the offence the person is suspected of committing).

Where a non-intimate sample is taken as a result of the suspect being charged, informed he/she is to be reported or following conviction for a recordable offence, he/she must be told of the reason why the sample is to be taken.

The person must be informed—before the sample is taken—that the sample may be subject to a 'speculative search' (Code D, para. 6.8) (**see para. 16.7.2**).

Recording the Authorisation

An officer of at least the rank of inspector authorisation may be given orally, but if so given, must be confirmed in writing as soon as practicable. The consent from the suspect must be given in writing (Code D, para. 6.10).

Other Information to be Recorded

Where a non-intimate sample is taken as a result of an officer of at least the rank of inspector's authority, the following information should be recorded:

- the *authorisation* by virtue of which the sample was taken;

- the *grounds* for the authorisation;

- the fact that the person has been informed that the sample may be subject to a *speculative search*.

This information must be recorded *as soon as possible* after the sample has been taken.

In other cases where a sample is taken without the person's consent, the reason shall be recorded as soon as practicable after the sample is taken.

Where a suspect is in police detention, the information shall be recorded in the custody record (Code D, paras 6.10 to 6.12).

Use of Force

Paragraph 6.7 of Code D provides that force may be used if necessary to obtain non-intimate samples in the circumstances described. Where force is used, a record should be made of the circumstances and those present at the time.

Taking a Non-intimate Sample

Where clothing needs to be removed in order to take a non-intimate sample, para. 6.9 of the Code D should be applied to prevent embarrassment.

16.7.4 | **Power to Require Persons to Attend a Police Station to Provide Samples**

In addition to the powers outlined, s. 63A of the Police and Criminal Evidence Act 1984 also provides for a constable to require a person to attend a police station for samples to be taken. The circumstances under which this requirement can be made are summarised as follows.

When Can the Requirement be Made?

A constable may make the requirement:

- where a person has been charged with a recordable offence or informed that he/she will be reported, or
- where the person has been convicted of a recordable offence

and, in either case, the person has not had a sample taken in the course of the investigation into the offence, or he/she has had a sample taken but it proved either unsuitable for the same means of analysis or the sample was insufficient.

The Period during which a Constable may Make the Requirement

The requirement to attend a police station must be made:

- within one month of the date of charge or of conviction; or
- within one month of the appropriate officer being informed that the sample is not suitable or has proved insufficient for analysis.

In making the requirement the officer:

- shall give the person at least seven days within which the person must attend; and
- may direct the person to attend at a specified time of day or between specified times of day.

Failure to Comply with the Requirement

Should a person fail to comply with the requirement, a constable may arrest the person without a warrant.

An appropriate officer is:

- the officer investigating the offence in the case of a person charged or told he/she will be reported;
- the officer in charge of the police station from which the investigation was conducted in the case of a person convicted.

For the corresponding power to take finger and palm prints, **see para. 16.5.**

16.7.5 Destruction of Samples

Code D, Annex F deals with the destruction and the speculative searches of fingerprints and samples. It is important that the Annex is followed particularly in relation to obtaining consent and explaining to volunteers what they are consenting to. Annex F, Note F1 provides suggested wordings that can be used when obtaining a person's consent to provide fingerprints or DNA samples for elimination purposes. It is important to use the correct wording depending on what the person has volunteered to, for example whether it is just to allow the fingerprint or sample to be used only for the purposes of a specific investigation; or for that investigation *and* retained by the police for future use. Such future use is limited to purposes related to the prevention or detection of crime, the investigation of an offence or the conduct of a prosecution in, as well as outside, the UK and may also be subject to a speculative search. This includes checking finger prints and samples against other fingerprints and DNA records held by, or on behalf of, the police and other law enforcement authorities in, as well as outside, the UK.

When fingerprints or DNA samples are taken from a person in connection with an investigation and the person is not suspected of having committed the offence, the fingerprints and/or sample must be destroyed as soon as they have fulfilled the purpose for which they were taken unless:

- they were taken for the purposes of an investigation of an offence for which a person has been convicted; and
- fingerprints or samples were also taken from the convicted person for the purposes of that investigation.

The reason why fingerprints and samples are retained is to allow for all fingerprints and samples in a case to be available for any subsequent miscarriage of justice investigation. They may not be used in the investigation of any offence or in evidence against the person who is, or would be, entitled to the destruction of the fingerprints and samples unless the person gives their written consent for their fingerprints or sample to be retained and used after they have fulfilled the purpose for which they were taken.

Annex F, para. 3 details what must be done when a person's fingerprints or sample are to be destroyed, this includes all copies of the fingerprints.

Annex F, para. 5 deals with the retention and destruction of fingerprints taken in connection with Immigration Service enquiries.

16.7.6 Terrorism Offences

There are additional powers and procedures for those suspects arrested in connection with terrorism which are contained in the Terrorism Act 2000 (as to which, **see General Police Duties, chapter 4**).

With the exception of fingerprints, non-intimate samples or intimate samples, a constable may take any steps which are reasonably necessary for:

- photographing the detained person,
- measuring him/her, or identifying him/her

(sch. 8, para. 2 to the 2000 Act).

Fingerprints and Non-intimate Samples

Fingerprints and non-intimate samples may be taken from a detained person only if they are taken by a constable either:

- with the consent of the detained person given in writing; or

- where he/she is detained at a police station and a police officer of at least the rank of superintendent authorises the fingerprints or sample to be taken; or
- where the person has been convicted of a recordable offence and, where a non-intimate sample is to be taken, he/she was convicted of the offence on or after 10 April 1995

(sch. 8, para. 10(1)–(4) to the 2000 Act).

Intimate Samples

An intimate sample may be taken from a detained person only if:

- he/she is detained at a police station;
- the appropriate consent is given in writing;
- a police officer of at least the rank of superintendent authorises the sample to be taken

(sch. 8, para. 10(5) to the 2000 Act).

An intimate sample other than a sample of urine or a dental impression may be taken only by a registered medical practitioner/registered health professional acting on the authority of a constable. An intimate sample which is a dental impression may be taken only by a registered dentist acting on the authority of a constable.

The grounds for which an authorisation may be given under the Terrorism Act 2000 are:

- the officer reasonably suspects that the person has been involved in an offence under any of the provisions mentioned in s. 40(1)(a) of the Terrorism Act 2000 and the officer reasonably believes that the fingerprints or sample will tend to confirm or disprove his/her involvement; or
- the officer is satisfied that the taking of the fingerprints or sample from the person is necessary in order to assist in determining whether he/she is or has been concerned in the commission, preparation or instigation of acts of terrorism (s. 40(1)(b) of the Terrorism Act 2000); or
- the officer is satisfied that the taking of fingerprints of the detained person will facilitate the ascertainment of that person's identity (or showing that he/she is not a particular person): and that person has refused to identify himself/herself or the officer has reasonable grounds for suspecting that that person is not who he/she claims to be.

Section 40(1)(a) of the Terrorism Act 2000 refers to offences of:

- membership to a proscribed organisation;
- arranging, managing or assisting in arranging or managing a meeting to support a proscribed organisation or to further the activities of a proscribed organisation;
- addressing a meeting for the purpose of encouraging support for a proscribed organisation or to further its activities;
- fund-raising for the purposes of terrorism;
- using and possessing money or other property for the purposes of terrorism or making arrangements for its use;
- money laundering;
- providing instruction or training in the making or use of weapons;
- directing terrorist organisation;
- possession of articles for terrorist purposes;

- collection or possession of information of a kind likely to be useful to a person committing or preparing an act of terrorism;
- inciting terrorism overseas.

Before fingerprints or a sample are taken from a person he/she must be informed that the authorisation has been given, the grounds upon which it has been given and, where relevant, of the nature of the offence in which it is suspected that he/she has been involved.

Where appropriate written consent to the taking of an intimate sample from a person is refused without good cause, in any proceedings against that person for an offence, the court, in determining whether to commit him for trial or whether there is a case to answer, may draw such inferences from the refusal as appear proper, and the court or jury, in determining whether that person is guilty of the offence charged, may draw such inferences from the refusal as appear proper.

It should be noted that s. 63A, as amended by the Criminal Justice and Police Act 2001, widens the extent that fingerprints and DNA profiles can be cross searched against those held by another UK or Island force. This has been extended to other police forces (for example, foreign police forces, the Ministry of Defence and the Armed Forces police forces) on the same basis that already exists between UK and Island forces. This also applies to fingerprints and samples obtained under the Terrorism Act 2000.

Where a sample proves to be insufficient there are provisions for obtaining further samples; this must be authorised by an officer of the rank of superintendent or above.

17 Interviews

17.1 Introduction

Much police time is spent interviewing witnesses and suspects. Confessions are often seen by the police to be an important part of the prosecution case but have frequently been a source of attack by the defence. The power imbalance between a detained person and his/her custodians has been an issue which has often brought into question the reliability of any confession, particularly as it had, until recently, been the right of an individual detainee to remain silent without any adverse inferences being drawn (**see chapter 10**). The PACE Codes of Practice C and E are intended to provide some protection to people being interviewed by police and lay down guidelines as to how interviews should be conducted. This protection means that confessions may be held to be inadmissible because of:

- the conduct of the interviewing officers (s. 76(2)(a) of the Police and Criminal Evidence Act 1984);
- the unreliability of the confession (s. 76(2)(b)); or
- unfairness in the proceedings (s. 78).

It may seem that the balance is in favour of the detained person. However the position now is that, while a person may still remain silent and the rules remain to preserve this right, inferences may now be drawn from a person's silence in some circumstances (**see chapter 10**).

It is not unusual for it to be alleged that officers have fabricated evidence or obtained a confession through trickery or by some kind of oppression. In order to provide safeguards against the risk of such evidence from questioning being obtained by oppression or in circumstances rendering it unreliable or obtained in a manner that breaches an individual's remaining right to silence, there are restrictions and guidelines on police questioning. These rules can be found throughout Codes C and E of the PACE Codes of Practice, giving guidance on the questioning of persons by police officers. Failure to follow these rules may lead to evidence being excluded and/or disciplinary charges and ultimately could lead to civil claims for compensation. For conduct that might lead to the exclusion of evidence, **see para. 13.3**. For police disciplinary proceedings, **see General Police Duties, chapter 1**.

17.2 What is an Interview?

Not all discussions between the police and members of the public will be protected or governed by the PACE Codes of Practice. Code C, para. 11.1A defines an interview as:

> . . . the questioning of a person regarding their involvement or suspected involvement in a criminal offence or offences which . . . must be carried out under caution.

KEYNOTE

Whether an interaction between a police officer and a member of the public is defined as an interview by the court can be crucial as to whether it will be admissible in evidence. It is therefore essential to understand the definition of an interview for the purposes of PACE and when a caution must be given and which caution must be given (for cautions, see para. 17.3).

If a person is asked questions for reasons *other than obtaining evidence about his/her involvement or suspected involvement in an offence*, this is not an interview (and a caution need not be given). (For the use of cautions, see para. 17.3.) This point is confirmed in the case of *R* v *McGuinness* [1999] Crim LR 318, where the court confirmed that it was only when a person was suspected of an offence that the caution must be administered before questioning. Consequently, in *R* v *Miller* [1998] Crim LR 209 the court held that asking a person the single question, 'Are these ecstasy tablets?' criminally implicated the person and therefore the conversation was an interview (i.e. it would not be necessary to ask such a question if there were no suspicion that the tablets were a controlled substance).

In *Whelehan* v *DPP* [1995] RTR 177, a police officer, without giving a caution, asked questions of a person, who was sitting in the driving seat of his stationary vehicle with the key in the ignition switch, to establish that the person had been drinking and had driven to the spot. The officer went on to require a breath test. The court held that the magistrates were entitled to rule that the constable's suspicion as to the commission of the offence arose only after taking the breath test and the caution had been correctly administered.

Whelehan should be compared with *R* v *Wyna*, 6 April 2000, unreported, where police had carried out a long-term surveillance operation. As a result of these observations the suspect was followed by police. He drove to central London where a man was seen to place an item in the boot of his car. The appellant then drove to the motorway heading north and was stopped by the police. A package containing over 4 kg of heroin was found in the boot. When the suspect was stopped, the reason given was that of speeding and when questioned about the drugs at the roadside he provided an innocent explanation. In this case even the Crown conceded that the police had reasonable grounds to suspect that the man had committed an arrestable offence when they stopped him at the roadside, and on that basis, under Code C, para. 10.1, they should have cautioned him immediately before asking him any questions.

Guidance on when questions do not amount to an interview is given by Code C, para. 10.1:

> ... A person need not be cautioned if questions are for other necessary purposes, e.g.:
>
> (a) solely to establish their identity or ownership of any vehicle;
>
> (b) to obtain information in accordance with any relevant statutory requirement ... ;
>
> (c) in furtherance of the proper and effective conduct of a search, e.g. to determine the need to search in the exercise of powers of stop and search or to seek co-operation while carrying out a search;
>
> (d) to seek verification of a written record as in paragraph 11.13;
>
> (e) when examining a person in accordance with the Terrorism Act 2000, schedule 7 and the Code of Practice for Examining Officers issued under that Act, schedule 14, paragraph 6.

KEYNOTE

Before a person can be interviewed about their involvement in an offence, that person must be cautioned. So it might be said that an interview is any questioning of a person after such time as a caution has been or should have been administered. Where a person is arrested for an offence, he/she must also be cautioned, as any questioning will amount to an interview (see General Police Duties, chapter 2).

17.3 **The Caution**

In *Murray* v *United Kingdom* (1996) 22 EHRR 29 it was held that adverse inferences may not be drawn from the silence of a person who wants legal advice if they have not been allowed an opportunity to receive it. As a result of this decision Code C, Annex C sets out the restriction on drawing adverse inferences from silence and the terms of the caution when the restriction applies. Adverse inferences from silence are restricted in some cases where the detainee has not had legal advice. In these cases the caution that must be given to the person has been amended in order to remove the infringement on the person's right to remain silent.

In all cases other than those where the restriction on drawing adverse inferences apply, the caution to be given is set out in Code C, para. 10.5:

> You do not have to say anything. But it may harm your defence if you do not mention when questioned something which you later rely on in Court. Anything you do say may be given in evidence.

The occasions where the alternative caution is required are set out in Code C, Annex C, para. 1, that is occasions where the restriction on drawing an adverse inference apply.

This restriction applies:

- to any detainee at a police station who has asked for legal advice and not been allowed an opportunity to consult a solicitor and has not changed their mind;

- to any detainee at a police station who has had their right to consult a solicitor suspended by an officer of the rank of superintendent or above (Code C, Annex B);

- where an officer of superintendent rank or above has authorised an interview without waiting for the detainee to consult with a solicitor as set out in Code C, para. 6.6(b)(ii);

- where the interview goes ahead without a solicitor, including a duty solicitor, because awaiting their arrival would cause unreasonable delay to the process of the investigation and the person has not changed their mind about wanting a solicitor (Code C, para. (6.6(b)(ii))

- where a person has been charged with, or informed they may be prosecuted for an offence and

  - has had brought to their notice a written statement made by another person or the content of an interview with another person which relates to that offence,

  - is interviewed about that offence, or

  - makes a written statement about that offence.

Annex C, para. 2 sets out the alternative terms of the caution to be used when the restriction on drawing adverse inferences from silence applies:

> You do not have to say anything, but anything you do say may be given in evidence.

The situation is likely to occur during a detainee's detention where it will be necessary to administer both of these cautions at various times during his/her detention. As there is a significant difference between them in relation to the right to silence, it will be important to make it clear which caution applies to the detainee during any interview or charge procedure. Guidance as to what the detainee should be told, is provided by Code C, Annex C, Note C2, this paragraph gives sample explanations that need to be explained to the detainee before the change is caution is given.

| Full caution already given (in most cases given when arrested) | → Detainee's access to legal advice restricted as per Code C, Annex C, para. 1. Need to give alternative caution | → Explain change in caution as set out at Code C, Annex C Note C2(a)(i) | → Give caution as set out at Annex C, para. 2 |

Full caution already given	→ Detainee has been charged but is further interviewed (Code C, Annex C, para. 1). Need to give alternative caution	→ Explain change in caution as set out at Code C, Annex C, Note C2(a) (ii)	→ Give caution as set out at Annex C, para. 2
Caution as set out at Annex C, para. 2, given	→ Detainee has now had access to a solicitor or changed their mind. Need to give alternative caution	→ Explain change in caution as set out at Code C, Annex C, Note C2(b)	→ Give caution Code C, para. 10.5

Where Code C, Annex C, para. 1 applies (i.e. the detainee has not been given access to a solicitor) and the detainee is charged with an offence or informed they may be prosecuted, the caution at Annex C, para. 2 should be used, on all other occasions the caution at Code C, para. l6.2 should be used:

> You do not have to say anything. But it may harm your defence if you do not mention now something which you later rely on in court. Anything you do say may be given in evidence.

If a person is questioned without being cautioned when a caution should have been given, any admissions made by that person are likely to be inadmissible in evidence. One of the main reasons for this is that a person has a right to remain silent and if the caution has not been given, the suspect has not been warned of this right nor of the risks of self-incrimination. Conversely, if a caution is not required and one is given, the person may not make admissions which he/she might otherwise have made. Consequently, it is important to be aware of when to administer a caution and, in cases of doubt, to err on the side of caution. Should an interview be excluded, this may have implications on other evidence obtained as a consequence of the confession (**see para. 13.2.2**).

An appropriate caution should be administered to all people who are:

- arrested for an offence, and/or
- where Code C, para. 10.1 applies.

Code C, para. 10.1 states:

> A person whom there are grounds to suspect of an offence, see Note 10A, must be cautioned before any questions about an offence, or further questions if the answers provide the grounds for suspicion, are put to them if either the suspect's answers or silence, (i.e. failure or refusal to answer or answer satisfactorily) may be given in evidence to a court in a prosecution....

KEYNOTE

If a person does not appear to understand the caution, the officer who has given it should go on to explain it in his/her own words (Code C, Note 10D).

The caution must be given where there are 'grounds to suspect the person of an offence'. Normally the 1984 Act and the Codes of Practice refer to 'reasonable grounds', whereas here the reference is simply to 'grounds'. This would suggest that the level of evidence/suspicion needed before a caution is given to a suspect may be *lower* than that needed to arrest the person. This would mean that a person may need to be cautioned when spoken to about offences for which there is no power of arrest or on occasions where there is a power of arrest but the officer's level of suspicion is not sufficient to justify an arrest (**see General Police Duties, chapter 2**).

The courts have given some guidance as to when a caution should be administered. There must be real *grounds* for suspicion; a mere hunch is not sufficient. The grounds have to be such as to lead to suspicion that an offence has been committed by that person. This view is confirmed in *Batley* v *DPP* (1998) *The Times*, 5 March, where the court accepted that, in general terms, where police officers had nothing more than a hunch that an offence was being committed, there would not be enough to activate the Code. However, it was necessary to caution a person before asking questions which went to the very heart of the issue as to whether he/she might be committing an offence, especially since the suspect was being invited to incriminate himself/herself.

In *Fox* v *United Kingdom* (1990) 13 EHRR 157, the court stated that reasonable suspicion arises from facts or information which would satisfy an objective observer that the person concerned may have committed the offence. Clearly there will be a need to record this information in detail to inform the court of the facts, as known at the time of the decision to caution or not to caution.

Further guidance was provided in *R* v *Smith* [2001] 1 WLR 1031 where the court held that establishing a reasonable suspicion was an objective test and an honest belief by a police officer was not required. Suspicion could take into account evidence that could not be adduced, such as hearsay. Except where evidence had been obtained in blatant breach of a statute, improperly obtained information could still be relied on.

Where the questions go beyond issues raised by Code C, para. 10.1 and go to the question of guilt, this is likely to be an interview for the purposes of the Police and Criminal Evidence Act 1984. In *Crown Prosecution Service* v *O'Shea*, 11 May 1998, unreported, police were called to a road traffic accident. O'Shea, the owner of the vehicle, was near the car, exhibiting signs of drunkenness and there was no one else in the vicinity who might have been driving the vehicle. The officer said to O'Shea the words, 'An accident has just happened that is alleged was your fault'. The court held that it was clear than when the officer had asked O'Shea whether he was driving his vehicle at the time of the accident, the officer had known that he was the owner of the vehicle and therefore the question was not solely to establish whether he was the owner. Accordingly, the thrust of the question was whether he had committed an offence. The defendant's subsequent answer was held to be inadmissible as the PACE Codes of Practice had not been complied with.

O'Shea can be contrasted with *R* v *Maguire* [1989] Crim LR 815 where the court held that Code C does not prevent a police officer from asking questions at or near the scene of the crime to elicit an explanation which if true or accepted, would clear the suspect.

Once a person has been cautioned, consideration of further cautions must be given. The need for additional cautions is provided for by the PACE Codes of Practice. In addition, in *R* v *Miller* [1998] Crim LR 209, the court said that one caution was not necessarily enough, and before other questions are asked of a suspect at a later stage, a further caution may be necessary.

In addition to the duty to caution a suspect, there will be occasions where a person arrested for an offence will have to be given a 'special warning' in interview. Special warnings are concerned with a person's right to silence (see ss. 34 to 37 of the Criminal Justice and Public Order Act 1994). As mentioned above, this will only apply where the detainee has had the opportunity to seek legal advice.

Unsolicited Comments

There will be occasions where suspects make unsolicited comments implicating them in an offence before they are suspected of any involvement and therefore before they are cautioned (or further cautioned if already suspected). Such statements are likely to be admissible provided the PACE Codes of Practice are complied with. Code C, paras 11.13 and 11.14 state:

11.13   A written record shall be made of any comments made by a suspect, including unsolicited comments, which are outside the context of an interview but which might be relevant to the offence. Any such record must be timed and signed by the maker. When practicable the suspect shall be given the opportunity to read that record and to sign it as correct or to indicate how they consider it inaccurate. See Note 11E

11.14   Any refusal by a person to sign an interview record when asked in accordance with this Code must itself be recorded.

Note 11E states:

When a suspect agrees to read records of interviews and other comments and sign them as correct, they should be asked to endorse the record with, e.g. 'I agree that this is a correct record of what was said' and add their signature. If the suspect does not agree with the record, the interviewer should record the details of any disagreement and ask the suspect to read these details and sign them to the effect that they accurately reflect their disagreement. Any refusal to sign should be recorded.

KEYNOTE

It is particularly important to record the comment and give the person an opportunity to see what has been recorded and to comment/endorse it. Where the person has had this opportunity and signs the record then it will strengthen the evidence and if he/she declines to sign it, this may assist in establishing what the defence case may be.

In *R* v *Miller* (above) the court held that Code C, para. 11.13 requires a written record, timed and signed by the suspect as correct or an opportunity for the suspect to indicate which parts were inaccurate.

Whilst it is suggested that this should be done at an early opportunity, in *Batley* v *DPP* (1998) *The Times*, 5 March, where it was held that as the Code did not require an *immediate* endorsement and no time factor was laid down, there was nothing to constrain the police from returning the next day to get their endorsement.

17.4 Interview of Person Not Under Arrest

If a person has not been arrested then he/she can be interviewed almost anywhere (but an officer intending to interview a person on private property must consider whether he/she is trespassing, **see General Police Duties, chapter 2**). If the interview with a person not under arrest takes place in a police station, Code C, para. 3.21 and Note 1A must be followed.

If the interview is to be with a juvenile, Code C, para. 11.16, gives guidance as to when interviews should take place at a juvenile's place of education. This should only be in exceptional circumstances and with the agreement of the principal or the principal's nominee. The juvenile's parent(s) or person(s) responsible for his/her welfare and the appropriate adult (if a different person) should be notified of the interview and be afforded reasonable time in which to attend. The principal or nominee can act as the appropriate adult where waiting for an appropriate adult would cause unreasonable delay. This is not the case where the juvenile is suspected of an offence against his/her educational establishment (Code C, para. 11.15). Code C, paras 11.18 to 11.20 and Note 11C outline the limited circumstances when a juvenile may be interviewed without an appropriate adult being present.

In cases where the person is not under arrest, certain information must be given to him/her. This is covered by Code C, para. 10.2 which states:

> Whenever a person not under arrest is initially cautioned, or reminded they are under caution, that person must at the same time be told they are not under arrest and are free to leave if they want to. See Note 10C

KEYNOTE

For the situation where a person is a police station voluntarily and not under arrest, see Code C, para. 3.21 (**see General Police Duties, chapter 2**).

When carrying out an interview, officers should be mindful of how they treat the person, this it is suggested, also applies to witnesses as well as suspects. For instance in *L* v *Reading Borough Council*, 12 March 2001, unreported, the court stated that it was arguable that when interviewing a young child victim there was an assumption of responsibility and a special relationship was created. Part of the responsibility was to protect the child from future harm that could ensue from the manner of the investigation. Following this line, failure to protect the victims/witnesses could lead to a claim for damages if they suffer harm.

17.5 **Interview of Person Under Arrest**

Any interview of a person who is under arrest must take place at a police station (Code C, para. 11.1) or other authorised place of detention unless waiting until the interview can be conducted at such a place is likely to:

- lead to interference with or harm to evidence connected with an offence or interference with or physical harm to other people or serious loss of, or damage to property; or

- lead to the alerting of other people suspected of having committed an offence but not yet arrested for it; or

- hinder the recovery of property obtained in consequence of the commission of an offence.

Code C requires that interviewing in any of these circumstances shall cease once the relevant risk has been averted or the necessary questions have been put in order to attempt to avert that risk (para. 11.1). There is a danger in these cases of continuing the interview past the point where the risk has been averted, this could lead to the whole interview being excluded.

The courts have recognised that there may be times when a person who is under arrest will be asked questions other than when at the police station. One such example is where the arrested person is present while officers search his/her address (**see General Police Duties, chapter 2**). In *R v Hanchard*, 6 December 1999, unreported, the court recognised that searches of premises could not be conducted in complete silence. The court stated that it would be unfair and unreasonable not to put any questions to owners of premises undergoing a search, however, what questions can be asked will be a matter of fact and degree in each individual case. Where questions go beyond that needed for the immediate investigation it would be a breach of the Codes. In *Hanchard*, the questions which were admissible included whether cannabis at the address belonged to the suspect and where a large quantity of money had come from.

If a person has been arrested by one police force on behalf of another and the lawful period of detention in respect of that offence has not yet begun (in accordance with s. 41 of the Police and Criminal Evidence Act 1984 (**see para. 15.4.5**)), no questions may be put to him/her about the offence while he/she is in transit between the forces except in order to clarify any voluntary statement made by him/her (Code C, para. 14.1).

If a person is in police detention at a hospital, he/she may not be questioned without the agreement of a responsible doctor (Code C, para. 14.2). If an interview does take place, the interviewing officer must inform the custody officer as the period will count to the total time spent in custody (Note 14A).

If questioning does take place in any of these circumstances it will affect the suspect's 'detention clock' (**see chapter 15**). The custody officer must be informed of such an interview as it may affect the lawfulness of the suspect's detention (**see para. 15.5.1**).

It is essential to comply with the rules on interviewing after arrest, as a failure could jeopardise any future admissions made in interview. In *R v Webster*, 12 December 2000, unreported, the police evidence was that during the search of his house the defendant, having been arrested but not cautioned, had made admissions as to where the drugs were located in his house and as to the amount of drugs that he possessed. No contemporaneous note was taken of the search. The defendant was then interviewed on the same basis as his answers to the questions which had been asked during the search. The court held that the later interview at the police station did not cure the breaches of the Codes of Practice which had occurred during the search and both interviews were excluded.

17.6 Person Charged with an Offence

Once a person has been charged with an offence generally he/she cannot be interviewed about the offence unless it is necessary:

- to prevent or minimise harm or loss to some other person or to the public; or

- to clear up an ambiguity in a previous answer or statement; or

- in the interest of justice that the person should have questions put to him/her and have an opportunity to comment on information concerning the offence which has come to light since he/she was charged or informed that he/she might be prosecuted.

It should be noted that the service of the Notice of Intended Prosecution under ss. 1 and 2 of the Road Traffic Offenders Act 1988 (**see Road Traffic, chapter 3**), does not amount to informing a person that he/she may be prosecuted for an offence and so does not preclude further questioning in relation to that offence (Code C, Note 16B).

If a person is interviewed for any other reason, the interview is likely to be inadmissible in evidence.

Where a person is interviewed after charge, Code C, para. 16.5 states:

> . . . Before any such interview, the interviewer shall:
>
> (a) caution the detainee, 'You do not have to say anything, but anything you do say may be given in evidence.';
>
> (b) remind the detainee about their right to legal advice.
>
> See Note 16B

This caution does not restrict the right to silence. It is not unusual for a person who has been charged with offences (and therefore his/her detention is for other reasons, e.g. because bail has been refused) to be paid a 'social visit' or to be spoken to for debrief intelligence purposes. Clearly there is a risk that the person may provide additional evidence about the offences for which he/she has been detained on other matters. *R v Williams* (1992) *The Times*, 6 February, recognised that this practice did occur but gave some guidance. The court held that investigating officers should avoid paying 'social visits' to people in custody whose conduct was under investigation. If, after being charged with an offence, a suspect of his/her own volition said that he/she wished to make a statement admitting or giving details of the offence, after properly cautioning the person and complying with the rest of the Codes of Practice, investigating officers were not debarred from recording what he/she had to say. Prior to a person being visited in his/her cell, the custody officer must give his/her authority and the visit must be recorded in the detained person's custody record.

17.7 When Must an Interview be Held?

Code C, para. 16.1 states:

> When the officer in charge of the investigation reasonably believes there is sufficient evidence to provide a realistic prospect of the detainee's conviction, see paragraph 11.6, they shall without delay, and subject to the following qualification, inform the custody officer who will be responsible for considering whether the detainee should be charged . . .

KEYNOTE

It is suggested that, in a case where a suspect has not been interviewed about an offence, Code C, para. 16.1, requires that person to be asked if he/she has anything further to say about the matter, in which case this will be an interview.

This view is supported by the case of *R v Pointer* [1997] Crim LR 676 which held that giving a suspect the opportunity to say something more when the officer already has enough evidence to charge is an interview within the definition of Code C, para. 11.1A, and, therefore, an event which attracts the protection of a caution, legal representation and tape recording.

Interviews in these circumstances are conducted to allow the suspect to make any additional comments and for the interviewing officers to follow up on those responses. If the interview is held for any other reason it is likely to be inadmissible. This was the case in *Pointer* where the court held that there was sufficient evidence to charge prior to the interview and consequently Code C, para. 16.1 had not been complied with. Such an interview may assist the investigating officer to make reasonable lines of enquiry which support the defence.

17.8 Conducting and Recording Interviews

The conduct of officers and the proper treatment of the suspect during an interview are essential if an interview is to be admissible in evidence. If an interview is not conducted properly, confessions made during the interview may be excluded (**see chapter 13**). The PACE Codes of Practice are there to afford suspects proper protection from false confessions and treatment which may lead a court to the conclusion that the confession may not be reliable. It is essential, therefore, that officers are fully aware of the relevant Codes and comply with them. For occasions when evidence may be excluded, **see chapter 13**. For evidential purposes interviews need to be recorded contemporaneously. An accurate record must be made of each interview with a person suspected of an offence, whether or not the interview takes place at a police station (Code C, para. 11.7).

Interviews fall into two main groups:

- those that are tape recorded; and

- those where the only record will be made in writing.

If a suspect makes unsolicited comments which are outside the context of an interview but which might be relevant to the offence, those comments should be recorded and Code C, para. 11.13 should be followed (**see chapter 13**). Code C, Note 11E gives guidance as to what must be included in the record and when the record should be made. As the relevance of the comment may not be obvious at the time it is made, it is suggested that all comments are recorded.

17.8.1 When Interviews Must Be Taped

The interviewing of suspects is governed by PACE Code of Practice E. Code E, paras 3.1 and 3.5 set out which interviews at a police station must be tape recorded. The most noticeable absence from this list is for interviews about matters which can only be tried summarily. These requirements do not *preclude* other interviews being tape recorded. Investigators may well be advised to tape record interviews concerning summarily only offences as it may be more difficult for the defence to suggest any confession was fabricated. If these interviews are tape recorded, they must follow the requirements of tape recorded interviews (see Code E, Note 3A).

The whole of each interview shall be recorded, including the taking and reading back of any statement (Code E, para. 3.5).

All interviews listed in Code E, para. 3.1 conducted at a police station must be tape recorded *unless* the custody officer authorises the interviewing officer not to tape record the interview. If the custody officer authorises the interview to go ahead without being tape recorded, the interview must be recorded in writing. A custody officer authorising this may have to justify the decision at court and the reasons for his/her decision should be recorded. Code E, para. 3.3 allows the custody officer to make this decision where:

- It is not reasonably practicable to tape record the interview because of:
  - failure of the equipment; or
  - the non-availability of a suitable interview room or recorder; and
  - the custody officer considers on reasonable grounds that the interview should not be delayed until the failure has been rectified or a suitable room or recorder becomes available
- or it is clear from the outset that no prosecution will ensue
- where the custody officer has authorised that the detainee can be interviewed in his/her cell (Code E, Para. 3.4).

Further, Code E, para. 3.1 does not apply to:

- certain interviews involving terrorism (Code E, para. 3.2).

For cases where a person objects to the interview being tape recorded, see Code E, para. 4.8.

As of September 2002, where persons are held in police detention at Basingstoke, Portsmouth, Southampton, Chatham, Gravesend, Tonbridge, Bromley, Colindale, Edmonton, Redditch, Telford, Worcester, Colchester, Harlow and Southend police stations any interviews held by police officers must be visually recorded. Codes of Practice for the visual recording of interviews have been produced for use at these police stations.

17.8.2 **Preparation before Interview at Police Station**

Preparation is essential before any interview (indeed it is the first step in the PEACE interviewing model). This preparation should include the following points:

- Decide where the interview will be conducted. Consider the availability of a room and the timing of the interview.
- The location must have a seat for the person being interviewed (Code C, para. 12.6) and should be adequately lit, heated and ventilated (Code C, para. 12.4). The detained person must also have clothing of a reasonable standard of comfort and cleanliness (Code C, para. 8.5). (It will be a question of fact as to what amounts to adequate clothing and it is suggested that if the clothing is such as to degrade the detained person or make him/her uncomfortable, it may lead to the confession being held to be unreliable.)
- If the interview is being taped, ensure that there are sufficient tapes for the anticipated length of the interview (or at least until the first break period). If the interview is being recorded in writing, ensure there are enough forms.
- If the interview is being taped, ensure the notice as set out in Code E, para. 4.19 is available to be given at the end of the interview.
- In deciding the timing of the interview, consideration must be given to the detainee's rest period, which should not be interrupted or delayed unless Code C, para. 12.2 applies. Where the interview goes ahead during the rest period under Code C, para. 12.2(a), a fresh rest period must be allowed. Before a detainee is interviewed, the custody officer, in consultation with the officer in charge of the investigation and appropriate health care professionals as necessary, shall assess whether the detainee is fit enough to be interviewed (Code C, para. 12.3 and Annex G.)
- If legal advice has been requested you must arrange for the legal representative to be present at the interview unless Code C, para. 6.6 applies.

- If a person has asked for legal advice and an interview is initiated in the absence of a legal adviser (e.g. where the person has agreed to be interviewed without his/her legal adviser being present or because of the urgent need to interview under Code C, para. 11.1), a record must be made in the interview record (Code C, para. 6.17).

- If an appropriate adult should be present, arrange for his/her attendance. (For the definition of appropriate adult, see Code C, para. 1.7.)

- If an interpreter is needed for the interview, arrange for his/her attendance (**see para 15.12**).

It is also important to draw up an interview plan and to include any relevant areas that may provide a general or specific defence (as to which, **see Crime, chapter 4**).

- Look at the evidence available and identify any significant statement or silence by the suspect in order that it can be put to him/her in interview (Code C, para. 11.4).

17.8.3   **Starting Interviews**

In order to interview a detained person, the interviewing officer must obtain permission from the custody officer. An entry must be made in the custody record to record that the interviewing officer accepts responsibility for the detained person. If the request to hand over the detained person is declined, the custody officer must record this fact and the reasons why on the custody record (Code C, para. 12.10). The responsibility for the detained person at this stage rests with the officer to whom the transfer is made and remains with this person until the detained person is returned to the custody officer (s. 39(2) of the Police and Criminal Evidence Act 1984). Section 39 of the 1984 Act states:

(2) If this custody officer, in accordance with any code of practise issued under this Act, transfers or permits the transfer of a person in police detention—
(a) to the custody of a police officer investigating an offence for which that person is in police detention; or
(b) to the custody of an officer who has charge of that person outside the police station, the custody officer shall cease in relation to that person to be subject to the duty imposed on him by subsection (1)(a) above; and it shall be the duty of the officer to whom the transfer is made to ensure that he is treated in accordance with the provisions of this Act and of any such codes of practice as are mentioned in subsection (1) above.

Before allowing a detainee to be interviewed the custody officer shall undertake a risk assessment in order to ensure that conducting the interview will not significantly harm the detainee's physical or mental state or that their physical or mental state might result in the them saying something in the interview about their involvement or suspected involvement in the offence being considered unreliable in subsequent court proceedings (Code C, Annex G, para. 1 and 2). The risk assessment should be done, where necessary, in consultation with the officer in charge of the investigation and appropriate health care professionals. Annex G, para. 3 sets out a number of factors that must be considered when conducting this risk assessment. Where risks are identified, the custody officer must determine what safeguards are needed to minimise those risks in order to allow the interview to take place. It should be remembered that vulnerable suspects listed at Code C, para. 11.18 must always be treated as if being at some risk during an interview and therefore may not be interviewed except in accordance with Code C, paras 11.18 to 11.20 (Code C, para. 12.3). Code C, Annex G provides guidance to help police officers and health care professionals assess whether a detainee might be at risk in an interview.

The risk assessment can be very important in terms of ensuring that any confession in an interview is admissible. In *R* v *Utip* (2003) unreported, the court held that the law required that where there were grounds to suspect mental illness, a defendant should be examined by a doctor to establish whether he/she was fit for interview. Where a defendant had been assessed as fit to be interviewed by a psychiatrist and had his/her interests protected by an appropriate adult and solicitor, there was no unfairness in allowing evidence of the interview to go before the jury.

17.8.4 Preliminary Issues for Interviews Not Being Tape Recorded

Before an interview begins the following points must be dealt with:

- Immediately before the commencement of the interview remind the suspect of his/her right to legal advice (Code C, para. 11.2) and make a note of this reminder and any response in the interview record.
- For the interview record, identify all officers present in the interview as required by Code C, para. 12.7.
- If an appropriate adult is present, inform that person of his/her role (Code C, para. 11.17).
- Administer the relevant caution (Code C, para. 10.1) (and re-administer where appropriate, **see para. 17.3**).

17.8.5 Preliminary Issues for Interviews Being Tape Recorded

Before an interview commences the following points must be dealt with:

- Break open tape seals in the presence of the suspect (Code E, para. 4.3).
- Load tapes in the presence of the suspect and set to record (Code E, para. 4.3).
- Inform the suspect about the tape recording in accordance with Code E, para. 4.4.
- Verbally identify all persons present at the interview for the tape (Code E, para. 4.4).
- Administer the relevant caution (Code E, para. 4.5) (and re-administer where appropriate, **see para. 17.3**).
- Remind the suspect of his/her right to free legal advice (Code E, para. 4.5 and Code C, paras 6.1 and 6.5) and ensure that the response is recorded on the tape (for instance a nod of the head would not be picked up by a tape recorder).

17.8.6 What Should be Disclosed to the Solicitor

It is important not to confuse the duty of disclosure to a person once charged with the need to disclose evidence to a suspect before interviewing them. After a person has been charged, and before trial, the rules of disclosure are clear (**see chapter 14**) and almost all material must be disclosed to the defence.

However, this is not necessarily the case at the interview stage of the investigation. There is no specific provision within the Police and Criminal Evidence Act 1984 for the disclosure of any information by the police at the police station, with the exception of the custody record and, in identification cases, the initial description given by the witnesses. Further, there is nothing within the Criminal Justice and Public Order Act 1994 that states that information must be disclosed before an inference from silence can be made. Indeed, in *R* v *Imran* [1997] Crim LR 754 the court held that it is totally wrong to submit that a defendant should be prevented from lying by being presented with the whole of the evidence against him/her prior to the interview.

In *R* v *Argent* [1997] Crim LR 346 the court dismissed the argument that an inference could not be drawn under s. 34 of the Criminal Justice and Public Order Act 1994 because there had not been full disclosure at the interview. However, the court did recognise that it may be a factor to take into account, but it would be for the jury to decide whether the failure to answer questions was reasonable.

In *R* v *Roble* [1997] Crim LR 449, the court suggested that an inference would not be drawn where a solicitor gave advice to remain silent where, for example, the interviewing officer had disclosed too little of the case for the solicitor usefully to advise his/her client, or where the nature of the offence, or the material in the hands of the police, was so complex or related to matters so long ago that no sensible immediate response was feasible.

It was not uncommon in the past for solicitors to advise on no comment interviews and this has been relied on by defendants to avoid adverse inferences being drawn from their silence. The courts and legal advisers are now very aware of the consequences of advising a suspect to offer no comment. In *R v Morgan* [2002] ECWA Crim 445, the Court of Appeal stated that a court was entitled to assume that a solicitor would advise his/her client about the adverse inferences rule. In *R v Ali* [2002] ECWA Crim 683, the court stated that the question was not whether the advice to remain silent was good advice but whether it provided an adequate reason for failing to answer questions.

There is a balance to be struck between providing the solicitor with enough information to understand the nature of the case against his/her client and keeping back material which, if disclosed, may allow the suspect the opportunity to avoid implicating himself/herself. For instance in *R v Thirlwell* [2002] EWCA Crim 286, the Court of Appeal agreed that the solicitor had not been entitled to provisional medical evidence as to possible causes of death in a murder case. The disclosure of material may well be a factor which the defendant relies on in showing that the failure to mention possible defences was reasonable. If the officers are not hoping to draw inferences from silence then tactically they may decide not to disclose as much information—it will be a question of fact in each case.

17.8.7 Conduct During Interview

All Interviews

- Code C, para. 11.5 reiterates the fact that officers must not act oppressively.

- If a complaint is made by the suspect concerning the provisions of the codes the interviewing officer must inform the custody officer and follow Code C, para. 12.9. If the complaint is not concerning the codes, Code E, Note 4F applies.

- Officers should only indicate the possible effect of refusing to answer questions or of answering questions if he/she is asked about those possible effects by the suspect *unless this is done as part of a special warning* (see Code C, paras 10.10, 10.11 and 11.15).

- Code E, para. 4.8 provides guidance where the person objects to the interview being taped.

- Code C, Note 11C reminds officers of the risks associated with the reliability of interviewing juveniles or people who are mentally disordered or otherwise mentally vulnerable.

At the start of the interview the investigating officer should put to the suspect any significant statement or silence which occurred before his/her arrival at the police station and ask the suspect whether he/she confirms the earlier statement or silence and whether he/she wishes to add anything. Code C, para. 11.4A defines a 'significant' statement or silence. This aspect of the interview is very important in terms of establishing whether the facts are disputed. If they are not disputed at this stage, it is unlikely that they will be challenged at any later court hearing and, if challenged, the defence will have to explain why this was not done at the time of the interview. The courts may also view this failure to put the statement to the suspect in a more sinister light. In *R v Allen*, 10 July 2001, unreported, the court were concerned that the police failed to put the admission to the suspect in interview, despite thorough questioning, which they felt clearly placed a question mark over its reliability. If the suspect remains silent in relation to a 'significant silence', that silence may give rise to an adverse inference being drawn under s. 34 of the Criminal Justice and Public Order Act 1994 if the person raises it in his/her defence at court. (As this is very important issue, it may be necessary to delay the interview until the arrest notes are completed or the officers witnessing the offence/arrest have been consulted to ensure that all matters are put to the suspect at this stage.) Consideration should be given to putting questions to a suspect who makes no comment, or even where the legal representative has stated that the suspect will make no comment, as this may allow the court to draw inferences against a defence that the suspect raises at court (**see para. 10.6.1**). The interviewer may wish to go through any significant statement or silence again if during earlier interviews adverse inferences could not be drawn.

Issues Specific to Tape Recorded Interviews

- If the equipment fails, rectify the fault quickly if possible. If this is not possible, look for an alternative recording machine or room. If none available, seek the authority of the custody officer to continue without the interview being tape recorded (see Code E, para. 4.15).

- If a tape breaks, follow Code E, Note 4H.

- When the tapes are removed from the recorder they must be retained (see Code E, para. 4.16) and the procedure at para. 4.18 followed.

- If you need to change tapes during interview, follow Code E, para. 4.11.

- If a suspect objects to the interview being tape recorded at any stage of the interview, the procedure in Code E, para. 4.8 must be followed and Note 4D should be taken into account in deciding whether to continue to record the interview on tape.

- If a suspect indicates that he/she wishes to tell the police about matters not connected with the offence(s) being investigated but does not wish this information to be recorded on tape, Code E, para. 4.10 requires this to be dealt with at the conclusion of the formal interview. Any comment by the suspect would still need to be recorded in writing.

Breaks

Breaks from interviewing must be made at recognised meal times or at other times that take account of when the person last had a meal (Code C, para. 12.8). Short breaks for refreshment must also be provided at intervals of approximately two hours. Code C, Note 12B gives guidance on how long breaks should be. Code C, para. 12.8 sets out the exceptions to the requirement to provide breaks. These exceptions exist where to break the interview would:

- involve a risk of harm to people or serious loss of, or damage to property;

- delay unnecessarily the person's release from custody; or

- otherwise prejudice the outcome of the investigation.

Any decision to delay a break during an interview must be recorded, with grounds, in the interview record (either on the written record or on the tape) (Code C, para. 12.12).

Solicitors and Legal Advice

A 'solicitor' for the purposes of the Codes of Practice means:

- a solicitor holding a current practising certificate;

- a trainee solicitor;

- a duty solicitor representative or an accredited representative included on the register of representatives maintained by the Legal Services Commission (Code C, para. 6.12).

Where a solicitor is available at the time the interview begins or while it is in progress, the solicitor must be allowed to be present while the person in interviewed (Code C, para. 6.8).

(This applies unless the suspect states that he/she does not want the solicitor to be present or where access is denied under s. 58 of the 1984 Act, see Code C, Annex B.)

If a solicitor arrives at the station to see a suspect, the suspect must be asked whether he/she would like to see the solicitor *regardless of what legal advice has already been received.* The solicitor's attendance and the suspect's decision must be recorded in the custody record (Code C, para. 6.15).

If the investigating officer considers that a solicitor is acting in such a way that he/she is unable properly to put questions to the suspect, he/she will stop the interview and consult an officer not below the rank of superintendent, if one is readily available, otherwise an officer not below the rank of inspector who is not connected with the investigation to decide whether that solicitor should be excluded from the interview. The interview may also have to be stopped in order to allow another solicitor to be instructed (Code C, para. 6.10). For the proper role of the legal representatives, see Code C, Note 6D. Code C, para. 6.6 sets out those occasions where a person can be interviewed without a solicitor being present even though he/she has requested a solicitor (**see para. 15.4.3**). Any authority to exclude a solicitor will need to be justified to the court if necessary (Code C, Note 6E).

With regard to the exclusion of a trainee/probationer solicitor this has to be considered in relation to the specific investigation and whether that person is likely to interfere with the investigation. The decision can take into account the character of the person. Internal advice could also provide guidance as to what the decision should be but the decision has to be made in relation to each individual case. It is not permissible to have blanket bans on such persons (*R* v *Chief Constable of the Northumbria Constabulary, ex parte Thompson* [2001] 1 WLR 1342).

If a request for legal advice is made during an interview, the interviewing officer must stop the interview straightaway and arrange for legal advice to be provided. If the suspect changes his/her mind again, the interview can continue provided Code C, para. 6.6 is complied with.

It is important to remember that Code C, para. 6.4 reminds officers that they should *not* try and dissuade the detained person from obtaining legal advice.

17.8.8   **When Must the Interview be Concluded?**

Guidance is provided by Code C, para. 11.6 as to when an interview should be concluded. Paragraph 11.6 states that the interview shall cease if the investigating officer considers that:

- all the questions relevant to obtaining accurate and reliable information about the offence have been put to the suspect, this includes allowing the suspect an opportunity to give an innocent explanation and asking questions to test if the explanation is accurate and reliable;
- has taken account of any other available evidence; and
- there is sufficient evidence to provide a realistic prospect of conviction for that offence if the person was prosecuted for it.

The investigating officer shall then bring the detained person before the custody officer for charge.

The interview may continue until the above conditions are satisfied with regard to other offences being investigated (Code C, para. 16.1).

It is important to remember that the interview should not be concluded at the point when there is sufficient evidence to prosecute but when there is sufficient evidence to provide a realistic prospect of conviction. (In *Prouse* v *DPP* [1999] All ER (D) 748 the question was said to be not how much evidence there is but the quality of it.) Once there is enough evidence to prosecute, it may still be necessary to cover those other points in the interview that may be relevant to the defence case (**see Crime, chapter 4**). If these points are not covered in the interview, the defence may surprise the prosecution case with matters that the prosecution have not covered or with issues that may result in the loss of an inference being drawn from the suspect's silence. This was considered in *R* v *McGuinness* [1999] Crim LR 318 where the court held that the words 'sufficient evidence to prosecute' and 'sufficient evidence for a prosecution to succeed' in Code C, para. 11.6 must involve some consideration of any explanation, or lack of one, from the suspect. It would depend on the facts of a case whether the stage where a suspect ought to be charged has been reached. As a word of caution, the court also said that under Code C, paras 16.1 and 11.6 it was not open for a suspect to be questioned beyond the point when he/she ought to have been charged. If the suspect was questioned beyond that point, then the interview was liable to be ruled inadmissible and the content would not be available to support the prosecution case.

Paragraph 3.4 of the Code of Practice to the Criminal Procedure and Investigations Act 1996 says that in conducting an investigation, the investigator should pursue all reasonable lines of enquiry, whether these point towards or away from the suspect. What is reasonable will depend on the particular circumstances. Interviewers should keep this in mind when deciding what questions to ask in an interview.

17.8.9 ## Special Groups

As a confession can be very damning evidence against a defendant, it is important to provide safeguards that give all suspects the same level of protection. The PACE Codes of Practice recognise certain groups as being in need of additional protection. These groups include juveniles, people who do not speak English, those suffering from a mental impairment and those who are deaf. Such suspects must not be interviewed without the relevant person being present.

For juveniles and those suffering from a mental impairment (or who appear to be such), an appropriate adult must be present (Code C, para. 11.15).

Under Code C, para. 13.2, a person capable of acting as interpreter is required where:

- the suspect has difficulty in understanding English;
- the interviewing officer cannot speak the person's own language; and
- the suspect wishes an interpreter to be present.

If the suspect appears to be deaf or there is any doubt about his/her hearing or speaking ability, an interpreter should be found (unless he/she agrees *in writing* to proceed without an interpreter) (Code C, para. 13.5). This requirement also applies in the case of the appropriate adult who appears to be deaf or there is doubt about his/her hearing or speaking ability (Code C, para. 13.6).

There are limited circumstances where an interview may be conducted without an interpreter or appropriate adult being present. These are set out in Code C, paras 11.1 and 11.15. Once those conditions no longer apply, the interview must be suspended until the appropriate person is present.

Where interpreters are required, Code C, paras 13.3 to 13.11 are to be followed.

If an interpreter who can translate straight from the detained person's language to English cannot be found then more than one interpreter should be used to bridge the language gap. It is the *interviewer* who is responsible for ensuring that the detained person can understand and be understood (*R* v *West London Youth Court, ex parte J* [2000] 1 All ER 823).

Taped Interviews and Special Groups

If the suspect is deaf or there is doubt about his/her hearing ability, a contemporaneous written record should be made as well as the tape recording. This record should be the same as where there is no taped record of the interview (Code E, para. 4.7).

17.8.10 **Special Warnings**

Now that inferences can be drawn from a suspect's silence (albeit in limited circumstances), it is necessary to warn the person of the dangers of remaining silent. For this reason the 'special warning' was introduced (**see para. 10.6.2**) where there is potentially incriminating evidence relating to objects, marks or substances; or relating to the accused's presence at a particular place. If the special warning is not given, inferences from silence will not be allowed to boost the prosecution case but the potentially incriminating evidence may still be admissible. Code C, paras 10.10 to 10.11 must be followed if any questions are to be put to the arrested suspect about:

- any object, marks or substances found on the him/her, or
- in or on his/her clothing or footwear, or
- otherwise in his/her possession, or
- in the place where he/she was arrested

(see s. 36 of the Criminal Justice and Public Order Act 1994).

These provisions also apply to any questions about why the suspect was:

- at the scene of the offence,
- at or near the time of the offence for which the constable who saw the suspect there arrested him/her, and
- unable to account for his/her presence at or near the scene of the offence

(see s. 37 of the Criminal Justice and Public Order Act 1994).

It must be made clear to the suspect what matters he/she is being asked to answer and the consequences of remaining silent on each occasion.

See **para. 17.3** and Code C, Annex C for occasions when special warnings and adverse inferences do not apply.

17.8.11 **Conclusion of Interview**

Written Interviews

- The person interviewed (and the appropriate adult or the suspect's solicitor if present during the interview (Code C, para. 11.12)) must be given an opportunity to read the interview record and to sign it as correct or to indicate the respects in which he/she considers it inaccurate (Code C, para. 11.11). If the person concerned cannot read or refuses to read the record or to sign it, the senior police officer present shall read it to him/her (Code C, para. 11.11). If there is any delay in recording the interview, if practicable, the suspect should still be given an opportunity to read the statement.

- Any refusal to sign the record must be recorded (Code C, para. 11.14).

- If an interpreter has been present at the interview, he/she should be given an opportunity to read the record and certify its accuracy (Code C, para. 13.7).

- If the person is in police detention, return him/her to the custody officer, informing that officer whether the Codes have been complied with, if any incidents occurred and whether there were any breaches of the Codes (s. 39(3) of the Police and Criminal Evidence Act 1984).

Tape Recorded Interviews

- The person interviewed must be offered the opportunity to clarify anything he/she has said during the interview and to add anything he/she may wish (Code E, para. 4.17). This may be important when the case comes to court and the defence try to explain why certain things were said during the interview.

- Turn off the tape and seal it with a master tape label (Code E, para. 4.18). If the seal on the tape needs to be broken for any reason, follow Code E, para. 6.2 or, if decision has been made not to institute criminal proceedings, follow Code E, para. 6.3.

- Sign the label and ask the suspect and any third party present to sign it also. If the suspect or third party refuses to sign it, an inspector, or if not available a custody officer, shall be called into the interview room and asked to sign it (Code E, para. 4.18).

- Hand the suspect the notice which explains the use which will be made of the tape recording and the arrangement for access to it (Code E, para. 4.19).

- Make a personal pocket book entry about the interview as required by Code E, para. 5.1 (see Code E, para. 1.10).

- Follow force standing orders or local procedures in relation to tape security whether or not the person is charged (Code E, paras 6.1 and 5.2).

17.9   Statements from Suspects

Statements under caution, particularly of a detained person, are less common than interviews. If a person has been interviewed on tape or an interview has been recorded contemporaneously in writing, a statement under caution should normally be conducted only at the person's express wish (Code C, Note 12A). A statement must not be elicited by the use of oppression (Code C, para. 11.5) and, if written at the police station, the statement must be on the correct forms (Code C, para. 12.13). Code C, Annex D sets out how the statement should be taken and matters that must be included in the statement whether it is written by the suspect or a police officer. See Code C, Annex C for restrictions on drawing inferences and the variable declarations the person must include in his/her statements.

When completing the statement, the person must always be invited to write down what he/she wants to say and should be allowed to do so without any prompting, except that a police officer may indicate which matters are material or question any ambiguity in the statement. In the case of a person making a statement in a language other than English, Code C, para. 13.4 states:

(a) the interpreter shall record the statement in the language it is made;

(b) the person shall be invited to sign it;

(c) an official English translation shall be made in due course

(in these cases, para. 13.4 means that the person will not be invited to write the statement themselves which is an exception to the guidance in Annex D).

A juvenile or a person who is mentally disordered or mentally vulnerable, *whether suspected or not*, must not be asked to provide or sign a written statement in the absence of the appropriate adult unless Code C, paras 11.1, 11.18 to 11.20 or Annex C applies (Code C, para. 11.15). Statements made by an accused under caution to the police are confidential. It is clearly implicit in the relationship between the police and the accused that the information, before being used in open court, is used only for the purposes for which it is provided and not for extraneous purposes, such as the media. However, the obligation of confidentiality (which is now included in the Police Code of Conduct; **see General Police Duties, chapter 1**) in respect of such a statement will be brought to an end where the contents of the statement are already in the public domain (*Bann* v *British Broadcasting Corporation and Another* (1998) 148 NLJ 979).

17.10 **Interviews on Behalf of Scottish Forces and Vice Versa**

The Crown Prosecution Service, in consultation with the Scottish Crown Office, has produced guidelines in relation to the potential admissibility of interview evidence when officers from England and Wales conduct interviews on behalf of Scottish forces and vice versa. These interviews relate to people subject to cross-border arrest as provided by ss. 136–140 of the Criminal Justice and Public Order Act 1994 (**see General Police Duties, chapter 2**).

17.10.1 **Suspects in Scotland: Interview Evidence Required for Prosecutions in England and Wales**

Under the legislation governing prosecutions in Scotland, the suspect is not entitled to legal representation during an interview. Suspects are not warned that a failure to answer questions may harm their defence. Failure to answer questions cannot harm their defence. Interviews under caution are, however, subject to guidelines which incorporate judicial precedent fairness to the accused.

In investigations of any great seriousness, English/Welsh constables should attend in Scotland, arrest the suspect and bring him/her back to their jurisdiction for interview. If such an arrest is made, the arrested person must be taken either to the nearest designated police station in England or a designated police station in a police area in England and Wales in which the offence is being investigated (s. 137(1) and (7)(a) of the 1994 Act).

Scottish officers do not have any statutory or common law powers to detain or arrest a suspect without warrant who is believed to have committed an offence in England and Wales. If there is insufficient evidence for the issue of a warrant, and the case is not sufficiently serious to justify officers travelling to Scotland, Scottish officers can be requested to invite the suspect to attend a police station on a voluntary basis for interview under caution.

When it has not been practicable for an English/Welsh constable to make an arrest, but a constable has gone to Scotland to interview a suspect following arrest or detention by a Scottish constable for Scottish offences, or a person has voluntarily agreed to be interviewed, the English/Welsh constable should comply, insofar as it is practical, with the PACE Codes of Practice, in particular:

- A suspect not under arrest or detention should be told that he/she is not under arrest or detention and that he/she is free to leave.

- A suspect should be told that he/she may seek legal advice and that arrangements are made for legal representation when required. An appropriate adult should also be present when interviewing a youth or a mentally disordered or mentally handicapped person.

- Administer an English/Welsh law caution. When appropriate officers should warn arrested suspects of the consequences of failure or refusal to account for objects, substances or marks (s. 36 of the 1994 Act) and the failure or refusal to account for their presence in a particular place (s. 37).

- Tape record the interview if possible.

- If it is not possible to tape record the interview, a contemporaneous written record of the interview should be made. The suspect must be given the opportunity to read the record and to sign it.

- Also, fingerprints etc. and non-intimate samples may be taken from an arrested or detained person with the authority of an officer of a rank no lower than inspector (s. 18 of the Criminal Procedure (Scotland) Act 1995).

Scottish constables interviewing suspects in Scotland when they are aware that the interview is required for a prosecution in England and Wales, should comply with Scottish law. In addition, in so far as it is practical:

- A suspect should be told that he/she may seek legal advice and that arrangements are made for legal representation when required. A solicitor may be present during any subsequent interview if the suspect requires. An appropriate adult should also be present when interviewing a youth or a mentally disordered or mentally handicapped person.

- When it is certain that the interview evidence will only be used in English/Welsh courts, the English/Welsh caution should be used.

- Tape record the interview if possible.

- If it is not possible to tape record the interview, a written contemporaneous record of the interview should be made. The suspect must be given the opportunity to read the record and to sign it.

English/Welsh officers should assist interviewing Scottish officers by providing a schedule of points to be covered in an interview. This could include a list of appropriate questions.

17.10.2   Suspects in England and Wales: Interview Evidence Required for Prosecutions in Scotland

- English officers do not have any statutory or common law powers to detain or arrest a suspect without warrant who is believed to have committed an offence in Scotland. If there is insufficient evidence for the issue of a warrant, and the case is not sufficiently serious to justify Scottish officers travelling to England or Wales to exercise their cross-border powers under the Act, English or Welsh officers can be requested to invite the suspect to attend an interview on a voluntary basis for interview under caution. See Code C, para. 1.12(i) and Code D, para. 2.17(iv).

- Where a Scottish officer has attended to interview the suspect, the Scottish form of caution should be given.

- English and Welsh constables interviewing suspects in England/Wales when they are aware that the interview is required for a prosecution in Scotland, should comply with the PACE Codes of Practice, save that a Scottish caution should be used in the following terms: 'You are not obliged to say anything but anything you do say will be noted and may be used in evidence.'

The use of the English/Welsh caution may render the interview inadmissible in Scotland.

Scottish officers should assist the interviewing officers by providing a schedule of points to be covered in an interview and a possible list of appropriate questions.

In all circumstances officers should ensure that suspects fully understand the significance of a caution or warning.

Appendix 1
The Code for Crown Prosecutors

1 Introduction

1.1   The decision to prosecute an individual is a serious step. Fair and effective prosecution is essential to the maintenance of law and order. Even in a small case a prosecution has serious implications for all involved—victims, witnesses and defendants. The Crown Prosecution Service applies the Code for Crown Prosecutors so that it can make fair and consistent decisions about prosecutions.

1.2   The Code helps the Crown Prosecution Service to play its part in making sure that justice is done. It contains information that is important to police officers and others who work in the criminal justice system and to the general public. Police officers should take account of the Code when they are deciding whether to charge a person with an offence.

1.3   The Code is also designed to make sure that everyone knows the principles that the Crown Prosecution Service applies when carrying out its work. By applying the same principles, everyone involved in the system is helping to treat victims fairly and to prosecute fairly but effectively.

2 General Principles

2.1   Each case is unique and must be considered on its own facts and merits. However, there are general principles that apply to the way in which Crown Prosecutors must approach every case.

2.2   Crown Prosecutors must be fair, independent and objective. They must not let any personal views about ethnic or national origin, sex, religious beliefs, political views or the sexual orientation of the suspect, victim or witness influence their decisions. They must not be affected by improper or undue pressure from any source.

2.3   It is the duty of Crown Prosecutors to make sure that the right person is prosecuted for the right offence. In doing so, Crown Prosecutors must always act in the interests of justice and not solely for the purpose of obtaining a conviction.

2.4   It is the duty of Crown Prosecutors to review, advise on and prosecute cases, ensuring that the law is properly applied, that all relevant evidence is put before the court and that obligations of disclosure are complied with, in accordance with the principles set out in this Code.

2.5   The CPS is a public authority for the purposes of the Human Rights Act 1998. Crown Prosecutors must apply the principles of the European Convention on Human Rights in accordance with the Act.

3 Review

3.1   Proceedings are usually started by the police. Sometimes they may consult the Crown Prosecution Service before starting a prosecution. Each case that the Crown Prosecution Service receives from the police is reviewed to make sure that it meets the evidential and public interest tests set out in this Code. Crown Prosecutors may decide to continue with the original charges, to change the charges, or sometimes to stop the case.

3.2 Review is a continuing process and Crown Prosecutors must take account of any change in circumstances. Wherever possible, they talk to the police first if they are thinking about changing the charges or stopping the case. This gives the police the chance to provide more information that may affect the decision. The Crown Prosecution Service and the police work closely together to reach the right decision, but the final responsibility for the decision rests with the Crown Prosecution Service.

4 The Code Tests

4.1 There are two stages in the decision to prosecute. The first stage is *the evidential test*. If the case does not pass the evidential test, it must not go ahead, no matter how important or serious it may be. If the case does meet the evidential test, Crown Prosecutors must decide if a prosecution is needed in the public interest.

4.2 This second stage is *the public interest test*. The Crown Prosecution Service will only start or continue with a prosecution when the case has passed both tests. The evidential test is explained in section 5 and the public interest test is explained in section 6.

5 The Evidential Test

5.1 Crown Prosecutors must be satisfied that there is enough evidence to provide a 'realistic prospect of conviction' against each defendant on each charge. They must consider what the defence case may be, and how that is likely to affect the prosecution case.

5.2 A realistic prospect of conviction is an objective test. It means that a jury or bench of magistrates, properly directed in accordance with the law, is more likely than not to convict the defendant of the charge alleged. This is a separate test from the one that the criminal courts themselves must apply. A jury or magistrates' court should only convict if satisfied so that it is sure of a defendant's guilt.

5.3 When deciding whether there is enough evidence to prosecute, Crown Prosecutors must consider whether the evidence can be used and is reliable. There will be many cases in which the evidence does not give any cause for concern. But there will also be cases in which the evidence may not be as strong as it first appears. Crown Prosecutors must ask themselves the following questions:

Can the evidence be used in court?

(a) Is it likely that the evidence will be excluded by the court? There are certain legal rules which might mean that evidence which seems relevant cannot be given at a trial. For example, is it likely that the evidence will be excluded because of the way in which it was gathered or because of the rule against using hearsay as evidence? If so, is there enough other evidence for a realistic prospect of conviction?

Is the evidence reliable?

(b) Is there evidence which might support or detract from the reliability of a confession? Is the reliability affected by factors such as the defendant's age, intelligence or level of understanding?

(c) What explanation has the defendant given? Is a court likely to find it credible in the light of the evidence as a whole? Does it support an innocent explanation?

(d) If the identity of the defendant is likely to be questioned, is the evidence about this strong enough?

(e) Is the witness's background likely to weaken the prosecution case? For example, does the witness have any motive that may affect his or her attitude to the case, or a relevant previous conviction?

(f) Are there concerns over the accuracy or credibility of a witness? Are these concerns based on evidence or simply information with nothing to support it? Is there further evidence which the police should be asked to seek out which may support or detract from the account of the witness?

5.4   Crown Prosecutors should not ignore evidence because they are not sure that it can be used or is reliable. But they should look closely at it when deciding if there is a realistic prospect of conviction.

6   The Public Interest Test

6.1   In 1951, Lord Shawcross, who was Attorney-General, made the classic statement on public interest, which has been supported by Attorneys-General ever since: 'It has never been the rule in this country—I hope it never will be—that suspected criminal offences must automatically be the subject of prosecution'. (House of Commons Debates, volume 483, column 681, 29 January 1951.)

6.2   The public interest must be considered in each case where there is enough evidence to provide a realistic prospect of conviction. A prosecution will usually take place unless there are public interest factors tending against prosecution which clearly outweigh those tending in favour. Although there may be public interest factors against prosecution in a particular case, often the prosecution should go ahead and those factors should be put to the court for consideration when sentence is being passed.

6.3   Crown Prosecutors must balance factors for and against prosecution carefully and fairly. Public interest factors that can affect the decision to prosecute usually depend on the seriousness of the offence or the circumstances of the suspect. Some factors may increase the need to prosecute but others may suggest that another course of action would be better.

The following lists of some common public interest factors, both for and against prosecution, are not exhaustive. The factors that apply will depend on the facts in each case.

Some common public interest factors in favour of prosecution

6.4   The more serious the offence, the more likely it is that a prosecution will be needed in the public interest. A prosecution is likely to be needed if:

(a) a conviction is likely to result in a significant sentence;

(b) a weapon was used or violence was threatened during the commission of the offence;

(c) the offence was committed against a person serving the public (for example, a police or prison officer, or a nurse);

(d) the defendant was in a position of authority or trust;

(e) the evidence shows that the defendant was a ringleader or an organiser of the offence;

(f) there is evidence that the offence was premeditated;

(g) there is evidence that the offence was carried out by a group;

(h) the victim of the offence was vulnerable, has been put in considerable fear, or suffered personal attack, damage or disturbance;

(i) the offence was motivated by any form of discrimination against the victim's ethnic or national origin, sex, religious beliefs, political views or sexual orientation, or the suspect demonstrated hostility towards the victim based on any of those characteristics;

(j) there is a marked difference between the actual or mental ages of the defendant and the victim, or if there is any element of corruption;

(k) the defendant's previous convictions or cautions are relevant to the present offence;

(l) the defendant is alleged to have committed the offence whilst under an order of the court;

(m) there are grounds for believing that the offence is likely to be continued or repeated, for example, by a history of recurring conduct; or

(n) the offence, although not serious in itself, is widespread in the area where it was committed.

Some common public interest factors against prosecution

6.5   A prosecution is less likely to be needed if:

(a) the court is likely to impose a nominal penalty;

(b) the defendant has already been made the subject of a sentence and any further conviction would be unlikely to result in the imposition of an additional sentence or order, unless the nature of the particular offence requires a prosecution;

(c) the offence was committed as a result of a genuine mistake or misunderstanding (these factors must be balanced against the seriousness of the offence);

(d) the loss or harm can be described as minor and was the result of a single incident, particularly if it was caused by a misjudgement;

(e) there has been a long delay between the offence taking place and the date of the trial, unless:
   • the offence is serious;
   • the delay has been caused in part by the defendant;
   • the offence has only recently come to light; or
   • the complexity of the offence has meant that there has been a long investigation;

(f) a prosecution is likely to have a bad effect on the victim's physical or mental health, always bearing in mind the seriousness of the offence;

(g) the defendant is elderly or is, or was at the time of the offence, suffering from significant mental or physical ill health, unless the offence is serious or there is a real possibility that it may be repeated. The Crown Prosecution Service, where necessary, applies Home Office guidelines about how to deal with mentally disordered offenders. Crown Prosecutors must balance the desirability of diverting a defendant who is suffering from significant mental or physical ill health with the need to safeguard the general public;

(h) the defendant has put right the loss or harm that was caused (but defendants must not avoid prosecution solely because they can pay compensation); or

(i) details may be made public that could harm sources of information, international relations or national security.

6.6   Deciding on the public interest is not simply a matter of adding up the number of factors on each side. Crown Prosecutors must decide how important each factor is in the circumstances of each case and go on to make an overall assessment.

The relationship between the victim and the public interest

6.7   The Crown Prosecution Service prosecutes cases on behalf of the public at large and not just in the interests of any particular individual. However, when considering the public interest test Crown Prosecutors should always take into account the consequences for the victim of the decision whether or not to prosecute, and any views expressed by the victim or the victim's family.

6.8   It is important that a victim is told about a decision which makes a significant difference to the case in which he or she is involved. Crown Prosecutors should ensure that they follow any agreed procedures.

Youths

6.9   Crown Prosecutors must consider the interests of a youth when deciding whether it is in the public interest to prosecute. However Crown Prosecutors should not avoid prosecuting simply because of the defendant's age. The seriousness of the offence or the youth's past behaviour is very important.

6.10   Cases involving youths are usually only referred to the Crown Prosecution Service for prosecution if the youth has already received a reprimand and final warning, unless the offence is so serious that neither of these were appropriate. Reprimands and final warnings are intended to prevent re-offending and the fact that a further offence has occurred indicates that attempts to divert the youth from the court system have not been effective. So the public interest will usually require a prosecution in such cases, unless there are clear public interest factors against prosecution.

Police cautions

6.11   These are only for adults. The police make the decision to caution an offender in accordance with Home Office guidelines.

6.12   When deciding whether a case should be prosecuted in the courts, Crown Prosecutors should consider the alternatives to prosecution. This will include a police caution. Again the Home Office guidelines should be applied. Where it is felt that a caution is appropriate, Crown Prosecutors must inform the police so that they can caution the suspect. If the caution is not administered because the suspect refuses to accept it or the police do not wish to offer it, then the Crown Prosecutor may review the case again.

7   Charges

7.1   Crown Prosecutors should select charges which:

(a) reflect the seriousness of the offending;

(b) give the court adequate sentencing powers; and

(c) enable the case to be presented in a clear and simple way.

This means that Crown Prosecutors may not always continue with the most serious charge where there is a choice. Further, Crown Prosecutors should not continue with more charges than are necessary.

7.2   Crown Prosecutors should never go ahead with more charges than are necessary just to encourage a defendant to plead guilty to a few. In the same way, they should never go ahead with a more serious charge just to encourage a defendant to plead guilty to a less serious one.

7.3   Crown Prosecutors should not change the charge simply because of the decision made by the court or the defendant about where the case will be heard.

8   Mode of Trial

8.1   The Crown Prosecution Service applies the current guidelines for magistrates who have to decide whether cases should be tried in the Crown Court when the offence gives the option and the defendant does not indicate a guilty plea. (See the 'National Mode of Trial Guidelines' issued by the Lord Chief Justice.) Crown Prosecutors should recommend Crown Court trial when they are satisfied that the guidelines require them to do so.

8.2   Speed must never be the only reason for asking for a case to stay in the magistrates' courts. But Crown Prosecutors should consider the effect of any likely delay if they send a case to the Crown Court, and any possible stress on victims and witnesses if the case is delayed.

9   Accepting Guilty Pleas

9.1   Defendants may want to plead guilty to some, but not all, of the charges. Alternatively they may want to plead guilty to a different, possibly less serious, charge because they are admitting only part of the crime. Crown Prosecutors should only accept the defendant's plea if they think the court is able to pass a sentence that matches the seriousness of the offending, particularly where there are aggravating features. Crown Prosecutors must never accept a guilty plea just because it is convenient.

9.2   Particular care must be taken when considering pleas which would enable the defendant to avoid the imposition of a mandatory minimum sentence. When pleas are offered, Crown Prosecutors must bear in mind the fact that ancillary orders can be made with some offences but not with others.

9.3   In cases where a defendant pleads guilty to the charges but on the basis of facts that are different from the prosecution case, and where this may significantly affect sentence, the court should be invited to hear evidence to determine what happened, and then sentence on that basis.

10   **Re-starting a Prosecution**

10.1   People should be able to rely on decisions taken by the Crown Prosecution Service. Normally, if the Crown Prosecution Service tells a suspect or defendant that there will not be a prosecution, or that the prosecution has been stopped, that is the end of the matter and the case will not start again. But occasionally there are special reasons why the Crown Prosecution Service will re-start the prosecution, particularly if the case is serious.

10.2   These reasons include:

(a) rare cases where a new look at the original decision shows that it was clearly wrong and should not be allowed to stand;

(b) cases which are stopped so that more evidence which is likely to become available in the fairly near future can be collected and prepared. In these cases, the Crown Prosecutor will tell the defendant that the prosecution may well start again; and

(c) cases which are stopped because of a lack of evidence but where more significant evidence is discovered later.

Appendix 2

Disclosure Extracts

CRIMINAL PROCEDURE AND INVESTIGATIONS ACT 1996: CODE OF PRACTICE UNDER PART II

Introduction

1.1 This code of practice is issued under part II of the Criminal Procedure and Investigations Act 1996 ('the Act'). It applies in respect of criminal investigations conducted by police officers which begin on or after the day on which this code comes into effect. Persons other than police officers who are charged with the duty of conducting an investigation as defined in the Act are to have regard to the relevant provisions of the code, and should take these into account in applying their own operating procedures.

1.2 This code does not apply to persons who are not charged with the duty of conducting an investigation as defined in the Act.

1.3 Nothing in this code applies to material intercepted in obedience to a warrant issued under section 2 of the Interception of Communications Act 1985, or to any copy of that material as defined in section 10 of that Act.

1.4 This code extends only to England and Wales.

Definitions

2.1 In this code:
- a *criminal investigation* is an investigation conducted by police officers with a view to it being ascertained whether a person should be charged with an offence, or whether a person charged with an offence is guilty of it. This will include
    - investigations into crimes that have been committed;
    - investigations whose purpose is to ascertain whether a crime has been committed, with a view to the possible institution of criminal proceedings; and
    - investigations which begin in the belief that a crime may be committed, for example when the police keep premises or individuals under observation for a period of time, with a view to the possible institution of criminal proceedings;
- charging a person with an offence includes prosecution by way of summons;
- an *investigator* is any police officer involved in the conduct of a criminal investigation. All investigators have a responsibility for carrying out the duties imposed on them under this code, including in particular recording information, and retaining records of information and other material;
- the *officer in charge of an investigation* is the police officer responsible for directing a criminal investigation. He is also responsible for ensuring that proper procedures are in place for recording information, and retaining records of information and other material, in the investigation;
- the *disclosure officer* is the person responsible for examining material retained by the police during the investigation; revealing material to the prosecutor during the investigation and any

criminal proceedings resulting from it, and certifying that he has done this; and disclosing material to the accused at the request of the prosecutor;

– the *prosecutor* is the authority responsible for the conduct of criminal proceedings on behalf of the Crown. Particular duties may in practice fall to individuals acting on behalf of the prosecuting authority;

– *material* is material of any kind, including information and objects, which is obtained in the course of a criminal investigation and which may be relevant to the investigation;

– material may be *relevant to an investigation* if it appears to an investigator, or to the officer in charge of an investigation, or to the disclosure officer, that it has some bearing on any offence under investigation or any person being investigated, or on the surrounding circumstances of the case, unless it is incapable of having any impact on the case;

– *sensitive material* is material which the disclosure officer believes, after consulting the officer in charge of the investigation, it is not in the public interest to disclose;

– references to *primary prosecution disclosure* are to the duty of the prosecutor under section 3 of the Act to disclose material which is in his possession or which he has inspected in pursuance of this code, and which in his opinion might undermine the case against the accused;

– references to *secondary prosecution disclosure* are to the duty of the prosecutor under section 7 of the Act to disclose material which is in his possession or which he has inspected in pursuance of this code, and which might reasonably be expected to assist the defence disclosed by the accused in a defence statement given under the Act;

– references to the disclosure of material to a person accused of an offence include references to the disclosure of material to his legal representative;

– references to police officers and to the chief officer of police include those employed in a police force as defined in section 3(3) of the Prosecution of Offences Act 1985.

General responsibilities

3.1   The functions of the investigator, the officer in charge of an investigation and the disclosure officer are separate. Whether they are undertaken by one, two or more persons will depend on the complexity of the case and the administrative arrangements within each police force. Where they are undertaken by more than one person, close consultation between them is essential to the effective performance of the duties imposed by this code.

3.2   The chief officer of police for each police force is responsible for putting in place arrangements to ensure that in every investigation the identity of the officer in charge of an investigation and the disclosure officer is recorded.

3.3   The officer in charge of an investigation may delegate tasks to another investigator or to civilians employed by the police force, but he remains responsible for ensuring that these have been carried out and for accounting for any general policies followed in the investigation. In particular, it is an essential part of his duties to ensure that all material which may be relevant to an investigation is retained, and either made available to the disclosure officer or (in exceptional circumstances) revealed directly to the prosecutor.

3.4   In conducting an investigation, the investigator should pursue all reasonable lines of inquiry, whether these point towards or away from the suspect. What is reasonable in each case will depend on the particular circumstances.

3.5   If the officer in charge of an investigation believes that other persons may be in possession of material that may be relevant to the investigation, and if this has not been obtained under paragraph 3.4 above, he should ask the disclosure officer to inform them of the existence of the investigation and to invite them to retain the material in case they receive a request for its disclosure. The disclosure officer should inform the prosecutor that they may have such material. However, the officer in charge of an investigation is not required to make speculative enquiries of other persons: there must be some reason to believe that they may have relevant material. That reason may come from information provided to the police by the accused or from other inquiries made or from some other source.

3.6   If, during a criminal investigation, the officer in charge of an investigation or disclosure officer for any reason no longer has responsibility for the functions falling to him, either his supervisor or the police officer in charge of criminal investigations for the police force concerned must assign someone else to assume that responsibility. That person's identity must be recorded, as with those initially responsible for these functions in each investigation.

Recording of information

4.1   If material which may be relevant to the investigation consists of information which is not recorded in any form, the officer in charge of an investigation must ensure that it is recorded in a durable or retrievable form (whether in writing, on video or audio tape, or on computer disk).

4.2   Where it is not practicable to retain the initial record of information because it forms part of a larger record which is to be destroyed, its contents should be transferred as a true record to a durable and more easily-stored form before that happens.

4.3   Negative information is often relevant to an investigation. If it may be relevant it must be recorded. An example might be a number of people present in a particular place at a particular time who state that they saw nothing unusual.

4.4   Where information which may be relevant is obtained, it must be recorded at the time it is obtained or as soon as practicable after that time. This includes, for example, information obtained in house-to-house enquiries, although the requirement to record information promptly does not require an investigator to take a statement from a potential witness where it would not otherwise be taken.

Retention of material

(a) Duty to retain material

5.1   The investigator must retain material obtained in a criminal investigation which may be relevant to the investigation. This includes not only material coming into the possession of the investigator (such as documents seized in the course of searching premises) but also material generated by him (such as interview records). Material may be photographed, or retained in the form of a copy rather than the original, if the original is perishable, or was supplied to the investigator rather than generated by him and is to be returned to its owner.

5.2   Where material has been seized in the exercise of the powers of seizure conferred by the Police and Criminal Evidence Act 1984, the duty to retain it under this code is subject to the provisions on the retention of seized material in section 22 of that Act.

5.3   If the officer in charge of an investigation becomes aware as a result of developments in the case that material previously examined but not retained (because it was not thought to be relevant) may now be relevant to the investigation, he should, wherever practicable, take steps to obtain it or ensure that it is retained for further inspection or for production in court if required.

5.4   The duty to retain material includes in particular the duty to retain material falling into the following categories, where it may be relevant to the investigation:

- crime reports (including crime report forms, relevant parts of incident report books or police officers' notebooks);
- custody records;
- records which are derived from tapes of telephone messages (for example, 999 calls) containing descriptions of an alleged offence or offender;

- final versions of witness statements (and draft versions where their content differs from the final version), including any exhibits mentioned (unless these have been returned to their owner on the understanding that they will be produced in court if required);

- interview records (written records, or audio or video tapes, of interviews with actual or potential witnesses or suspects);

- communications between the police and experts such as forensic scientists, reports of work carried out by experts, and schedules of scientific material prepared by the expert for the investigator, for the purposes of criminal proceedings;

- any material casting doubt on the reliability of a confession;

- any material casting doubt on the reliability of a witness;

- any other material which may fall within the test for primary prosecution disclosure in the Act.

5.5   The duty to retain material falling into these categories does not extend to items which are purely ancillary to such material and possess no independent significance (for example, duplicate copies of records or reports).

(b) Length of time for which material is to be retained

5.6   All material which may be relevant to the investigation must be retained until a decision is taken whether to institute proceedings against a person for an offence.

5.7   If a criminal investigation results in proceedings being instituted, all material which may be relevant must be retained at least until the accused is acquitted or convicted or the prosecutor decides not to proceed with the case.

5.8   Where the accused is convicted, all material which may be relevant must be retained at least until:

- the convicted person is released from custody, or discharged from hospital, in cases where the court imposes a custodial sentence or a hospital order;

- six months from the date of conviction, in all other cases.

If the court imposes a custodial sentence or hospital order and the convicted person is released from custody or is discharged from hospital earlier than six months from the date of conviction, all material which may be relevant must be retained at least until six months from the date of conviction.

5.9   If an appeal against conviction is in progress when the release or discharge occurs, or at the end of the period of six months specified in paragraph 5.8, all material which may be relevant must be retained until the appeal is determined. Similarly, if the Criminal Cases Review Commission is considering an application at that point in time, all material which may be relevant must be retained at least until the Commission decides not to refer the case to the Court of Appeal, or until the Court determines the appeal resulting from the reference by the Commission.

5.10   Material need not be retained by the police as required in paragraph 5.8 if it was seized and is to be returned to its owner.

Preparation of material for prosecutor

(a) Introduction

6.1   The officer in charge of the investigation, the disclosure officer or an investigator may seek advice from the prosecutor about whether any particular item of material may be relevant to the investigation.

6.2   Material which may be relevant to an investigation, which has been retained in accordance with this code, and which the disclosure officer believes will not form part of the prosecution case, must be listed on a schedule.

6.3   Material which the disclosure officer does not believe is sensitive must be listed on a schedule of non-sensitive material. The schedule must include a statement that the disclosure officer does not believe the material is sensitive.

6.4   Any material which is believed to be sensitive must be either listed on a schedule of sensitive material or, in exceptional circumstances, revealed to the prosecutor separately.

6.5   Paragraphs 6.6 to 6.11 below apply to both sensitive and non-sensitive material. Paragraphs 6.12 to 6.14 apply to sensitive material only.

(b)   Circumstances in which a schedule is to be prepared

6.6   The disclosure officer must ensure that a schedule is prepared in the following circumstances:

- the accused is charged with an offence which is triable only on indictment;
- the accused is charged with an offence which is triable either way, and it is considered either that the case is likely to be tried on indictment or that the accused is likely to plead not guilty at a summary trial;
- the accused is charged with a summary offence, and it is considered that he is likely to plead not guilty.

6.7   In respect of either way and summary offences, a schedule may not be needed if a person has admitted the offence, or if a police officer witnessed the offence and that person has not denied it.

6.8   If it is believed that the accused is likely to plead guilty at a summary trial, it is not necessary to prepare a schedule in advance. If, contrary to this belief, the accused pleads not guilty at a summary trial, or the offence is to be tried on indictment, the disclosure officer must ensure that a schedule is prepared as soon as is reasonably practicable after that happens.

(c)   Way in which material is to be listed on schedule

6.9   The disclosure officer should ensure that each item of material is listed separately on the schedule, and is numbered consecutively. The description of each item should make clear the nature of the item and should contain sufficient detail to enable the prosecutor to decide whether he needs to inspect the material before deciding whether or not it should be disclosed.

6.10   In some enquiries it may not be practicable to list each item of material separately. For example, there may be many items of a similar or repetitive nature. These may be listed in a block and described by quantity and generic title.

6.11   Even if some material is listed in a block, the disclosure officer must ensure that any items among that material which might meet the test for primary prosecution disclosure are listed and described individually.

(d)   Treatment of sensitive material

6.12   Subject to paragraph 6.13 below, the disclosure officer must list on a sensitive schedule any material which he believes it is not in the public interest to disclose, and the reason for that belief. The schedule must include a statement that the disclosure officer believes the material is sensitive. Depending on the circumstances, examples of such material may include the following among others:

- material relating to national security;
- material received from the intelligence and security agencies;
- material relating to intelligence from foreign sources which reveals sensitive intelligence gathering methods;
- material given in confidence;
- material which relates to the use of a telephone system and which is supplied to an investigator for intelligence purposes only;

- material relating to the identity or activities of informants, or under-cover police officers, or other persons supplying information to the police who may be in danger if their identities are revealed;

- material revealing the location of any premises or other place used for police surveillance, or the identity of any person allowing a police officer to use them for surveillance;

- material revealing, either directly or indirectly, techniques and methods relied upon by a police officer in the course of a criminal investigation, for example covert surveillance techniques, or other methods of detecting crime;

- material whose disclosure might facilitate the commission of other offences or hinder the prevention and detection of crime;

- internal police communications such as management minutes;

- material upon the strength of which search warrants were obtained;

- material containing details of persons taking part in identification parades;

- material supplied to an investigator during a criminal investigation which has been generated by an official of a body concerned with the regulation or supervision of bodies corporate or of persons engaged in financial activities, or which has been generated by a person retained by such a body;

- material supplied to an investigator during a criminal investigation which relates to a child or young person and which has been generated by a local authority social services department, an Area Child Protection Committee or other party contacted by an investigator during the investigation.

6.13   In exceptional circumstances, where an investigator considers that material is so sensitive that its revelation to the prosecutor by means of an entry on the sensitive schedule is inappropriate, the existence of the material must be revealed to the prosecutor separately. This will apply where compromising the material would be likely to lead directly to the loss of life, or directly threaten national security.

6.14   In such circumstances, the responsibility for informing the prosecutor lies with the investigator who knows the detail of the sensitive material. The investigator should act as soon as is reasonably practicable after the file containing the prosecution case is sent to the prosecutor. The investigator must also ensure that the prosecutor is able to inspect the material so that he can assess whether it needs to be brought before a court for a ruling on disclosure.

Revelation of material to prosecutor

7.1   The disclosure officer must give the schedules to the prosecutor. Wherever practicable this should be at the same time as he gives him the file containing the material for the prosecution case (or as soon as is reasonably practicable after the decision on mode of trial or the plea, in cases to which paragraph 6.8 applies).

7.2   The disclosure officer should draw the attention of the prosecutor to any material an investigator has retained (whether or not listed on a schedule) which may fall within the test for primary prosecution disclosure in the Act, and should explain why he has come to that view.

7.3   At the same time as complying with the duties in paragraphs 7.1 and 7.2, the disclosure officer must give the prosecutor a copy of any material which falls into the following categories (unless such material has already been given to the prosecutor as part of the file containing the material for the prosecution case):

- records of the first description of a suspect given to the police by a potential witness, whether or not the description differs from that of the alleged offender;

- information provided by an accused person which indicates an explanation for the offence with which he has been charged;

- any material casting doubt on the reliability of a confession;

- any material casting doubt on the reliability of a witness;

- any other material which the investigator believes may fall within the test for primary prosecution disclosure in the Act.

7.4   If the prosecutor asks to inspect material which has not already been copied to him, the disclosure officer must allow him to inspect it. If the prosecutor asks for a copy of material which has not already been copied to him, the disclosure officer must give him a copy. However, this does not apply where the disclosure officer believes, having consulted the officer in charge of the investigation, that the material is too sensitive to be copied and can only be inspected.

7.5   If material consists of information which is recorded other than in writing, whether it should be given to the prosecutor in its original form as a whole, or by way of relevant extracts recorded in the same form, or in the form of a transcript, is a matter for agreement between the disclosure officer and the prosecutor.

Subsequent action by disclosure officer

8.1   At the time a schedule of non-sensitive material is prepared, the disclosure officer may not know exactly what material will form the case against the accused, and the prosecutor may not have given advice about the likely relevance of particular items of material. Once these matters have been determined, the disclosure officer must give the prosecutor, where necessary, an amended schedule listing any additional material:

- which may be relevant to the investigation,

- which does not form part of the case against the accused,

- which is not already listed on the schedule, and

- which he believes is not sensitive,

unless he is informed in writing by the prosecutor that the prosecutor intends to disclose the material to the defence.

8.2   After a defence statement has been given, the disclosure officer must look again at the material which has been retained and must draw the attention of the prosecutor to any material which might reasonably be expected to assist the defence disclosed by the accused; and he must reveal it to him in accordance with paragraphs 7.4 and 7.5 above.

8.3   Section 9 of the Act imposes a continuing duty on the prosecutor, for the duration of criminal proceedings against the accused, to disclose material which meets the tests for disclosure (subject to public interest considerations). To enable him to do this, any new material coming to light should be treated in the same way as the earlier material.

Certification by disclosure officer

9.1   The disclosure officer must certify to the prosecutor that, to the best of his knowledge and belief, all material which has been retained and made available to him has been revealed to the prosecutor in accordance with this code. He must sign and date the certificate. It will be necessary to certify not only at the time when the schedule and accompanying material is submitted to the prosecutor, but also when material which has been retained is reconsidered after the accused has given a defence statement.

Disclosure of material to accused

10.1   If material has not already been copied to the prosecutor, and he requests its disclosure to the accused on the ground that:

– it falls within the test for primary or secondary prosecution disclosure, or

– the court has ordered its disclosure after considering an application from the accused,

the disclosure officer must disclose it to the accused.

10.2   If material has been copied to the prosecutor, and it is to be disclosed, whether it is disclosed by the prosecutor or the disclosure officer is a matter for agreement between the two of them.

10.3   The disclosure officer must disclose material to the accused either by giving him a copy or by allowing him to inspect it. If the accused person asks for a copy of any material which he has been allowed to inspect, the disclosure officer must give it to him, unless in the opinion of the disclosure officer that is either not practicable (for example because the material consists of an object which cannot be copied, or because the volume of material is so great), or not desirable (for example because the material is a statement by a child witness in relation to a sexual offence).

10.4   If material which the accused has been allowed to inspect consists of information which is recorded other than in writing, whether it should be given to the accused in its original form or in the form of a transcript is a matter for the discretion of the disclosure officer. If the material is transcribed, the disclosure officer must ensure that the transcript is certified to the accused as a true record of the material which has been transcribed.

10.5   If a court concludes that it is in the public interest that an item of sensitive material must be disclosed to the accused, it will be necessary to disclose the material if the case is to proceed. This does not mean that sensitive documents must always be disclosed in their original form: for example, the court may agree that sensitive details still requiring protection should be blocked out, or that documents may be summarised, or that the prosecutor may make an admission about the substance of the material under section 10 of the Criminal Justice Act 1967.

ATTORNEY-GENERAL'S GUIDELINES: DISCLOSURE OF INFORMATION IN CRIMINAL PROCEEDINGS

Introduction

1.   Every accused person has a right to a fair trial, a right long embodied in our law and guaranteed under Article 6 of the European Convention on Human Rights. A fair trial is the proper object and expectation of all participants in the trial process. Fair disclosure to an accused is an inseparable part of a fair trial.

2.   The scheme set out in the Criminal Procedure and Investigations Act 1996 (the Act) is designed to ensure that there is fair disclosure of material which may be relevant to an investigation and which does not form part of the prosecution case. Disclosure under the Act should assist the accused in the timely preparation and presentation of their case and assist the court to focus on all the relevant issues in the trial. Disclosure which does not meet these objectives risks preventing a fair trial taking place.

3.   Fairness does, however, recognise that there are other interests that need to be protected, including those of victims and witnesses who might otherwise be exposed to harm. The scheme of the Act protects those interests. It should also ensure that material is not disclosed which overburdens the participants in the trial process, diverts attention from the relevant issues, leads to unjustifiable delay, and is wasteful of resources.

4.   These guidelines build upon the existing law to help to ensure that the legislation is operated more effectively. In some areas guidance is given which goes beyond the requirements of the legislation, where experience has suggested that such guidance is desirable.

General principles

Investigators and disclosure officers

5.   Investigators and disclosure officers must be fair and objective and must work together with prosecutors to ensure that disclosure obligations are met. A failure to take action leading to proper disclosure may result in a wrongful conviction. It may alternatively lead to a successful abuse of process argument or an acquittal against the weight of the evidence.

6.   In discharging their obligations under the statute, code, common law and any operational instructions, investigators should always err on the side of recording and retaining material where they have any doubt as to whether it may be relevant.

7.   An individual must not be appointed as disclosure officer, or continue in that role, if that is likely to result in a conflict of interest, for instance, if the disclosure officer is the victim of the alleged crime which is the subject of criminal proceedings. The advice of a more senior officer must always be sought if there is doubt as to whether a conflict of interest precludes an individual acting as the disclosure officer. If thereafter the doubt remains, the advice of a prosecutor should be sought.

8.   Disclosure officers, or their deputies, must inspect, view or listen to all material that has been retained by the investigator, and the disclosure officer must provide a personal declaration to the effect that this task has been done. The obligation does not apply, however, in the circumstances set out in paragraph 9 below.

9.   In some cases, out of an abundance of caution, investigators seize large volumes of material which may not, because of its source, general nature or other reasons, seem likely ever to be relevant. In such circumstances, the investigator may consider that it is not an appropriate use of resources to examine such large volumes of material seized on a precautionary basis. If such material is not examined by the investigator or disclosure officer, and it is not intended to examine it, but the material is nevertheless retained, its existence should be made known to the accused in general terms at the primary stage and permission granted for its inspection by him or his legal advisers. A section 9 statement will be completed by the investigating officer or disclosure officer describing the material by general category and justifying it not having been examined. This statement will itself be listed as unused material and automatically disclosed to the defence.

10.   In meeting the obligations in paragraph 6.9 and 8.1 of the Code, it is crucial that descriptions by disclosure officers in non-sensitive schedules are detailed, clear and accurate. The descriptions may require a summary of the contents of the retained material to assist the prosecutor to make an informed decision on disclosure. The same applies to sensitive schedules, to the extent possible without compromising the confidentiality of the information.

11.   Disclosure officers must specifically draw material to the attention of the prosecutor for consideration where they have any doubt as to whether it might undermine the prosecution case or might reasonably be expected to assist the defence disclosed by the accused.

12.   Disclosure officers must seek the advice and assistance of prosecutors when in doubt as to their responsibility, and must deal expeditiously with requests by the prosecutor for further information on material which may lead to disclosure.

Prosecutors generally

13.   Prosecutors must do all that they can to facilitate proper disclosure, as part of their general and personal professional responsibility to act fairly and impartially, in the interests of justice. Prosecutors must also be alert to the need to provide advice to disclosure officers on disclosure issues and to advise on disclosure procedure generally.

14.   Prosecutors must review schedules prepared by disclosure officers thoroughly and must be alert to the possibility that material may exist which has not been revealed to them. If no schedules have been provided, or there are apparent omissions from the schedules, or documents or other

items are insufficiently described or are unclear, the prosecutor must at once take action to obtain properly completed schedules. If, following this, prosecutors remain dissatisfied with the quality or content of the schedules they must raise the matter with a senior officer, and if necessary, persist, with a view to resolving the matter satisfactorily.

15.   Where prosecutors have reason to believe that the disclosure officer has not discharged the obligation in paragraph 8 to inspect, view or listen to material, they must at once raise the matter with the disclosure officer and, if it is believed that the officer has not inspected, viewed or listened to the material, request that it be done.

16.   When the prosecutor or disclosure officer believes that material might undermine the prosecution case or assist the defence case, for instance in the case of records of previous statements by witnesses, prosecutors must always inspect, view or listen to the material and satisfy themselves that the prosecution can properly be continued. Their judgment as to what other material to inspect, view or listen to will depend on the circumstances of each case.

17.   Prosecutors should inform the investigator if, in their view, reasonable and relevant lines of further inquiry exist.

18.   Prosecutors should not adduce evidence of the contents of a defence statement other than in the circumstances envisaged by section 11 of the Act or to rebut alibi evidence. Where evidence may be adduced in these circumstances, this can be done through cross-examination as well as through the introduction of evidence. There may be occasions when a defence statement points the prosecution to other lines of inquiry. Further investigation in these circumstances is possible and evidence obtained as a result of inquiring into a defence statement may be used as part of the prosecution case or to rebut the defence.

19.   Prosecutors must ensure that they record in writing all actions and decisions they make in discharging their disclosure responsibilities, and this information is to be made available to the prosecution advocate if requested or if relevant to an issue.

20.   In deciding what material should be disclosed (at any stage of the proceedings) prosecutors should resolve any doubt they may have in favour of disclosure, unless the material is on the sensitive schedule and will be placed before the court for the issue of disclosure to be determined.

21.   If prosecutors are satisfied that a fair trial cannot take place because of a failure to disclose which cannot or will not be remedied, they must not continue with the case.

Prosecution advocates

22.   Prosecution advocates should use their best endeavours to ensure that all material that ought properly to be made available is either presented by the prosecution or disclosed to the defence. However, the prosecution cannot be expected to disclose material if they are not aware of its existence. As far as is possible, prosecution advocates must place themselves in a fully informed position to enable them to make decisions on disclosure.

23.   Upon receipt of instructions, prosecution advocates should consider as a priority all the information provided regarding disclosure of material. Prosecution advocates should consider, in every case, whether they can be satisfied that they are in possession of all relevant documentation and that they have been instructed fully regarding disclosure matters. Decisions already made regarding disclosure should be reviewed. If as a result the advocate considers that further information or action is required, written advice should be promptly provided setting out the aspects that need clarification or action. If necessary and where appropriate a conference should be held to determine what is required.

24.   The prosecution advocate must continue to keep under review until the conclusion of the trial decisions regarding disclosure. The prosecution advocate must in every case specifically consider whether he or she can satisfactorily discharge the duty of continuing review on the basis of the material supplied already, or whether it is necessary to inspect further material or to reconsider material already inspected.

25.   Prior to the commencement of a trial, the prosecuting advocate should always make decisions on disclosure in consultation with those instructing him and it is desirable that the disclosure officer should also be consulted. After a trial has started, it is recognised that in practice consultation on disclosure issues may not be practicable; it continues to be desirable, however, whenever this can be achieved without affecting unduly the conduct of the trial.

26.   The practice of 'counsel to counsel' disclosure should cease: it is inconsistent with the requirement of transparency in the prosecution process.

Defence practitioners

27.   A defence statement should set out the nature of the defence, the matters on which issue is taken and the reasons for taking issue. A comprehensive defence statement assists the participants in the trial to ensure that it is fair. It provides information that the prosecutor needs to identify any remaining material that falls to be disclosed at the secondary stage. The more detail a defence statement contains the more likely it is that the prosecutor will make a properly informed decision about whether any remaining material might assist the defence case, or whether to advise the investigator to undertake further inquiries. It also helps in the management of the trial by narrowing down and focusing the issues in dispute. It may result in the prosecution discontinuing the case. Defence practitioners should be aware of these considerations in advising their clients.

28.   Defence solicitors should ensure that statements are agreed by the accused before being served. Wherever possible, the accused should sign the defence statement to evidence his or her agreement.

Involvement of other agencies

(a) Material held by Government departments or other Crown bodies

29.   Where it appears to an investigator, disclosure officer or prosecutor that a Government department or other Crown body has material that may be relevant to an issue in the case, reasonable steps should be taken to identify and consider such material. Although what is reasonable will vary from case to case, prosecutors should inform the department or other body of the nature of its case and of relevant issues in the case in respect of which the department or body might possess material, and ask whether it has any such material. Departments in England and Wales have established Enquiry Points to deal with issues concerning the disclosure of information in criminal proceedings. Further guidance for prosecutors and investigators seeking information (including documents) from Government departments or other Crown bodies may be found in the pamphlet 'Giving Evidence or Information about suspected crimes: Guidance for Departments and Investigators' (March, 1997, Cabinet Office).

(b) Material held by other agencies

30.   There may be cases where the investigator, disclosure officer or prosecutor suspects that a nongovernment agency or other third party (for example, a local authority, a social services department, a hospital, a doctor, a school, providers of forensic services) has material or information which might be disclosable if it were in the possession of the prosecution. In such cases consideration should be given as to whether it is appropriate to seek access to the material or information and if so, steps should be taken by the prosecution to obtain such material or information. It will be important to do so if the material or information is likely to undermine the prosecution case, or assist a known defence.

31.   If the investigator, disclosure officer or prosecutor seeks access to the material or information but the third party declines or refuses to allow access to it, the matter should not be left. If despite any reasons offered by the third party it is still believed that it is reasonable to seek production of the material or information, and the requirements of section 2 of the Criminal Procedure (Attendance of Witnesses) Act 1965 or as appropriate section 97 of the Magistrates Courts Act 1980 are satisfied, then the prosecutor or investigator should apply for a witness summons causing a representative of the third party to produce the material to the Court.

32. Information which might be disclosable if it were in the possession of the prosecution which comes to the knowledge of investigators or prosecutors as a result of liaison with third parties should be recorded by the investigator or prosecutor in a durable or retrievable form (for example potentially relevant information revealed in discussions at a child protection conference attended by police officers).

33. Where information comes into the possession of the prosecution in the circumstances set out in paragraphs 30–32 above, consultation with the other agency should take place before disclosure is made: there may be public interest reasons which justify witholding disclosure and which would require the issue of disclosure of the information to be placed before the court.

Disclosure prior to primary disclosure under the CPIA 1996

34. Prosecutors must always be alive to the need, in the interests of justice and fairness in the particular circumstances of any case, to make disclosure of material after the commencement of proceedings but before the prosecutor's duty arises under the Act. For instance, disclosure ought to be made of significant information that might affect a bail decision or that might enable the defence to contest the committal proceedings.

35. Where the need for such disclosure is not apparent to the prosecutor, any disclosure will depend on what the defendant chooses to reveal about the defence. Clearly, such disclosure will not normally exceed that which is obtainable after the duties under the 'Act' arise.

Primary disclosure

36. Generally, material can be considered to potentially undermine the prosecution case if it has an adverse effect on the strength of the prosecution case. This will include anything that tends to show a fact inconsistent with the elements of the case that must be proved by the prosecution. Material can have an adverse effect on the strength of the prosecution case:

   (a) by the use made of it in cross-examination; and
   (b) by its capacity to suggest any potential submissions that could lead to:
      (i) the exclusion of evidence;
      (ii) a stay of proceedings;
      (iii) a court or tribunal finding that any public authority had acted incompatibly with the defendant's rights under the ECHR.

37. In deciding what material might undermine the prosecution case, the prosecution should pay particular attention to material that has potential to weaken the prosecution case or is inconsistent with it. Examples are:

   i. Any material casting doubt upon the accuracy of any prosecution evidence.
   ii. Any material which may point to another person, whether charged or not (including a co-accused) having involvement in the commission of the offence.
   iii. Any material which may cast doubt upon the reliability of a confession.
   iv. Any material that might go to the credibility of a prosecution witness.
   v. Any material that might support a defence that is either raised by the defence or apparent from the prosecution papers. If the material might undermine the prosecution case it should be disclosed at this stage even though it suggests a defence inconsistent with or alternative to one already advanced by the accused or his solicitor.
   vi. Any material which may have a bearing on the admissibility of any prosecution evidence.

It should also be borne in mind that while items of material viewed in isolation may not be considered to potentially undermine the prosecution case, several items together can have that effect.

38. Experience suggests that any item which relates to the defendant's mental or physical health, his intellectual capacity, or to any ill-treatment which the defendant may have suffered when in the investigator's custody is likely to have the potential for casting doubt on the reliability of an accused's purported confession, and prosecutors should pay particular attention to any such item in the possession of the prosecution.

Secondary disclosure

39. Prosecutors should be open, alert and promptly responsive to requests for disclosure of material supported by the comprehensive defence statement. Conversely, if no defence statement has been served or if the prosecutor considers that the defence statement is lacking specific and/or clarity, a letter should be sent to the defence indicating that secondary disclosure will not take place or will be limited (as appropriate), and inviting the defence to specify and/or clarify the accused's case. The prosecutor should consider raising the issue at a preliminary hearing if the position is not resolved satisfactorily to enable the court to give directions.

40. Experience suggests that material of the description set out below might reasonably be expected to be disclosed to the defence where it relates to the defence being put forward. Accordingly, following the delivery of a defence statement and on receipt of a request specifically linking the material sought with the defence being put forward, such linked material should be disclosed unless there is good reason not to do so. However, if defences put forward in a defence statement are inconsistent within the meaning of section 11 of the Act, then the preceding guidance set out in this paragraph will not apply. Conversely, if material of the description set out below might undermine the prosecution case, and does not justify an application to the court to withhold disclosure, prosecutors must disclose it at the primary stage. The material is:

   i. Those recorded scientific or scenes of crime findings retained by the investigator which:
      relate to the defendant; and
      are linked to the point at issue; and
      have not previously been disclosed.

   ii. where identification is or may be in issue, all previous descriptions of suspects, however recorded, together with all records of identification procedures in respect of the offence(s) and photographs of the accused taken by the investigator around the time of his arrest;

   iii. information that any prosecution witness has received, has been promised or has requested any payment or reward in connection with the case;

   iv. plans of crime scenes or video recordings made by investigators of crime scenes;

   v. names, within the knowledge of investigators, of individuals who may have relevant information and whom investigators do not intend to interview;

   vi. records which the investigator has made of information which may be relevant, provided by any individual (such information would include, but not be limited to, records of conversation and interviews with any such person).

Disclosure of video recordings or scientific findings by means of supplying copies may well involve delay or otherwise not be practicable or desirable, in which case the investigator should make reasonable arrangements for the video, recordings or scientific findings to be viewed by the defence.

Applications for non-disclosure in the public interest

41. Before making an application to the court to withhold material which would otherwise fall to be disclosed, on the basis that to disclose would not be in the public interest, a prosecutor should aim to disclose as much of the material as he properly can (by giving the defence redacted or edited copies of summaries).

42. Prior to or at the hearing, the court must be provided with full and accurate information. The prosecution advocate must examine all material which is the subject matter of the application and

make any necessary enquiries of the prosecutor and/or investigator. The prosecutor (or representative) and/or investigator should attend such applications.

Summary trial

43.   The prosecutor should, in addition to complying with the obligations under the CPIA, provide to the defence all evidence upon which the Crown proposes to rely in a summary trial. Such provision should allow the accused or their legal advisers sufficient time properly to consider the evidence before it is called. Exceptionally, statements may be withheld for the protection of witnesses or to avoid interference with the course of justice.

Material relevant to sentence

44.   In all cases the prosecutor must consider disclosing in the interests of justice any material which is relevant to sentence (e.g. information which might mitigate the seriousness of the offence or assist the accused to lay blame in whole or in part upon a co-accused or another person).

Applicability of these guidelines

45.   These guidelines should be adopted with immediate effect in relation to all cases submitted in future to the prosecuting authorities in receipt of these guidelines. They should also be adopted as regards cases already submitted to which the Act applies, so far as they relate to stages in the proceedings that have not yet been reached.

JOINT POLICE AND CPS DISCLOSURE PROJECT (JOPI) GUIDELINES

SECTION TWO: POLICE ACTIONS

Introduction

2.1   This section contains instructions and guidance explaining how police officers should meet the requirements of the Act and the Code. The Code provides the framework for the roles of police officers in the disclosure process, and it forms the basis of this guidance. These instructions should also be read in conjunction with the Manual of Guidance for the Preparation, Processing and Submission of Files and other agreements on operational issues reached between ACPO and the CPS.

Roles and responsibilities

2.2   The **chief officer of police** for each police force is responsible for putting in place arrangements to ensure that in every investigation the identity of the officer in charge of an investigation and that of the disclosure officer is recorded.

2.3   An investigator, a disclosure officer, and an officer in charge of an investigation perform different functions. The three roles may be performed by different people or by one person. The person who is performing the role of disclosure officer and officer in charge of the investigation must be identifiable.

2.4   Where the three roles are undertaken by more than one person, close consultation between them will be essential to ensure compliance with the statutory duties imposed by the Act and the Code.

2.5   The **officer in charge of the investigation** is responsible for directing an investigation. This officer's responsibilities under the Act and the Code are to:

- account for any general policies followed in the investigation

- ensure that all reasonable steps are taken for the purposes of the investigation and, in particular, that all reasonable lines of enquiries are pursued

- ensure that proper procedures are in place for recording and retention of material obtained in the course of the investigation

- appoint the disclosure officer

- ensure that tasks delegated to civilians employed by the police force have been carried out in accordance with the requirements of the Code

- ensure that material which is relevant to an investigation is retained and recorded in a durable and retrievable form

- ensure that all retained material is either made available to the disclosure officer, or in exceptional circumstances revealed directly to the prosecutor

- ensure that all practicable steps are taken to recover any material that was inspected and not retained, if as a result of developments in the case it later becomes relevant.

2.6   An **investigator** is any police officer or civilian employee involved in a criminal investigation. All officers, including those who may not view themselves as investigators, have a responsibility for carrying out the duties imposed under the Code. All officers, in particular must retain material obtained in a criminal investigation which is either created or discovered during the investigation, and which may be relevant to the investigation.

2.7   The investigator must notify the disclosure officer of the existence and whereabouts of material that has been retained.

2.8   The **disclosure officer** (or **officers**, see paragraphs 2.164–66 below) has a statutory duty to discharge disclosure responsibilities throughout a criminal investigation. The officer(s) must:

- examine, inspect, view or listen to all material that has been retained by the investigator and that does not form part of the prosecution case unless the material comes within paragraph 9 of the Attorney General's Guidelines 2000 (see paragraph 2.145 below)

- create schedules that fully describe the material

- identify to the prosecutor all material which might undermine the prosecution case

- pass the schedules to the prosecutor

- at the same time, supply to the prosecutor a copy of material falling into any of the categories described in paragraph 7.3 of the Code and copies of the documents described in 2.120 below, if the prosecutor does not have them already

- consult with and allow the prosecutor to inspect the retained material

- review the schedules and the retained material after the defence statement has been received, identify to the prosecutor material that might reasonably be expected to assist the accused's defence, and supply a copy of any such material not already provided

- certify that all retained material has been revealed to the prosecutor in accordance with the Code at both the primary and secondary stages of prosecution disclosure

- schedule and reveal to the prosecutor any relevant additional unused material pursuant to the continuing duty of disclosure

- where the prosecutor requests disclosure of any material to the accused, give the accused a copy of the material or allow the accused to inspect it.

2.9   The disclosure officer may be a police officer or a civilian. In order to perform the duties under the Code properly, the disclosure officer will need to become fully familiar with the facts and background to the case. The investigator(s) and the officer in charge of the investigation (where these roles are performed by a different individual to the disclosure officer) must provide assistance to the disclosure officer in performing this function.

2.10   In some cases it will be desirable to appoint a disclosure officer at the outset of the investigation. In making this decision, the officer in charge of the investigation should have regard to the nature and seriousness of the case, the volume of material which may be obtained or created, and the likelihood of a committal or a not guilty plea. If not appointed at the start of an investigation, a disclosure officer must be appointed in sufficient time to be able to prepare the unused material schedules for inclusion in the full file submitted to CPS.

2.11   An individual must not be appointed as disclosure officer, or continue in that role, if that is likely to result in a conflict of interest, for instance, if the disclosure officer is the victim of the alleged crime which is the subject of criminal proceedings. The advice of a more senior officer must always be sought if there is doubt as to whether a conflict of interest precludes an individual acting as the disclosure officer. If thereafter the doubt remains, the advice of the prosecutor should be sought.

2.12   The officer in charge of an investigation may delegate certain tasks to civilians employed by the police such as SOCO and fingerprint officers. The officer in charge of an investigation must ensure that those tasks have been carried out in accordance with the Code.

Retention

2.13   The Code requires that material of any kind, including information and objects, which is **obtained in the course of a criminal investigation and which may be relevant to the investigation** must be retained.

2.14   If material with an evidential value has been destroyed, there is a danger that a court may stop the prosecution for abuse of process. Thus while it is not necessary to retain every item obtained or generated during the course of an investigation, any doubt should be resolved in favour of retention.

2.15   Material includes information given orally. Where relevant material is not recorded in any way, it will need to be reduced into a suitable form (see paragraphs 2.28 onwards below).

2.16   Material which may be **relevant to the investigation** is defined in the Code as anything that: **has some bearing on any offence under investigation or any person being investigated, or to the surrounding circumstances of the case, unless it is incapable of having any impact on the case.**

2.17   Care is needed when exercising judgement and discretion to decide what should be retained. Material or information which may not appear to have any significance at the outset of an investigation may have a bearing at a later stage.

2.18   The issue of relevance is especially important where an investigator is considering whether to throw something away, or to return an item to the owner, or not to record information; or where not keeping material or recording information would result in the permanent loss or alteration of the material (as with control room tapes, shop videos etc).

2.19   In discharging their obligations under the Act, Code, Attorney General's Guidelines, the common law and these operational instructions, investigators should always err on the side of recording and retaining material where they have any doubt as to whether it may be relevant.

2.20   Factors that may influence the decision to record information or retain material may be the size of the enquiry, the number of potential suspects, and the stage that the enquiry has reached. Early in an enquiry it may not be possible to make a considered decision on the relevance of an item until later in the case when the facts are clearer. However, considerations that the investigator should bear in mind will include:

- whether the information adds to the total knowledge of how the offence was committed, who may have committed it, and why

- whether the information could support an alternative explanation, given the current understanding of events surrounding the offence
- what the potential consequences will be if the material is not preserved.

2.21   If there is any question whatsoever that the material or information might have an impact on the case, either now or at some time in the future, the investigator should exercise his judgement in favour of recording and retaining the material.

2.22   Negative results can sometimes be as significant to an investigation as positive ones. It is impossible to define precisely when a negative result may be significant, as every case is different. However it will include the result of any enquiry that differs from what might be expected, given the prevailing circumstances. An example is given in paragraph 4.3 of the Code. Not only must material or information which points towards a fact or an individual be retained, but also that which casts doubt on the suspect's guilt, or implicates another person. Examples of negative information include:

- a CCTV camera that did not function, had no videotape loaded or did not record the crime/location/suspect. This comprises three separate and distinct scenarios for potential negative information, but it is only the last of these that may usually be considered relevant
- where a number of people present at a particular location at the particular time that an offence is alleged to have taken place state they saw nothing unusual
- where a finger-mark from a crime scene cannot be identified as belonging to a known suspect, or is of insufficient value to determine identity
- any other failure to match a crime scene sample with one taken from a known suspect.

2.23   Material may come into an investigator's possession during an investigation, or be generated during the course of the investigation: for example an interview record. Whatever the source, if it is relevant, it must be retained. If it is not possible or practicable to retain an item, a copy or a photograph may be taken. In indictable cases, and those other cases where a not guilty plea is likely, investigators should seek the advice of the officer in charge of the investigation, and if necessary, the prosecutor, particularly when the investigator is minded to return any material to its owner or otherwise dispose of it.

2.24   A **criminal investigation** is defined in the Code as an investigation conducted by a police officer with a view to it being ascertained whether a person should be charged with an offence, or whether a person charged with an offence is guilty of it.

2.25   This includes investigations which are begun in the belief that a crime is about to be committed. For example, a surveillance operation is part of an investigation even if it is directed to a target without there being a specific offence in mind.

2.26   This means that information and material arising out of operations conducted purely for intelligence purposes **might become disclosable** (subject to Public Interest Immunity (PII) considerations). Officers involved in intelligence operations should regularly and actively consider whether the information that they have impacts upon any live investigations or prosecutions, and if so, act quickly to ensure it is brought to the attention of the disclosure officer and prosecutor.

2.27   Particular categories of material that **must** be retained are listed in paragraph 5.4 of the Code. The list is not exhaustive, and there may be other material which requires retaining because it may be relevant. Examples of specific items which fall into these categories are listed in Annex D and the disclosure wall chart.

Recording of information

2.28   It is important to record promptly any information from any source, which might later become relevant to the investigation. A record should be made at the time the information is obtained, or as soon as practicable after that time.

2.29   It is the responsibility of the officer in charge of the investigation to ensure that the material is recorded in a durable or retrievable form, for instance, in writing, on video or audio tape, or computer disk.

2.30   Sometimes it is not practicable to retain the initial record because it forms part of a larger record which is to be destroyed, for example, control room audio tapes, custody suite video tapes, traffic car videos of speeding offences, or other similar recordings. Where this is the situation, the officer in charge of the investigation should identify information that should be retained, and ensure that it is transferred accurately to a durable and more easily stored form before the tapes are destroyed.

2.31   Investigators should be alert to the potential relevance and evidential value of information contained in messages that might not normally be retained; for example, running commentaries and details of pursuit. Investigators should also consider making a record of conversations with experts and other investigators, where the information discussed is likely to be relevant to the case.

2.32   Whether in original or copy form, details of preserved messages should be listed on the schedule(s) in the normal way.

Information recorded on computer

2.33   It is difficult to give clear-cut guidance on the approach to be adopted when dealing with information recorded on computer, owing to the wide range of investigative computer systems employed throughout the Police Service. But many computer systems (for example, HOLMES) generate material in the form of hard copy. This should be treated in the same way as relevant material from any other source.

2.34   The prosecutor will need to be informed of the use of such systems, and any hard copies produced listed on the schedules by the disclosure officer. Local arrangements may need to be agreed as to the means by which the prosecutor can inspect material held on computer systems. Where material is to be disclosed to the defence under the Act, supervised access to a terminal screen may be appropriate. Material may be supplied on a disk where this is acceptable to the accused and the disclosure officer.

2.35   Information contained in emails may amount to relevant unused material, particularly if the information is not recorded elsewhere. It should be recorded, retained and scheduled in the same way as other relevant material. (Where however, emails are intercepted under section 17 of the Regulation of Investigatory Powers Act 2000, disclosure is specifically prohibited.)

2.36   On a major crime enquiry, investigators may find it helpful to identify potentially sensitive material at the input stage. The final decision as to sensitivity at this stage will be the responsibility of the officer in charge of the investigation.

Recovering material not retained

2.37   Material may be examined during the course of an investigation, but not retained because it does not appear to be relevant at that stage. This will include material that has been returned to its owner without a copy being taken.

2.38   If during the lifetime of a case, the officer in charge of an investigation becomes aware that such material may become relevant as a result of new developments, paragraph 5.3 of the Code will apply. That officer should take steps to recover the material wherever practicable, or ensure that it is preserved by the person in possession of it.

Material in the possession of third parties

2.39   The Act only imposes duties of disclosure upon the investigator and the prosecutor. The term 'third party' applies to any person or agency who does not have a duty under the Act.

2.40   A third party has no obligation under the Act to reveal material to the investigator or to the prosecutor, nor is there any duty on the third party to retain material which may be relevant to the investigation. In some circumstances, the third party may not be aware of the investigation or prosecution.

2.41   However, there is a duty under the Code for an investigator to pursue all reasonable lines of enquiry, whether these point towards or away from a suspect. What is reasonable will depend upon the particular case, but it may include enquiries as to the existence of material relevant to the investigation in the possession of a third party. It is not necessary to make speculative enquiries, but frequently the existence of the material will be known or can be deduced from the circumstances. For example, where a child witness is in the care of the local authority, the social services may have relevant material relating to the allegation under investigation.

2.42   If the officer in charge of the investigation, the investigator or the disclosure officer suspects that a third party holds material that may be relevant to the investigation, that person or body should be told of the investigation. They should be alerted to the need to preserve relevant material. Consideration should be given as to whether it is appropriate to seek access to the material, and if so, steps should be taken to obtain such material. It will be important to do so if the material or information is likely to undermine the prosecution case, or to assist a known defence. A letter should be sent to the third party together with the explanatory leaflet, specimens of which are at Annex J.

2.43   The disclosure officer should inform the prosecutor of the identity of the third party and the nature of the material the third party is believed to possess by way of the MG6. In some circumstances it may be appropriate for the disclosure officer and the investigator to consider with the prosecutor whether the third party should be approached and further material sought or inspected.

2.44   If material relevant to the investigation comes to the knowledge of the investigator or is inspected or obtained from a third party, it will become unused material or information within the terms of the Code. This applies particularly to relevant information conveyed verbally by the third party. This should be recorded in a durable or retrievable form (for example potentially relevant information revealed in discussions at a child protection conference attended by police officers). It will have to be recorded on the appropriate schedule and revealed to the prosecutor in the usual way.

2.45   Where access to the material is declined or refused by the third party and the investigator believes that it is reasonable to seek production of the material before a suspect is charged because he or she believes it is likely to be relevant evidence and of substantial value, the investigator should consider making an application under Schedule 1 of the Police and Criminal Evidence Act (PACE) 1984, (Special Procedure Material). The investigator may seek advice of the prosecutor before such an application is made.

2.46   Where there are proceedings before a court and the requirements of section 2 of the Criminal Procedure (Attendance of Witnesses) Act 1965 or section 97 of the Magistrates' Court Act 1980 as appropriate are satisfied, then the investigator or the prosecutor should apply for a witness summons causing a representative of the third party to produce the material to the court.

2.47   The statutory requirements in 2.46 above are more stringent than those for the primary and secondary disclosure tests. Items sought under the summons procedure must be 'likely to be material evidence,' (which the House of Lords in *R v Derby Magistrates' Court ex parte B* [1995] 4 All ER 526 has construed to mean 'immediately admissible *per se*.') Accordingly, there should be consultation between the investigator and the prosecutor before any application to the court is made to assess whether it can properly proceed. (The transcript of *R v Brushett* (2001) Crim LR 471, illustrates an approach, commended by the Court of Appeal, where a pragmatic and co-operative stance was taken by social services and material revealed to the prosecution.)

2.48   Any reports prepared by a third party at the request of the investigator and supplied to the investigator will also be subject to the requirements of the Act relating to disclosure.

2.49   Where material is obtained from third parties, the investigator should discuss with them whether any sensitivities attach to the material that might influence whether it is used as evidence, or otherwise disclosed to the defence, or whether there may be public interest reasons that justify withholding disclosure. The third party's view must be passed to the prosecutor using the MG6.

2.50   Where material is held by a Government department or other Crown body that may be relevant to an issue in the case, reasonable steps should be taken to identify and consider such material. Investigators and disclosure officers should refer to paragraph 3.145 below for the procedure to follow.

Retention periods

2.51   Paragraphs 5.6 to 5.10 of the Code provide for the period of retention. This is the minimum period of retention and individual force policy may provide for a longer period.

2.52   Material seized under the provisions of PACE will be subject to the retention provisions of section 22 PACE.

Preparation of schedules

2.53   The disclosure officer is responsible for preparing the schedules and submitting them to the prosecutor. The schedules, dated by the disclosure officer, should be submitted to the prosecutor with a full file.

2.54   It is not necessary to maintain schedule(s) of unused material from the start of all investigations. During the course of the investigation it may not be possible to decide whether particular material will eventually form part of the prosecution case, or will remain unused. In some cases there may be advantages in starting the schedule(s) at an early stage. The officer in charge of the investigation will need to consider at what stage the schedules should be prepared, and when to appoint a disclosure officer.

2.55   Where working schedules or draft lists have been created as the enquiry progressed, the disclosure officer must check the contents and consolidate the items into two schedules for the prosecutor listing:

> any non-sensitive unused material (MG6C)
>
> any sensitive unused material (MG6D).

2.56   Draft schedules or lists used to prepare the final schedule need not be retained or listed on the MG6C.

2.57   Any comments, observations or explanations about the contents of the schedules should be made on the MG6, which should accompany the submission of the MG6C and MG6D. The disclosure officer must also indicate on the MG6E whether the investigation started before 1 April 1997. This will be of relevance to the prosecutor in deciding how to go about disclosing material to the accused, see **Pre-CPIA investigations** at paragraphs 1.48–49 above.

2.58   **All** items of material relevant to the investigation must be listed on one of the above schedules for the prosecutor, unless the material is so sensitive that it cannot even be listed on a schedule. This is dealt with at paragraph 2.86 below.

2.59   The table at Annex D provides some help as to whether the material should be listed as sensitive or otherwise. If in doubt, consult the prosecutor.

2.60   Correspondence or advice between the CPS and the police should not ordinarily be listed on either schedule, see paragraph 2.85 below.

2.61   As a general rule, pure opinion or speculation, for example police officers' theories about who committed the crime, is not unused material. However, if the opinion or speculation is based on some other information or fact, not otherwise apparent to the prosecutor, that information or fact might well be relevant to the investigation and should be notified to the prosecutor in accordance with these instructions.

2.62   Where the disclosure officer is unsure whether an item is relevant to the investigation and thus requires listing on a schedule, the prosecutor should be consulted as soon as practicable.

The non-sensitive material schedule

2.63   Non-sensitive unused material should be listed on the MG6C. **This form will be disclosed to the defence.**

2.64   In the description column of every schedule, each item should be individually listed and consecutively numbered throughout all schedules. Thus, where continuation sheets are used or additional schedules sent in later submissions, item numbering must be consecutive to all items on earlier schedules.

2.65   The descriptions in non-sensitive schedules should be detailed, clear and accurate. **They should include a summary of the contents of the retained material to allow the prosecutor to make an informed decision on disclosure.** The same applies to sensitive schedules to the extent possible without compromising the confidentiality of the information. It is not sufficient merely to refer to a document by way of a form number which may be meaningless outside the Police Service. Example schedules are given on the disclosure wall chart.

2.66   In cases where there are many items of a similar or repetitive nature (messages for example) it is permissible to describe them by quantity and generic title. However, inappropriate use of generic listing (such as 'correspondence 1.4.02 to 10.12.02') is likely to lead to requests from the prosecutor and the defence to see the items. This may result in wasted resources and unnecessary delay. The preparation of properly detailed schedules at this stage will save time and resources throughout the disclosure process, and will promote confidence in its integrity.

2.67   When items are described by generic titles or quantities, the disclosure officer must ensure that items which might meet the test for disclosure are listed individually.

2.68   The disclosure officer should keep a copy of the schedules that are sent to the prosecutor, in case there are any queries that need to be resolved. A copy will also assist the disclosure officer to keep track of the items listed, should the schedules need to be updated.

Phoenix input documents

2.69   Frequently, Phoenix input documents and fingerprint forms contain information that replicates exactly that which appears in other documents which have been used as evidence or are unused material. Not all information recorded on Phoenix forms will be material relevant to the investigation within the meaning of the Code: for example, information recorded for intelligence purposes only.

2.70   However, there will be circumstances where relevant information on these documents does not appear elsewhere, or is inconsistent with other material. Where this occurs, the disclosure officer should seek advice from the prosecutor as to whether the material may be relevant before listing the item on a schedule. A copy of the document should be sent to the prosecutor. The disclosure officer should explain why the information is thought to be relevant in the particular case.

2.71   It will not normally be necessary to list these documents on a schedule unless the prosecutor considers that they may be relevant. The prosecutor will decide whether the material is relevant, and whether it requires disclosure to the accused under the Act. If the item is relevant, but does not require disclosure to the accused, the prosecutor will request that it be added to the appropriate schedule.

2.72   If the document contains relevant information that must be disclosed to the accused because it undermines the prosecution case, or assists the defence at secondary stage, the prosecutor and the disclosure officer may need to consider whether the document should be edited if it contains sensitive material.

Offences taken into consideration (TICs)

2.73   Offences not charged but prepared as matters to be taken into consideration by the court on sentence will be treated in accordance with the Manual of Guidance. Normally, material relating to TICs need not be scheduled as individual items. However, if the investigating officer or the disclosure officer forms the view that a confession is unreliable, and this undermines the prosecution case, the CPS must be informed using the MG6. In this event the material relating to proposed TICs should be listed in the same way as all other unused material.

The sensitive material schedule

2.74   This schedule should be used to reveal to the prosecutor the existence of unused material which the disclosure officer, after consulting with the officer in charge of the investigation, believes should be withheld from the defence because it is not in the public interest to disclose it. Such material must none the less be revealed to the prosecutor.

2.75   The disclosure officer must list such material on the MG6D, and indicate on the form why the item(s) should not be disclosed. **This form will not be disclosed to the defence**.

2.76   In those cases where there is no sensitive unused material, the disclosure officer should endorse and sign an MG6D to this effect and should submit this with the MG6C and MG6E.

2.77   It is not possible to provide an exhaustive list of items which may be withheld. The proper test to apply is whether disclosure of the item would cause **real harm to the public interest**. Some examples are given at paragraph 6.12 of the Code.

2.78   Some items by their very nature will reveal why disclosure should be withheld, for example, information concerning intelligence sources. Others require more explanation. Careful attention to this element of the schedule will avoid further enquiries and consequent delay. Both the 'Description of item' and the 'Reasons for sensitivity' sections must contain sufficient information to enable the prosecutor to make an informed decision as to whether or not the material itself should be viewed. Schedules containing insufficient information will be returned by the prosecutor. If there is any doubt about the sensitivity of the material, the prosecutor should be consulted.

2.79   The police and CPS will always take care to protect intelligence information and information given to the police in confidence. That will be so whether or not it is thought likely that the court will order its disclosure. If the investigator is unsure whether information was given in confidence, the position should be clarified with the person who provided the information.

2.80   When the schedule and any material is sent to the prosecutor, a protective marking should be applied to it consistent with the level of sensitivity of its contents. This will determine the manner in which the material is conveyed to, and stored by the CPS. Reference should be had to the police policy guidance issued in October 2001 as to the detailed categorisation of different types of sensitive material as **Restricted**, **Confidential**, **Secret** or **Top Secret**. Guidance is given in Annex K below.

2.81   In deciding sensitivity it is important to bear in mind that the sensitivity of the schedule and the sensitivity of the information may differ. It may be possible to describe a highly sensitive piece of material adequately on the schedule without disclosing the information (for example, a name), which makes the material sensitive. The security marking will depend on what is being submitted to the prosecutor; if the material itself is to accompany the schedule the material will determine the marking. If the schedule alone is submitted the content of the schedule will determine its security marking.

2.82   Sensitive unused material and schedules relating to informants, observation posts or undercover operations will normally be treated as **Confidential**. They should be sent to the prosecutor in a sealed envelope marked 'Sensitive unused material—**Confidential** and bearing the name and URN of the defendant(s). Any other material which the police consider to meet the requirements of a **Confidential** marking should be submitted in the same way.

2.83   If a third party gives material to investigators, or allows material to be inspected, but indicates that material is sensitive in any way, the material must be listed on the MG6D. The third party's view must be passed on to the prosecutor via the MG6.

2.84   In order to make a proper assessment of the material which is said to be sensitive, the prosecutor will need either to see the material or part of it, or to be fully informed of its contents. In many cases it will be possible to attach a copy of the material (or part of it) to the schedule. But there will be occasions when this will not be feasible, either because the bulk of the material makes it impractical, or because the material is too sensitive to be copied and transmitted. In this event it will be for the disclosure officer to make arrangements with the prosecutor to view the material with an appropriate level of physical and personal security.

2.85   There is no need to list reports, advice or other communications between the CPS and police. Most in themselves will have no bearing on the case and thus will not be relevant. Those that are relevant will usually be protected by PII. When in doubt, guidance should be sought from the prosecutor.

Handling highly sensitive material

2.86   **All** relevant sensitive unused material should be included on the MG6D unless the exceptional circumstances identified in paragraph 6.13 of the Code exist. Paragraph 6.13 recognises that there may be material of such sensitivity that it would be inappropriate even to list it on the MG6D. Examples of such highly sensitive material would include information that, should it be compromised, would:

- lead directly to the loss of life
- directly threaten national security.

The small number of such cases where this situation may arise are likely to involve investigations into organised crime or into terrorist offences. This material is likely to be in the **Secret** or **Top Secret** categories.

2.87   Where there is unused material that is so sensitive that it cannot be itemised on the MG6D but the disclosure officer is aware of it, the disclosure officer should refer to the existence of such material on the MG6D without identifying it. The disclosure officer should notify the prosecutor of the existence of such material as soon as possible after a full file has been submitted to the prosecutor and should identify the person holding the material to enable the prosecutor to contact that person to discuss the nature of the material and to arrange to inspect it. Inspection should be at an appropriate location having regard to the sensitivity of the material.

2.88   Where the material in question is considered by police to be too sensitive even for a reference to its existence to be included on the MG6D, or it is considered too sensitive to reveal to the disclosure officer, the person holding the material should make contact with the prosecutor to discuss the material which **must** be viewed by the prosecutor.

2.89   It is likely that there will need to be an early consultation to discuss whether sensitive material may require disclosure and to decide whether the direction of the court should be sought. Where the police contend that material comes within paragraph. 2.86 above, initial contact with the CPS to discuss the material should be with the appropriate Unit Head or Special Casework Lawyer.

Applications to the court: sensitive material

2.90   The prosecutor has a duty under the Act to consider whether sensitive material might undermine the prosecution case or assist the defence. Where the prosecutor decides that the sensitive material requires disclosure to the accused because it falls within the tests set out in the Act, and the prosecutor in consultation with the police considers that disclosure should be withheld on public interest grounds, the direction of the court must be sought.

2.91 Before an application is made to the court, the prosecutor will need to consult the police. This should take place at a senior level, and a senior officer (who may be independent of the investigation) should be involved (see paragraphs 3.120 and 3.123 for levels of authority). Others may also be consulted, including the officer in charge of the investigation, and in Crown court cases, the prosecution advocate.

2.92 Consultation will include a careful examination of the circumstances of the case and the nature of the sensitive material. In particular, the prosecutor will require information dealing with the following issues:

- the reasons why the material is said to be sensitive
- the degree of sensitivity said to attach to the material, in other words, why it is considered that real harm would be caused to the public interest by disclosure
- the consequences of revealing to the defence
  (i) the material itself
  (ii) the category of the material
  (iii) the fact that an application is being made
- the significance of the material to the issues in the trial
- the involvement of any third parties in bringing the material to the attention of the police
- where the material is likely to be the subject of an order for disclosure, what the police view is regarding continuance of the prosecution.

2.93 For consultation to be effective, the officer in charge of the investigation should ensure that the prosecutor is provided with the information necessary to make a proper decision on how the application is to be made. This should be in documentary form, unless the information is so sensitive that it would be inappropriate to put it into writing.

2.94 On the basis of the information provided at the consultation, the prosecutor will decide whether an application should be made, and the form of application required. The editing of a document, or other methods of disclosing the relevant information without compromising the sensitive material may be considered appropriate.

2.95 Following consultation, the prosecutor will set out in writing the submission to be made to the court (see paragraph 3.124 below). The submission will be signed by the prosecutor (at Unit Head or Special Casework Lawyer level), and by a Detective Chief Inspector, unless a Detective Inspector has specific delegated authority to do so. The officer will state that to the best of his or her knowledge and belief the assertions of fact on which the submission is based are correct. The officer may be required to attend court to give evidence in support of the application.

Editing

2.96 Some documents may contain a mixture of sensitive and non-sensitive material. For example, a witness address or personal telephone number may appear on a document that otherwise is entirely non-sensitive.

2.97 In these cases there may be no objection to the sensitive part being blocked out, using a dark marker pen (not correcting fluid), on the copy document which is to be sent to the prosecutor. The original should not be marked in any way. A description of the document should be listed on the MG6C. (The unedited version should **not** be listed on the MG6D, but made available to the prosecutor for inspection if required). The prosecutor should be informed of the nature of the edited material, if not obvious, on the MG6.

2.98 Decisions about editing documents should only be made after consultation between the disclosure officer and the prosecutor, other than for the simple deletion of the personal addresses or telephone numbers of witnesses.

Amending the schedules

2.99   On occasions it may be necessary to amend the schedules. When the schedules are first submitted with a full file, the disclosure officer may not know exactly what material the prosecutor intends to use as part of the prosecution case. The prosecutor may create unused material by extracting statements or documents from the evidence bundle, in which case the prosecutor may disclose material directly to the defence without waiting for the disclosure officer to amend the schedule, but should advise the officer accordingly. Police officers should ensure that obviously non-evidential material is not included in the evidence bundle.

2.100   The prosecutor is required to advise the disclosure officer of: items listed on the MG6C that should properly be on the MG6D; any apparent omissions or amendments required; where there are insufficient or unclear descriptions; or where there has been a failure to provide schedules at all. The disclosure officer must then take all necessary remedial action and provide properly completed schedules to the prosecutor. Failure to do so may result in the matter being raised with a senior officer.

2.101   The Code places the responsibility for creating the schedules and keeping them accurate and up to date on the disclosure officer. Consequently, the prosecutor will not amend them. In these circumstances the prosecutor will inform the disclosure officer of the changes required, and will return the schedules for amendment where appropriate.

2.102   The disclosure officer should effect the amendments promptly and return the amended or fresh schedules to the prosecutor as soon as possible with an MG6E as appropriate.

Continuing duties

2.103   The duties of revelation to the prosecutor and disclosure to the accused are continuing obligations. Any new material coming to light after primary or secondary disclosure has been completed should be treated in the same way as earlier material. The new material should be listed on a further MG6C, MG6D or a continuation sheet. To avoid confusion, numbering of items submitted at a later stage must be consecutive to those on the previously submitted schedules.

2.104   A further MG6E should also be submitted irrespective of whether or not any of the new material is considered by the disclosure officer to come within the appropriate primary or secondary disclosure test.

Revelation of the material to the prosecutor: common law

2.105   Investigators and disclosure officers must be mindful of the prosecutor's duty, in the interests of justice and fairness in the particular circumstances of any case, to make disclosure of material after the commencement of proceedings but **before** the duty arises under the Act. For instance, the investigator or disclosure officer must inform the prosecutor of significant information, such as a victim's previous convictions, that might affect a bail decision or that might enable the defence to contest committal proceedings.

2.106   Similarly, the investigator or disclosure officer must reveal to the prosecutor any material that is relevant to sentence (for example, information which might mitigate the seriousness of the offence or assist the defendant in laying blame in whole or in part upon a co-defendant or another).

Revelation of the material to the prosecutor: primary stage

2.107   Revealing material to the prosecutor does not mean automatic disclosure to the defence. The prosecutor will only disclose material to the defence if it falls within the tests for disclosure set out in the Act. If the material is sensitive, and must otherwise be disclosed under the Act, the prosecutor will either apply to the court for a ruling as to whether the public interest requires disclosure or disclose the material after consultation with police or withdraw the prosecution.

2.108   The MG6C will be disclosed to the defence at primary stage.

2.109   Revelation to the prosecutor involves:

- promptly sending the completed schedules
- pointing out any material which might undermine the prosecution case and therefore fall within the test for primary disclosure
- copying certain material to the prosecutor (see paragraphs 2.119–2.125 below)
- allowing the prosecutor to inspect material.

2.110   Disclosure at the primary stage requires the disclosure of material which **in the prosecutor's opinion might undermine the case for the prosecution**. The disclosure officer will need to carefully check the material listed on **both** schedules and assist the prosecutor to identify anything which **potentially** might need disclosing to the defence. The case against each accused must be considered separately.

2.111   In large or complicated cases or in any case where particular difficulties are anticipated, an early discussion between the disclosure officer or the officer in charge of the investigation, the prosecutor and prosecution advocate, if instructed, may be extremely beneficial. For example, they may agree to look at the material together before the schedules are prepared. In such circumstance, the disclosure officer or the officer in charge of the investigation, should not hesitate to contact the prosecutor for advice.

2.112   The disclosure officer should bring to the prosecutor's attention any material which might have the potential to undermine the prosecution case. Examples will include:

- records of previous convictions and cautions for prosecution witnesses (see Annex A and Annex B)
- any other information which casts doubt on the reliability of a witness or on the accuracy of any prosecution evidence
- any motives for the making false of allegations by a prosecution witness
- any material which may have a bearing on the admissibility of any prosecution evidence
- the fact that a witness has sought, been offered or received a reward
- any material that might go to the credibility of a prosecution witness
- any information which may cast doubt on the reliability of a confession. Any item which relates to the defendant's mental or physical health, his intellectual capacity, or to any ill-treatment which the defendant may have suffered when in the investigators custody is likely to have the potential for casting doubt on the reliability of a purported confession
- information that a person other than the defendant was or might have been responsible or which points to another person whether charged or not (including a co-defendant) having involvement in the commission of the offence.

2.113   Any material that has an adverse effect on the strength of the prosecution case should be pointed out by the disclosure officer. This will include anything that may weaken an essential part of the prosecution case. Any material that supports or is consistent with a defence put forward in interview or before charge or which is apparent from the prosecution papers should be provided to the prosecutor at this stage. It also includes anything that points away from the defendant, such as information about a possible alibi. If the material might undermine the prosecution case it should be brought to the prosecutor's attention at this stage even though it suggests a defence inconsistent with or alternative to the one already advanced by the defendant or solicitor. Items of material viewed in isolation may not be considered to have potential to undermine the prosecution case, however several items together can have that effect.

2.114   Such material must be brought to the prosecutor's attention regardless of any views about the accuracy or truth of the information, although where appropriate the disclosure officer may express an opinion on what weight should be given to it.

2.115   A wide interpretation should be given when identifying material that might fall within the test. A thorough and careful check at primary stage may save time later on. The disclosure officer should consult with the prosecutor where necessary to help identify material that may require disclosure at this stage, and must specifically draw material to the attention of the prosecutor where the disclosure officer has any doubt as to whether it might have potential to undermine the prosecution case.

2.116   Disclosure officers must deal expeditiously with requests by the prosecutor for further information on material which may lead to disclosure.

2.117   The MG6E should be used to draw the attention of the prosecutor to material that might undermine the prosecution case. The disclosure officer should also explain on form MG6E (by referring to the relevant item's number on the schedule) why he or she has come to that view. The MG6C itself should not be marked or highlighted in any way, as it will be provided to the defence.

2.118   Where it is the case that the disclosure officer believes there is no material that might have the potential to undermine the prosecution case, the officer should endorse the MG6E in the following terms: '**I have reviewed all the material which has been retained and made available to me and there is nothing to the best of my knowledge and belief that might undermine the prosecution case.**'

2.119   As well as describing the material on the schedule(s), there is a duty to copy certain material to the prosecutor. The types of material that should **always** be sent are described in paragraph 7.3 of the Code.

2.120   In addition to this, and as an aid to prosecutors in their case review function, copies of the crime report and the log of messages should also be routinely copied to the prosecutor in every case in which a full file is provided. (These documents are known in different police forces by different names, for example OIS or CAD for the log of messages.)

2.121   The documents should be fully described in accordance with 2.65 above to enable a properly informed decision by the prosecutor as to disclosure.

2.122   If the disclosure officer believes that these documents might have the potential to undermine the prosecution case, they should be listed on the MG6E in the usual way. However, copies should be provided to the prosecutor irrespective of whether they are considered to be potentially disclosable to the defence.

2.123   The copy of the crime report and log of messages should be edited by the police in accordance with paragraphs 2.96 and 2.97 above, before they are sent to the prosecutor. If it is impossible to edit any sensitive parts of the material, then it should be listed on the MG6D and be sent to the prosecutor with that schedule.

2.124   **Revealing this material to the prosecutor does not mean it will be automatically disclosed to the defence.** The prosecutor will only disclose unused material if it falls within the test for disclosure set out in the Act, and will advise the police of any such decision by endorsing the MG6C with reasons as to why the material meets the disclosure test.

2.125   This requirement to routinely reveal the crime report and the log of messages does not prejudice any other locally agreed arrangements between the police and the CPS that allow for the similar treatment of other additional categories or types of document.

2.126   The task of indicating material that might undermine the prosecution case, and the submission of copies of that material, involves a proper consideration of all the retained material. That obligation cannot be discharged by simply sending to the prosecutor material which has not been so considered.

2.127   Considering the unused material against the primary disclosure test does not mean that material not thought to be capable of undermining the prosecution case can be omitted from the schedule(s). **All retained unused material or information must be scheduled**, save in those rare cases where paragraphs 2.86–2.89 apply.

2.128   A prosecutor may ask to inspect material, or request a copy of material where one has not been sent. The disclosure officer is responsible for arranging this. Material should be copied to the prosecutor on request unless it is too sensitive or too bulky, or can only be inspected. This applies to both stages of disclosure.

2.129   After the prosecutor has considered each schedule, it will be endorsed with the decisions as to whether each listed item will be disclosed to the defence. A copy of the endorsed schedule will be sent to the disclosure officer.

Revelation of material to the prosecutor: secondary stage

2.130   The prosecutor will give the disclosure officer a copy of any defence statement received as soon as possible following its receipt.

2.131   The defence statement should set out the nature of the defence in general terms, indicate the matters on which the defendant takes issue with the prosecution and the reasons why he takes issue. There may be a note from the prosecutor, providing guidance on what material might have to be disclosed at the secondary stage, advice on whether any further lines of enquiry need to be followed (for example, where an alibi has been given) or suggestions for when the officer reconsiders the unused material. These may arise where the prosecutor (unlike the disclosure officer) is aware of issues raised by the defence during the progress of the case, for example at bail hearings or during committal proceedings.

2.132   At the secondary stage, the prosecutor must serve upon the defence material which might be reasonably expected to assist the accused's defence as disclosed by the defence statement. This must be done as soon as reasonably practicable after receipt of the defence statement.

2.133   The disclosure officer should promptly look again at the retained material and must draw the attention of the prosecutor to any material which **might reasonably be expected to assist the accused's defence as disclosed by the defence statement**. Both sensitive and non-sensitive material must be considered.

2.134   Material that might assist the defence may already have been identified at primary stage. It will include anything that might help the defence in preparing or presenting their case, as outlined in the defence statement. The disclosure officer should consult with the prosecutor where necessary to help identify any material which may require disclosure at this stage, as for primary disclosure.

2.135   The disclosure officer's observations should be submitted to the prosecutor on a fresh MG6E. If there is no material that the disclosure officer believes will assist the defence, the disclosure officer should endorse the second MG6E in the following terms: '**I have reviewed all the retained material made available to me and there is nothing to the best of my knowledge and belief to assist the defence in the light of the defence statement.**'

2.136   Any items that might assist should be referred to by quoting the item number from the schedule(s). If material identified has not previously been supplied to the prosecutor, a copy should be forwarded by the disclosure officer, except where the material is considered to be too sensitive to copy and arrangements are to be made for the prosecutor to inspect the material.

2.137   The disclosure officer should ensure that it is clear that the MG6E has been completed in response to a defence statement (secondary disclosure). The disclosure officer should explain why the material might reasonably be expected to assist the defence. The disclosure officer must sign and date the MG6E to comply with paragraph 9.1 of the Code.

2.138   The defence statement may on occasion point the prosecution to other lines of inquiry, for example, the investigation of an alibi, or where forensic expert evidence is involved. The disclosure officer should inform the officer in charge of the investigation and copy the defence statement to him or her, together with any advice provided by the prosecutor, if appropriate. Further investigation in these circumstances is possible and evidence obtained as a result of inquiring into a defence statement may be used as part of the prosecution case or to rebut the defence. However, an investigator should not show a defence statement to a witness. The extent to which the detail of a defence case statement is made known to a witness will depend upon the extent to which it is necessary to clarify the issues disputed by the defence, assist the prosecutor to identify any further disclosable material and/or to identify any further reasonable lines of inquiry. The officer should seek guidance from the prosecutor if there is any doubt as to permissible usage of the defence statement in conducting further inquiries.

2.139   If enquiries are carried out in response to the defence statement, the disclosure officer in consultation with the officer in charge of the investigation should notify the prosecutor of the results of those enquiries. This should be done on an MG20, and given to the prosecutor together with any additional schedules and a further MG6E as appropriate. If no enquiries were made, particularly when the defence statement has given details of an alibi, the disclosure officer should explain why.

2.140   Once the prosecutor has decided whether there is material that should be disclosed at secondary stage, a letter will be sent to the defence. The disclosure officer will be sent a copy of the letter, which will contain details of any items that require disclosure.

Large or complex cases

2.141   Some investigations may involve a large quantity of material, both used and unused. Examples of cases where this may occur include the following:

- substantial frauds
- large scale conspiracies
- drug related offences involving manufacture, importation or supply
- homicide or other major enquiries.

2.142   Such cases will inevitably need close and early liaison between the disclosure officer and the prosecutor. Where appropriate, they may agree to look at the material together before the schedules are prepared. Alternatively, they may need to work closely to identify material listed on the schedules that may require disclosure under the Act, and to agree arrangements for its disclosure to the accused. Such early discussion between the Police and the prosecutor may be extremely beneficial to effective case preparation.

2.143   In any cases where there is a large amount of unused material, it may not be possible or desirable to copy all necessary material to the prosecutor. The disclosure officer should inform the prosecutor that a large quantity of material exists, and should make any necessary arrangements to facilitate inspection of the items by the prosecutor.

2.144   The disclosure officer and the prosecutor must consider the unused material, and decide what items require disclosure to the accused. Once a decision has been reached on what should be disclosed, the disclosure officer and the prosecutor may agree that it would be more practicable to allow the defence to inspect all or part of the material that should be disclosed. This is more likely to occur at secondary stage in cases where there is potentially a lot of material that may assist the defence put forward, but it may occur at primary stage.

2.145   In some cases, investigators may seize large volumes of material that may not, for whatever reason, seem likely ever to be relevant. In such circumstances, the investigator may consider that it is not an appropriate use of resources to examine such large volumes of material seized on a precautionary basis. If such material is not examined by the investigator or disclosure officer, and it is not intended to examine it, but the material is nevertheless retained, its existence should be made known to the accused in general terms at the primary stage and permission granted for its inspection by him or his legal advisers. A section 9 statement will be completed by the investigator or the disclosure officer describing the material by general category and justifying it not having been examined. This statement will itself be listed as unused material and automatically disclosed to the defence.

2.146   The prosecutor should be informed of any arrangements made with the defence and should also be informed of defence requests for copies of items. The disclosure officer must comply with defence requests for copies unless it is neither practicable nor desirable. Examples of such circumstances are given in paragraph 10.3 of the Code.

Certification by disclosure officer

2.147   The disclosure officer is required to certify to the prosecutor that: **To the best of my knowledge and belief, all material which has been retained and made available to me has been inspected, viewed or listened to (other than unexamined irrelevant material) and revealed to the prosecutor in accordance with the Criminal Procedure and Investigations Act 1996, Code of Practice and the Attorney General's Guidelines 2000.** The purpose of certification is to provide an assurance to the prosecutor on behalf of the police investigating team that all relevant material has been identified, considered and revealed to the prosecutor.

2.148   The officer in charge of the investigation must ensure that all relevant material that has been retained is either made available to the disclosure officer, or in exceptional circumstances revealed directly to the prosecutor. The disclosure officer must be able to perform the duties of scheduling the material and revealing it to the prosecutor accurately and efficiently.

2.149   The disclosure officer must make certification when the schedules are submitted at primary stage, and again at secondary stage when a defence statement has been supplied and the retained material is reviewed again. The signed and dated MG6E should be used to provide certification to the prosecutor at both stages.

2.150   If the disclosure officer is uncertain as to whether all the retained material has been made available, enquiries should be made of the officer in charge of the investigation to resolve the matter.

Disclosure to the accused

2.151   Disclosure of material that falls within the tests for disclosure to the accused can be achieved either by copying the item, or by allowing the accused to inspect it. Where the item to be disclosed is a document, and has been copied to the CPS, the prosecutor will usually copy it to the defence.

2.152   There will be situations where this is not possible or appropriate, for example where the quality of the copy supplied is inadequate, or where the item is in a form requiring specialist copying equipment (such as audio or video tapes), or where the prosecutor considers that the material is not suitable for copying for other reasons (such as the sexual content). Sometimes it will not be possible to copy the item at all, for example where the item is a physical object.

2.153   In these circumstances the prosecutor may decide that the item should be inspected, or that the disclosure officer should arrange for a copy to be given to the defence. Where the item is a video or an audio tape, the police will be responsible for providing copies.

2.154   The prosecutor will indicate on the MG6C whether the item is to be disclosed by way of inspection, and should discuss with the disclosure officer the appropriate method of disclosure before that decision is taken. Where the prosecutor requests that the item to be disclosed should be made available for the accused (or his legal representative) to inspect, the disclosure officer is responsible for arranging this.

2.155   If the accused asks for a copy of any material which he has been allowed to inspect, the disclosure officer must give it to him, unless in the opinion of the disclosure officer it is either not practicable or desirable. Examples of these circumstances are given in paragraph 10.3 of the Code.

2.156   Where a copy of any disclosable item is given to the accused, the disclosure officer should inform the prosecutor, and supply a copy to the prosecutor, if one has not already been provided. It is important that a careful record is kept by the disclosure officer of what items are inspected by or copied to the accused or his legal representatives.

2.157   For information that is not recorded in writing, the disclosure officer may decide in what form the material should be disclosed. If a transcript is provided, the disclosure officer must ensure that the transcript is certified as a true record, for example by way of a short statement by the transcriber. It is not necessary for the disclosure officer to personally certify the accuracy of the transcript.

Summary trials

2.158   In summary trials, the time available for the investigator and the prosecutor to carry out their respective functions under the Act will be limited, particularly where the accused is in custody.

2.159   To make best use of available time, it is therefore essential that:

- potential not guilty pleas are identified so that the preparation of full files can start as soon as possible
- file upgrades are commenced as soon as possible
- full files should be submitted on time, complete with the schedules and copies of any items that must be supplied to the prosecutor.

2.160   In summary trials, the defence need not provide a defence statement. This means that there may not be a secondary stage to prosecution disclosure, and no opportunity to provide assisting material. In the interests of justice, the identification of material which might undermine the prosecution case should be interpreted as widely as possible.

2.161   In summary only matters, there is no requirement to provide schedules unless and until a formal not guilty plea is entered by the accused. However, as soon as the police receive notification of a not guilty plea in such cases, all appropriate disclosure schedules should be prepared and submitted to the prosecutor. This also applies to minor traffic offences.

Special problems with disclosure

2.162   There are a number of difficult areas that require specific and detailed guidance in relation to the handling of material for disclosure purposes. These are dealt with in the following annexes:

- previous convictions and disciplinary findings against police officers: Annex A
- previous convictions and cautions against other prosecution witnesses: Annex B
- debriefing sessions: Annex E
- pre-trial meetings with witnesses: Annex F
- financial investigation material: Annex G
- scientific support disclosure: Annexes H and I
- third party material procedures: Annex J
- the security of sensitive material schedules and unused material: Annex K (**Restricted**).

2.163   Investigators and disclosure officers should refer to the appropriate annex when dealing with these issues.

2.164   There will occasionally be cases where the unused material is revealed to the prosecutor by someone other than the disclosure officer. In some cases, for example, where the police investigation has been intelligence led, there may be an additional disclosure officer appointed just to deal with intelligence material which, by its very nature, is likely to be sensitive.

2.165   Where more than one disclosure officer has been appointed to deal with different aspects of the case, a **principal disclosure officer** should be identified as the single point of contact for the prosecutor. Where an officer other than the principal disclosure officer submits a disclosure schedule to the prosecutor, that officer should inform the principal disclosure officer.

2.166   Where the prosecutor consults with the principal disclosure officer, for example, when he provides a copy of the defence statement, the principal disclosure officer should inform any other officer who has provided unused material schedules to the prosecutor.

ANNEX J THIRD PARTY PROCEDURES

Explanatory leaflet on the principles and procedures relating to third parties under the Criminal Procedures and Investigation Act 1996 and the disclosure of material in their possession.

Letter from the Police Disclosure Officer to Local Authority Legal Department.

AN EXPLANATORY LEAFLET ON THE PRINCIPLES AND PROCEDURES RELATING TO THIRD PARTIES UNDER THE CRIMINAL PROCEDURE AND INVESTIGATIONS ACT 1996 AND THE DISCLOSURE OF MATERIAL IN THEIR POSSESSION

Introduction

1.   This document explains the procedures to be followed by the prosecution in seeking to obtain relevant material held by individuals and organisations that are regarded as third parties in criminal proceedings.

2.   The law governing material held by third parties is contained in the Criminal Procedure and Investigations Act 1996 (CPIA) and the Attorney General's Guidelines published in November 2000.

Who are third parties?

3.   In the course of an investigation to determine whether an offence has been committed, the police may become aware of relevant material in the possession of persons or organisations which may have a bearing on the investigation. It is only the investigator and the prosecutor who have statutory duties of revelation and disclosure under the CPIA. All other categories of persons are third parties so far as the conduct of the case is concerned.

The Legal Requirements of the Prosecution

4.   Every accused person has a right to a fair trial, a right enshrined in our law and guaranteed under the European Convention on Human Rights. This right to a fair trial is fundamental and the accused's right to fair disclosure is an inseparable part of it.

5.   The scheme set out in the CPIA is designed to ensure that there is fair disclosure of material to the accused which may be relevant to an investigation and which does not form part of the

prosecution case. This is known as 'unused material'. Fairness does, however, recognise that there are other interests that need to be protected, including those of the victims and witnesses who might otherwise be exposed to harm. The CPIA protects those interests.

6.   Investigators are under a duty to pursue all reasonable lines of enquiry, whether these point towards or away from the accused. What is reasonable in each case will depend on the particular circumstances. Investigators and prosecutors must do all they can to facilitate proper disclosure, as part of their general and professional responsibility to act fairly and impartially, in the interests of justice.

7.   Where you possess material, which has not been obtained by the police, they are under a duty to inform you of the existence of the investigation and to invite you to retain the material in case they receive a request for its disclosure. Where the police inspect material with your agreement and do not retain it, they are under a duty to record details of that material and to reveal it to the prosecutor.

8.   Where you do not allow the prosecution access to the material, the prosecution may apply to the court for a witness summons, and if granted would require you to attend court to produce the material to the court. Application for a witness summons will only be made where the prosecution considers that the material sought is likely to be material to the proceedings. You do have the right to make representations to the court against the issue of a witness summons.

9.   Where the relevant material held by you or owned by you but in the possession of the prosecution is sensitive, in that it is not in the public interest to disclose, then the prosecution will treat that material in confidence. Where that material might undermine the prosecution case or might reasonably assist the defence case, a public interest immunity application must be made to prevent disclosure to the defence. Where you have an interest in that material, the prosecution is under a duty to notify you in writing of the time and place of any public interest immunity application. You have a right to make representations to the court.

10.   Failure by the prosecution to take action leading to the disclosure of relevant material may result in a wrongful conviction or dismissal of the proceedings.

The Prosecution Procedures in dealing with Third Parties

11.   In the course of an investigation, the investigator will write to you setting out the circumstances of the case and specifying the relevant material that he believes is in your possession.

12.   Where you acknowledge that you hold relevant material which may have some bearing on the issues in the case, the investigator will request a copy from you or request to inspect the material.

13.   Where you provide the material to the police in the course of the investigation, the police will discuss with you whether any sensitivity attaches to the material. Your view will be passed on to the Crown Prosecution Service.

14.   Where the material is sensitive, and a public interest immunity application is made to withhold the material from the defence, you have a right to make representations to the court on issues of the sensitivity of the material. The Crown Prosecution Service will notify you of the time and place of the application.

15.   Where you refuse to provide all or part of the material, or refuse to allow the police to inspect it, the police will request you to retain the material in case they receive a request for its disclosure or the court later requires the material to be disclosed.

16.   Where an accused has been charged with an offence and you have refused to reveal the material to the police, or failed to respond to the request for the material, the Crown Prosecution Service may consider applying to the court for a witness summons. The procedure relating to witness summonses is set out below.

Rules relating to witness summonses in the Crown Court (Criminal Procedure (Attendance of Witnesses) Act 1965)

17.   An application for a summons for a person to produce a document or thing to the court must be made in writing, where the trial has not commenced, to the appropriate officer of the Crown Court. The application should contain:

- A brief description of the required document or thing;
- Reasons why the person will not voluntarily produce it;
- Reasons why the document or thing is likely to be material evidence;
- A supporting affidavit setting out the charge and specifying: the evidence which will enable the person to identify it; the grounds for believing that the person is likely to be able to produce the document or thing; and the grounds for believing that it will be material evidence.

18.   A copy of the application and the supporting affidavit will be served on the person by the Crown Prosecution Service/Police. It will inform the person of their right to make representations in writing and at the hearing, and that they have 7 days to inform the court if they wish to make representations.

19.   If the person does not request a hearing, the appropriate officer of the Crown Court will refer the papers to the judge. The judge will decide whether or not to issue a witness summons in the light of the information before him.

20.   If the person requests a hearing, the court will set a time, place and date and will notify both the person and the Crown Prosecution Service. The hearing shall be in private unless the judge directs otherwise.

21.   Where the person produces the document or thing prior to the hearing of the summons, the Crown Prosecution Service will notify the court that the requirements imposed by the summons are no longer needed.

22.   A person may make an application to the Crown Court to make a summons which has been issued ineffective on the grounds that he had not received a notice of application to issue the summons and that he had not been present or represented at any hearing of the application and would not be able to produce any document or thing likely to be material evidence.

Rules Relating to Witness Summonses in the Magistrates' Court

23.   If the proceedings are before the Magistrates' Court, an application can be made for a witness summons for a person to produce a document or thing under section 97 or 97A (committal proceedings) of the Magistrates' Court Act 1980.

24.   Where an indictable only offence has been sent to the Crown Court and before service of the prosecution case, an application can be made to the Magistrates' Court for a person to produce a document or other exhibit, Schedule 3, paragraph 4 of the Crime and Disorder Act 1998.

DRAFT LETTER TO THIRD PARTIES

Dear Sir/Madam

REQUEST FOR DISCLOSURE OF MATERIAL HELD BY...
( ) Police are conducting a criminal investigation into allegations made against *(name and address, if appropriate, of the alleged offender)*.
The allegations being investigated are, in general terms, that *(set out the nature of the allegations and the issues in the case)*.

I believe that you hold material which may be relevant to the investigation, namely *(set out what material it is believed the third party holds)*.

The reasons why I am seeking access to this material is because I believe that *(list the reasons which may include; material which might affect the credibility and reliability of a witness; material which might undermine the prosecution case; and material which might reasonably assist the defence case)*.

I would be grateful if you would confirm whether or not you hold any such material and if so, whether you are prepared to disclose it for the purposes of the investigation. I would also be grateful if you could let me know whether you consider the material to be sensitive and the reasons for any sensitivity.

If you object to disclosing the material, I would be grateful if you could specify your reasons.

I request that you retain the material in case the court requires you to disclose some or all of the material.

I enclose for your assistance, an explanatory leaflet that sets out the role of the prosecution in dealing with material in the possession of third parties. It explains what will happen with the material if you disclose it. Further, it explains what may happen if you refuse to disclose it.

It would be of great assistance if you could reply by *(insert date)*.

If you wish to discuss this request, or any further information, please do not hesitate to contact me on *(insert contact number)*.

Thank you in advance for your assistance.

Yours faithfully,

(Officer in charge of the investigation/investigator/disclosure officer).

Appendix 3

Home Office Circular 31/2002: Deaths in Police Custody: Guidance to the Police on Pre-inquest Disclosure

This note provides revised guidance to Chief Officers about the disclosure of documentary evidence to interested persons in advance of inquest hearings which concern deaths in police custody. It has been prepared in consultation with representatives of the Association of Chief Police Officers, the Metropolitan Police, the Police Federation, the Superintendents' Association, the Police Complaints Authority, the Coroners Society, Liberty, Inquest and others who have expertise in relevant issues.

Background

2. Home Office Circular 20/1999 was issued to clarify various issues in relation to the pre-inquest disclosure of documentary evidence which had been under consideration for some time. The updated version of the Circular reflects experience of operating the system, but the essential issues remain largely unchanged. Chief Officers may be aware that there is a fundamental review of the Coroners' Service underway. At least until that review has been completed there is no intention to alter the limited requirement of an inquest to ascertain who the deceased was, and how, when and where he came by his death. The existing prohibition on the attribution of civil or criminal responsibility remains, as does the restriction on commenting on matters outside the remit of the inquest.

3. Inquests are non-adversarial. There are in law no parties to the matter, and no issues to be litigated between them. However, where a death occurs in controversial circumstances, it can be difficult to avoid an adversarial approach arising, particularly where the deceased was in legal custody.

4. In such circumstances, disclosure of information held by the authorities in advance of the hearing should help to provide reassurance to the family of the deceased and other interested persons that a full and open police investigation has been conducted, and that they and their legal representatives will not be disadvantaged at the inquest. Advance disclosure may also remove a source of friction between interested persons and facilitate concentration on the facts surrounding the death. Experience has shown that pre-hearing disclosure in cases relating to deaths in police custody has been useful in allaying suspicions that matters are being deliberately concealed by the police which might otherwise have distracted attention from the real issues and made it more difficult for inquests to achieve the purpose required in law.

5. Chief Officers are advised, therefore, that there should continue to be as great a degree of openness as possible, and that disclosure of documentary material to interested persons before the inquest hearing should be normal practice in the cases described in paragraph 7 below. In all cases Chief Officers will want to consider whether there are compelling reasons why certain documents, or parts of documents, may not be disclosed. But there should always be a strong presumption in favour of openness.

6. Our understanding from the review is that it is common practice in most forces to keep bereaved families fully informed during the course of the investigation. We consider that this is

essential good practice which should be followed in all cases. It is important to establish contact with the bereaved family as early as possible and keeping them fully informed will help to allay any fears that matters are being concealed by the police, particularly in the more controversial cases.

Scope

7.   This guidance applies to all cases of deaths of a member of the public during or following contact with the police which the police are required to report to the Home Office. A full definition of such deaths is at Annex A.

Extent of disclosure

8.   The courts have established that statements taken by the police and other documentary material produced by the police during the investigation of a death in police custody are the property of the force commissioning the investigation. The Coroner has no power to order the pre-inquest disclosure of such material, and limited powers to prevent such disclosure. Disclosure will therefore be on a voluntary basis.

9.   All the material which is supplied to the Coroner should normally be made available to all those whom the Coroner considers to be interested persons.

10.   There are some kinds of material which require particular consideration when pre-inquest disclosure is being arranged:

(i)   There may in some cases be a question of whether disclosure of certain material might have an impact on possible subsequent proceedings, whether criminal, civil or disciplinary. This is likely to arise, however, only in exceptional cases. Where the material might have an impact on subsequent criminal proceedings, the matter should be discussed with the Crown Prosecution Service. These reasons would only justify withholding of documents, or parts of documents, where there was a genuine risk, not simply a remote possibility, that disclosure would have a prejudicial effect.

(ii)   There may be material which contains sensitive or personal information about the deceased, or unsubstantiated allegations about the deceased, or other material which may cause concern or distress to the family of the deceased. Such material should be handled with appropriate care and sensitivity, particularly over the way in which such material is disclosed to the family of the deceased. The handling of such material should be discussed with the family or the family's legal representatives.

(iii)   Personal information about third parties which is not material to the inquest—for example, the addresses of witnesses—should be deleted from documents to be disclosed. The names of witnesses should not be disclosed where an application to the Coroner for anonymity is being considered.

(iv)   Where disclosure of material which is not likely to be called in evidence is contemplated, it may be preferable to arrange for interested persons to view the material in advance, rather than the material being copied and provided directly to them, on the grounds that such material is generally not likely to be relevant.

(v)   Any person who is asked to give a statement during the course of the police investigation of a death in custody should be made aware that his/her statement may be used in the context of an inquest and may therefore be disclosed in accordance with this guidance. That can readily be done by a declaration to that effect at the beginning of the statement.

11.   Where any of paragraphs 10(i)–(iv) above apply, Chief Officers should seek the views of the Coroner concerned about how pre-inquest disclosure should best be handled. This would be consistent with the Coroner's role in controlling the conduct of the inquest. It would also enable

account to be taken of any concerns that the Coroner might have regarding possible prejudice to the inquest hearing. However, consulting the Coroner on specific issues should *not* be used as an opportunity to delay the whole disclosure process. In cases where the Coroner decides to hold a pre-inquest hearing, that may provide an opportunity for the handling of disclosure to be discussed. It should be emphasised, however, that the Coroner has no power to order or prohibit disclosure of material which is in the possession of the police.

12.   Disclosure of the investigating officer's report will not normally be expected to form part of the pre-inquest disclosure. That does not mean, however, that it is impossible for such a report to be disclosed where a Chief Officer considers that it would be right to do so. Where contemplating such disclosure, the Chief Officer should consider carefully, with the benefit of legal advice, whether it is in the public interest for the report to be disclosed to interested persons in whole or in part. The Chief Officer should also seek the views of others with an interest in the report, including the Police Complaints Authority in supervised investigations and the Crown Prosecution Service. Where a Chief Officer decides to disclose the investigating officer's report, expressions of opinion by the investigating officer and his or her recommendations and conclusions should be redacted.

Confidentiality

13.   Pre-inquest disclosure to interested persons should be on a confidential basis, solely for the purpose of enabling interested persons to prepare for the inquest. That should be explained to and should be clearly understood by all interested persons when disclosure takes place.

14.   Interested persons other than the police, including the family of the deceased, who have in their possession material about the death not otherwise disclosed to the police or the Coroner, should at the same time bring it to the attention of the Coroner and offer to provide similar pre-inquest disclosure to other interested persons.

Timing and costs

15.   The precise timing of pre-inquest disclosure in a particular case will depend on the particular circumstances. It should be noted that in most cases the custody record and pathologist's report are disclosed prior to full pre-inquest disclosure. There will be cases on which CPS advice is sought on whether criminal proceedings are appropriate. In such cases, in order to avoid prejudice to a criminal trial, disclosure should not take place until either the CPS have advised against a prosecution or any criminal proceedings have finished. Subject to that proviso it is recommended that arrangements should normally be made for pre-inquest disclosure to take place as soon as the Chief Officer is satisfied that the material may be disclosed and in any case not less than 28 days before the date of the inquest proceedings. However, where possible, pre-inquest disclosure should be made as far in advance as possible. It is *not* good practice to delay disclosure to the 28 day point where there is no good reason to do so.

16.   It is not anticipated that pre-inquest disclosure of documentary material will involve substantial additional costs. Indeed pre-inquest disclosure, through saving unnecessary adjournments and avoiding unnecessary suspicion, should actually save time and associated costs in many cases. The police should normally meet the costs of any reproduction of documents which is necessary for disclosure to interested persons.

Annex A

1.   Deaths of a member of the public during or following police contact must be reported to the Home Office, Police Leadership and Powers Unit (PLPU) within 48 hours of the death. Forces are also required to report the outcome of any Coroner's inquest into the death. PLPU maintain

a continuous record of all reported deaths and seek confirmation of the details and circumstances of each death with the force concerned prior to publication.

2.   The definition of a death of a member of the public during or following police contact was revised on 1 April 2002 in order to provide greater clarity and avoid confusion.

Category 1—Fatal road traffic incidents involving the police

This definition covers all deaths of members of the public resulting from road traffic incidents involving the police, both where the person who dies is in a vehicle and where they are on foot.

Category 2—Fatal shooting incidents involving the police

This definition covers circumstances where police fire the fatal shots.

Category 3—Deaths in or following custody

This definition covers the deaths of persons who have been arrested or otherwise detained by the police. It also includes deaths occurring whilst a person is being arrested or taken into detention. The death may have taken place on police, private or medical premises, in a public place or in a police or other vehicle.

Deaths in the following circumstances are amongst those covered by the definition:

- where the person dies in or on the way to hospital (or some other medical premises) following or during transfer from police detention;
- where the person dies after leaving police detention and there is a link between that detention and the death;
- where the person is being detained for the purposes of exercising a power to stop and search;
- where the death is of a child or young person detained for their own protection;
- where the person is in the care of the police having been detained under the Mental Health Act 1983;
- where the person is in police custody having been arrested by officers from a police force in Scotland exercising their powers of detention under section 137(2) of the Criminal Justice and Public Order Act 1994;
- where the person is in police custody having been arrested under section 3(5) of the Asylum and Immigration Appeals Act 1993;
- where the person is in police custody having been served a notice advising them of their detention under powers contained in the Immigration Act 1971;
- where the person is a convicted or remanded prisoner held in police cells on behalf of the Prison Service under the Imprisonment (Temporary Provisions) Act 1980.

Category 4—Deaths during or following other types of contact with the police

This definition covers circumstances where the person dies during or after some form of contact with the police which did not amount to detention and there is a link between that contact and the death. Examples of deaths which would be covered by the definition are as follows:

- where the person is actively attempting to evade arrest and the death occurs otherwise than as the result of a road traffic incident;

- where there is a siege situation, including where a person shoots himself, or another, whilst police are in attendance;
- where a person is present at a demonstration and is struck by a police baton and subsequently dies.

Deaths which follow police contact but which are not linked to that contact would not be covered. For example:

- Those attending police stations as innocent visitors or witnesses who are not suspects;
- Those which occur in a police vehicle which is being used as an ambulance to transport a dying person to hospital quickly, but not under the circumstances described under the category *'Deaths in police custody'*;
- Those where police attend the scene of an incident where a person, who has not been detained, has received fatal injuries.

Notes

- The above categorisations cannot be considered completely exhaustive. Cases will still have to be considered individually to decide whether and how they should be recorded;
- The term 'police' includes police civilians as well as police officers;
- Deaths involving off-duty police personnel are not included.

Appendix 4

National Standards for Cautioning (Revised)

Aims

1. The purposes of a formal caution are—
   — to deal quickly and simply with less serious offenders;
   — to divert them from unnecessary appearance in the criminal courts; and
   — to reduce the chances of their re-offending.

Note 1A   A caution is not a form of sentence. It may not be made conditional upon the satisfactory completion of a specific task such as reparation or the payment of compensation to the victim. Only the courts may impose such requirements.

Decision to caution

2. A formal caution is a serious matter. It is recorded by the police; it should influence them in their decision whether or not to institute proceedings if the person should offend again; and it may be cited in any subsequent court proceedings. In order to safeguard the offender's interests, the following conditions must be met before a caution can be administered—
   — there must be *evidence of the offender's guilt* sufficient to give a realistic prospect of conviction;
   — the offender must *admit the offence*;
   — the offender (or, in the case of a juvenile, his parents or guardian) must understand the significance of a caution and give *informed consent* to being cautioned.

Note 2A   Where the evidence does not meet the required standard, a caution cannot be administered.

Note 2B   A caution will not be appropriate where a person does not make a clear and reliable admission of the offence (for example if intent is denied or there are doubts about his mental health or intellectual capacity).

Note 2C   If an offence is committed by a juvenile under the age of 14, it is necessary to establish that he knew that what he did was seriously wrong.

Note 2D   In practice consent to the caution should not be sought until it has been decided that cautioning is the correct course. The significance of the caution must be explained: that is, that a record will be kept of the caution, that the fact of a previous caution may influence the decision whether or not to prosecute if the person should offend again, and that it may be cited if the person should subsequently be found guilty of an offence by a court. In the case of a juvenile this explanation must be given to the offender in the presence of his parents or guardian, or other appropriate adult. The special needs of other vulnerable groups should also be catered for, in accordance with the Code of Practice for the Detention, Treatment and Questioning of Persons by Police Officers.

Public interest considerations

3.   If the first two of the above requirements are met, consideration should be given to whether a caution is in the public interest. The police should take into account the public interest principles described in the Code for Crown Prosecutors.

Note 3A   There should be a presumption in favour of not prosecuting certain categories of offender, such as elderly people or those who suffer from some sort of mental illness or impairment, or a severe physical illness. Membership of these groups does not, however, afford absolute protection against prosecution, which may be justified by the seriousness of the offence.

Note 3B   Two factors should be considered in relation to the offender's attitude towards his offence: the wilfulness with which it was committed and his subsequent attitude. A practical demonstration of regret, such as apologising to the victim and/or offering to put matters right as far as he is able, may support the use of a caution.

Note 3C   The experience and circumstances of offenders involved in group offences can vary greatly, as can their degree of involvement. Although consistency and equity are important considerations in the decision whether to charge or caution, each offender should be considered separately. Different disposals may be justified.

Views of the victim

4.   Before a caution can be administered it is desirable that the victim should normally be contacted to establish—

— his or her view about the offence;

— the nature and extent of any harm or loss, and their significance relative to the victim's circumstances;

— whether the offender has made any form of reparation or paid compensation.

Note 4A   If a caution is being, or likely to be, considered its significance should be explained to the victim.

Note 4B   In some cases where cautioning might otherwise be appropriate, prosecution may be required in order to protect the victim from further attention from the offender.

Note 4C   If the offender has made some form of reparation or paid compensation, and the victim is satisfied, it may no longer be necessary to prosecute in cases where the possibility of the court's awarding compensation would otherwise have been a major determining factor. *Under no circumstances should police officers become involved in negotiating or awarding reparation or compensation.*

Administration of a caution

5.   A formal caution should be administered in person by a police officer, and wherever practicable at a police station. A juvenile must always be cautioned in the presence of a parent, guardian or other appropriate adult. Members of other vulnerable groups must be treated in accordance with Code of Practice C.

Note 5A   The officer administering the caution should be in uniform and normally of the rank of inspector or above. In some cases, however, a Community Liaison Officer or Community Constable might be more appropriate, or in the inspector's absence the use of a sergeant might be justified. Chief Officers may therefore wish to consider nominating suitable 'cautioning officers'.

Note 5B   Where the person is elderly, infirm or otherwise vulnerable, a caution may be administered less formally, perhaps at the offender's home and in the presence of a friend or relative or other appropriate adult.

Recording cautions

6.   All formal cautions should be recorded and records kept as directed by the Secretary of State. The use of cautioning should also be monitored on a force-wide basis.

Note 6A   Formal cautions should be cited in court if they are relevant to the offence under consideration. In presenting antecedents, care should be taken to distinguish between cautions and convictions, which should usually be listed on separate sheets of paper.

THE CRIME AND DISORDER ACT 1998
FINAL WARNING SYSTEM

Sections 65–66

The new final warning scheme, which includes police reprimands and warnings, will replace cautions for young offenders. The warning is to be accompanied by intervention to reduce the likelihood of re-offending.

- The new system has been introduced in order to end the practice of repeat cautioning, which led to inconsistency which in turn undermined public confidence. It also ensures that each offence committed by a young offender will be met with a progressive response designed to prevent any further offending.

- Under the final warning scheme the only response available to the police in dealing with offending by young people, short of prosecution, will be a police reprimand or a final warning. The current cautioning system will remain for adults.

- Reprimands will be available for first-time minor offences. Any re-offending will result in either a final warning or charge. In the most serious cases a final warning may be appropriate for a first offence. Apart from in exceptional circumstances, any further offending after a final warning has been issued will result in a charge.

- After receiving a warning a young offender is referred to a youth offending team without delay. The youth offending team will then assess the offender to determine whether a rehabilitation programme aimed at preventing re-offending is appropriate and, in the vast majority of cases, provide such a programme.

- The courts' use of conditional discharge for young offenders who have previously received a warning is restricted. Unless there are exceptional circumstances relating directly to the offence or offender, the option of a conditional discharge will not be open to the courts where they are sentencing the offender for a crime committed within two years of receiving a warning.

Appendix 5

PACE Code of Practice for the Detention, Treatment and Questioning of Persons by Police Officers (Code C)

This Code applies to people in police detention after midnight on 31st March 2003, notwithstanding that their period of detention may have commenced before that time.

1 General

1.1 All persons in custody must be dealt with expeditiously, and released as soon as the need for detention no longer applies.

1.1A A custody officer must perform the functions in this Code as soon as practicable. A custody officer will not be in breach of this Code if delay is justifiable and reasonable steps are taken to prevent unnecessary delay. The custody record shall show when a delay has occurred and the reason. See *Note 1H*.

1.2 This Code of Practice must be readily available at all police stations for consultation by:

- police officers
- detained persons
- members of the public.

1.3 The provisions of this Code:

- include the *Annexes*
- do not include the *Notes for Guidance*.

1.4 If an officer has any suspicion, or is told in good faith, that a person of any age may be mentally disordered or otherwise mentally vulnerable, in the absence of clear evidence to dispel that suspicion, the person shall be treated as such for the purposes of this Code. See *Note 1G*

1.5 If anyone appears to be under 17, they shall be treated as a juvenile for the purposes of this Code in the absence of clear evidence that they are older.

1.6 If a person appears to be blind, seriously visually impaired, deaf, unable to read or speak or has difficulty orally because of a speech impediment, they shall be treated as such for the purposes of this Code in the absence of clear evidence to the contrary.

1.7 'The appropriate adult' means, in the case of a:

- (a) juvenile:
    - (i) the parent, guardian or, if the juvenile is in local authority or voluntary organisation care, or is otherwise being looked after under the Children Act 1989, a person representing that authority or organisation;
    - (ii) a social worker of a local authority social services department;
    - (iii) failing these, some other responsible adult aged 18 or over who is not a police officer or employed by the police.

(b) person who is mentally disordered or mentally vulnerable: See Note 1D
  (i)   a relative, guardian or other person responsible for their care or custody;
  (ii) someone experienced in dealing with mentally disordered or mentally vulnerable people but who is not a police officer or employed by the police;
  (iii) failing these, some other responsible adult aged 18 or over who is not a police officer or employed by the police.

1.8   If this Code requires a person be given certain information, they do not have to be given it if at the time they are incapable of understanding what is said, are violent or may become violent or in urgent need of medical attention, but they must be given it as soon as practicable.

1.9   References to a custody officer include those performing the functions of a custody officer.

1.9A   When this Code requires the prior authority or agreement of an officer of at least inspector or superintendent rank, that authority may be given by a sergeant or chief inspector authorised to perform the functions of the higher rank under the Police and Criminal Evidence Act 1984 (PACE), section 107.

1.10   Subject to *paragraph 1.12,* this Code applies to people in custody at police stations in England and Wales, whether or not they have been arrested, and to those removed to a police station as a place of safety under the Mental Health Act 1983, sections 135 and 136. *Section 15* applies solely to people in police detention, e.g. those brought to a police station under arrest or arrested at a police station for an offence after going there voluntarily.

1.11   People in police custody include anyone detained under the Terrorism Act 2000, Schedule 8 and section 41, having been taken to a police station after being arrested under the Terrorism Act 2000, section 41. In these cases, reference to an offence in this Code includes the commission, preparation and instigation of acts of terrorism.

1.12   This Code's provisions do not apply to people in custody:
  (i)   arrested on warrants issued in Scotland by officers under the Criminal Justice and Public Order Act 1994, section 136(2), or arrested or detained without warrant by officers from a police force in Scotland under section 137(2). In these cases, police powers and duties and the person's rights and entitlements whilst at a police station in England or Wales are the same as those in Scotland;
  (ii)   arrested under the Immigration and Asylum Act 1999, section 142(3) in order to have their fingerprints taken;
  (iii) whose detention is authorised by an immigration officer under the Immigration Act 1971;
  (iv)   who are convicted or remanded prisoners held in police cells on behalf of the Prison Service under the Imprisonment (Temporary Provisions) Act 1980;
  (v)   detained for examination under the Terrorism Act 2000, Schedule 7 and to whom the Code of Practice issued under that Act, Schedule 14, paragraph 6 applies;
  (vi)   detained for searches under stop and search powers except as required by Code A.

The provisions on conditions of detention and treatment in *section 8* and *9* must be considered as the minimum standards of treatment for such detainees.

1.13   In this Code:
  (a) 'designated person' means a person other than a police officer, designated under the Police Reform Act 2002, Part 4 who has specified powers and duties of police officers conferred or imposed on them;
  (b) reference to a police officer includes a designated person acting in the exercise or performance of the powers and duties conferred or imposed on them by their designation.

1.14   If a power conferred on a designated person:
  (a) allows reasonable force to be used when exercised by a police officer, a person exercising that power has the same entitlement to use force;
  (b) includes power to use force to enter any premises, that power is not exercisable by that designated person except:
    (i) in the company, and under the supervision, of a police officer;

(ii) for the purpose of:
- saving life or limb; or
- preventing serious damage to property.

1.15   Nothing in this Code prevents the custody officer, or other officer given custody of the detainee, from allowing civilian support staff who are not designated persons to carry out individual procedures or tasks at the police station if the law allows. However, the officer remains responsible for making sure the procedures and tasks are carried out correctly in accordance with the Codes of Practice. Any such civilian must be:

(a) a person employed by a police authority maintaining a police force and under the control and direction of the Chief Officer of that force;

(b) employed by a person with whom a police authority has a contract for the provision of services relating to persons arrested or otherwise in custody.

1.16   Designated persons and other civilian support staff must have regard to any relevant provisions of the Codes of Practice.

1.17   References to pocket books include any official report book issued to police officers or civilian support staff.

Notes for guidance

1A   Although certain sections of this Code apply specifically to people in custody at police stations, those there voluntarily to assist with an investigation should be treated with no less consideration, e.g. offered refreshments at appropriate times, and enjoy an absolute right to obtain legal advice or communicate with anyone outside the police station.

1B   A person, including a parent or guardian, should not be an appropriate adult if they:

- *are*
    - *~ suspected of involvement in the offence*
    - *~ the victim*
    - *~ a witness*
    - *~ involved in the investigation*
- *received admissions prior to attending to act as the appropriate adult.*

Note: If a juvenile's parent is estranged from the juvenile, they should not be asked to act as the appropriate adult if the juvenile expressly and specifically objects to their presence.

1C   If a juvenile admits an offence to, or in the presence of, a social worker or member of a youth offending team other than during the time that person is acting as the juvenile's appropriate adult, another appropriate adult should be appointed in the interest of fairness.

1D   In the case of people who are mentally disordered or otherwise mentally vulnerable, it may be more satisfactory if the appropriate adult is someone experienced or trained in their care rather than a relative lacking such qualifications. But if the detainee prefers a relative to a better qualified stranger or objects to a particular person their wishes should, if practicable, be respected.

1E   A detainee should always be given an opportunity, when an appropriate adult is called to the police station, to consult privately with a solicitor in the appropriate adult's absence if they want.

1F   A solicitor or independent custody visitor (formerly a lay visitor) present at the police station in that capacity may not be the appropriate adult.

1G   'Mentally vulnerable' applies to any detainee who, because of their mental state or capacity, may not understand the significance of what is said, of questions or of their replies. 'Mental disorder' is defined in the Mental Health Act 1983, section 1(2) as 'mental illness, arrested or incomplete development of mind, psychopathic disorder and any other disorder or disability of mind'. When the custody officer has any doubt about the mental state or capacity of a detainee, that detainee should be treated as mentally vulnerable and an appropriate adult called.

1H   Paragraph 1.1A is intended to cover delays which may occur in processing detainees e.g. if:

- *a large number of suspects are brought into the station simultaneously to be placed in custody;*
- *interview rooms are all being used;*
- *there are difficulties contacting an appropriate adult, solicitor or interpreter.*

1I   The custody officer must remind the appropriate adult and detainee about the right to legal advice and record any reasons for waiving it in accordance with section 6.

2   Custody records

2.1   A separate custody record must be opened as soon as practicable for each person brought to a police station under arrest or arrested at the station having gone there voluntarily. All information recorded under this Code must be recorded as soon as practicable in the custody record unless otherwise specified. Any audio or video recording made in the custody area is not part of the custody record.

2.2   If any action requires the authority of an officer of a specified rank, subject to *paragraph 2.6A*, their name and rank must be noted in the custody record.

2.3   The custody officer is responsible for the custody record's accuracy and completeness and for making sure the record or copy of the record accompanies a detainee if they are transferred to another police station. The record shall show the:

- time and reason for transfer;
- time a person is released from detention.

2.4   A solicitor or appropriate adult must be permitted to consult a detainee's custody record as soon as practicable after their arrival at the station and at any other time whilst the person is detained. Arrangements for this access must be agreed with the custody officer and may not unreasonably interfere with the custody officer's duties.

2.4A   When a detainee leaves police detention or is taken before a court they, their legal representative or appropriate adult shall be given, on request, a copy of the custody record as soon as practicable. This entitlement lasts for 12 months after release.

2.5   The detainee, appropriate adult or legal representative shall be permitted to inspect the original custody record after the detainee has left police detention provided they give reasonable notice of their request. Any such inspection shall be noted in the custody record.

2.6   Subject to *paragraph 2.6A*, all entries in custody records must be timed and signed by the maker. Records entered on computer shall be timed and contain the operator's identification.

2.6A   Nothing in this Code requires the identity of officers or civilian support staff to be recorded or disclosed:

- (a) in the case of enquiries linked to the investigation of terrorism; or
- (b) if the officer or civilian support staff reasonably believe recording or disclosing their name might put them in danger.

In these cases, they shall use their warrant or other identification numbers and the name of their police station. See *Note 2A*

2.7   The fact and time of any detainee's refusal to sign a custody record, when asked in accordance with this Code, must be recorded.

Note for guidance

2A   The purpose of paragraph 2.6A(b) is to protect those involved in serious organised crime investigations or arrests of particularly violent suspects when there is reliable information that those arrested or their associates may threaten or cause harm to those involved. In cases of doubt, an officer of inspector rank or above should be consulted.

3 Initial action

(a) Detained persons—normal procedure

3.1   When a person is brought to a police station under arrest or arrested at the station having gone there voluntarily, the custody officer must make sure the person is told clearly about the following continuing rights which may be exercised at any stage during the period in custody:

(i)   the right to have someone informed of their arrest as in *section 5;*

(ii)   the right to consult privately with a solicitor and that free independent legal advice is available;

(iii)   the right to consult these Codes of Practice. See *Note 3D*

3.2   The detainee must also be given:

- a written notice setting out:
  - ~ the above three rights;
  - ~ the arrangements for obtaining legal advice;
  - ~ the right to a copy of the custody record as in *paragraph 2.4A;*
  - ~ the caution in the terms prescribed in *section 10.*

- an additional written notice briefly setting out their entitlements while in custody, see *Notes 3A* and *3B.*

Note: The detainee shall be asked to sign the custody record to acknowledge receipt of these notices. Any refusal must be recorded on the custody record.

3.3   A citizen of an independent Commonwealth country or a national of a foreign country, including the Republic of Ireland, must be informed as soon as practicable about their rights of communication with their High Commission, Embassy or Consulate. See *section 7*

3.4   The custody officer shall:

- note on the custody record any comment the detainee makes in relation to the arresting officer's account but shall not invite comment. If the custody officer authorises a person's detention the detainee must be informed of the grounds as soon as practicable and before they are questioned about any offence;

- note any comment the detainee makes in respect of the decision to detain them but shall not invite comment;

- not put specific questions to the detainee regarding their involvement in any offence, nor in respect of any comments they may make in response to the arresting officer's account or the decision to place them in detention. Such an exchange is likely to constitute an interview as in *paragraph 11.1A* and require the associated safeguards in *section 11.*

See *paragraph 11.13* in respect of unsolicited comments.

3.5   The custody officer shall:

(a)   ask the detainee, whether at this time, they:
  - (i)   would like legal advice, see *paragraph 6.5;*
  - (ii)   want someone informed of their detention, see *section 5;*

(b)   ask the detainee to sign the custody record to confirm their decisions in respect of (*a*);

(c)   determine whether the detainee:
  - (i)   is, or might be, in need of medical treatment or attention, see *section 9;*
  - (ii)   requires:
    - an appropriate adult;
    - help to check documentation;
    - an interpreter;

(d)   record the decision in respect of (*c*).

3.6   When determining these needs the custody officer is responsible for initiating an assessment to consider whether the detainee is likely to present specific risks to custody staff or themselves. Such assessments should always include a check on the Police National Computer, to be carried out as soon as practicable, to identify any risks highlighted in relation to the detainee. Although such assessments are primarily the custody officer's responsibility, it may be necessary for them to consult and involve others, e.g. the arresting officer or an appropriate health care professional, see *paragraph 9.13*. Reasons for delaying the initiation or completion of the assessment must be recorded.

3.7   Chief Officers should ensure that arrangements for proper and effective risk assessments required by *paragraph 3.6* are implemented in respect of all detainees at police stations in their area.

3.8   Risk assessments must follow a structured process which clearly defines the categories of risk to be considered and the results must be incorporated in the detainee's custody record. The custody officer is responsible for making sure those responsible for the detainee's custody are appropriately briefed about the risks. If no specific risks are identified by the assessment, that should be noted in the custody record. See *Note 3E* and *paragraph 9.14*

3.9   The custody officer is responsible for implementing the response to any specific risk assessment, e.g.:

- reducing opportunities for self harm;
- calling a health care professional;
- increasing levels of monitoring or observation.

3.10   Risk assessment is an ongoing process and assessments must always be subject to review if circumstances change.

3.11   If video cameras are installed in the custody area, notices shall be prominently displayed showing cameras are in use. Any request to have video cameras switched off shall be refused.

(b) Detained persons—special groups

3.12   If the detainee appears deaf or there is doubt about their hearing or speaking ability or ability to understand English, and the custody officer cannot establish effective communication, the custody officer must, as soon as practicable, call an interpreter for assistance in the action under *paragraphs 3.1–3.5*. See *section 13*.

3.13   If the detainee is a juvenile, the custody officer must, if it is practicable, ascertain the identity of a person responsible for their welfare. That person:

- may be:
  - ~ the parent or guardian;
  - ~ if the juvenile is in local authority or voluntary organisation care, or is otherwise being looked after under the Children Act 1989, a person appointed by that authority or organisation to have responsibility for the juvenile's welfare;
  - ~ any other person who has, for the time being, assumed responsibility for the juvenile's welfare.
- must be informed as soon as practicable that the juvenile has been arrested, why they have been arrested and where they are detained. This right is in addition to the juvenile's right in *section 5* not to be held incommunicado. See *Note 3C*

3.14   If a juvenile known to be subject to a court order under which a person or organisation is given any degree of statutory responsibility to supervise or otherwise monitor them, reasonable steps must also be taken to notify that person or organisation (the 'responsible officer'). The responsible officer will normally be a member of a Youth Offending Team, except for a curfew order which involves electronic monitoring when the contractor providing the monitoring will normally be the responsible officer.

3.15   If the detainee is a juvenile, mentally disordered or otherwise mentally vulnerable, the custody officer must, as soon as practicable:

- inform the appropriate adult, who in the case of a juvenile may or may not be a person responsible for their welfare, as in *paragraph 3.13*, of:
  - ~ the grounds for their detention;
  - ~ their whereabouts.
- ask the adult to come to the police station to see the detainee.

3.16   It is imperative a mentally disordered or otherwise mentally vulnerable person, detained under the Mental Health Act 1983, section 136, be assessed as soon as possible. If that assessment is to take place at the police station, an approved social worker and a registered medical practitioner shall be called to the station as soon as possible in order to interview and examine the detainee. Once the detainee has been interviewed, examined and suitable arrangements made for their treatment or care, they can no longer be detained under section 136. A detainee must be immediately discharged from detention under section 136 if a registered medical practitioner, having examined them, concludes they are not mentally disordered within the meaning of the Act.

3.17   If the appropriate adult is:

- already at the police station, the provisions of *paragraphs 3.1* to *3.5* must be complied with in the appropriate adult's presence;
- not at the station when these provisions are complied with, they must be complied with again in the presence of the appropriate adult when they arrive.

3.18   The detainee shall be advised that:

- the duties of the appropriate adult include giving advice and assistance;
- they can consult privately with the appropriate adult at any time.

3.19   If the detainee, or appropriate adult on the detainee's behalf, asks for a solicitor to be called to give legal advice, the provisions of *section 6* apply.

3.20   If the detainee is blind, seriously visually impaired or unable to read, the custody officer shall make sure their solicitor, relative, appropriate adult or some other person likely to take an interest in them and not involved in the investigation is available to help check any documentation. When this Code requires written consent or signing the person assisting may be asked to sign instead, if the detainee prefers. This paragraph does not require an appropriate adult to be called solely to assist in checking and signing documentation for a person who is not a juvenile, or mentally disordered or otherwise mentally vulnerable (see *paragraph 3.15*).

(c) Persons attending a police station voluntarily

3.21   Anybody attending a police station voluntarily to assist with an investigation may leave at will unless arrested. If it is decided they shall not be allowed to leave, they must be informed at once that they are under arrest and brought before the custody officer, who is responsible for making sure they are notified of their rights in the same way as other detainees. If they are not arrested but are cautioned as in *section 10,* the person who gives the caution must, at the same time, inform them they are not under arrest, they are not obliged to remain at the station but if they remain at the station they may obtain free and independent legal advice if they want. They shall be told the right to legal advice includes the right to speak with a solicitor on the telephone and be asked if they want to do so.

3.22   If a person attending the police station voluntarily asks about their entitlement to legal advice, they shall be given a copy of the notice explaining the arrangements for obtaining legal advice. See *paragraph 3.2*

(d) Documentation

3.23   The grounds for a person's detention shall be recorded, in the person's presence if practicable.

3.24   Action taken under *paragraphs 3.12* to *3.20* shall be recorded.

Notes for guidance

3A   The notice of entitlements should:

- *list the entitlements in this Code, including:*
  - *~ visits and contact with outside parties, including special provisions for Commonwealth citizens and foreign nationals;*
  - *~ reasonable standards of physical comfort;*

~ *adequate food and drink;*
~ *access to toilets and washing facilities, clothing, medical attention, and exercise when practicable.*

- *mention the:*
  ~ *provisions relating to the conduct of interviews;*
  ~ *circumstances in which an appropriate adult should be available to assist the detainee and their statutory rights to make representation whenever the period of their detention is reviewed.*

3B   In addition to notices in English, translations should be available in Welsh, the main minority ethnic languages and the principal European languages, whenever they are likely to be helpful.

3C   If the juvenile is in local authority or voluntary organisation care but living with their parents or other adults responsible for their welfare, although there is no legal obligation to inform them, they should normally be contacted, as well as the authority or organisation unless suspected of involvement in the offence concerned. Even if the juvenile is not living with their parents, consideration should be given to informing them.

3D   The right to consult the Codes of Practice does not entitle the person concerned to delay unreasonably any necessary investigative or administrative action whilst they do so. Examples of action which need not be delayed unreasonably include:

- *procedures requiring the provision of breath, blood or urine specimens under the Road Traffic Act 1988 or the Transport and Works Act 1992*

- *searching detainees at the police station*

- *taking fingerprints or non-intimate samples without consent for evidential purposes.*

3E   Home Office Circular 32/2000 provides more detailed guidance on risk assessments and identifies key risk areas which should always be considered.

4   Detainee's property

(a) Action

4.1   The custody officer is responsible for:

(a) ascertaining what property a detainee:
   (i) has with them when they come to the police station, whether on:
      - arrest or re-detention on answering to bail;
      - commitment to prison custody on the order or sentence of a court;
      - lodgement at the police station with a view to their production in court from prison custody;
      - transfer from detention at another station or hospital;
      - detention under the Mental Health Act 1983, section 135 or 136;
   (ii) might have acquired for an unlawful or harmful purpose while in custody;

(b) the safekeeping of any property taken from a detainee which remains at the police station.

The custody officer may search the detainee or authorise their being searched to the extent they consider necessary, provided a search of intimate parts of the body or involving the removal of more than outer clothing is only made as in *Annex A*. A search may only be carried out by an officer of the same sex as the detainee. See *Note 4A*

4.2   Detainees may retain clothing and personal effects at their own risk unless the custody officer considers they may use them to cause harm to themselves or others, interfere with evidence, damage property, effect an escape or they are needed as evidence. In this event the custody officer may withhold such articles as they consider necessary and must tell the detainee why.

4.3   Personal effects are those items a detainee may lawfully need, use or refer to while in detention but do not include cash and other items of value.

(b) Documentation

4.4   The custody officer is responsible for recording all property brought to the police station which a detainee had with them, or had taken from them on arrest. The detainee shall be allowed to check and sign the record of property as correct. Any refusal to sign shall be recorded.

4.5   If a detainee is not allowed to keep any article of clothing or personal effects, the reason must be recorded.

Notes for guidance

4A   PACE, Section 54(1) and paragraph 4.1 require a detainee to be searched when it is clear the custody officer will have continuing duties in relation to that detainee or when that detainee's behaviour or offence makes an inventory appropriate. They do not require every detainee to be searched, e.g. if it is clear a person will only be detained for a short period and is not to be placed in a cell, the custody officer may decide not to search them. In such a case the custody record will be endorsed 'not searched', paragraph 4.4 will not apply, and the detainee will be invited to sign the entry. If the detainee refuses, the custody officer will be obliged to ascertain what property they have in accordance with paragraph 4.1.

4B   Paragraph 4.4 does not require the custody officer to record on the custody record property in the detainee's possession on arrest if, by virtue of its nature, quantity or size, it is not practicable to remove it to the police station.

4C   Paragraph 4.4 does not require items of clothing worn by the person be recorded unless withheld by the custody officer as in paragraph 4.2.

5   Right not to be held incommunicado

(a) Action

5.1   Any person arrested and held in custody at a police station or other premises may, on request, have one person known to them or likely to take an interest in their welfare informed at public expense of their whereabouts as soon as practicable. If the person cannot be contacted the detainee may choose up to two alternatives. If they cannot be contacted, the person in charge of detention or the investigation has discretion to allow further attempts until the information has been conveyed. See *Notes 5C* and *5D*

5.2   The exercise of the above right in respect of each person nominated may be delayed only in accordance with *Annex B*.

5.3   The above right may be exercised each time a detainee is taken to another police station.

5.4   The detainee may receive visits at the custody officer's discretion. See *Note 5B*

5.5   If a friend, relative or person with an interest in the detainee's welfare enquires about their whereabouts, this information shall be given if the suspect agrees and *Annex B* does not apply. See *Note 5D*

5.6   The detainee shall be given writing materials, on request, and allowed to telephone one person for a reasonable time, see *Notes 5A* and *5E*. Either or both these privileges may be denied or delayed if an officer of inspector rank or above considers sending a letter or making a telephone call may result in any of the consequences in:

(a) *Annex B paragraphs 1* and *2* and the person is detained in connection with an arrestable or serious arrestable offence; or

(b) *Annex B paragraphs 8* and *9* and the person is detained under the Terrorism Act 2000, Schedule 7 or section 41

For the purposes of this paragraph, any reference to a serious arrestable offence in *Annex B* includes an arrestable offence. However, nothing in this paragraph permits the restriction or denial of the rights in *paragraphs 5.1* and *6.1*.

5.7   Before any letter or message is sent, or telephone call made, the detainee shall be informed that what they say in any letter, call or message (other than in a communication to a solicitor) may be read or listened to and may be given in evidence. A telephone call may be terminated if it is being abused. The costs can be at public expense at the custody officer's discretion.

(b) Documentation

5.8   A record must be kept of any:

(a) request made under this section and the action taken;

(b) letters, messages or telephone calls made or received or visit received;

(c) refusal by the detainee to have information about them given to an outside enquirer. The detainee must be asked to countersign the record accordingly and any refusal recorded.

Notes for guidance

5A   A person may request an interpreter to interpret a telephone call or translate a letter.

5B   At the custody officer's discretion, visits should be allowed when possible, subject to having sufficient personnel to supervise a visit and any possible hindrance to the investigation.

5C   If the detainee does not know anyone to contact for advice or support or cannot contact a friend or relative, the custody officer should bear in mind any local voluntary bodies or other organisations who might be able to help. Paragraph 6.1 applies if legal advice is required.

5D   In some circumstances it may not be appropriate to use the telephone to disclose information under paragraphs 5.1 and 5.5.

5E   The telephone call at paragraph 5.6 is in addition to any communication under paragraphs 5.1 and 6.1.

6   Right to legal advice

(a) Action

6.1   Unless *Annex B* applies, all detainees must be informed that they may at any time consult and communicate privately with a solicitor, whether in person, in writing or by telephone, and that free independent legal advice is available from the duty solicitor. See *paragraph 3.1, Note 6B* and *Note 6J*

6.2   Not Used

6.3   A poster advertising the right to legal advice must be prominently displayed in the charging area of every police station. See *Note 6H*

6.4   No police officer should, at any time, do or say anything with the intention of dissuading a detainee from obtaining legal advice.

6.5   The exercise of the right of access to legal advice may be delayed only as in *Annex B*. Whenever legal advice is requested, and unless *Annex B* applies, the custody officer must act without delay to secure the provision of such advice. If, on being informed or reminded of this right, the detainee declines to speak to a solicitor in person, the officer should point out that the right includes the right to speak with a solicitor on the telephones. If the detainee continues to waive this right the officer should ask them why and any reasons should be recorded on the custody record or the interview record as appropriate. Reminders of the right to legal advice must be given as in *paragraphs 3.5, 11.2, 15.4, 16.4 and 16.5* and Code D, *paragraphs 3.17(ii)* and *6.3*. Once it is clear a detainee does not want to speak to a solicitor in person or by telephone they should cease to be asked their reasons. See *Note 6K*

6.6   A detainee who wants legal advice may not be interviewed or continue to be interviewed until they have received such advice unless:

(a) *Annex B* applies, when the restriction on drawing adverse inferences from silence in *Annex C* will apply because the detainee is not allowed an opportunity to consult a solicitor; or

(b) an officer of superintendent rank or above has reasonable grounds for believing that:
    (i) the consequent delay might:
- lead to interference with, or harm to, evidence connected with an offence;
- lead to interference with, or physical harm to, other people;
- lead to serious loss of, or damage to, property;
- lead to alerting other people suspected of having committed an offence but not yet arrested for it;
- hinder the recovery of property obtained in consequence of the commission of an offence.

    (ii) when a solicitor, including a duty solicitor, has been contacted and has agreed to attend, awaiting their arrival would cause unreasonable delay to the process of investigation.

Note: In these cases the restriction on drawing adverse inferences from silence in *Annex C* will apply because the detainee is not allowed an opportunity to consult a solicitor;

(c) the solicitor the detainee has nominated or selected from a list:
    (i)   cannot be contacted;
    (ii) has previously indicated they do not wish to be contacted; or
    (iii) having been contacted, has declined to attend; and

the detainee has been advised of the Duty Solicitor Scheme but has declined to ask for the duty solicitor.

In these circumstances the interview may be started or continued without further delay provided an officer of inspector rank or above has agreed to the interview proceeding.

Note: The restriction on drawing adverse inferences from silence in *Annex C* will not apply because the detainee is allowed an opportunity to consult the duty solicitor;

(d) the detainee changes their mind, about wanting legal advice.

In these circumstances the interview may be started or continued without delay provided that:

    (i) the detainee agrees to do so, in writing or on tape; and
    (ii) an officer of inspector rank or above has inquired about the detainee's reasons for their change of mind and gives authority for the interview to proceed.

Confirmation of the detainee's agreement, their change of mind, the reasons for it if given and, subject to *paragraph 2.6A,* the name of the authorising officer shall be recorded in the taped or written interview record. See *Note 6I.* Note: In these circumstances the restriction on drawing adverse inferences from silence in *Annex C* will not apply because the detainee is allowed an opportunity to consult a solicitor if they wish.

6.7   If *paragraph 6.6(b)(i)* applies, once sufficient information has been obtained to avert the risk, questioning must cease until the detainee has received legal advice unless *paragraph 6.6(a), (b)(ii), (c)* or *(d)* applies.

6.8   A detainee who has been permitted to consult a solicitor shall be entitled on request to have the solicitor present when they are interviewed unless one of the exceptions in *paragraph 6.6* applies.

6.9   The solicitor may only be required to leave the interview if their conduct is such that the interviewer is unable properly to put questions to the suspect. See *Notes 6D and 6E*

6.10   If the interviewer considers a solicitor is acting in such a way, they will stop the interview and consult an officer not below superintendent rank, if one is readily available, and otherwise an officer not below inspector rank not connected with the investigation. After speaking to the solicitor, the officer consulted will decide if the interview should continue in the presence of that solicitor. If they decide it should not, the suspect will be given the opportunity to consult another solicitor before the interview continues and that solicitor given an opportunity to be present at the interview. *See Note 6E*

6.11   The removal of a solicitor from an interview is a serious step and, if it occurs, the officer of superintendent rank or above who took the decision will consider if the incident should be reported to the Law Society. If the decision to remove the solicitor has been taken by an officer below superintendent rank, the facts must be reported to an officer of superintendent rank or above who will similarly consider whether a report to the Law Society would be appropriate. When the solicitor concerned is a duty solicitor, the report should be both to the Law Society and to the Legal Services Commission.

6.12 'Solicitor' in this Code means:

- a solicitor who holds a current practising certificate
- a trainee solicitor;
- a duty solicitor representative;
- an accredited representative included on the register of representatives maintained by the Legal Services Commission.

6.12A A non-accredited or probationary representative sent to provide advice by, and on behalf of, a solicitor shall be admitted to the police station for this purpose unless an officer of inspector rank or above considers such a visit will hinder the investigation and directs otherwise. Hindering the investigation does not include giving proper legal advice to a detainee as in *Note 6D*. Once admitted to the police station, *paragraphs 6.6* to *6.10* apply.

6.13 In exercising their discretion under *paragraph 6.12A*, the officer should take into account in particular:

- whether:
  - ~ the identity and status of the non-accredited or probationary representative have been satisfactorily established;
  - ~ they are of suitable character to provide legal advice, e.g. a person with a criminal record is unlikely to be suitable unless the conviction was for a minor offence and not recent.
- any other matters in any written letter of authorisation provided by the solicitor on whose behalf the person is attending the police station. See *Note 6F*

6.14 If the inspector refuses access to a non-accredited or probationary representative or a decision is taken that such a person should not be permitted to remain at an interview, the inspector must notify the solicitor on whose behalf the representative was acting and give them an opportunity to make alternative arrangements. The detainee must be informed and the custody record noted.

6.15 If a solicitor arrives at the station to see a particular person, that person must, unless *Annex B* applies, be so informed whether or not they are being interviewed and asked if they would like to see the solicitor. This applies even if the detainee has declined legal advice or, having requested it, subsequently agreed to be interviewed without receiving advice. The solicitor's attendance and the detainee's decision must be noted in the custody record.

(b) Documentation

6.16 Any request for legal advice and the action taken shall be recorded.

6.17 A record shall be made in the interview record if a detainee asks for legal advice and an interview is begun either in the absence of a solicitor or their representative, or they have been required to leave an interview.

Notes for guidance

6A In considering if paragraph 6.6(b) applies, the officer should, if practicable, ask the solicitor for an estimate of how long it will take to come to the station and relate this to the time detention is permitted, the time of day (i.e. whether the rest period under paragraph 12.2 is imminent) and the requirements of other investigations. If the solicitor is on their way or is to set off immediately, it will not normally be appropriate to begin an interview before they arrive. If it appears necessary to begin an interview before the solicitor's arrival, they should be given an indication of how long the police would be able to wait before 6.6(b) applies so there is an opportunity to make arrangements for someone else to provide legal advice.

6B A detainee who asks for legal advice should be given an opportunity to consult a specific solicitor or another solicitor from that solicitor's firm or the duty solicitor. If advice is not available by these means, or they do not want to consult the duty solicitor, the detainee should be given an opportunity to choose a solicitor from a list of those willing to provide legal advice. If this solicitor is unavailable, they may choose up to two alternatives. If these attempts are unsuccessful, the custody officer has discretion to allow further attempts until a solicitor has been contacted and agrees to provide legal advice. Apart from carrying out these duties, an officer must not advise the suspect about any particular firm of solicitors.

6C   Not Used

6D   A detainee has a right to free legal advice and to be represented by a solicitor. The solicitor's only role in the police station is to protect and advance the legal rights of their client. On occasions this may require the solicitor to give advice which has the effect of the client avoiding giving evidence which strengthens a prosecution case. The solicitor may intervene in order to seek clarification, challenge an improper question to their client or the manner in which it is put, advise their client not to reply to particular questions, or if they wish to give their client further legal advice. Paragraph 6.9 only applies if the solicitor's approach or conduct prevents or unreasonably obstructs proper questions being put to the suspect or the suspect's response being recorded. Examples of unacceptable conduct include answering questions on a suspect's behalf or providing written replies for the suspect to quote.

6E   An officer who takes the decision to exclude a solicitor must be in a position to satisfy the court the decision was properly made. In order to do this they may need to witness what is happening.

6F   If an officer of at least inspector rank considers a particular solicitor or firm of solicitors is persistently sending non-accredited or probationary representatives who are unsuited to provide legal advice, they should inform an officer of at least superintendent rank, who may wish to take the matter up with the Law Society.

6G   Subject to the constraints of Annex B, a solicitor may advise more than one client in an investigation if they wish. Any question of a conflict of interest is for the solicitor under their professional code of conduct. If, however, waiting for a solicitor to give advice to one client may lead to unreasonable delay to the interview with another, the provisions of paragraph 6.6(b) may apply.

6H   In addition to a poster in English, a poster or posters containing translations into Welsh, the main minority ethnic languages and the principal European languages should be displayed wherever they are likely to be helpful and it is practicable to do so.

6I   Paragraph 6.6(d) requires the authorisation of an officer of inspector rank or above to the continuation of an interview when a detainee who wanted legal advice changes their mind. It is permissible for such authorisation to be given over the telephone, if the authorising officer is able to satisfy themselves about the reason for the detainee's change of mind and is satisfied it is proper to continue the interview in those circumstances.

6J   Whenever a detainee exercises their right to legal advice by consulting or communicating with a solicitor, they must be allowed to do so in private. This right to consult or communicate in private is fundamental. Except as allowed by the Terrorism Act 2000, Schedule 8, paragraph 9, if the requirement for privacy is compromised because what is said or written by the detainee or solicitor for the purpose of giving and receiving legal advice is overheard, listened to, or read by others without the informed consent of the detainee, the right will effectively have been denied. When a detainee chooses to speak to a solicitor on the telephone, they should be allowed to do so in private unless this is impractical because of the design and layout of the custody area or the location of telephones. However, the normal expectation should be that facilities will be available, unless they are being used, at all police stations to enable detainees to speak in private to a solicitor either face to face or over the telephone.

6K   A detainee is not obliged to give reasons for declining legal advice and should not be pressed to do so.

7   Citizens of independent Commonwealth countries or foreign nationals

(a) Action

7.1   Any citizen of an independent Commonwealth country or a national of a foreign country, including the Republic of Ireland, may communicate at any time with the appropriate High Commission, Embassy or Consulate. The detainee must be informed as soon as practicable of:

- this right;
- their right, upon request, to have their High Commission, Embassy or Consulate told of their whereabouts and the grounds for their detention. Such a request should be acted upon as soon as practicable.

7.2   If a detainee is a citizen of a country with which a bilateral consular convention or agreement is in force requiring notification of arrest, the appropriate High Commission, Embassy or Consulate shall be informed as soon as practicable, subject to *paragraph 7.4*. The countries to which this applies as at 1st April 2003 are listed in *Annex F*.

7.3   Consular officers may visit one of their nationals in police detention to talk to them and, if required, to arrange for legal advice. Such visits shall take place out of the hearing of a police officer.

7.4   Notwithstanding the provisions of consular conventions, if the detainee is a political refugee whether for reasons of race, nationality, political opinion or religion, or is seeking political asylum, consular officers shall not be informed of the arrest of one of their nationals or given access or information about them except at the detainee's express request.

(b) Documentation

7.5   A record shall be made when a detainee is informed of their rights under this section and of any communications with a High Commission, Embassy or Consulate.

Note for guidance

7A   *The exercise of the rights in this section may not be interfered with even though Annex B applies.*

8   Conditions of detention

(a) Action

8.1   So far as it is practicable, not more than one detainee should be detained in each cell.

8.2   Cells in use must be adequately heated, cleaned and ventilated. They must be adequately lit, subject to such dimming as is compatible with safety and security to allow people detained overnight to sleep. No additional restraints shall be used within a locked cell unless absolutely necessary and then only restraint equipment, approved for use in that force by the Chief Officer, which is reasonable and necessary in the circumstances having regard to the detainee's demeanour and with a view to ensuring their safety and the safety of others. If a detainee is deaf, mentally disordered or otherwise mentally vulnerable, particular care must be taken when deciding whether to use any form of approved restraints.

8.3   Blankets, mattresses, pillows and other bedding supplied shall be of a reasonable standard and in a clean and sanitary condition. See *Note 8A*

8.4   Access to toilet and washing facilities must be provided.

8.5   If it is necessary to remove a detainee's clothes for the purposes of investigation, for hygiene, health reasons or cleaning, replacement clothing of a reasonable standard of comfort and cleanliness shall be provided. A detainee may not be interviewed unless adequate clothing has been offered.

8.6   At least two light meals and one main meal should be offered in any 24 hour period. See *Note 8B*. Drinks should be provided at meal times and upon reasonable request between meals. Whenever necessary, advice shall be sought from the appropriate health care professional, see *Note 9A*, on medical and dietary matters. As far as practicable, meals provided shall offer a varied diet and meet any specific dietary needs or religious beliefs the detainee may have. The detainee may, at the custody officer's discretion, have meals supplied by their family or friends at their expense. See *Note 8A*

8.7   Brief outdoor exercise shall be offered daily if practicable.

8.8   A juvenile shall not be placed in a police cell unless no other secure accommodation is available and the custody officer considers it is not practicable to supervise them if they are not placed in a cell or that a cell provides more comfortable accommodation than other secure accommodation in the station. A juvenile may not be placed in a cell with a detained adult.

(b) **Documentation**

8.9 A record must be kept of replacement clothing and meals offered.

8.10 If a juvenile is placed in a cell, the reason must be recorded.

8.11 The use of any restraints on a detainee whilst in a cell, the reasons for it and, if appropriate, the arrangements for enhanced supervision of the detainee whilst so restrained, shall be recorded. See *paragraph 3.9*

Notes for guidance

8A The provisions in paragraph 8.3 and 8.6 respectively are of particular importance in the case of a person detained under the Terrorism Act 2000, immigration detainees and others likely to be detained for an extended period. In deciding whether to allow meals to be supplied by family or friends, the custody officer is entitled to take account of the risk of items being concealed in any food or package and the officer's duties and responsibilities under food handling legislation.

8B Meals should, so far as practicable, be offered at recognised meal times, or at other times that take account of when the detainee last had a meal.

9 **Care and treatment of detained persons**

(a) **General**

9.1 Nothing in this section prevents the police from calling the police surgeon or, if appropriate, some other health care professional, to examine a detainee for the purposes of obtaining evidence relating to any offence in which the detainee is suspected of being involved. See *Note 9A*

9.2 If a complaint is made by, or on behalf of, a detainee about their treatment since their arrest, or it comes to notice that a detainee may have been treated improperly, a report must be made as soon as practicable to an officer of inspector rank or above not connected with the investigation. If the matter concerns a possible assault or the possibility of the unnecessary or unreasonable use of force, an appropriate health care professional must also be called as soon as practicable.

9.3 Detainees should be visited at least every hour. If no reasonably foreseeable risk was identified in a risk assessment, see *paragraphs 3.6–3.10,* there is no need to wake a sleeping detainee. Those suspected of being intoxicated through drink or drugs or whose level of consciousness causes concern must, subject to any clinical directions given by the appropriate health care professional, see *paragraph 9.13:*

- be visited and roused at least every half hour
- have their condition assessed as in *Annex H*
- and clinical treatment arranged if appropriate

See *Notes 9B, 9C* and *9H*

9.4 When arrangements are made to secure clinical attention for a detainee, the custody officer must make sure all relevant information which might assist in the treatment of the detainee's condition is made available to the responsible health care professional. This applies whether or not the health care professional asks for such information. Any officer or civilian support staff with relevant information must inform the custody officer as soon as practicable.

(b) **Clinical treatment and attention**

9.5 The custody officer must make sure a detainee receives appropriate clinical attention as soon as reasonably practicable if the person:

(a) appears to be suffering from physical illness; or

(b) is injured; or

(c) appears to be suffering from a mental disorder; or

(d) appears to need clinical attention.

This applies even if the detainee makes no request for clinical attention and whether or not they have already received clinical attention elsewhere. If the need for attention appears urgent, e.g. when indicated as in *Annex H,* the nearest available health care professional or an ambulance must be called immediately. See *Note 9C*

9.6 *Paragraph 9.5* is not meant to prevent or delay the transfer to a hospital if necessary of a person detained under the Mental Health Act 1983, section 136. See *Note 9D.* When an assessment under that Act takes place at a police station, see *paragraph 3.16,* the custody officer must consider whether an appropriate health care professional should be called to conduct an initial clinical check on the detainee. This applies particularly when there is likely to be any significant delay in the arrival of a suitably qualified medical practitioner.

9.7 If it appears to the custody officer, or they are told, that a person brought to a station under arrest may be suffering from an infectious disease or condition, the custody officer must take reasonable steps to safeguard the health of the detainee and others at the station. In deciding what action to take, advice must be sought from an appropriate health care professional. See *Note 9E.* The custody officer has discretion to isolate the person and their property until clinical directions have been obtained.

9.8 If a detainee requests a clinical examination, an appropriate health care professional must be called as soon as practicable to assess the detainee's clinical needs. If a safe and appropriate care plan cannot be provided, the police surgeon's advice must be sought. The detainee may also be examined by a medical practitioner of their choice at their expense.

9.9 If a detainee is required to take or apply any medication in compliance with clinical directions prescribed before their detention, the custody officer must consult the appropriate health care professional before the use of the medication. Subject to the restrictions in *paragraph 9.10,* the custody officer is responsible for the safekeeping of any medication and for making sure the detainee is given the opportunity to take or apply prescribed or approved medication. Any such consultation and its outcome shall be noted in the custody record.

9.10 No police officer may administer or supervise the self-administration of controlled drugs of the types and forms listed in the Misuse of Drugs Regulations 2001, Schedule 1, 2 or 3. A detainee may only self-administer such drugs under the personal supervision of the registered medical practitioner authorising their use. Drugs listed in Schedule 4 or 5 may be distributed by the custody officer for self-administration if they have consulted the registered medical practitioner authorising their use, this may be done by telephone, and both parties are satisfied self-administration will not expose the detainee, police officers or anyone else to the risk of harm or injury.

9.11 When appropriate health care professionals administer drugs or other medications, or supervise their self-administration, it must be within current medicines legislation and the scope of practice as determined by their relevant professional body.

9.12 If a detainee has in their possession, or claims to need, medication relating to a heart condition, diabetes, epilepsy or a condition of comparable potential seriousness then, even though *paragraph 9.5* may not apply, the advice of the appropriate health care professional must be obtained.

9.13 Whenever the appropriate health care professional is called in accordance with this section to examine or treat a detainee, the custody officer shall ask for their opinion about:

- any risks or problems which police need to take into account when making decisions about the detainee's continued detention;
- when to carry out an interview if applicable; and
- the need for safeguards.

9.14 When clinical directions are given by the appropriate health care professional, whether orally or in writing, and the custody officer has any doubts or is in any way uncertain about any aspect of the directions, the custody officer shall ask for clarification. It is particularly important that directions concerning the frequency of visits are clear, precise and capable of being implemented. See *Note 9F.*

(c) **Documentation**

9.15   A record must be made in the custody record of:

(a) the arrangements made for an examination by an appropriate health care professional under *paragraph 9.2* and of any complaint reported under that paragraph together with any relevant remarks by the custody officer;

(b) any arrangements made in accordance with *paragraph 9.5;*

(c) any request for a clinical examination under *paragraph 9.8* and any arrangements made in response;

(d) the injury, ailment, condition or other reason which made it necessary to make the arrangements in (*a*) to (*c*), see *Note 9G;*

(e) any clinical directions and advice, including any further clarifications, given to police by a health care professional concerning the care and treatment of the detainee in connection with any of the arrangements made in (*a*) to (*c*), see *Note 9F;*

(f) if applicable, the responses received when attempting to rouse a person using the procedure in *Annex H,* see *Note 9H.*

9.16   If a health care professional does not record their clinical findings in the custody record, the record must show where they are recorded. See *Note 9G.* However, information which is necessary to custody staff to ensure the effective ongoing care and well being of the detainee must be recorded openly in the custody record, see *paragraph 3.8* and *Annex G, paragraph 7.*

9.17   Subject to the requirements of *Section 4,* the custody record shall include:

- a record of all medication a detainee has in their possession on arrival at the police station;

- a note of any such medication they claim to need but do not have with them.

Notes for guidance

9A   A 'health care professional' means a clinically qualified person working within the scope of practice as determined by their relevant professional body. Whether a health care professional is 'appropriate' depends on the circumstances of the duties they carry out at the time.

9B   Whenever possible juveniles and mentally vulnerable detainees should be visited more frequently.

9C   A detainee who appears drunk or behaves abnormally may be suffering from illness, the effects of drugs or may have sustained injury, particularly a head injury which is not apparent. A detainee needing or dependent on certain drugs, including alcohol, may experience harmful effects within a short time of being deprived of their supply. In these circumstances, when there is any doubt, police should always act urgently to call an appropriate health care professional or an ambulance. Paragraph 9.5 does not apply to minor ailments or injuries which do not need attention. However, all such ailments or injuries must be recorded in the custody record and any doubt must be resolved in favour of calling the appropriate health care professional.

9D   Whenever practicable, arrangements should be made for persons detained for assessment under the Mental Health Act 1983, section 136 to be taken to a hospital. There is no power under that Act to transfer a person detained under section 136 from one place of safety to another place of safety for assessment.

9E   It is important to respect a person's right to privacy and information about their health must be kept confidential and only disclosed with their consent or in accordance with clinical advice when it is necessary to protect the detainee's health or that of others who come into contact with them.

9F   The custody officer should always seek to clarify directions that the detainee requires constant observation or supervision and should ask the appropriate health care professional to explain precisely what action needs to be taken to implement such directions.

9G   Paragraphs 9.15 and 9.16 do not require any information about the cause of any injury, ailment or condition to be recorded on the custody record if it appears capable of providing evidence of an offence.

9H   The purpose of recording a person's responses when attempting to rouse them using the procedure in Annex H is to enable any change in the individual's consciousness level to be noted and clinical treatment arranged if appropriate.

10 **Cautions**

(a) **When a caution must be given**

10.1   A person whom there are grounds to suspect of an offence, see *Note 10A*, must be cautioned before any questions about an offence, or further questions if the answers provide the grounds for suspicion, are put to them if either the suspect's answers or silence, (i.e. failure or refusal to answer or answer satisfactorily) may be given in evidence to a court in a prosecution. A person need not be cautioned if questions are for other necessary purposes, e.g.:

 (a) solely to establish their identity or ownership of any vehicle;

 (b) to obtain information in accordance with any relevant statutory requirement, see *paragraph 10.9;*

 (c) in furtherance of the proper and effective conduct of a search, e.g. to determine the need to search in the exercise of powers of stop and search or to seek co-operation while carrying out a search;

 (d) to seek verification of a written record as in *paragraph 11.13;*

 (e) when examining a person in accordance with the Terrorism Act 2000, Schedule 7 and the Code of Practice for Examining Officers issued under that Act, Schedule 14, paragraph 6.

10.2   Whenever a person not under arrest is initially cautioned, or reminded they are under caution, that person must at the same time be told they are not under arrest and are free to leave if they want to. See *Note 10C*

10.3   A person who is arrested, or further arrested, must be informed at the time, or as soon as practicable thereafter, that they are under arrest and the grounds for their arrest, see *Note 10B*.

10.4   A person who is arrested, or further arrested, must also be cautioned unless:

 (a) it is impracticable to do so by reason of their condition or behaviour at time;

 (b) they have already been cautioned immediately prior to arrest as in *paragraph 10.1.*

(b) **Terms of the cautions**

10.5 The caution which must be given on:

 (a) arrest;

 (b) all other occasions before a person is charged or informed they may be prosecuted, see *section 16,*

should, unless the restriction on drawing adverse inferences from silence applies, see *Annex C*, be in the following terms:

"You do not have to say anything. But it may harm your defence if you do not mention when questioned something which you later rely on in Court. Anything you do say may be given in evidence."

See *Note 10G*

10.6   *Annex C, paragraph 2* sets out the alternative terms of the caution to be used when the restriction on drawing adverse inferences from silence applies.

10.7   Minor deviations from the words of any caution given in accordance with this Code do not constitute a breach of this Code, provided the sense of the relevant caution is preserved. See *Note 10D*

10.8   After any break in questioning under caution, the person being questioned must be made aware they remain under caution. If there is any doubt the relevant caution should be given again in full when the interview resumes. See *Note 10E*

10.9   When, despite being cautioned, a person fails to co-operate or to answer particular questions which may affect their immediate treatment, the person should be informed of any relevant consequences and that those consequences are not affected by the caution. Examples are when a person's refusal to provide:

 • their name and address when charged may make them liable to detention;

 • particulars and information in accordance with a statutory requirement, e.g. under the Road Traffic Act 1988, may amount to an offence or may make the person liable to a further arrest.

(c) Special warnings under the Criminal Justice and Public Order Act 1994, sections 36 and 37

10.10   When a suspect interviewed at a police station or authorised place of detention after arrest fails or refuses to answer certain questions, or to answer satisfactorily, after due warning, see *Note 10F*, a court or jury may draw such inferences as appear proper under the Criminal Justice and Public Order Act 1994, sections 36 and 37. Such inferences may only be drawn when:

(a) the restriction on drawing adverse inferences from silence, see *Annex C*, does not apply; and

(b) the suspect is arrested by a constable and fails or refuses to account for any objects, marks or substances, or marks on such objects found:
- on their person;
- in or on their clothing or footwear;
- otherwise in their possession; or
- in the place they were arrested;

(c) the arrested suspect was found by a constable at a place at or about the time the offence for which that officer has arrested them is alleged to have been committed, and the suspect fails or refuses to account for their presence there.

When the restriction on drawing adverse inferences from silence applies, the suspect may still be asked to account for any of the matters in (*b*) or (*c*) but the special warning described in *paragraph 10.11* will not apply and must not be given.

10.11   For an inference to be drawn when a suspect fails or refuses to answer a question about one of these matters or to answer it satisfactorily, the suspect must first be told in ordinary language:

(a) what offence is being investigated;

(b) what fact they are being asked to account for;

(c) this fact may be due to them taking part in the commission of the offence;

(d) a court may draw a proper inference if they fail or refuse to account for this fact;

(e) a record is being made of the interview and it may be given in evidence if they are brought to trial.

(d) Juveniles and persons who are mentally disordered or otherwise mentally vulnerable

10.12   If a juvenile or a person who is mentally disordered or otherwise mentally vulnerable is cautioned in the absence of the appropriate adult, the caution must be repeated in the adult's presence.

(e) Documentation

10.13   A record shall be made when a caution is given under this section, either in the interviewer's pocket book or in the interview record.

Notes for guidance

10A   There must be some reasonable, objective grounds for the suspicion, based on known facts or information which are relevant to the likelihood the offence has been committed and the person to be questioned committed it.

10B   An arrested person must be given sufficient information to enable them to understand they have been deprived of their liberty and the reason they have been arrested, e.g. when a person is arrested on suspicion of committing an offence they must be informed of the suspected offence's nature, when and where it was committed. If the arrest is made under the general arrest conditions in PACE, section 25, the grounds for arrest must include an explanation of the conditions which make the arrest necessary. Vague or technical language should be avoided.

10C   The restriction on drawing inferences from silence, see Annex C, paragraph 1, does not apply to a person who has not been detained and who therefore cannot be prevented from seeking legal advice if they want, see paragraph 3.21.

10D   If it appears a person does not understand the caution, the person giving it should explain it in their own words.

10E   It may be necessary to show to the court that nothing occurred during an interview break or between interviews which influenced the suspect's recorded evidence. After a break in an interview or at the beginning of a subsequent interview, the interviewing officer should summarise the reason for the break and confirm this with the suspect.

10F   The Criminal Justice and Public Order Act 1994, sections 36 and 37 apply only to suspects who have been arrested by a constable or Customs and Excise officer and are given the relevant warning by the police or customs officer who made the arrest or who is investigating the offence. They do not apply to any interviews with suspects who have not been arrested.

10G   Nothing in this Code requires a caution to be given or repeated when informing a person not under arrest they may be prosecuted for an offence. However, a court will not be able to draw any inferences under the Criminal Justice and Public Order Act 1994, section 34, if the person was not cautioned.

11   Interviews—general

(a) Action

11.1A   An interview is the questioning of a person regarding their involvement or suspected involvement in a criminal offence or offences which, under *paragraph 10.1,* must be carried out under caution. Whenever a person is interviewed they must be informed of the nature of the offence, or further offence. Procedures under the Road Traffic Act 1988, section 7 or the Transport and Works Act 1992, section 31 do not constitute interviewing for the purpose of this Code.

11.1   Following a decision to arrest a suspect, they must not be interviewed about the relevant offence except at a police station or other authorised place of detention, unless the consequent delay would be likely to:

(a) lead to:
  - interference with, or harm to, evidence connected with an offence;
  - interference with, or physical harm to, other people; or
  - serious loss of, or damage to, property;

(b) lead to alerting other people suspected of committing an offence but not yet arrested for it; or

(c) hinder the recovery of property obtained in consequence of the commission of an offence.

Interviewing in any of these circumstances shall cease once the relevant risk has been averted or the necessary questions have been put in order to attempt to avert that risk.

11.2   Immediately prior to the commencement or re-commencement of any interview at a police station or other authorised place of detention, the interviewer should remind the suspect of their entitlement to free legal advice and that the interview can be delayed for legal advice to be obtained, unless one of the exceptions in *paragraph 6.6* applies. It is the interviewer's responsibility to make sure all reminders are recorded in the interview record.

11.3   Not Used

11.4   At the beginning of an interview the interviewer, after cautioning the suspect, see *section 10,* shall put to them any significant statement or silence which occurred in the presence and hearing of a police officer or civilian interviewer before the start of the interview and which have not been put to the suspect in the course of a previous interview. See *Note 11A.* The interviewer shall ask the suspect whether they confirm or deny that earlier statement or silence and if they want to add anything.

11.4A   A significant statement is one which appears capable of being used in evidence against the suspect, in particular a direct admission of guilt. A significant silence is a failure or refusal to answer a question or answer satisfactorily when under caution, which might, allowing for the restriction on drawing adverse inferences from silence, see *Annex C,* give rise to an inference under the Criminal Justice and Public Order Act 1994, Part III.

11.5   No interviewer may try to obtain answers or elicit a statement by the use of oppression. Except as in *paragraph 10.9,* no interviewer shall indicate, except to answer a direct question, what action will be taken by the police if the person being questioned answers questions, makes a statement or refuses to do either. If the person asks directly what action will be taken if they answer questions, make a statement or refuse to do either, the interviewer may inform them what action the police propose to take provided that action is itself proper and warranted.

11.6   The interview or further interview of a person about an offence with which that person has not been charged or for which they have not been informed they may be prosecuted, must cease when the officer in charge of the investigation:

(a) is satisfied all the questions they consider relevant to obtaining accurate and reliable information about the offence have been put to the suspect, this includes allowing the suspect an opportunity to give an innocent explanation and asking questions to test if the explanation is accurate and reliable, e.g. to clear up ambiguities or clarify what the suspect said;

(b) has taken account of any other available evidence; and

(c) the officer in charge of the investigation, or in the case of a detained suspect, the custody officer, see *paragraph 16.1,* reasonably believes there is sufficient evidence to provide a realistic prospect of conviction for that offence if the person was prosecuted for it. See *Note 11B*

This paragraph does not prevent officers in revenue cases or acting under the confiscation provisions of the Criminal Justice Act 1988 or the Drug Trafficking Act 1994 from inviting suspects to complete a formal question and answer record after the interview is concluded.

(b) Interview records

11.7   (a) An accurate record must be made of each interview, whether or not the interview takes place at a police station

(b) The record must state the place of interview, the time it begins and ends, any interview breaks and, subject to *paragraph 2.6A,* the names of all those present; and must be made on the forms provided for this purpose or in the interviewer's pocket book or in accordance with the Codes of Practice E or F;

(c) Any written record must be made and completed during the interview, unless this would not be practicable or would interfere with the conduct of the interview, and must constitute either a verbatim record of what has been said or, failing this, an account of the interview which adequately and accurately summarises it.

11.8   If a written record is not made during the interview it must be made as soon as practicable after its completion.

11.9   Written interview records must be timed and signed by the maker.

11.10   If a written record is not completed during the interview the reason must be recorded in the interview record.

11.11   Unless it is impracticable, the person interviewed shall be given the opportunity to read the interview record and to sign it as correct or to indicate how they consider it inaccurate. If the person interviewed cannot read or refuses to read the record or sign it, the senior interviewer present shall read it to them and ask whether they would like to sign it as correct or make their mark or to indicate how they consider it inaccurate. The interviewer shall certify on the interview record itself what has occurred. See *Note 11E*

11.12   If the appropriate adult or the person's solicitor is present during the interview, they should also be given an opportunity to read and sign the interview record or any written statement taken down during the interview.

11.13   A written record shall be made of any comments made by a suspect, including unsolicited comments, which are outside the context of an interview but which might be relevant to the offence. Any such record must be timed and signed by the maker. When practicable the suspect shall be given the opportunity to read that record and to sign it as correct or to indicate how they consider it inaccurate. See *Note 11E*

11.14   Any refusal by a person to sign an interview record when asked in accordance with this Code must itself be recorded.

(c) Juveniles and mentally disordered or otherwise mentally vulnerable people

11.15   A juvenile or person who is mentally disordered or otherwise mentally vulnerable must not be interviewed regarding their involvement or suspected involvement in a criminal offence or offences, or asked to provide or sign a written statement under caution or record of interview, in the absence of the appropriate adult unless *paragraphs 11.1, 11.18 to 11.20* apply. See *Note 11C*

11.16   Juveniles may only be interviewed at their place of education in exceptional circumstances and only when the principal or their nominee agrees. Every effort should be made to notify the parent(s) or other person responsible for the juvenile's welfare and the appropriate adult, if this is a different person, that the police want to interview the juvenile and reasonable time should be allowed to enable the appropriate adult to be present at the interview. If awaiting the appropriate adult would cause unreasonable delay, and unless the juvenile is suspected of an offence against the educational establishment, the principal or their nominee can act as the appropriate adult for the purposes of the interview.

11.17   If an appropriate adult is present at an interview, they shall be informed:

- they are not expected to act simply as an observer; and
- the purpose of their presence is to:
  - ~ advise the person being interviewed;
  - ~ observe whether the interview is being conducted properly and fairly;
  - ~ facilitate communication with the person being interviewed.

(d) Vulnerable suspects—urgent interviews at police stations

11.18   The following persons may not be interviewed unless an officer of superintendent rank or above considers delay will lead to the consequences in *paragraph 11.1(a) to (c)*, and is satisfied the interview would not significantly harm the person's physical or mental state (see Annex G):

(a) a juvenile or person who is mentally disordered or otherwise mentally vulnerable if at the time of the interview the appropriate adult is not present;

(b) anyone other than in *(a)* who at the time of the interview appears unable to:
   - appreciate the significance of questions and their answers; or
   - understand what is happening because of the effects of drink, drugs or any illness, ailment or condition;

(c) a person who has difficulty understanding English or has a hearing disability, if at the time of the interview an interpreter is not present.

11.19   These interviews may not continue once sufficient information has been obtained to avert the consequences in *paragraph 11.1(a) to (c)*.

11.20.   A record shall be made of the grounds for any decision to interview a person under *paragraph 11.18*.

Notes for guidance

11A   Paragraph 11.4 does not prevent the interviewer from putting significant statements and silences to a suspect again at a later stage or a further interview.

11B   The Criminal Procedure and Investigations Act 1996 Code of Practice, paragraph 3.4 states 'In conducting an investigation, the investigator should pursue all reasonable lines of enquiry, whether these point towards or away from the suspect. What is reasonable will depend on the particular circumstances.' Interviewers should keep this in mind when deciding what questions to ask in an interview.

11C Although juveniles or people who are mentally disordered or otherwise mentally vulnerable are often capable of providing reliable evidence, they may, without knowing or wishing to do so, be particularly prone in certain circumstances to provide information that may be unreliable, misleading or self-incriminating. Special care should always be taken when questioning such a person, and the appropriate adult should be involved if there is any doubt about a person's age, mental state or capacity. Because of the risk of unreliable evidence it is also important to obtain corroboration of any facts admitted whenever possible.

11D Juveniles should not be arrested at their place of education unless this is unavoidable. When a juvenile is arrested at their place of education, the principal or their nominee must be informed.

11E Significant statements described in paragraph 11.4 will always be relevant to the offence and must be recorded. When a suspect agrees to read records of interviews and other comments and sign them as correct, they should be asked to endorse the record with, e.g. 'I agree that this is a correct record of what was said' and add their signature. If the suspect does not agree with the record, the interviewer should record the details of any disagreement and ask the suspect to read these details and sign them to the effect that they accurately reflect their disagreement. Any refusal to sign should be recorded.

12 **Interviews in police stations**

(a) **Action**

12.1   If a police officer wants to interview or conduct enquiries which require the presence of a detainee, the custody officer is responsible for deciding whether to deliver the detainee into the officer's custody.

12.2   Except as below, in any period of 24 hours a detainee must be allowed a continuous period of at least 8 hours for rest, free from questioning, travel or any interruption in connection with the investigation concerned. This period should normally be at night or other appropriate time which takes account of when the detainee last slept or rested. If a detainee is arrested at a police station after going there voluntarily, the period of 24 hours runs from the time of their arrest and not the time of arrival at the police station. The period may not be interrupted or delayed, except:

- (a) when there are reasonable grounds for believing not delaying or interrupting the period would:
  - (i)   involve a risk of harm to people or serious loss of, or damage to, property;
  - (ii)   delay unnecessarily the person's release from custody;
  - (iii)   otherwise prejudice the outcome of the investigation;
- (b) at the request of the detainee, their appropriate adult or legal representative;
- (c) when a delay or interruption is necessary in order to:
  - (i)   comply with the legal obligations and duties arising under *section 15;*
  - (ii)   to take action required under *section 9* or in accordance with medical advice.

If the period is interrupted in accordance with *(a)*, a fresh period must be allowed. Interruptions under *(b)* and *(c)*, do not require a fresh period to be allowed.

12.3   Before a detainee is interviewed the custody officer, in consultation with the officer in charge of the investigation and appropriate health care professionals as necessary, shall assess whether the detainee is fit enough to be interviewed. This means determining and considering the risks to the detainee's physical and mental state if the interview took place and determining what safeguards are needed to allow the interview to take place. See *Annex G*. The custody officer shall not allow a detainee to be interviewed if the custody officer considers it would cause significant harm to the detainee's physical or mental state. Vulnerable suspects listed at *paragraph 11.18* shall be treated as always being at some risk during an interview and these persons may not be interviewed except in accordance with *paragraphs 11.18* to *11.20.*

12.4   As far as practicable interviews shall take place in interview rooms which are adequately heated, lit and ventilated.

12.5   A suspect whose detention without charge has been authorised under PACE, because the detention is necessary for an interview to obtain evidence of the offence for which they have been arrested, may choose not to answer questions but police do not require the suspect's consent or agreement to interview them for this purpose. If a suspect takes steps to prevent themselves being questioned or further questioned, e.g. by refusing to leave their cell to go to a suitable interview room or by trying to leave the interview room, they shall be advised their consent or agreement to interview is not required. The suspect shall be cautioned as in *section 10,* and informed if they fail or refuse to co-operate, the interview may take place in the cell and that their failure or refusal to co-operate may be given in evidence. The suspect shall then be invited to co-operate and go into the interview room.

12.6   People being questioned or making statements shall not be required to stand.

12.7   Before the interview commences each interviewer shall, subject to *paragraph 2.6A,* identify themselves and any other persons present to the interviewee.

12.8   Breaks from interviewing should be made at recognised meal times or at other times that take account of when an interviewee last had a meal. Short refreshment breaks shall be provided at approximately two hour intervals, subject to the interviewer's discretion to delay a break if there are reasonable grounds for believing it would:
   (i)   involve a:
       • risk of harm to people;
       • serious loss of, or damage to, property;
   (ii)   unnecessarily delay the detainee's release;
   (iii) otherwise prejudice the outcome of the investigation.

See *Note 12B*

12.9   If during the interview a complaint is made by or on behalf of the interviewee concerning the provisions of this Code, the interviewer should:
   (i)   record it in the interview record;
   (ii)   inform the custody officer, who is then responsible for dealing with it as in *section 9.*

(b) Documentation

12.10   A record must be made of the:
   • time a detainee is not in the custody of the custody officer, and why
   • reason for any refusal to deliver the detainee out of that custody

12.11   A record shall be made of:
   (a)   the reasons it was not practicable to use an interview room; and
   (b)   any action taken as in *paragraph 12.5.*

The record shall be made on the custody record or in the interview record for action taken whilst an interview record is being kept, with a brief reference to this effect in the custody record.

12.12   Any decision to delay a break in an interview must be recorded, with reasons, in the interview record.

12.13   All written statements made at police stations under caution shall be written on forms provided for the purpose.

12.14   All written statements made under caution shall be taken in accordance with *Annex D.* Before a person makes a written statement under caution at a police station they shall be reminded about the right to legal advice. See *Note 12A*

Notes for guidance

12A   It is not normally necessary to ask for a written statement if the interview was recorded or taped at the time and the record signed by the interviewee in accordance with paragraph 11.11. Statements under caution should normally be taken in these circumstances only at the person's express wish. A person may however be asked if they want to make such a statement.

12B Meal breaks should normally last at least 45 minutes and shorter breaks after two hours should last at least 15 minutes. If the interviewer delays a break in accordance with paragraph 12.8 and prolongs the interview, a longer break should be provided. If there is a short interview, and another short interview is contemplated, the length of the break may be reduced if there are reasonable grounds to believe this is necessary to avoid any of the consequences in paragraph 12.8(i) to (iii).

13 Interpreters

(a) General

13.1   Chief officers are responsible for making sure appropriate arrangements are in place for provision of suitably qualified interpreters for people who:

- are deaf;
- do not understand English.

(b) Foreign languages

13.2   Unless *paragraphs 11.1, 11.18 to 11.20* apply, a person must not be interviewed in the absence of a person capable of interpreting if:

(a) they have difficulty understanding English;

(b) the interviewer cannot speak the person's own language;

(c) the person wants an interpreter present.

13.3   The interviewer shall make sure the interpreter makes a note of the interview at the time in the person's language for use in the event of the interpreter being called to give evidence, and certifies its accuracy. The interviewer should allow sufficient time for the interpreter to note each question and answer after each is put, given and interpreted. The person should be allowed to read the record or have it read to them and sign it as correct or indicate the respects in which they consider it inaccurate. If the interview is tape-recorded or visually recorded, the arrangements in Code E or F apply.

13.4   In the case of a person making a statement other than in English:

(a) the interpreter shall record the statement in the language it is made;

(b) the person shall be invited to sign it;

(c) an official English translation shall be made in due course.

(c) Deaf people and people with speech difficulties

13.5   If a person appears to be deaf or there is doubt about their hearing or speaking ability, they must not be interviewed in the absence of an interpreter unless they agree in writing to being interviewed without one or *paragraphs 11.1, 11.18 to 11.20* apply.

13.6   An interpreter should also be called if a juvenile is interviewed and the parent or guardian present as the appropriate adult appears to be deaf or there is doubt about their hearing or speaking ability, unless they agree in writing to the interview proceeding without one or *paragraphs 11.1, 11.18 to 11.20* apply.

13.7   The interviewer shall make sure the interpreter is allowed to read the interview record and certify its accuracy in the event of the interpreter being called to give evidence. If the interview is tape-recorded or visually recorded, the arrangements in Code E or F apply.

(d) Additional rules for detained persons

13.8   All reasonable attempts should be made to make the detainee understand that interpreters will be provided at public expense.

13.9 If *paragraph 6.1* applies and the detainee cannot communicate with the solicitor because of language, hearing or speech difficulties, an interpreter must be called. The interpreter may not be a police officer or civilian support staff when interpretation is needed for the purposes of obtaining legal advice. In all other cases a police officer or civilian support staff may only interpret if the detainee and the appropriate adult, if applicable, give their agreement in writing or if the interview is tape-recorded or visually recorded as in Code E or F.

13.10 When the custody officer cannot establish effective communication with a person charged with an offence who appears deaf or there is doubt about their ability to hear, speak or to understand English, arrangements must be made as soon as practicable for an interpreter to explain the offence and any other information given by the custody officer.

(e) Documentation

13.11 Action taken to call an interpreter under this section and any agreement to be interviewed in the absence of an interpreter must be recorded.

14 Questioning—special restrictions

14.1 If a person is arrested by one police force on behalf of another and the lawful period of detention in respect of that offence has not yet commenced in accordance with PACE, section 41 no questions may be put to them about the offence while they are in transit between the forces except to clarify any voluntary statement they make.

14.2 If a person is in police detention at a hospital they may not be questioned without the agreement of a responsible doctor. See *Note 14A*.

Note for guidance

14A *If questioning takes place at a hospital under paragraph 14.2, or on the way to or from a hospital, the period of questioning concerned counts towards the total period of detention permitted.*

15 Reviews and extensions of detention

(a) Persons detained under PACE

15.1 The review officer is responsible under PACE, section 40 for periodically determining if a person's detention, before or after charge, continues to be necessary. This requirement continues throughout the detention period and except as in *paragraph 15.10*, the review officer must be present at the police station holding the detainee. See *Notes 15A* and *15B*

15.2 Under PACE, section 42, an officer of superintendent rank or above who is responsible for the station holding the detainee may give authority any time after the second review to extend the maximum period the person may be detained without charge by up to 12 hours. Further detention without charge may be authorised only by a magistrates' court in accordance with PACE, sections 43 and 44. See *Notes 15C, 15D* and *15E*

15.3 Before deciding whether to authorise continued detention the officer responsible under *paragraphs 15.1* or *15.2* shall give an opportunity to make representations about the detention to:

   (a) the detainee, unless in the case of a review as in *paragraph 15.1*, the detainee is asleep;

   (b) the detainee's solicitor if available at the time; and

   (c) the appropriate adult if available at the time.

15.3A Other people having an interest in the detainee's welfare may also make representations at the authorising officer's discretion.

15.3B   Subject to *paragraph 15.10,* the representations may be made orally in person or by telephone or in writing. The authorising officer may, however, refuse to hear oral representations from the detainee if the officer considers them unfit to make representations because of their condition or behaviour. See *Note 15C*

15.4   Before conducting a review or determining whether to extend the maximum period of detention without charge, the officer responsible must make sure the detainee is reminded of their entitlement to free legal advice, see *paragraph 6.5,* unless in the case of a review the person is asleep.

15.5   If, after considering any representations, the officer decides to keep the detainee in detention or extend the maximum period they may be detained without charge, any comment made by the detainee shall be recorded. If applicable, the officer responsible under *paragraph 15.1* or *15.2* shall be informed of the comment as soon as practicable. See also *paragraphs 11.4* and *11.13*

15.6   No officer shall put specific questions to the detainee:

- regarding their involvement in any offence; or
- in respect of any comments they may make;
  - ~ when given the opportunity to make representations; or
  - ~ in response to a decision to keep them in detention or extend the maximum period of detention.

Such an exchange could constitute an interview as in *paragraph 11.1A* and would be subject to the associated safeguards in *section 11* and, in respect of a person who has been charged, *paragraph 16.5.* See also *paragraph 11.13.*

15.7   A detainee who is asleep at a review, see *paragraph 15.1,* and whose continued detention is authorised must be informed about the decision and reason as soon as practicable after waking.

(b) Persons detained under the Terrorism Act 2000

15.8   In terrorism cases:

(a) the powers and duties of the review officer are in the Terrorism Act 2000, Schedule 8, Part II;

(b) a police officer of at least superintendent rank may apply to a judicial authority for a warrant of further detention under the Terrorism Act 2000, Schedule 8, Part III.

(c) Telephone review of detention

15.9   PACE, section 40A provides that the officer responsible under section 40 for reviewing the detention of a person who has not been charged, need not attend the police station holding the detainee and may carry out the review by telephone if:

(a) it is not reasonably practicable for the officer to be present;

(b) PACE, section 45A, in respect of the use of video conferencing facilities, does not apply or it is not reasonably practicable to use such facilities.

See *Note 15F*

15.10   When a telephone review is carried out, an officer at the station holding the detainee shall be required by the review officer to fulfil that officer's obligations under PACE section 40 or this Code by:

(a) making any record connected with the review in the detainee's custody record;

(b) if applicable, making a record in (*a*) in the presence of the detainee; and

(c) giving the detainee information about the review.

15.11   When a telephone review is carried out, the requirement in *paragraph 15.3* will be satisfied:

(a) if facilities exist for the immediate transmission of written representations to the review officer, e.g. fax or email message, by giving the detainee an opportunity to make representations:

(i) orally by telephone; or

(ii) in writing using those facilities; and

(b) in all other cases, by giving the detainee an opportunity to make their representations orally by telephone.

(d) Documentation

15.12   It is the officer's responsibility to make sure all reminders given under *paragraph 15.4* are noted in the custody record.

15.13   The grounds for, and extent of, any delay in conducting a review shall be recorded.

15.14   When a telephone review is carried out, a record shall be made of:

(a) the reason the review officer did not attend the station holding the detainee;

(b) the place the review officer was;

(c) the method representations, oral or written, were made to the review officer, see *paragraph 15.11*.

15.15   Any written representations shall be retained.

15.16   A record shall be made as soon as practicable about the outcome of each review or determination whether to extend the maximum detention period without charge or an application for a warrant of further detention or its extension. If *paragraph 15.7* applies, a record shall also be made of when the person was informed and by whom. If an authorisation is given under PACE, section 42, the record shall state the number of hours and minutes by which the detention period is extended or further extended. If a warrant for further detention, or extension, is granted under section 43 or 44, the record shall state the detention period authorised by the warrant and the date and time it was granted.

Notes for guidance

15A   Review officer for the purposes of:

- *PACE, sections 40 and 40A means, in the case of a person arrested but not charged, an officer of at least inspector rank not directly involved in the investigation and, if a person has been arrested and charged, the custody officer;*

- *the Terrorism Act 2000, means an officer not directly involved in the investigation connected with the detention and of at least inspector rank, for reviews within 24 hours of the detainee's arrest or superintendent for all other reviews.*

15B   The detention of persons in police custody not subject to the statutory review requirement in paragraph 15.1 should still be reviewed periodically as a matter of good practice. The purpose of such reviews is to check the particular power under which a detainee is held continues to apply, any associated conditions are complied with and to make sure appropriate action is taken to deal with any changes. This includes the detainee's prompt release when the power no longer applies, or their transfer if the power requires the detainee be taken elsewhere as soon as the necessary arrangements are made. Examples include persons:

(a) *arrested on warrant because they failed to answer bail to appear at court;*

(b) *arrested under the Bail Act 1976, section 7(3) for breaching a condition of bail granted after charge;*

(c) *in police custody for specific purposes and periods under the Crime (Sentences) Act 1997, Schedule 1;*

(d) *convicted, or remand prisoners, held in police stations on behalf of the Prison Service under the Imprisonment (Temporary Provisions) Act 1980, section 6;*

(e) *being detained to prevent them causing a breach of the peace;*

(f) *detained at police stations on behalf of the Immigration Service.*

The detention of persons remanded into police detention by order of a court under the Magistrates' Courts Act 1980, section 128 is subject to a statutory requirement to review that detention. This is to make sure the detainee is taken back to court no later than the end of the period authorised by the court or when the need for their detention by police ceases, whichever is the sooner.

15C   In the case of a review of detention, but not an extension, the detainee need not be woken for the review. However, if the detainee is likely to be asleep, e.g. during a period of rest allowed as in paragraph 12.2, at the latest time a review or authorisation to extend detention may take place, the officer should, if the legal obligations and time constraints permit, bring forward the procedure to allow the detainee to make representations. A detainee not asleep during the review must be present when the grounds for their continued detention are recorded and must at the same time be informed of those grounds unless the review officer considers the person is incapable of understanding what is said, violent or likely to become violent or in urgent need of medical attention.

15D   An application to a Magistrates' Court under PACE, sections 43 or 44 for a warrant of further detention or its extension should be made between 10am and 9pm, and if possible during normal court hours. It will not usually be practicable to arrange for a court to sit specially outside the hours of 10am to 9pm. If it appears a special sitting may be needed outside normal court hours but between 10am and 9pm, the clerk to the justices should be given notice and informed of this possibility, while the court is sitting if possible.

15E   In paragraph 15.2, the officer responsible for the station holding the detainee includes a superintendent or above who, in accordance with their force operational policy or police regulations, is given that responsibility on a temporary basis whilst the appointed long-term holder is off duty or otherwise unavailable.

15F   The provisions of PACE, section 40A allowing telephone reviews do not apply to reviews of detention after charge by the custody officer or to reviews under the Terrorism Act 2000, Schedule 8, Part II in terrorism cases. When video conferencing is not required, they allow the use of a telephone to carry out a review of detention before charge if it is not reasonably practicable for the review officer to attend the station holding the detainee, e.g. when severe weather conditions or an unforeseen operational emergency prevent the review officer from attending. The procedure under PACE, section 42 must be done in person.

16 **Charging detained persons**

(a) **Action**

16.1   When the officer in charge of the investigation reasonably believes there is sufficient evidence to provide a realistic prospect of the detainee's conviction, see *paragraph 11.6*, they shall without delay, and subject to the following qualification, inform the custody officer who will be responsible for considering whether the detainee should be charged. See *Notes 11B* and *16A*. When a person is detained in respect of more than one offence it is permissible to delay informing the custody officer until the above conditions are satisfied in respect of all the offences, but see *paragraph 11.6*. If the detainee is a juvenile, mentally disordered or otherwise mentally vulnerable, any resulting action shall be taken in the presence of the appropriate adult if they are present at the time. See *Note 16B and 16C*

16.2   When a detainee is charged with or informed they may be prosecuted for an offence, see *Note 16B*, they shall, unless the restriction on drawing adverse inferences from silence applies, see *Annex C*, be cautioned as follows:

'You do not have to say anything. But it may harm your defence if you do not mention now something which you later rely on in court. Anything you do say may be given in evidence.'

Annex C, paragraph 2 sets out the alternative terms of the caution to be used when the restriction on drawing adverse inferences from silence applies.

16.3   When a detainee is charged they shall be given a written notice showing particulars of the offence and, subject to *paragraph 2.6A*, the officer's name and the case reference number. As far as possible the particulars of the charge shall be stated in simple terms, but they shall also show the precise offence in law with which the detainee is charged. The notice shall begin:

'You are charged with the offence(s) shown below.' Followed by the caution.

If the detainee is a juvenile, mentally disordered or otherwise mentally vulnerable, the notice should be given to the appropriate adult.

16.4   If, after a detainee has been charged with or informed they may be prosecuted for an offence, an officer wants to tell them about any written statement or interview with another person relating to such an offence, the detainee shall either be handed a true copy of the written statement or the content of the interview record brought to their attention. Nothing shall be done to invite any reply or comment except to:

(a)   caution the detainee, *'You do not have to say anything, but anything you do say may be given in evidence.';* and

(b)   remind the detainee about their right to legal advice.

16.4A   If the detainee:

* cannot read, the document may be read to them

* is a juvenile, mentally disordered or otherwise mentally vulnerable, the appropriate adult shall also be given a copy, or the interview record shall be brought to their attention

16.5   A detainee may not be interviewed about an offence after they have been charged with, or informed they may be prosecuted for it, unless the interview is necessary:

* to prevent or minimise harm or loss to some other person, or the public

* to clear up an ambiguity in a previous answer or statement

* in the interests of justice for the detainee to have put to them, and have an opportunity to comment on, information concerning the offence which has come to light since they were charged or informed they might be prosecuted

Before any such interview, the interviewer shall:

(a)   caution the detainee, *'You do not have to say anything, but anything you do say may be given in evidence.';*

(b)   remind the detainee about their right to legal advice.

See *Note 16B*

16.6   The provisions of *paragraphs 16.2* to *16.5* must be complied with in the appropriate adult's presence if they are already at the police station. If they are not at the police station then these provisions must be complied with again in their presence when they arrive unless the detainee has been released.

See *Note 16C*

16.7   When a juvenile is charged with an offence and the custody officer authorises their continued detention after charge, the custody officer must try to make arrangements for the juvenile to be taken into the care of a local authority to be detained pending appearance in court unless the custody officer certifies it is impracticable to do so or, in the case of a juvenile of at least 12 years old, no secure accommodation is available and there is a risk to the public of serious harm from that juvenile, in accordance with PACE, section 38(6). See *Note 16D*

(b) Documentation

16.8   A record shall be made of anything a detainee says when charged.

16.9   Any questions put in an interview after charge and answers given relating to the offence shall be recorded in full during the interview on forms for that purpose and the record signed by the detainee or, if they refuse, by the interviewer and any third parties present. If the questions are tape recorded or visually recorded the arrangements in Code E or F apply.

16.10   If it is not practicable to make arrangements for a juvenile's transfer into local authority care as in *paragraph 16.7*, the custody officer must record the reasons and complete a certificate to be produced before the court with the juvenile. See *Note 16D*

Notes for guidance

16A   The custody officer must take into account alternatives to prosecution under the Crime and Disorder Act 1998, reprimands and warning applicable to persons under 18, and in national guidance on the cautioning of offenders, for persons aged 18 and over.

16B   The giving of a warning or the service of the Notice of Intended Prosecution required by the Road Traffic Offenders Act 1988, section 1 does not amount to informing a detainee they may be prosecuted for an offence and so does not preclude further questioning in relation to that offence.

16C   There is no power under PACE to detain a person and delay action under paragraphs 16.2 to 16.5 solely to await the arrival of the appropriate adult. After charge, bail cannot be refused, or release on bail delayed, simply because an appropriate adult is not available, unless the absence of that adult provides the custody officer with the necessary grounds to authorise detention after charge under PACE, section 38.

16D   Except as in paragraph 16.7, neither a juvenile's behaviour nor the nature of the offence provides grounds for the custody officer to decide it is impracticable to arrange the juvenile's transfer to local authority care. Similarly, the lack of secure local authority accommodation does not make it impracticable to transfer the juvenile. The availability of secure accommodation is only a factor in relation to a juvenile aged 12 or over when the local authority accommodation would not be adequate to protect the public from serious harm from them. The obligation to transfer a juvenile to local authority accommodation applies as much to a juvenile charged during the daytime as to a juvenile to be held overnight, subject to a requirement to bring the juvenile before a court under PACE, section 46.

ANNEX A—INTIMATE AND STRIP SEARCHES

A   Intimate search

1.   An intimate search consists of the physical examination of a person's body orifices other than the mouth. The intrusive nature of such searches means the actual and potential risks associated with intimate searches must never be underestimated.

(a) Action

2.   Body orifices other than the mouth may be searched only if authorised by an officer of inspector rank or above who has reasonable grounds for believing that:

   (a) the person may have concealed on themselves
      (i) anything which they could and might use to cause physical injury to themself or others at the station; or
      (ii) a Class A drug which they intended to supply to another or to export; and

   (b) an intimate search is the only means of removing those items.

2A.   The reasons an intimate search is considered necessary shall be explained to the person before the search begins.

3.   An intimate search may only be carried out by a registered medical practitioner or registered nurse, unless an officer of at least inspector rank considers this is not practicable and the search is to take place under *paragraph 2(a)(i)*, in which case a police officer may carry out the search. See *Notes A1 to A5*

3A.   Any proposal for a search under *paragraph 2(a)(i)* to be carried out by someone other than a registered medical practitioner or registered nurse must only be considered as a last resort and when the authorising officer is satisfied the risks associated with allowing the item to remain with the detainee outweigh the risks associated with removing it. See *Notes A1 to A5*

4. An intimate search under:

- *paragraph 2(a)(i)* may take place only at a hospital, surgery, other medical premises or police station
- *paragraph 2(a)(ii)* may take place only at a hospital, surgery or other medical premises and must be carried out by a registered medical practitioner or a registered nurse

5. An intimate search at a police station of a juvenile or mentally disordered or otherwise mentally vulnerable person may take place only in the presence of an appropriate adult of the same sex, unless the detainee specifically requests a particular adult of the opposite sex who is readily available. In the case of a juvenile the search may take place in the absence of the appropriate adult only if the juvenile signifies in the presence of the appropriate adult they do not want the adult present during the search and the adult agrees. A record shall be made of the juvenile's decision and signed by the appropriate adult.

6. When an intimate search under *paragraph 2(a)(i)* is carried out by a police officer, the officer must be of the same sex as the detainee. A minimum of two people, other than the detainee, must be present during the search. Subject to *paragraph 5*, no person of the opposite sex who is not a medical practitioner or nurse shall be present, nor shall anyone whose presence is unnecessary. The search shall be conducted with proper regard to the sensitivity and vulnerability of the detainee.

(b) Documentation

7. In the case of an intimate search the custody officer shall as soon as practicable, record:

- which parts of the detainee's body were searched
- who carried out the search
- who was present
- the reasons for the search including the reasons to believe the article could not otherwise be removed
- the result.

8. If an intimate search is carried out by a police officer, the reason why it was impracticable for a registered medical practitioner or registered nurse to conduct it must be recorded.

B Strip search

9. A strip search is a search involving the removal of more than outer clothing. In this Code, outer clothing includes shoes and socks.

(a) Action

10. A strip search may take place only if it is considered necessary to remove an article which a detainee would not be allowed to keep, and the officer reasonably considers the detainee might have concealed such an article. Strip searches shall not be routinely carried out if there is no reason to consider that articles are concealed.

The conduct of strip searches

11. When strip searches are conducted:

- (a) a police officer carrying out a strip search must be the same sex as the detainee;
- (b) the search shall take place in an area where the detainee cannot be seen by anyone who does not need to be present, nor by a member of the opposite sex except an appropriate adult who has been specifically requested by the detainee;
- (c) except in cases of urgency, where there is risk of serious harm to the detainee or to others, whenever a strip search involves exposure of intimate body parts, there must be at least two people present other than the detainee, and if the search is of a juvenile or mentally

disordered or otherwise mentally vulnerable person, one of the people must be the appropriate adult. Except in urgent cases as above, a search of a juvenile may take place in the absence of the appropriate adult only if the juvenile signifies in the presence of the appropriate adult that they do not want the adult to be present during the search and the adult agrees. A record shall be made of the juvenile's decision and signed by the appropriate adult. The presence of more than two people, other than an appropriate adult, shall be permitted only in the most exceptional circumstances;

(d) the search shall be conducted with proper regard to the sensitivity and vulnerability of the detainee in these circumstances and every reasonable effort shall be made to secure the detainee's co-operation and minimise embarrassment. Detainees who are searched shall not normally be required to remove all their clothes at the same time, e.g. a person should be allowed to remove clothing above the waist and redress before removing further clothing;

(e) if necessary to assist the search, the detainee may be required to hold their arms in the air or to stand with their legs apart and bend forward so a visual examination may be made of the genital and anal areas provided no physical contact is made with any body orifice;

(f) if articles are found, the detainee shall be asked to hand them over. If articles are found within any body orifice other than the mouth, and the detainee refuses to hand them over, their removal would constitute an intimate search, which must be carried out as in *Part A*;

(g) a strip search shall be conducted as quickly as possible, and the detainee allowed to dress as soon as the procedure is complete.

(b) Documentation

12. A record shall be made on the custody record of a strip search including the reason it was considered necessary, those present and any result.

Notes for guidance

A1   Before authorising any intimate search, the authorising officer must make every reasonable effort to persuade the detainee to hand the article over without a search. If the detainee agrees, a registered medical practitioner or registered nurse should whenever possible be asked to assess the risks involved and, if necessary, attend to assist the detainee.

A2   If the detainee does not agree to hand the article over without a search, the authorising officer must carefully review all the relevant factors before authorising an intimate search. In particular, the officer must consider whether the grounds for believing an article may be concealed are reasonable.

A3   If authority is given for a search under paragraph 2(a)(i), a registered medical practitioner or registered nurse shall be consulted whenever possible. The presumption should be that the search will be conducted by the registered medical practitioner or registered nurse and the authorising officer must make every reasonable effort to persuade the detainee to allow the medical practitioner or nurse to conduct the search.

A4   A constable should only be authorised to carry out a search as a last resort and when all other approaches have failed. In these circumstances, the authorising officer must be satisfied the detainee might use the article for one or more of the purposes in paragraph 2(a)(i) and the physical injury likely to be caused is sufficiently severe to justify authorising a constable to carry out the search.

A5   If an officer has any doubts whether to authorise an intimate search by a constable, the officer should seek advice from an officer of superintendent rank or above.

ANNEX B—DELAY IN NOTIFYING ARREST OR ALLOWING ACCESS TO LEGAL ADVICE

A   Persons detained under PACE

1. The exercise of the rights in *Section 5* or *Section 6*, or both, may be delayed if the person is in police detention, as in PACE, section 118(2), in connection with a serious arrestable offence,

has not yet been charged with an offence and an officer of superintendent rank or above, or inspector rank or above only for the rights in *Section 5*, has reasonable grounds for believing their exercise will:

    (i)   lead to:
- interference with, or harm to, evidence connected with a serious arrestable offence; or
- interference with, or physical harm to, other people; or

   (ii) lead to alerting other people suspected of having committed a serious arrestable offence but not yet arrested for it; or

 (iii) hinder the recovery of property obtained in consequence of the commission of such an offence.

2. These rights may also be delayed if the serious arrestable offence is:

    (i)   a drug trafficking offence and the officer has reasonable grounds for believing the detainee has benefited from drug trafficking, and the recovery of the value of the detainee's proceeds from drug trafficking will be hindered by the exercise of either right;

   (ii) an offence to which the Criminal Justice Act 1988, Part VI (confiscation orders) applies and the officer has reasonable grounds for believing the detainee has benefited from the offence, and the exercise of either right will hinder the recovery of the value of the:
- property obtained by the detainee from or in connection with the offence
- pecuniary advantage derived by the detainee from or in connection with it.

3.   Authority to delay a detainee's right to consult privately with a solicitor may be given only if the authorising officer has reasonable grounds to believe the solicitor the detainee wants to consult will, inadvertently or otherwise, pass on a message from the detainee or act in some other way which will have any of the consequences specified under *paragraphs 1 or 2*. In these circumstances the detainee must be allowed to choose another solicitor. See *Note B3*

4.   If the detainee wishes to see a solicitor, access to that solicitor may not be delayed on the grounds they might advise the detainee not to answer questions or the solicitor was initially asked to attend the police station by someone else. In the latter case the detainee must be told the solicitor has come to the police station at another person's request, and must be asked to sign the custody record to signify whether they want to see the solicitor.

5.   The fact the grounds for delaying notification of arrest may be satisfied does not automatically mean the grounds for delaying access to legal advice will also be satisfied.

6.   These rights may be delayed only for as long as grounds exist and in no case beyond 36 hours after the relevant time as in PACE, section 41. If the grounds cease to apply within this time, the detainee must, as soon as practicable, be asked if they want to exercise either right, the custody record must be noted accordingly, and action taken in accordance with the relevant section of the Code.

7.   A detained person must be permitted to consult a solicitor for a reasonable time before any court hearing.

B   Persons detained under the Terrorism Act 2000

8.   The rights as in *sections 5* or *6*, may be delayed if the person is detained under the Terrorism Act 2000, section 41 or Schedule 7, has not yet been charged with an offence and an officer of superintendent rank or above has reasonable grounds for believing the exercise of either right will:

    (i)   lead to:
- interference with, or harm to, evidence connected with a serious arrestable offence;
- interference with, or physical harm to, other people; or

   (ii) lead to the alerting of other people suspected of having committed a serious arrestable offence but not yet arrested for it; or

 (iii) hinder the recovery of property:
- obtained in consequence of the commission of such an offence; or
- in respect of which a forfeiture order could be made under that Act, section 23;

(iv) lead to interference with the gathering of information about the commission, preparation or instigation of acts of terrorism; or

(v) by alerting any person, make it more difficult to prevent an act of terrorism or secure the apprehension, prosecution or conviction of any person in connection with the commission, preparation or instigation of an act of terrorism.

9. These rights may also be delayed if the officer has reasonable grounds for believing:

(a) the detainee:

(i) has committed an offence to which the Criminal Justice Act 1988, Part VI (confiscation orders) applies;

(ii) has benefited from the offence; and

(b) the exercise of either right will hinder the recovery of the value of that benefit.

10. In these cases *paragraphs 3 (with regards to the consequences specified at paragraphs 8 and 9), 4* and *5* apply.

11. These rights may be delayed only for as long as is necessary but not beyond 48 hours from the time of arrest if arrested under section 41, or if detained under the Terrorism Act 2000, Schedule 7 when arrested under section 41, from the beginning of their examination. If the above grounds cease to apply within this time the detainee must as soon as practicable be asked if they wish to exercise either right, the custody record noted accordingly, and action taken in accordance with the relevant section of this Code.

12. In this case *paragraph 7* applies.

C Documentation

13. The grounds for action under this Annex shall be recorded and the detainee informed of them as soon as practicable.

14. Any reply given by a detainee under *paragraphs 6* or *11* must be recorded and the detainee asked to endorse the record in relation to whether they want to receive legal advice at this point.

D Cautions and special warnings

When a suspect detained at a police station is interviewed during any period for which access to legal advice has been delayed under this Annex, the court or jury may not draw adverse inferences from their silence.

Notes for guidance

B1 Even if Annex B applies in the case of a juvenile, or a person who is mentally disordered or otherwise mentally vulnerable, action to inform the appropriate adult and the person responsible for a juvenile's welfare if that is a different person, must nevertheless be taken as in paragraph 3.13 and 3.15.

B2 In the case of Commonwealth citizens and foreign nationals, see Note 7A.

B3 A decision to delay access to a specific solicitor is likely to be a rare occurrence and only when it can be shown the suspect is capable of misleading that particular solicitor and there is more than a substantial risk that the suspect will succeed in causing information to be conveyed which will lead to one or more of the specified consequences.

ANNEX C—RESTRICTION ON DRAWING ADVERSE INFERENCES FROM SILENCE AND TERMS OF THE CAUTION WHEN THE RESTRICTION APPLIES

(a) The restriction on drawing adverse inferences from silence

1.   The Criminal Justice and Public Order Act 1994, sections 34, 36 and 37 as amended by the Youth Justice and Criminal Evidence Act 1999, section 58 describe the conditions under which adverse inferences may be drawn from a person's failure or refusal to say anything about their involvement in the offence when interviewed, after being charged or informed they may be prosecuted. These provisions are subject to an overriding restriction on the ability of a court or jury to draw adverse inferences from a person's silence. This restriction applies:

   (a) to any detainee at a police station, see *Note 10C* who, before being interviewed, see *section 11* or being charged or informed they may be prosecuted, see *section 16*, has:

   (i)   asked for legal advice, see *section 6, paragraph 6.1;*

   (ii) not been allowed an opportunity to consult a solicitor, including the duty solicitor, as in this Code: and

   (iii) not changed their mind about wanting legal advice, see *section 6, paragraph 6.6(d)*

   Note the condition in (ii) will

   ~ apply when a detainee who has asked for legal advice is interviewed before speaking to a solicitor as in *section 6, paragraph 6.6(a)* or *(b).*

   ~ not apply if the detained person declines to ask for the duty solicitor, see *section 6, paragraphs 6.6(c)* and *(d);*

   (b) to any person charged with, or informed they may be prosecuted for, an offence who:

   (i)   has had brought to their notice a written statement made by another person or the content of an interview with another person which relates to that offence, see *section 16, paragraph 16.4;*

   (ii) is interviewed about that offence, see *section 16, paragraph 16.5;* or

   (iii) makes a written statement about that offence, see *Annex D paragraphs 4* and *9.*

(b) Terms of the caution when the restriction applies

2.   When a requirement to caution arises at a time when the restriction on drawing adverse inferences from silence applies, the caution shall be:

'You do not have to say anything, but anything you do say may be given in evidence.'

3.   Whenever the restriction either begins to apply or ceases to apply after a caution has already been given, the person shall be re-cautioned in the appropriate terms. The changed position on drawing inferences and that the previous caution no longer applies shall also be explained to the detainee in ordinary language. See *Note C2*

Notes for guidance

C1   The restriction on drawing inferences from silence does not apply to a person who has not been detained and who therefore cannot be prevented from seeking legal advice if they want to, see paragraphs 10.2 and 3.15.

C2   The following is suggested as a framework to help explain changes in the position on drawing adverse inferences if the restriction on drawing adverse inferences from silence:

   (a) begins to apply:

   'The caution you were previously given no longer applies. This is because after that caution:

   (i)   you asked to speak to a solicitor but have not yet been allowed an opportunity to speak to a solicitor.' See paragraph 1(a); or

   (ii) you have been charged with/informed you may be prosecuted.' See paragraph 1(b).

   'This means that from now on, adverse inferences cannot be drawn at court and your defence will not be harmed just because you choose to say nothing. Please listen carefully to the caution I am

about to give you because it will apply from now on. You will see that it does not say anything about your defence being harmed.'

(b) *ceases to apply before or at the time the person is charged or informed they may be prosecuted, see paragraph 1(a);*

'The caution you were previously given no longer applies. This is because after that caution you have been allowed an opportunity to speak to a solicitor. Please listen carefully to the caution I am about to give you because it will apply from now on. It explains how your defence at court may be affected if you choose to say nothing.'

ANNEX D—WRITTEN STATEMENTS UNDER CAUTION

(a) Written by a person under caution

1. A person shall always be invited to write down what they want to say.

2. A person who has not been charged with, or informed they may be prosecuted for, any offence to which the statement they want to write relates, shall:

(a) unless the statement is made at a time when the restriction on drawing adverse inferences from silence applies, see Annex C, be asked to write out and sign the following before writing what they want to say:

'I make this statement of my own free will. I understand that I do not have to say anything but that it may harm my defence if I do not mention when questioned something which I later rely on in court. This statement may be given in evidence.';

(b) if the statement is made at a time when the restriction on drawing adverse inferences from silence applies, be asked to write out and sign the following before writing what they want to say;

'I make this statement of my own free will. I understand that I do not have to say anything. This statement may be given in evidence.'

3. When a person, on the occasion of being charged with or informed they may be prosecuted for any offence, asks to make a statement which relates to any such offence and wants to write it they shall:

(a) unless the restriction on drawing adverse inferences from silence, see *Annex C,* applied when they were so charged or informed they may be prosecuted, be asked to write out and sign the following before writing what they want to say:

'I make this statement of my own free will. I understand that I do not have to say anything but that it may harm my defence if I do not mention when questioned something which I later rely on in court. This statement may be given in evidence.';

(b) if the restriction on drawing adverse inferences from silence applied when they were so charged or informed they may be prosecuted, be asked to write out and sign the following before writing what they want to say:

'I make this statement of my own free will. I understand that I do not have to say anything. This statement may be given in evidence.'

4. When a person, who has already been charged with or informed they may be prosecuted for any offence, asks to make a statement which relates to any such offence and wants to write it they shall be asked to write out and sign the following before writing what they want to say:

'I make this statement of my own free will. I understand that I do not have to say anything. This statement may be given in evidence.';

5. Any person writing their own statement shall be allowed to do so without any prompting except a police officer or civilian interviewer may indicate to them which matters are material or question any ambiguity in the statement.

(b) Written by a police officer or civilian interviewer

6.   If a person says they would like someone to write the statement for them, a police officer, or civilian interviewer shall write the statement.

7.   If the person has not been charged with, or informed they may be prosecuted for, any offence to which the statement they want to make relates they shall, before starting, be asked to sign, or make their mark, to the following:

(a) unless the statement is made at a time when the restriction on drawing adverse inferences from silence applies, see *Annex C*:

'I, _____, wish to make a statement. I want someone to write down what I say. I understand that I do not have to say anything but that it may harm my defence if I do not mention when questioned something which I later rely on in court. This statement may be given in evidence.'

(b) if the statement is made at a time when the restriction on drawing adverse inferences from silence applies:

'I, _____, wish to make a statement. I want someone to write down what I say. This statement may be given in evidence.'

8.   If, on the occasion of being charged with or informed they may be prosecuted for any offence, the person asks to make a statement which relates to any such offence they shall before starting be asked to sign, or make their mark to, the following:

(a) unless the restriction on drawing adverse inferences from silence applied, see *Annex C*, when they were so charged or informed they may be prosecuted:

'I, _____, wish to make a statement. I want someone to write down what I say. I understand that I do not have to say anything but that it may harm my defence if I do not mention when questioned something which I later rely on in court. This statement may be given in evidence.';

(b) if the restriction on drawing adverse inferences from silence applied when they were so charged or informed they may be prosecuted:

'I, _____, wish to make a statement. I want someone to write down what I say. This statement may be given in evidence.'

9.   If, having already been charged with or informed they may be prosecuted for any offence, a person asks to make a statement which relates to any such offence they shall before starting, be asked to sign, or make their mark to:

'I, _____, wish to make a statement. I want someone to write down what I say. This statement may be given in evidence.'

10.   The person writing the statement must take down the exact words spoken by the person making it and must not edit or paraphrase it. Any questions that are necessary, e.g. to make it more intelligible, and the answers given must be recorded at the same time on the statement form.

11. When the writing of a statement is finished the person making it shall be asked to read it and to make any corrections, alterations or additions they want. When they have finished reading they shall be asked to write and sign or make their mark on the following certificate at the end of the statement:

'I have read the above statement, and I have been able to correct, alter or add anything I wish. This statement is true. I have made it of my own free will.'

12.   If the person making the statement cannot read, or refuses to read it, or to write the above mentioned certificate at the end of it or to sign it, the person taking the statement shall read it to them and ask them if they would like to correct, alter or add anything and to put their signature or make their mark at the end. The person taking the statement shall certify on the statement itself what has occurred.

ANNEX E—SUMMARY OF PROVISIONS RELATING TO MENTALLY DISORDERED AND OTHERWISE MENTALLY VULNERABLE PEOPLE

1. If an officer has any suspicion, or is told in good faith, that a person of any age may be mentally disordered or otherwise mentally vulnerable, or mentally incapable of understanding the significance of

questions or their replies that person shall be treated as mentally disordered or otherwise mentally vulnerable for the purposes of this Code. See *paragraph 1.4*

2. In the case of a person who is mentally disordered or otherwise mentally vulnerable, 'the appropriate adult' means:

(a) a relative, guardian or other person responsible for their care or custody;

(b) someone experienced in dealing with mentally disordered or mentally vulnerable people but who is not a police officer or employed by the police;

(c) failing these, some other responsible adult aged 18 or over who is not a police officer or employed by the police.

See *paragraph 1.7(b) and Note 1D*

3. If the custody officer authorises the detention of a person who is mentally vulnerable or appears to be suffering from a mental disorder, the custody officer must as soon as practicable inform the appropriate adult of the grounds for detention and the person's whereabouts, and ask the adult to come to the police station to see them. If the appropriate adult:

• is already at the station when information is given as in *paragraphs 3.1 to 3.5* the information must be given in their presence

• is not at the station when the provisions of *paragraph 3.1 to 3.5* are complied with these provisions must be complied with again in their presence once they arrive.

See *paragraphs 3.15 to 3.17*

4. If the appropriate adult, having been informed of the right to legal advice, considers legal advice should be taken, the provisions of *section 6* apply as if the mentally disordered or otherwise mentally vulnerable person had requested access to legal advice. See *paragraph 3.19* and *Note E1*

5. The custody officer must make sure a person receives appropriate clinical attention as soon as reasonably practicable if the person appears to be suffering from a mental disorder or in urgent cases immediately call the nearest health care professional or an ambulance. It is not intended these provisions delay the transfer of a detainee to a place of safety under the Mental Health Act 1983, section 136 if that is applicable. If an assessment under that Act is to take place at a police station, the custody officer must consider whether an appropriate health care professional should be called to conduct an initial clinical check on the detainee. See *paragraph 9.5* and *9.6*

6. It is imperative a mentally disordered or otherwise mentally vulnerable person detained under the Mental Health Act 1983, section 136 be assessed as soon as possible. If that assessment is to take place at the police station, an approved social worker and registered medical practitioner shall be called to the station as soon as possible in order to interview and examine the detainee. Once the detainee has been interviewed, examined and suitable arrangements been made for their treatment or care, they can no longer be detained under section 136. A detainee should be immediately discharged from detention if a registered medical practitioner having examined them, concludes they are not mentally disordered within the meaning of the Act. See *paragraph 3.16*

7. If a mentally disordered or otherwise mentally vulnerable person is cautioned in the absence of the appropriate adult, the caution must be repeated in the appropriate adult's presence. See *paragraph 10.12*

8. A mentally disordered or otherwise mentally vulnerable person must not be interviewed or asked to provide or sign a written statement in the absence of the appropriate adult unless the provisions of *paragraphs 11.1 or 11.18 to 11.20* apply. Questioning in these circumstances may not continue in the absence of the appropriate adult once sufficient information to avert the risk has been obtained. A record shall be made of the grounds for any decision to begin an interview in these circumstances. See *paragraphs 11.1, 11.15* and *11.18 to 11.20*

9. If the appropriate adult is present at an interview, they shall be informed they are not expected to act simply as an observer and the purposes of their presence are to:

• advise the interviewee

• observe whether or not the interview is being conducted properly and fairly

• facilitate communication with the interviewee

See *paragraph 11.17*

10. If the detention of a mentally disordered or otherwise mentally vulnerable person is reviewed by a review officer or a superintendent, the appropriate adult must, if available at the time, be given an opportunity to make representations to the officer about the need for continuing detention. See *paragraph 15.3*

11. If the custody officer charges a mentally disordered or otherwise mentally vulnerable person with an offence or takes such other action as is appropriate when there is sufficient evidence for a prosecution this must be done in the presence of the appropriate adult. The written notice embodying any charge must be given to the appropriate adult. See *paragraphs 16.1 to 16.4A*

12. An intimate or strip search of a mentally disordered or otherwise mentally vulnerable person may take place only in the presence of the appropriate adult of the same sex, unless the detainee specifically requests the presence of a particular adult of the opposite sex. A strip search may take place in the absence of an appropriate adult only in cases of urgency when there is a risk of serious harm to the detainee or others. See *Annex A, paragraphs 5* and *11(c)*

13. Particular care must be taken when deciding whether to use any form of approved restraints on a mentally disordered or otherwise mentally vulnerable person in a locked cell. See *paragraph 8.2*

Notes for guidance

E1 *The purpose of the provision at paragraph 3.19 is to protect the rights of a mentally disordered or otherwise mentally vulnerable detained person who does not understand the significance of what is said to them. If the detained person wants to exercise the right to legal advice, the appropriate action should be taken and not delayed until the appropriate adult arrives. A mentally disordered or otherwise mentally vulnerable detained person should always be given an opportunity, when an appropriate adult is called to the police station, to consult privately with a solicitor in the absence of the appropriate adult if they want.*

E2 *Although people who are mentally disordered or otherwise mentally vulnerable are often capable of providing reliable evidence, they may, without knowing or wanting to do so, be particularly prone in certain circumstances to provide information that may be unreliable, misleading or self-incriminating. Special care should always be taken when questioning such a person, and the appropriate adult should be involved if there is any doubt about a person's mental state or capacity. Because of the risk of unreliable evidence, it is important to obtain corroboration of any facts admitted whenever possible.*

E3 *Because of the risks referred to in Note E2, which the presence of the appropriate adult is intended to minimise, officers of superintendent rank or above should exercise their discretion to authorise the commencement of an interview in the appropriate adult's absence only in exceptional cases, if it is necessary to avert an immediate risk of serious harm. See paragraphs 11.1, 11.18 to 11.20*

ANNEX F—COUNTRIES WITH WHICH BILATERAL CONSULAR CONVENTIONS OR AGREEMENTS REQUIRING NOTIFICATION OF THE ARREST AND DETENTION OF THEIR NATIONALS ARE IN FORCE AS AT 1 APRIL 2003

Armenia

Austria

Azerbaijan

Belarus

Belgium

Bosnia-Herzegovina

Bulgaria

China*

Croatia

Cuba

Czech Republic

Denmark

Egypt

France

Georgia

German Federal Republic

Greece

Hungary

Italy

Japan

Kazakhstan

Macedonia

Mexico	Spain
Moldova	Sweden
Mongolia	Tajikistan
Norway	Turkmenistan
Poland	Ukraine
Romania	USA
Russia	Uzbekistan
Slovak Republic	Yugoslavia
Slovenia	

* Police are required to inform Chinese officials of arrest/detention in the Manchester consular district only. This comprises Derbyshire, Durham, Greater Manchester, Lancashire, Merseyside, North South and West Yorkshire, and Tyne and Wear.

ANNEX G—FITNESS TO BE INTERVIEWED

1.   This Annex contains general guidance to help police officers and health care professionals assess whether a detainee might be at risk in an interview.

2.   A detainee may be at risk in an interview if it is considered that:

(a) conducting the interview could significantly harm the detainee's physical or mental state;

(b) anything the detainee says in the interview about their involvement or suspected involvement in the offence about which they are being interviewed **might** be considered unreliable in subsequent court proceedings because of their physical or mental state.

3. In assessing whether the detainee should be interviewed, the following must be considered:

(a) how the detainee's physical or mental state might affect their ability to understand the nature and purpose of the interview, to comprehend what is being asked and to appreciate the significance of any answers given and make rational decisions about whether they want to say anything;

(b) the extent to which the detainee's replies may be affected by their physical or mental condition rather than representing a rational and accurate explanation of their involvement in the offence;

(c) how the nature of the interview, which could include particularly probing questions, might affect the detainee.

4.   It is essential health care professionals who are consulted consider the functional ability of the detainee rather than simply relying on a medical diagnosis, e.g. it is possible for a person with severe mental illness to be fit for interview.

5.   Health care professionals should advise on the need for an appropriate adult to be present, whether reassessment of the person's fitness for interview may be necessary if the interview lasts beyond a specified time, and whether a further specialist opinion may be required.

6.   When health care professionals identify risks they should be asked to quantify the risks. They should inform the custody officer:
   • whether the person's condition:
     ~ is likely to improve
     ~ will require or be amenable to treatment; and
   • indicate how long it may take for such improvement to take effect

7.   The role of the health care professional is to consider the risks and advise the custody officer of the outcome of that consideration. The health care professional's determination and any advice or recommendations should be made in writing and form part of the custody record.

8.   Once the health care professional has provided that information, it is a matter for the custody officer to decide whether or not to allow the interview to go ahead and if the interview

is to proceed, to determine what safeguards are needed. Nothing prevents safeguards being provided in addition to those required under the Code. An example might be to have an appropriate health care professional present during the interview, in addition to an appropriate adult, in order constantly to monitor the person's condition and how it is being affected by the interview.

ANNEX H—DETAINED PERSON: OBSERVATION LIST

1. If any detainee fails to meet any of the following criteria, an appropriate health care professional or an ambulance must be called.

2. When assessing the level of rousability, consider:

Rousability—can they be woken?

- go into the cell
- call their name
- shake gently

Response to questions—can they give appropriate answers to questions such as:

- What's your name?
- Where do you live?
- Where do you think you are?

Response to commands—can they respond appropriately to commands such as:

- Open your eyes!
- Lift one arm, now the other arm!

3. Remember to take into account the possibility or presence of other illnesses, injury, or mental condition, a person who is drowsy and smells of alcohol may also have the following:

- Diabetes
- Epilepsy
- Head injury
- Drug intoxication or overdose
- Stroke

Appendix 6

PACE Code of Practice for the Identification of Persons by Police Officers (Code D)

This code has effect in relation to any identification procedure carried out after midnight on 31st March 2003.

1 Introduction

1.1   This Code of Practice concerns the principal methods used by police to identify people in connection with the investigation of offences and the keeping of accurate and reliable criminal records.

1.2   Identification by witnesses arises, e.g., if the offender is seen committing the crime and a witness is given an opportunity to identify the suspect in a video identification, identification parade or similar procedure. The procedures are designed to:

- test the witness' ability to identify the person they saw on a previous occasion
- provide safeguards against mistaken identification.

While this Code concentrates on visual identification procedures, it does not preclude the police making use of aural identification procedures such as a 'voice identification parade', where they judge that appropriate.

1.3   Identification by fingerprints applies when a person's fingerprints are taken to:

- compare with fingerprints found at the scene of a crime
- check and prove convictions
- help to ascertain a person's identity.

1.4   Identification by body samples and impressions includes taking samples such as blood or hair to generate a DNA profile for comparison with material obtained from the scene of a crime, or a victim.

1.5   Taking photographs of arrested people applies to recording and checking identity and locating and tracing persons who:

- are wanted for offences
- fail to answer their bail.

1.6   Another method of identification involves searching and examining detained suspects to find, e.g., marks such as tattoos or scars which may help establish their identity or whether they have been involved in committing an offence.

1.7   The provisions of the Police and Criminal Evidence Act 1984 (PACE) and this Code are designed to make sure fingerprints, samples, impressions and photographs are taken, used and retained, and identification procedures carried out, only when justified and necessary for preventing, detecting or investigating crime. If these provisions are not observed, the application of the relevant procedures in particular cases may be open to question.

2   **General**

2.1   This Code must be readily available at all police stations for consultation by:

- police officers
- detained persons
- members of the public

2.2   The provisions of this Code:

- include the *Annexes*
- do not include the *Notes for guidance*.

2.3   Code C, paragraph 1.4, regarding a person who may be mentally disordered or otherwise mentally vulnerable and the *Notes for guidance* applicable to those provisions apply to this Code.

2.4   Code C, paragraph 1.5, regarding a person who appears to be under the age of 17 applies to this Code.

2.5   Code C, paragraph 1.6, regarding a person who appears blind, seriously visually impaired, deaf, unable to read or speak or has difficulty orally because of a speech impediment applies to this Code.

2.6   In this Code:

- 'appropriate adult' means the same as in Code C, paragraph 1.7,
- 'solicitor' means the same as in Code C, paragraph 6.12

and the *Notes for guidance* applicable to those provisions apply to this Code.

2.7   References to custody officers include those performing the functions of custody officer.

2.8   When a record of any action requiring the authority of an officer of a specified rank is made under this Code, subject to *paragraph 2.18*, the officer's name and rank must be recorded.

2.9   When this Code requires the prior authority or agreement of an officer of at least inspector or superintendent rank, that authority may be given by a sergeant or chief inspector who has been authorised to perform the functions of the higher rank under PACE, section 107.

2.10   Subject to *paragraph 2.18*, all records must be timed and signed by the maker.

2.11   Records must be made in the custody record, unless otherwise specified. References to 'pocket book' include any official report book issued to police officers or civilian support staff.

2.12   If any procedure in this Code requires a person's consent, the consent of a:

- mentally disordered or otherwise mentally vulnerable person is only valid if given in the presence of the appropriate adult
- juvenile, is only valid if their parent's or guardian's consent is also obtained unless the juvenile is under 14, when their parent's or guardian's consent is sufficient in its own right. If the only obstacle to an identification procedure in *section 3* is that a juvenile's parent or guardian refuses consent or reasonable efforts to obtain it have failed, the identification officer may apply the provisions of *paragraph 3.21*. See *Note 2A*.

2.13   If a person is blind, seriously visually impaired or unable to read, the custody officer or identification officer shall make sure their solicitor, relative, appropriate adult or some other person likely to take an interest in them and not involved in the investigation is available to help check any documentation. When this Code requires written consent or signing, the person assisting may be asked to sign instead, if the detainee prefers. This paragraph does not require an appropriate adult to be called solely to assist in checking and signing documentation for a person who is not a juvenile, or mentally disordered or otherwise mentally vulnerable (see Note 2B and Code C *paragraph 3.15*).

2.14   If any procedure in this Code requires information to be given to or sought from a suspect, it must be given or sought in the appropriate adult's presence if the suspect is mentally disordered, otherwise mentally vulnerable or a juvenile. If the appropriate adult is not present when the information is first given or sought, the procedure must be repeated in the presence of the appropriate adult when they arrive. If the suspect appears deaf or there is doubt about their hearing or speaking ability or ability to understand English, and effective communication cannot be established, the information must be given or sought through an interpreter.

2.15 Any procedure in this Code involving the participation of a person (whether as a suspect or a witness) who is mentally disordered, otherwise mentally vulnerable or a juvenile, must take place in the presence of the appropriate adult. However, the adult must not be allowed to prompt any identification of a suspect by a witness.

2.16 References to:

- 'taking a photograph', include the use of any process to produce a single, still, visual image

- 'photographing a person', should be construed accordingly

- 'photographs', 'films', 'negatives' and 'copies' include relevant visual images recorded, stored, or reproduced through any medium

- 'destruction' includes the deletion of computer data relating to such images or making access to that data impossible.

2.17 Except as described, nothing in this Code affects the powers and procedures:

(i) for requiring and taking samples of breath, blood and urine in relation to driving offences, etc, when under the influence of drink, drugs or excess alcohol under the:
  - Road Traffic Act 1988, sections 4 to 11
  - Road Traffic Offenders Act 1988, sections 15 and 16
  - Transport and Works Act 1992, sections 26 to 38;

(ii) under the Immigration Act 1971, Schedule 2, paragraph 18, for taking photographs and fingerprints from persons detained under that Act, Schedule 2, paragraph 16 (Administrative Controls as to Control on Entry etc.); for taking fingerprints in accordance with the Immigration and Asylum Act 1999; sections 141 and 142(3), or other methods for collecting information about a person's external physical characteristics provided for by regulations made under that Act, section 144;

(iii) under the Terrorism Act 2000, Schedule 8, for taking photographs, fingerprints, skin impressions, body samples or impressions from people:
  - arrested under that Act, section 41,
  - detained for the purposes of examination under that Act, Schedule 7, and to whom the Code of Practice issued under that Act, Schedule 14, paragraph 6, applies ('the terrorism provisions')

  See *Note 2C*;

(iv) for taking photographs, fingerprints, skin impressions, body samples or impressions from people who have been:
  - arrested on warrants issued in Scotland, by officers exercising powers under the Criminal Justice and Public Order Act 1994, section 136(2)
  - arrested or detained without warrant by officers from a police force in Scotland exercising their powers of arrest or detention under the Criminal Justice and Public Order Act 1994, section 137(2), (Cross Border powers of arrest etc.).

Note: In these cases, police powers and duties and the person's rights and entitlements whilst at a police station in England and Wales are the same as if the person had been arrested in Scotland by a Scottish police officer.

2.18 Nothing in this Code requires the identity of officers or civilian support staff to be recorded or disclosed:

(a) in the case of enquiries linked to the investigation of terrorism;

(b) if the officers or civilian support staff reasonably believe recording or disclosing their names might put them in danger.

In these cases, they shall use warrant or other identification numbers and the name of their police station. See *Note 2D*

2.19   In this Code:

(a) 'designated person' means a person other than a police officer, designated under the Police Reform Act 2002, Part 4, who has specified powers and duties of police officers conferred or imposed on them;

(b) any reference to a police officer includes a designated person acting in the exercise or performance of the powers and duties conferred or imposed on them by their designation.

2.20   If a power conferred on a designated person:

(a) allows reasonable force to be used when exercised by a police officer, a designated person exercising that power has the same entitlement to use force;

(b) includes power to use force to enter any premises, that power is not exercisable by that designated person except:

(i) in the company, and under the supervision, of a police officer; or

(ii) for the purpose of:

- saving life or limb; or
- preventing serious damage to property.

2.21   Nothing in this Code prevents the custody officer, or other officer given custody of the detainee, from allowing civilian support staff who are not designated persons to carry out individual procedures or tasks at the police station if the law allows. However, the officer remains responsible for making sure the procedures and tasks are carried out correctly in accordance with the Codes of Practice. Any such civilian must be:

(a) a person employed by a police authority maintaining a police force and under the control and direction of the Chief Officer of that force;

(b) employed by a person with whom a police authority has a contract for the provision of services relating to persons arrested or otherwise in custody.

2.22   Designated persons and other civilian support staff must have regard to any relevant provisions of the Codes of Practice.

Notes for guidance

2A   For the purposes of paragraph 2.12, the consent required from a parent or guardian may, for a juvenile in the care of a local authority or voluntary organisation, be given by that authority or organisation. In the case of a juvenile, nothing in paragraph 2.12 requires the parent, guardian or representative of a local authority or voluntary organisation to be present to give their consent, unless they are acting as the appropriate adult under paragraphs 2.14 or 2.15. However, it is important that a parent or guardian not present is fully informed before being asked to consent. They must be given the same information about the procedure and the juvenile's suspected involvement in the offence as the juvenile and appropriate adult. The parent or guardian must also be allowed to speak to the juvenile and the appropriate adult if they wish. Provided the consent is fully informed and is not withdrawn, it may be obtained at any time before the procedure takes place.

2B   People who are seriously visually impaired or unable to read may be unwilling to sign police documents. The alternative, i.e. their representative signing on their behalf, seeks to protect the interests of both police and suspects.

2C   Photographs, fingerprints, samples and impressions may be taken from a person detained under the terrorism provisions to help determine whether they are, or have been, involved in terrorism, as well as when there are reasonable grounds for suspecting their involvement in a particular offence.

2D   The purpose of paragraph 2.18(b) is to protect those involved in serious organised crime investigations or arrests of particularly violent suspects when there is reliable information that those arrested or their associates may threaten or cause harm to the officers. In cases of doubt, an officer of inspector rank or above should be consulted.

3 Identification by witnesses

3.1 A record shall be made of the suspect's description as first given by a potential witness. This record must:

(a) be made and kept in a form which enables details of that description to be accurately produced from it, in a visible and legible form, which can be given to the suspect or the suspect's solicitor in accordance with this Code; and

(b) unless otherwise specified, be made before the witness takes part in any identification procedures under *paragraphs 3.5* to *3.10, 3.21* or *3.23*.

A copy of the record shall where practicable, be given to the suspect or their solicitor before any procedures under *paragraphs 3.5* to *3.10, 3.21* or *3.23* are carried out. See *Note 3E*

(a) Cases when the suspect's identity is not known

3.2 In cases when the suspect's identity is not known, a witness may be taken to a particular neighbourhood or place to see whether they can identify the person they saw. Although the number, age, sex, race, general description and style of clothing of other people present at the location and the way in which any identification is made cannot be controlled, the principles applicable to the formal procedures under *paragraphs 3.5* to *3.10* shall be followed as far as practicable. For example:

(a) where it is practicable to do so, a record should be made of the witness' description of the suspect, as in paragraph 3.1(a), before asking the witness to make an identification;

(b) care must be taken not to direct the witness' attention to any individual unless, taking into account all the circumstances, this cannot be avoided. However, this does not prevent a witness being asked to look carefully at the people around at the time or to look towards a group or in a particular direction, if this appears necessary to make sure that the witness does not overlook a possible suspect simply because the witness is looking in the opposite direction and also to enable the witness to make comparisons between any suspect and others who are in the area; See *Note 3F*

(c) where there is more than one witness, every effort should be made to keep them separate and witnesses should be taken to see whether they can identify a person independently;

(d) once there is sufficient information to justify the arrest of a particular individual for suspected involvement in the offence, e.g., after a witness makes a positive identification, the provisions set out from paragraph 3.4 onwards shall apply for any other witnesses in relation to that individual. Subject to *paragraphs 3.12* and *3.13*, it is not necessary for the witness who makes such a positive identification to take part in a further procedure;

(e) the officer or civilian support staff accompanying the witness must record, in their pocket book, the action taken as soon as, and in as much detail, as possible. The record should include: the date, time and place of the relevant occasion the witness claims to have previously seen the suspect; where any identification was made; how it was made and the conditions at the time (e.g., the distance the witness was from the suspect, the weather and light); if the witness's attention was drawn to the suspect; the reason for this; and anything said by the witness or the suspect about the identification or the conduct of the procedure.

3.3 A witness must not be shown photographs, computerised or artist's composite likenesses or similar likenesses or pictures (including 'E-fit' images) if the identity of the suspect is known to the police and the suspect is available to take part in a video identification, an identification parade or a group identification. If the suspect's identity is not known, the showing of such images to a witness to obtain identification evidence must be done in accordance with *Annex E*.

(b) Cases when the suspect is known and available

3.4 If the suspect's identity is known to the police and they are available, the identification procedures set out in paragraphs 3.5 to 3.10 may be used. References in this section to a suspect being 'known' mean there is sufficient information known to the police to justify the arrest of a particular person for suspected involvement in the offence. A suspect being 'available' means they are immediately available or will be within a reasonably short time and willing to take an effective part in at least one of the following which it is practicable to arrange;

- video identification;
- identification parade; or
- group identification.

Video identification

3.5   A 'video identification' is when the witness is shown moving images of a known suspect, together with similar images of others who resemble the suspect. See paragraph 3.21 for circumstances in which still images may be used.

3.6   Video identifications must be carried out in accordance with *Annex A*.

Identification parade

3.7   An 'identification parade' is when the witness sees the suspect in a line of others who resemble the suspect.

3.8   Identification parades must be carried out in accordance with *Annex B*.

Group identification

3.9   A 'group identification' is when the witness sees the suspect in an informal group of people.

3.10   Group identifications must be carried out in accordance with *Annex C*.

Arranging identification procedures

3.11   Except for the provisions in *paragraph 3.19*, the arrangements for, and conduct of, the identification procedures in paragraphs 3.5 to 3.10 and circumstances in which an identification procedure must be held shall be the responsibility of an officer not below inspector rank who is not involved with the investigation, 'the identification officer'. Unless otherwise specified, the identification officer may allow another officer or civilian support staff, see *paragraph 2.21*, to make arrangements for, and conduct, any of these identification procedures. In delegating these procedures, the identification officer must be able to supervise effectively and either intervene or be contacted for advice. No officer or any other person involved with the investigation of the case against the suspect, beyond the extent required by these procedures, may take any part in these procedures or act as the identification officer. This does not prevent the identification officer from consulting the officer in charge of the investigation to determine which procedure to use. When an identification procedure is required, in the interest of fairness to suspects and witnesses, it must be held as soon as practicable.

Circumstances in which an identification procedure must be held

3.12   Whenever:

(i)   a witness has identified a suspect or purported to have identified them prior to any identification procedure set out in paragraphs 3.5 to 3.10 having been held; or

(ii)   there is a witness available, who expresses an ability to identify the suspect, or where there is a reasonable chance of the witness being able to do so, and they have not been given an opportunity to identify the suspect in any of the procedures set out in paragraphs 3.5 to 3.10,

and the suspect disputes being the person the witness claims to have seen, an identification procedure shall be held unless it is not practicable or it would serve no useful purpose in proving or disproving whether the suspect was involved in committing the offence. For example, when it is not disputed that the suspect is already well known to the witness who claims to have seen them commit the crime.

3.13 Such a procedure may also be held if the officer in charge of the investigation considers it would be useful.

Selecting an identification procedure

3.14 If, because of paragraph 3.12, an identification procedure is to be held, the suspect shall initially be offered either a video identification or identification unless:

a) a video identification is not practicable; or

b) an identification parade is both practicable and more suitable than a video identification; or

c) paragraph 3.16 applies.

The identification officer and the officer in charge of the investigation shall consult each other to determine which option is to be offered. An identification parade may not be practicable because of factors relating to the witnesses, such as their number, state of health, availability and travelling requirements. A video identification would normally be more suitable if it could be arranged and completed sooner than an identification parade.

3.15 A suspect who refuses the identification procedure first offered shall be asked to state their reason for refusing and may get advice from their solicitor and/or if present, their appropriate adult. The suspect, solicitor and/or appropriate adult shall be allowed to make representations about why another procedure should be used. A record should be made of the reasons for refusal and any representations made. After considering any reasons given, and representations made, the identification officer shall, if appropriate, arrange for the suspect to be offered an alternative which the officer considers suitable and practicable. If the officer decides it is not suitable and practicable to offer an alternative identification procedure, the reasons for that decision shall be recorded.

3.16 A group identification may initially be offered if the officer in charge of the investigation considers it is more satisfactory than a video identification or an identification parade and the identification officer considers it practicable to arrange.

Notice to suspect

3.17 Unless *paragraph 3.20* applies, before a video identification, an identification parade or group identification is arranged, the following shall be explained to the suspect:

(i) the purposes of the video identification, identification parade or group identification;

(ii) their entitlement to free legal advice; see Code C, paragraph 6.5;

(iii) the procedures for holding it, including their right to have a solicitor or friend present;

(iv) that they do not have to consent to or co-operate in a video identification, identification parade or group identification;

(v) that if they do not consent to, and co-operate in, a video identification, identification parade or group identification, their refusal may be given in evidence in any subsequent trial and police may proceed covertly without their consent or make other arrangements to test whether a witness can identify them, see *paragraph 3.21*

(vi) whether, for the purposes of the video identification procedure, images of them have previously been obtained, see *paragraph 3.20*, and if so, that they may co-operate in providing further, suitable images to be used instead;

(vii) if appropriate, the special arrangements for juveniles;

(viii) if appropriate, the special arrangements for mentally disordered or otherwise mentally vulnerable people;

(ix) that if they significantly alter their appearance between being offered an identification procedure and any attempt to hold an identification procedure, this may be given in evidence if the case comes to trial, and the identification officer may then consider other forms of identification, see *paragraph 3.21* and *Note 3C*;

(x)   that a moving image or photograph may be taken of them when they attend for any identification procedure;

(xi)   whether, before their identity became known, the witness was shown photographs, a computerised or artist's composite likeness or similar likeness or image by the police; see *Note 3B*

(xii) that if they change their appearance before an identification parade, it may not be practicable to arrange one on the day or subsequently and, because of the appearance change, the identification officer may consider alternative methods of identification; see *Note 3C*

(xiii) that they or their solicitor will be provided with details of the description of them as first given by any witnesses who are to attend the video identification, identification parade, group identification or confrontation, see *paragraph 3.1*.

3.18   This information must also be recorded in a written notice handed to the suspect. The suspect must be given a reasonable opportunity to read the notice, after which, they should be asked to sign a second copy to indicate if they are willing to co-operate with the making of a video or take part in the identification parade or group identification. The signed copy shall be retained by the identification officer.

3.19   The duties of the identification officer under *paragraphs 3.17* and *3.18* may be performed by the custody officer or other officer not involved in the investigation if:

(a) it is proposed to hold an identification procedure at a later date, e.g., if the suspect is to be bailed to attend an identification parade; and

(b) an inspector is not available to act as the identification officer, see *paragraph 3.11*, before the suspect leaves the station.

The officer concerned shall inform the identification officer of the action taken and give them the signed copy of the notice. See *Note 3C*

3.20   If the identification officer and officer in charge of the investigation suspect, on reasonable grounds that if the suspect was given the information and notice as in *paragraphs 3.17* and *3.18*, they would then take steps to avoid being seen by a witness in any identification procedure, the identification officer may arrange for images of the suspect suitable for use in a video identification procedure to be obtained before giving the information and notice. If suspect's images are obtained in these circumstances, the suspect may, for the purposes of a video identification procedure, co-operate in providing suitable new images to be used instead, see *paragraph 3.17(vi)*.

(c) Cases when the suspect is known but not available

3.21   When a known suspect is not available or has ceased to be available, see *paragraph 3.4*, the identification officer may make arrangements for a video identification (see Annex A). If necessary, the identification officer may follow the video identification procedures but using **still** images. Any suitable moving or still images may be used and these may be obtained covertly if necessary. Alternatively, the identification officer may make arrangements for a group identification. See *Note 3D*. These provisions may also be applied to juveniles where the consent of their parent or guardian is either refused or reasonable efforts to obtain that consent have failed (see *paragraph 2.12*).

3.22   Any covert activity should be strictly limited to that necessary to test the ability of the witness to identify the suspect.

3.23   The identification officer may arrange for the suspect to be confronted by the witness if none of the options referred to in paragraphs 3.5 to 3.10 or 3.21 are practicable. A 'confrontation' is when the suspect is directly confronted by the witness. A confrontation does not require the suspect's consent. Confrontations must be carried out in accordance with Annex D.

3.24   Requirements for information to be given to, or sought from, a suspect or for the suspect to be given an opportunity to view images before they are shown to a witness, do not apply if the suspect's lack of co-operation prevents the necessary action.

(d)   Documentation

3.25   A record shall be made of the video identification, identification parade, group identification or confrontation on forms provided for the purpose.

3.26   If the identification officer considers it is not practicable to hold a video identification or identification parade requested by the suspect, the reasons shall be recorded and explained to the suspect.

3.27   A record shall be made of a person's failure or refusal to co-operate in a video identification, identification parade or group identification and, if applicable, of the grounds for obtaining images in accordance with *paragraph 3.20*.

(e)   Showing films and photographs of incidents and information released to the media

3.28   Nothing in this Code inhibits showing films or photographs to the public through the national or local media, or to police officers for the purposes of recognition and tracing suspects. However, when such material is shown to potential witnesses, including police officers, see *Note 3A*, to obtain identification evidence, it shall be shown on an individual basis to avoid any possibility of collusion, and, as far as possible, the showing shall follow the principles for video identification if the suspect is known, see *Annex A*, or identification by photographs if the suspect is not known, see *Annex E*.

3.29   When a broadcast or publication is made, see *paragraph 3.28*, a copy of the relevant material released to the media for the purposes of recognising or tracing the suspect, shall be kept. The suspect or their solicitor shall be allowed to view such material before any procedures under *paragraphs 3.5* to *3.10, 3.21* or *3.23* are carried out, provided it is practicable and would not unreasonably delay the investigation. Each witness involved in the procedure shall be asked, after they have taken part, whether they have seen any broadcast or published films or photographs relating to the offence or any description of the suspect and their replies shall be recorded. This paragraph does not affect any separate requirement under the Criminal Procedure and Investigations Act 1996 to retain material in connection with criminal investigations.

(f)   Destruction and retention of photographs and images taken or used in identification procedures

3.30   PACE, section 64A, provides powers to take photographs of suspects detained at police stations and allows these photographs to be used or disclosed only for purposes related to the prevention or detection of crime, the investigation of offences or the conduct of prosecutions by, or on behalf of, police or other law enforcement and prosecuting authorities inside and outside the United Kingdom. After being so used or disclosed, they may be retained but can only be used or disclosed for the same purposes.

3.31   Subject to *paragraph 3.33*, the photographs (and all negatives and copies), of suspects not detained and any moving images, (and copies), of suspects whether or not they have been detained which are taken for the purposes of, or in connection with, the identification procedures in *paragraphs 3.5* to *3.10, 3.21* or *3.23* must be destroyed unless the suspect:

(a) is charged with, or informed they may be prosecuted for, a recordable offence;

(b) is prosecuted for a recordable offence;

(c) is cautioned for a recordable offence or given a warning or reprimand in accordance with the Crime and Disorder Act 1998 for a recordable offence; or

(d) gives informed consent, in writing, for the photograph or images to be retained for purposes described in *paragraph 3.30*.

3.32   When *paragraph 3.31* requires the destruction of any photograph or images, the person must be given an opportunity to witness the destruction or to have a certificate confirming the destruction if they request one within five days of being informed that the destruction is required.

3.33   Nothing in *paragraph 3.31* affects any separate requirement under the Criminal Procedure and Investigations Act 1996 to retain material in connection with criminal investigations.

Notes for guidance

3A   Except for the provisions of Annex E, paragraph 1, a police officer who is a witness for the purposes of this part of the Code is subject to the same principles and procedures as a civilian witness.

3B   When a witness attending an identification procedure has previously been shown photographs, or been shown or provided with computerised or artist's composite likeness, or similar likenesses or pictures, it is the officer in charge of the investigation's responsibility to make the identification officer aware of this.

3C   The purpose of paragraph 3.19 is to avoid or reduce delay in arranging identification procedures by enabling the required information and warnings, see sub-paragraphs 3.17(ix) and 3.17(xii), to be given at the earliest opportunity.

3D   Paragraph 3.21 would apply when a known suspect deliberately makes themself 'unavailable' in order to delay or frustrate arrangements for obtaining identification evidence. It also applies when a suspect refuses or fails to take part in a video identification, an identification parade or a group identification, or refuses or fails to take part in the only practicable options from that list. It enables any suitable images of the suspect, moving or still, which are available or can be obtained, to be used in an identification procedure.

3E   When it is proposed to show photographs to a witness in accordance with Annex E, it is the responsibility of the officer in charge of the investigation to confirm to the officer responsible for supervising and directing the showing, that the first description of the suspect given by that witness has been recorded. If this description has not been recorded, the procedure under Annex E must be postponed. See Annex E paragraph 2.

3F   The admissibility and value of identification evidence obtained when carrying out the procedure under paragraph 3.2 may be compromised if:

(a) before a person is identified, the witness' attention is specifically drawn to that person; or

(b) the suspect's identity becomes known before the procedure.

4   Identification by fingerprints

(A)   Taking fingerprints in connection with a criminal investigation

(a) General

4.1   References to 'fingerprints' means any record, produced by any method, of the skin pattern and other physical characteristics or features of a person's:

(i) fingers; or

(ii) palms.

(b)   Action

4.2   A person's fingerprints may be taken in connection with the investigation of an offence only with their consent or if *paragraph 4.3* applies. If the person is at a police station consent must be in writing.

4.3   PACE, section 61, provides powers to take fingerprints without consent from any person over the age of ten years:

(a) under section 61(3)(a), from a detainee at a police station if authorised by an officer of at least inspector rank who has reasonable grounds for suspecting that person is involved in a criminal offence and for believing their fingerprints will tend to confirm or disprove involvement, or assist in establishing their identity (including showing that they are not a particular person), or both. However, authority may not be given solely to establish the person's identity unless they have refused to identify themselves or the authorising officer has reasonable grounds to suspect the person is not who they claim to be.

(b) under section 61(3)(b), from a detainee at a police station who has been charged with a recordable offence, see *Note 4A*, or informed they will be reported for such an offence if, in the course of the investigation of that offence:

    (i) they have not had their fingerprints taken; or

    (ii) the fingerprints taken do not constitute a complete set of their fingerprints or some, or all, of the fingerprints are not of sufficient quality to allow satisfactory analysis, comparison or matching;

(c) under section 61(4A), from a person who has been bailed to appear at a court or police station if the person:

    (i) has answered to bail for a person whose fingerprints were taken previously and there are reasonable grounds for believing they are not the same person; or

    (ii) who has answered to bail claims to be a different person from a person whose fingerprints were previously taken;

and in either case, the court or an officer of inspector rank or above, authorises the fingerprints to be taken at the court or police station;

(d) under section 61(6), from a person who has been:

    (i) convicted of a recordable offence;

    (ii) given a caution in respect of a recordable offence which, at the time of the caution, the person admitted; or

    (iii) warned or reprimanded under the Crime and Disorder Act 1998, section 65, for a recordable offence.

4.4   PACE, section 27, provides power to:

(a) require the person as in *paragraph 4.3(d)* to attend a police station to have their fingerprints taken if the:

    (i) person has not been in police detention for the offence and has not had their fingerprints taken in the course of the investigation of that offence; or

    (ii) fingerprints that were taken from the person in the course of the investigation of that offence, do not constitute a complete set or some, or all, of the fingerprints are not of sufficient quality to allow satisfactory analysis, comparison or matching; and

(b) arrest, without warrant, a person who fails to comply with the requirement.

Note: The requirement must be made within one month of the date the person is convicted, cautioned, warned or reprimanded and the person must be given a period of at least 7 days within which to attend. This 7 day period need not fall during the month allowed for making the requirement.

4.5   A person's fingerprints may be taken, as above, electronically.

4.6   Reasonable force may be used, if necessary, to take a person's fingerprints without their consent under the powers as in *paragraphs 4.3* and *4.4*.

4.7   Before any fingerprints are taken with, or without, consent as above, the person must be informed:

(a) of the reason their fingerprints are to be taken;

(b) of the grounds on which the relevant authority has been given if the powers mentioned in *paragraph 4.3(a)* or *(c)* apply;

(c) that their fingerprints may be retained and may be subject of a speculative search against other fingerprints, see *Note 4B*, unless destruction of the fingerprints is required in accordance with *Annex F, Part (a)*; and

(d) that if their fingerprints are required to be destroyed, they may witness their destruction as provided for in *Annex F, Part (a)*.

(c)   Documentation

4.8   A record must be made as soon as possible, of the reason for taking a person's fingerprints without consent. If force is used, a record shall be made of the circumstances and those present.

4.9   A record shall be made when a person has been informed under the terms of *paragraph 4.7(c)*, of the possibility that their fingerprints may be subject of a speculative search.

(B)   Taking fingerprints in connection with immigration enquiries

Action

4.10   A person's fingerprints may be taken for the purposes of Immigration Service enquiries in accordance with powers and procedures other than under PACE and for which the Immigration Service (not the police) are responsible, only with the person's consent in writing or if *paragraph 4.11* applies.

4.11   Powers to take fingerprints for these purposes without consent are given to police and immigration officers under the:

(a)   Immigration Act 1971, Schedule 2, paragraph 18(2), when it is reasonably necessary for the purposes of identifying a person detained under the Immigration Act 1971, Schedule 2, paragraph 16 (Detention of person liable to examination or removal);

(b)   Immigration and Asylum Act 1999, section 141(7)(a), from a person who fails to produce, on arrival, a valid passport with a photograph or some other document satisfactorily establishing their identity and nationality if an immigration officer does not consider the person has a reasonable excuse for the failure;

(c)   Immigration and Asylum Act 1999, section 141(7)(b), from a person who has been refused entry to the UK but has been temporarily admitted if an immigration officer reasonably suspects the person might break a condition imposed on them relating to residence or reporting to a police or immigration officer, and their decision is confirmed by a chief immigration officer;

(d)   Immigration and Asylum Act 1999, section 141(7)(c), when directions are given to remove a person:
   • as an illegal entrant,
   • liable to removal under the Immigration and Asylum Act 1999, section 10,
   • who is the subject of a deportation order from the UK;

(e)   Immigration and Asylum Act 1999, section 141(7)(d), from a person arrested under UK immigration laws under the Immigration Act 1971, Schedule 2, paragraph 17;

(f)   Immigration and Asylum Act 1999, section 141(7)(e), from a person who has made a claim:
   • for asylum
   • under Article 3 of the European Convention on Human Rights; or

(g)   Immigration and Asylum Act 1999, section 141(7)(f), from a person who is a dependant of someone who falls into (b) to (f) above.

4.12   The Immigration and Asylum Act 1999, section 142(3), gives a police and immigration officer power to arrest, without warrant, a person who fails to comply with a requirement imposed by the Secretary of State to attend a specified place for fingerprinting.

4.13   Before any fingerprints are taken, with or without consent, the person must be informed:

(a)   of the reason their fingerprints are to be taken;

(b)   the fingerprints, and all copies of them, will be destroyed in accordance with *Annex F, Part B*.

4.14   Reasonable force may be used, if necessary, to take a person's fingerprints without their consent under powers as in *paragraph 4.11*.

4.15   *Paragraphs 4.1* and *4.8* apply.

Notes for guidance

4A   References to 'recordable offences' in this Code relate to those offences for which convictions, cautions, reprimands and warnings may be recorded in national police records. See PACE, section 27(4). The recordable offences current at the time when this Code was prepared, are any offences which carry a sentence of imprisonment on conviction (irrespective of the period, or the age of the offender or actual sentence passed) as well as the non-imprisonable offences under the Street Offences Act 1959, section 1 (loitering or soliciting for purposes of prostitution), the Telecommunications Act 1984, section 43 (improper use of public telecommunications systems), the Road Traffic Act 1988, section 25 (tampering with motor vehicles), the Malicious Communications Act 1988, section 1 (sending letters, etc. with intent to cause distress or anxiety) and others listed in the National Police Records (Recordable Offences) Regulations 2000.

4B Fingerprints or a DNA sample (and the information derived from it) taken from a person arrested on suspicion of being involved in a recordable offence, or charged with such an offence, or informed they will be reported for such an offence, may be subject of a speculative search. This means the fingerprints or DNA sample may be checked against other fingerprints and DNA records held by, or on behalf of, the police and other law enforcement authorities in, or outside, the UK, or held in connection with, or as a result of, an investigation of an offence inside or outside the UK. Fingerprints and samples taken from a person suspected of committing a recordable offence but not arrested, charged or informed they will be reported for it, may be subject to a speculative search only if the person consents in writing. The following is an example of a basic form of words:

> *"I consent to my fingerprints and DNA sample and information derived from it being retained and used only for purposes related to the prevention and detection of a crime, the investigation of an offence or the conduct of a prosecution either nationally or internationally.*
>
> *I understand that my fingerprints or this sample may be checked against other fingerprint and DNA records held by or on behalf of relevant law enforcement authorities, either nationally or internationally.*
>
> *I understand that once I have given my consent for the sample to be retained and used I cannot withdraw this consent."*

See Annex F regarding the retention and use of fingerprints taken with consent for elimination purposes.

5   Examinations to establish identity and the taking of photographs

(A)   Detainees at police stations

(a)   Searching or examination of detainees at police stations

5.1 PACE, section 54A (1), allows a detainee at a police station to be searched or examined or both, to establish:

(a) whether they have any marks, features or injuries that would tend to identify them as a person involved in the commission of an offence and to photograph any identifying marks, see *paragraph 5.5*; or

(b) their identity, see *Note 5A*.

A person detained at a police station to be searched under a stop and search power, see Code A, is not a detainee for the purposes of these powers.

5.2   A search and/or examination to find marks under section 54A (1) (a) may be carried out without the detainee's consent, see *paragraph 2.12*, only if authorised by an officer of at least inspector rank when consent has been withheld or it is not practicable to obtain consent, see *Note 5D*.

5.3   A search or examination to establish a suspect's identity under section 54A (1) (b) may be carried out without the detainee's consent, see *paragraph 2.12*, only if authorised by an officer of at least inspector rank when the detainee has refused to identify themselves or the authorising officer has reasonable grounds for suspecting the person is not who they claim to be.

5.4   Any marks that assist in establishing the detainee's identity, or their identification as a person involved in the commission of an offence, are identifying marks. Such marks may be photographed with the detainee's consent, see *paragraph 2.12*; or without their consent if it is withheld or it is not practicable to obtain it, see *Note 5D*.

5.5   A detainee may only be searched, examined and photographed under section 54A, by a police officer of the same sex.

5.6   Any photographs of identifying marks, taken under section 54A, may be used or disclosed only for purposes related to the prevention or detection of crime, the investigation of offences or the conduct of prosecutions by, or on behalf of, police or other law enforcement and prosecuting authorities inside, and outside, the UK. After being so used or disclosed, the photograph may be retained but must not be used or disclosed except for these purposes, see *Note 5B*.

5.7   The powers, as in *paragraph 5.1*, do not affect any separate requirement under the Criminal Procedure and Investigations Act 1996 to retain material in connection with criminal investigations.

5.8   Authority for the search and/or examination for the purposes of *paragraphs 5.2* and *5.3* may be given orally or in writing. If given orally, the authorising officer must confirm it in writing as soon as practicable. A separate authority is required for each purpose which applies.

5.9   If it is established a person is unwilling to co-operate sufficiently to enable a search and/or examination to take place or a suitable photograph to be taken, an officer may use reasonable force to:

(a)   search and/or examine a detainee without their consent; and

(b)   photograph any identifying marks without their consent.

5.10   The thoroughness and extent of any search or examination carried out in accordance with the powers in section 54A must be no more than the officer considers necessary to achieve the required purpose. Any search or examination which involves the removal of more than the person's outer clothing shall be conducted in accordance with Code C, Annex A, paragraph 11.

5.11   An intimate search may not be carried out under the powers in section 54A.

(b)   Photographing detainees at police stations

5.12   Under PACE, section 64A, an officer may photograph a detainee at a police station:

(a)   with their consent; or

(b)   without their consent if it is:
 (i)   withheld; or
 (ii)   not practicable to obtain their consent.

See *Note 5E*

and *paragraph 5.6* applies to the retention and use of photographs taken under this section as it applies to the retention and use of photographs taken under section 54A, see *Note 5B*.

5.13   The officer proposing to take a detainee's photograph may, for this purpose, require the person to remove any item or substance worn on, or over, all, or any part of, their head or face. If they do not comply with such a requirement, the officer may remove the item or substance.

5.14   If it is established the detainee is unwilling to co-operate sufficiently to enable a suitable photograph to be taken and it is not reasonably practicable to take the photograph covertly, an officer may use reasonable force:

(a)   to take their photograph without their consent; and

(b)   for the purpose of taking the photograph, remove any item or substance worn on, or over, all, or any part of, the person's head or face which they have failed to remove when asked.

5.15   For the purposes of this Code, a photograph may be obtained without the person's consent by making a copy of an image of them taken at any time on a camera system installed anywhere in the police station.

(c)   Information to be given

5.16   When a person is searched, examined or photographed under the provisions as in *paragraph 5.1* and *5.12*, or their photograph obtained as in *paragraph 5.15*, they must be informed of the:

(a)   purpose of the search, examination or photograph;

(b)   grounds on which the relevant authority, if applicable, has been given; and

(c)   purposes for which the photograph may be used, disclosed or retained.

This information must be given before the search or examination commences or the photograph is taken, except if the photograph is:

    (i) to be taken covertly;

    (ii) obtained as in *paragraph 5.15*, in which case the person must be informed as soon as practicable after the photograph is taken or obtained.

(d) Documentation

5.17   A record must be made when a detainee is searched, examined, or a photograph of the person, or any identifying marks found on them, are taken. The record must include the:

    (a) identity, subject to paragraph 2.18, of the officer carrying out the search, examination or taking the photograph;

    (b) purpose of the search, examination or photograph and the outcome;

    (c) detainee's consent to the search, examination or photograph, or the reason the person was searched, examined or photographed without consent;

    (d) giving of any authority as in *paragraphs 5.2* and *5.3*, the grounds for giving it and the authorising officer.

5.18   If force is used when searching, examining or taking a photograph in accordance with this section, a record shall be made of the circumstances and those present.

(B) Persons at police stations not detained

5.19   When there are reasonable grounds for suspecting the involvement of a person in a criminal offence, but that person is at a police station **voluntarily** and not detained, the provisions of *paragraphs 5.1* to *5.18* should apply, subject to the modifications in the following paragraphs.

5.20   References to the 'person being detained' and to the powers mentioned in *paragraph 5.1* which apply only to detainees at police stations shall be omitted.

5.21   Force may not be used to:

    (a) search and/or examine the person to:

        (i) discover whether they have any marks that would tend to identify them as a person involved in the commission of an offence; or

        (ii) establish their identity, see *Note 5A*;

    (b) take photographs of any identifying marks, see *paragraph 5.4*; or

    (c) take a photograph of the person.

5.22   Subject to *paragraph 5.24*, the photographs or images, of persons not detained, or of their identifying marks, must be destroyed (together with any negatives and copies) unless the person:

    (a) is charged with, or informed they may be prosecuted for, a recordable offence;

    (b) is prosecuted for a recordable offence;

    (c) is cautioned for a recordable offence or given a warning or reprimand in accordance with the Crime and Disorder Act 1998 for a recordable offence; or

    (d) gives informed consent, in writing, for the photograph or image to be retained as in *paragraph 5.6*.

5.23   When *paragraph 5.22* requires the destruction of any photograph or image, the person must be given an opportunity to witness the destruction or to have a certificate confirming the destruction provided they so request the certificate within five days of being informed the destruction is required.

5.24   Nothing in *paragraph 5.22* affects any separate requirement under the Criminal Procedure and Investigations Act 1996 to retain material in connection with criminal investigations.

Notes for guidance

5A   The conditions under which fingerprints may be taken to assist in establishing a person's identity, are described in Section 4.

5B   Examples of purposes related to the prevention or detection of crime, the investigation of offences or the conduct of prosecutions include:

(a) *checking the photograph against other photographs held in records or in connection with, or as a result of, an investigation of an offence to establish whether the person is liable to arrest for other offences;*

(b) *when the person is arrested at the same time as other people, or at a time when it is likely that other people will be arrested, using the photograph to help establish who was arrested, at what time and where;*

(c) *when the real identity of the person is not known and cannot be readily ascertained or there are reasonable grounds for doubting a name and other personal details given by the person, are their real name and personal details. In these circumstances, using or disclosing the photograph to help to establish or verify their real identity or determine whether they are liable to arrest for some other offence, e.g. by checking it against other photographs held in records or in connection with, or as a result of, an investigation of an offence;*

(d) *when it appears any identification procedure in section 3 may need to be arranged for which the person's photograph would assist;*

(e) *when the person's release without charge may be required, and if the release is:*
  (i) *on bail to appear at a police station, using the photograph to help verify the person's identity when they answer their bail and if the person does not answer their bail, to assist in arresting them; or*
  (ii) *without bail, using the photograph to help verify their identity or assist in locating them for the purposes of serving them with a summons to appear at court in criminal proceedings;*

(f) *when the person has answered to bail at a police station and there are reasonable grounds for doubting they are the person who was previously granted bail, using the photograph to help establish or verify their identity;*

(g) *when the person arrested on a warrant claims to be a different person from the person named on the warrant and a photograph would help to confirm or disprove their claim;*

(h) *when the person has been charged with, reported for, or convicted of, a recordable offence and their photograph is not already on record as a result of (a) to (f) or their photograph is on record but their appearance has changed since it was taken and the person has not yet been released or brought before a court.*

5C   There is no power to arrest a person convicted of a recordable offence solely to take their photograph. The power to take photographs in this section applies only where the person is in custody as a result of the exercise of another power, e.g. arrest for fingerprinting under PACE, section 27.

5D   Examples of when it would not be practicable to obtain a detainee's consent, see paragraph 2.12, to a search, examination or the taking of a photograph of an identifying mark include:

(a) *when the person is drunk or otherwise unfit to give consent;*

(b) *when there are reasonable grounds to suspect that if the person became aware a search or examination was to take place or an identifying mark was to be photographed, they would take steps to prevent this happening, e.g. by violently resisting, covering or concealing the mark etc and it would not otherwise be possible to carry out the search or examination or to photograph any identifying mark;*

(c) *in the case of a juvenile, if the parent or guardian cannot be contacted in sufficient time to allow the search or examination to be carried out or the photograph to be taken.*

5E   Examples of when it would not be practicable to obtain the person's consent, see paragraph 2.12, to a photograph being taken include:

(a) *when the person is drunk or otherwise unfit to give consent;*

(b) *when there are reasonable grounds to suspect that if the person became aware a photograph, suitable to be used or disclosed for the use and disclosure described in paragraph 5.6, was to be taken, they would take steps to prevent it being taken, e.g. by violently resisting, covering or distorting their face etc, and it would not otherwise be possible to take a suitable photograph;*

(c) when, in order to obtain a suitable photograph, it is necessary to take it covertly; and

(d) in the case of a juvenile, if the parent or guardian cannot be contacted in sufficient time to allow the photograph to be taken.

6 Identification by body samples and impressions

(A) General

6.1 References to:

(a) an 'intimate sample' mean a dental impression or sample of blood, semen or any other tissue fluid, urine, or pubic hair, or a swab taken from a person's body orifice other than the mouth;

(b) a 'non-intimate sample' means:
  (i) a sample of hair, other than pubic hair, which includes hair plucked with the root, see *Note 6A*;
  (ii) a sample taken from a nail or from under a nail;
  (iii) a swab taken from any part of a person's body including the mouth but not any other body orifice;
  (iv) saliva;
  (v) a skin impression which means any record, other than a fingerprint, which is a record, in any form and produced by any method, of the skin pattern and other physical characteristics or features of the whole, or any part of, a person's foot or of any other part of their body.

(B) Action

(a) Intimate samples

6.2 PACE, section 62, provides that intimate samples may be taken under:

(a) section 62(1), from a person in police detention only:
  (i) if a police officer of inspector rank or above has reasonable grounds to believe such an impression or sample will tend to confirm or disprove the suspect's involvement in a recordable offence, see *Note 4A*, and gives authorisation for a sample to be taken; and
  (ii) with the suspect's written consent;

(b) section 62(1A), from a person not in police detention but from whom two or more non-intimate samples have been taken in the course of an investigation of an offence and the samples, though suitable, have proved insufficient if:
  (i) a police officer of inspector rank or above authorises it to be taken; and
  (ii) the person concerned gives their written consent. See *Notes 6B* and *6C*

6.3 Before a suspect is asked to provide an intimate sample, they must be warned that if they refuse without good cause, their refusal may harm their case if it comes to trial, see *Note 6D*. If the suspect is in police detention and not legally represented, they must also be reminded of their entitlement to have free legal advice, see Code C, *paragraph 6.5*, and the reminder noted in the custody record. If *paragraph 6.2(b)* applies and the person is attending a station voluntarily, their entitlement to free legal advice as in Code C, *paragraph 3.21* shall be explained to them.

6.4 Dental impressions may only be taken by a registered dentist. Other intimate samples, except for samples of urine, may only be taken by a registered medical practitioner or registered health care professional.

(b)   Non-intimate samples

6.5   A non-intimate sample may be taken from a detainee only with their written consent or if *paragraph 6.6* applies.

6.6   A non-intimate sample may be taken from a person without consent in accordance with PACE. The principal circumstances provided for are as follows:

(a)   under section 63(3), from a person in police detention, or police custody on the authority of a court, if a police officer of inspector rank or above has reasonable grounds to believe the sample will tend to confirm or disprove the suspect's involvement in a recordable offence, see *Note 4A*, and gives authorisation for a sample to be taken. However, the officer may not give authorisation to take a non-intimate sample consisting of a skin impression if a skin impression of the same part of the body has already been taken from that person in the course of the investigation of the offence and the impression previously taken is not one that has proved insufficient;

(b)   under section 63(3A), from a person charged with a recordable offence or informed they will be reported for such an offence: and
  (i)   that person has not had a non-intimate sample taken from them in the course of the investigation; or
  (ii)   if they have had a sample taken, it proved unsuitable or insufficient for the same form of analysis, see *Note 6B*; or

(c)   under section 63(3B), from a person convicted of a recordable offence after the date on which that provision came into effect. PACE, section 63A, describes the circumstances in which a police officer may require a person convicted of a recordable offence to attend a police station for a non-intimate sample to be taken.

6.7   Reasonable force may be used, if necessary, to take a non-intimate sample from a person without their consent under the powers mentioned in *paragraph 6.6*.

6.8   Before any intimate sample is taken with consent or non-intimate sample is taken with, or without, consent, the person must be informed:

(a)   of the reason for taking the sample;

(b)   of the grounds on which the relevant authority has been given, including, if appropriate, the nature of the suspected offence;

(c)   that the sample or information derived from the sample may be retained and subject of a speculative search, see *Note 6E*, unless their destruction is required as in *Annex F*, Part A.

6.9   When clothing needs to be removed in circumstances likely to cause embarrassment to the person, no person of the opposite sex who is not a registered medical practitioner or registered health care professional shall be present, (unless in the case of a juvenile, mentally disordered or mentally vulnerable person, that person specifically requests the presence of an appropriate adult of the opposite sex who is readily available) nor shall anyone whose presence is unnecessary. However, in the case of a juvenile, this is subject to the overriding proviso that such a removal of clothing may take place in the absence of the appropriate adult only if the juvenile signifies, in their presence, that they prefer the adult's absence and they agree.

(c)   Documentation

6.10   A record of the reasons for taking a sample or impression and, if applicable, of its destruction must be made as soon as practicable. If force is used, a record shall be made of the circumstances and those present. If written consent is given to the taking of a sample or impression, the fact must be recorded in writing.

6.11   A record must be made of a warning given as required by *paragraph 6.3*.

6.12   A record shall be made of the fact that a person has been informed as in *paragraph 6.8(c)* that samples may be subject of a speculative search.

Notes for guidance

6A   When hair samples are taken for the purpose of DNA analysis (rather than for other purposes such as making a visual match), the suspect should be permitted a reasonable choice as to what part of the body the hairs are taken from. When hairs are plucked, they should be plucked individually, unless the suspect prefers otherwise and no more should be plucked than the person taking them reasonably considers necessary for a sufficient sample.

6B (a)   An insufficient sample is one which is not sufficient either in quantity or quality to provide information for a particular form of analysis, such as DNA analysis. A sample may also be insufficient if enough information cannot be obtained from it by analysis because of loss, destruction, damage or contamination of the sample or as a result of an earlier, unsuccessful attempt at analysis.

(b)   An unsuitable sample is one which, by its nature, is not suitable for a particular form of analysis.

6C   Nothing in paragraph 6.2 prevents intimate samples being taken for elimination purposes with the consent of the person concerned but the provisions of paragraph 2.12 relating to the role of the appropriate adult, should be applied. Paragraph 6.2(b) does not, however, apply where the non-intimate samples were previously taken under the Terrorism Act 2000, Schedule 8, paragraph 10.

6D   In warning a person who is asked to provide an intimate sample as in paragraph 6.3, the following form of words may be used:

"You do not have to provide this sample/allow this swab or impression to be taken, but I must warn you that if you refuse without good cause, your refusal may harm your case if it comes to trial."

6E   Fingerprints or a DNA sample and the information derived from it taken from a person arrested on suspicion of being involved in a recordable offence, or charged with such an offence, or informed they will be reported for such an offence, may be subject of a speculative search. This means they may be checked against other fingerprints and DNA records held by, or on behalf of, the police and other law enforcement authorities in or outside the UK or held in connection with, or as a result of, an investigation of an offence inside or outside the UK. Fingerprints and samples taken from any other person, e.g. a person suspected of committing a recordable offence but who has not been arrested, charged or informed they will be reported for it, may be subject to a speculative search only if the person consents in writing to their fingerprints being subject of such a search. The following is an example of a basic form of words:

"I consent to my fingerprints/DNA sample and information derived from it being retained and used only for purposes related to the prevention and detection of a crime, the investigation of an offence or the conduct of a prosecution either nationally or internationally.

I understand that this sample may be checked against other fingerprint/DNA records held by or on behalf of relevant law enforcement authorities, either nationally or internationally.

I understand that once I have given my consent for the sample to be retained and used I cannot withdraw this consent."

See Annex F regarding the retention and use of fingerprints and samples taken with consent for elimination purposes.

ANNEX A—VIDEO IDENTIFICATION

(a)   General

1.   The arrangements for obtaining and ensuring the availability of a suitable set of images to be used in a video identification must be the responsibility of an identification officer, who has no direct involvement with the case.

2.   The set of images must include the suspect and at least eight other people who, so far as possible, resemble the suspect in age, height, general appearance and position in life. Only one suspect shall

appear in any set unless there are two suspects of roughly similar appearance, in which case they may be shown together with at least twelve other people.

3.   The images used to conduct a video identification shall, as far as possible, show the suspect and other people in the same positions or carrying out the same sequence of movements. They shall also show the suspect and other people under identical conditions unless the identification officer reasonably believes:

(a)   because of the suspect's failure or refusal to co-operate or other reasons, it is not practicable for the conditions to be identical; and

(b)   any difference in the conditions would not direct a witness' attention to any individual image.

4.   The reasons identical conditions are not practicable shall be recorded on forms provided for the purpose.

5.   Provision must be made for each person shown to be identified by number.

6.   If police officers are shown, any numerals or other identifying badges must be concealed. If a prison inmate is shown, either as a suspect or not, then either all, or none of, the people shown should be in prison clothing.

7.   The suspect or their solicitor, friend, or appropriate adult must be given a reasonable opportunity to see the complete set of images before it is shown to any witness. If the suspect has a reasonable objection to the set of images or any of the participants, the suspect shall be asked to state the reasons for the objection. Steps shall, if practicable, be taken to remove the grounds for objection. If this is not practicable, the suspect and/or their representative shall be told why their objections cannot be met and the objection, the reason given for it and why it cannot be met shall be recorded on forms provided for the purpose.

8.   Before the images are shown in accordance with *paragraph 7*, the suspect or their solicitor shall be provided with details of the first description of the suspect by any witnesses who are to attend the video identification. When a broadcast or publication is made, as in *paragraph 3.28*, the suspect or their solicitor must also be allowed to view any material released to the media by the police for the purpose of recognising or tracing the suspect, provided it is practicable and would not unreasonably delay the investigation.

9.   The suspect's solicitor, if practicable, shall be given reasonable notification of the time and place the video identification is to be conducted so a representative may attend on behalf of the suspect. If a solicitor has not been instructed, this information shall be given to the suspect. The suspect may not be present when the images are shown to the witness(es). In the absence of the suspect's representative, the viewing itself shall be recorded on video. No unauthorised people may be present.

(b)   Conducting the video identification

10.   The identification officer is responsible for making the appropriate arrangements to make sure, before they see the set of images, witnesses are not able to communicate with each other about the case or overhear a witness who has already seen the material. There must be no discussion with the witness about the composition of the set of images and they must not be told whether a previous witness has made any identification.

11.   Only one witness may see the set of images at a time. Immediately before the images are shown, the witness shall be told that the person they saw on a specified earlier occasion may, or may not, appear in the images they are shown and that if they cannot make a positive identification, they should say so. The witness shall be advised that at any point, they may ask to see a particular part of the set of images or to have a particular image frozen for them to study. Furthermore, it should be pointed out to the witness that there is no limit on how many times they can view the whole set of images or any part of them. However, they should be asked not to make any decision as to whether the person they saw is on the set of images until they have seen the whole set at least twice.

12.   Once the witness has seen the whole set of images at least twice and has indicated that they do not want to view the images, or any part of them, again, the witness shall be asked to say whether the individual they saw in person on a specified earlier occasion has been shown and, if so, to

identify them by number of the image. The witness will then be shown that image to confirm the identification, see *paragraph 17*.

13.   Care must be taken not to direct the witness' attention to any one individual image or give any indication of the suspect's identity. Where a witness has previously made an identification by photographs, or a computerised or artist's composite or similar likeness, the witness must not be reminded of such a photograph or composite likeness once a suspect is available for identification by other means in accordance with this Code. Nor must the witness be reminded of any description of the suspect.

14.   After the procedure, each witness shall be asked whether they have seen any broadcast or published films or photographs, or any descriptions of suspects relating to the offence and their reply shall be recorded.

(c)   **Image security and destruction**

15.   Arrangements shall be made for all relevant material containing sets of images used for specific identification procedures to be kept securely and their movements accounted for. In particular, no-one involved in the investigation shall be permitted to view the material prior to it being shown to any witness.

16.   As appropriate, *paragraph 3.30* or *3.31* applies to the destruction or retention of relevant sets of images.

(d)   **Documentation**

17.   A record must be made of all those participating in, or seeing, the set of images whose names are known to the police.

18.   A record of the conduct of the video identification must be made on forms provided for the purpose. This shall include anything said by the witness about any identifications or the conduct of the procedure and any reasons it was not practicable to comply with any of the provisions of this Code governing the conduct of video identifications.

ANNEX B—IDENTIFICATION PARADES

(a)   **General**

1.   A suspect must be given a reasonable opportunity to have a solicitor or friend present, and the suspect shall be asked to indicate on a second copy of the notice whether or not they wish to do so.

2.   An identification parade may take place either in a normal room or one equipped with a screen permitting witnesses to see members of the identification parade without being seen. The procedures for the composition and conduct of the identification parade are the same in both cases, subject to *paragraph 8* (except that an identification parade involving a screen may take place only when the suspect's solicitor, friend or appropriate adult is present or the identification parade is recorded on video).

3.   Before the identification parade takes place, the suspect or their solicitor shall be provided with details of the first description of the suspect by any witnesses who are attending the identification parade. When a broadcast or publication is made as in *paragraph 3.28*, the suspect or their solicitor should also be allowed to view any material released to the media by the police for the purpose of recognising or tracing the suspect, provided it is practicable to do so and would not unreasonably delay the investigation.

(b)   **Identification parades involving prison inmates**

4.   If a prison inmate is required for identification, and there are no security problems about the person leaving the establishment, they may be asked to participate in an identification parade or video identification.

5. An identification parade may be held in a Prison Department establishment but shall be conducted, as far as practicable under normal identification parade rules. Members of the public shall make up the identification parade unless there are serious security, or control, objections to their admission to the establishment. In such cases, or if a group or video identification is arranged within the establishment, other inmates may participate. If an inmate is the suspect, they are not required to wear prison clothing for the identification parade unless the other people taking part are other inmates in similar clothing, or are members of the public who are prepared to wear prison clothing for the occasion.

(c) Conduct of the identification parade

6. Immediately before the identification parade, the suspect must be reminded of the procedures governing its conduct and cautioned in the terms of Code C, paragraphs 10.5 or 10.6, as appropriate.

7. All unauthorised people must be excluded from the place where the identification parade is held.

8. Once the identification parade has been formed, everything afterwards, in respect of it, shall take place in the presence and hearing of the suspect and any interpreter, solicitor, friend or appropriate adult who is present (unless the identification parade involves a screen, in which case everything said to, or by, any witness at the place where the identification parade is held, must be said in the hearing and presence of the suspect's solicitor, friend or appropriate adult or be recorded on video).

9. The identification parade shall consist of at least eight people (in addition to the suspect) who, so far as possible, resemble the suspect in age, height, general appearance and position in life. Only one suspect shall be included in an identification parade unless there are two suspects of roughly similar appearance, in which case they may be paraded together with at least twelve other people. In no circumstances shall more than two suspects be included in one identification parade and where there are separate identification parades, they shall be made up of different people.

10. If the suspect has an unusual physical feature, e.g., a facial scar, tattoo or distinctive hairstyle or hair colour which cannot be replicated on other members of the identification parade, steps may be taken to conceal the location of that feature on the suspect and the other members of the identification parade if the suspect and their solicitor, or appropriate adult, agree. For example, by use of a plaster or a hat, so that all members of the identification parade resemble each other in general appearance.

11. When all members of a similar group are possible suspects, separate identification parades shall be held for each unless there are two suspects of similar appearance when they may appear on the same identification parade with at least twelve other members of the group who are not suspects. When police officers in uniform form an identification parade any numerals or other identifying badges shall be concealed.

12. When the suspect is brought to the place where the identification parade is to be held, they shall be asked if they have any objection to the arrangements for the identification parade or to any of the other participants in it and to state the reasons for the objection. The suspect may obtain advice from their solicitor or friend, if present, before the identification parade proceeds. If the suspect has a reasonable objection to the arrangements or any of the participants, steps shall, if practicable, be taken to remove the grounds for objection. When it is not practicable to do so, the suspect shall be told why their objections cannot be met and the objection, the reason given for it and why it cannot be met, shall be recorded on forms provided for the purpose.

13. The suspect may select their own position in the line, but may not otherwise interfere with the order of the people forming the line. When there is more than one witness, the suspect must be told, after each witness has left the room, that they can, if they wish, change position in the line. Each position in the line must be clearly numbered, whether by means of a number laid on the floor in front of each identification parade member or by other means.

14. Appropriate arrangements must be made to make sure, before witnesses attend the identification parade, they are not able to:

  (i)   communicate with each other about the case or overhear a witness who has already seen the identification parade;

  (ii) see any member of the identification parade;

  (iii) see, or be reminded of, any photograph or description of the suspect or be given any other indication as to the suspect's identity; or

  (iv) see the suspect before or after the identification parade.

15. The person conducting a witness to an identification parade must not discuss with them the composition of the identification parade and, in particular, must not disclose whether a previous witness has made any identification.

16. Witnesses shall be brought in one at a time. Immediately before the witness inspects the identification parade, they shall be told the person they saw on a specified earlier occasion may, or may not, be present and if they cannot make a positive identification, they should say so. The witness must also be told they should not make any decision about whether the person they saw is on the identification parade until they have looked at each member at least twice.

17. When the officer or civilian support staff (see paragraph 3.11) conducting the identification procedure is satisfied the witness has properly looked at each member of the identification parade, they shall ask the witness whether the person they saw on a specified earlier occasion is on the identification parade and, if so, to indicate the number of the person concerned, see *paragraph 28*.

18. If the witness wishes to hear any identification parade member speak, adopt any specified posture or move, they shall first be asked whether they can identify any person(s) on the identification parade on the basis of appearance only. When the request is to hear members of the identification parade speak, the witness shall be reminded that the participants in the identification parade have been chosen on the basis of physical appearance only. Members of the identification parade may then be asked to comply with the witness' request to hear them speak, see them move or adopt any specified posture.

19. If the witness requests that the person they have indicated remove anything used for the purposes of *paragraph 10* to conceal the location of an unusual physical feature, that person may be asked to remove it.

20. If the witness makes an identification after the identification parade has ended, the suspect and, if present, their solicitor, interpreter or friend shall be informed. When this occurs, consideration should be given to allowing the witness a second opportunity to identify the suspect.

21. After the procedure, each witness shall be asked whether they have seen any broadcast or published films or photographs or any descriptions of suspects relating to the offence and their reply shall be recorded.

22. When the last witness has left, the suspect shall be asked whether they wish to make any comments on the conduct of the identification parade.

(d) Documentation

23. A video recording must normally be taken of the identification parade. If that is impracticable, a colour photograph must be taken. A copy of the video recording or photograph shall be supplied, on request, to the suspect or their solicitor within a reasonable time.

24. As appropriate, *paragraph 3.30* or *3.31*, should apply to any photograph or video taken as in *paragraph 23*.

25. If any person is asked to leave an identification parade because they are interfering with its conduct, the circumstances shall be recorded.

26.   A record must be made of all those present at an identification parade whose names are known to the police.

27.   If prison inmates make up an identification parade, the circumstances must be recorded.

28.   A record of the conduct of any identification parade must be made on forms provided for the purpose. This shall include anything said by the witness or the suspect about any identifications or the conduct of the procedure, and any reasons it was not practicable to comply with any of this Code's provisions.

ANNEX C—GROUP IDENTIFICATION

(a)   General

1.   The purpose of this Annex is to make sure, as far as possible, group identifications follow the principles and procedures for identification parades so the conditions are fair to the suspect in the way they test the witness' ability to make an identification.

2.   Group identifications may take place either with the suspect's consent and co-operation or covertly without their consent.

3.   The location of the group identification is a matter for the identification officer, although the officer may take into account any representations made by the suspect, appropriate adult, their solicitor or friend.

4.   The place where the group identification is held should be one where other people are either passing by or waiting around informally, in groups such that the suspect is able to join them and be capable of being seen by the witness at the same time as others in the group. For example people leaving an escalator, pedestrians walking through a shopping centre, passengers on railway and bus stations, waiting in queues or groups or where people are standing or sitting in groups in other public places.

5.   If the group identification is to be held covertly, the choice of locations will be limited by the places where the suspect can be found and the number of other people present at that time. In these cases, suitable locations might be along regular routes travelled by the suspect, including buses or trains or public places frequented by the suspect.

6.   Although the number, age, sex, race and general description and style of clothing of other people present at the location cannot be controlled by the identification officer, in selecting the location the officer must consider the general appearance and numbers of people likely to be present. In particular, the officer must reasonably expect that over the period the witness observes the group, they will be able to see, from time to time, a number of others whose appearance is broadly similar to that of the suspect.

7.   A group identification need not be held if the identification officer believes, because of the unusual appearance of the suspect, none of the locations it would be practicable to use satisfy the requirements of *paragraph 6* necessary to make the identification fair.

8.   Immediately after a group identification procedure has taken place (with or without the suspect's consent), a colour photograph or video should be taken of the general scene, if practicable, to give a general impression of the scene and the number of people present. Alternatively, if it is practicable, the group identification may be video recorded.

9.   If it is not practicable to take the photograph or video in accordance with *paragraph 8*, a photograph or film of the scene should be taken later at a time determined by the identification officer if the officer considers it practicable to do so.

10.   An identification carried out in accordance with this Code remains a group identification even though, at the time of being seen by the witness, the suspect was on their own rather than in a group.

11.   Before the group identification takes place, the suspect or their solicitor shall be provided with details of the first description of the suspect by any witnesses who are to attend the identification. When a broadcast or publication is made, as in *paragraph 3.28*, the suspect or their solicitor should also be allowed to view any material released by the police to the media for the purposes of recognising or tracing the suspect, provided that it is practicable and would not unreasonably delay the investigation.

12.   After the procedure, each witness shall be asked whether they have seen any broadcast or published films or photographs or any descriptions of suspects relating to the offence and their reply recorded.

(b)   Identification with the consent of the suspect

13.   A suspect must be given a reasonable opportunity to have a solicitor or friend present. They shall be asked to indicate on a second copy of the notice whether or not they wish to do so.

14.   The witness, the person carrying out the procedure and the suspect's solicitor, appropriate adult, friend or any interpreter for the witness, may be concealed from the sight of the individuals in the group they are observing, if the person carrying out the procedure considers this assists the conduct of the identification.

15.   The person conducting a witness to a group identification must not discuss with them the forthcoming group identification and, in particular, must not disclose whether a previous witness has made any identification.

16.   Anything said to, or by, the witness during the procedure about the identification should be said in the presence and hearing of those present at the procedure.

17.   Appropriate arrangements must be made to make sure, before witnesses attend the group identification, they are not able to:

(i)   communicate with each other about the case or overhear a witness who has already been given an opportunity to see the suspect in the group;

(ii)   see the suspect; or

(iii)   see, or be reminded of, any photographs or description of the suspect or be given any other indication of the suspect's identity.

18.   Witnesses shall be brought one at a time to the place where they are to observe the group. Immediately before the witness is asked to look at the group, the person conducting the procedure shall tell them that the person they saw may, or may not, be in the group and that if they cannot make a positive identification, they should say so. The witness shall be asked to observe the group in which the suspect is to appear. The way in which the witness should do this will depend on whether the group is moving or stationary.

Moving group

19.   When the group in which the suspect is to appear is moving, e.g. leaving an escalator, the provisions of *paragraphs 20* to *24* should be followed.

20.   If two or more suspects consent to a group identification, each should be the subject of separate identification procedures. These may be conducted consecutively on the same occasion.

21.   The person conducting the procedure shall tell the witness to observe the group and ask them to point out any person they think they saw on the specified earlier occasion.

22.   Once the witness has been informed as in *paragraph 21* the suspect should be allowed to take whatever position in the group they wish.

23.   When the witness points out a person as in *paragraph 21* they shall, if practicable, be asked to take a closer look at the person to confirm the identification. If this is not practicable, or they cannot

confirm the identification, they shall be asked how sure they are that the person they have indicated is the relevant person.

24.   The witness should continue to observe the group for the period which the person conducting the procedure reasonably believes is necessary in the circumstances for them to be able to make comparisons between the suspect and other individuals of broadly similar appearance to the suspect as in *paragraph 6*.

Stationary groups

25.   When the group in which the suspect is to appear is stationary, e.g. people waiting in a queue, the provisions of *paragraphs 26* to *29* should be followed.

26.   If two or more suspects consent to a group identification, each should be subject to separate identification procedures unless they are of broadly similar appearance when they may appear in the same group. When separate group identifications are held, the groups must be made up of different people.

27.   The suspect may take whatever position in the group they wish. If there is more than one witness, the suspect must be told, out of the sight and hearing of any witness, that they can, if they wish, change their position in the group.

28.   The witness shall be asked to pass along, or amongst, the group and to look at each person in the group at least twice, taking as much care and time as possible according to the circumstances, before making an identification. Once the witness has done this, they shall be asked whether the person they saw on the specified earlier occasion is in the group and to indicate any such person by whatever means the person conducting the procedure considers appropriate in the circumstances. If this is not practicable, the witness shall be asked to point out any person they think they saw on the earlier occasion.

29.   When the witness makes an indication as in *paragraph 28*, arrangements shall be made, if practicable, for the witness to take a closer look at the person to confirm the identification. If this is not practicable, or the witness is unable to confirm the identification, they shall be asked how sure they are that the person they have indicated is the relevant person.

All cases

30.   If the suspect unreasonably delays joining the group, or having joined the group, deliberately conceals themselves from the sight of the witness, this may be treated as a refusal to co-operate in a group identification.

31.   If the witness identifies a person other than the suspect, that person should be informed what has happened and asked if they are prepared to give their name and address. There is no obligation upon any member of the public to give these details. There shall be no duty to record any details of any other member of the public present in the group or at the place where the procedure is conducted.

32.   When the group identification has been completed, the suspect shall be asked whether they wish to make any comments on the conduct of the procedure.

33.   If the suspect has not been previously informed, they shall be told of any identifications made by the witnesses.

(c)   Identification without the suspect's consent

34.   Group identifications held covertly without the suspect's consent should, as far as practicable, follow the rules for conduct of group identification by consent.

35.   A suspect has no right to have a solicitor, appropriate adult or friend present as the identification will take place without the knowledge of the suspect.

36.   Any number of suspects may be identified at the same time.

(d) Identifications in police stations

37. Group identifications should take place in police stations only for reasons of safety, security or because it is not practicable to hold them elsewhere.

38. The group identification may take place either in a room equipped with a screen permitting witnesses to see members of the group without being seen, or anywhere else in the police station that the identification officer considers appropriate.

39. Any of the additional safeguards applicable to identification parades should be followed if the identification officer considers it is practicable to do so in the circumstances.

(e) Identifications involving prison inmates

40. A group identification involving a prison inmate may only be arranged in the prison or at a police station.

41. When a group identification takes place involving a prison inmate, whether in a prison or in a police station, the arrangements should follow those in *paragraphs 37* to *39*. If a group identification takes place within a prison, other inmates may participate. If an inmate is the suspect, they do not have to wear prison clothing for the group identification unless the other participants are wearing the same clothing.

(f) Documentation

42. When a photograph or video is taken as in *paragraph 8* or *9*, a copy of the photograph or video shall be supplied on request to the suspect or their solicitor within a reasonable time.

43. *Paragraph 3.30* or *3.31*, as appropriate, shall apply when the photograph or film taken in accordance with *paragraph 8* or *9* includes the suspect.

44. A record of the conduct of any group identification must be made on forms provided for the purpose. This shall include anything said by the witness or suspect about any identifications or the conduct of the procedure and any reasons why it was not practicable to comply with any of the provisions of this Code governing the conduct of group identifications.

ANNEX D—CONFRONTATION BY A WITNESS

1. Before the confrontation takes place, the witness must be told that the person they saw may, or may not, be the person they are to confront and that if they are not that person, then the witness should say so.

2. Before the confrontation takes place the suspect or their solicitor shall be provided with details of the first description of the suspect given by any witness who is to attend. When a broadcast or publication is made, as in *paragraph 3.28*, the suspect or their solicitor should also be allowed to view any material released to the media for the purposes of recognising or tracing the suspect, provided it is practicable to do so and would not unreasonably delay the investigation.

3. Force may not be used to make the suspect's face visible to the witness.

4. Confrontation must take place in the presence of the suspect's solicitor, interpreter or friend unless this would cause unreasonable delay.

5. The suspect shall be confronted independently by each witness, who shall be asked "Is this the person?". If the witness identifies the person but is unable to confirm the identification, they shall be asked how sure they are that the person is the one they saw on the earlier occasion.

6. The confrontation should normally take place in the police station, either in a normal room or one equipped with a screen permitting a witness to see the suspect without being seen. In both cases, the procedures are the same except that a room equipped with a screen may be used only when the suspect's solicitor, friend or appropriate adult is present or the confrontation is recorded on video.

7.   After the procedure, each witness shall be asked whether they have seen any broadcast or published films or photographs or any descriptions of suspects relating to the offence and their reply shall be recorded.

ANNEX E—SHOWING PHOTOGRAPHS

(a) Action

1.   An officer of sergeant rank or above shall be responsible for supervising and directing the showing of photographs. The actual showing may be done by another officer or civilian support staff, see *paragraph 3.11*.

2. The supervising officer must confirm the first description of the suspect given by the witness has been recorded before they are shown the photographs. If the supervising officer is unable to confirm the description has been recorded they shall postpone showing the photographs.

3.   Only one witness shall be shown photographs at any one time. Each witness shall be given as much privacy as practicable and shall not be allowed to communicate with any other witness in the case.

4.   The witness shall be shown not less than twelve photographs at a time, which shall, as far as possible, all be of a similar type.

5.   When the witness is shown the photographs, they shall be told the photograph of the person they saw may, or may not, be amongst them and if they cannot make a positive identification, they should say so. The witness shall also be told they should not make a decision until they have viewed at least twelve photographs. The witness shall not be prompted or guided in any way but shall be left to make any selection without help.

6.   If a witness makes a positive identification from photographs, unless the person identified is otherwise eliminated from enquiries or is not available, other witnesses shall not be shown photographs. But both they, and the witness who has made the identification, shall be asked to attend a video identification, an identification parade or group identification unless there is no dispute about the suspect's identification.

7.   If the witness makes a selection but is unable to confirm the identification, the person showing the photographs shall ask them how sure they are that the photograph they have indicated is the person they saw on the specified earlier occasion.

8.   When the use of a computerised or artist's composite or similar likeness has led to there being a known suspect who can be asked to participate in a video identification, appear on an identification parade or participate in a group identification, that likeness shall not be shown to other potential witnesses.

9.   When a witness attending a video identification, an identification parade or group identification has previously been shown photographs or computerised or artist's composite or similar likeness (and it is the responsibility of the officer in charge of the investigation to make the identification officer aware that this is the case), the suspect and their solicitor must be informed of this fact before the identification procedure takes place.

10.   None of the photographs shown shall be destroyed, whether or not an identification is made, since they may be required for production in court. The photographs shall be numbered and a separate photograph taken of the frame or part of the album from which the witness made an identification as an aid to reconstituting it.

(b) Documentation

11.   Whether or not an identification is made, a record shall be kept of the showing of photographs on forms provided for the purpose. This shall include anything said by the witness about any identification or the conduct of the procedure, any reasons it was not practicable to comply with any of the provisions of this Code governing the showing of photographs and the name and rank of the supervising officer.

12.   The supervising officer shall inspect and sign the record as soon as practicable.

ANNEX F—FINGERPRINTS AND SAMPLES — DESTRUCTION AND SPECULATIVE SEARCHES

(a) Fingerprints and samples taken in connection with a criminal investigation

1. When fingerprints or DNA samples are taken from a person in connection with an investigation and the person is not suspected of having committed the offence, see *Note F1*, they must be destroyed as soon as they have fulfilled the purpose for which they were taken unless:

   (a) they were taken for the purposes of an investigation of an offence for which a person has been convicted; and

   (b) fingerprints or samples were also taken from the convicted person for the purposes of that investigation.

However, subject to *paragraph 2*, the fingerprints and samples, and the information derived from samples, may not be used in the investigation of any offence or in evidence against the person who is, or would be, entitled to the destruction of the fingerprints and samples, see *Note F2*.

2. The requirement to destroy fingerprints and DNA samples, and information derived from samples, and restrictions on their retention and use in *paragraph 1* do not apply if the person gives their written consent for their fingerprints or sample to be retained and used after they have fulfilled the purpose for which they were taken, see *Note F1*.

3. When a person's fingerprints or sample are to be destroyed:

   (a) any copies of the fingerprints must also be destroyed;

   (b) the person may witness the destruction of their fingerprints or copies if they ask to do so within five days of being informed destruction is required;

   (c) access to relevant computer fingerprint data shall be made impossible as soon as it is practicable to do so and the person shall be given a certificate to this effect within three months of asking; and

   (d) neither the fingerprints, the sample, or any information derived from the sample, may be used in the investigation of any offence or in evidence against the person who is, or would be, entitled to its destruction.

4. Fingerprints or samples, and the information derived from samples, taken in connection with the investigation of an offence which are not required to be destroyed, may be retained after they have fulfilled the purposes for which they were taken but may be used only for purposes related to the prevention or detection of crime, the investigation of an offence or the conduct of a prosecution in, as well as outside, the UK and may also be subject to a speculative search. This includes checking them against other fingerprints and DNA records held by, or on behalf of, the police and other law enforcement authorities in, as well as outside, the UK.

(b) Fingerprints taken in connection with Immigration Service enquiries

5. Fingerprints taken for Immigration Service enquiries in accordance with powers and procedures other than under PACE and for which the Immigration Service, not the police, are responsible, must be destroyed as follows:

   (a) fingerprints and all copies must be destroyed as soon as practicable if the person from whom they were taken proves they are a British or Commonwealth citizen who has the right of abode in the UK under the Immigration Act 1971, section 2(1)(b);

   (b) fingerprints taken under the power as in *paragraph 4.11(g)* from a dependant of a person in *4.11 (b)* to *(f)* must be destroyed when that person's fingerprints are to be destroyed;

   (c) fingerprints taken from a person under any power as in *paragraph 4.11* or with the person's consent which have not already been destroyed as above, must be destroyed within ten years of being taken or within such period specified by the Secretary of State under the Immigration and Asylum Act 1999, section 143(5).

Notes for guidance

F1   Fingerprints and samples given voluntarily for the purposes of elimination play an important part in many police investigations. It is, therefore, important to make sure innocent volunteers are not deterred from participating and their consent to their fingerprints and DNA being used for the purposes of a specific investigation is fully informed and voluntary. If the police or volunteer seek to have the sample or fingerprints retained for use after the specific investigation ends, it is important the volunteer's consent to this is also fully informed and voluntary.

Examples of consent for:

- *DNA/fingerprints - to be used only for the purposes of a specific investigation;*
- *DNA/fingerprints - to be used in the specific investigation **and** retained by the police for future use.*

*To minimise the risk of confusion, each consent should be physically separate and the volunteer should be asked to sign one or the other, **not both**.*

- *(a) DNA:*

  - *(i) DNA sample taken for the purposes of elimination or as part of an intelligence-led screen and to be used only for the purposes of that investigation and destroyed afterwards:*

    "I consent to my DNA/mouth swab being taken for forensic analysis. I understand that the sample will be destroyed at the end of the case and that my profile will only be compared to the crime stain profile from this enquiry. I have been advised that the person taking the sample may be required to give evidence and/or provide a written statement to the police in relation to the taking of it".

  - *(ii) DNA sample to be retained on the National DNA database and used in the future:*

    "I consent to my DNA sample and information derived from it being retained and used only for purposes related to the prevention and detection of a crime, the investigation of an offence or the conduct of a prosecution either nationally or internationally."

    "I understand that this sample may be checked against other DNA records held by, or on behalf of, relevant law enforcement authorities, either nationally or internationally".

    "I understand that once I have given my consent for the sample to be retained and used I cannot withdraw this consent."

- *(b) Fingerprints:*

  - *(i) Fingerprints taken for the purposes of elimination or as part of an intelligence-led screen and to be used only for the purposes of that investigation and destroyed afterwards:*

    "I consent to my fingerprints being taken for elimination purposes. I understand that the fingerprints will be destroyed at the end of the case and that my fingerprints will only be compared to the finger-prints from this enquiry. I have been advised that the person taking the fingerprints may be required to give evidence and/or provide a written statement to the police in relation to the taking of it."

  - *(ii) Fingerprints to be retained for future use:*

    "I consent to my fingerprints being retained and used only for purposes related to the prevention and detection of a crime, the investigation of an offence or the conduct of a prosecution either na-tionally or internationally".

    "I understand that my fingerprints may be checked against other records held by, or on behalf of, relevant law enforcement authorities, either nationally or internationally."

    "I understand that once I have given my consent for my fingerprints to be retained and used I can-not withdraw this consent."

F2   The provisions for the retention of fingerprints and samples in paragraph 1 allow for all fingerprints and samples in a case to be available for any subsequent miscarriage of justice investigation.

Appendix 7

PACE Code of Practice on Tape Recording Interviews with Suspects (Code E)

This code applies to interviews carried out after midnight on 31st March 2003, notwithstanding that the interview may have commenced before that time.

1 General

1.1   This Code of Practice must be readily available for consultation by:
- police officers
- detained persons
- members of the public.

1.2   The *Notes for Guidance* included are not provisions of this Code.

1.3   Nothing in this Code shall detract from the requirements of Code C, the Code of Practice for the detention, treatment and questioning of persons by police officers.

1.4   This Code does not apply to those people listed in Code C, *paragraph 1.12*.

1.5   The term:
- 'appropriate adult' has the same meaning as in Code C, *paragraph 1.7*
- 'solicitor' has the same meaning as in Code C, *paragraph 6.12*.

1.6   In this Code:
- (a) 'designated person' means a person other than a police officer, designated under the Police Reform Act 2002, Part 4 who has specified powers and duties of police officers conferred or imposed on them;
- (b) any reference to a police officer includes a designated person acting in the exercise or performance of the powers and duties conferred or imposed on them by their designation.

1.7   If a power conferred on a designated person:
- (a) allows reasonable force to be used when exercised by a police officer, a designated person exercising that power has the same entitlement to use force;
- (b) includes power to use force to enter any premises, that power is not exercisable by that designated person except:
  - (i) in the company, and under the supervision, of a police officer; or
  - (ii) for the purpose of:
    - saving life or limb; or
    - preventing serious damage to property.

1.8   Nothing in this Code prevents the custody officer, or other officer given custody of the detainee, from allowing civilian support staff who are not designated persons to carry out individual procedures or tasks at the police station if the law allows. However, the officer remains responsible for making sure the procedures and tasks are carried out correctly in accordance with these Codes. Any such civilian must be:

(a) a person employed by a police authority maintaining a police force and under the control and direction of the Chief Officer of that force; or

(b) employed by a person with whom a police authority has a contract for the provision of services relating to persons arrested or otherwise in custody.

1.9   Designated persons and other civilian support staff must have regard to any relevant provisions of the Codes of Practice.

1.10   References to pocket book include any official report book issued to police officers or civilian support staff.

1.11   References to a custody officer include those performing the functions of a custody officer.

2   Recording and sealing master tapes

2.1   Tape recording of interviews shall be carried out openly to instil confidence in its reliability as an impartial and accurate record of the interview.

2.2   One tape, the master tape, will be sealed in the suspect's presence. A second tape will be used as a working copy. The master tape is either of the two tapes used in a twin deck machine or the only tape in a single deck machine. The working copy is either the second/third tape used in a twin/triple deck machine or a copy of the master tape made by a single deck machine. See *Notes 2A* and *2B*.

2.3   Nothing in this Code requires the identity of officers or civilian support staff conducting interviews to be recorded or disclosed:

(a) in the case of enquiries linked to the investigation of terrorism; or

(b) if the interviewer reasonably believes recording or disclosing their name might put them in danger.

In these cases interviewers should use warrant or other identification numbers and the name of their police station. See *Note 2C*.

Notes for guidance

2A   The purpose of sealing the master tape in the suspect's presence is to show the tape's intergrity is preserved. If a single deck machine is used the working copy of the master tape must be made in the suspect's presence and without the master tape leaving their sight. The working copy shall be used for making further copies if needed.

2B   Reference to 'tapes' includes 'tape', if a single deck machine is used.

2C   The purpose of paragraph 2.3(b) is to protect those involved in serious organised crime investigations or arrests of particularly violent suspects when there is reliable information that those arrested or their associates may threaten or cause harm to those involved. In cases of doubt, an officer of inspector rank or above should be consulted.

3   Interviews to be tape recorded

3.1   Subject to *paragraphs 3.3* and *3.4*, tape recording shall be used at police stations for any interview:

(a) with a person cautioned under Code C, *section 10* in respect of any indictable offence, including an offence triable either way; see *Note 3A*

(b) which takes place as a result of an interviewer exceptionally putting further questions to a suspect about an offence described in *paragraph 3.1(a)* after they have been charged with, or told they may be prosecuted for, that offence, see Code C, *paragraph 16.5*

(c) when an interviewer wants to tell a person, after they have been charged with, or informed they may be prosecuted for, an offence described in *paragraph 3.1(a)*, about any written statement or interview with another person, see Code C, *paragraph 16.4*.

3.2 The Terrorism Act 2000 makes separate provision for a Code of Practice for the tape recording of interviews of those arrested under Section 41 or detained under Schedule 7 of the Act. The provisions of this Code do not apply to such interviews.

3.3 The custody officer may authorise the interviewer not to tape record the interview when it is:

(a) not reasonably practicable because of equipment failure or the unavailability of a suitable interview room or recorder and the authorising officer considers, on reasonable grounds, that the interview should not be delayed; or

(b) clear from the outset there will not be a prosecution.

Note: In these cases the interview should be recorded in writing in accordance with Code C, *section 11*. In all cases the custody officer shall record the specific reasons for not tape recording. See *Note 3B*.

3.4 If a person refuses to go into or remain in a suitable interview room, see Code C *paragraph 12.5*, and the custody officer considers, on reasonable grounds, that the interview should not be delayed the interview may, at the custody officer's discretion, be conducted in a cell using portable recording equipment or, if none is available, recorded in writing as in Code C, *section 11*. The reasons for this shall be recorded.

3.5 The whole of each interview shall be tape recorded, including the taking and reading back of any statement.

Notes for guidance

3A Nothing in the Code is intended to preclude tape recording at police discretion of interviews at police stations with people cautioned in respect of offences not covered by paragraph 3.1, or responses made by persons after they have been charged with, or told they may be prosecuted for, an offence, provided this Code is complied with.

3B A decision not to tape record an interview for any reason may be the subject of comment in court. The authorising officer should be prepared to justify that decision.

4 **The interview**

(a) **General**

4.1 The provisions of Code C:

- *sections 10 and 11*, and the applicable *Notes for Guidance* apply to the conduct of interviews to which this Code applies
- *paragraphs 11.7 to 11.14* apply only when a written record is needed.

4.2 Code C, *paragraphs 10.10, 10.11* and Annex C describe the restriction on drawing adverse inferences from a suspect's failure or refusal to say anything about their involvement in the offence when interviewed or after being charged or informed they may be prosecuted, and how it affects the terms of the caution and determines if and by whom a special warning under sections 36 and 37 can be given.

(b) **Commencement of interviews**

4.3 When the suspect is brought into the interview room the interviewer shall, without delay but in the suspect's sight, load the recorder with clean tapes and set it to record. The tapes must be unwrapped or opened in the suspect's presence.

4.4   The interviewer should tell the suspect about the tape recording. The interviewer shall:

(a) say the interview is being tape recorded

(b) subject to *paragraph 2.3*, give their name and rank and that of any other interviewer present

(c) ask the suspect and any other party present, e.g. a solicitor, to identify themselves

(d) state the date, time of commencement and place of the interview

(e) state the suspect will be given a notice about what will happen to the tapes.

See *Note 4A*

4.5   The interviewer shall:

• caution the suspect, see Code C, *section 10*

• remind the suspect of their entitlement to free legal advice, see Code C, *paragraph 11.2*.

4.6   The interviewer shall put to the suspect any significant statement or silence; see Code C, *paragraph 11.4*.

(c)   Interviews with deaf persons

4.7   If the suspect is deaf or is suspected of having impaired hearing, the interviewer shall make a written note of the interview in accordance with Code C, at the same time as tape recording it in accordance with this Code. See *Notes 4B* and *4C*

(d)   Objections and complaints by the suspect

4.8   If the suspect objects to the interview being tape recorded at the outset, during the interview or during a break, the interviewer shall explain that the interview is being tape recorded and that this Code requires the suspect's objections be recorded on tape. When any objections have been tape recorded or the suspect has refused to have their objections recorded, the interviewer shall say they are turning off the recorder, give their reasons and turn it off. The interviewer shall then make a written record of the interview as in Code C, *section 11*. If, however, the interviewer reasonably considers they may proceed to question the suspect with the tape still on, the interviewer may do so. See *Note 4D*

4.9   If in the course of an interview a complaint is made by or on behalf on the person being questioned concerning the provisions of this Code or Code C, the interviewer shall act as in Code C, *paragraph 12.9*. See *Notes 4E* and *4F*

4.10   If the suspect indicates they want to tell the interviewer about matters not directly connected with the offence and they are unwilling for these matters to be tape recorded, the suspect should be given the opportunity to tell the interviewer at the end of the formal interview.

(e)   Changing tapes

4.11   When the recorder shows the tapes have only a short time left, the interviewer shall tell the suspect the tapes are coming to an end and round off that part of the interview. If the interviewer leaves the room for a second set of tapes, the suspect shall not be left unattended. The interviewer will remove the tapes from the tape recorder and insert the new tapes which shall be unwrapped or opened in the suspect's presence. The tape recorder should be set to record on the new tapes. To avoid confusion between the tapes, the interviewer shall mark the tapes with an identification number immediately they are removed from the tape recorder.

(f)   Taking a break during interview

4.12   When a break is taken, the fact that a break is to be taken, the reason for it and the time shall be recorded on tape.

4.12A   When the break is taken and the interview room vacated by the suspect, the tapes shall be removed from the tape recorder and the procedures for the conclusion of an interview followed; see *paragraph 4.18*.

4.13   When a break is a short one and both the suspect and an interviewer remain in the interview room, the tape recorder may be turned off. There is no need to remove the tapes and when the interview recommences the tape recording should continue on the same tapes. The time the interview recommences shall be recorded on tape.

4.14   After any break in the interview the interviewer must, before resuming the interview, remind the person being questioned that they remain under caution or, if there is any doubt, give the caution in full again. See *Note 4G*

(g)   Failure of recording equipment

4.15   If there is an equipment failure which can be rectified quickly, e.g. by inserting new tapes, the interviewer shall follow the appropriate procedures as in *paragraph 4.11*. When the recording is resumed the interviewer shall explain what happened and record the time the interview recommences. If, however, it will not be possible to continue recording on that tape recorder and no replacement recorder is readily available, the interview may continue without being tape recorded. If this happens, the interviewer shall seek the custody officer's authority as in *paragraph 3.3*. See *Note 4H*

(h)   Removing tapes from the recorder

4.16   When tapes are removed from the recorder during the interview, they shall be retained and the procedures in *paragraph 4.18* followed.

(i)   Conclusion of interview

4.17   At the conclusion of the interview, the suspect shall be offered the opportunity to clarify anything he or she has said and asked if there is anything they want to add.

4.18   At the conclusion of the interview, including the taking and reading back of any written statement, the time shall be recorded and the tape recorder switched off. The interviewer shall seal the master tape with a master tape label and treat it as an exhibit in accordance with force standing orders. The interviewer shall sign the label and ask the suspect and any third party present during the interview to sign it. If the suspect or third refuse to sign the label an officer of at least inspector rank, or if not available the custody officer, shall be called into the interview room and asked, subject to *paragraph 2.3*, to sign it.

4.19   The suspect shall be handed a notice which explains:
- how the tape recording will be used

- the arrangements for access to it

- that if the person is charged or informed they will be prosecuted, a copy of the tape will be supplied as soon as practicable or as otherwise agreed between the suspect and the police.

Notes for guidance

4A   For the purpose of voice identification the interviewer should ask the suspect and any other people present to identify themselves.

4B   This provision is to give a person who is deaf or has impaired hearing equivalent rights of access to the full interview record as far as this is possible using audio recording.

4C   The provisions of Code C, section 13 on interpreters for deaf persons or for interviews with suspects who have difficulty understanding English continue to apply. However, in a tape recorded interview the requirement on the interviewer to make sure the interpreter makes a separate note of the interview applies only to paragraph 4.7 (interviews with deaf persons).

4D   The interviewer should remember that a decision to continue recording against the wishes of the suspect may be the subject of comment in court.

4E   If the custody officer is called to deal with the complaint, the tape recorder should, if possible, be left on until the custody officer has entered the room and spoken to the person being interviewed. Continuation or termination of the interview should be at the interviewer's discretion pending action by an inspector under Code C, paragraph 9.2.

4F   If the complaint is about a matter not connected with this Code or Code C, the decision to continue is at the interviewer's discretion. When the interviewer decides to continue the interview, they shall tell the suspect the complaint will be brought to the custody officer's attention at the conclusion of the interview. When the interview is concluded the interviewer must, as soon as practicable, inform the custody officer about the existence and nature of the complaint made.

4G   The interviewer should remember that it may be necessary to show to the court that nothing occurred during a break or between interviews which influenced the suspect's recorded evidence. After a break or at the beginning of a subsequent interview, the interviewer should consider summarising on tape the reason for the break and confirming this with the suspect.

4H   If one of the tapes snaps during the interview it should be sealed as a master tape in the suspect's presence and the interview resumed where it left off. The unbroken tape should be copied and the original sealed as a master tape in the suspect's presence, if necessary after the interview. If equipment for copying the unbroken tape is not readily available, both tapes should be sealed in the suspect's presence and the interview begun again. If the tape breaks when a single deck machine is being used and the machine is one where a broken tape cannot be copied on available equipment, the tape should be sealed as a master tape in the suspect's presence and the interview begun again.

5   After the interview

5.1   The interviewer shall make a note in their pocket book that the interview has taken place, was tape recorded, its time, duration and date and the master tape's identification number.

5.2   If no proceedings follow in respect of the person whose interview was recorded, the tapes must be kept securely as in *paragraph 6.1* and *Note 6A*.

Note for guidance

5A   Any written record of a tape recorded interview should be made in accordance with national guidelines approved by the Secretary of State.

6   Tape security

6.1   The officer in charge of each police station at which interviews with suspects are recorded shall make arrangements for master tapes to be kept securely and their movements accounted for on the same basis as material which may be used for evidential purposes, in accordance with force standing orders. See *Note 6A*

6.2   A police officer has no authority to break the seal on a master tape required for criminal trial or appeal proceedings. If it is necessary to gain access to the master tape, the police officer shall arrange for its seal to be broken in the presence of a representative of the Crown Prosecution Service. The defendant or their legal adviser should be informed and given a reasonable opportunity to be present. If the defendant or their legal representative is present they shall be invited to reseal and sign the master tape. If either refuses or neither is present this should be done by the representative of the Crown Prosecution Service. See *Notes 6B* and *6C*

6.3   If no criminal proceedings result or the criminal trial and, if applicable, appeal proceedings to which the interview relates have been concluded, the chief officer of police is responsible for establishing arrangements for breaking the seal on the master tape, if necessary.

6.4   When the master tape seal is broken, a record must be made of the procedure followed, including the date, time, place and persons present.

Notes for guidance

6A   This section is concerned with the security of the master tape sealed at the conclusion of the interview. Care must be taken of working copies of tapes because their loss or destruction may lead to the need to access master tapes.

6B   If the tape has been delivered to the crown court for their keeping after committal for trial the crown prosecutor will apply to the chief clerk of the crown court centre for the release of the tape for unsealing by the crown prosecutor.

6C   Reference to the Crown Prosecution Service or to the crown prosecutor in this part of the Code should be taken to include any other body or person with a statutory responsibility for prosecution for whom the police conduct any tape recorded interviews.

Appendix 8
Flow Charts

Strip Searches

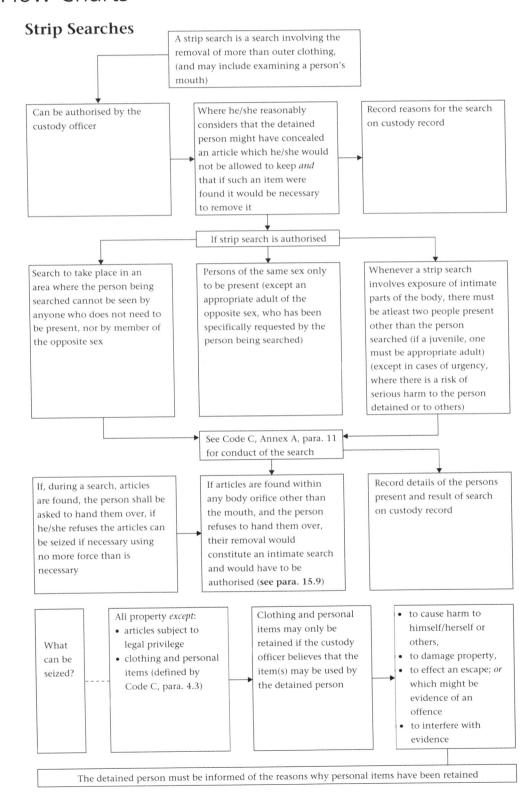

A strip search is a search involving the removal of more than outer clothing, (and may include examining a person's mouth)

Can be authorised by the custody officer

Where he/she reasonably considers that the detained person might have concealed an article which he/she would not be allowed to keep *and* that if such an item were found it would be necessary to remove it

Record reasons for the search on custody record

If strip search is authorised

Search to take place in an area where the person being searched cannot be seen by anyone who does not need to be present, nor by member of the opposite sex

Persons of the same sex only to be present (except an appropriate adult of the opposite sex, who has been specifically requested by the person being searched)

Whenever a strip search involves exposure of intimate parts of the body, there must be atleast two people present other than the person searched (if a juvenile, one must be appropriate adult) (except in cases of urgency, where there is a risk of serious harm to the person detained or to others)

See Code C, Annex A, para. 11 for conduct of the search

If, during a search, articles are found, the person shall be asked to hand them over, if he/she refuses the articles can be seized if necessary using no more force than is necessary

If articles are found within any body orifice other than the mouth, and the person refuses to hand them over, their removal would constitute an intimate search and would have to be authorised (**see para. 15.9**)

Record details of the persons present and result of search on custody record

What can be seized?

All property *except*:
- articles subject to legal privilege
- clothing and personal items (defined by Code C, para. 4.3)

Clothing and personal items may only be retained if the custody officer believes that the item(s) may be used by the detained person

- to cause harm to himself/herself or others,
- to damage property,
- to effect an escape; *or* which might be evidence of an offence
- to interfere with evidence

The detained person must be informed of the reasons why personal items have been retained

Intimate Searches

Definition	An 'intimate search' is a search which consists of the physical examination of a person's body orifices other than the mouth

Who can authorise	An officer of the rank of inspector or above	Has reasonable grounds for believing that the detained person has concealed	• an article which could cause physical injury to the detained person or others at the police station; or • a class A drug which the detained person intended to supply to another or to export	that an intimate search is the only practicable means of removing it.

If authority is given	Can be given orally but must be confirmed in writing as soon as practicable (in the custody record)	Reasons why intimate search considered 'necessary' must be explained to person

For searches which are for:	*an article which could cause physical injury to the detained person or others at the police station*	*a class A drug which the detained person intended to supply to another or to export*

Where can take place?	• police station • hospital • surgery • other medical premises	• hospital • surgery • other medical premises

Who can conduct	• a registered medical practitioner • registered nurse • police officer of the same sex if an officer of at least the rank of inspector considers that it is not practicable to use a nurse or medical practitioner	• a registered medical practitioner • registered nurse

Who should be present?	Only people who need to be present and they must be of the same sex except for a doctor, nurse or appropriate adult

What must be recorded?	The custody officer must record which parts of the person's body were searched, who carried out the search and why, who was present, the reasons for the search and its result

What can be seized?	All property *except*: • articles subject to legal privilege • clothing and personal items (defined by Code C, para. 4.3)	Clothing and personal items may only be retained if the custody officer believes that the item(s) may be used by the detained person	• to cause harm to himself/herself or others, • to damage property, • to effect an escape; *or* which might be evidence of an offence • to interfere with evidence

The detained person must be informed of the reasons why personal items have been retained

Level of Search

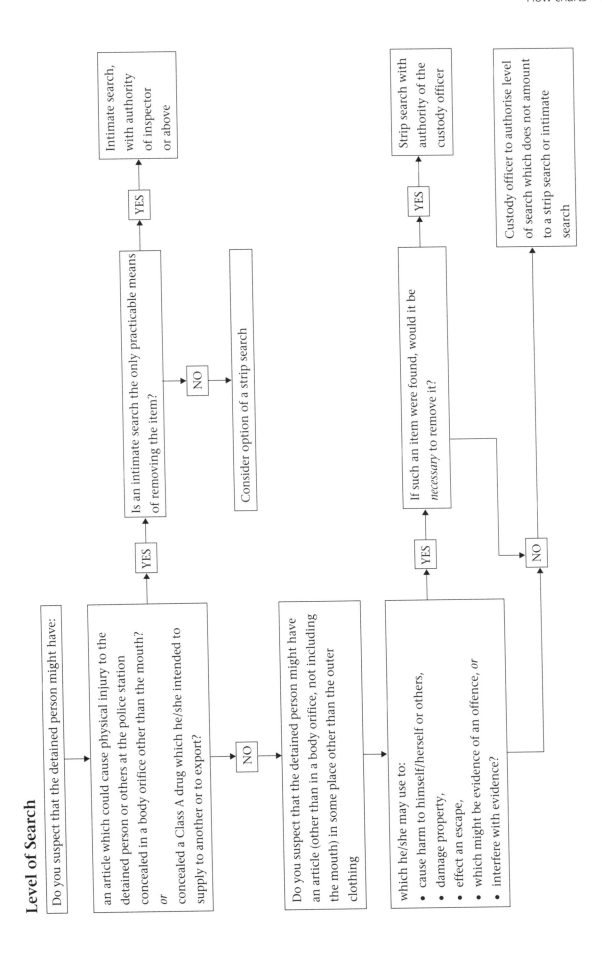

Do you suspect that the detained person might have:

an article which could cause physical injury to the detained person or others at the police station concealed in a body orifice other than the mouth?

or

concealed a Class A drug which he/she intended to supply to another or to export?

YES → Is an intimate search the only practicable means of removing the item?

YES → Intimate search, with authority of inspector or above

NO → Consider option of a strip search

NO →

Do you suspect that the detained person might have an article (other than in a body orifice, not including the mouth) in some place other than the outer clothing

which he/she may use to:
- cause harm to himself/herself or others,
- damage property,
- effect an escape,
- which might be evidence of an offence, *or*
- interfere with evidence?

YES → If such an item were found, would it be *necessary* to remove it?

YES → Strip search with authority of the custody officer

NO → Custody officer to authorise level of search which does not amount to a strip search or intimate search

Medical Care of Detained Persons

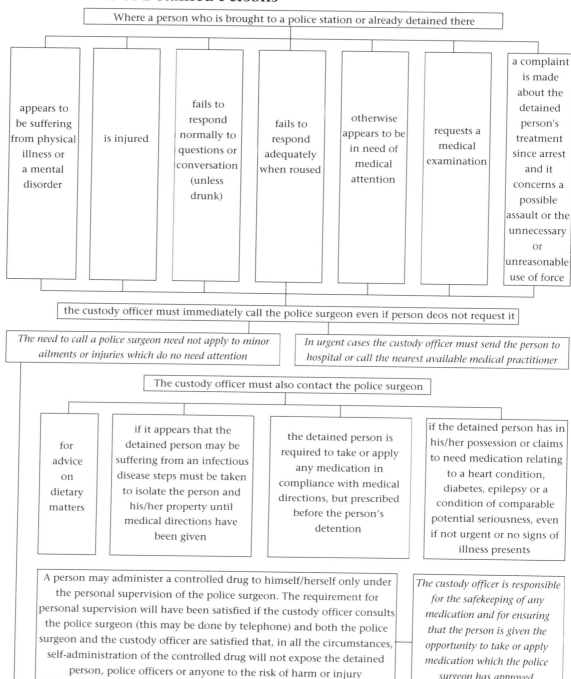

Where a person who is brought to a police station or already detained there

- appears to be suffering from physical illness or a mental disorder
- is injured
- fails to respond normally to questions or conversation (unless drunk)
- fails to respond adequately when roused
- otherwise appears to be in need of medical attention
- requests a medical examination
- a complaint is made about the detained person's treatment since arrest and it concerns a possible assault or the unnecessary or unreasonable use of force

the custody officer must immediately call the police surgeon even if person deos not request it

The need to call a police surgeon need not apply to minor ailments or injuries which do no need attention

In urgent cases the custody officer must send the person to hospital or call the nearest available medical practitioner

The custody officer must also contact the police surgeon

- for advice on dietary matters
- if it appears that the detained person may be suffering from an infectious disease steps must be taken to isolate the person and his/her property until medical directions have been given
- the detained person is required to take or apply any medication in compliance with medical directions, but prescribed before the person's detention
- if the detained person has in his/her possession or claims to need medication relating to a heart condition, diabetes, epilepsy or a condition of comparable potential seriousness, even if not urgent or no signs of illness presents

A person may administer a controlled drug to himself/herself only under the personal supervision of the police surgeon. The requirement for personal supervision will have been satisfied if the custody officer consults the police surgeon (this may be done by telephone) and both the police surgeon and the custody officer are satisfied that, in all the circumstances, self-administration of the controlled drug will not expose the detained person, police officers or anyone to the risk of harm or injury

The custody officer is responsible for the safekeeping of any medication and for ensuring that the person is given the opportunity to take or apply medication which the police surgeon has approved

A record must be made of:
- any arrangements made for an examination by a police surgeon
- any request for a medical examination, of the arrangements for any examination made, and of any medical directions to the police
- of all medication that a detained person has in his/her possession on arrival at the police station
- any medication the detained person claims he/her needs but does not have with him/her
- police surgeon's clinical findings
- all ailments or injuries must be recorded in the custody record

If in any doubt, the police surgeon should be asked to attend

VULNERABLE SUSPECTS

A detained person at a police station or other authorised place of detention who:

| is heavily under the influence of drink or drugs | is a juvenile | is mentally disordered or mentally handicapped | has difficulty in understanding English | has a hearing disability |

must not be interviewed until

| he/she is in a fit state | an appropriate adult is in attendance | an interpreter is in attendance |

unless an officer of the rank of superintendent or above considers that the dealy will:

| lead to interference with, or harm to evidence connected with, an offence or interference with or physical harm to other people | lead to the alerting of other people suspected of having committed an offence but not yet arrested for it | hinder the recovery of property obtained in consequence of the commission of an offence |

Interviewing in any of these circumstances shall cease once sufficient information has been obtained to avert the immediate risk

This procedure should only be used in *exceptional cases of need.*
The officer must be satisfied that the interview with the vulnerable suspect will not significantly harm the peron's physical or mental state.

Appendix 9

Home Office Circular 32/2000: Detainee Risk Assessment

Annex A

Risk Assessment of Persons Entering Police Custody

1   All persons entering police custody should be assessed to consider whether they are likely to present specific risks, either to staff or to themselves.

2   Such assessments are primarily the responsibility of the custody officer, but it will frequently be necessary to consult others such as the arresting officer and the police surgeon.

3   The results of risk assessments should be incorporated in detainees' custody records. Such recording procedures should refer specifically to each risk category included in paragraph 5 and to the responses to the questions in paragraph 6. The record should highlight identified risks in such a way as to be obvious to all those responsible for the detainee's custody. Details of such risks should be given and reports attached where appropriate. Where no specific risks are identified by the assessment, that should be noted in the custody record.

4   Risk assessment is an ongoing process and assessments must always be subject to review where circumstances change. Where the circumstances of risk in relation to a detainee change, a new PER Form must be completed.

5   Specific risk categories which must always be considered are as follows. Further details relevant to each category are in the guidance at Annex C which covers the completion of the PER Form. Much of that guidance is equally applicable to the documenting of risks in the custody record.

Medical/Mental Condition

Medication Issued

Special Needs

First Aid Given

Violence

Conceals Weapons

Escape Risk

Hostage Taker

Stalker/Harasser

Racial Motivation

Sex Offence

Drug/Alcohol Issues

Suicide/Self Harm

Injuries

Vulnerable

Force/Restraint Used

CS Spray Used.

6   The following questions must be asked of every person entering police custody.

    i   Do you have any illness or injury?

    ii   Have you seen a doctor or been to a hospital for this illness/injury?

    iii Are you taking or supposed to be taking any tablets/medication?

    iv What are they? What are they for?

    v   Are you suffering from any mental health problems or depression?

    vi Have you ever tried to harm yourself?

7   It is the custody officer's responsibility to determine the response to any specific risk assessment. For example, in terms of calling the police surgeon or instigating extra levels of monitoring or observation.

Annex B

PER - PART A

TICK APPROPRIATE BOX: **NO KNOWN RISK** ☐ **RISK** ☐ (PROVIDE DETAILS BELOW)

PRISONER NOT FOR RELEASE ☐ REASON: _____

PERSONAL DETAILS

PRISON NO: [   ] OR PNC ID NO: [   ]

SURNAME: [   ] FORENAME(S): [   ]

ALIAS(ES): [   ] DOB: [   ] UNDER 18: ☐

SEX: MALE: ☐ FEMALE: ☐ ETHNICITY: WHITE: ☐ BLACK: ☐ ASIAN: ☐ MIXED: ☐ CHINESE/OTHER: ☐

ESCORT DETAILS

FROM		TO	
FROM		TO	

RISK CATEGORIES (TICK AND ATTACH REPORTS WHERE APPROPRIATE)

MEDICAL

MEDICAL CONDITION ☐
MENTAL CONDITION ☐
MEDICATION ISSUED
WITH PRISONER ☐
WITH ESCORT ☐
SPECIAL NEEDS ☐
FIRST AID GIVEN ☐

NO KNOWN RISK ☐

SECURITY

VIOLENCE ☐
CONCEALS WEAPONS ☐
ESCAPE RISK ☐
HOSTAGE TAKER ☐
STALKER/HARASSER ☐
RACIAL MOTIVATION ☐
SEX OFFENCE ☐

NO KNOWN RISK ☐

OTHER

DRUGS/ALCOHOL ISSUES ☐
SUICIDE/SELF HARM ☐
INJURIES ☐
VULNERABLE ☐
FORCE/RESTRAINT USED ☐
CS SPRAY USED ☐
FIRST AID GIVEN ☐
OTHER ☐
NO KNOWN RISK ☐

PRISON AND ESCORT CONTRACTORS USE ONLY

SIGNED	SIGNED	SIGNED
NAME (CAPS)	NAME (CAPS)	NAME (CAPS)
DATE	DATE	DATE

FURTHER INFORMATION ABOUT RISK

POLICE USE ONLY

SIGNED
NAME (CAPS)
DATE

REPORTS(S) ATTACHED ☐ PRE CONS ☐ HANDCUFF REQUEST ☐ IMMIGRATION DETENTION AUTHORITY ☐

PRISONER PROPERTY

CODE	SEAL/SERIAL NO.	OUT	IN
		☐	☐
		☐	☐
		☐	☐
		☐	☐
		☐	☐
		☐	☐

CASH
OUT £
IN £

LAST MEAL GIVEN/OFFERED

TIME:

ATTACH
PHOTO
IF AVAILABLE
(TOP COPY ONLY)

PRISONER AND PROPERTY RECEIVED **BY** ESCORT .... SIGNED .... DATE ....

PRISONER AND PROPERTY RECEIVED **FROM** ESCORT .... SIGNED .... DATE ....

PER - PART B

RECORD OF EVENTS : DATE

INCIDENT REPORT ATTACHED ☐

SURNAME: _____ FORENAME(S): _____

PRISON NO: _____ PNC ID NO: _____

TIME	DETAILS	NAME (CAPS)	SIGNED	SIGNIFICANT EVENTS (TICK)

Produced in the UK for Tactica Solutions De806937 5/00

MEALS (STATE TIME)	BREAKFAST	LUNCH	DINNER
TIME GIVEN / OFFERED			
REFUSED			
REASON			

NEXT APPEARANCE AND COURT DATE: .... TIME .... COURT ....

Annex C

Completing the Prisoner Escort Record (PER) Form

Part A

1 At a police station, the PER should be completed by or under the supervision of the custody officer. The following guidance is intended to assist with that process and works through the form in order.

Overall Risk Assessment

2 One of the boxes at the top of the form must be ticked to indicate either 'Risk' or 'No Known Risk'. This should be done *after* the detailed consideration of Risk Categories in the box below has been completed.

Prisoner Not for Release

3 This box is generally for use by the Prison Service, but should be ticked by the police where it is clear that the detainee should not be released from custody in any circumstances. For example, where the detainee is a serving prisoner who is temporarily in police custody. In such cases the reason should be stated in the space provided.

Personal Details

4 Surname, forenames, known aliases and date of birth should be entered, as should details of sex and ethnicity. The 5-box ethnicity classification is in accord with the main categories within the 2001 Population Census system. The 'Mixed' box is to be used for persons who are of mixed racial background, e.g. White and Asian. The 'Chinese/Other' box is to be used for persons who come from one ethnic group other than White, Black or Asian.

5 Where the detainee has a PNC ID number, that should be included in the space provided. Prison number is primarily a matter for the Prison Service, but there may be occasions when it is known to the police officer completing the form. Where the detainee is under the age of 18, the box provided should be ticked to highlight that fact.

Escort Details

6 This section should be completed with the details available prior to the detainee's departure on escort.

Risk Categories

7 These are divided into three sets—Medical, Security and Other. That reflects the fact that in prisons the responsibility for assessing specific sets of risks is clearly divided between different groups of staff. The form allows for that. **However, a police officer filling in the PER only has to sign the Risk Categories box *once*, using the box identified for *'police use only'* within this section of the form.**

8 The officer completing the PER must consider the individual risk categories in turn and tick the box against each category that applies. **Whenever a box is ticked, additional details should be entered in the 'Further information about risk' section and reports attached where appropriate.** (It may be necessary to continue Further Information' on a separate report which must then be attached to the Part A.) If no known risks in a specific set are identified, the officer should tick the 'No Known Risk' box at the bottom of the relevant column. Once the assessment is completed the officer should sign and date the box identified for police use and then reflect the assessment by ticking either the 'Risk' or 'No Known Risk' box at the top of the form.

9   In completing the PER, the responsible officer will often be drawing from the structured risk assessment that should be carried out in respect of *all* detainees entering police custody (see Annex A). S/he may also need to liaise with medical personnel and other colleagues such as the arresting officer.

Medical Risks

Medical/Mental Condition

10   Where the custody officer is aware that there may be medical risks to record, this should normally be done in consultation within the relevant medical, psychiatric or healthcare staff. It will not be normal practice to record information about medical conditions on the face of the PER, unless that is essential to ensure the health and safety of the detainee or others. For example, it will not be appropriate to record the fact that a detainee may be HIV positive, since escorts will assume this may apply to any detainee in their charge. **However, communicable diseases *should* be recorded to safeguard others who may come into contact with the detainee.**

11   Confidential medical information should generally be attached to the PER in a sealed envelope, marked with an indication of its contents, that can be opened in an emergency. However, it is important that essential information about the need for ongoing medical care, observation or examination should be included on the PER or in open attachments. That is to avoid the detainee and escorts being exposed to unnecessary risk or harm. It may frequently be appropriate to attach a copy of a Detained Persons Medical Report Form in a standard agreed format.

Medication Issued

12   Where medication has been issued, the PER must indicate whether the detainee and/or the escort have received instructions about its administration or whether specific instructions for medical personnel have been provided. Where a Detained Persons Medication Form in a standard agreed format is available, it should be used to inform the PER and a copy should be attached for reference.

Special Needs

13   This box is to be used if the detainee has a disability or has special transport or care requirements due to medical treatment or an on-going medical condition that may affect the safety of the detainee or escorting staff during the escort. Clear details of the specific condition applicable will be particularly helpful for those escorting and/or receiving the detainee.

First Aid Given

14   Has first aid been applied to the detainee at any stage, either before arrival at the police station or while detained there? If so, details should be provided as concisely as possible. The police may tick *either* of the two boxes (one entry is listed in the Other section of risk categories). [The Prison Service require two separate listings.]

Security Risks

Violence

15   This should apply where, for example, the detainee has a history of violent behaviour or has recently committed an assault on a member of police staff or a fellow detainee.

Conceals Weapons

16   This should be ticked if the detainee has a history of concealing weapons or is considered likely to do so whilst in detention.

Escape Risk

17   This should be ticked where the detainee's custodial history or behaviour suggest that they present an escape risk or where intelligence is available to that effect.

Hostage Taker

18   This covers where the detainee is a known hostage taker or where information exists to suggest they may attempt to take a hostage.

Stalker / Harasser

19   Does the detainee have a restraining order or a civil injunction against them under current stalking and/or harassment legislation? Is the detainee likely to attempt to harass or intimidate witnesses?

Racial Motivation

20   Does the detainee have a history of racially motivated offences or have they been racially motivated to assault other detainees whilst in custody?

Sex Offence

21   Is the detainee a known or suspected sex offender, particularly with regard to offences against children?

Other Risks

Drug / Alcohol Issues

22   Is drug or alcohol abuse an **immediate** factor in the treatment / handling of the detainee? Is there an active dependency to be taken account of? Could the detainee have needles or drugs concealed upon them? Again, this is an area where input from medical staff may be important.

Suicide / Self Harm

23   **This is a very important category and should be ticked whenever the custody officer has any belief or suspicion that the detainee may try and harm themselves.** That may arise from a whole range of factors, including the detainee's past or current behaviour, their stated intentions, their mood or the circumstances in which they entered custody. Liaison with medical staff will often be relevant to completing this entry.

Injuries

24   Does the detainee have any visible or known injuries prior to departure on escort?

Vulnerable

25   Is the detainee particularly vulnerable to interference or assault by other detainees or even by members of the public? That may derive from the general nature or specific circumstances of the offence in relation to which they are being held. The attitude of associates or co-defendants may also be relevant.

Force / Restraint Used

26   Has force or restraint been used, either during arrest or while the detainee has been in custody?

CS Spray Used

27   Has CS been used at any stage in the process leading up to the detainee entering custody or since they have been in custody?

First Aid Given

28   See paragraph 14. The police may tick either entry.

Other

29   This is a 'catch all' box for risks which are not covered by any of the other categories. If this box is ticked, it will be necessary to provide details in the section for 'Further information about risk'.

Attachments

Report(s)

30   The box should be ticked whenever report(s) expanding on specific risks are attached to the PER.

Pre-cons

31   Pre-convictions should be attached when readily available and this box ticked.

Handcuff Request

32   This should be ticked (and a copy of the appropriate form attached) where it is necessary to make an application to the Crown Prosecution Service for the detainee to wear handcuffs in court during their appearance.

Immigration Detention Authority

33   Detainees held on behalf of the immigration authorities will be accompanied by a form authorising their detention on that basis. The form should be attached to the PER and the relevant box ticked. Such detainees may be vulnerable because of their race.

Detainee's Property

34   Property will normally be transported in sealed bags or containers and the seal numbers should be recorded. The Prison Service uses property codes, but this column will not generally be relevant for the police.

35   Each sealed bag/container should be recorded by ticking on departure and on arrival at the final destination. Cash amounts transported outside sealed bags/containers should be specifically recorded on departure and arrival.

36   The person in charge of the escort should sign to indicate receipt of the detainee and of recorded property and cash at the point of departure. The person finally accepting the detainee at the end of the last leg of the escort should sign to indicate receipt of the detainee and of recorded property and cash from the escorting staff.

Time of last meal prior to departure

37   It is helpful for escorting staff to know when the detainee was last fed or if a meal has been offered and refused (and the reason, if known). The time of the relevant meal should be recorded here.

Photograph

38   Where a photograph of the detainee is available, it should be attached to the ***top copy*** of the PER (Part A) where indicated. Ideally, this will be small enough so as to avoid obscuring other parts of the form.

Part B—Record of Events

39   While the Record of Events should always be linked to Part A of the PER, it will not always be physically part of the same document. Therefore, to ensure any necessary cross-referencing, it is essential that the Record of Events includes the detainee's surname, forename(s), PNC and/or Prison Number(s).

40   The Record should be used to document key events such as departures, arrivals and handovers of responsibility. It should also include any notable incidents and any new information arising in relation to the detainee. Particular attention should be paid to anything bearing on the risk assessment of the detainee. Significant events should be highlighted by a tick in the final column and, if it is necessary to attach an incident report, the box referring to that should be ticked.

41   If a significant *new* risk becomes apparent during escort, details should be given on the Record of Events. Part A of the PER should be updated as necessary.

Other Information

Meals

42   The time of meals given or offered during escort should be recorded, as should any refusal and the reason for it.

Next Appearance and Court

43   Escorting staff should ensure these details are entered before leaving court. Where there is to be a further court appearance but the date is not yet known, the space should be marked DTBF (date to be fixed).

Index